HISTORY OF MUSLIM SPAIN

Sahibzada Masud-ul-Hassan Khan Sabri

M.A. (History, Pol.Science, English, Economics)
Hindi & Arabic (d) LLB. (Pb)

Adam Publishers & Distributors
Delhi - 110 006

Adam Publishers & Distributors
Exporters & Importers
Shandar Market Chitli Qabar, Delhi - 110006
Ph: (O) 3271690, 3282550;
Fax: 3267510; (R) 91-553953
E-mail: apd@bol.net.in
Web: www.adampublishers.com

Revised Edition: 2000
ISBN 81-7435-183-3

Computerised Setting by:
Sangam Computers
Delhi-53
Ph: 2173670

Printed & Bound In India
Published by: S. Sajid Ali for
Adam Publishers & Distributors
Shandar Market, Chitli Qabar,
Delhi - 110 006

Dedicated to

Hazrat Muhammad Noor khan
Afghan Yusufzai

(A. Rohila Chief)

CONTENTS

Sr. No.	Chapter	Page No.

Contents

PREFACE

The present book has been prepared with hard labour and research, so that the students could get high mark in the examinations. It is according to the syllabus of M.A. History of Universities and departmental examinations. Nothing has been left all the topics on Islamic Spain has been discussed frequently and in detail. Some matter has also been collected from important documents, reports, statements and other precious books on the subject.

I hope this book will prove a precious document in Theory and practice of History.

I am grateful to Mr. Nusrat Hassan Khan who helped me in preparing this book.

S. M. H. Khan

Author

CHAPTER 1

PRE-ISLAMIC GEOGRAPHY

The Iberian Peninsula (Spain and Portugal) is roughly the same size as Burma. The Peninsula is cut off from France and remainder of Europe by the lofty chain of the Pyrenees. In the south, the straits of Gibraltar between Spain and Africa are only a few miles wide. The Peninsula consists of a high plateau, called the Meseta, bounded by a line of fold mountains on the north (The Pyrenees and the Cantabian mountains) and also on the south (the Siesra Nevada). The plateau has been cut into deeply by a number of rivers. One river, the Ebro, flows into the Mediterranean Sea, the remainder flow into the Atlantic Ocean. The important ones are the Douro, Tagus, Guadiana and Guadalquivir. The north-western and northern parts of the Peninsula have a good rainfall all the year round and belong to the climate region of North-Western Europe. But the rest of the Peninsula has a tropical Mediterranean climate. The rainfall is heaviest on the western side, and it is there that the Mediterranean woodlands of cork oak flourish. The eastern coast is dry all the year, being in the rain-shadow of the Meseta.

The mountainous north coast stretches from the Cantabrian Mountains to the sea. It is richest and most densely populated part of Spain. Maize grows in the valleys, the rich grasslands amongst the hills are well suited to cattle whilst the mountains are covered with pine forests. But great wealth of the region

lies in its minerals, especially coal and iron. Bilbao and
Santander both export good quality iron ore much of it goes to
Great Britain. The coalfields are round Oniedo.

The Meseta or Plateau covers the greater part of Spain.
Its southern edge forms the Sierra Morena. Much is too dry or
too infertile for cultivation. On the richer soils wheat is grown
and milled at Vallodolid. Large numbers of sheep are kept and
are noted for their fine wool. Madrid the capital of Spain is in
the centre of the plateau nearly in the geographical centre of
the country and so a convenient centre for government.

Southern Spain does not suffer from the cold winters of
the plateau and sub-tropical plants flourish. Oranges and lemons
and the vine all flourish; the region is famous both for wine
and for dried grapes or raisins. But the region is dry and where
possible, is irrigated. Both sugarcane and sugar-beef are grown
on irrigated land. Iron is mined in the Sierra Nevada, copper
near Huelva; and there are other minerals. The fine old town of
Seville is the largest in the region and although seventy miles
from the sea the principal port. The old port of Cadiz is now
little used. Malaga serves the southern slopes of the Sierra
Nevada. Gibraltar, the "Key of the Mediterranean" is a very
important port of Spain. The town is built on the eastern side
of a small rocky Peninsula the rock of Gibraltar and has a five
harbours.

The Mediterranean Coastlands are famous for their fruits-
grapes, olives, oranges, and lemons. The coastlands lie in the
rainshadow of the plateau and so are dry but the hillsides are
carefully terraced and any available river water used for
irrigation, Valencia and Cartagena are fruit ports; Muscia is an
inland centre. But more important is Barcelona, the largest
port and chief manufacturing centre of Spain. Cotton and
woollen goods and machinery are made. The Ebro Basin opens

out on to the Mediterranean coast. It is colder the coast and the centre is bridge town of Saragossa.

Spain like Portugal was once the centre of a great Empire but the old colonies, including a large part of South America, have become independent. Meanwhile Spain itself is comparatively undeveloped and until recently has remained backward amongst the countries of Europe.

The Pyrenees form a very marked barrier between Spain and France. It is only with difficulty that a railway has been built round the eastern end and another round the western end. Spain is thus greatly cut off by natural barriers from the rest of Europe and has come more under the influence of the Moors of North Africa. Several of the cities were built by Moor like Murcia. Madrid is the natural centre of the railways of the Peninsula. The principal export of Spain are wine, fruits, metals and ores.

PRE-ISLAMIC HISTORY OF SPAIN

Ancient Spain : Though an inhospitable land, Spain has a very old history. It began in the dim ages of the primitive times. The first people who settled in ancient Spain were the Iberians, who came into Spain from North Africa more than two thousands years before Christ. This is the reason why the Peninsula came to be known as Iberian Peninsula. The Iberians belonged to the Hamitic race, a white race of North Africa, distantly related to the Semitic race to which belong the Arabs and Laws. After the Iberians came the Greeks the Phoenicians and Earthagians. The established colonies on the coast of the Mediterranean Sea. Next came the Romans, in the pursuit of the Earthagians, whom they defeated and drove out of Spain nearly two centuries before Christ. They subdued whole of the Peninsula and made it a province of their empire. They ruled it for next six centuries. They called it Hispanian a name by which Peninsula was also known to the Arab writers.

When the Romans adopted Christianity, they introduced it in their Spain possessions also. Indeed, the Romans left a deep imprint on the language, culture, law, administration and religion of the people of Spain. Like their religion Christianity, Spanish language was also thoroughly Latinised language of the Romans, hence called Romans later on.

During 409 A.D. three tribes of German Suevi Alans and Vandals attacked the Roman province of Spain and occupied many areas of Spain. While the Suevis captured central and western areas of Spain. The tribe of Vandals conquered and settled the fertile valley of the river Baeticer, as the Guadalquivir was called then. It came to be called Vandalusia the land of the Vandals. In course of time, Vandalusisa became Andalusia.

When later the Arabs conquered it, they Arabicised it all, Al-Andalus which was the name by which Islamic Spain was known to the Muslim rulers and people. In their new territories however the Vandals did not live long.

They were defeated and driven across the strait of Gibraltar into North Africa by the another Germanic tribe called Visigoths or Western Goths. But Andalusia remained for ever the name of this region.

CIRCUMSTANCES THAT LED TO THE CONQUEST OF SPAIN

Religious Condition

The followers of the primitive belief "Nature Worship" were the sons of the soil. They were quelled and persecuted by the Goths. The Gothic king Ricard (586-601 A.D.) disapproving the Arian form of Christianity accepted the Catholicism and made it state religion. It preached orthodoxy and intolerance towards other beliefs. Forcible conversion was the ignoble feature of the government. They were superior to the Christian both educationally and economically held a high position in the society. The persistent attempt of the Catholic Church for the conversion of the Jews was not satisfactory. It was however in 611 A.D. in the regime of the Gothic King Sisebut that under the royal decree the Jews were to be forcibly baptised on pain of death, banishment and the confiscation of both movable and immovable property. The forcible conversion of 90 thousand Jews and their frequent persecutions created a general hatred, bitterness and discontent not only among the Jews but also among other people of Saner views. According to Edwyn the Jews were forbidden by law to celebrate the circumcision and marriage ceremonies and other social rituals according to their religion. The child had to be baptised and in case of default the parents were awarded 100 lashes. Their lands were forfeited and their heads were well-shaven for a more *deplorable* when the 12 Church Council passed a decree of the mass conversion, to hammer their trade and industry.. The life had become so miserable that they had no other alternative but to approach their brethren in North Africa who lived a very happy and prosperous life there under the Muslims, for appropriate solution. The climax of injustice and intolerance was in 694 A.D., when the church council issued a decree for the general sale of the Jews to slavery except children under seven years of age who were to be baptised forcibly. Their unsuccessful revolt supported by the Berber Jews of North Africa and settlers across the Strait of Gibraltar, resulted in their general massacre. Their female folk were given to the Christians as slaves. Thus the Jews who once occupied a higher position in society became the most wretched soul always praying for the days of deliverance.

Social Condition

The entire population was divided into various social groups by the crown and the church.

The crown, the church, the princes, the lords or nobles formed one group. The burgers, the serfs and the slaves formed the second group. The first was the ruling class while the second the subject class.

The social order was like the caste system of the Hinduism. The Goths who ruled Spain for 200 years did not care to eradicate the social evils which prevailed under the Romans rather they allowed them to glow and grow. Parochialism, self-centredness, music, dance, drinking and gambling formed the idea even the priestly class was not an exception.

One of the visigothic kings, named Leoviglid (568-88) was the first ruler who abolished the ban on intermarriages between the Visigoths and the native Hispano-Romans. Thus began the fusion of the two peoples. But it was on class basis. The Visigothic nobles married with the richer people among the Hispano-Romans, who constituted a new aristocracy, called the "upper classes" or classes elevadas. To the upper classes also belonged the ecclesiastical hierarchy, the bishops and archbishops of the catholic church, who began to play a considerable role in the administration and government of the visigothic kingdom. Like the nobles, the bishops also participated in the councils and worked as high functionaries of the kingdom. Thus the fusion of the two peoples was further cemented by the catholic religion. Thus the victors were vanquished by the subject people. Thereafter the Hispano Romans developed a strong loyalty to the Visigothic monarchy. Even in law, the Germanic law was dicarded in favour of the Hispano-Roman Law.

The condition of the lower class or slaves was miserable

beyond imagination. Marriage was not allowed to the slaves without the permission of the master. They lived like Chattler. A free man possessed 4000 to 8000 slaves. The tenants who had no tenancy right had till the fields and provide money for the Spanish aristocracy which was indulged in all conceivable social views.

Economic Condition

The economy of the country was adjudged with the wealth, in the treasuries of the Crown the church and the nobles. The entire produce of the agricultural lands, tilled and maintained by the serf and slaves. The lands and tilled were under control of land lords. The privileged class was exempt from taxation. The middle class had to bear the entire burden of it. The heavy taxes were imposed on the traders and industrialists. So the factories and mills were closed down and the merchants gave up their profusions.

Political Conditions: The kings were have to be elected by their Tribal Chiefs, nobles and church. The elective principle remained sound during visigothic kingdom because it was tribolistic, but when it became a territorial kingdom, with Toledo its capital, the elective principle became a source of political weakness, which resulted plots and intrigues at the election of new king. There was no law of hereditary succession that is why the intrigues were common. The church tried to initiate these evils and introduced the ceremony of anointing a new king after his election, thus giving him a sacred character and to make known to all that; he was under God's protection. Royal councils were set up attended by bishops, nobles and chiefs. In the cities system of self-government was prevailed. Provinces were administered by dulles, judges and counts etc. Germinatic tribal laws were abolished and Hispano-Roman laws, (Liber Judicionum) were introduced.

Thus there was a regular struggle for power. The governors of distant provinces had become almost independent. The centre was unable to control the situation. Army was busy plotting against the rulers. There was a situation of revolt everywhere. Roderick assumed the rein after the murder of king, Witiza (702 AD) Roderick's policy incurred the displeasure of the aristocracy and the church. The ecclesiastical group became powerful and the aristocracy joined hands with it.

The seduction and molestation of Florinda, the daughter of Count Julian, the governor of Ceuta, by Poderick worsened the condition of the country. Count Julian invited the Muslims to Spain by way of revenge and received a good response.

The Muslims were welcomed as Saviours of the wretched and discontended citizens.

Jews: Jews were subjected to cruel persecutions by the rulers of Spains. Repressive injunctions were formulated against them and in 613 AD, all the Jews were ordered to adopt Christianity otherwise their properties would be confiscated and they have to leave the country. Their children were forcibly snatched from their parents and were brought up as Christians. Every new king had to *swear* upon his carnation for persecution of the Jews. In persecution of the Jews, in 694 AD the Jews rose in rebellion, but failed.

As a result the Jews welcomed the Arabs as their saviours, and all Jewish city of Ducena assisted the Arabs.

If we study the History, we will find that on many occasions the Jews helped Muslims, but unfortunately bigoted Muslims under the influence of false propaganda of the bigoted Christians and bishops, hates the Jews, though they are also human beings and believe in One God.

CHAPTER 2

THE CONQUEST OF SPAIN

Khalifa Abu Bakr and Khalifa Umer were busy quelling the revolt and subjugating the neighbouring countries, like Persia and the Byzantine empire. In 27 A.H. that the Third Khalifa Usman ordered Abdullah-bin-Nafe-bin-Abdul Qais and Abdullah-bin-Nafe-bin-Hasin to attack on Constantinople to find easy route to Spain. The invasion was partially successful.

Second invasion of Spain was made during the regime of Khalifa, Muawiyah, headed by Muawiyah-bin-Khadij the Amir of Africa. The effective invasion was made during the regime of Walid-bin-Abdul-Malik (705-715 A.D.) by Tariq-bin-Ziad, 30th April 711 A.D. Shawwal 92 A.H.

The Arabs did not invade Spain: they were invited to do so by a disgruntle group among the Visigothic rulers. Some of them escaped to North Africa and sought the help of Musa bin Nusayr against Roderic, through the intercession of Count Julian. He had conceived a bitter hatred against Roderic because of the ill-treatment of his daughter, Florinda. "It was the custom at that time to rear lads and maidens who were children of the high officials in the king's court; and there was then among the maidens of the king's chamber a daughter of Count Julian, who was very beautiful". Roderic, infatuated with her beauty, once violated her chastity. She complained to her father about it, who then resolved to avenge his daughter's dishonour. Disguising his real feelings, the Count visited Roderic's court in order to bring his daughter back but without rousing King's suspicions. When taking leave, the king asked him for some African falcons, to which the Count said, "the next time I return to Spain I promise to bring you some hawks the like of which your Majesty has never seen!" Unsuspecting his ill-will, the king could not catch the hint of what Count Julian had planned against him.

Count visited Musa bin Nusayr, the governor of Qayrowan, and invited him to invade Roderic's kingdom and remove him from the throne. He also told Musa that valuable booty and beautiful captives could be acquired in Spain. He thus planned to avenge his daughter's wrong. On his part, Musa was willing to comply with the Count's wishes. But before launching his invasion, he sought Khalifa Walid's permission. Khalifa was at first reluctant to grant the permission, for he did not like to send his troops across the sea into an unknown land. At last he gave his consent to his governor's request. With this opened a new chapter in the history of Islam and of Spain.

Musa first decided to probe the situation in this country. Accordingly, in July, 710, he first sent a small force of about four hundred men under the command of one of his Berber freedmen, named Tariq to reconnoitre southern Spain, nearest to North Africa. Tariq landed at a place on the southern coast of which later came to be known after him as Jabal al-Tariq. On his return, he reported that conditions were suitable in the country for sending a force. So, Musa sent an army of seven thousand men, all Berbers except 300 Arabs, to invade Spain under the command of his trusted Berber freedman named Tariq bin Ziyad, in April, 711 A.D.

Tariq's troops crossed the narrow starlit between Spain

and North Africa in four boats provided by Count Julian. They landed at a rocky promontory on the southern coast of Spain to the east of the city of Algeciras, The place later came to be known as Jabl at-Tariq, the Rock of Tariq or Gibraltar in English. The Arab army then marched on Algeciras, which they captured without any difficulty. It became the base of their campaign. Being informed of Spanish preparation, Musa reinforced Tariq's army with another 5000 troops, almost all Berbers. Tariq had thus twelve thousand men under his command before he advanced further into Spain. At this critical juncture, Roderic was engaged in a campaign against the Basque rebels in the extreme north of his kingdom. On hearing of Tariq's landing, he summoned his vassals to a war against the Arabs. He thus collected a large army, variously estimated from 25,000 to 100,000 strong. According to Ibn Khaldun, the number was 40,000 men. With this large force, Roderic marched against the invaders. The two armies came face to face with each other on the banks of river, Barbate.

Barbate Battle: On meeting the Arab troops, Roderic started hostilities. His army was about four times larger than that of the Muslims, and was fighting on its own soil. Obviously, the contest was unequal. Knowing his numerical weakness, Tariq roused the morale of his troops.

Tariq was right: though Roderic's army was larger, there was disaffection among his troops. His two wings were commanded by Witiza's partisans. Unaware of all this, but eager to give battle to the invaders, King Roderic crossed the river and engaged the Muslims on their side of the river. The battle lasted for about a week. At a critical moment, Witiza's sons and brothers deserted the King along with their men and joined Count Julian, the Arabs' ally. The Arabs attacked with redoubled fury and routed Roderic's army. Most of his horsemen fled across the river, but many of them were drowned in it. King

Roderic also fled from the battle-field and was heard no more. Perhaps he too was drowned in the river while crossing it. The Arabs had won a victory. They captured many thousand of the fleeing Visigoths and a huge booty. Visigothic army was shattered and offered little or no resistance to Arab advance.

What he received in reply was a rebuke. Musa warned him against any further advance and ordered him to stay where he was till Musa had joined him. Really, when he sent Tariq, he had thought that he would, at best, win an indecisive victory and would call for help. Instead, Tariq had won a resounding victory, which Musa had himself expected to win. Tariq and his Berber troops had captured vast spoils. Musa sent letter to Tariq and ordered him to stay where he was and wait till he had joined him.

Maghith ar-Rumi commanded the detachment which marched on Cordova, he conquered the city after two months of resistance by its Gothic defenders.

The second detachment, under Qais bin Qesadi, marched towards Elvira and captured it. Next captured Malaga and thus reopened the way to North Africa and Qayrowan.

Muslims appointed Jews as their administrators and left a garrison to help the administrators in maintaining peace and order. In fact, Jews and common people welcomed the Muslims. They opened the gates of their cities to welcome the Muslims as their liberators from Gothic oppression. Where there were no Jews, the Muslims appointed one of the Hispano-Romans as administrator, because they too were disaffected.

Conquest of Toledo: Toledo lay in the centre of the central highlands. Being the capital of the Visigothic kingdom, it was expected that they would resist Tariq stoutly. But as usual, the common people and Jews were ready to welcome the Arabs.

Tariq offered the Christian defenders highly favourable terms, so they opened its gates without fighting. According to the terms, all inhabitants surrendered their weapons and horses to the Muslims. Those who wished to leave the city were allowed to do so, while those who elected to stay were assured the security of life and property. They were free to worship in their own way. Nothing was taken from them: there were no captives and no slavery. Only they were required to pay Jazia, or poll-tax. Tariq captured the treasures of the Gothic rulers including the golden table, reputed to be the table of Solomon.

Handing over the administration of Toledo to Bishop Oppas, a brother of the former king, Witiza, Tariq advanced towards Guadalajara in the north-eastern region of Spain. Musa invaded Spain.

Other Conquests:

The battle of Guadlete frightened the Christians to face the Muslim army in open combat. It gave a deadly blow to the socio-political structure of the Visigoths. Elvira and Archidona were subduced. Tariq advanced towards Toledo, the Gothic capital through Ejica which capitulated easily.

Thus the whole of Spain, Valencia, Almeria with its capital Orihuela, held by Theodonier were brought to subjection. Theodonier was however allowed to retain his governorship on payment of tributes and loyalty to the Muslim government. Toledo fell without much resistance. By the end of 711 A.D. almost half of Spain including the central and eastern part of the country was conquered by Tariq.

Tariq captured Sadonia, Cadiz, Almadover, an important city in the west of Cordonia. Carmona 25 miles from Seville was subjugated. Seville however entered into a peace treaty by paying tribute and protection tax with loyalty to the Khalifa.

The Christian aristocracy had collected a big force at Eliga. The battle of Eliga was the second great. Eliga was subjugated. The Christians moved to Toledo for the second test.

The subjection of cities was obligatory for the conquerors to provide the subjects with all facilities of basic needs, Eliga was newly conquered, the Muslims had not set up their administrative foot firmly, yet they were not unmindful of their duties to humanity.

Tariq dug a canal known as Ayn Tariq from the adjoining river, four miles away only to meet the basic human need.

Tariq left for Cordova with Mughis-al-Rumi and staying there for nine days advanced towards Toledo, leaving the command in the hands of Mughis.

Guided by a shepherd, Mughis reached the walls of the fort. One soldier climbed the fig tree by the side of the wall and dropped the rope which helped others climb the wall. The soldiers opened the gate and entered the city. Cordova was thus annexed, in October 712 A.D.

Fall of Jaliqa and Asturias paved the way for the annexation of Toledo. Tariq then marched to Guadala-Jara, a hilly tract. He crossing it passed through a hillpass known as Fajj. Tariq reached Maeda and got possession of the Book and Rehl said to have been the Book of Soloman. He reached Galicia after annexing Maya. It was here that he heard the arrival of Musa. He therefore returned to Toledo to receive him.

Musa and Tariq: Let us now return to Musa once again. A month after the capture of Merida in July 713, Musa marched not against the Goths but against his insubordinate lieutenant, Tariq, in order to put a bridle on him. The two met in August, 713, at a place near Talavera to the west of Toledo, on the river Tagus, where Tariq had moved to meet his master. Tariq had been sitting idle at Toledo, because Musa had ordered him not to march against the Goths any further. He thus hoped to conquer North Spain and to show the Khalifa that he had the honour to subdue far greater part of Spain than Tariq did. When the two met at Talavera, Tariq descended from his horse and marched on foot to Musa still on his horse. Musa was furious and hurled abuses at him and demanded why did he not obey the orders of his superior? "Why did you enter and penetrate the land without my orders? I only sent you to make a foray and then return." Tariq remained calm and restraint and pointed out that military situation required his advance, which Musa would have himself approved if he had known it, and that he did this all for the glory of Islam. He added further that he had captured large spoils in the service of Islam and said, "I am only of your subordinate commanders. Whatever I had gained and conquered is in your name and will be counted as your achievement." Musa was to some extent pacified by Tariq's conciliatory reply and both then repaired to Toledo.

It was in Rajab 93 A.H., June 712 A.D., that Musa with 18000 troops landed in the island of Khizra, Algeciras. Count Julian also joined him with other Gothic Princes. Musa took the north western-coastal route and conquered Mediara Sidonica, Carmona and Swiller, the seat of the Government under the Romans. Nicha (Huelva), Bija and Merida were also annexed, in June 713 A.D. He then moved to Toledo to meet Tariq where a grand reception was awaiting him.

Musa and Tariq, then marched towards Aragon. Count Fortun the governor of Argon embraced Islam and was allowed to continue in his office. Several other cities like Saragossa, Barcelona, Asturica, Legio and Amaya, the capital of Cantabria were annexed. The whole of Spain was subjugated. Barcelona, Pamplona, Lerida, Huesca, Geronaand Tortona acknowledging the Muslim sovereignty agreed to pay tribute in lieu of internal freedom.

Musa and Tariq, conquered Languidoc Narbone, Avignon (Avennis) Lubdun and Lyon.

Pepin of the Carolingian Qarlab, being defeated by the Muslims, took refuge in the frontier cities on the Rhone.

Musa was planning to annex the whole of southern Europe and was awaiting the approval of the Khalifa Walid. Unfortunately the Khalifa was losing his health fastly and the news of the army's hardships in Narbone had told further upon his health. He therefore did not approve of the proposal of Musa to return to Damascus through Europe and Asia Minor after subjugating the South-Eastern Europe.

Musa therefore turned to North-Western Spain and compelling the guerillas to surrender persued Pelayo the guerilla chief who had taken refuge in Covadonga the rocky defiles of Austurias who however escaped and proved a menace in future.

MUSA AND TARIQ LEFT FOR DAMASCUS

Only three years after their landing on the coast of south Spain, Tariq and Musa were recalled to Damascus by the orders of Khalifa al-Walid in the autumn of 714. They reached Damascus in February, 715, leading a long train of camels, loaded with vast treasures and beautiful damsels of Spain, the daughters of the Visigothic kings and nobles, whom they presented to the Khalifa and his nobles as their *kanizees*. It is, however, an unsolved riddle why did al-Walid recall his generals who were even then winning brilliant victories in Spain and were preparing to advance on the Frankish kingdom of the Merovingians? Al-Walid died before Musa and Tariq reached

Damascus. His successor, Sulaiman, received them coolly and treated them harshly. They were soon disgraced and thrown into a dungeon. This treatment is also inexplicable. Sulaiman favoured the Yemani tribes and Musa was a Yemeni, Arabi. After Sulaiman's death, Musa and Tariq were released by the next Khalifa, Umar II, but they were not honoured. They were last seen begging in the streets of Damascus and died in obscurity. Thus did the Umayyads reward their great generals who had extended their empire from Sind to Spain a veritable tri-continental empire, indeed, the largest in the history of Islam.

Arabs Speedy Conquest: Tariq's and Musa's victories in Spain were spectacular. Both of them were brave soldiers and competent generals. However the Arabs' victories were also helped by the weaknesses of the Visigothic kingdom, which we have analysed in the previous chapter. The Jews were hostile to the Visigoths due to the Catholic Church, the common people in the towns and villages, were doubly oppressed both by the nobles and the bishops. Lastly, a civil war raged between Roderic, and the sons and family of the previous king, Witiza, which led to the Arab intervention. After their initial resistance in the battle on the river Guadalete, the Visigoths put up no further resistance anywhere in the Peninsula. On the contrary, many a townspeople themselves opened the gates and welcomed the Arabs as their liberators from Visigothic tyranny. The Jews, the merchant class of the kingdom, who had suffered cruelly at the hands of the Visigothic kings and bishops, also joined their compatriots in welcoming the Arabs, who rescued them from centuries of the Christian persecutions. Real losers were the Visigothic nobles: they lost their all. Only a few of them escape to Asturias, in the extreme north-western corner of the Peninsula. If Tariq's victorious advance had not been checked by the Khalifa's orders, he would have captured the whole of Asturias. But Arab history is filled with strange quirks of fate. Musa and

Tariq's sudden recall saved Asturias for the Christians. From there, afterwards they launched their attacks against the Muslims, as we shall describe later on.

The Effects: We shall now briefly describe the families of those Gothic nobles who themselves or their descendants accepted Islam and played a great role in the history of Islamic Spain.

When Musa was recalled, the Count, as also the sons and partisans of Witiza, the former king of Spain, accompanied him. Khalifa Sulaiman received Count Julian with great honours. He was similarly treated by the Arabs when he returned to Spain. Vast lands were conferred upon him, which remained in the possession of his descendants. Count Julian remained Christian and so did his son, Peter. But his grandson became a Muslim and adopted the name of Abdullah. Count Julian's family always remained popular among the Spanish Muslims.

Another group of the Christian supporters of the Arabs, the sons and family members of the king, Witiza, were also greatly honoured by them. His son, Achila, was granted a thousand villages in eastern Spain, where he lived happily ever after. Bishop Oppas, a brother of the king, was appointed as the first governor of Toledo after Tariq captured it. Artabast became the Christian Count of Cordova. The title was transmitted to his Muslim descendant, named Abu Sa'id. Another son of Witiza, named Almund, became the count of Seville and was allotted a thousand villages as his estate in south-eastern Spain. He had a daughter Sara and two sons. When he died, his brother, Artabast, tried to seize his lands from his children. But Khalifa Hisham intervened and restored the properties to his children. Nevertheless, Artabast always remained as a counsellor of the rulers of Cordova. When Abdur Rahmen I became the Amir of Cordova, Artabast also won his favours and retained the title of the count and of the lands. Princess Sara, the niece of Artabast, was a brave lady. When her uncle seized her property on the death of her father, she decided to put her case before the Khalifat at Damascus. Though a girl of eighteen, she chartered a ship and sailed from Spain to Syria and appealed to Khalifa Hisham for justice who granted her suit. After winning her case, she married a young Arab noble, named Isa Bin Azahim and came back to Spain with him. Among her descendants were both Muslims and Christians. Long after, one of her descendants, named Mary, became the mother of Abdur Rahman III, one of the greatest rulers of Islamic Spain. This showed the tolerance of the Muslim rulers towards their Christian subjects. When Musa and Tariq conquered Saragossa, a powerful Gothic noble, Count Fortunia of Tarazona and Bojra, near Tudela, came over to Islam, They too retained their extensive possessions along the right bank of the river Ebro for about two centuries. In fact, during this period, they became the defenders of the Upper March (*Thaghr al-Aqsa*) of Islamic Spain. In the fratricidal wars of the Arabs, Banu Qazi sided with the Modarite faction as against the Yemenites. When the Umayyad Caliphate became weak, Banu Qazi ruler, Musa II, governed Saragossa as an autonomous prince. As in other cases, the Muslim Banu Qazi intermarried with the Christian nobles in their neighbourhood, who ruled the valleys between the Ebro and the Pyranees.

The Arab conquest of Visigothic Spain ushered in a social revolution. First of all, the privileged classes of the Visigothic nobles, and clergy lost completely their former power. Almost all the nobles lost their lands, who then became peasant proprietors. This change gave a boost to agricultural production, which had languished under the Visigoths. It was one reason why agriculture flourished so much in Muslim Spain.

The Jews benefited most from Muslim conquest. Though

once a flourishing community under the Visigoths, the Jews had suffered much persecution at the hands of the bigoted Bishops and other churchmen and were driven out of the country in thousands. The Muslim conquerors, however, granted them protection and security from all kinds of persecutions and granted them freedom of worship and trade. The Jews were often appointed to high positions under the new rulers. As traders and merchants, they became once again a very prosperous community in the country.

The lot of the serfs also improved. They became peasant proprietors,. As Muslims they became equal of their masters. Many of them even migrated to towns, where they became artisans and craftsmen. Moreover, as owners of the lands they tilled, they worked hard and increased agricultural production, which made Muslim Spain a prosperous country.

The settlement of Muslims, the erection of mosques and buildings; the division of the country into various provinces, and districts for administrative purposes left no doubt in the minds of the Visigoths that their downfall was permanent and the Muslims were the masters.

The Muslim laws of toleration, equality, fraternity, justice and equity, universal brotherhood, recognition of basic human rights, abolition of Roman system of slavery, freedom of speech religious freedom and the right of appeal even against the highest, were promulgated. New churches were built. The Jews had their own sinagogues to perform their religious ceremonies without any hindrance. Both the Jews and Christians were governed by their own religious laws by their own judges appointed by the Amirs.

GOVERNORS
Abdul Aziz-bin-Musa
(713 AD.—715 AD.)

Musa in obedience to the royal call hurried to the Capital appointing his son Abdul Aziz as Amir (Governor) of Spain.

Abdul Aziz had outlined such an administrative system which ensured the permanency of the newly conquered land. Bearing well in mind the causes of the defeat of Roderick, he won the hearts of the people by introducing the Islamic principles in letter and spirit. He shaped the entire social and political structure on Islamic democratic principles.

Abdul Aziz set up an advisory council consisting of pious and able persons from amongst the communities other than Muslims also. It framed rules and regulations for the estate-income and expenditure. It could levy taxes upto 12 dirhams a years.

Judicial and criminal courts were headed by Judges. Muslim laws governed the country. The non-Muslims however were governed in religious matters by their own heads appointed by the Amir.

The land reformation act was the landmark in the history of Spain. Tenancy right was given to the peasants. Irrigation system was organized a new to yield better and more standard-crop. The revenue was mild and the collection method was easy. In case of failure of crops special remission was allowed to the cultivators.

Trade and industry were specially encouraged. The problem of bread and butter was so nicely solved that the basic need was available for all. The national exchequer therefore became very sound and strong.

Hospitals, education centres, inns and rest houses were run by the government for the people and were free.

The administration of the country was so logical just and impartial that no room for complaints was left for any.

The table however turned with the accession of Sulaiman bin-Abdul Malik who regarded the son of Musa a menace for him.

Abdul Aziz's marriage with Egilona (Um-e-Asim) the widow of Roderick gave an opportunity for his opponents to prepare a case against him. Sulaiman who disliked him from the very beginning got him beheaded by Habib-ibne-Ubaida while saying his prayer and his head was presented to Musa in prison, Rajab 97 A.H.

Ayub-bin-Habib Lakhmi
(August 716 A.D.)

After Abdul Aziz when Spain was without any Amir, rebellion broke out at many places so, the Muslims elected Ayub the nephew of Musa (sister's son) as Amir in Zil-Hajj 97 or in.

Ayub was a seasoned soldier and tried lieutenant of Musa. He changed the capital from Seville to Cordova. With the opening of schools, colleges and libraries. Cordova became the seat of learning which later on became the renowned university of Europe. In Courts justice was done according to Muslim laws. Special attention was given to the construction of new buildings which marked the Hispano-Arab architecture. Military cantonments were set up for the establishment of peace in the cities. He established peace and punished the murderer of Abdul Aziz. Corrupt officials were brought to books.

He made a tour of the country, contacted the people ranks and removed the elements of discontent.

He could not satisfy the hatred of Sulaiman because of his being a near relation of Musa. His election was therefore not approved by the Khalifa and Hur-bin-Abdur-Rahman Saqfi was appointed in his place.

Hur-bin-Abdur-Rahman Saqfi (716 AD.—718 A.D.)

Hur was incapable administrator. Both the Christians and the Muslims were annoyed of him for his injustice and un-scheduled high-handedness. It was due to his bad administration that Pelayo an officer of Rodericks' army who was a hostage in Cordova, fled away. He defeated Alqama at Covadonga (718 A.D/98 A.H.) and established an independent estate in Asturias. The Khalifa Abdul Aziz dismissed him for his bad administration and despotic rule.

Samah-bin-Malik-Alkhulani (718 A.D.—721 A.D.)

Samah was appointed Governor of Spain by Umer bin-Abdul Aziz, the Khalifa. He was kind, just, impartial and an one-eyed statesman. He freed all innocent persons. He compensated them both in kind and cash.

Samah reviewed the entire revenue system and introduced easy positive measures for the improvement of national exchequer. He made a census of the country which not only indicated the population but also a detailed account of trade, industry, chief crops and area of arable and non-arable land. Irrigation system was improved to ensure better yield. A survey of the mineral products was also made and was organized in a manner which enriched the country all the more. To facilitate the communication; roads and bridges were repaired with new additions. The bridge of Cordova was reconstructed. A grand mosque was built in Saragossa.

Septimania a dependency of the Visigothic kingdom was annexed, 720 A. D. It was known as the country of seven cities— Narbona, Agde, Bezier, Iodeve, Carcassone, Nimes and' Maguelone. He suffered martyrdom in the battle of Toulous (Talushaha).

Abdur-Rahmen-bin-Abdullah Ghafiqui (721 A D.)

After the martyrdom of Samah the army nominated Abdur Rehman as Amir, who saved tactfully the army in the battle of Toulouse to the utter dismay of the Duke of Aquitaine.

He was very popular in the army. He however fell a victim. He ruled over Spain only for six months.

Anbass-bin-Sahim Kalbi (721 AD.—725 A.D.)

Anbasa was a wise administrator and brave soldier. After the assumption of office he engaged himself in setting right the internal affairs of the country. He ended the local intrigues and punished the intriguers in time.

He persuaded the large number of Muslim families of Africa and Syria to settle down in Spain to balance the population. The Berbers were specially settled, Agricultural lands were given to them to adopt agriculture as a profession.

After resolving the internal disorder, Anbasa quelled the rebellion of the Province of Tac-Aconna. He, crushing the Christians in the Rhone valley swayed over layons. The beautiful French city Biyons was also annexed, and Burgandy was swayed over.

The annexation of Carcasoma was a great blow to Southern France. A treaty was however signed and the Christians agreed to pay annual tribute to the Muslim government with the following, conditions:—

1. Half of Carcassona was to be governed by the Muslim government of Narbanna. The other half under the direct supervision of Narbonne government. The protection Tax was to be paid annually, and they had to remain loyal to the Muslim government both in time of war and peace.

2. The Province of Septimania was also annexed. His mild and just treatment with the hostages and prisoners captivated the hearts of the Christians which strengthened the Muslim position in Southern France all the more.

It was in September 725 A.D. that the city of Autun in North West France, was conquered.

While returning to the capital, the Muslims were attacked stealthily from the rear and Anbassa fell fighting in the field (Shaban 107 A.H., January 726 A.D.) according to Arabs.

After the martyrdom of Anbasa the governorship became a bone of contention for the Arab settlers in the newly conquered country. Some five persons assumed the office one after the other but all proved a failure. (a) Azra-bin-Abdullah Fahri remained in office for a few months (725 A.D. (2) Yahya-bin-Salma (107 A.H/725 A.D.) was deposed (3) Usman-bin-Ali Ibaida (109 A.H/726 A.D.) elected by the army, remained in the office for five months only. (4) Usman-bin-Abi Nasa Khasami (110 A.H./727) A.D. and Huzaifa-bin-Ahwas Qaisi (111 A.H./728 A.D.) were deposed, while Haisam-bin-Ubaid Kalabi, (111 A.H./729 A.D.) was killed by Banu Kalb.

Muhammad-bin-Abdullah Ashjaii (111 A.H./729 A.D.)
remained in office for a few months only.

Abdur Rahman al-Ghafiqi
(731-732)

Abdur Rahman al-Ghafiqi was appointed as the governor
of the province in 731 by Khalifa Hisham. The changing of the
governor was to maintain law and order. During these years of
anarchy, Pelayo the Gothic noble who had taken refuge in the
mountains of Astruous acquired great strength.

The people of Spain were worried on the disorders of the
province so they hailed the appointment of Abdur Rahman. He
was the most patriotic governor the province ever had under
the Umayyad Khalifas. He was also a military commander. He
had equal influence with both the Modhar and Yemeni Arabs
in the province. The people and soldiers loved him because of
his gentle spirit and justice.

First Abdur Rahman turned his attention to the
administration of the province. He toured various cities and
heard the complaints of the people. He dismissed the careless
officers and appointed competent persons. He restored the
churches to the Christians which had been seized by the
Muslims.

Battle of Tours

Abdur Rahman was a genius. He explored a new route to
the West of the Pyrenees for the conquest of Europe. In 732
A.D. he crossing Pamplona entered France through
Roncesvalles' pass. Arabs on the Rhone capitulated after a tough
resistance. Bordeux, Burgandy, Lyon, Basancon and Sens were
also annexed.

Eudus being defeated on the bank of the Carrone reached Poitiers and moved northward to the vicinity of Tours. Poitiers was 62 miles from Tours. Eudues had entered into an alliance with the Frankish king Charles the son of Pepin of Heristal. He collected a huge army and met the Muslim army on Saturday, October 732 A. D. 114 A.H. on the plain between Tours and Poitiers at the bank of the loire. Abdur Rahman, following the technique of the Battle of Uhad had posted a fair number of his troops at strategic points with dear instructions to the soldiers not to leave their positions at any cost. The Christians had almost lost the field but the greedy Berbers forgetting the order, engaged in collecting the booty. This proved fatal and the dislocated troops were attacked from the rear. Thus the Muslims lost the win. Abdur Rahman could not re-assemble his troops to order, and he fell fighting in the field. In the middle of October 732 the army of Abdur Rahman reached the river Loire two hundreds kilometers away from Pads the capital of France. Suddenly there Frankish force confronted him having marched south stealthily without the Arabs being aware of their approach. The exact site of the battle field is now unknown. The Muslim army consisted of Arabs and Barbers with the Berbers being more numerous. The Muslim camp was at some distance from the battlefield. The camp was full of the captives including beautiful Frenkish women, whom the Arabs had captured and great booty, plundered from the churches and moasteries, which contained large quantities of gold and other precious goods, donated to them by generations of worshippers.

The battle lasted for seven days. The first five days, however were spent in skirmishes. On the sixth day, fighting began in night earnest and raged the whole day: the combatants parted only when the darkness of night made fighting difficult. Next day the battle was renewed early morning with redoubled fury. By midday, the Muslims were winning. But in the afternoon, an event occurred which turned the tables on them. Someone in the Muslim army rained the alarm that the Muslim soldiers quitted fighting and rushed to the camp to save their plundered booty. Their general Abdur Rehman pleaded with them not to stop fighting, but no one paid heed to him. At this critical juncture, a frank attacked Abdur Rehman with his lance and killed him. The death of their commander dishearted the remaining Muslim army and it withdrew to its camp. Night had already fallen which prevented the Franks from pursuing them. During, the night, furious disputes broke out the Muslim commanders and their soldiers. No commander of the stature of Abdur Rehman was left. Most commanders, more worried about their booty, decided to flee from the battlefield in the darkness of the night rather than to flight the Franks next day. Among them the disorderly Berbers were in majority. In short the Muslims broke their camp and fled across the Pyrenees.

Charles and his Franks moved next day towards the Muslim camp with great caution, believing that the stillness in the Muslim camp might be a stratagem of war. But when they found the camp empty, their joy was boundless: they had won a battle which they were about to lose. Some of the Frankish commanders wanted to pursue the fleeing enemy. But the cautious Charles Martel forbade them. The Franks, instead, fell upon the wounded Muslims and killed them in cold blood. Thus ended the battle of Tours on the 23rd of October, 732.

Abdul Malik-bin-Qatn Fahri
(732–734 A.D.)

Abdul Malik-bin-Qatn Fahri was no fit person. He could neither end the internal administrative disorder nor could lead his expedition to France successfully.

Aqbabin Hajjaj Sloohi
(735-738 A.D.)

Aqba-bin-Hajjaj Slooli took the reins of the government after the deposition of Qatn Fahri.

For the re-establishment the strength of Muslim arms he fortified the strategic points and annexed important cities, Volence, Trois Chateaux and Donzre and threatened the central part of France. Aqba faced heroically the combined forces of Charles Martel and Liuprand, king of the Lombards. The Christian forces while retreating adopted the escorthearth policy and burnt a number of important cities, to ashes. Aqba was however not dejected but his recall to Africa by Ubaidullah the Governor General of Africa to put down the serious insurrection of the Berbers, gave relief to the Christians.

Abdul Malik-bin-Qatn Fahri
(739–742 A.D.)

Second time Abdul Malik took over the administration for the country. The Berbers of Aragon, Galicia and Estre Medora were ready for revolt. Besides, Alfanso the son-in-law of Pelayo, taking advantage of the internal disorder in the Muslim Camp had made himself master of Galacia. Abdul Malik was planning to punish him but the Berbers revolt had to be crushed first which threatened, the very existence of the empire. One contingent of the Berber force was to attack Cordova, the other on Toledo and the third on Al-Jazra. Hisham-bin-Abdul Malik had despatched a strong contingent of 30 thousand soldiers to Africa to chastise the Berbers, but Kulsoom-bin-Ayaz the Syrian commander was killed. The next commander Balj Bin Bashar confined himself in the fort of Sibta. Later on to avoid the Berbers he forced his way into Spain with his Syrian troops. His entry into Spain was however allowed by Abdul Malik on

some conditions. The Berbers in the mean time had resolved to
drive away the Arabs from the Peninsula to establish a Berber
Kingdom. The Berbers with the help of Balj were defeated.
Balj however became a menace and refused to leave Spain and
keep up the contract. Abdul Malik now had to face a new trouble.
The defeated Berbers formed an alliance with Balj and Salaba.
Abdul Malik was defeated by Balj in the battle at Martoola and
took refuge in Cordova, The people of Cordova opened the city
gate treacherously and Balj occupied the city. Abdul Malik was
hanged on the bridge of Cordova. Balj now declared himself
Amir of Spain.

Balj-bin-Bashar Qusairi
(742–742 A.D.)

The Syrians and the Berbers both were against Balj. A
large number of Syrians were with Salaba. Ummayya bin Abdul
Malik and Abdur Rahman-bin Aqba supported by their Berber
friends marched to Cordova with a troop of 20 thousand. A
fierce battle was fought near the fort of Rahlia and Balj was
killed by Abdur Rahman with the deadly strike of his spear.
Salaba however, to get rid of Abdur Rahman the claimant of
the governorship, despatched one contingent to Marida and one
to Cordova and declared himself as Governor of Spain on the
point of sword.

Salaba-bin-Salama Alameli
(742–743 A.D.)

Salaba was a very cruel man. His hatred towards the Arabs
was exemplary. Salaba was responsible for the general-massacre
of a large number of eminent Arabs and their families. He was
however deposed by Hanzala-bin-Safvan Kalbi the Governor
General of Africa.

Abdul Khattar Husam-bin-Zarrar Kalbi
(743–746 A.D.)

The whole of Muslim Spain was the hotbed of civil war and anarchy. So Abdul Khattar took over the reins of the government.

He devoted himself to the restoration of peace and order on stable basis. Slaba along with turbulent chiefs was exiled to Africa. In order to end the tribal rivalries and jealousness he allocated different cities for each rival group and kept the various tribes engaged in their own affairs. The Palestinian were settled in Sidonia and Algeciras. The district of Regio was reserved for the Jordanians and Elvira for the Syrians of Damascus. The Qinnisrians and Emessaians were settled in the districts of Jean, Nsiebla and Sevill. The Egyptians were rehabilitated in Beja and Murcia. This new rehabilitation policy brought to an end the frequent exchange of swords between the various rival groups.

There was an underground selfish and mischievous group headed by Sumail-bin-Hatim who was a claimant for the governorship of Siragossa. He belonged to the tribe of Qais while Sumail came from Banu Kalb. Sumail therefore fanned up the tribal jealousy. Umayya and Qatn the sons of Abdul Malik-bin Qatn were also trying to regain their lost power. Sawaba-bin-Salma Haddani was also working against Khattar.

Khattar was guilty of undue favouritism to his friends and supporters and that he had compelled the judge to change the judgement in favour of convict. The efforts of Khattar to win failed. The rebels in the meantime had nominated Sawaba as their Amir. Khattar leaving Cordova advanced to punish Sumail. Khattar was defeated in the battle of Secunda and killed.

Yousuf-bin-Abdur Rahman Alfahri
(747–756 A.D.)

Spain was gutted with the fire of tribal jealousy and civil war. Yousuf bin-Abdur Rahman commanded respect and confidence of the people, his previous records were fine and heroic. It was he who could finalize the treaty with Duke of Marseilles. He had defended heroically the attacks of Charles Martle against Narbone.

He had his own independent neutral policy and believed in justice and toleration.

Yousuf however had to face new miscreants. Yahya son of Haris, a claimant of the governorship was appeased by the award of governorship of Regio. His removal from office, for his maladministration, brought a very fierce civil war in its bag. Abdul Khattar also was on the side of Yahya. Peace was however concluded with the effort of Yousuf and Sumail. The Amir was to be elected only once a year. Sumail refused to accept a Yamanite as Amir. Yousuf being an honest man tried to abide by the treaty but was helpless before Sumail. He therefore leaving the office went to Eluria. Alfahri at the request of Sumail assumed the office of the Governor once again. The battle of Secanda was so fierce that the streets of Cordova even, were turned into a stream of blood. Khattar and Ibne Haris were killed and Alfahri became a popular governor.

Sumail ruled the country through Alfahri. To get rid of such treacherous persons, Alfahri packed Sumail away to Saragossa as governor and Ahmad-bin-Amir as the chief of Seville. This chamberlain-policy did not prove effective and Alfahri could not save the country from internal disorders. Amir Abdani a prominent chief of Cordova and Hubab Zahri, another chief of Saragossa were supporters of the Abbasides. Saragossa was besieged (753 A.D.) and Sumail was helpless. Abdullah bin-Ali a chief of the Kalb tribe hurried to the help of Sumail and was also joined by Sulaiman the chief of this Bani Ka'ab. Four hundred Mudarites also came out to help Sumail. Amir Abdari and Hubab Zahri had to raise the siege (755 A.D.)

The new-Muslim class was in majority constituting the whole of the productive classes. The economy of the country was controlled by this class. A considerable group of new-Muslims in the towns belonged to rich and noble families. The Arabs for their superiority complex and the Berbers for their nature and conquest-complex hated the Muslim converts and did not condescend to recognize their equality in status-social or political. Moreover conversion was discouraged— a clear breach of Muslim law—due to the fear of loss to the treasury. In some cases the protection tax was collected from the converts on the false plea of hypocrisy clearly opposed to the shariat and sunna. Neither the governor of Spain nor the Governor General of Africa and not even the Khalifa could control the situation. The grave situation could have been averted for the good, had the Khalifa followed the policy of Umer-bin-Abdul Aziz, Sharih-bin Hayan the governor of Egypt tried in vain to convince Umer for levying sea tax of new-Muslims pleading heavy loss to the treasury, Umer told him point-blank that Islam was more dear to him than the state-bank. Simultaneously Hajaj the Governor of Iraq was ordered to reduce the Jazya almost to nullity. The annual revenue then was only two crores and 80 lacs but it increased to twelve crores and 40 lacs with practical and sincere development projects. Thus the people were happy and contented.

Arabs intoxicated with vain vanity, unmindful of the consequences, invited trouble both for themselves and the country, by incurring the displeasure of the new-Muslims. Their sons were called sons of the slaves. Lucrative and responsible posts were reserved for the Arabs and Berbers. They therefore revolted which worried the government all the more.

The Khalifa of Damascus failed to unite the various rival groups. The period (732 to 755 A.D. was the period of anarchy and disorder and as many as 15 Governors were appointed, Alfanso I of Austrias taking advantage of the internal troubles compelled the Arabs to withdraw from nearly quarter of the country.

The Umayyad caliphate in Syria was encircled by the Abbaside movement. On June 9, 947 A.D. the long-planned revolt broke-out when Abu Muslim of Khurasan in coalition with Abdul-Abbas, unfurled the black banner and entered Marw, the capital of Khurasan. The Governor Nasr-Ibne-Sayyar, getting no aid from Marwan II, had to yield. The battle of the Zab, a tributory of the Tigris, January, 750A.D. sealed the fate of the Syrian empire and Abdul Abbas enthroned himself as Khalifa.

The Christians were planning to overthrow the newly conquered land on one hand, and the Arab chiefs of Spain on the other were intriguing against Alfahri to win the favour of Al-Abbas. The letter of Ibne-Amr to the Abbaside- Khalifa was timely detected by Yousuf Alfahri which foiled the hopes of Amr to get the governor's chair.

Christians availing of the opportunity had raised their heads. Pepin, the short son and successor of Charles Martel attacked the Muslim zone in 752 A.D. The Franks plundered the Muslim cities of Agde, Beziers and Lodov They killed the Muslims regardless of sex, and age, Mosques schools, hospitals and welfare centres were burnt to ashes. Narbone was captured by the Franks (759 A.D.) The loss of Muslim possessions in France was followed by the withdrawal from the hilly parts of northern Spain, Pelayo, taking advantage of the engagement of the Muslims in civil war in Spain, established the kingdom of the Austurias. Their stability in France was already threatened by Charles Martel and his successors.

Alfahri could not cope with the situation successfully at all points. He was greatly perturbed to hear the news of the attack Abdur Rahman Addakhil on Spain, He was therefore pondering over carving out a new policy which could save his position and power.

Civil Wars:

At the end of this lesson, I shall discuss over the role of Berber's revolt in Spanish history and discuss on the civil wars of Spain (Islamic).

Berber revolt : The Berbers in Spain had come, as we said in the previous chapter, with Tariq bin Ziyad. They too had grievances against the Spanish Arabs. Though their share in the conquest of Spain was equal, if not greater, the Arabs had captured lion's share of it. While the Arabs had possessed the fertile valleys and plains in the new province, the Berbers were left with the barren valleys in the highlands of the Peninsula. Then came the Kharijis who incited them to revolt by their egalitarian preachings. The Berber revolt in North Africa and the news of their victory over the Arabs were sufficient to incite the Berbers in Spain to revolt against the Arabs, whom they regarded as tyrants. The Berbers of Galacia, Merida, Talavera and other places combined their forces and marched against Toledo in central Spain, Cordova and Medina Sidonia in the south. Confronted with the Berber rebels, the governor, Abdul Malik, relented in his bitter hatred of the Syrian troops in North Africa. He sent three ships to bring them across the Straits into Spain, but on the promise that once the war with the Berbers was over, they would again return to Africa. The Syrians under Balj ibn Bishr then crossed the Straits and combined their forces with the Arabs in Spain under Abdul Malik and defeated the Berbers in a battle near

Medina Sidonia. Then the combined Arab army drove the Berbers away from Cordova, the Spanish capital. Finally, the Berbers around Toledo were also defeated by the Arabs. The Syrians captured great amount of spoils from the Berbers.

Abdul Malik then reminded Balj and his Syrians of their promise in an agreement with him that they would return to North Africa after revolt of the Spanish Berbers had been crushed. But they had no desire to do so. Abdul Malik then committed a mistake. He refused to provide the Syrians the ships to ferry them over the Straits, as he had promised under the agreement with them. The Syrians revolted, defeated and drove Abdul Malik out of Cordova and proclaimed Balj as the governor on September 20, 741. Abdul Malik had kept a few Syrian chiefs as hostages. One of them, a Yemenite, died in captivity. The Syrian chiefs came to Cordova and demanded Abdul Malik's head for their dead companion. When their governor, Balj, refused to punish the old Abdul Malik, the Yemenite group among the Syrians accused him of favouring Abdul Malik, for he was also a Modarite. Fearing to alienate the support of his Syrian troops, Balj had Abdul Malik killed. This touched off a war between the Syrians and the Spanish Arabs. Besides the death of Abdul Malik, yet another cause of war was the declared intention of the Syrians, the new Arab group, to settle in the fertile valleys of Spain. This was really a war between the old Arab settlers and the new colonisers. But, as it was Arab wont, the civil war between the two Arab groups was fought in the name of the Modarites and the Yemenites of old. It was to decide as to which of them would be the masters of the Peninsula.

The First Civil War:

On the death of Abdul Malik, his sons, Omayya and Qatn, revolted simultaneously at Merida and Saragossa, in the west and east of the Peninsula. They became the leaders of told Spanish Arabs. Their erstwhile enemies, the Berbers, also joined them, not because any love was lost between them, but because the Berbers hope to crush the Syrians first and then fall upon their Arabs allies. The Lakhmite tribe, under Abdur Rahman bin Al Hawa, the governor of Narbonne, joined the Spanish Arabs, Balj, with his 12,000 Syrians, gave battle to the combined Arab and Berber force. He, was wounded and defeated. He returned to Cordova, where he died of his wounds. The Yeminite group among the Syrian then proclaimed Thalaba, a Yemenite as the governor of Spain. He defeated the Arab, and Berber confederates and brought with him 10,000 prisoners to Cordova, where he sold them as slaves; something unprecedented among the Arabs, for they never sold their, fellow-Arab captives as slaves. There upon, the moderates among both the rival parties appealed to Hazala, Governor-General of Qaysowan to appoint a new governor, who would restore peace in the Peninsula. For a new danger had appeared on the northern horizons, viz., the incursion into Islamic Spain by the Christian of the North, who threatened to take advantage of the Muslims dissensions. Hanzala sent a Yemenite, Abdul Khattar, as the new governor with instructions to pecify the Peninsula. He gave state lands to the Syrian; and ordered the Christian serfs to pay their new masters one-third of the State share of the produce. The Syrians rival the Mediness rebels under Abdul Malik, were also induced to return to their lands and live there peacefully. Thus Abdul Malik's descendants, Banu'Judd, settled at Seville and Bani Qasim in the province of Valencia on the coast of eastern Spain. Yet another Medinese elan, the Bani Ahmer descendants of Saad bin Ubayda who was the leader of the Ansar of Medina and a candidate of caliphate immediately after the death of Holy Prophet (peace be upon him) settled in Elvira and became the rulers of Granada, when the whole of the remaining Peninsula had been conquered by the Christians of the north.

Second Civil War

Abdul Khattar ruled for four years. But then a new civil war broke out again among the Qaisite and Kelbite Arabs. It was due to Khattar's character, which was a mixture of opposite now conciliatory now cruel. He acted towards the Qaisites so cruelly that it led to a civil war. Once he ill-treated a Kinanite among the Qaisies. Their chief, Sumay Ibn Hatim bin Shimir, complained to the governor for his bias towards his kinsmen, the Kelbites, and demanded justice for the Kinannite. The governor insulted him and drove him out of his palace in Cordova with the help of his Kelbites, Sumayl got the support of the two Yemenite tribes, Lakhmites and Judhamites on the promise that one of their chiefs would be proclaimed governor. Then the Qaisites, the Lakhmites and Judhamites jointly marched against Abu'l Khattar the governor. In the battle on the banks of the river Guadalete, the governor's Yemenites fought half-heartedly. He was defeated, captured and imprisoned in a prison in Cordova. Thalaba, the chief of the Judhamites, became the new governor. When he died after a year his son Amer claimed Emirate (governorship). But Sumail chose a Qaisite Yousuf bin Abdur Rahman al-Fahri, as the governor, in 747, for he believed that he himself had not prestige enough to be the governor. But it was a dual control because while Yousuf was the governor his decisions were made by Sumayl.

Yousuf dismissed the Yemenite deputy governor of Regio, Yahya Ibn Haraith. He rose in revolt against Yousuf and the Yemenite tribes joined him. Yousuf and Sumail got the support of the Qaisite tribes. The two armies fought a battle at Scunda, opposite Cordova, on the river Quadalquivir. When the Kelbs (Yamenities) were on the point of winning the battle, Yousuf on the advice of Sumail, summoned the common people of Cordova to their support. It was something the Arab rulers of Spain had not done before. But it opened the gate to the common people of the capital into its politics.

Third Civil War : In 750, Yousuf the nominal ruler of Spain asked Sumail to appoint him as the governor of the province of Saragossa. He arrived in Saragossa, accompanied by his clients, his slaves and 200 Syrians. But, instead of wreaking vengeance on the Kelbites (Yemenites) he had to show great mercy and compassion towards them. The reason was the outbreak of a great famine in Spain, which made the life sorrowful of all its people. The famine lasted for five years, caused numerous deaths and reduced the people to great hardship and misery. During a time of calamity, all men are brothers, Yousuf, who had come with the intent to suppress the Kelbites, rendered aid and relief to them, as well as to the Qaisites.

After the end of famine the old rivalry of the two tribes revived. The Yemenites believed that being the first Arabs to come and conquer Spain, they had the right to the supremacy of the province, while the Syrians (Qaisites) being late-comers, were merely intruders and usurpers. An ambitious Qaisite noble, Amir, claimed governorship in 755, because he was appointed to it by the Abbasid Khalifa, who had overthrown the Umayyads in 750. Amir then marched towards Saragossa in order to join the Yemenites, who were in revolt against Sumail. Sumail then appealed to the Qaisite chiefs to support him in his war with their mortal enemies, the Yemenites.

Sumail marched towards Toledo, he received the news of the landing of an Umayyad prince, Abdur Rahman, on the south coast of Spain.

CHAPTER 3

ADMINISTRATION UNDER THE GOVERNOR'S RULE

Cordova : In 719, Cordova became the capital. The Arabs never had a liking for Toledo. It was partly because of its association with the Visigothic rulers, but mainly because it was situated in the arid and bitterly cold highlands of central Spain. Cordova had several advantages. It was situated in the sunny south of Spain, climatically akin to the Middle East and North Africa, the homelands of the Arabs and the Berbers. It was situated in the heart of the fertile basin of the Guadalquivir, or *Al-Andalus* of the Arabs. It was full of flourishing towns and cities. It was much nearer to the port-cities, like Cadiz, Malaga and others, on the southern coast of Spain, which linked Spain to the Muslim East and North Africa both by sea and land routes. During the five centuries Cordova became a great centre of trade and industry, arts and earning, poetry, literature and architecture as we shall describe in subsequent chapters.

Provincial Division : Islamic Spain was divided into five lesser provinces.

1. Andalusia : Andalusia comprised the 'basin of the Guadalquivir and lay between the northern plateau and the sea in the south of the Peninsula. The Arabs called it al-Andalus. It was the name which they used also for the whole of Islamic

Spain, and it was most fertile and flourishing region. Its ports in the south linked it closely with North Africa and even with Qayrowan, Egypt and other eastern lands of the Islamic world.

2. Toledo : It was only a provincial capital in Islamic Spain, for the reasons we have mentioned above. This Province extended from Lusitania to its west, the Mediterranean Sea to its east, the river Douro to its north and the Guadalquivir to its south. It was severely cold for nine months during winter and hot sultry in the three months of summer. The Province of Toledo lay on the upper reaches of the river Tagus. Besides it contained such important towns as Segovia on a tributary of the Douro.

3. Lusitania : It was in the west and Galacia in the north-west corner of the Peninsula. It was situated in the lower reaches of the rivers Tagus and Douro (Duero). Merida, Beja, Lisbon, Coimbra, Astorga, Salamanca were its important towns.

4. Saragossa : The province of Saragona extended from the river Douro to the mountain ranges of the Pyrenees, with Saragossa as its capital, situated on the river Ebro. Under the Umayyad governors it was a base for Muslim invasions of the lands of the Franks. Its important cities were Saragossa, Tortosa, Terragona, Barcelona etc.

5. Septimania : It consisted of seven cities, hence called Septimania, namely Narbonne, Caracasonne, Agde, Nimes, Bezien, Lodeve and Maguelone. The Pyrenees then became the boundary between the Frankish Empire and Islamic Spain. The Franks now and then raided Muslim territories in the province of Saragossa, but most of the time they incited the Christians of the north to revolt against the Muslim rulers.

Social and Demographic Changes in Islamic Spain under the Umayyad Governors : Forty-two year rule of the

Umayyad governors brought about many social and demographic changes in the Peninsula, which greatly determined the evolution and development of the Islamic civilization and culture in the Peninsula.

Islam endeavoured to overcome the conflictive nature of the Arab tribal society by unifying them under its banner. Under the Umayyad Khalifas, however, there was a recrudescence of the pre Islamic tribalism. But it became more fragmentary rather than segmentary i.e. the conflictive element became preponderant over segmentary the co-operative. When they settled in newly conquered lands, they were more liable to quarrel, not only with their rival groups, but also within themselves. It divided the Arab tribes into ever smaller groups. They combined with each other only to establish the hegemony and supremacy of their *pro tempore* alliance. But this alliance was liable to be as transient as the politics of the tribes. Like the tribes, political alliance was so fragile as to split up into component units, whether they were tribes, or clans or subclans. The political alliance was for the purpose of controlling the office of the governor. The Governor-General at Qayrowan and even the Khalifa in the distant Damascus, more often than not, respected the wishes of the victorious alliance of Arab tribes in the kaleidoscope of the Spanish tribal politics; sometimes it was the Kelbites, at other times the Qaisite, sometimes the wider tribal groupings of the Modarites and Himyarites, and at other time, the coalition of the Kelbites and Qaisites as was the Medinite alliance under the governor, Abdul Malik ibn Qatn, because they were the dominant, ruling groups. But whosoever the allies, they were always challenged by their rival tribes or tribal groupings. The result, in any case, was political instability and, consequently, very quick changes of governors: many of them did not hold office for more than couple of months.

Berber tribal system : The Berber tribal system was as

segmentary in organization. And it remained so even after their conquest of Spain. The reason was that the Spanish Berber tribes had freshly come into Spain and their new homeland was in close proximity to their ancestral homeland across the Strait of Gibraltar. The Berber tribes remained as segmentary as they were in Africa before. Moreover, as they were surrounded by the Arab tribes and also by hostile Christians, they were united amongst themselves. There was yet another difference between the two tribal peoples. The Berbers were simple people. Being tantrum tribesmen, when not fighting, they drove their herds of sheep to the mountains in summer and descended into the valleys and plains in winter. Their belief in Islam was simple and they were inclined to follow the saints and visit shrines.

Arab Settlement : The Arabs under Musa bin Nusayr were mostly Yemenite tribes. They were organized into troops to fight in the cause of Islam. They were stationed in separate quarters in the conquered cities or towns, They were meant to fight against the infidels or on expanding the frontiers of Islam. So they were not settled on lands, which were left in the possession of their Christian owners, who were required to land tax and poll tax. From the taxes thus collected in the public treasury, the soldiers of Islam were paid stipends according to their service in the cause of Islam and their ranks. Consequently, the soldiers could not be paid stipends at the old rates. The Yemenite tribes, therefore, demanded that lands should be distributed among them. But at this very time came the Qaisite tribes under Balj bin Bishr from across North Africa. They had come not as soldiers of Islam but as colonisers in Muslim Spain: for they openly declared that they wanted entry to settle on the lands in the Peninsula. That was why their entry into Spain was so bitterly opposed by the Arabs of the first wave, who regarded Spain as their patrimony, for they had conquered it. The internecine wars finally came to an end when Abu'l

Khattar was appointed as governor by the Governor-General of Qayrowan in 743 with the express instructions to reconcile the warring Arab tribes and to pacify them.

The Yemenite of Kelbite Arabs who had come with Musa bin Nusayr also returned to the regions where they were stationed. They settled in these regions permanently.

Biladiun : Most of the Arabs who came into Spain did not bring their women with them. Instead, they married with the native women. In course of time, their descendants were called Biladiun for these Arabs had settled in the various towns and cities.

Muwalladun : They were called *Muwalladun* or the origin of Muwalladun however, lay in an ancient custom among the Arabs. It was an old Arab custom that no outsider could live in an Arab tribe without becoming its client or Maula, (plural Mawali). Many Christians in Muslim Spain accepted Islam and became the Mawali of one or the other Arab tribe. In one sense, it strengthened the tribe, because the number of its warriors increased. But in the long run, it was a source of tension between the Mawali and their Arab patrons, because the Mawali had lesser privileges than the Arabs. For instance, their stipend was lesser than that of the Arabs. Afterwards, the use of the term Mawali ceased, for the distinction between the Arabs and their clients no longer existed. The Mawali then mixed with another class of Muslims in Spain, called Muwalludun or the native born Muslims. The Muwalladun were, therefore, a mixed class. It originated from three different groups of Spanish Muslims. They were, firstly, the descendants of the old Mawali; secondly, the children of the Spanish Christians who accepted Islam; and thirdly, the descendants of the Spanish Christian women, whom the Arab settlers married. As we said above, unlike the Visigothic Germans, the Arab conquerors of Spain did not bring their womenfolk with them, Instead, they took the Spanish Christian women as their wives and concubines. The children of these women were, originally, called Muwalladun or Born-Muslims. In course of time, however, all the three elements came to be known as Muwalludun, as they constituted the majority of the Muslims in Spain, more numerous than the Arabs or Berbers, they dominated the political, economic, commercial and social life in Islamic Spain of the later periods.

Other Citizens : The Jews were freed from the cruel persecutions to which they were subjected by both the Visigothic rulers and their bishops, partly because of their religion and partly because they were a rich mercantile community. The Jews obtained the right to practise their religion freely without any fear of persecution. They re-established contact with Jewish merchant colonies in the cities and towns of North Africa, which enabled the Spanish Jews to carry trade with their fellow-religionists in North Africa and other parts of the Islamic world. Indeed, they became international traders. While the Muslims and Christians fought and killed each other, the Jews carried on trade and commerce peacefully, becoming richer with every passing day.

The Muslim rulers did not interfere in the beliefs of their Christian subjects. The Christians had their own judges to administer their personal laws, their own magistrates to settle their disputes, and their own headman to collect taxes from them. Moreover, lands were left in the possession of the Christian land-owners. They were required only to pay land revenue for their lands and poll tax. Furthermore, the churches remained in Christian possession and the bishops who had a great hold on their fellow-Christians, continued to enjoy their authority over them. In short, the Christians continued to practice their religion and culture and to speak their Roman language.

CHAPTER 4

KHILAFAT PERIOD

ABDUL RAHMAN III AL-NASIR
(912–961 A.D.)

Abdul Rahman ascended the throne of Cordova after the death of his grandfather Abdullah at the age of 22.

The accession of Abdul-Rahman to the throne of Cordova was not by virtue of his being a direct claimant, but purely on compassionate ground. His father Muhammad, the rightful heir to the throne fell a victim to the insane intrigues of his brother Prince Mutrif who had seduced the Amir so cunningly with his black lies that a very severe punishment awaited for Prince Muhammad. To save his life Muhammad took shelter with Ibne-Hafsoon which strengthened the suspicion of the Amir all the more. He however returned to Cordova on being granted amnesty by the Amir.

Prince Mutrif hatched out such a furious scheme which resulted in the imprisonment of Muhammad in the palace. As ill-luck would have it, Mutrif was to act as Deputy Amir in the absence of Amir Abdullah who had to go out of the capital for sometime. The cruel Mutrif achieved his aim by ending the life of Muhammad by poison. Amir Abdullah was so much moved with the death of his son that he nominated Muhammad's son

Abdul Rahman as his successor. Prince Abdul Rahman was then of 20 days only. The babe–heir apparent–was brought up under the direct supervision of his grandfather. Mutrif was awarded death punishment by₀ the Amir for murdering Prince Muhammad.

When only 17, Abdul Rahman was ordered by the Amir to look to the affairs of the Imarat. Inspite of his being so young he conducted the various affairs so confidently and judiciously that all the people of the empire irrespective of ranks liked him too much and admitted the maturity of his mind. This is why no voice was raised at his assuming the charge of the Imarat at such a young age.

Condition of Spain. At the time of Abdul Rahman's accession, the condition of Muslim Spain was deplorable. The authority of the Amirs was virtually confined to Cordova, while almost all the provinces and districts of the Emirate were in the hands of the Arab or Muwallad or Christian rebels and the Christian kings of the north had pushed as far south as the rivers Douro and Ebro. In the mountains of Regio, Ibne Hafsun, now known by his Christian name Samuel, the old and inveterate enemy of the Emirate, was still powerful, and had powerful allies, both Christians and Muslims. He was in league with the Fatimid rulers of Tunisia. Though Shia, they laid claim to the overlordship of the Caliphate. Among the native Muslims, his allies were the powerful Beni Hajjaj, who ruled Seville and Carmona. In Algarve, an Arab chief was dominant. The provinces of Elvira, Granada, Algeciras, Medina Sidonia, Moron, Jaen, Murcia, Tadmir in central and eastern Andalusia, various Muslim and Christian rebels were in power. Badajoz in the west was still ruled by a son of Ibne Merwan.

Death of Abdullah : After a reign of twenty four years, Abdullah died on October 15, 912, at the age of sixty-eight.

Only the last nine years of his reign were free from any danger
to his throne. His grandson, Abdul Rahman, son of Muhammad,
his eldest son, ascended the throne.

Abdullah had come to power by poisoning his abler
brother, Munzir, to death. He had kept himself on his tottering
throne by cowardly behaviour towards his enemies, whether of
his kingdom, his religion or of his race. He was cruel, vile and
despicable. He was feeble in policy and governance. But a lucky
turn in the battle of Polei saved his kingdom for him and for his
descendants a century more to come. Toledo was as usual in
the control of the rebels, who were aided by both the king of
Leon and by the Beni Qasis of Saragossa.

In spite of these revolts, however, a change had come all
over the Peninsula. The rebels were not what they had been a
generation earlier, under Amir Abdullah. First of all, the Arab
aristocracy, the most arrogant element among the disloyal, had
lost its illustrious chiefs, like Sa'd ibne Judi, Koraib ibne Khalfun
and Ibrahim Ibn Haik, who had died in 911. Among the new
leaders there was none to take the place or play the role of the
old leaders.

The Spanish Muslims and Christians, the Muwalladun
and the Mozarabs, had also lost their will to revolt. Though
still rebellious, they had not the old enthusiasm to fight the
hated Arab rule of the Amirs, especially of the young Amir
Abdul Rehman. Their leaders had also grown old and their
fervour to challenge the Arab rulers had evaporated. The old
grievances which had made their fathers to revolt against the
oppressive rule of the Arabs had been replaced by new ones,
not against the rulers, but against their own fellows, for many
of the leaders of the Spanish party had become brigands,
plundering indiscriminately all wayfarers. The rank and file in
the Spanish party had more grievances than their leaders who

could satisfy their grievances by loot and plunder, but the common people among them could not do so. On the contrary, they saw every day that in the continuing civil war, both the royal troops and the insurgents often destroyed their farms and fields, uprooted their fruit-trees, and burnt their houses and villages to the ground, and yet their fellow-Spaniards could not win a decisive victory over the Amir's troops. What disheartened the rebellious Spaniards most was a series of reverses they suffered at the hands of the royalist army. The feelings of despair were felt as much in the mountains as also in the towns, where disruption of trade and industry inclined the towns-people towards peace with the Sultan. Such was the case in towns like Jaen, Elvira, Archidona, Sidonia, etc.

In the mountains of Serrania of Regio, where Ibn Hafsun's partisans were dominant, there was no gloom and despondency, yet signs of weariness and discouragement were perceptible. The change in mood was reflected in the lack of eagerness to flock under the banner of Ibne Hafsun, which used to attract the mountaineers in great numbers a decade or two ago. That was the reason why Ibne Hafsun now relied more on the Berber mercenaries recruited from Tangier in North Africa. But they were the least reliable soldiers. They looked upon the war as a sort of commercial activity and were always ready to change sides when the enemy offered to pay them more. Money, not fighting, was their interest. With such troops, a man like -Ibne Hafsun could not win a kingdom, And they had now to deal with a man like Abd Rehman.

Factor of Religions : Another significant factor was the change in the nature of war. Before Abd Rehman, war between the Sultan and the Spanish rebels was of racial nature, that is, between the ruling Arabs and the Muslim and Christians' Spaniards, who hated to be ruled by haughty and arrogant foreigners. But at the end of Abdullah's reign, the war had assumed more religious character. Formerly, a rebel leader, like Ibne Hafsun, did not enquire what the religion of a man was who offered to fight under him: all were welcomed, whether Christians or Muslims. But a change came when Ibne Hafsun became Christian as well as many of his allies, like Ibne Mastana. What was more, Ibne Hafsun or Samuel, as he now called himself, showed confidence only in Christians, whom he appointed to high and lucrative posts under him. Thus all his governors and generals were now Christians. In his capital and important cities, like Bobastro, Archidona, he followed the same policy of driving out their Muslim populations and settling them with Christians. Thus Bolbastro became a hotbed of Christian fanaticism. Now his zeal for Christianity and hatred towards Islam was a stumbling block to the Muwalladun or Spanish Muslims, who were reluctant to join with him and against the Amir of Cordova. They were deeply attached to their faith, which they had imbibed from the Arabs, to whom they now felt grateful. Moreover, they knew very well that once Christians became the dominant power in Spain, they would be reduced to the same miserable condition of serfs, as they were under the Christian Visigoths. These were the reasons why the Spanish Christians and Muslims regarded each other with jealousy and suspicion. Indeed, the two groups had fought in various places with genocidal consequences: if the Christians won, they put the Muslims to the sword and when the Muslims won, they did the same to the Christians. In such conditions, the Spanish Muslims were inclined to go over to the side of the Sultan, whenever he appeared at the gates of their cities.

Submission of Rebels:

Amir Abdul Rahman took only three months in the organization of the administration and the army. The people were filled with the feelings of acclamation, sincerity and obedience when they saw the Amir leaving Cordova with a strong army under his personal command, for quelling the rebellious chiefs all over the country. Many of the vassals joined the Amir with their force, wealth and resources (April, 923 A.D.). Ecija, Jaene and Elvira submitted easily. Notable chiefs like Said-bin-Huzail the chief of Monteleon Fortress in Jaene, Ibne-Saleba, chief of Cazlona and Ishaque bin-Ibrahim the chief Mentesa submitted to the Amir and paid homage to him. His march to Elvira was easy until he reached Finanah, which fell to the Amir after an easy skimish. The Berbers of the Bani Mahallab of Elvira were also brought to submission. The fort of Monte Rubbio a very important frontier fort of Jane and Elvira was captured and the Christian bandits were crushed for ever. The fall of Monte Rubio broke the necks of all the neighbouring chiefs leaving no alternative but to acknowledge the suzerainty of Cordova.

Important Christian fortresses like Juviles, Salborena, San Estevan de-Gormaz and Bena Forata were annexed.

After establishing his authority in the south the Amir crushed the Arab Shaikh Aslami the chief of Alicante (928 A.D.) who was brought to Cordova as a prisoner along with his family.

Merida and Beja were forced to submission. The new-Muslim chief of Oksonoba in the province of Algrane, Khalaf- bin-Bakr also submitted.

Banu Hajjaj of Seville:

After the death of Ibrahim bin Hajjaj, Seville remained under the possession of his eldest son Abdul Rahman while Carmona was under his younger son Muhammad. If so happened that after the death of Abdul Rahman in 301 A.H., 913 A.D. Muhammad tried to capture Seville. The people on the other hand declared Ahmad bin Muslim a cousin of Muhammad, as the chief of Seville. Muhammad bin Ibrahim sought the help of Amir Abdul Rahman III, who besieged Seville forthwith. Ahmed-bin-Muslima duly helped by Ibne Hafsoon met the royal force on the right bank of the Guadalquivir. The combined forces of Ahmad and Ibne Hafsoon met with crushing defeat. Ibne Hafsoon fled away and took shelter in his fort of Babastro. Ahmad ibne Muslima began to negotiate peace through Badr the minister of Cordova. Peace was however concluded on honourable terms. The royal force entered Seville and Muhammad bin-Ibrahim went to Carmona and raised the standard of rebellion. At this juncture Qasim-bin-Walid Kalbi intervened and brought Muhammad to Cordova. He was appointed as Deputy chief of Carmona. He was also awarded the title of Hajib Kabir. Thus he was reconciled and became faithful to the Amir.

Toledo Subjugated:

Primarily the Amir tried to win over the people by persuations and reasonings but they refused to come to terms. When all the peace negotiations failed, the Amir marched against Toledo, with a strong army under his personnel command. He besieged Toledo very firmly. He built up a strong fortress called Al-Fatah on a hillock just opposite Toledo. The siege lasted for two years. He further blockaded the supply of food and water to Toledo which resulted in the out break of famine. King Ordono of leon and Galacia who came to help Toledo, was defeated hopelessly (320 A.H; 932 A.D.) Toledo the last stronghold of the rebels in the Middle March fell to Cordova. Thus the Arabs, the Berbers and the Spaniards were fully crushed and were compelled to submit to the Amir. The enemies succumbed and yielded before the authority of Cordova.

Christians:

The success of Abdul Rahman III, within the country did

not end his worries altogether. He had yet to face the Christian powers, which were constant source of trouble for his precursors as well as for him. He therefore outlined a strong foreign policy to end the external activities with calculated steps. His first strike was reserved for the Christian chief of the North while the second was for the Fatimids in North Africa and the Mediterranean sea.

The Christian chiefs of the North were in possession of a string of forts along the frontiers which formed a barrier against Cordova. The Christians of the North, the Basques, the Aragonese and the Castillions remained unsubdued.

It was in 914 A.D. that Ordono II. (Urdoon) let the Leonese to devastate Merida. They also burnt the suberbs of Talavera, and played unthinkable atrocities at Alanje, putting the civil population to the swords irrespective of age and sex. Children and young females were enslaved and molested.

It was in 304 AH. 916 AD. that Abdul Rahman despatched a force under Ahmad-bin-Abi Abdah to chastise Ordono II. He was defeated but the Leonese devastated the suberbs of Talavera and burnt the cities. Ahmad bin-Abi Abdah marched against the Leonese (911 AD.). Unfortunately the Berbers and the Spaniards treacherously fled away from the battle field and Ahmad could not win even at the cost of his life.

Abdul Rahman III, hearing the defeat of the royal forces and the martyrdom of Ahmad-bin-Abdah was greatly shocked.

He therefore immediately sent a strong force under Hajib Badr in 305 A.H. 918 A.D. who defeated the king of Leon twice at Mustonia. It was in 308 A.H; 920 A.D. that the Amir advanced towards Osma which was possessed by Ordono II. The fortresses of Castro Moris, Alcabilla and Clunia were devastated by Ordono II. On the approach of the royal force, the enemies fled away leaving their possessions for the Amir.

Abdullah-bin-lope, the governor of Tudela was deputed to check the intrusion of the Leonese. The Amir then advanced towards Navaree and crossed the Ebro without resistance. Sancho King of Navaree and his ally Ordono were crushed by the royal army at Val-de-Jun Quiras. Bishop Dulcidus of Salamanca and Bishop Hermoguis of Tuy were captivated. On the return of the Amir to Cordova after three months with triumph the Christians raised their heads again.

It was in 923 A.D., 311 A.H. that Ordono II and Sancho captured Najera and Viguera. They killed a large number of Muslims. Many women and children were made captives. Abdul Rahman rushed to the field and crushed them badly. He punished well the Basques and the Leones. He entered Pamplona the capital of Navaree and broke their strength by destroying many important fortresses. Sancho was left alone, on account of the death of Ordono, to face the royal army, simply to meet humiliating defeat. Thus the kingdom fell to the Amir who proclaimed himself as Amir-ul-Momenin, Al-Nasir-le-Din-Allah (16th January or 12th June 929 A.D., 23rd Zi-qada 316 A.H.)

Khalifat's Establishment :

Customarily Amir-ul-Momenin is the custodian of the holy cities of Mecca and Medina. Abdul Rahman III was not of course the custodian of the holy cities but he was completed by the circumstances to assume the title to stabilise the superiority of Islam. His assumption of the role and title of Amir-ul-Momenin was quite appropriate in view of the titular Eastern caliphate which dwindled day by day and the Abbaside rule was confined to Baghdad only. The provincial chiefs were almost independent. A parallel caliphate was formed by the Fatimide of Egypt which threatened Andalusia. Al-Nasir had brought Andalusia to a much higher position than it had ever enjoyed before. He had conducted successful Jihads against the Christians. Inspite of being nearer to the holy cities of Mecca and Medina, the Abbaside caliphate was powerless to protect the holy cities and maintain their honour dignity and prestige. Al-Nasir was indeed fully capable to protect the holy cities from Cordova inspite of its situation in the West. The geographical barriers and distance of the east and west were cemented by the powerful empire of Cordova. His choice of the title "Al-Nasir-le-Din-Allah", defender of the religion of God, was quite true and logical in view of his inflicting successive crushing defeats on the Zionists and Christians of Europe and establishing the might of Islam, both in the west and the east.

Christian's Rise:

Alfanso IV the ruler of Leon turned a monk and abdicated in favour of his brother Romero II. After some time Alfanso denouncing the ascetic life occupied the throne of Leon. Romero made him a captive and blinded him miserably. Romero II raided the Muslim cities. The Khalifa therefore devastated Bargos the capital of Castile and captured it.

Muhammad-bin-Hashim Tajbud (Tajbi) was the governor of Saragossa. In view of the faithfulness of Bani Hashim, the Cordovan government had allowed them to retain the governorship on the principle of heredity. Banu Hashim had earned the confidence of Khalifa Al-Nasir as well. However, Muhammad-bin-Hashim switched over to the side of Romero II and rebelled against the Khalifa (321 A.H.; 934 A.D.). They also made an alliance with Garcia the minor ruler of Navaree under Queen Regent Tots. Practically the whole of the North was to be faced by the Khalifa, who defeated Banu Hashim and the Christians at Calatayud (324 A.H., 937 A.D.). About 34 fortresses were captured. The supporters of Navaree and Saragossa had to surrender. Muhammad-bin-Hashim was granted amnesty and was awarded with the restoration of the governorship of Saragossa. The Queen Regent Tota (Thueda) of Navaree used for peace and acknowledged the suzerainty of the Khalifa.

Barring Leon and a part of Catalonia the whole of Spain submitted to Abdul Rahman III.

Alhandega's Battle :

The Galicians, the Basques and Leon revolted again (327 A.H; 939 A.D.). The Khalifa therefore determined to crush the rebels fully and with this end in view he collected a huge army: one lac slaves called Saqalibah and the Arabs. The command was given to a slave general Najda Saqlabi. The Arabs did not approve of the appointment of the Slave general because of their superior blood and status. They were so much disgusted with the appointment that they preferred defeat to victory but the Khalifa who hated the concept of blood superiority did not mind the Arab's dissension.

The Khalifa advanced towards Leon and the royal force reached Simancas south of modern Valladolid. The fort of Zamora was besieged, which was defended by several strong walls and a large deep ditch. Just in the thick of fight, the Arabs left the field and retreated to be ruined. The Leonese persued them hotly. Many of the Arabs fell in the ditch and died. The slaves fought bravely but could not set the line in order which was disordered by the abrupt desertion of the disloyal Arabs. A very sanguinary battle was fought on the banks of the Torones near a village Al- Khandaq (Sp. Al-handega) South of Salamanca. Najdah, the general was killed and the Khalifa reached Cordova with a handful of his loyal soldiers numbering 49 only. This was the first defeat in the life of the Khalifa which was due to the disloyalty of the Arabs only. The Khalifa however, resolved to avenge the defeat. He therefore deputed Ahmad-bin-Yahya, the governor of Badjoz (329 A.H.; 940 A.D.) to check the advance of the Leonese. A fresh force was despatched to quell the Galacians and the Basques. Between 944 to 947 A.D. the royal army penetrated into the Castilian territories. In the meantime the city walls of Medina-Salim (Medina Celi) were fully repaired to be used as a strong fort against Castilia. With the death of Romero II in 239 A.H; 950 A.D. Civil war began among the Christians. The Khalifa strengthening his position all the more, threatened the Christian territories in the North. The king of Leon the Queen regent of Navaree and the counts of Castile and Barcelona acknowledging the suzerainty of the Khalifa agreed to pay annual tribute and to hand over or dismantle their fortresses on the Muslim frontiers.

Medinaceli or Madina-al-Salim, the newly repaired city was given the status of a province to form a link with Castile and also to act as a bulwork.

Thus the Muslim frontier in the North ran from Lerida on the Atlantic to the mouth of the Ebro.

Sancho and Queen Regent Tutah in Cordova:

Ordono III died in August 956 A.D. His successor Sancho the Fat refused to accept the treaty concluded by Ordono III. Ahmad-bin-Yahya the governor of Toledo defeated him in 957 A.D. Not only that, but Sancho was driven out by the Leonese duly helped by Fernan Carizaliz; the chief of Castile and Ordono IV. Sancho went to Pamplona to take refuge with the queen regent Tutah of Navaree. Sancho was left without a sincere friend. He therefore appealed to the Khalifa for help against his rival cousin Ordono IV. While the negotiations were on, the Khalifa sent his personal physician Hasdai-bin-Shaprut to treat Sancho of his corpulence. Hasdai was a Jew and also Inspector General of Customs of Cordova. He was a great diplomat also.

He handled the situation so diplomatically that Sancho and Queen Tulah his grandmother visited Cordova and in lieu of royal help agreed to surrender ten fortresses.

In order to keep up the terms of the treaty, the royal force captured Zamora (959 A.D.) and Oviedo for Sancho the following year. Thus the authority of Sancho was re-established in Leon, Galacia and Navaree with the active military support of the Khalifa. Sancho became a vassal of the Khalifa. The acknowledgment of the Umayyad sovereignty (960 A.D.) by Leon brought the Muslim expansion to the limit and the conquest of the Iberian Peninsula was in a way completed.

Fatimids : The Fatimids were a group of extremist Shi'ites, known as Ismails. Like other Shi'ites they also claimed that the Ahl-al-Bayt, i.e. the descendants of Ali and Fatimah, alone had the legitimate right to be Khalifas and Imams of the whole Islamic world and that the Abbasid Khalifas were usurpers, who should, therefore, be overthrown and the rule of the Ahl al-bayt be established. They also claimed to be the descendants of Fatimah, the daughter of the Holy Prophet (PBUH), and hence they were Fatimids. Their claim was false. They had organized a powerful secret propaganda system to win the Muslims in various parts of the Abbasid caliphate, in order to realise their aims.

They also claimed that Mahdi would come who would abolish all injustices in the world and bring peace and prosperity to all. This was also a Sunni belief. But the Shi'ites declared that their Imam would be the promised Mahdi. In 884, the Ismaili sect of the extremist Shia sent a *da'i* or missionary, named Abu Abdullah al-Shi'i, to North Africa to win over the Berbers to their cause. He won over the Ketamah tribe of the Berbers in eastern Ifriqia, who became, his followers. They captured various towns belonging to the last Aghlabi ruler. Later another Ismaili da'i, Ubaidallah, came to the Ketamah to lead them to victory. Abu Abdullah, having made himself master of the Aghlabi capital, Raqqadah, near Qayrowan, and after apelling the Aghlabi ruler, Ziayadat Allah, in March, 909, proclaimed Ubaidallah as *Mahdi* and *Amir al-Momineen* and *Khalifa* on January 15, 910, at Raqqadah. Thus was established the Fatimid caliphate in North Africa. But they considered it only as a base from where they planned to invade Abbasid caliphate, after collecting a large army and immense resources to this end. With this purpose in view, they extended their power into three directions, that is, into al-Maghrib or western Africa and Spain, into Sicily and other Mediterranean islands, and finally, into Egypt. They had built their capital at Mahdiyya, near Qayrowan. But when they conquered Egypt in 969, they founded Cairo (Al-Qahira) which became their new capital. With this their interest in al-Mughrib and Spain waned and later vanished. But during the Mahdiyya period of their rule, they proved to be a great danger to Abd Rehman III on many counts, religious, political and geographical.

The Fatimid claims to universal caliphate was a peril to all Muslim States, but particularly so to Muslim Spain. Though all Spanish Muslims-Arabs Berbers, and Muwalladun, were Sunnis, but the belief in the advent of Mahdi was common among them especially among the poorer classes who expected their miserable existence to be ameliorated by Mahdi's promise of justice and prosperity for all, while to many a rich Muslim it provided an opportunity to capture political power by claiming himself to be the promised Mahdi. Besides this danger, Abd Rehman had to face yet another. As soon as the Fatimids had come to power in North Africa they opened negotiations with Ibne Hafsoon, who offered to recognize the Fatimid Khalifa as his sovereign. However, before the two enemies of Abd Rehman could conclude an alliance, their negotiations broke down. But the Fatimids were not discouraged. Their spies, in the guise of merchants, travelled all over Muslim Spain, and reported back to their master about the conditions in Spain. One of them was Ibne Hawkal, the well-known Arab geographer. In his report, he wrote:

> "That which chiefly astonishes foreigners when they set foot on this Peninsula, is the fact that it is still ruled by the Umayyad sovereigns; that the inhabitants are spiritless, servile and cowards, they are wretched horsemen and are wholly incapable of defending themselves against disciplined troops: and yet our masters–on whom be the blessings of god-will know the true worth of this country how great is the revenue it yields, and what are its beauties and delights."

If the Fatimids had invaded Spain, they would have won many people over to them, for they believed in the advent of Mahdi. Even before the Fatimids rose to power in Africa, a prince, Muhammad ibn Muawiya, had proclaimed himself a Mahdi in 901. He collected a large Berber following around him in Zamora. He was, however, defeated. Soon after Abd Rehman ascended the throne, a prince of royal blood, Ahmad ibne Ishaq, revolted in 916. He opened negotiations with the Fatimids to surrender Spain to them. But his plot was discovered. He was arrested and condemned to death as a Shi'ite and executed in 916.

War with the Fatimids :

Although Abd Rehman was himself never at war with the Fatimids, nevertheless, his vassals in North Africa did fight many battles with them. The Fatimids were bent upon the conquest of Mauritania, as North-Western Africa was called then. This was a danger signal for Abd Rehman, for he knew that as soon as they had accomplished their mission in North Africa, they would turn their arms against him. Therefore, he decided to support its rulers against the Fatimids so to make it a buffer state between them and Spain. He could not go to war with them at the moment, because he had to deal with the rebels at home and the Christians in the North. He supported such princes in North Africa as were ready to defend themselves against Fatimid ambitions. The Arab rulers of Nakur was the first such prince. The Umayyads of Spain had cordial relations with them since long. In 917, the Fatimid Khalifa, Ubaidullah, wrote to Sa'id II, the then ruler of Nakur, to submit to him so that justice and prosperity might come to his little kingdom. In his reply, Sa'd II not only refused to submit to the Fatimids, but also wrote some verses in which he ridiculed their claims to be Fatimids. When Ubaidullah received his insulting reply, he ordered his general, Massala, the Governor of Tahort, to attack Nakur. Said II, though bent with age, marched out to meet him. But he was defeated and killed by Massala, when one of his officers went over to the enemy. Sa'id's three sons, fled to Malaga on the coast of Spain. Abdul Rahman received them hospitably. Instead of going to Cordova, they preferred to stay in Malaga, which was nearer to their country, and waited for an opportunity to regain it. Their opportunity came six months later, when Massala left Nakur for Tahort and left a small garrison in the city under Jalul. The three brothers agreed among themselves to run a sort of marathon race: that is, whoever of the brothers would reach Nakur first would become its ruler. Salih, the youngest brother, reached Nakur first. He was joyfully received by the people and proclaimed as the Amir. However, he recognized Abdul Rahman as his sovereign.

In 1929, when Abdul Rahman had assumed the title of 'Khalifa' his attention was again directed towards Africa.

Muhammad ibn Khazer, the chief of the Berber tribe of
Maghrawa, had defeated the Fatimid general, Massala, and killed
him with his own hands. But to protect himself from the Fatimid
reprisals, he recognized the sovereignty of Abdul Rahman over
the whole of Central Maghrib (the districts of Oran and Algeirs
in modern times). Abdul Rahman also succeeded in winning
over to his side Ibn Abi'l-Afia, the chief of the Miknesa, from
the Fatimids and persuaded him surrender the possession of
Ceuta, on the African coast, in 931.

His Misconception of West European Feudalism : In
the Middle Ages, the strength and stability of the kingdom or
empire depended on the loyalty of its troops and of other high
officials. In medieval Europe, the evolution of feudalism ensured
the loyalty of the royal army which consisted exclusively of the
knights and Bassals of a feudal lord, and 'through him, of his
overlord, who was called a king, emperor or the like. It also
obviated the need for regular administrators, appointed by the
king, because every feudal lord, big or small, was also a judge
and an administrator of his fief or landed estate. Thus European
feudalism fulfilled two purposes: it provided an army of life-long
soldiers, for war was the be-all and end-all of every feudal
noble and knight, and also a system of local administration.
Feudal state in Europe was a sort of contractual state, in which
the king or emperor was not the master of his nobles but their
equal, or rather the first among the equals. He had some rights
and obligations towards them, just as they had also some rights
and obligations towards him. When the German envoy explained
this nature of European feudalism to Abdul Rahman, the Khalifa
said:

> Your king is, I grant, a wise and able
> monarch, but one feature of his statesmanship
> does not commend itself to me: instead of
> retaining the government entirely in his own

hands, he admits his vassals to a share of it. He even places them in possession of his provinces, thinking thereby to attach them to himself. This is a grave error. Condescension to the nobility has no other effect than that of nourishing their pride and their propensity to rebel."

The defects which Abdul Rahman had pointed out were true of his and of other Muslim kingdoms. Feudalism in them did not evolve beyond the initial forms of tribal feudalism, which always ended in feudal anarchy and revolts of the land-owning tribal chiefs. Confronted with such a situation, Abdul Rahman and his predecessors had tried to overcome their lawlessness, firstly, by centralising all authority in their own hands, thus instituting an absolutist and autocratic monarchy, and secondly, by appointing slaves in their military and administrative systems. In other words, instead of relying on freemen and citizens of their kingdoms for these purposes, as did the Christians rulers in Spain and Europe, Muslim rulers recruited slaves, freedmen and foreign mercenaries in their armed forces and administration, with disastrous consequences for their successors, and kingdoms.

Death:

The Khalifa died on October 16, 961, at the age of seventy years.

Character:

Abdul Rahman III was gifted with extraordinary administrative ability. He proved himself a great leader possessed of all rare qualities to win the hearts of the people. He was very daring and industrious. As an enlightened sovereign, he was never harsh or imprudent. He was rather mild, generous and just. He was a man of grasp and nothing escaped his attention.

He followed the footsteps of Hazrat Umar, the great, and Umar-bin-Abdul Aziz and did not allow any unauthorised taxes. He kept a vigilant eye on every item of the country's affair and cared honestly for the welfare of the people. He did not believe in amassing wealth in the national exchequer at the cost of the rate-payers.

A great defender of the Faith, he fought the unbelievers for the solidarity of Islam, but he was not intolerant. Both the Christians and the Jews were allowed to practice their religions freely. He did not even oppose the idea of entrusting with the highest post of Justice to a non-Muslim of excellent character and will.

He was never led by passion ever in the darkest moment an attribute seldom found in a despotic monarch. His royal council was represented by all class of learned persons irrespective of religious beliefs and ideologies.

Himself an accomplished Alim, Faqih and poet, he had great respect for men of knowledge and education. Being a great patroniser of education, he welcomed men of letters to his court. Qazi Munzir-bin-Saeed-al-Baluti (878-965 A.D.) the renowned theologian, Ahmad-bin-Abde-Rabbehi the historian and author of Iabul-Farid, Abul Qasim-bin-Abbas Al-Zahravi adored the Darbar of the Khalifa. Cordova then was the intellectual centre of Europe.

Achievements:

The achievements of Al-Nasir need a detailed classification. Before doing so, one should note that his was the golden period in the history of Muslim Spain. He got the throne at a time when the country was shrouded with rebellions, chaos and confusion. He had to fight inch by inch for consolidating the empire. His military operations of 18 years surmounted all the difficulties and hurdles which surrounded his throne. With the use of sword he applied his talents as well. He won over many lawless persons and rebels tactfully and reduced the power of the Arab and Berber rebels artfully. The Christians were taught a good lesson both in the field and outside and were compelled to use for peace.

Abdul Rahman III had outlined his administration on sound principles of Islamic Justice and equity, fraternity and brotherhood. The welfare of the people was to be always kept in view. The Khalifa who was all powerful did not allow any interference from any quarter. The nobles, the courtiers, the vassals and the officers had to look to their own assigned domain. Transgressors were liable to severe punishment.

The appointments of high officials were made by the Khalifa purely on merit basis irrespective of beliefs or groups.

The rebels, the bandits the law-breakers and conspirators were dealt with severely. The breeders of parochialism were never spared.

The Arabs had no superiority over the non-Arabs. All had to live peacefully and behave well with each other. Besides the royal guards, a strong militia was maintained and kept ready to meet the exigency. Besides the salary, the soldiers were awarded agricultural lands as a mark of encouragement.

The nobles were granted Jagirs and were allowed to keep a small army to maintain peace and order and also to supply soldiers to Cordova, on call.

No free manual labour could be taken from the farmers and slaves by any person.

His monarchy was in a way coloured with an agreeable form of democracy speaking weal of a Welfare-State.

To maintain equilibrium, if the secretaries here appointed from notable Arab families, other equally important posts were filled in by meritorious slaves and freedmen.

Badr-bin-Ahmad a freedman was in great confidence of the Khalifa while Ahmad-bin-Shuhayd enjoyed the rank and salary of Zul-wazaratain.

Overhauling the entire economic structure, the caliph built up the economy of the country which aimed at forming an opulant common-people society. To do so he did not hesitate to reduce the regular taxes and abolish the unwarranted taxes.

In order to compensate the loss in revenue, he tapped other natural resources of the country, like agriculture, minerals, trade and industry.

According to Ibne Asir the State income from revenue was 54 lacs 80 thousand dinars and 65 thousand dinars from the shops. Besides the 5th part of the booty was beyond limit. A fair amount of revenue was collected from the import and export duty, as well.

The state revenue inclusive of the protection income was divided into three parts. One-third was spent on the royal militia, one-third on public buildings and one-third was deposited in the treasury. The national exchequer was always full of gold. Two crores gold coins (dinars) served as reserve currency in the treasury in 340 A.H., 951 A.D. Muhammad bin-Jawhar, Ahmad bin-Isa-bin-Abi Abdah, Abdul Rahman, bin Abdullah-al-Zajjali and Ahmad bin Muhammad-bin-Albi Qamus were talented treasures.

The revised revenue policy improved the condition of the people economically and strengthened the position of the national exchequer. Ibne-Hoqal, the eminent historians, but an open enemy of Cordova, had to admit the superiority of the fiscal policy of the Khalifa and also the availability of all commodities at a much cheaper rate.

The Khalifa believed that the commodities could be made available at cheaper rates, if agriculture was improved to give the best yield in abundance. With the implementation of new methods of agriculture and horticulture, the production of better crops was guaranteed. Not an inch of land was kept waste. The vegetables were grown in abundance in Cordova, Mercia and other places and were sold at awfully cheaper rates. Even the hilly tracts were brought under cultivation. Cultivation was done according to the quality of the land. Water system was organized through canals, rivulets and wells. Agriculture had so much improved that crops and fruits were exported to other cities of Europe.

The population of the country increased day by day till it reached 3 crores. The population of Cordova was more than 10 lacs.

Three thousand new villages were populated in the valley of the Guadalquivir.

Communication was yet another item which awaited the royal attention. With the growth of trade, industry and agriculture easy means of communication was a necessity, both through land and water. Old roads were therefore repaired and new ones were constructed. New bridges were also constructed on villages-rivulets and streams. Ferry system was introduced and stabilized. A large number of inns (hotels) were constructed for easy and cheap accommodation of travellers and merchants. Armed guards were placed at outposts and on highways for the maintenance of peace and safety for the travellers and traders. The efficiency of the police guaranteed the safety of the travellers and merchants at all routes dangerous or non-dangerous.

Transmission of news and letters were done by the relays of horses stationed at every outpost. Watch Towers along the coast lines watched the movements of the enemies.

Hospitals with outdoor and indoor patients were attended properly by doctors (Hakims) nurses and attendants. Destitutes rest houses and orphanage were constructed in numbers. Special horse carriages were provided in each welfare centre to meet the emergency.

The development of trade and industry was the natural outcome of the growth of agriculture. The affluence of the country turned its attention to the establishment of industry for further promotion of trade to capture the European as well as the Asian markets. The government also took special interest in the establishment of industries at various places. Numerous industries of silk, cotton, wool, leather and metals were established in Cordova, Seville and Almeria. With the development of industries both the people and the national exchequer became all the more prosperous. The silk industry gave birth to a new side-industry of silk-worms breeding. There were about 3000 agrarians in the province of Cordova alone who had a flourishing silk-worms breeding-farms–a side business–which made their fiscal position stronger than ever.

Cordova alone had about 30 thousand weavers. Almeria and Seville surpassed Cordova in weaving. The Khalifa was greatly pleased with the textile fabrics prepared at Zahra presented to him by Ibne-Shuhayd, Dibaj a kind of silk cloth noted for its beauty and colour was produced in Spain, then unknown to the world. Silk cloth for the royal use was much superior to those of the royal clothes of the Abbasides. Silk cloths and cloths of daily use were sold very cheap in the open market.

Main roads were named after the various flourishing

industries to add to the grandeur of the country. Parchment industry was greatly encouraged and Elvira produced silk goods and Cuenca produced fine carpets.

Weapons came from Toledo, pottery from Calayud hides from Saragossa, leather, tapestries and books from Cordova. Almost all the finished goods were exported to other parts of Europe and Asia which not only earned the foreign exchange but added to the glory of the country. The Muslim Spanish currency was more stable and valuable than the dollar of today. The metal works had earned the admiration of the world for manufacturing fine swords, armours, lamps and iron gate etc. The leather-work has even today kept alive the name of Cordova in Europe and elsewhere. Gold, silver, quicksilver and iron mines were available, and worked out and used properly. Querries were on in regard to marbles and other precious stones.

Daine, a coastal city of Alicante and Calatayud were famous for pottery-industry.

The trade of Spain was carried on by merchant-fleets, The land route was used for France and other European countries. The sea route was adopted for the Mediterranean-islands, coastal cities, Tunisia, Egypt and other eastern countries. Trade had gone to such a height that the merchant-ships numbered above one thousand. Several trade agencies of Spanish merchants were established in distant placer, to facilitate the sale and purchase of goods and commodities. The government earned a lot from the import and export duty. Protection to the traders, importers and exporters were guaranteed by the government.

The national revenue was 6,24,000 dinars eighteen times more than what it was in the reign of Abdul Rahman I. The prosperity of the country and the people could be judged from the fact that the people rode on mules and horses instead of journeying on foot.

The Khalifa Abdul Rahman was a great patroniser of all branches of education,–art, science, and literature. He felt pleasure in spending one third of the state income on education alone.

Himself a poet, he developed and patronised the art so much that even an ordinary peddler was a standard poet.

Eminent scholars from different parts of the world flocked in Cordova and received the bounty of the Khalifa.

Ibne Massarah (d. 931 A.D.) the philosopher, Ibne Ahmar the historian (d, 969 A.D.) Ahmad-bin-Nasr, (d. 944 A.D.) Muslema-bin Al-Qasim (d. 964 A.D.) the astronomers, Arib-bin-Saeed and Yayha-bin-Ishaque, the physicians enhanced the glory of Spain.

The Khalifa did not believe in orthodoxy, especially in the field of education. He received men of letters and learning with respect irrespective of beliefs and ideologies.

He encouraged the translation of the Greek philosophy, science and literature into Arabic and tried to evince out a new Philosophy on modern thoughts of the day. He encouraged research work in all branches of learning by eminent scholars of the day.

Hasdai-bin-Shahpurt (945–070) the Jewish physician, diplomat and philosopher held the confidence of the Khalifa. He also held the coveted post of finance minister. Nicholas and Abu-Al-Raees were yet other philosophers of repute.

The translation into Arabic of Discords the Greek work on botany by the Greek scholar Nicholas assisted by Hasadi opened a line for the study of Greek science for the students in Spain.

Ibne-Hawqal, the geographer of the Fatimide court visited

Cordova and was so much impressed by the development of Cordova in particular and Spain in general, that inspite of his being a deadly enemy of the Spanish caliphate, could not resist the temptation of eulogising the grand development of the country in all fields, specially the various branches of learning and culture.

Ibne-Masarah, taking advantage of the liberty of the Khalifa, established a school of mysticism and propagated the Greek philosophy, just opposed to the Maliki views. The library-science was also encouraged. A large number of libraries, public and private were established and run under eminent scholars. Special training was imparted for maintaining the libraries. Cataloguing system was done on scientific methods.

Ibne-al-Ahmar wrote the famous biography of the Khalifa which was kept in the royal library. Several printed copies of the same were kept for people's use in public libraries of the country *Kitabul-Awqat-al-Sanat* written by Abul Hassan Arib-bin-Saeed was a gem for the royal library.

Ibne-Qautia, the author of *Iftetah-al-Undulus* earned a name as a historian of the age. The *Cronica-dal-Moro Rasis* of Ahmad Al Razi (d. 953 A.D.) became the basis of Spanish document.

The study of medicine with all research facilities was carried on under eminent physicians. The domain of mathematics was covered by Abu Ghalib, Abu Ayub and others.

Summit scholars of Qirwa and philologists of Baghdad like Abu Abd-al-Qab were welcomed in Cordova with honour and respect.

It may however be noted that it was during the regime of Abdul Rahman II that transition of Greek works on different subjects into Arabic was undertaken successfully. Library was well organized. Abdul Rahman III re-organised and sytematised the work begun by Abdul Rahman II. Schools and colleges were opened in numbers in every city and village. Education was imparted with free lodging and boarding.

Ibne-Abd-Rabbehi the composer of *lqdul Farid*, (The unique necklace) a unique anthology, added to the literary glory of Andulusia.

Ibne Hani (d. 973 A.D.) the Mutanabbi of the west had adored the court as a poet. He being banished from Spain on the charge of heresy, took refuge under the Fatimids. He composed a poem on the warships of Al-Muiz the Fatimid Khalifa.

Muwash Shah a new form of poetic composition was invented in Spain by Muqaddam bin-Muafa or Mohammed bin Mahmood who lived in a village Cabra near Cordova in the early part of the tenth century. The innovation was greatly admired and followed in the country.

The rythmic style of Arabic prose work became so popular that the original Spanish prose embellished with the style.

The Khalifa being an ardent lover of art and architecture could be very well called the great architect of Spain. He constructed a large number of beautiful public buildings but Al-Zahra excelled all.

It is said that the money spent on the construction of Al-Zahra was primarily to be spent for ransoming the Muslim prisoners and captives in the hands of the Christians. Since none could be traced, the Khalifa was at a fix to find out the real use of the left over money. At the suggestion of his most beloved slave girl Al-Zahra, he agreed to construct a palace after her name to be one of the wonders of the world. It was in 324 A.H. Nov. 936 A.D. that the foundation stone was laid down by the Khalifa himself. It stood northwest of Cordova, some three miles away, on one of the projections of the Sierra Morena, Jabal-al-Urus, overlooking the Guadalquivir. The city was named as Madinatul Zahra and the palace as Alzahra after the name of the beloved queen of the Khalifa. It was a mile long and half a mile wide. It was surrounded by a huge wall with 5000 gates. The construction which was begun by Abdul Rahman III was completed by Al-Hakam II in 365 A.H., 975 A.D. Ten thousand labourers and eighteen thousand pack-mules and camels were employed daily. The average annual expenditure was two lacs dinars. The Madina-Al-Zahra had three divisions. The palace, the Harem the Seraglio and the fort were located on the upper terrace whereas the grand mosque with three reception rooms and the servants-residence were on the lower terrace. The middle terrace was reserved for gardens and games reserve.

The mosque was completed in five years (Friday 329 A.H. 22nd January, 941 A.D.). The first Juma prayer was led by Qazi Abu Abdullah-bin Abi Isa attended by the Khalifa Abdul Rahman III and the public.

The Al-Zahra palace had 750 gates with 4316 pillars. Precious stones and valuable construction materials were imported from Byzantium, Carthage, Utica, Narbonne and Tarragona. 140 marble pillars were brought from Constantinople and African cities, 19 pillars from the Fankish kingdom. Rome and the Spanish quarries also took part in the supply of pillars. Tarragona and Almeria supplied white marbles.

Marble pillars from Africa were brought under the care of the chief architects Abdullah, Hasan-bin-Muhamed and Ali-bin-Jafar. A fair number of marble pillars were presented to the Khalifa by the king of France and Constantinople. The freight was paid at the rate of 10 dinars per pillar.

A very big fountain made of gilded bronze with human figures's base reliefs of exquisite beauty and workmanship was brought from Constantinople by Ahmad the Greek and Bishop Rabi. The other fountain a smaller one, made of green marble came from Syria. The fountains were fixed in Salon-de-loscalifas and the Patiode-Al-Mumis, (Qasre-Almunis).

The Khalifa's special room's roofs and walls were all exquisitely gilded. The palace hall with eight beautifully gilded doors had a mercury tank which was wrought so artfully that the sun rays failing through the doors on the tank presented a dazzling light to the enjoyment of all. The gilded tank served the royal bath-tub, was surrounded by 12 pieces of statuary of gold and precious stones carved into statues of various animals emitting water from their mouths. The audience hall was dome-like supported by marble columns inlaid with precious stones.

A gilded statue of the Khalifa's beloved queen AI-Zahra was set up at the main gate of the palace.

It is said that the Khalifa was much annoyed with remarks of the queen,—the palace by the side of the black mountain, gave a glimpse of a beloved by the side of negro. The Khalifa therefore ordered for drilling out the entire hill. But as the order was purely sentimental, he planted a beautiful garden on the hill to obliterate the grim look.

The palace had 13 thousand house-hold servants. Besides there were six thousand maid servants for the queen alone. Slaves and eunuchs numbered 3350. A special acquarium called Bahirat-Alzahra was a wonder indeed. 12,000 loaves were given daily to the fish; According to Maqri there were Qasr-ul-Mashooq, Qasrul-Suroor, Qasrul-Taj, Qasrul Damishq, which spoke of the grandeur of Undulusia under Khalifa Abdul Rahman III.

The stately minaret erected on the northern side of the court of Oranges in the Grand Mosque of Cordova was nothing less than a wonder. With a height of 108 ft. and 27 sq. ft. in girth made of highly polished and engraved stone brought from North Africa spoke of the architectural taste of the Khalifa. 26,530 dinars were spent on the construction of the minaret. The grand mosque was improved with re-innovation under the supervision of Abul Jafal-al-Asqalabi, a famous slave engineer, 1000 olive-oil lamps were lighted daily. There were 300 servants to look after the maintenance of the mosque.

The installation of running water plant for the city latrines was a novel innovation of the age. Public baths were numerous. The water reservoirs of the city were always kept ready for supply of clean and sweet water.

The city of Cordova was divided into five districts with 21 suberbs. Mosques and public markets were numerous. The total area was about 51 square miles. Alcazaba fort stood in the centre of the city. The water being channelled from the Sierra de-Cordova, to the palace was distributed to the city and the suberbs through lead pipes.

Cordova was the most cultured city in Europe. The travellers were filled with awe and admiration by the progress of the city. Its innumerable magnificent buildings, 21 subers, 70 libraries, large number of book stalls, mosques, palaces, paved streets fully illuminated by street-lights, schools, colleges and hostels earned the admiration of all. According to John. W. Draper in his history of the intellectual development of Europe:

> "Seven hundred years this time there was not
> so much as one public lamps in London",
> and "in Paris centuries subsequently, whoever
> stepped over his threshold on a rainy day

stepped up to his ankles in mud". "When
the university of Oxford still looked upon
bathing as a heathen custom, generation of
· Cordovan scientists had been enjoying baths
in luxurious establishments"

To quote Hitti

"Whenever the rulers of Leon, Navaree or
Barcelona needed surgeon, an architect, a
master-singer or a dressmaker, it was to
Cordova that they applied."

The fame of Cordova had penetrated almost every part of
Europe. A Saxon nun of Germany called it "Jewel of the world"
as described by Horotsvitha in Scriptors Maron Germanicarum.

The bold straight and independent policy of the Khalifa
not only closed the chapter of internal troubles and disorders
for good but also sealed the foreign in roads and crushed the
enemies all over, with the result that they were impertinent to
establish friendly relations with Cordova.

The supremacy of Cordova was acknowledged by the
Christian-world. The Khalifa acted many a time as arbitrator
to settle the Christian kings' disputes. Constantinople, Germany,
France, Italy and other kingdoms took it an honour to establish
ambassadorial relations with Cordova. The embassy of
Constantinople (336 A.H. 947 A.D.) was received in pomp in
the palace of Alzahra.

According to Ibne Khaldun the ambassador of king
Constantine was bewildered and bewitched by the grandeur of
the royal court. It is worthwhile mentioning that the Khalifa
though an independent despotic monarch, unlike modern rulers,
never missed the opportunity of establishing the authority of
Islam on any occasion specially in ceremonial congregation of

foreigners of opposite-beliefs. After the king Constantine's letter was presented to the Khalifa by the ambassador, orators like Aby Ali Al Qali Baghdadi spoke of the sovereignty of Allah and the beauty of Islam.

Munzir-bin-Saeed Balooti further impressed the Khalifa and the august audiance by him eloquent extempore speech. The Khalifa therefore appointed him as the chief Qazi.

The Khalifa in return sent Hisham-bin-Kalib Jasliq to Constatinople with valuable presents to strengthen the ties of friendly relations.

King Ukoh or Hugo of Provence, the Frank's king beyond the Pyrenees and Caldob (Charles the simple) the king of Eastern France established friendly relations through embassies. Italy also signed a friendly pact with Cordova.

The Salv countries, the Christians of North of Rome felt elated by establishing direct friendly relations with Cordova and acted according to the advice of the Khalifa. Rabi ibne-Zayad (Recemund) the ambassador of the Khalifa at the court of Otto the great of Germany was very popular. He was a scholar of Latin and Arabic. He helped Luifrand or Luiprand in the compilation of his history, 'The Antapodosis'. The Khalifa's personal physician Hasdibin-Shaprut was sent to Queen Regent Tota of Navaree and king Ordono IV of Leon, as ambassador. The protocol system of the Khalifa was so perfect and sincere that Europe of the day was eager to establish ambassadorial relations with Cordova.

It may be noted that the growing weakness of the Abbasides, the growing power of the Saljuks and the strength of the Fatimids had brought the then Europe on the verge of collapse, both internally and externally. Europe therefore had no other alternative but to look to the Spanish Caliphate to act as a bulwark to secure their obscure destinies.

The Khalifa Abdul Rahman was fully alive to the causes of the weakness of the government of his precursors. Though an absolute monarch, he did not forget his vicegerency to the Almighty God and the responsibilities imposed on him by God. His first duty was to blend the diverse ideologies and outlooks into one single unit based on the teachings of Islam.

He condemned the blood and racial superiority of the Arabs. He convinced them all that greatness lies in piety (*Ittiqa*) only. All dominant positions were open for all, purely on merit basis. The Arabs and the Spaniards the Serfs and the slaves were at par with each other. There was thus a corporate life and the Muslims were tolerant to other communities. Edwyn Hole could not appreciate the composition of the homogeneous compound in one part of Europe when the other parts were wrapped up in sharp divisions of race and beliefs. Antipathy dates back to the evolution of man. It may lit called instinctive as well, The ameliorative efforts has however, never been neglected by the successive community of man and even the partial success cannot be depricated. The Khalifa therefore deserved full credit for establishing the true national Islamic spirit in a land which was beset with all social evils.

The Arabs, the Berbers, the Spaniards, the Jews the Christians, the slaves, the orientals, soldiers, merchants, and farmers, were cemented into one group of nation to work and stand for the country shoulder to shoulder, and neck to neck.

The overhauling of the entire military organization was yet a very wise and bold step towards the solidification of the nation and the country.

His army, Jund or Saqalibah chiefly consisted of the slaves. The Spanish slaves, called Saqalibah from Spanish esclavo were sold for a thousand dinar each. Primarily Saqaliah or Salavia was used for the war prisoners of the German tribe of esclav.

With the march of time and the popularity of the salve trade all the slaves were called Saqalebah. The Jews were the chief slave traders. They had a factory where boys of tender age were made eunuchs and were sold at high prices. The slaves were also brought by the pirates from France, Germany, Lombardy, Italy and Galacia and Africa.

The jund of pre-Abdul Rahman days, being based on tribal units, the Amirs could not claim their loyalty to them. On the contrary they were loyal to the tribal chiefs who were their direct employers. The Amirs therefore set up their own body guards increasing the number from time to time but ineffective to control the tribal chiefs and maintain peace and order in the country.

The Khalifa Abdul Rahman therefore reduced the influence of the Arab chiefs by creating a group of wealthy middle class and by raising a strong army of slaves or Saqaleba who were responsible to the Khalifa direct. The Saqalibas or the foreign mercinaries, served in the army and in the Harem always looking for the interest of the Khalifa. They were promoted to high posts ignoring the Arab rights. Najda Saqalabi was appointed Commander-in-Chief in 327 A.H., 938-9 A.D to the disgust of the Arab nobility. The collosal loss of Muslim army was of course due to the treachery of the Arabs but the Khalifa instead of being harrassed, stood up with full determination to crush the Arab aristocracy. This he did through the Saqualibah organization. The number of the Saqlebah varied from 3750 to 13750.

Besides, the Khalifa had 15,000 regular troops at his direct command.

He spend a huge amount on Defence and, kept the soldiers fully contented and happy which guaranteed a firm and strong government.

CHAPTER 5

HISHAM II
(976 A.D.)

Hisham II succeeded his father Hakam II at the age of 12 in 355 A.H; 976 A.D. under the title of Al-Muaiid. Scott is of opinion that he was 14 at the time of his accession.

Jafer-bin-Usman Mushafi and Muhammad-bin-Abi Amir were appointed guardians of Hisham by his father, Hakam at the time of his death.

His mother Sultana Subh called Aurora, a Basque by birth acted as the Queen regent. The saqlibah opposed the accession of Hisham on the ground of his age and wanted to install Al-Mughira the brother of Hakam on the throne. They also opposed Al-Mus-hafi to hold the office of the Grand Vazir. The leaders of the Saqaleba, Faiq al-Nizami and Jawadhar favoured the accession of Al-Mughira.

Al-Mushafi, the Hajib, conspired to kill Al-Mughira which was ultimately done by Muhammad-bin-Abi Amir. The Saqalibas' scheme having thus failed, Hisham II was declared king and the people offered *Baiat* to him. Queen Subh the queen-mother became the regent while Mushafi and Ibne-Abi Amir became Prime Minister (Hajib) and minister respectively.

The slaves who were organizing secret revolutions were

crushed diplomatically by the remission of taxes on olive oil which earned the admiration and loyalty of the people for the minor caliph Jozar and Faiq the Saqaliba leaders were punished. Jozar had to resign his post and Faiq was driven out of Cordova.

The minor caliph was virtually confined in the palace and the government was run by the queen Regent and Ibne-Abi Amir.

Muhammad-bin-Amir was born about 942 A.D. and had settled in Cordova in his youth. His father was an eminent lawyer of Cordova. His mother Burayah, daughter of Yahya-bin-Zakaryah-al-Tamimi, a magistrate of Cordova, was a talented lady. His forefathers were attached to the royal court, and were greatly respected.

Ibne-Abi Amir however had not enjoyed the affluent days of his precursors.

He was a self made man and rose to the highest position mainly due to his own effort.

After obtaining the degree of Law from the University of Cordova, he adopted the profession of petition-writer in the Court of Muhammad Al-Salim the Qazi of Cordova. He maintained a well established office at the palace-gate, Fortune favoured him and he was introduced to the queen Regent Subh by one of her palace eunuchs who happened to be well-acquainted with him.

Having earned the admiration of the queen, he was appointed a steward of the estate of her elder son Abdul Rehman on 15 Dinars per month. (February 976 A.D.) at the age of 26.

Later on he held different higher posts, such as, the steward of the Queen's estate, Collector of tithes and inheritance duties at Seville and Superintendent of the mint at Cordova. He earned the confidence of the Ibne- Hudayr the finance minister, by getting the embezzlement charges set aside by compiling the accounts talently. He was later on appointed as Sahebul-Shurta, police officer (361 A.H; 972 A.D.) of Cordova. He got a still higher post of controller-general of Finance and the chief Qazi of Mauritania. His marriage to Asmah, the daughter of General Ghalib paved his way for positions of eminence in the long run, till at last he became the guardian of the young crown prince, Hisham. He became all the more popular by repulsing the Christians (Rajab 366 A.H; February, 977) and returned to the capital with large booty.

Ibn Abi Amir: Muhammad ibn Abi Amar belonged to a Yemeni tribe of Ma'afer and to the family of Beni Ibne Amir. The family belonged not to Arab aristocracy, but to Arab gentry. Many of its members had held important, though not great, offices in the Umayyad State. The founder of the family, Abdul Malik, was one of the few Arab nobles who accompanied Tariq bin Ziyad in 711, when he invaded Visigothic Spain. Indeed, he was the first officer to capture a Spanish town even before the Battle of Barbate which gave the Muslims victory over the Visigoths. As a result of his services, the castle of Torrax, near Algeciras, in southern Spain, was allotted to him, which remained in the possession of his family. His descendants, however, lived mostly at Cordova, where they held judicial and other minor offices. Ibne Abi Amir's grandfather, also called Muhammad, was the Qazi of Seville. He had married a daughter of Yahya Ibne Ishaq, a wazir and physician of Abdul Rehman Ill. His father, Abdullah, surnamed Abu Hafs, was of religious turn of mind. He was well-versed in Islamic religion and had travelled to the Holy Places in Arabia for Hajj. But, while on his way back home, he breathed his last in Africa. Ibne Abi Amir's mother was called Boraiha. As it was the tradition of his family, Ibne Abi Amir did not stay long on his family estate.

While still young, he came to Cordova, where he joined the University of Cordova. In the University, he studied Islamic theology and law. But he had also an interest in history, philosophy and literature. In all these branches of knowledge he became very proficient. His real interest, however lay in politics. Having read the history of the Arab, and other nations and rulers, he conceived an all-engrossing ambition to become a ruler of Spain. Being a young man of great talents, and ambitions, he once boasted before his friends of his plan to become a ruler of Spain when they were gossiping under a tree in the lawn of the University. Boundlessly ambitious, he had tremendous self-confidence in his powers and abilities to realize his plans. Knowing that power comes by being near the place of the caliph, he sought an employment which would keep him as near to the court as possible. With this object, he became a petition-writer, with his office near the gate of the palace, through which people went in and out of the palace.

Ibne Abi Amir's beginning was modest, but his plans were sound. Many of the servants and slaves of the royal harem passed through the gate. Soon he got a subordinate post in the court of the Qazi of Cordova, in the days of Hakam II. The Qazi was not satisfied with the work of his young assistant, who appeared to him as an absent-minded young man of unorthodox views, The Qazi complained about him to the Wazir Mus'hafi and requested him to provide him with some other job. Hakam II was in need of a steward to look after the property of his eldest son, Abdul Rehman, and the Wazir recommended the name of Ibne Abi Amir. As the prince was only a child of five, his property was really supervised by his mother, Subh, the favourite wife of caliph Hakam II. Thus the young steward came into the service of the inner circle of the court. With this, indeed, he had put his foot on the first rung of the ladder of power, which he knew very well to what heights it would enable

him to climb. Although the Qazi had found him a
good-for-nothing, absent minded young man, Ibne Abi Amir
was not at all so. He knew the modern art of how to win friends
and influence people. He was a hard-working, painstaking,
resourceful and resolute young man, who was at once pliant,
cautious, crafty and courteous, and, if, need be, unscrupulous.
He could also converse captivatingly. By his polished courtesy
and charming manners, he soon won the good opinion of the
Sultana Subh. On February 23, 967, he was appointed the
steward of the property of Abdul Rehman, when he was 26
years of age. He pleased Subh so much that she appointed him
steward of her own property. And then, within a year, he was
made the Master of the Mint, This office provided him control
over large sums of money, which he used not only in the interests
of the State, but also to advance his own interests. Once
Muhammad Ibne Aflah, a client (mawla) of the Umayyad
Caliphs and a court functionary, visited him at the Mint and
requested him to exchange a bridle studded with jewels for a
sum, for he was deep in debt owing to heavy expenditures he
had incurred on the marriage of his daughter. Ibne Abi Amir at
once ordered his men to weigh the bridle and the bit and gave a
large sum of silver coins in exchange for the two, which was
sufficient to pay his debts and yet the surplus was enough to
make him a rich man once again. Afterwards, Ibne Aflah became
his admirer. In this way, Ibne Abi Amir collected a party devoted
to him.

Above all, he won the heart of the Sultana Subh by his
single-minded devotion to her interests. Once he presented her
a silver model of a palace. She was so much pleased with it that
she was afterwards never weary of singing praises of him before
caliph Hakam. But Ibne Abi Amir did not neglect other inmates
of the royal harem, who were also charmed by his liberality,
and good manners. They were so much full of praise for him

that the caliph once remarked, "I do not understand how this young man has gained the hearts of the ladies of the harem. I lavish on them everything they desire, and yet they praise no other gift except his." The Caliph suspected embezzlement of public moneys by the Master of the Mint. One day he summoned him to the palace to render account of the public funds to him. He satisfied the Caliph fully, which enhanced the Caliph's good opinion about him and was entrusted by the Caliph with new duties. In February, 968, he was made the trustee of vacant estates; in July, 970, he was appointed steward to Hisham, who was a heir to the throne; in February, 972, he was made the Commander of the second regiment of the Caliph's bodyguard, who was also the Chief of the City Police (Shurtah) of Cordova, although he was then only thirty-one years of age. He was now rich enough to build a palate of his own, where he entertained liberally all kinds of visitors, high or low, officers and courtiers, These people were always full of praises for him.

A new opportunity opened his way to still greater heights. It was the most of the chief justice of Mauritania in western Africa. As we have said in the previous chapter, in August, 972, Hakam II despatched an army under Muhammad Ibne Qasim Ibne Tomlos to teach Ibne Kennun, the pro-Fatimid ruler of north-west Africa, a lesson. Ibne Tomlos defeated him in a battle near Tangier, but was later defeated and killed by Ibne Kennun. Hakam then sent a new army under another general, Ghalib to Africa. Ibne Kennun tried to resist him. But Ghalib won victory over him both by feat of arms and by liberally bribing his officers and tribal chiefs. Though Hakam was happy over the news of victory, but he was worried by huge sums spent by Ghalib to win over Ibne Kennun's men. In order to check the wastage of public funds, Hakam sent Ibne Abi Amir to North Africa as Chief Justice of Mauritania, with instructions to keep an eye on the doings of his generals and other military officers, especially over their financial dealings.

Ibne Abi Amir's task was very difficult. If he audited the accounts of the generals strictly, they would be angry with him, especially Ghalib, who was then the most influential commander in Umayyad Spain. But if he did not, the Caliph would be displeased. In spite of difficulties, Ibne Abi Amir fulfilled his duties so tactfully and skilfully that both sides were pleased with his performance. Military officers were all praise for him, while he won friends among the tribal chiefs. What was more, he freely mixed with the rank and file of the Spanish army and won their affection. The first-hand experience of the military life stood him in good stead later on, as we shall see. So far as the campaign against Ibne Kennun was concerned, Ghalib succeeded in defeating him and compelled him to capitulate. Other Idrisid princes did the same. Thus by September, 974, Umayyad arms were victorious all over Western Africa and Ghalib returned to Cordova amidst tremendous welcome. Two years later, Hakam died and his younger son, Hisham, became the boyish Caliph.

His Wazarat: After the assassination of the prince Mughira and the accession of the young Hisham to the throne, Sultana Subh was proclaimed as regent to the young Caliph. The people of Cordova seemed to be reconciled to the idea of regency of a woman. But the eunuchs, of the royal household were not happy over the turn of events. They stirred the people of Cordova against Mus'hafi and his friends. Ibne Abi Amir was the first to notice their discontent and advised Mus'hafi to bring the young Caliph before the people and to win their favour by abolishing some taxes. Accordingly, on October 7, 976, Minister Mus'hafi first made himself as Hajib or Prime Minister, with Ibne Abi Amir as a Wazir and took Hisham on horseback through the streets of Cordova, escorted by a large body of troops and accompanied by Ibne Abi Amir. At the same time the tax on oil was abolished, which had pinched the poorer classes most. As

Ibne Abi Amir had taken special rare to make all these measures public, especially the abolition of the oil-tax, he became very popular among the people as a true friend of the poor. He then crushed the influence of the royal eunuchs who were not happy with the accession of Hisham, and were conspiring against the government of Hajib Mus'hafi. Ibne Abi Amir was, however not the man to rest content with the high office of a Wazir. He was resolved to become the sole ruler of Spain, Now Hajib Mus'hafi was in his way. He must, therefore, be removed. He could do so only by winning favours of the whole people of Spain. The ever-aggressive Christians of the North provided him with this opportunity.

Breaking their treaties with Hakam, they attacked his kingdom when he fell ill during the last days of his life. A renegade, Abu'l Ahwas Mann, of the family of the Tojibi Quraysh of Saragoss, helped them. They captured several Muslim fortresses on the frontiers. The weakness of the central government, arising from the events of accession of Hisham, further emboldened them and they pushed their raids even up to the very gates of Cordova. The Christian raids not only upset the regent, Sultana Subh, but also disquieted the people of the capital. They blamed the new government for their inactivity to check Christian raids.

Informed of Sultana Subh's fears, Mus'hafi convened a conference of his viziers, in which it was decided that an army would be sent against the Christians. But the question was as to who should command it. No vizier was ready to do so, for the risk of defeat was very great. At this Ibne Abi Amir said, "I am ready to lead the troops, provided I am provided a sum of one hundred thousand dinars".

One of the viziers objected to the sum asked by him. Ibne Abi Amir said, "Very well, you take two hundred thousand and command the army yourself". The vizier was silenced. It was then decided to grant the money and the command of an army to Ibne Abi Amir. It may be mentioned here that Ibne Abi Amir was a civilian officer and had no military training at all. His only experience of warfare was the tete-a-tete he had with the military officers of General Ghalib's army in north-western Africa a couple of years ago. Be it as it may, Ibne Abi Amir marched out of Cordova in February, 977, at the head of an army. He raised the morale of his soldiers by lavishly spending the subsidy granted to him. He then crossed the frontier and inflicted a defeat on the Christians at Alhama, near Simancas, where a few years earlier, Ramiro II had defeated the Muslims. Loaded with large booty, he returned to Cordova in April, 977, where he was welcomed by the Cordovans heartily. His star was now rising. He was popular with the people and had won the affections of the troops by lavishly spending on them money and the booty he had captured. They were now heart and soul for him. Thus from a Qazi, Ibne Abi Amir had become, almost overnight, a general, and a wonderful general at that, as later events would show.

Military Expeditions:

His military expeditions against the Christians were highly successful. The revolt of the Galicians and the Basques just after the death of Al-Hakam II was crushed. The alliance of Romero III of Lon with Garcia count of castile and Sancho Abarca of Pamplona (Navaree) was broken and the enemies met with rushing defeat (371 A.H., 981 A.D.) His assumption of the title of Al-Mansoor be-Allah (981 A.D.) was quite justified and appropriate. He captured Barcelona (6th July 985 A.D.) and Count Borrel was defeated badly. The revolt of the Leonese under Bermidu II (988 A.D.) was quelled to extend the Muslim-frontiers to the Pyreneses again. His general Asqalajah, quelled the rebellion of Hasan-bin-Ghannum, the Idrisid ruler of Morocco. He was successful in Mauritania and reduced the major part of North Africa to subjection.

It is said that he led his expedition against the Christians annually which had frightened them so much that they had no courage to uproot the Muslim flag planted by Al-Mansoor on a hillock of a Christian town.

It was in 997 A.D. that the might of Al-Mansoor was all the more acknowledged by his successful attack on Galicia by sea. He thus ruled over the coastal region of north Africa in the south and the Cantaberian sea after conquering Leon and Santiago-de-Compostela in the north. According to Ibne-Khaldoon he undertook 52 successful campaigns against the Christians.

He is said to have assumed the title of Syed (Lord) and Malik-al-Karim (The generous ruler) also (996 A.D.).

Death :

On his way back from the battle of Castile, against Riouja, he fell ill and died on 27th Ramzan 392 A.H,, 10th August, 1002 A.D at the age of 61. He was buried in Medina-celi.

It is said that he used to preserve the battle-field-dust on his uniform in separate bags to dust his body after his death denoting his Jihad against the unbelievers for the glory of Islam. He was wrapped in the cotton cloth coffin woven by his daughters from the cotton grown in his own inherited cotton field.

Character:

Al-Mansoor was a highly ambitious, sagacious, diplomat, statesman and warrior of Europe in the 10th century. It was he who saved the country from its fall during the decaying period of Al-Hisham II, the minor caliph. He crippled the Christians of Leon, Navaree and Barcelona to such a degree that his name was enough to terrorise them. He did not believe in treaties and preferred to negotiate the terms in the battle fields. As a disciplinarian, he maintained strict discipline in all civil and military departments.

He was a just ruler and a great upholder of justice, but to achieve his own end he did not tolerate the least clash of interest at any stage whatsoever. He was loyal to his ownself and to none; not even to his benefactors Sultana Subh or his father-in-law General Ghalib nor even Mus'hafi who always held him in his confidence. The establishment of the Amirid-caliphate was the realization of the dream of his young life in the university of Cordova.

His policy of apprisement towards the orthodox Ulema by putting to fire rare collections on philosophy and other subjects in the library of Al-Hakam II cannot be overlooked. His copying of the Holy Quran may not be attributed to his religious fervancy like King Nasiruddin and Emperor Aurangzeb but simply to obliterate the hatred of the Ulema for him.

Achievements:

Al-Mansoor during his regime brought the country on a very prosperous footing. After establishing his position abroad, he looked to the material welfare of the country and the people. He made a survey of the developments under AI-Nasir and Al-Mustansir and finding no room left for him, he satisfied himself with widening old roads, constructing new ones with bridges to facilitate the military move and also to nourish trade and industry. The bridges across the Gevil at Ejica and over the Gudalquiver in Cordova facilitated the general communication.

He enlarged the mosque of Cordova by adding eight more naves to it. He himself took part as a labourer in the construction work.

He built a magnificent city east of Cordova called Madina-al-Zahira in 368 A.H; 978 A.D. He transferred the treasure from the Caliph's palace to it and made him a pauper. All the government offices were located there. He himself held his courts there and all official ceremonies were held there. His efforts to outshine Al-Zahra however could not be achieved for its being a wonder by itself.

Spain which had already reached the height of her glory under Al-Nasir and Al-Mustansir and also the first world power, retained her prestige, honour, fame and solidarity under Al-Mansoor the great. Cordova, in the words of a nun Hortsuitha of Gandersheim (d. 1002 A.D.) was "a fair ornament, a venerable city, well cultured, rich, illustrious and renowned for all resources particularly in the seven streams of knowledge and famous for victories".

He was a patron of learning and culture. He encouraged and fostered the Arab culture and civilization with a view to arbicise Spain on the pattern of Zaryab.

He welcomed scholars of various subjects and patronised them with bounties. It is said that forty one poets and historians accompanied him in his Catalonian campaign. Abdul Ala Sa'aid-bin-Hasan of Baghdad was very prominent then.

Al-Mansoor popularised the study of mathematics, astronomy and astrology by establishing well equipped Madrasa for the purpose. Abdul Qasim Maslama-al-Majriti (d. 1004-7 A.D.) was the celebrated teacher of astrology. He wrote a book on the Astrolab and also a commercial arithmetic. Abdul Rehman Ishaque-bin-Haytham, the personal physician of Al-Mansoor worked on Omitives and laxatives. His works on medicine are very valuable.

Al-Fusus of Said of Baghdad was dedicated to Mansoor

who was rewarded 1000 Dinars. The employment of Abu-al-Wahid-bin-Mansoor, a historian and paleaographist to compare, correct and collate the manuscripts in his library, testifies the patronage of Hajib for learning.

To pacify the Fuqaha he was intolerant to the free thinkers and philosophers and even allowed a large number of books of Al-Hakam's library to be put to fire, but later on he encouraged them to a great deal. He married a daughter of Sancho III, king of Navaree and declared Sunday as the rest-day on the plea of his Christian soldiers being a majority a very injudicious decision of a man who always fought for the superiority of Islam.

Ibne Abi Amir was famous for his justice. It is said that once his youngest son whipped a poor boy. His father complained to Abi Amir. He therefore ordered his son to be whipped accordingly who died of sharp strokes.

Abi Amir wept bitterly saying that he loved justice more than the life of his own son.

Thus all sorts of oppressions were unknown and peace reigned supreme. Theft, robbery, and high-handedness could not be traced in the country. The rule of Abi Amir was the stamp of justice and equity.

His Personality:

Al-Mansoor was one of the most lovable personalities in the history of Islamic Spain. It was not only because of his fifty or more campaigns against his enemies in all of which he was victorious, though he was not trained for a military career, nor only because he rose from the humble position of a petition-writer at the gate of the royal palace to that of the supreme ruler of the whole Iberian Peninsula, but also because of his many acts of justice and his onscientious effort not to commit any injustice against anyone, high or low, rich or poor,

Christian or Muslim, Arab or Berber. Dozy writes, "If we find ourselves obliged to condemn the means which Almanzor employed in the pursuit of sovereignty, we are also compelled to admit that he made noble use of his power once he had achieved it." We may conclude his history with the words inscribed on his tomb by his Muslim admirers:

His history in his deeds you may trace,
As tho'he stood before you face to face.

CHAPTER 6

ABDUR REHMAN THE ENTERER
(756–788 A.D.)

Abdur Rehman was born in 113 A.H, at Ulya or St. Hinadair a city in the vicinity of Damascus. His father Muaviyay died at the age of 21 in 118 A.H. Abdur Rehman therefore was brought up under the direct care and patronage of his grandfather, Caliph Hisham, who had a mind to nominate him as his successor.

Abdur Rehman was only 10 years of age that Muslima the brother of Hisham met him at the gate of the Rusafa palace, the residence of Hisham in Qinsirin. Muslima was a profound scholar of astrology and astronomy. He had predicted the greatness of Abdur Rehman which evidently became an established truth.

The proclamation of the Abbaside caliphate, Rabiul Awwal (132 A.H./March 750 A.D.) brought a great calamity for the house of the Umayyads. A general massacre of the Umayyads was ordered by Al-Saffah (the blood shedder). Almost all the royal members were killed. Aban-bin-Muaviya-bin-Hisham was deprived of his one hand and one leg and paraded in Damascus. The graves of all the Umayyad caliphs were dug out; their corpses were desecrated and hanged. The graves of Muaviyah I and Umer bin-Abdul Aziz were however spared. Abdur Rehman was only 19 years of age that he witnessed the havoc played by the Abbasides. He managed to escape with his brother Yahya-bin-Muaviyah and went underground in a village in Qinsirin. Al-Saffah after killing Aban-bin Muaviyah a brother of Abdur Rehman and Yahya-bin-Muaviyah, his cousin, proclaimed a general amnesty for the Umayyads. It was nothing but a political trap. Believing the proclamation, a large number of the Umayyads came out of their hidden shelters. All of them, nearly 70 in number, were caught and put to sword at the banks of the Abi Fitras 12 miles from Ramla. Abdur Rehman sent a detective of his own to survey the situation. He hurried back to convey the gruesome murder of the Umayyads but he and Yahya the brother of Abdur Rehman were killed by the chasing horsemen, Abdur Rehman, luckily was out a hunting. Abdur Rehman took shelter in a dense forest on the bank of the Euphrates, along with his family. One day Sulaiman his son was playing in the village field that he came trembling with fear to his father Abdur Rehman who was suffering from eye-trouble. On enquiry he knew of the chase of the Abbaside soldiers for him. He therefore leaving his family with his freed-man Badr dropped down in the Euphrates to swim it over to the other side. His brother only 13 years of age also followed him. When he reached the other side of the Euphrates, he saw the severed head of his innocent brother who being unable to face the strong current of the river and fully believing the words of the Abbaside soldiers for amnesty had returned to the bank. Abdur Rehman hiding himself in a village of Palestine awaited the arrival of his family with Badr. He staying there for sometime reached Africa on the assurance of Abdur Rehman-Habib Alfahri, a relation of Yousuf Alfahri the governor of Spain. Bin-Habib till then had not acknowledged the sovereignty of Al-Abbas. He was rather ambitious for proclaiming his independence. With the arrival of Abdur Rehman in Africa as a state-guest, Bin-Habib recollected the prediction of Muslima, and was so much perturbed that he resolved to hand over Abdur Rehman to Al-Abbas to earn his favour and secure his chair. Abdul Rehman guessed the plan and fled away incognito. For full five years he kept on changing his stay from one place to the other–sometime in Barqa, sometime with the Amir Tahoorat and sometime with the Berber tribe of Maknasa. He then decided to take shelter with the Berber tribe Banu Nafossa, his mother's clan. This tribe stood for his full active support. Here he could find time to survey the possibility of carving an avenue for himself. He decided to test his stars on the soil of Spain which was then engaged in civil war and the country was out of the control of the government. There was no chance of direct intervention by Al-Abbas who was awfully busy in his own affairs in Syria. He also hoped that many of the Syrian settlers favoured the Umayyads and will welcome him. Abu Usman, Ubaidullah-bin-Usman and Abdullah-bin-Khalid-bin-Aban commanded respect and influence in Elvira. Abdur Rehman sent a letter through his trusted man Badr to Abu Usman requesting him to rise to his support and restore the lost honour of the Umayyads. The letters had the full details of the havoc played by Al-Saffah and was so pathetic that Abu Usman wept bitterly and assured Badr of his support to the prince. Abu Usman prevailed over other chiefs of Spain and enlisted their support for prince, Abdur Rehman. The delay in the return of Badr disturbed the mental peace of the prince who had moved from the Banu Nafoosa to the tribe of Banu Mughila on the ocean-coast. While surveying the ocean with his naked eyes desperately, he was filled with joy coupled with the feelings of hope and dismay, when he saw the barge of Badr heading hastily to the shore. Badr after paying his respects to the prince acquainted him with the whole affairs, Badr was accompanied by selected chiefs of Spain who paying homage to the prince welcomed him to the land conquered by his predecessors.

Abu-Ghalib Tamam was the first chief, introduced to the prince followed by other tribal heads.

The news of Abdur Rehman's expedition, spread like the wild fire. Five hundred eminent horsemen of Banu Nafoosa formed his first contingent. Abdur Rehman who wandered for five years as a fugitive, had now 1000 soldiers at his command. The Spanish chiefs had brought with them heavy wealth in the shape of gold and silver coins, which was distributed among the various Berber tribes just to gain their favour and support.

Abdur Rehman with his army landed on the shore of Spain at Almonicar port, (Rabiul Awwal 138 A.H.). He was accorded a royal welcome at the port. Eminent nobles like Abu Usman, Abu Khalid, Yusuf-bin-Bakht, Abu Ubaida Husain-bin-Malik Kalbi and many others were present on the port to receive him. He stayed in the Garden of Alfantin, a palace of Abdullah-bin-Khalid near the city of Lusha between Arjazoona and Elvira.

Yousuf Al-Fahri, the governor of Spain was engaged in the affairs of Saragossa and Austurias. The country was overtaken by famine. The murder of Amir and Hubab Zuhri had caused the rise of the Yamanites against Al-Fahri. It was at this critical moment that a special messenger of his wife Umme-Usman waited on him with her letter which disclosed the entry of Abdur Rehman into Spain, his stay with Abu Usman and the defeat of the deputy governor of Elvira. Yousuf therefore in consultation with Sumail sent a goodwill mission which consisted of Ubaid, Khalid and Isa. These three persons laden with 1000 Dinars, Jewels, fine clothes, male and female slaves, horses mules, two each, proceeded on their peace mission to Abdul Rehman. When they reached Orch, Isa who wanted to misappropriate the presents stayed in Orch on the promise of sending the presents on successful talks. Both Ubaid and Khalid had pictured the prince as a forlorn, helpless, poverty striken and miserable man. They were rather amazed, puzzled and dismayed to find the prince in pomp and grandeur. The talk however failed and Khalid was imprisoned for his loose talk.

It was on the Ist Shawwal 138 A.H—8th March 756 A.D. that Abdur Rehman entered Archidona the Capital of Ragio where he was declared Amir and the religious Sermon was read in his name and all those present there. Isa-bin-Musawar the governor of Ragio and Jidar-bin-Umar Qaisi and other took the oath of allegiance to the new Amir.

The Battle of Masarah, May 13, 756: After landing on the Spanish coast, Abdur Rehman received the support and loyalty of the Yemenites and also of some Berber tribes in southern Spain. Yousuf and Sumail, the real rulers of Spain, tried to win him over by offering him large gifts and the offer of the estate which his grandfather, Hisham, had allocated to him while Abdur Rehman was still a child. But Abdur Rehman had not come to Spain to live quietly on his landed estate: he had come to rule the province which he believed was his for it was a province of the Umayyad Caliphate. So he spurned all offers of Yousuf and Sumail, who then made preparations for a war with him. In the meanwhile, the Yemenite tribes had proclaimed Abdur Rehman as the Amir of Spain. Then he marched on Cordova. On the way, he was welcomed by the people of Seville as the new Amir. The rival armies of Abdur Rehman and Yousuf and Sumail met at Masarah, near Cordova. Before fighting began, Abdur Rehman told his troops that those who had no heart to fight could go in peace. As none left him, he addressed them as thus:

> Tomorrow is Friday and the feast of Eid ul Azha. The two forces are the sons of Qays arrayed against the tribes of Yemen. Let this day be the same as that of Marj Rahit (At

Marj Rahit in Syria the Umayyads under
Merwan had defeated their enemies and
secured their Caliphate once again).

The battle then began with great fury. The shrewd Sumail knew well that if defeated, he and Yousuf would lose their all. He tried to kill Abdur Rehman, for he knew that he alone had united the Yemenites and the Berbers against his Qaisites. If killed, his supporters would have no leader left to fight. He made a determined attack on the Intruder, but failed. Then Abdur Rehman's cavalry defeated Yousufs right wing. He fled from the battlefield towards Cordova. But Abdur Rehman was hard on his heals. He entered Cordova, where he was proclaimed the Amir of Spain. Thus the fugitive prince had at last realised his dream. In July 756, both Yousuf and Sumail surrendered to Abdur Rehman, who then became the sole ruler of Spain. He assumed the title of Amir. Although he did not recognise the authority of the Abbaside Caliphs, he did not take the title of "Ameer ul Momineen" or "Khalifa", for he still believed in the unity of the Ummah, and did not want to split it into warring loyalties. In a poem of his own composing, Abdur Rehman described how he won the kingdom:

*I, and I alone, driven by a consuming anger, bared a
two-edged sword,*

*Crossed the desert and furrowed the sea, mastering waves
and waste-land,*

*I won a kingdom, gave it strength, and built a mosque for
prayer;*

I rallied a disbanded army and peopled deserted cities.

Trouble by Yousuf and Sumail:

Abdur Rehman was not yet the undisputed master of the whole of Muslim Spain. The Christian nobility was attempting an insurrection on one hand and the Arab aristocracy was planning for setting up an oligarchy on the other. While the new Amir was discussing with his lieutenants the repression plan, he was conveyed of the rebellious gestures of Yousuf and Sumail. Abdur Rehman the son of Yousuf joined his father with 500 soldiers and reached Merida. At Toledo, Sumail with his own forces joined Yousuf. Sumail and Yousuf played havoc in the neighbourhood of Elvira. The combined forces reached Jaen and captured Elvira. The governor of Elvira, Jabir-bin-Ula was defeated and took shelter in the mountains. Abdur Rehman hearing the fall of Elvira, appointing Abu Usman as governor of Cordova and Umayya-bin-Zaid the former secretary of Yousuf, as his own secretary, marched on to Elvira to punish Yousuf. Learning the advance of Amir Abdur Rehman, he (Yousuf) sent his son Abu Zaid to attack Cordova and himself waited for Abdur Rehman in the fort of Mantisha.

Abu Usman was, however defeated and took refuge in the mosque, who later on surrendered himself to Abu Zaid on the assurance of the safety of his life. Abu Zaid, had no strength enough to keep Cordova under his control permanently. He therefore thought it wise to return to Elvira with his family. Abdur Rehman who was greatly shocked to hear the news, was not discouraged. He immediately appointed Amir-bin-Ali as governor of Cordova who managed the administration of Cordova successfully.

Abdur Rehman stayed in a village Armina to threaten Elvira. Yousuf and Sumail, both were so much overawed that they lost not only courage but wisdom too and preferred to enter into a peace treaty for the second time. Things could have been otherwise if resistance could have been continued. The Amir himself was trying to evade the scuffle for two major reasons—the insurgence of the Christians and the imprisonment of Abu Usman his chief supporter.

Yousuf however submitted in Safar 139 A.H., July 756 A.D. The treaty envisaged the following:

(a) Yousuf and Sumail were allowed to retain their properties—movable or immovable—without any risk whatsoever. All were given general amnesty.

(b) Abu Zaid and Abdul Aswad the two sons of Yousuf were kept as hostages till the restortion of complete law and order in the country.

(c) Yousuf will stay in the eastern part of Cordova and will report himself daily to the royal court.

(d) Khalid bin-Zaid and Abu Usman were freed.

This treaty did not last for more than two years. Both Abdur Rehman and Yousuf were suspicious of each other. Yousuf decided to try his luck for the third time. He fled to Merida. The two sons of Yousuf were therefore thrown in prison.

Yousuf who was encouraged and helped by the people of Merida and Toledo was able to collect an army of 20,000. Hearing the advance of Abdur Rehman, Yousuf moved to Seville. Abdul Malik-bin-Merwan the governor of Seville preferred to stay in the fort. Yousuf laid siege to the fort. But he changed his mind and advanced to Burj-e-Usama to fight Abdur Rehman there. The governor of Seville Abdul Malik chased Yousuf who was defeated in the famous battle of Loxa (141 A.H./758 A.D.) Yousuf now wandered from place to place till he was killed by Abdullah-bin-Umar Ansari a villager of Toledo. Sumail preferred to end his life by poison in the prison.

The death of Yousuf did not end the trouble of Abdur Rehman, Abdul Aswad Muhammad-bin-Yousuf feigning himself blind for full 18 years in the prison managed to escape away from jail, (168 A.H./782 A.D.). The Fahris and the Qaisis

joined him at Toledo. He then advanced to Cordova with a
strong army. He was however defeated at Qastaloona in the
province of Jaen. Abdul Aswad was not discouraged. He faced
the royal army just the next year, 169 A.H., but luck did not
favour him. He died in Toledo, (171 A.H./786 A.D.). After a
continued struggle of 33 years for power, Yousuf's family
succumbed for ever.

Toledo's Affairs:

Eversince the arrival of Amir Abdur Rehman in Spain, a
strong group was against him. Yousuf had a strong hold there
and Toledo was the centre of his insurgent activities.

Hisham-bin-Urwah the former governor of Toledo declared
himself independent in 761 A.D. Toledo was therefore besieged
and had to surrender. His son was kept as a hostage. Hisham
revolted again in 764 A.D. and his refusal to submission caused
the death of his son. Toledo fell to Amir Abdur Rehman and
the rebel leaders were hanged in Cordova.

The Yamanites' Disloyalty in the South:

Abdur Rehman was disliked both by the Yamanites and
the Berbers due to his paternal ascendancy. It was in 143 A.H;
760 A.D. that Arzaq-bin-Noman Ghassani capturing Medina
Sidonia and Seville made himself strong in the Southern part
of Spain. Abdur Rehman however defeated Ghassani and
beheaded him without delay. Abu-Sabbah, a Yamanite chief
and governor of Seville was deposed and killed, (706 A.D.) for
his rebellious activities after the battle of Masarah. The result
was obvious. Many of the Yamanites chiefs and relations of
Abu Sabbah, such as Abdul Ghaffar-bin-Hamid, Amr-bin-Talut,
Abul Kulthoom-bin-Yasub and Hayat-bin-Mulamis rose in open
revolt and put a large number of the Mudarites to sword. Abdur
Rehman therefore hastened to meet the rebels in 774 A.D. on

the bank of the Mayasar (Bembezar) in the province of Cordova. The Berbers however refrained from raising their sword against. Abdur Rehman who was a lineal of their own through his mother. The Yamanites met with crushing defeat and Niebla the rebel chief was killed which closed the chapter of rebellions of the Yamanis in the south.

The Unsuccessful Efforts of Abbasides:

Although Abdur Rehman was the independent ruler of Spain he did pay due respect the Abbaside Caliphs for their being the custodian of the holy cities of Mecca and Madina. It was in this spirit that he had read the Khutba in the name of Abbaside Caliph in the mosque of Cordova. It so happened that Abdul Malik an Umayyad, narrated to Abdur Rehman, the atrocities and brutalities of the Abbasides to the Ummayads, so pathetically that Abdur Rehman stopped the recitation of the Khutba in the name of the Abbaside Caliph. He however remained content with the title of 'AMIR' as he believed that Muslims cannot have two Khalifas at a time according to Shariat.

The Caliph Al-Mansoor with no lawful excuse invaded Spain to drive away the Umayyads from the peninsula whom he considered a menace to the Caliphate. Al-bin-Mughis Yahsubi a trusted lieutenant of Al-Mansoor and a prominent leader of Africa landed in the province of Beja, (146 A.H; 763 A.D.), and hoisted the Black Flag of the Abbasides there. With a strong army constituted of the Yamins, the Egyptians settlers and prominent chiefs, such as Wasit-bin-Ala-bin-Mughis and Mughis-bin-Qatn; Yahsoobi invaded Seville. Ala being unable to resist Amir Abdur Rehman retreated to Carnova. Badr foiled the plan of Ghayas-bin-Alqama Al-Lakhmi of Sidonia of joining Ala, who had besieged Carmona. The siege lasted for two months. The army of Ala suffered heavily from food scarcity. The surprise night-attack of Amir Abdur Rehman with only

700 soldiers spread a great confusion in the Ala's camp. Ala was killed with 7,000 of his Berber supporters. Ala's head along with other chiefs heads was sent to Caliph Al-Mansoor through a merchant to Qirwan. It is also said that Mansoor was then at Mecca. Looking the heads he exclaimed in rage 'Thank God' the Satan is beyond the ocean'.

Berber Revolts

As we have said above, the Berber tribes had settled in both the western and eastern provinces of the Peninsula. The first to revolt were the Berbers of the eastern province. They were instigated by a Berber school-master, named Shakya. His revolt continued for ten years. In the meanwhile, the Berbers of the west also revolted and became masters of Merida, Coria and other towns. A desultary war raged with the Berber rebels for six years. At the same time, the Yemenites revolted in the west to avenge Abu Sabbah's death. They were joined by the Marabout's (i.e. Shakya's) troops. These revolts came to an end in 774. But a new danger appeared on the north-east frontiers of the Islamic Spain, namely the invasion by Charlemagne, the Emperor of the Franks.

Charlemagne's Invansion and the Chansonde Roland:

Charlemagne, the emperor of the franks, considered himself as a great champion of Christianity. As such there could be no greater service to the cause of Christianity thus the destruction of the Islamic Spain, then rampant with endless revolts. Charlemagne was, indeed, in league with the Abbaside Caliph of Baghdad, on the one side and with some Muslim rebels in the province of Saragossa, on the other. When defeated by the loyal troops of the Amir, one of the rebels, Sulaiman al-Kalbi, fled across the Pyrenees and sought the help of the Frankish Emperor in 777. Next year, Charlemagne invaded

Spain, partly to drive out Islam from Spain, but mainly to extend his empire into the Iberian Peninsula.

Collecting a vast army, Charlemagne crossed the Pyrenees and carried everything before him till he reached the walls of Saragossa. It was defended by Hussain bin Yahya al-Ansari, who repulsed the Frankish assault. Suspecting foul play. Charlemagne captured the renegade Sulaiman and took him back to his dominions. But while crossing the Pyresees through the pass of Roncesvalles, his rear suffered a disastrous defeat at the hands of his fellow-Christians, the Basques and the Gascons. The reason was that while crossing the Pyrenees into Spain he first met not the Muslims but the Basques and other Christians of Spain, on whom he inflicted a defeat at Pamplona. The Spanish Christians resented Charlemagne's invasion of their land as much as did the Spanish Muslims. Their defeat at Pamplona rankled in their hearts.

Diplomacy of Christians:

It may be noted with interest that eversince the conquest of Spain, the Muslim rulers had been tolerant towards the Christians. The royal blood was respected and the common blood too enjoyed freedom like the Muslim subjects. Many of the Christian prince who were oppressed and deprived of their principalities by Roderick, were given their due place and awarded back their confiscated land and property. Inspite of all facilities granted to them by the Muslim rulers, they were not true to them. They were in search of the opportunity and never failed to prove faithless by interfering in the internal affairs. They were a constant source of trouble for the Cordovan government either by open revolt or secret intrigues.

They could be well-located with the Indian government and other powers posing friendship with our country but always busy in positive intrigues against us.

Abdul Rehman therefore could not be an exception. It was between 765 and 768 A.D. that Caliph Mansoor established friendly relations with the Frankish Emperor simply to use him against the Ummayad Imarat in Spain. This detrimental policy of the Abbaside rulers remained unrectified in future also. The Abbaside Caliph being himself unable to defeat the ambitions of Amir Abdur Rehman entered into a secret pact with Charlemagne, king of France to surrender to him the major part of Spain, if he could defeat the new Amir. He was assured of full support by the Caliph to this effect. The coalition of the Arab chiefs and Charlemagne was the outcome of the caliph's sanguinary policy against the newly established Imarat of Spain. Harun-Al-Rashid the renowned Abbaside Caliph who was more powerful and represented a higher culture than Charlemagne, prompted by self-interest and hostility to the Umayyads of Spain, exchanged embassies and presents with the Christian king of France only to use him for the attainment of his evil design. The presents, it is said, included the famous clock unknown to the then Europe. Charlemagne marched with confidence but courted failure and defeat. He was disastrously repulsed at Saragossa (162 A.H./778 A.D.). Besides, the break up of the Arab coalition and the march of wittikind to the French capital after conquering Duetz and other cities on the Rhine, confused Charlemagne so much that he had no other alternative but to run away homeward. The Basques taught him a good lesson by annihilating his army in the valley of Roncesvaus, or Ronces. A fair number of military officers was killed. The famous Roland Prefect of March of Britanny was also put to sword.

The Christian powers thus paralised, preferred to refrain from subversive activities openly in future. Amir Abdur Rehman kept a watch on them and thought friendly, kept them at bay.

Thus both the Abbasides and the Christians failed miserably in overthrowing the Umayyads from Spain.

Achievements of Enterer

The establishment of a glorious dynasty to last for generations was no less an achievement of Abdur Rehman who wandered from place to place for years forlorn and forsaken, in tattered clothes for the safety of his life. The subjugation of Spain was so quick and speedy that it may be termed "dramatic" which bestowed upon him the coveted title of the "Falcon of the Quraish", to the disappointment of Caliph Mansoor. He had studied well the turbulent factors and crushed them all in gradual steps. The Fihrites, the Yamanites, and the selected groups of Berbers were brought to submission for all times. The Christian princes and the neighbouring Christian ruler of France were tackled intelligently. Although an imperialist by nature, character and inheritance, he believed in "Shoora" or advisory council to uphold the democratic way of disposing a subject. He therefore wanted to establish such an empire in the west which could be a combination of monarchy and Islamic democracy. To achieve his aim he devoted himself to uniting the various rival group very intelligently. He curbed the despotic tendency of the Arab chiefs and brought the Berbers and the Spanish Muslims to the upper strata to balance the society and eradicate the evils of the blood-superiority complex. He gave rights and privileges to all based on justice and equity. Every man had a free access to him. Once a poor man came to him and demanded justice and due help for the poor, widows and orphans.

The Amir assured him of all help according to Sharia: and asked him to send all such persons to him to get the relief as prescribed by the Qur'an and Sunna.

He had laid the foundation of an administration which aimed at winning the hearts of the people through justice, kindness and benevolence.

Once an ordinary man pulling down the reins of the horse of the Amir, on the thoroughfare of Cordova, narrated the injustice done to him by the Qazi (Judge). The Amir summoned the Qazi immediately there on the spot and asked him to do justice to the man. Large number of people congregated there and he delivering an eloquent lecture on justice exhorted the congregation to build up character and demand justice at all costs.

He believed in military despotism. He therefore curbed the power of the Arab chiefs by raising his own army of Berbers and new-Muslims whom he showered with wealth and concessions. He had eminent Commander-in-chiefs, like Badr, Tamam-bin-Alqama, Habib-bin-Abdul Malik-al-Qarshi, Asim-bin-Muslim Saqfi and others. Evidence is there, that on many occasions, he himself led the army in person and fought like an ordinary soldier in the battle-field.

He kept a vigilant eye on the administration of the country and was all ears even to the minutes point. Due to the most antagonistic behaviour of caliph Mansoor, he stopped khutba in his name and assumed the title of Amirul Muslimin, and retained the prestige of the Abbaside caliph to be called as Khalifat-ul-Muslimin.

The entire kingdom was divided into' six provinces each, under a governor, who was necessarily the head of the army.

The provincial ministers and other officers were under the provincial governors. The police, judiciary and prison were the central subjects. The centre had a number of departments Secretariat, Ministry, Judiciary, Police, Military judicial courts, and Revenue.

There was an advisory council consisted of men of letters and character. Later on the councillors were called 'Wazir" or minister. The institution of wizarat (ministry) was foreign to the Umayyads of Syria but it came down to the Spanish Umayyads from the Abbasides who got it from Persia.

The Ummal or revenue collectors were placed under a Secretary incharge of the revenue of the country. Correspondence-incharge was the other secretary. Each secretary had a number of assistants to conduct the work systematically with prompt and speedy disposal.

Mention may be made of Abu Usman; Abdullah-bin-Khalid; Abu-Ubaida, Shaheed-bin-Isa-bin-Shaheed; Abdus Salam Rumi; Salaba-bin-Ubaid-bin-Nizam Jizami and Asim-bin-Muslim Saqfi, who held the posts of Councillors or Wazirs, Abdul Malik Mervani was the Chairman of the Council or the Grand Wazir.

Abu Usman and Abdullah-bin-Khalid were incharge of the correspondence departments until regular arrangements were made. Umayya-bin-Yazid was Katib or Secretary.

The judiciary had two separate chief judges, each having a separate independent department. One was called "Qazi of the Civilians and the other Qazi of the armed forces: Besides the Chief Judge, there were other judges in all cities to decide the cases. Each military cantonment likewise had a judge or Qazi. The Qazis accompanied the army units in the battle fields.

Yahya-bin-Yazid Yahsubi who held the post of Qazi-ul-Jama'at during the governorship of Yousuf was allowed to continue and confirmed, in his post by the Amir. After his death, with the approval of the Advisory Council the Amir appointed Masab-bin-lmran or Said- bin-Bashir as chief judge of Cordova in his place.

Before his entry into Spain, the governor was also called Amir. Abdur Rehman, who was a modest man, retained the old title. He did not assume the more pretentious title of Amir

ul Momineen or the Commander of the Faithful, "out of respect
for the seat of the Caliphate, which was still the abode of Islam
and the meeting-place of the Arabian tribes", writes the Arab
historian, Ibne al-Athir. For a long time, he read the Khutbah
at the Friday public prayers in the name of the Abbaside Caliphs,
though lesser men than him had read the Khutbah in their own
names soon after their revolt. It was only two years before his
death, after he had to face several revolts by men instigated by
the Abbaside caliphs, that he stopped in 786 invoking the name
of the Caliph in the Friday khutbahs.

Abdur Rehman had his own court of justice to hear the
parties and decide the cases. All were allowed to see him in the
Darbar or royal court to say any thing they liked. Appeal of all
cases was made to the Amir.

The Amir paid special attention to the organization of the
army. The number of the soldiers went up to one lac. It was
divided into two parts–Cavalry and Infantry.

The Chief of the Infantry Saheb-er-Rajala was Abdul
Hameed-bin-Ghanim and Chief of Cavalry Saheb-ul-Khail was
Sama'ah.

The navy was already strong during the governor's period
and the Amir made it all the more strong.

Abu Sulaiman Dawood Ansari was incharge of the
National Flag, a very covatable position indeed.

The police department "Shurta" was well-established and
worked efficiently. The I.G. Police was called Sahebul Shurta
and was a member of the Advisory Council.

Each government paper had to be authenticated with the
Royal Seal. The officer-in-charge was called Lord Privy Seal.

Amir Abdur Rehman was a versatile genius. He was a
man of knowledge and a high class poet. He was master of

astronomy and astrology. It was an honour for him to sit among the learned and poets. Learned people from distant places used to call on him and got rewards. He was much impressed by Shaikh Ghazi and Sheikh Abu Musa Havari who were eminent theologians. It was at the instance of Sheikh Ghazi that the theological system of Imam Malik was introduced in Spain.

During his brief period of peace Abdur Rehman initiated a number of welfare schemes. Unlike the tendency and practice in the modern age, he revised the gradation of all service ranks and enhanced their salaries without any clamour or protest. The entire service structure was so overhauled that genuine satisfaction prevailed among the service class and corruption was unthinkable.

New methods for the improvement of cultivation were adopted. The cultivators were provided with all facilities and better yield was guaranteed which ensured a balanced exchequer.

The interest of Addakhil was not limited only to the material welfare and progress of the people. He was keenly impatient to improve the spiritual and religious attachment of the people as a whole.

He brought a number of eminent architects and engineers with him who submitted the plan of the famous mosque of Cordova. He himself made certain additions and alterations in the plan and then ordered for the construction of the great mosque. It is said that more than two lacs gold coins were spent on its construction. It was 600 feet in length and 100 feet in breadth. It had 19 arches from north to south and 38 arches from east to west. It had 193 pillars of white marble and 19 big gates. The gates facing south were covered with gold and engravings of holy Quranic ayat. The golden Minar was 240 feet high, and the domes were covered with gold. There was special arrangement for light. Three hundred maunds of olive oil and perfumes, per year, were utilised for the purpose. A lamp made of pure gold, burnt permanently at the MIMBER; the Sermon's pulpit.

Unfortunately this great mosque was turned into a Christian catherdral by Ferdinand III in 1236 A.D. just after the collapse of the Muslim Empire in Spain. It is still known as "Lamezequita" (the mosque). This is a living evidence of the hostile attitude of the Christians towards the Muslims who always gave due regard to their religious sentiments.

The construction of a huge bridge over the Guadalquiver, later on enlarged to seventeen arches is a living testimony of the achievement of the Amir.

The construction of a paved foot-path on the bank of the Guadalquiver leading to the Cordova bridge from the Algazar the Secretariat house, was a new idea for the age.

Education was one of the main subjects of attention for the Amir. He constructed new schools and colleges for imparting higher education in all subjects. Free lodging and boardings were provided in the hostels. Primary education was arranged in mosques. Theology was also taught in mosques. Special grant was allocated for the expenditure on the subject. Eminent Scholars of different subjects were employed on rich salaries and commanded respect and honour.

Inns were innumerable where the tourists were lodged and boarded free of charge. Cash help was also given to the needy. A number of stately buildings were constructed to enhance the national grandeour. He diligently and successfully fashioned out national mould which depicted a fine combination of Arabs, Hispano-Arabs and Gothic architectural systems.

He inaugurated the intellectual movement which made Muslim Spain centre of culture for Europe as a whole to last for centuries. Bilat Razrif the palace of Cordova was enlarged and beautified.

Just close to Cordova he built a garden-palace called Muawiyat-ul- Rusafa after the villa of his grand father Hisham, at Damascus.

The supply of water to the city was under his direct supervision. He had organized new canal systems throughout his empire. The water-supply was free to all.

The Amir is said to be a good horticulturist. He was specially interested in gardening and helped those who adopted it as a profession. He had brought flowers, fruit-plants and seeds from Syria, Iraq, Egypt and other places. He had planted the date-tree himself to adore the recollection of east. He had composed a beautiful poem which spoke of his love for the date tree and the Rusafa Palace. He planted the pomegranate, the peach and other plants and flower plants, all imported from different climes. A regular nursery was organized in the palace to supply the well-nursed plants to other places of Spain to encourage the plantation scheme. His sister Ume-Asbagh had sent to him the plant of a pomegranate of exquisite flavour and colour.

He established a mint at Cordova to strike coins on the pattern of those issued from Damascus.

The city walls of Cordova, originally built by Samah-bin-Malik-Alkhulani in 720 A.D. was reconstructed with seven gates.

Public and private baths were built in every city–a project then unknown to the Christian world.

Inspite of the fact that the Amir was mostly engaged in warfare, he did find time to look into other matters of public interest. He saw that Art and letters flourished in Spain. He patronised all private, enterprises in the field. Literary figures like, Abu-al-Mutahash-Sha the poet, Shaikh Abu Musa Hawari, the legist, Shaikh Ghazi-bin-Qais the theologian and linguist adored the royal Court, Allama Ghazi had brought *Al-Mowattah* of Imam Malik-bin-Anas (715-792 A.D.) to Spain. *Al-Mowattah* was studied and discussed in the royal court which resulted in the introduction of Maliki doctrines in Spain.

The Amir was fond of songs and was very much impressed by the song of Afza one of his singing-girls.

It may however be noted that the growth of civilization and culture was all due to the patriotic administration of the Muslin, rulers of Spain. Had the Muslims been away from this part of Europe, the present Europe, rather the Christian world, would have been moving in the dark and the present growth in civilization and culture would have been delayed for centuries.

Death

Thus all the risings and conspiracy which disturbed his reign, were completely crippled and crushed and the power of the driven and homeless Umayyads began to rise in the western horizon. But the reviver of the power did not live long to enjoy the work of his life. He died in 683 A.D. after a reign of thirty-three years.

Character

Abdur Rehman had proved himself a great general and conqueror. His triumph earned him the praise even of his enemies. It was no small credit that a homeless wanderer had founded a great empire and united under his sceptre a realm which seemed already parcelled out amongst the petty chieftains. He was an able administrator. Himself a poet, Abdur Rehman was a patron of learning and arts. He adorned Cordova with many magnificent building. Though able and energetic, he was cruel and vindictive. Under his despotic rule, no honourable-man would enter his service. Abdur Rehman did not assume the title of *Amirul Mumenin* but was pleased with the simple title *Amir*.

Abdur Rehman was a lover of trees and flowers, especially of Syria. He cultivated different varieties of them in his pleasure garden, Rusafah, and advised his nobles also to do so,

Saud Khan Rohilla says that Abdur Rehman had 150 sons by his different wives.

HISHAM ABDUR REHMAN

Hisham, Abdur Rehman's, second son, born of his favourite slavegirl, Hulal, was preferred by him as his successor due to his pious qualities. Hisham was found of the company of the learned, theologians, poet and historians, while his elder brother, Sulaiman, lived in the company of sychophants, fools and cowards. Moreover, Hulal, his mother interceded on his behalf with Abdur Rehman. So he selected him to be his successor and appointed him as the governor of Merida so that he would have experience of administration. When the Amir died, Hisham was away from Cordova, but was proclaimed Amir on reaching the capital.

Brother's Animosity

The eldest son Sulaiman, the governor of Toledo did not accept the succession of his younger brother Hisham. Abdullah, another brother who had conducted the funeral-prayer of Abdur Rehman in Cordova offering homage in absentia to Hisham, had declared his Imarat. A large number of the people followed suit. Sulaiman having strong hold in Toledo instigated the people to rise against Hisham. He also won over Abdullah who in the beginning was a great supporter of his brother Hisham, joined Sulaiman at Toledo.

Hisham hurried to Toledo and besieged it, Sulaiman leaving the city to his son and his brother Abdullah advanced towards Cordova. He deputed his son Umaid Al Malik to encounter Sulaiman and himself threatened Toledo by the siege.

Cordovans who adored Hisham faithfully stopped Sulaiman at Secunda, who being sand wished, met with crushing defeat. Hisham returned to Cordova after a siege of two months of Toledo. His brother Abdullah came back to Cordova and was welcomed by Hisham.

Sulaiman had collected a strong for under the command of his force in Theodomir. Hisham therefore despatched a formidable army under son Muawiyah. Sulaiman was defeated (174 A.H./790 A.D.) and fled away to Valencia. Sulaiman remaining unidentified for several months sued for amnesty. Hisham pardoned him and allowed him to migrate with his family, on his own request. He was allowed to take away all his belongings and valuables. He was also given 60 thousand Dinars as the share of the inheritance of his father. He settled down in Tangir among the Berbers.

Eastern Spain's Revolts:

Taking advantage of Hisham's engagements with his rebel brothers, Said-bin-Husain-bin-Yahya-Alansari the Yamanite leader and governor of Tortosa rose in revolt in 172 A.H./788 A.D. Yousuf Qaisi, the Tax Collector was expelled from Tortosa. Musa-bin-Fortunio and Spanish Muslim gathering the Mudarites around him, defeated the Yamanites. Saeed was killed. Tortosa was occupied by Fortunio in the name of the Amir of Cordova.

Encouraged by revolt of Said other chiefs rose in revolt. Matrooh-bin-Sulaiman-bin-Yaqzan rebelled at Barcelona. So was the case with Saragossa Heusca, and Taragona. The defeat of Musa at the hands of Matrooh had a very adverse effect. The rebel chiefs like Bahlol-bin-Maklook and Mutrif caused a great havoc.

Hisham however despatched a formidable force under the Command of Abu Usman-Ubaidullah-bin-Usman, the governor of Valencia against the rebels (175 A.H. 791 A.D.). The rebels were fully crushed and Matrooh was killed by his own supporters. Musa-bin Fortunio was awarded the governorship of Saragossa.

France's Invasion:

The disloyal Christian chiefs, a permanent source of trouble for the Cordovan government, compelled Hisham to close the source by putting effective check on the Franks who were responsible for the fomentation and the organization of the raids. The then French government played the part of the present governments just to upset the administration of other countries.

It was in (176 A.H./792 A.D.) that Hisham despatched a formidable army under Abu Usman to invade the Southern provinces of France.

One contingent under Abdul Malik-bin-Abdul Waheed attacked Cerdagen (792 A.D.) The Franks were defeated at Narbone which was the capital of the Muslim government in Septimania (South France). Gerona the key-city to the Pyrenees was also annexed.

The Duke of Tortosa, William was defeated at the Orbina to leave a number of important cities to the Muslims.

Another column of the Muslim army under Abdul Karim-bin-Abdul Waheed invaded Austurias and Galicia. Bermudo I the king of Austuria and his nephew Alfanso II who led the Austurians and Galicians met with crushing defeat. Bermudo I was defeated by Yusuf- bin-Bakht and Alfanso by Abdul Karim. Charlemagne had no courage to come to the rescue of the Christians.

Maliki doctrines of Maliki :

Hisham was a learned man and an eminent theologian. His study of *Al-Mowatta* of Imam Malik was very vast and sound. Shaikh Ghazi, an authority on the Maliki doctrines was able to convince Hisham's father to the acceptance of the sect. Hisham, was also a follower of the Maliki sect and did much in introducing the Maliki doctrines to the empire. He was a true disciple of Imam Malik-bin Anas and requested him, to settle down in Spain, to avoid the oppression of the Abbasides but he did not agree.

Hisham encouraged the students of theology to journey to Medina to learn the Science of theology by Imam Malik-bin-Anas.

Yahya-bin-Yahya and Isa-bin-Dinar the Spanish pupils of Imam Malik did much for spreading the doctrine Isa-bin-Dinar earned the title of "Wise man of Undulusia" by Imam Malik.

Important ecclesiastical posts were given to Imam Malik's disciples. *Al-Mowatta*, the great book of Imam Malik was taught in all schools and colleges.

Hisham out of his devotion to the Maliki sect, did not hesitate offering his apology to the Maliki Ulema for any fault pointed out by them. The Maliki Ulema created a bit of hatred among the Christians for their being treated intolerantly. The Amir however was fully tolerant. This shortsightedness of the Maliki Ulema did not prove conducive to conversion to Islam. Their activities was not confined to the religious field alone, rather they had originated a religious-cum-political party entirely suicidal to the progress and solidarity of the empire.

Character:

Hisham was a pious man and a just kind ruler. He visited the patients and attended the funeral ceremonies. He was a poet and often sat in the poets' congregation. He was a true follower of the Maliki doctrines. He always offered his prayers in the mosque. He can be well compared with Umar-bin-Abdul Aziz in all respects. Imam Malik was so much impressed by him that he wished his presence in Medina.

He desired the mosques to be well attended. He very often sent money in bags to be distributed to the needy in the mosques. Even in rains he himself carried bags of Dirhams to distribute among the widows and pardah-nashin ladies. He very often went round the streets of Cordova to know the conditions of the people. He was a great philanthropist, and he felt pleasure in helping the needy irrespective of sect or community. Basic needs were provided affluently by law to every citizen of the empire. The absolute monarchy of the age was much better than the democracy of today.

It is said that impressed by the verdict of a sooth-sayer, Zibbi, that his rule will last only for about eight years, he gave up his interest in the empire and confined himself to prayers, only, is not correct. It is to be noted carefully that the true Muslim looks first to Akhirat and then to Duniya (world), but does not forsake, Duniya for Akhirat as Asceticism is not allowed in Islam. Hisham being a pious man cared more for the Akhirat but was not unmindful of the heavy duties of the empire, imposed on him by God. He had no pessimistic view of life. He believed in piety (*Itteqa*) and therefore could not afford to ignore the safety of his life after death.

Eminent historians like–Ibne Khaldoon, Ibne Asir, Maqri, Ibnul Qotia and many others are unanimous in their verdict of Hisham's pious character, impartial judgements, God-fearing nature and solid administration.

Achievements:

During the brief period of his rule, Hisham responded

well to the keen desire of his father in building up the newly
founded empire on a sound footing. Right from the day of his
enthronement, was surrounded by unrest and chaos, which he
faced heroically and weathered the storm successfully. He foiled
the plan of the Christians by invading South France and punishing
the rebel chiefs thoroughly. Alfanso II was silenced for good.
He faced all odds with heroic patience.

He devoted himself to the development of cultural and
social life on piety basis. He did not tolerate corrupt persons.
The collection of Zaka'at and Sadqa was organized and unlawful
tax was prohibited.

The judges were men of knowledge and of tested character.
Musab-bin-Imran the chief justice of Cordova was noted for
his high and impartial sense of justice. His secretary
Mohammad-bin-Bashir was an exemplary figure of knowledge
and peity.

A faithful of Hisham, and inhabitant of Jaene was heavily
penalised and fined along with his whole Kanani tribe for the
murder of an unknown person. He was alleged with the murder
and was heavily fined. Hisham, gave him his valuable necklace
to pay the fine. He, instead, demanded justice. Hisham therefore
saw his father and requested him to do justice. The case was
re-opened and the accused was found not guilty. Sulaiman was
warned and admonished by the caliph.

Hisham, like Umar-bin-Abdul Aziz did not believe in
enriching the national exchequer by heavy undue taxes. He on
the other hand devised ways and means for the development of
agriculture, horticulture, trade and commerce to stabilize the
finance of the government.

He rebuilt the bridge of the Guadalquiver originally
constructed by Sama Al-Khulani and constructed new roads

and streets to facilitate communications. He like his father had great interest with architecture. He built a number of new stately buildings and completed the construction of the great mosque of Cordova, at the cost of 60 thousand Dinars.

Hisham's Death:

Hisham died in 796 and was succeed by his son, Hakam. Al-Maqqari writes, 'Hisham is counted among the good and virtuous monarchs, full of military ardour and Zeal for the promotion of the faith". He completed the construction of the Grand Mosque, began by his father, Abdur Rehman I. His subjects called him "*arradha*" and *al-adil*". He built ribats or fortresses in the North, occupied by warriors fighting in the sense of Islam and waged was against the Christian forces there.

Character:

Hisham died in the year 180 A.H./796 A.D. after a reign of eight years. He was a just and generous ruler, "truly religious and a model of virtue". His acts of piety were numberless and in him the indigent and the oppressed found their protector. He used to walk at night through the streets of Cordova in the guise of a simple man to know the complaints of the poor. He also visited the sick and would often go forth on stormy nights to carry food to some pious invalid and to watch beside his bed. He distributed money among those good souls whom rain and cold could not deter from attending the mosques at night time. Though he was just, mild and amiable, he showed sufficient firmness when his throne was threatened by the conspirators and rebels. He rebuilt the bridge of Cordova and completed the Cathedral mosque begun by his father. Indeed he was a benevolent ruler.

CHAPTER 7

AL-HAKAM I
(796-822)

Al-Hakam ruled for 26 years. But his long reign was full of troubles, caused by the rebellions were suppressed soon, but others lasted for several years. His enemies were, firstly, his own uncle, Sulaiman and Abdullah, secondly, his nobles, thirdly, the northern Christians: fourthly the Franks, and lastly a new enemy, namely the Maliki Faqihs and the Muwalladun of Cordova, who had joined hands with the Faqihs,

Unpopularity of Ulema:

Hakam, a young and energetic ruler of high spirits, did not agree with the rigid enunciations of the Ulema or theologians on all principles of Fiqah leading to the threshold of asceticism. He being himself in profound possession of the knowledge of Fiqah opposed the ideology of renunciation and life in Usrat hard-pressed life. He propounded the theory, God has ordained comfortable life, for you all.

The theologians could not brook the proposition which could threatened their superior hold not only in ecclesiastical matters but also in the crown affairs. The conflict between the Amir and the theologians was quite logical. He therefore did not condescend to leave them unbridled. They on the other felt much disturbed with the curtailment or the power which they wore enjoying since the days of Hisham.

Hakam was surrounded with young wise minds and lived in pomp and grandeur. The theologians described it as skepticism and opposed him tooth and nail. They denounced him in public and from the pulpit as irreligious Amir. They accused him of drinking and opposed the employment of negroes as his bodyguards,

The neo-Muslims or Muwalids were staunch followers of the theologains. Yahya-bin-Yahya the most eminent of all the Fuqaha (theologians) of the time had plotted with the help of the Muwalids, to seat Mohammad-bin-Qasim known as Alshamash on the throne of Cordova. Alshamash divulged the plot to Hakam as he did not consider the step of the religious leaders, sound arid judicious. Many nobles and notable Fuqaha who were the leaders of the plot, were killed. It may be noted that Hakam punished only those Ulema and Fuqaha, who in the religious garb, exposed themselves to exploit the innocent people just to gain their own ends. Throughout his reign, Hakam paid due respect to such Ulema and Fuqaha who were busy establishing and widening the Islamic tenets in the country.

War with his uncles:

Within a year of his accession to the throne his uncles, Sulaiman and Abdullah, again invaded Spain and occupied various towns in the south. First Abdullah came in 797, but a year later Sulaiman also did so, Supported by some Berber tribes, among whom he was popular. Hakam sent troops against them. However, they gave him trouble for several years. At, past Sulaiman was defeated and killed, while Abdullah was pardoned. Afterwards, he lived in Cordova. His sons were appointed to high offices by Hakam and his successors.

Ditch's Episoder

Toledo the former Visigothic capital was mostly inhabited by the neo-Muslims or Muwalids and the disloyal Christian minority. The neo-Muslims who controlled the economy and the society of Toledo, were dissatisfied with the Arabs because of their preferential treatment with them, whereas the crippled cunning Christian minority longed for regaining the lost empire, by exploitation and hoodwinding, Both the renegades and the Christians were chronic rebels. A Christian poet Gharbib Talili was the inspiring soul for revolts, and a black nuisance for the government. The neo-Muslims and the Christians formed a coalition and revolted under the banner of Ubaida bin Hameed who proclaimed his independence at Toledo like the advance post of France. Borei, a Frankish noble was the first lord of the Principality. Cardona and Gerona, the chief cities of the principality were refuge of the Christians. The unlawful principality had the active support of the Christian powers, who disregarding the international protocol, acknowledged its independence and garrisoned it with their trained soldiers. They brought in, a huge of number of outlaws and robbers who ravaged the Muslim frontier cities and drove away the Muslims from their homes. The bandits were investitured with knighthoods and were also given lands free of cost. Thus the no man's land became an abode of highway men, outlaws and robbers who with the open support of the king of France became a regular menace for Cordova.

It was in 801 A.D. that the Franks in their assembly decided to annex Barcelona.

The count of Gerona laid siege to the city while William, count of Toulouse stood with his army to check and prevent the relief expected from Cordova. Zaid (Zardon) the governor had to surrender and cacate the town, due to the shortage of food and the non-availability of any relief from the Cordovan headquarter. The governor Zaid was put to humiliation. The female folks were dishonoured in the streets. The Muslims were thus enslaved by the Christians who were always treated tolerantly by the Muslim rulers. Thus encouraged, the Franks annexed Huesca and Tarragona.

Hakam was so busy in quelling the internal revolts in Cordova that he could not move out of the capital. The power seeking Ulema instead of helping him fanned up the renegades and did all what they could do, even through Fatwas, to dethrone Hakam. The Amir however subdued the insurgents and hurried up stop the mischiefs of the Christians. In the meantime he heard of the revolt of the selfish aristocracy of Toledo. He therefore leaving a division of his army to protect Toledo, advanced to meet the Franks. The news of the advance of the Amir broke the hearts of the Franks. The Amir recaptured Saragossa and other lost towns. The Franks were driven out across the Ebro Barcelona did not remain under the Franks yoke.

After the return of the Amir to Cordova, the Franks attack Toledo (803 A.D.) but they had to flee away with the approach of a fresh handful of Muslim soldiers from the capital. The Franks proclaiming a crusade besieged Tortosa (192 A.H; 806 A.D.) twice but the crusaders fled away in disgrace. The crown prince Abdul Rahman inflicted such a crushing defeat on Louis, the commander-in-chief of the Christian army that he fled away in a state of misery coupled with fear and awe.

It was in 197 A.H; 812 A.D. that the Franks invaded Spain and captured Lusitania, a city ill-guarded. But the Amir himself chased the intruders and drove them to the French borders and captured a number of important cities in the north. The Franks now had courage to face the Muslims in the open field. They kept on attacking the weak points of the borders of northern Spain.

Charlemagne, the French king, negotiated for truce in 810 A.D. The truce of Aix-la-Chapelle which was the third truce lasted only for three years. Charalemagne used for peace which was concluded in 200 A.H.; 816 A.D. and the Franks had no courage to cause disturbance in the lifetime of the Amir.

It may however be noted that Hakam had no desire to invade the Christian's principalities for any aggressive or aggrandizing design. He was compelled by the provocations of the Christians to take up arms against them. It was in 196 A.H., 811 A.D. that the Christians attacked a peaceful Muslim caravan in the Guadalajara (Ariac) and killed all except a woman whom they carried away with them. She being put to unthinkable tortures and humiliations by the socalled Christian knight, bewailed, groaned and moaned only to make a provision for their enjoyment, laughter and amusements. In her distress she cried for help and succour to Amir Hakam. The woeful tragedy was carried to the Amir by the poet Abbas through his verses. The Amir was so much impressed by the tragic incident that he advanced for her help. The Christian criminals were cut to pieces and she was recovered from their custody. He now invaded and annexed other Christian cities just to subdue their evil designs against the Muslims in future. This once again reminded the invasion of Sind by Mohammed bin Qasim against Raja Dahir who provoked the Muslim spirit of fraternity and brotherhood by attacking the Muslim-merchantship and putting the ladies to humiliation, torture and disgrace.

Beja and Merida

Asbagh, the son of his uncle Abdullah was brother-in-law of Hakam. He was governor of Merida. The dismissal of a minister by Asbagh caused misunderstanding between the Amir and Asbagh. The Amir being convinced with the report of the dismissed minister about the rebellious planning of Asbagh, dismissed him who actually rose in revolt. He therefore advanced to Merida (806 A.D.) but the intercession of his sister saved the worsening situation. Asbagh was pardoned and also restored his former position.

Hasam-bin-Wahb and Walid rebelled at Beja (807 and 817 A.D.) only to be crushed and crippled.

Cordovans' insurrection of Cordovans

Hakam as the crown-prince was very popular among the Ulema, fuqaha and the people. The education and the training that he had through his pious father were not obliterated from his mind. He, however being a man of independent did not like to be subordinated and dominated by the views of such theologians who deemed their interference in the estate affairs, a matter of right. He believed in the Maliki doctrines and had great respect for the Ulema and Fuqaha, but unlike his father he was not prepared to offer apology to them on the pretence of wrong interpretation of Fiqah. He actually wanted to fix their domain and did not approve of any trespass. His alleged addiction to wine, which is still to be authenticated, may be attributed as an answer to the unlawful rising of the Ulema against him, who even plotted to depose him.

The people were, regularly and openly, instigated and infuriated by the Ulema through Fatawa to rise against the Amir. The people therefore raising slogans in his presence did not refrain even from pelting him (187 A.H; 803 A.D.).

Those Ulema and Fuqaha, who virtually controlled the Imarat during the reign of Hisham, conspired to install an Umayyad prince Mohammad-bin-Qasim, better known as al-Shamas, on the throne of Cordova. As-Shamass however divulged the secret to the Amir. All such Ulema and Fuqaha assembled in the house of Al-Shams. A trusted slave of the

Amir named Barnat and an officer were in the adjoining room, unknown to insurgents, to note down the proceedings of the secret meeting. Ali Shamas asked them to declare their names loudly. The officer of the Amir noted their names and struck the pen so harshly that the sound could be heard even from outside. Many were caught on the spot and many fled away, Yahaya-bin-Yahya iaisi and Isa-bin-Dinar, the theologians could escape but Yaha-bin-Nasar-Yahsibi, Musa-bin-Salim Khulani, ibne Ali kale, Abu Yahya Zakarya Matr Ghassani, the pillars of the Maliki Sect, were arrested. All of them including other 72 conspirators were put to sword in front of the palace.

The consequence, however, was sanguinary. The followers of the Ulema, comprised of the major population of Cordova, could not tolerate the massacre of the eminent theologians who were regarded as pillars of Islamic faith.

The people therefore became all the more serious in accomplishing the mission of the Ulema. A wave of disdain and contempt swelled up so high that the people called him 'Oh! Drunkard' even from the pulpit, openly. Hakam was not unaware of the rising. He relied chiefly on his body guards who were despised by the people. Hakam displeased the people all the more by enhancing taxes.

Once the Amir was insulted to his face, by the Cordovans, on his way to the mosque for prayer. Talut the theologian was the ring-leader.

It was in Ramzan 198 A.H. May 814 A.D. that royal bodyguard killed on armourer who had delayed the delivery of his sword given to him for polishing.

The Cordovans being highly infuriated cried out Al-Salah (War- war) and surrounded the palace. Many of the body-guards were cut to pieces by the armed mob. The Amir shut himself in the palace which encouraged mob all the more. He was however not at all nervous rather he had engineered plan which struck deep the advancing rebels.

He asked his servant Yazaanto to perfume his hair and body profusely. The servant was dumb and mute at the order but beckoned to the riotous mob.

He understood the servants gesture and said,

"Today-victory or death-If I am killed, the insurgents will easily recognise me by the extraordinary perfume of my head"

He then asked his cousin Ubaidullah to force his way through the rebels and set fire to the Arrabal-de-Sur, abode of the rebels, south of the Guadalquiver. When the houses were ablaze, the mob hurried to their houses to extinguish the fire and save their families. Just then the Amir attacked the rebels so furiously that they were cut to pieces and fled away confusion. Hakam was overfurious and ordered for the general massacre of the rebels. The massacre lasted for full three days. It was however at the special request of Abdul Karim-bin-Mughis that the massacre stop-order was proclaimed.

At least 300 traitors and 36 leaders were hanged in the Alcazar at the Babul Suda, the fixed place for execution.

Some 8000 families had to quit Cordova. They settled down at Fez in Morocco, the capital of Idris II the descendant of Hazart Ali. Later on 15000 families migrated from Cordova to Alexandria and from there to Crete to found a kingdom under Abu Hafs, 'Umar-al-Baluti which lasted till 991 A.D.

It may be noted that the tragedy was not an eyeopener either for the Arabs of Qirwan or Cordova. Their hatred with each other was so deep that a wall has to be constructed to mark their separated settlement.

Hakam had indeed a remarkable land force. He worked
for the establishment of strong navy to guarantee the safety of
his possessions in Spain and France. The Arab navy was not
inferior to other naval forces, but was match to the landforce.
Hakam paid special attention to the improvement of navy. The
unsuccessful in vasion on Sardinia (808 A.D.) and Corsica
caused the strengthening of the naval force. Corsica was captured
(813 A.D.) It was in 818 A.D. that the Islands of Iviza, Majorca
and Sardinia were captured. The Balearic Islands were also
annexed. Thus the Muslim naval force established its superiority
over the Christian navy.

Death

Hakam died of fever on 26th Zulhaj 206 A.H; May 822
A.D. at the age of 52 after a rule of 26 years.

Character

Hakam was kind and just ruler. He was neither obstinate
nor irreligious but did not tolerate undue interference in the
state-affairs by any section of the people. He gave due respect,
due share and due position to all deserving persons. He never
transgressed of domain of justice.

The house of a poor woman stood by the palace of the
Amir and provided obstacle in the expansion prógramme of the
palace. The woman was not prepared to sell it away or part
with at any cost. When all persuations failed the chief architect
demolished the house and completed the palace-plan. She filed
a suit against the Amir. The Amir went to the palace for
inspecting the garden and the building. The Qazi also followed
him with empty bags. He sought the permission of the Amir to
fill the waste earth in the bags. He filled the bags accordingly
but the bags were so heavy that he could not lift them up. The
Amir therefore, himself tried to assist him but his strength failed.

The Qazi then exclaimed "Oh! Amir-ul Mominin, your strength has failed to lift up the small bag of earth, how would you lift up the land of the woman on your weak shoulder on the Day of Judgement?" The Amir wept bitterly and gave away the entire portion of the palace along with its belongings to the woman and sought her pardon.

Hakam was a pious man and never indulged himself in major sins. His liking for fine clothes or perfumes or hunting pastime should not have been declared blasphamous and irreligious just to pollute the public mind. Still then, Hakam did not show the least sign of disdain against such group of Muftis. He of course, desisted to play a stooge in the hands of a handful of self-centred Ulema, like his father Hisham, who were power-thirsty and wielded authority, during the regime of his father. His love for poetry, music and light amusement was not foreign to the Muslim ruler of Syria and Baghdad. His affiliation with wine was just the reaction of the unconsidered steps taken by those Ulema who were deprived of their political hold over the Amir. If the conduct of Hakam is scanned judiciously, no reason can be assigned to plot against the Imarat itself. According to the custom of the age he could have been charged in the open court before the Qazi, which was not done at all.

Ibne Hazam considered him a tyrant but he did not go into the details of the causes which compelled Hakam to subdue the revolt by force. Could he be called a "wise ruler" by allowing the rebels to play havoc in the capital and thereby inviting the Christian enemies to overthrow the empire?

Conspiracy has always been the unpardonable act of treason. The conspirators, political leaders, religious heads, foreign or internal agents, bind the ruler to trap them to death.

The Umayyad empire founded by Al-Dakhil at the cost of

percious lives was going to be doomed at the hands of his co-religionists. When all peaceful negotiations failed. Hakam had no alternative but to resort to the use of arms. In the heat of the moment eminent theologians like Abu Bakr Zakaria and many others were killed. Hakam considered the safety and the solidarity of the empire more important than any. All obstacles had to be removed at all costs.

His reverence to the Ulema and Fuqaha was too deep without doubt. His clemency to them was evident. Many of the theologians who had taken active part in the revolt were pardoned and allowed to settle in Spain except Cordova. Their property and posts were restored to them. Talut-bin-Ahmad Jobbar was also pardoned and reinstated in his lost position.

Hakam loved to sit in the company of Ulema and Fuqaha and took active part in religious discourses. He encouraged and patronised all intellectual activities in the religious field. Asadiyya the codified work of the Maliki doctrines by Asad-bin-Alfirat was introduced in Spain by Isa-bin- Dinar (800 A.D.) with the approval of Hakam. Zayad-bin-Abdul-Rahman was his favourite Faqih.

Music is not heresy. Evidence is there that it had open entry to the recognised pious societies since long. Modern pious societies have also accorded their recognition to it.

Poets have played a very important role in all ages of human civilization and culture. They have been inseparable partisans in building up the national character, will and integrity. They have been a source of inspiration in the battle field, on one hand, and in the social field, on the other. Hakam's respect for poets was not based on luxury. He learned history, war episodes, administrative tales and methods of the various rulers from the eminent poets of the kingdom just to weigh his own methods.

Achievements

The twenty six years reign of Hakam was full of internal, revolts, intrigues, conspiracies and foreign invasions. Hakam a man of mettle, surmounted all the oppositions, internal or external, successfully. A man of elegant disposition, did not allow himself to be led by undue clemency. He was a good blend of mildnesss and rigour.

He was kind, tolerant and just to all but he did not spare those who took the law in their hands. He always voted for the oppressed. The tax collector of Elvira, Rabi was punished for his oppression and injustice to the Christian tenets, (206 A.H; 821 A.D.)

His first consideration was safeguard his kingdom, against all odds. He entered into effective alliance with the Idrisids of Morocco (806 A.D.) to safeguard his country against the Frankish attacks.

All the state-departments were under the direct supervision of Hakam himself.

He had a well established secret intelligence department of his own which kept him well-informed of all the events, happenings and affairs of each house of his kingdom. Besides, there was a public espionage department attached with police.

He increased the number of troops and paid them regular salaries. A regular troop of 5,000 Mamluks were always in attention in Cordova. Besides, 2,000 Mamluks troops, posted on the banks of the Gualdquiver, guarded the places. The troops were placed in two camps, with ten Arifs (Commander) in each.

His military strength and logical tactics brought peace in the country and Charlmagne had to sue for peace and finally entered into a peace treaty which afforded and opportunity for solidifying the state-affairs.

Rabi Ibne-Teodulfo, a Christian, held the important Post of tax collector. The total revenue was 6,00,000 Dinars a year.

Eminent Ulema were his councillors or Wazirs. Mention may be made of Allama Ishaque-Munzir, Allama Abbas-ibne-Abdullah, Abdul Karim-ibne-Mughis and Saeed-ibne-Husain, in this connection.

Eminent theologians like Umar-ibne-Bashir, Bashir-ibne-Qatn, Abdullah-bin-Musa and Hameed-ibne-Muahmmad-ibne-Yahya were appointed judges of Cordova in succession.

After the death of Ibne-Imran the office of the Chief justice was conferred upon Mohammad Ibne-Bashir whose father Saeed-ibne-Bashir was investitured with rank by Amir Abdul Rahman II. He was noted for his piety and impartial justice. His son followed the foot- prints of his illustrious father, to the great satisfaction of Amir Hakam.

Whatever opinion may be formed of Hakam, there is no denying the fact that he strengthened the kingdom so solidly that no room was left open either for external or internal risings. His successors could rule smoothly if they adhered to the Principles of Amir Hakam.

CHAPTER 8

ABDUL RAHMAN II
(822-852 A.D.)

Accession : On the death of his father, al-Hakam, Abdul Rahman II ascended the throne. In his advice to his son and successor, Hakam had said:

"peaceful are the provinces which I hand down to you, O my son! They are a couch on which you may repose undisturbed: 'I have taken care that no rebellion shall break in upon your sleep"

Hakam's prediction proved to be true to a great extent. Abdul Rahman II's reign of 30 years was, comparatively, far more peaceful than that of his father. It was a period of prosperity, which Muslim Spain had not enjoyed before. But it was also a period when the Christians, both within the kingdom and on its northern borders, began to challenge the rule of the Muslims more successfully than ever before.

Tribal Scuffles:

The Yamanites and the Mudarits once again stood into scuffles with teacher in Tudmir (822 A.D.). The tribal jealousy and hatred coupled with the sectarian ideological inconsistency turned into regular tribal feuds to last for about three years. The Amir therefore transferred the government seat from Lorca in Tudmir to Mercia which had transferred a number of influential officers to the new seat. This policy was not effective for long. It was however in 210 A.H. that he asked Abul-Shamakh Muhammad-bin-Ibrahim the leader of the Mudarites to maintain peace and keep hostages at Cordova. Abul Shamakh was to serve the royal army.

The tribal skirmishes were however brought to an end by the royal forces in 828 A.D., 213 A.H.

Merida & Toledo's Revolts:

Merida and Toledo, with Christian majority, were hatching grounds of rebellions duly incubated by Louis the gentle, the son of Charlimagne.

The Jews and the Christians both hated the Muslims and were always a nuisance to the State. They set up a traitor, the former Tax-Collector, Mahmood-ibne-Abdul Jabbar to lead the revolt organised by them, on the false plea of taxation on articles of daily use. Louis the Frankish king regardless of the international law and ettiquette interfered with the internal affairs of the Muslim government and instigated the people through a secret letter, to rise in revolt, assuring them of his active support.

The Muslims since yore, have been subjected to such underhand enemical dealings by the non-Muslims who inspite of being disposed of well, did not deter from their nefarious activities. The great Ottoman Empire was shared to pieces on the table of Europe and Turkey was declared the "Sick man of Europe but instead, it emerged out as "Strong man of Europe". The great Mughal Empire fell a prey to the foreign anti-Muslim and palace intrigues. 'Quislings agglomerated around the intriguers, intruders and unfaithfuls.

Luis kindled the rebellion but the miscreants were forced to submit leaving 7000 casualties in the field. Mahmood escaped to Saragossa but was put to sword by Alfanso II (225 A.H; 840 A.D.) a good reward for the traitor.

Toledo the hot-bed of revolts, rebelled once again under the leadership of Hashim, a black-smith, in 829 A.H; 207 A.H.

Hashim originally a Christian neo-muslim, collecting a strong army of rebels duly supported by Louis and the local Christians, plundered the Arabs and Berbers' houses.

He devastated Cantalonia, and the Fort of Amrus. He had become so powerful that the frontier governor Muhammad Ibne-Wasim could not check his advance. He attacked Santobria and defeated the Berbers in several skirmishes.

It was in 831 A.D. that Abdul Rahman himself had to attend to the rebels in person. A fierce battle took place in the west of Haz-e-Semiua. Hashim was killed. The rebels were either killed or fled away. Toledo was however unsubdued till the Amir deputed his brother Umayya-bin-Hakam with a strong force in 834 A.D. to subdue it. Umayya laid siege to the city but to no effect. He stationed his army in the fort of Colatrava and returned to Cordova, leaving the command in the hands of Abu Ayyoub Maisara. After the departure of Umayya, the people of Toledo invaded the fort but they were ruthlessly killed by the royal forces. The rebels shut themselves in the city of Toledo The rebellions now went in series till Walid-bin-Hakam crushed the insurgents totally on 16th June 837 A.D. or Shaban 223 A.H; 838 A.D.).

The people of Toledo were granted general amnesty. Administration was reorganised on strong footing and trusted people were posted on key posts. The fort of Amroos was rebuilt and strongly garrisoned.

Sporadic risings, a regular feature of the age, were curbed down effectively. The revolt of Habiba, a Berber chief, in

Algecars (236 A.H. 850 A.D.) was crushed. The rising of
Muhammad-bin Isa, in Theodomir was crushed by
Abbas-bin-Walid (235 A.H; 849 A.D.) The revolts in Beja and
Takarna were also crushed. (211 A.H; 826 A.D.)

Norman Invasion:

In 844, a new enemy appeared off the coasts of Spain,
namely the Normans or Northmen. The Arabs called them
Majus, a name they applied to all non-Muslims enemies. The
Normans were vikings, who dwelt in Scandinavia, in the north
of Europe. They were pagans or no-christians. Christianity
spread in Scandinavia much later than in countries of Western
Europe. They were a seafaring and piratical people. In their
long ships, they sailed from their northern regions and attacked
cities and towns on the coasts England, Scotland, France and
other countries, during the ninth century. In 844, they first
appeared off the coast off of Lusitania and plundered Lisbon
and then attacked Cadiz. They came to these cities in their
small boats and plundered them. Then they sailed up the river
Guadalquivir and attacked and plundered Seville. The Amir
sent an army against them, which drove them out of Seville and
Medina Sidonia. At the same time, the Amir ordered his navy
to attack the piratical invaders on the sea and drove them away.
A shipyard was set up at Seville, coastal towns were fortified
and watch-towers were built along the coasts. These measures
put a stop to the menace of the Norman invaders for some
time, although they continued to terrorise the peoples of France,
England and other countries of Europe.

Inroads of Christians:

Just after the accession of Abdul Rahman, the Christian
chiefs worked out a secret plan for attacking the Muslim
territories. Alfanso II, the chief of Leon raided Madinut-al-Salam

or Medinaceli and Argon. Alfanso II was joined by other Christian chiefs of the North. Count Borel of the Gottic March raided lerida and plundered the city. Amir Abdul Rahman therefore despatched a strong force in the command of Abdul Karim-bin-Abdul Wahid to attack Barcelona. Barcelona was besieged, many of the Christian forts were annexed. The Christians were thoroughly crushed who acknowledging the Amir's suzerainty agreed to pay the Jaziya or protection Tax. All the Muslim prisoners were freed (208 A.H; 823 A.D.). The Amir being tired of the frequent Christian raids decided to stop their unwholesome practice for good. A strong army under the command of Ubaidullah-bin-Abdul Rahman I, marched against Barcelona in 210 A.H; 825 A.D. The Christians were confined in the city, it was however in 212 A.H; 827 A.D. that Barcelona was subdued. The Christians were forced to remain confined within the four walls of the city.

The Muslim frontier provinces of Huesca and Saragossa were on the border line of the Basques territory of Navaree in Northern Spain. The count of Navaree was a subsurvient to the king of France. He declared his independence and established friendly relations with Cordova on ambassadorial level. The Amir agreed to protect him against the French and the external aggression and the count of Navaree in turn was to provide all possible facilities to the Amir for crossing the Pyrenees to invade France.

In the meantime, a Gothic Lord Aizon being displeased with the behaviour of the Frankish government allied himself with the Cordovan Government. He sent his brother to the Amir to seek military help against France. Lord Aizon with the help of the Muslim army invaded the territories around Barcelona and Garronne. The north eastern possession of France were routed well. The French and the count of Barcelona retreated in miserable state.

The Christians having mustered strength marched under the command of Louis (839 A.D.) to invade Medina Sidonia. Furtoon-bin-Musa the Governor of the frontier provinces plundered the Christian army and forced it to surrender.

The death of Louis in 840 A.D. brought disorder and confusion in the Christian camp. The sons of Louis, Pepin and Charles the Bald drew swords for the possession of Languedoc. The Amir was watching the situation with interest. The Christians had broken the treaty of Galacia which provided an opportunity for the Amir to attack Galacia. A number of forts were captured. The expedition against Galacia was taken up the following year (841 A.D.) by the Amir's son Mutarrif, who compelled the Christians army to retire senselessly.

The Muslim army entered province through the estuary of the Rhone. Musa the Governor or Tudela in Navaree attacked Ceradgne and marched into central France through the Seines the Loire and the Garonne. A section of the Muslim army advanced from Urgal and Rivagorsa into France. William, the count of Toulouse with the help of the Amir captured Barcelona. He also defeated Charles the Bald and annexed the Catalonian towns.

Romero II succeeded Alfanso II in 842 A.D; 227 A.H. He instead of taking lessons from the previous crushing defeats raised arms against Cordova. The Amir primarily tried to convince him through peaceful methods but the hot-headedness of Romero worsened the situation. The Amir therefore invaded, Galacia (231 A.H; 845 A.D.) and penetrated as far as Leon a city in North Spain. Romero was reconciled with the defeat. His son Ordino who succeeded him in 849 A.D. 235 A.H. had remained content with his own principality of Leon and had no courage to avenge the defeat of his father.

It may be noted that the Muslim navy invaded the French

coasts very successfully and also the vicinity of Marsailles. The Franks were thus crushed at every point and had to acknowledge the Muslim superiority.

Musa son of Musa

Musa-bin-Musa was appointed by Amir, Abdul Rahman II as the Governor of Tudela to safeguard the frontiers (226 A.H; 841 A.D.). He crossing the border captured Narbonne and gave a crushing defeat to the Christians. Musa was very popular there. An army officer Jarir-bin-Mufiq was jealous of him. Jarir on one occasion insulted him in the Darbar of Cordova. Musa therefore, in the heat of the moment rushed to Tudela and declared his independence. Banu Qasis were his chief supporters. Haris-bin-Barigh (228 A.H; 843 A.D.) advanced with a strong army from Cordova to punish him. Musa was defeated in the field of Gerga. His son Alb was killed in the battle of Gerga. Haris then advanced towards Tudela. Musa entered into a peace treaty and went to Arnedo. Musa with the help of the king of Navarra defeated Haris in the battle of Arnedo. Haris was made a captive.

Hearing the news of the defeat of Haris, Amir Abdul Rahman sent his son Muhammed to punish Musa. Muhammad-bin-Abdul Rahman besieged Tudela (229 A.H; 843 A.D.) and compelled Musa to surrender. Prince Muhammad pardoned Musa of his fault and reinstated him to his former post. The prince then marched to Navarra to punish the king for his treachrous breach of the peace treaty by helping Musa. He raided Pampilona, the capital city. The king was killed in the battle and things were set right.

After the departure of the Prince, Musa revolted once again. He however surrendered to the royal force and sent his son Ismail, as a hostage to Cordova. After sometime Ismail, escaped from Cordova and reached Tudela. Musa revolted again

the third time (846 A.D.) Prince Muhammad hurried to Tudela.
On his approach Musa implored for mercy. He was however
pardoned with the restoration of his post. Musa thence forward
remained loyal to the crown and performed his duties faithfully.

Ambassadorial Relations:

Eversince the establishment of the Umayyad Empire in
Spain, the Abbaside caliphs were trying to overthrow it by hooks
and crooks. They, failing in the battlefield, persuaded the
European Christian kings to drive away the Umayyad rulers
from the European soil. Exchange of presents and gifts were
made between the king of France and the Abasside Caliph.
Both Mansoor and Rashid did all what they could do to
overthrow the Muslim kingdom of Spain. The Umayyad Amirs
of Spain, however had no such malicious designs against the
Abbaside Caliph. They on the other hand acknowledged their
superiority by calling them "Khalifatul Muslimin" and also by
reciting Khutba in their names from the pulpit. Had the Abbaside
Caliphs not worked adversely for the Muslim Spain Empire,
the Umayyads would not have met such a dark fate on pain of
the extinction of the Muslim name from the soil of Spain which
they ruled for centuries.

Theophilus the Emperor of Constantinople was not happy
with the Caliph Al-Motasim. He also knew of the unfriendly
relations between Cordova and Baghdad. He therefore sent an
embassy (840 A.D.) to Amir Abdul Rahman II with rich presents
seeking his help and coalition against the Abbaside Caliph.
Inspite of his preoccupations in his own kingdom, the Amir
could have made an effort to regain the lost empire of Syria,
his homeland, but he preferred to be content with the European
soil simply because he abhored to strike his own co-religionist
for appeasing the Spirit of revenge. The Amir however received
the embassy with due respect and honour and in return he sent

Yahya-bin-Hakam al-Ghazal with rich and valuable presents to Constantinople. He remained content with the cultural and commercial treaty with the Byzantine Kingdom.

The Amir also received an embassy from the Count of Navarra, a subserviant to France, who had declared his independence being dissatisfied with the treatment of the French Emperor. The Amir did not disappoint the embassy and concluded a treaty to protect the Count from external aggression. The Count in return agreed to provide the Cordovan army with all facilities to invade France through the Pyrenees. The Treaty of Navarra was an effective blow on the malicious designs of the Christians.

The Fanatics' Movement:

With the advent of the Muslims in Spain, the Jews and the common people who were the main targets of the tyranny and persecution by the Christian rulers and the church, found a new life and succour. The Christians also were given due place and respect. Both the Jews and the Christians enjoyed a high place in the society in all the important towns of the empire specially in Cordova, the Capital city. They enjoyed full religious freedom and held key posts in the administration without prejudice. They were very sound, economically and high socially. They represented even the embassies to other European kingdoms.

They were so much lured by the Muslim culture, elegance and eloquence of the Arabic language that they did not only adopt the Muslim way of life but embraced the language as their own. They expressed contempt for Latin and Hebrew texts. A number of their religious books were translated into Arabic.

The enlightened Jews and the Christians were conscious of their inferiority in all fields of Arts, science literature, social

customs, manners, public dealings and the principles of equity
and justice. They felt pleasure in adopting the Arab costumes,
They were known as "Mustaribs" (one who adopts the Arabic
language and costumes). This enlightened class lived in Cordova,
Seville Saragossa, Toledo and other cities, kith and kin with
the Arabs.

There was however a Fanatic disloyal group of the
Christians which hated the Muslims and had not acknowledged
the Muslim kingdom honestly in their hearts. This group had
the support of the church, as well, and despired the Mustaribs.

It may be remembered that Spain was the last country in
Europe to be christianized as a whole. A number of the pagan
districts had embraced Islam. The Visigothic Arianism had
accepted the Muslim doctrines. This factual and ideological
drift of the natives towards the Muslim tenets distressed the
church too much. All the organisations of the church were
crushed in the battle fields.

Having failed in the open combats the church resorted to
a very ignoble plot of striking the religious sentiments of the
Muslims by vilifying the holy Prophet (peace be upon him)
publicly.

The vilifiers were headed by Eulogius, a priest and a
wealthy friend of his Alvaro. Eulogius was in love with Flora,
a Christian girl born of a Muslim father. He enticed her to his
plan just to earn the sympathy of other Christians and also to
lure the Zealots by her company.

The vilifiers were ignored in the beginning. The Zealots
were encouraged by this ignorance of the government, all the
more. The government therefore had to take steps to stop the
frenzy.

It may be noted that the "Mustaribs" who were enlightened

and learned Christians did not approve of the agitation which they regarded as irreligious embraced Islam on their own accord, and many joined them also. It was due to the unwise policy of a group of the priestly class that the number of the neo-Muslims increase all the more.

Death :

Abdul Rahman II died of fever after a reign of 30 years at the, age of 62 in 852 A.D. He had nominated his eldest son Muhammad as his successor, in his life time.

Character of Abdul Rahman II

He was a wise and sagacious ruler, endowed with administrative acumen, military farsightedness and political insight. He was loved by the poor people and so called Abul Maskeen. He was excessively fond of women and married many of them so the number of his children was about one hundred. He was fond of music and art and patronised great musicians like Zirhab. Spanish people were also affected by his love for music. Moreover he was a kind-hearted person. He was influenced by powerful man and women around him who defrauded him of his treasure.

Achievements:

The major part of the 30 years rule of Abdul Rahman was full of internal and foreign troubles; but he overcame them all successfully and tactfully. He not only established the solidarity of the empire, but gave it a positive prosperity. The people were, happy and prosperous. According to Ibne Khuldoon, Spain under Abdul Rahman II joined peace, tranquillity and affluence. The cultural and social developments of Spain owe much to the Amir. He reorganised the administrative system in a manner which could suit all minds of the country and acceptable to all shades of opinion.

The advisory Council sat in the palace with Amir in the chair. All matters pertaining to the kingdom were discussed and debated freely. The Prime Minister was called Hajib. Ordinarily he used to be the senior most member of the Council. The Amir paid special attention to the courts of justice and did not like the delay in deciding the cases with impartial justice. He was very careful in appointing the Qazis or Judges. Only men of character, knowledge and piety were investitured with the rank. He had much regard for Yahya bin-Yahya, a great theologian of the Maliki doctrines, The efficient working of the royal mint was guaranteed and the use of the official seal was systematised.

All the important appointments were made by the Amir himself who was very cautious and rigid in making the selection.

The finance department was a separate one, placed under the Finance Minister called Shaikhul-Khazzan. Musa-bin Jadir the Finance Minister was noted for his abilities in Finance. He had introduced the Budget system, duly approved by the Amir, which had to be followed rigidly. Once the Amir sanctioned an amount to Zaryab, as a reward. There was no such provision in the budget. Musa bin-Jadir, the Finance Minister, placed the matter before the Amir in such a clever manner that he agreed with the minister, and paid the amount from his own personal budget.

The establishment of a shipyard gave a strong navy to the country. Spain was thus freed from the attacks of the Norman pirates. The coastal cities became safe and flourished well, and added wealth to the national exchequer.

The annual revenue increased from 6 to 15 lacs Dinars a year.

His advisory council, headed by Abdul Karim-bin-Mughis

the Prime Minister and other ministers like Isa bin Shahid, Abdul Rahman-bin-Rustom, Yousuf-bin-Bakht and Mohammad-bin-Salam, became very popular for its impartial judgements and for conducting the affairs of the country talently not only for the good of the crown but for the people as a whole.

Love for art and architecture was his ancestral legacy. He was blended with the aesthetic sense so much that he liked to beautify the whole kingdom. Beautiful gardens were laid out-on the banks of the Guadalquiver. The roads and streets of Cordova had rows of beautiful rose-flowers on their sides. The planning was mathematical and geometrical.

Water supply of sweet water to Cordova and other cities was regular and efficient. Beautiful fountains were erected in all squares, with marbles paths and flowers around them. New roads were laid to facilitate the communication. Mosques were built not only in the cities but also in distant villages. The Jam-e-Masjids of Jaen and Seville spoke of the fine Arab Architecture. In order to enlist his name in the construction of the Mosque of Cordova, he planned for adding two porches to it. The project was however completed by his son Muhammad I.

The frontier towns destroyed and damaged by flood (827 A.D,) were repaired and reconstructed. The fortification of all the coastal towns was made with the postings of well-equipped guards. The watch-towers watched the movements of the enemies ships in the Atlantic Ocean.

The shipyard at Seville built a number of new ships to strengthen the navy.

All the projects of the Amir were for the good of the country and the prosperity of the people. There is no instance of levying new taxes to meet the projects. The royal treasury was there to help the nation.

On the outbreak of a severe famine, all the taxes were remitted. Public granaries were opened. The helpless and the needy got food and meals free. A separate department was set up to provide all facilities to the famine-striken. The Amir himself on many occasions inspected the working.

Abdul Rahman II, a patron of Science, Literature and Philosophy, sent his agents to distant places to collect rare books specially work on the Greek philosophy. Abbas-bin-Nasib brought Arabic translations of Persian and Greek works from Mesopotamia. The poems (Qasaed) of Habib-bin-Aus was brought to Cordova by Ibnul- Musanna. Musanna had been the tutor of the Amir and also of his sons Muhammad and Umar. An Arabic School of Translation was set up in Cordova. The Greek works on science, philosophy and administration were translated into Arabic and introduced into the country. The Amir had set huge botanical and zoological gardens. Large number of Plants and animals were brought from the East and elsewhere. His agents travelled all over the world in search of rare collections and brought them to Cordova, at royal price.

It may be noted that the school of translation, then unknown to Europe, had a very salutary effect upon the progress of culture in those days. Arabic language pined its popularity in Europe and the Muslim political thought and culture could be dissiminated in other parts of Europe through the students coming from abroad who were educated in the Cordovan Schools, colleges and university. The translation work was done on very large scale by eminent scholars. Research facilities were available. The research-students were put on translation work also.

This translation-institution was so highly recognised that even after the fall of Muslim Spain, Europe adopted the method on the same pattern. The English imitated it by founding a similar institution in the Fort William at Calcutta. The huge botanical and zoological gardens of Calcutta and other places in modern Europe and Asia are the reminiscence of the Muslim contributions in Spain.

Education, a very important portfolio, was under the direct care of the Amir. Large number of schools, primary and secondary were set up in every town and village where education was imparted with free lodging and boarding. Each school had a well furnished library. Public and private libraries were in abundance.

Special institutions for destitutes were established in all places, maintained by the government. Beggers were unknown Occupation was provided to skilled and non skilled persons by the State. Cottage industries were encouraged.

The court of the Amir was a blend of Perso-Arab manners and customs. It was full of pomp and grandeur. Clothes were fashioned out anew, according to the yearly season. The court life as well as the palace life was full of pomp and luxury. The luxuries living of the Abbasides in the East could be very well matched with the Umayyads' living in the West during the days of Abdul Rahman II.

It is interesting to note that inspite of all affluence, luxury and pomp, Abdul Rahman never led a licentious life. He followed the Shara very strictly and was always prepared to undergo even the severest punishment for any fault against the Shara. One day in the month of Ramzan, the Amir admitted his transgression of law in the holy month, to Imam Yahya and asked him about the compensation. Imam Yahya, asked him to observe fasting for 60 days consecutively, which the Amir conceded.

After the court was over, other Ulema told Yahya that the compensation could be the other way easier according to the Shara. Qazi Yahya silenced them saying that the head of the

State should be awarded the severest punishment for even a petty fault to subdue his ego and also a lesson for the public.

Abdul Rahman brought intelligent reformation not only in the administrative machinery but also in daily life. He introduced fashionable reforms in dress and mode of living. The manufacturing of silk-cloths and embroidery work was much encouraged. Fine silk cloths were marked with the names of the manufacturers. Clothes for royal use were indicated with special embroidered mark.

The Amir took special interest in Public works. New Hospitals were constructed where free medicines and treatments were provided for the patients. There was good arrangements for both indoor and outdoor patients. Drugs were imported from the East but mostly from Baghdad. The Hospitals were placed under the Public Health Department and were run by the government. The sanitation was very uptodate and high. Sweet water was supplied to Cordova, in every house through the lead pipes whereas the filthy water was flown to the river through separate pipes. Public baths were numerous. Cleanliness reached a high level. Roads and streets were cleaned by Kannas (Sweepers) before dawn regularly. Lighting arrangement in all cities and towns and even in villages was perfect. Capital cities enjoyed a flood of light. Lamp-posts were erected at small distances every where. Due to the use of olive oil the dour was pleasant and agreeable.

A section of the public health department called Baldiya or Municipality looked to such city affairs.

Life was decent and fashionable and Cordova was then regarded as the Jem of all the cities of Europe.

Foreign Policy:

Abdur Rahman's reign was beset with internal and external

troubles. Local revolts, frontier troubles, Christians' fanatic movement, Norman inroads and French attacks had threatened the very solidarity of the empire. Abdur Rahman tackled all the problems very successfully. He was however not satisfied with timely defeat of the foreigners. He therefore took positive steps to remove the foreign menace for ever.

He having reviewed the policy of his precursers he outlined his foreign policy on "live and let live" basis. He laid a great emphasis on the establishment of permanent peace without resorting to arms.

In order to safeguard his frontiers he raised 'the number of the armed forces and equipped them with the latest weapons. He set up a shipyard at Seville which built war and merchant ships at high speed. The strength of the navy disheartened the pirates and other European navy so much that they had no courage to look maliciously at the Muslim coasts. The movements of the enemies on the Atlantic were watched by the Watch-Towers.

The Arab merchants had safe voyage and conducted their business safely.

The Amir being fully aware of the enemical behaviour of the Abbaside caliph and of the ulterior motive of his friendly relations with the French king, established ambassadorial contacts with other European powers to counteract the conspiracy.

The Abbaside caliph apprehended the attack of the Spanish Umayyads on Africa and the king of France considered the Cordovan empire as a menace for France. Both of them therefore considered the Amir of Spain as their common enemy. Thus the bilateral defence agreement was inevitable.

To neutralise their basic plan, Abdul Rahman readily acknowledged the independence of the count of Navarra. The treaty between Cordova and Navarra was a hard political blow on France.

Similarly, his treaty with Theophilus, the successor of Michael the emperor of Constnatinople (840 A.D.) foiled the hopes of the Abbaside Caliph. The foreign policy of Abdul Rahman was so successful and effective that the enemies were chopfallen.

The Gems of the Court of Amir:

Abdul Rahman a great patron of Art, literature and Science was endowed with the aesthetic sense of the highest order. He himself, a poet had great regard for poets. He appreciated beauty and music.

Under his munificent patronage Cordova became the coveted seat of civilization and culture. Eminent scholars of all subjects, theology, religion, arts, science, engineering, medicine, astronomy, astrology poetry etc. flocked in the capital and received very generous welcome by the Amir himself.

Let us glitter our minds for a while, with the sparks of the few of the gems.

Yahya-bin-Yahya, an eminent scholar of theology was authority on the Maliki doctrines. He was highly respected by the Amir who used to consult him in ecclesiastical matters.

Ubaidullah the grand son of the illustrious Badr was a great literary figure and also a great poet. He was in confidence with the Amir. Abdul Rahman bin-Shimr was another poet who had earned a name for his poetical talents.

Abdul Karim-bin-Mughis the Prime Minister, Isa-bin-Sahid, Abdul Rahman bin Rustam, Yousuf-bin-Bakht and

Muhammad bin Salam, the talented ministers added to the glory of the kingdom.

Judair, the Shaikhul Khazzan, the chief of the Finance department, raised the economy of the country to the highest pitch without burdening the people's pockets with undue taxes.

Abdul Hasan-Ali-bin-Nafe popularly known as Zaryab the melodious musician was an asset to the court. Originally a Persian, he had settled in Baghdad. He was a student of Ibrahim Al-Moosab (according to Maqri) or Isac Al-Moosali. Looking to the talents of Zaryab, Isac trained him in the art so perfectly that he had the largest number of fans around him.

Once Moosali presented Zaryab to the caliph Haroon-al-Rashid. The caliph was so highly impressed by his performance that he was ordered to attend the music-court on other occasions also.

He had captivated the hearts of the caliph and the audience by his self-originated tune on his own self-made instrument.

Moosali apprehending his own fall in the royal court asked him to leave Baghdad immediately. He therefore left for North Africa to try his luck there.

Ibnul-Qutaiba is of the opinion that the flight of Zaryab from Baghdad to Ifriqiah followed the succession of Mamoon who was not happy with the musician and his arrival in Baghdad from Merve (819 A.D.) necessitated his flight in Maghrib (Ifriqiah). The Aghlabid ruler, Ziadatullah I (816-837 A.D.) welcomed him to Qirwan. As ill luck would have it, Zaryab sang of the famous poet "Antara" with the opening verse "If mother were as black as a crow". Ziadat's mother was of dark complexion, perhaps a Negress, quite unknown to Zaryab. He was however spared of his life to migrate to Spain.

Here, one is reminded of an interesting incident in the

Darbar of Emperor Aurangzeb. The emperor was not a recorded poet but approved poetry as an important art. Once a poet was granted audiance in the Darbar to recite a poem of his own. The verse opened with (in Urdu) "*a taj daulat ber musarat*" "O! the crown of wealth on your head" Aurangzeb stopped him and did not allow him to complete even the first line and asked him .... "are you conversant with prosody?" On receiving the reply in the negative he was spared of his life and had to leave the court dejected and dismayed.

Zaryab left Qirwan for Spain in 821 A.D. but as ill-luck would have it Hakam I breathed his last and Zaryab lost the hope of getting an entry to the generous court of the Amir Fortune however favoured him and he was introduced to Abdul Rahman II by a renowned Jewish musician Mansur. He was appointed as a court musician on an annual stipend of 24,000 Dinars with additional allowances in the shape of rewards on Festive Occasions.

Zaryab was not only a singer and musician but also a poet, a historian, a geographer and an astronomer. He is also said to have been a literary figure and well-versed in Fiqah.

The period of Abdul Rahman was the period of renaissance in aspects of social and cultural life of the day. Zaryab, so to say, was an asset in reforming the social and cultural life of Cordova, to the keen desire of the Amir. The combination of the Persian refinements and decency in food, customs and manners with those of Arabs was greatly appreciated and adopted by the society as a whole. The refined improvements in the public and private baths and toilets were all the more appreciated.

The establishment of music schools in Spain brought a great change in the Muslim social thoughts.

Zaryab's method of teaching music to his pupils was unique

and funny. The beginner had to tie his waist tightly with a turban with a wooden piece three inches in length in between, his jaws to cry with full force emitting the sound 'Ah' or ya Hajjam.

Zaryab invented a new and peculiar instrument of five strings much better than "Ubul-al-Shabut!' the perfect lute of Zalat a renowned singer of Baghdad.

Zaryab had also introduced new fashions in dress and the mode of living. He had fashioned out silken and woollen dresses to suit the seasons. The gents and ladies costumes were designed delicately and artfully to indicate a fine blend of the Perso-Arab cut with a tinge the Byzantine style.

Zaryab was thus a very important personality of the kingdom and had considerably influence on the Amir as well.

Impressed by his talents, the Amir often consulted him in matters of state and his opinion carried weight. Encouraged by this honour, Zaryab tried for a post of Qazi in Cordova on the ground of his being accomplished in the science of theology. The Amir turned down his request for his being a better singer than a theologian. Thence forward the Amir did not allow him to cross the boundary of his limit.

Nasr a Spanish slave of the Amir was a convert. He could not speak Arabic and was called the Mute. He was very clever, cunning and shrewd. Having earned the favour of Sultana Taroob, came 'close to the Amir as well. Both Taroob and Nasr had great influence in the administration of the country.

His plot to poison Prince Muhammad the crown prince, at the instigation of Taroob was discovered. He was therefore ordered by the Amir to swallow the poison himself to end his life.

Queen Taroob was noted for her beauty both in Europe and Asia. Abdul Rahman was not only fond of her but loved her to the core of his heart. She was a very clever lady. She was over greedy by nature. No wealth could satisfy her lust for riches. She was the weakness of the Amir. She had a great say in the administration also. In order to give a continuity to her power, she plotted to poison Muhammad the crown prince just to pave way for the accession of her son Abdullah. Out of the forty five sons of Abdul Rahman, Muhammad was not only the eldest but also a talented young prince. The queen prepared Nasr to do the job and promised her big fortune. Nasr prepared a scheme to end first the life of the Amir by poison. With this end in view he approached Hurrani the court physician and offered him a heavy bribe. Hurrani accepted the bribe but informed the Amir about the plot. The Amir became cautious of Nasr, his most trusted slave. One day when Nasr talked about the stimulating medicine, the Amir asked him to take it first. He had no courage to refuse and got the best award of his treachery.

There were yet two other slave girls. Hakam and Dishfa who were greatly admired by the Amir. Both of them were accomplished singers and musicians. They were noted for beauty. Their knowledge of history, and philosophy was very solid. Hakam was the title bestowed upon the slave girl Jaria, by the Amir, because of her talents in literature and poetry.

The impartial critics of history are unanimous in their verdict of declaring the reign of Abdul Rahman as the reign of peace and prosperity. They give credit to the Amir for his successful efforts for quelling the internal disorders and crushing the external attacks, simultaneously. Like a statesman, he did not overlook the interest of the people and the progress of their country. He brought a very agreeable revolution in the civic life of the people through such reforms which changed the entire set up. The Perso-Hispano-Arab culture introduced by the Amir suited the people of all ranks without any discrimination. Thus Spain grew with a new thought which guaranteed peace progress and prosperity for all.

The enemies being badly discouraged in the battlefield, emerged with the severest religious coloured fanatic intrigue but even then they could not deprive the Muslim Spain from moulding the minds of the people to adopt the reforms with civic sense to highten its glory to the Zenith.

His interest in arts, science and learning : Equally significant with his war and foreign policy was Abdul Rahman's lavish patronage of the artists, scientists and philosophers.

First of all, we shall mention Abu'l Hasan ibn Ali, surnamed Ziryab, whose life we have sketched above, We shall now briefly describe his influence on arts and music, fashion and style of life first on the court of Abdul Rahman and on Cordova where he lived all his life and, eventually, on the whole of Spain, medieval and modern, Islamic or Christian, Ziryab, originally native of Iraq, born perhaps of Persian parents, brought with him from the East an improved version of the traditional Arab instrument of music, called all 'ud or lute. It consisted of four strings, dyed black, yellow, white, and red, representing the four "humours of ancient Greek, namely black bile, yellow bile, phlegm string, which he called the soul, for it made music more harmonious, while the four stringed lute had a jarring effect on the ears of the music-lovers. It was this improved lute which he brought with him to Cordova, with which he gladdened the hearts of Abdul Rahman and of his harem and courtiers and of the nobles of al-Andalus, who flocked into Cordova. Moreover, Ziryab had composed one thousand songs, though, al-Maqqari says, some of them were composed by Ptolemy, (the great astronomer, geographer, mathematician and musicians of the ancient hellenist Greece), Ziryab "influenced the whole subsequent development of popular music and dance in Spain by introducing musical forms from Persia", 'as for example Flamencok, so popular even today in southern Spain. Ziryab even changed the dining habits of the Cordovans. Formerly they used to drink wine from the heavy goblets of gold and silver. But he introduced the goblets of crystal. He also taught them to take their food, not with all the foods laid on the table, or on dastarkhwan, as we do in Indian Peninsula even today, but in separate courses one after the other; this method of dining became popular among the Spanish Christians and thence among other nations of Europe in subsequent ages. Ziryab also introduced many dishes of his own devising, some of which were long after, known after him, especially be made of fish and meatballs. He even popularized shaving among men and introduced toothpaste, he taught the people to change their hair style:

> "Henri Terrasse, that most perceptive guide
> to the arts and manners of Moorish Spain,
> finds it difficult to believe that one man could
> so profoundly have modified the habits of a
> whole city, but nevertheless concludes that
> Ziryab symbolizes the oriental influence
> which pervades al-Andalus at the time and
> have become part of a common Spanish
> heritage."

Abbas ibn Firnas was scientist attached to the court of Abdul Rahman II. He was an astronomer and an experimentalist. He made many startling inventions. For example, he constructed a flying machine out of a light frame to which he attached feathers to function as wings. It is said that the machine remained airborne for some time. He made a globe of glass which could change from clear to cloudy at will.

Another courtier in Abdul Rahman's entourage was Yahya ibn Hakam al-Ghazzal. He was a man of great learning and a poet. He was also interested in botany. He went to Constantinople, the Byzantine capital, as an ambassador of Abdul Rahman to the Byzantine emperor Theophilus, in 840. On return, he brought with him a sapling of the fig tree of a rare quality, which came to be called "donegal fig" in Al Andalus. The story of how he brought the sapling from Constantinople to Cordova would illustrate the difficulties of international restrictions between Muslim and Christian countries. He saw the fig there and admired it. It was forbidden to take anything from Constantionple. He took the green figs and put them between his books and warped them. On his departure from Constantinople, he was searched, but no sign was found of it. When he arrived in Cordova he planted the sapling and watered it carefully. When it bore fruit, he went to the Amir, Abdul Rahman II, and showed it to him. When the Amir asked him about its name. AlGhazzal replied:

"I do not know what its name is except that when the one who picks it and gives some of it to someone he says, Dunahu qawli' which means 'O my lord, look!'" and so the Commander of the Muslims named it Dunaqal"

In the last years of his life, al-Ghazzal was banished from Cordova and lived in his native-town, Jaen, for he had lampooned the Maliki faqih, Yahya, in verse thus:

Why is it that one only finds rich faqihs? I should like to know from where their wealth proceeds.

CHAPTER 9

MUHAMMAD-I BIN ABDUL RAHMAN II (852-886 A.D.)

Accession: The accession of Muhammad I to the throne was in a way dramatic. A group of historians believe that Abdul Rahman had left no will either in favour of his eldest son Muhammad or his son Abdullah. His sudden death therefore confused the accession case. The circumstancial evidence show in the later period of his life, could not afford to ignore the succession problem in his lifetime to create trouble for the empire.

The mother of Abdullah Queen Taroob was his weakness but he was not prepared to put the kingdom at stake by nominating Abdullah who loved to be indulged in wine and music with no political and administrative insight. Moreover the Amir became disgustingly overcautious by the poison-plot of Queen Taroob and nominated his eldest son Muhammad, the crown prince as his lawful successor. Public announcement could not however be made due to the serious illness of the Amir and it remained confined in the palace. It may also be noted that the Amir inspite of his mad love with Queen Taroob did not allow her any role in the country's affairs. To him the palace and the throne were two separate apartments with no room to communicate with each other. Had there been a will or an expressed desire of the Amir in favour of Abdullah, the necessity of deeping the death of the Amir a secret was frivolous.

There is no doubt that the two princes were diametrically opposed to each other in character, temperament and disposition. If Abdullah was recklessly extravagent and loved luxurious, excessive and fast life, Muhammad was just the contrast.

The palace slaves who lived on the bounty of queen Taroob and her son Abdullah were naturally interested in prince Abdullah and were afraid of the rigidity of prince Muhammad.

The deadbody of the Amir was locked up in a palace room and Queen Taroob was preparing the ground for her son. All the palace slaves and guards favoured Abdullah except Abdul Mufarrah who informed prince Muhammad through a slave Sadun to hurry up to the palace to meet the situation. Prince Muhammad clad in female dress entered the palace. He had however to disclose his identity to the palace guards on their refusal to accept him as the daughter of the prince. He entered the palace early dawn. All were bewildered his succession to throne. A large number of the palace people offered homage to the prince and thus Muhammad overcame the palace intrigue just in time.

Revolt in Toledo. Soon after the accession of Muhammad I the people of Toledo revolted in 852. The Toledan Christians had deep sympathies with the Zealots of Cordova, whose leader, Eulogies they elected as the archbishop of Toledo. But the new sultan did not sanction his election. He marched against the toledans at the head of a large army and laid siege to the city, which lasted for two years. At last in 854, the Toledans, revolt was crushed by a ruse. But the revolted again five years later. It was caused by the execution of Elogius in Cordova. This time they were supported again by the king of Leon. They were between the sultan's forces and the rebellious goledans dragged on for several years. At last in 873, Sultan, Muhammad I was compelled to enter into a treaty with them. He recognised their republican form of government on the payment of a yearly tribute.

The Christian Zealots:

The monastry of Tabnos was the Zealot's centre. Abdul Rahman II had crushed the talions mildy. They remained silent in his time but raise their heads again during the rule of Muhammad. Eulogus life was spared by Abul-Rahman and being indebted to him, gave new life to the fanatic movement against Church Office, by the Zealots. He sought help of Charles the Bald, the king of France. The Bald sent his agents Uswad and Odilard to survey the situation (858 A.D.) Muhammad-I took drastic steps against the ringleaders. Eulogius, Alvaro and Lecoritia were hanged (March 859 A.D.) for villifying the holy Prophet (Peace be upon him) in the open court of the Qazi. The sober Christian community disliked the Zealots and felt relief with the award for the punishment to the ringleaders.

Hanbalis & Malikis:

The Maliki doctrine had gained ground in Spain and had special patronage of Amir Hisham. The followers of other doctrines did not like the dominance of the Maliki Ulema. The general disorders during the reign of Muhammad-I encouraged the followers of Imam Hanbal to force the Hanbali views. Public debates instead of resolving the dispute, created hatred and bitterness. The Amir however intervened and pacified both the parties.

The independence of Banu-Qasi:

Inspite of all efforts of the rulers of Spain, the traditional superiority complex of the Arabs could not be erased effectively.

The neo-Muslims and the Berbers inspite of their being powerful in social, economic and political fields could not claim equality with the Arabs. This notion of superiority was highly pinching for neo-Muslims and the Berbers. A number of neo-Muslims belonged to royal families and they could not brook the bloodboasting of the Arabs which was neither Islamic nor the demand of the age. Ambitious persons were impatient to have either an independent or semi-independent principalities of their own.

The accession of Muhammad I brought an opportunity for Banu Qasi to declare their independence in Aragon. Banu Qasi were those converts who belonged to the royal visigothic family. They had settled down in Aragon.

Musa II was an ambitious. He taking the advantage of the internal disorder, declared his independence. He captured Tudela, Huesca and Saragossa. The Christians of Toledo joined hands with him. His son Lope, the Commander-in-Chief of the Toledoan army was virtually the master of Toledo, Musa had become so popular and strong that he was regarded as the third king of Spain. The king of France sent valuable presents to him as a mark of friendship. The sudden death of Musa II (248 A.H; 862 A.D.) weakened the newly established independent principality and Amir Muhammad was successful in annexing Saragossa and Toledo for Cordova. After a few years the Banu Qasi raised arms against Cordova led by the son of Musa. The royal army was driven out of the terriledged Aragon as an independent territory. Cordova was helpless.

Revolt of Ibn Merwan : Ibn Merwan, a Muwallad, revolted in Galacia in the west of the peninsula and established an independent principality. But when the Sultan marched against him, he surrendered to him. He was brought to Cordova. Some time later, he was one day insulted by Hashim, the favourite wazir of Muhammad. He left Cordova and captured a castle near merida, the provincial centre of the west. He was again besieged by the royal troops and submitted to the Sultan on the condition that he would be allowed to go to Badajoz. He again revolted and called upon the Muwalladun of Merida and other places in the west to join with him. He then preached a new religion which was an amalgam of Islam and Christianity. He formed an alliance with Alfonso III, the king of Leon, who was "the natural ally of all rebels against the sultan", so Dozy puts it. Ibn Merwan declared himself to be the mortal enemy of the Arabs and Berbers, whom he considered as the enemies of his country. Muhammad then sent an army against him under the command of his son, Munzir, and his favourite wazir, Hashim. But he inflicted heavy losses on the royal army and captured Hashim, Ibn Merwan sent Hashim, as a war booty, to the king of Leon, Alfonso III. The Sultan paid one hundred thousand ducats to Alfonso as Hashim's ransom. Ibn Merwan advanced on Seville and laid waste the districts of Seville and Niebla. At last, the Sultan made peace with him by ceding Badajoz to him.

Galacia and Navaree:

Taking advantage of the internal disorders, the king of France breaking the peace-treaty concluded with Abdul Rahman II (223 A.H; 847 A.D.) invaded and pluddered the frontier cities. The Galacians and the Navarees who were in league with the French king, rebelled and annexed a major part of the Muslim land. Muhammad despatched a force from Cordova and also ordered the governors of Saragossa and Merida to end the frontier troubles. In the meantime the Hanblis and the Malikis were scuffing with each other. This scuffle had taken such a serious turn that it had threatened the very peace of Cordova. Muhammad-I therefore could not attend the royal force against Galacia and Navaree, in person, and preferred to settle the disputes of the two strong religious groups to stop further deterioration in the administration of the capital.

The royal army under the command of the governor of Saragossa and Merida was however successful in stopping the frontier inroads. Navaree the land of the Basques was attached by the royal force in 861 A.D. and its capital Pamplona fell to Cordova. Thus the Gothic March or Spanish March turned into a bloody war field. The Christians retreated to their fortresses.

After the return of Munzir to Cordova, the Christians came out again and plundered the northern part of Muslim Spain. Many towns and cities were burnt to ashes by them. Lusitania and Leutra suffered much. Amir Muhammad therefore marched in person with a strong force and compelled the Christians ruler of Leon (865 A.D.) to surrender unconditionally.

Just the following year a peace-treaty was concluded with Charles the Bald who got back Calatonia on condition of guaranteeing his support to Cordova and keeping himself away from the rebels in all respects.

Norman Inroads:

The Normanpirates were greatly dejected by their defeat by Abdul Rahman-II (239 A.H; 843 A.D.). The Muslim fleet was a terror for them. They however watched with interest the internal and external disorders and rebellions in the country. In the meantime they being instigated and encouraged by the Christians planned to plunder the coastal cities. They invaded, with 70 ships (859 A.D.) Malaga and Seville and devasted other coastal towns. On the approach of the royal fleet they fled away with heavy loss.

Muhammad-I suspected the intrigue of Galicia in the Norman raids. He therefore ordered Abdul Hamid-bin-Mughis to attack Galicia. Mughis with a fleet of light ships sailed down the Gudalquiver but as the light fleet entered the Atlantic ocean it was encircled by heavy storm. The fleet could not resist the fury of the storm and there was no other alternative but to suspend the sail for the smooth season.

Character and Achievements of Muhammad-I

During Muhammad's reign an internal crisis had overtaken the Ummayad Emirate. He was a weak and narrow-minded ruler. His greed and selfishness had oriented many of his subjects. However, the Maliki faqihs supported him, for he had crushed the movement of the Christian Fanatics with a strong hand and put an end to their movement. In desperation against the continuous Christian revolts, he ordered the destruction of many Christian Churches in his capital. Muhammad was a patron of learning and "a lover of science" writes Ibn al Athir. "He was discreet and wise, and well-versed in the rules of administration". But Bozy's opinion of his character nearest the point.

> "While the insurgents had shown themselves brave and resourceful, the Sultan had proved himself both weak and cowardly. Every concession granted to the rebels, every treaty made with them, had tended to diminish the prestige so necessary for inspiring respect in an unsubdued and disaffected population much more numerous than their conquerors".

CHAPTER 10

UMAR-BIN-HAFSOON

Umar-bin-Hafsoon, a descendant of a visigothic count was born in 246 A.H., in Yzoute (Hisne Ote) or Iznate (Hisn Ante) a village in Ronda. His father Hafs-bin-Umar-bin-Jafer al-Islami lived in the north-east of Malaga as a landlord. Jafer-bin-Damya-bin Fargoos was the first man of the line who embraced Islam during the rule of Hakam-I. Hafs the father of Umar was not only a landlord but a business man also and later on was called Hafsoon.

His son Umar was just a contrast to the mild and gentle disposition of his father. He was hot-headed and ill-tempered. His father left Iznate with his only son who was charged with the murder of a local officer, to Serrania de Ronda at the foot of Mount Bobastro, just to save him from the clutches of the law. Umar, an incorrigle urchin, joined a band of the brigands. His father therefore turned him out of his house, and refused to provide any protection for him. Umar therefore fled away to Tahirat (Tahort) in North Africa, and stayed with a tailor, an acquaintance of his father.

He however, did not consider safe his stay at Tahirat as he suspected the prince of Tahirat the Ummayad client of handing him over to the court of law. In this state of fear and confusion he was recognised by a Christian priest who having diluted him

with the false prediction of the crown of Undulisia goaded him
to sail immediately for Spain. The priest, a very cunning zealot
seeing in him the leading qualities of the brigands, anticipated
the fulfillment of his fulsome designs, through a fresh inroad
by the frustrated outlaw Ibne-Hafsoon.

It was in 880 A.D. that Hafsoon returned to Spain and
was welcomed by his uncle Nazahir. Here he raised a gang of
40 notorious farmers and stayed in an old deserted Roman castle
known as El-Castillon. The mountaineers of Elvira flocked
round him and accepted him as their leader.

He started plundering the adjoining towns and villages.
He even looted the royal granary. The governor of Regio failed
to stop his inroads. He was however defeated by the Prime
Minister Hashim and was compelled to surrender. The Amir,
on the recommendation of Hashim appointed him as a military
officer. (883 A.D.) While in the royal army, he proved his mettle
against the Bani Qasi and the Asturians.

Walid-ibne-Ghanim the prefect of city of Cordova was a
rival of Hashim, the Prime Minister. He disliked all who were
in good books with Hashim. Ibne Hafsoon therefore could not
be an exception. Ghanim, wilfully supplied poor-quality ration
to the troops of Ibne Hafsoon. Hisham turned a deaf ear to his
complaint. Ibne Hafsoon taking it as direct insult, and
disconnecting himself with the royal army (884 A.D.) joined
the robbers, gang to avenge the insult and make himself master
of the land. Establishing himself in Babastro he denounced
Muhammad's rule and took up army against him. He was not
only a robber but had also a diplomatic brain. He earned the
sympathy of the neo-Muslims by promising them a high status
in life by relieving them of the servitude of the Arabs. A large
number of neo-Muslim and fortune seekers flocked around him.
Thus he was able to form an independent principality in the

hilly tracts with peace and order. He used to address the congregation and infused hatred for the Arabs and the Amir. His speech was carried through various lips to Cordova and other places which worked well for poisoning the people's mind. He was thus a robber, a leader and a ruler.

He plundered the neighbouring districts of Jaen and Iznajar. His preachings had no relevancy with his action. Neither the Muslims nor the neo-Muslims were spared of his plunderings.

Ibne Hafsoon however had to submit to the royal army under Zayd-bin-Qasim and implored for amnesty. On being pardoned, he came, out with a treacherous plan and attacked the royal army at night killing Zayd-bin.Qasim.

Hearing the treachery of Ibne-Hafsoon, Prince Al-Munzir advanced with a strong army to punish him (June 886 A.D.)

In the meantime Abdul Malik a chief of Al-bama fort confronted the royal force and fought to death. Ibne Hafsoon came to his rescue only to escape away severely wounded with life.

The death of Muhammad and the internal troubles that Al-Munzir had to face, provided relief for Ibne Hafsoon. He could find time to re-organise himself to face the new Amir Al-Munzir. The new Amir was a terror for Ibne-Hafsoon and he was afraid of him.

Al-Munzir, known for his prudent and proven generalship, sparing Umar for the time being, crushed and killed Ayshun a neo-Muslim chief of Archidona and an ally of Umar. He then, after having crushed the Banu Matroob of the Sierra-de-Priego, the chief supporter of Umar, besieged Bobastro (888 A.D.) the stronghold of Ibne-Hafsoon. The cunning rebel submitted to the Amir and agreed to pay tribute. His submission was only an act of treachery. He attacked the royal force on its way back to Cordova, from the rear. The Amir therefore besieged Bobastro in person and the defeat of Ibne-Hafsoon was certain and guaranteed. But as ill-luck would have it, the Amir fell a pray to the palace intrigue. He was poisoned to death by his own doctor at the enticed instigation of his brother Abdullah. Ibne-Hafsoon was thus spared to challenge Abdullah and Abdul Rahman Ill.

The chaotic condition of Spain encouraged Ibne-Hafsoon, all the more. He was the most formidable of all the rebels. Amir Abdullah therefore tried to subdue him by force. In a forty day's campaign (889 A.D.) Amir Abdullah could capture a few villages but calculating his own weakness due to the internal disorders in the country, he tried to win over the rebel by allowing him to rule the territory in his possession as a permanent and independent representative of the Amir. The supporters of Ibne-Hafsoon, who were mostly robbers and free booters did not appreciate the peace treaty.

Ibne Mastana one of the chief supporter of Ibne-Hafsoon attacked Abu Harb the Berber chief of Algicars, plundered the city and captured the fortress.

Amir Abdullah despatched a force under the command Ibrahim-bin-Humair Amvi and asked Ibne-Hafsoon to join to help Ibrahim. Ibne-Hafsoon entered into a secret pact with Ibne-Mastana of Jean with the result that Ibrahim along with other royal officer was imprisoned. The Christians of Cordova extended their support to Ibne-Hafsoon to threaten Cordova by strengthening his position in the north.

Count Servando, who enjoyed the confidence of the Amir rebelled and joined Ibne-Hafsoon. The count was killed in a skirmish but Ibne-Hafsoon captured Ejica and Polei. All the important forts south of the Guadalquiver were occupied by him. The provinces Elvira and Jean were governed by the Ibne-Hafsoon alone.

Intoxicated with power, Ibne-Hafsoon planned to rule the whole of Muslim Spain. He therefore requested Ibne Aghlab the Abbaside Governor of North Africa to get the approval of the Abbaside caliph Motazid-Billah for investituring him as the governor of Undulusia. He knew that his dream of ruling over Muslim Spain could be realized by establishing his authority over the Arabs which was not possible without winning the favour of the caliph. Inspite all differences with the Cordovan government, Ibne Aghlab did not like the slaughter of the Arabs by a man whose dishonesty and treachery was more than obvious. Ibne Aghlab who was in close study of the length of his insurrections and the motive behind it was true in adjudging him a faithless convert who sought an opportunity of restoring the Christian rule in disguise.

Ibne-Hafsoon in the meantime had made a stronghold in Eliga and Polei. Cordova was then facing a very hard time. The capital like frontier city, was a prey to the plunderers and robbers.

The royal treasury once renowned for its solvency had become hopelessly insolvent that even the salaries could not be disbursed the staff of all ranks. Amir Abdullah having failed to control the deteriorating condition tried to appease Ibne-Hafsoon by offering peace on favourable terms but he turned down the peace offer of the Amir.

The Amir, feeling much humiliated, decided to punish the rebel in the open field to establish the superiority of the Arab sword once again.

Abdul Malik-bin Umayyah marched towards Polei with fourteen thousand soldiers (4000 regular, 10,000 new recruits).

The two armies met at Polei (Friday April 16, 891 A.D.) Ibne-Hafsoon was defeated and sheltered himself in the Fort of Polei. Many of his soldiers fled to Ejica. Ibne-Hafsoon and his right hand, the treacherous Ibne Mastana, vacating Polei and Archidona escaped to Cabra. The fortress of Polei was placed at the disposal of the Amir. A huge quantity of war equipments and immense wealth were amassed to compensate the emptiness of the royal treasury. Ejica was also captured. Jean also submitted to the Amir whose authority was re- established in the south. Had the Amir been himself present in the battle of Police, the bravery of the soldiers would have been augmented to annex Bobastro the chief strong hold of Ibne-Hafsoon.

The battle of Polei regained the lost prestige of Cordova and the Amir became popular among the people. The terror of Ibne Hafsoon was wiped out from the hearts of the people.

Ibne-Hafsoon being disappointed with his defeat at Polei and the cold attitude of the Ibne-Aghlab, the Abbaside governor of North Africa, had no other alternative but to sue for peace. Instead giving his own son as a hostage, according to the terms of treaty, he sent his adopted son to cover cunningly the treaty. The refusal of Amir Abdullah to accept his adopted son as hostage, gave way to a few fight.

Raising a strong army of bandits and Christian mercenaries, duly supported by the Christian chiefs he attacked and plundered the Muslim territories (892 A.D.). He captured almost all his lost possessions except Polei and Ejica. The Arab leader Saeed-bin-Judi of Elvira was defeated. Thus Elvira and Jaen were occupied by him. The royal force, due to the incapability of the Amir, had to face defeat at all points.

Ibne-Hafsoon intoxicated with his unexpected success and power recollected the prediction of the Christian priest of Tahirat in North Africa. He, therefore considering it an opportune time planned to re-establish the Christian rule in Spain. It was in 286 A.H.; 899 A.D. that he declared his retreat to Christianity with his family, which he had so artfully concealed for long.

Just to pave way for the restoration of the Christian power in Spain, by creating hatred and bitterness within the Muslim-fold against the Amir.

The reading of Ibne-Aghlab, the Abbaside governor of North Africa, about the apostastic leanings of Ibne-Hafsoon came to be true and he was fully justified in ignoring his debaced request. Ibne-Hafsoon could be well termed as Lawrance of Undulusia.

His apostacy bore no fruit for him. Neither the Arabs nor the Spanish Muslims were prepared to be led and ruled by a Christian.

The Christians went over to the side of Ibne-Hafsoon, whereas the Muslims stood for the support of the Amir.

This gave a turn to a crusade. Many of his Muslim supporters and officers-like Yahya-bin-Anatole, Awasaja-bin-al-Khali, the Berber chief of Cante and many others submitted to the Amir. The people in general rose to the side of Amir Ibne-Hafsoon lost his prestige in no time and courted defeat at every point. He therefore tried once again to gain the confidence of the Arabs. With this end in view he entered into alliance with Ibrahim-bin-Hajjaj the chief of Seville. He was however looking for an opportunity to conclude peace with the Amir. Amir Abdullah who was devrid of the heroic qualities of his illustrious predecessors concluded a peace treaty with Ibne-Hafsoon in 901 A.D., 289 A.H. only to allow further nuisance in the kingdom.

According to the terms of the treaty four hostages including Ibne Mastana the chief of Preiego and Khalaf his paymaster were to remain in Cordova. Abdul Rahman the son of Ibne Hajjaj was also among the hostages. Ibne Hajjaj in the meantime entered into an alliance with the Banu Qasi and the king of

Leon-a threatening alliance for Amir Abdullah. The Amir therefore restored his son to him to win his confidence. It was done at the instance of his minister Badr. Thus the rising in Seville came to an end and the western parts of Spain also submitted to Cordova right from Algeciras to Niable.

The accession of Abdul Rahman III (912 A.D.) brought new hopes for the country. He earned the confidence in the people by establishing peace based on justice and equity. He dealt with the rebels talently and artfully. He looked to the welfare of the people more than anything else.

Ibne-Hafsoon became very cautious with the accession of Abdul Rahman III. Being disappointed with the desertion of the people of Regio he appointed the Berbers of Africa on rich salaries to adjust the uncertain condition of his army. He also acknowledged the suzerainty of the Fatmide ruler Ubaid Al-Shii to enlist his support against Cordova.

The retreat of Ibne-Mastana, his best friend and supporter, to Christianity caused further indignation in the Muslim camp.

Ibne-Hafsoon who had assumed the Christian name Samuel tried his best to win over the descendants of the serfs and slaves, but they recollecting the atrocities of the Gothic rule did not join his call. Ibne-Hafsoon had the support of the African mercinaries and Christians.

Ibne-Shaliah, a neo-Muslim chief recaptured Cazlona, a strong fortress in the province of Jaen. Being defeated on the right bank of the Guadalquiver Samuel (Ibne-Hafsoon) met Abdul Rahman III at Regio. Abdul Rahman III inspite of stiff resistance by the Christians reached Tolox, Samuel faced the royal army very stubbornly but to no effect and Tolox had to surrender.

Thus the long insurrection of Ibne-Hafsoon, which had

threatened the very existence of the Muslim empire in Spain was thoroughly crushed by Abdul Rahman, III compelling the rebel to die a traitor in 917 A.D; 304 A.H.

Samuel had four sons, Jafar, Sulaiman, Abdul Rahman and Hafs. Jafar who succeeded his father, stayed, in Bobastro. The Amir besieged Bobastro and entered the fort as a conqueror. He however implored the Amir for amnesty and agreed to pay tribute (306 A.H; 919 A.D.). He was however killed by his own Christian soldiers (307 A.H., 920 A.D.) His brother Sulaiman broke the peace treaty and was killed in a battle by a royal soldier (314 A.H.; 927 A.D.). The Amir who was not prepared to grant more concessions to the rebel family annexed Bobastro and appointed Hafs on a responsible military post.

Thus ended the Bani Hafsoon line which had trembled the empire. Bobastro which had resisted Cordova for the last fifty years was brought to complete subjugation.

Ibne-Hafsoon or Samuel a skilled hypocrite was hopelessly treacherous and selfish. He hated the Muslim faith from the core of his heart and was planning very diplomatically, cunningly, and artfully to get the restoration of the Christian rule in Spain.

Being a man of great ability and military skill, he won over the people, both Muslims and non-Muslims, feigning sincerity to them. He did not disclose his innate malicious hatred to the Muslims and wanted to overburden them with the Christian load, through their own weighty sword. He even tried to outwit the Abbaside caliph, feigning his obedience to him and also to the Fatmide king, acknowledging his suzerainty.

His declaration of his retreat to Christianity with family clearly proves that his motives were not obscure as Hole says. He being overconfident of his power, miscalculated the force of the Muslim faith and embraced shameful ruin and annihilation. Ibne Izhari is right to remark him "Prop of the infidels, crown of hypocrites", cunning breeder of discord, discontent and hatred."

He can be very well located with Abdullah bin-Ubai, Kanana bin-Bashir and Saudan bin Hamran of the early period of Hijra.

CHAPTER 11

MUNZIR
(886–888)

Accession : On the death of Muhammad-I his son Munzir ascended the throne. He had been trained in administration and warfare during the life time of his father. He had fought against many rebels successfully, in the north against Banu Qasi. In the west against Ibne Merwan and in the south against Umar Ibne Hafsun, with whom he was still at war.

War with Ibne Hafsun:

After his accession, Munzir left the capital at the head of an army against the Muwallad rebel, Umar bin Hafsun. Archidona the capital of the Regio province was captured. He then besieged Babastro, the strong hold of Ibne Hafsun. The rebel then submitted to the Sultan. But he revolted soon after the Sultan had departed for his capital. Munzir again marched against him. But he died in suspicious circumstances, while fighting near Bobastro in 888.

Character:

Munzir was brave and enterprising Sultan. He would have subdued all the rebels. But his life was cut short when he had been on the throne for only two years. He was succeeded by his brother Abdullah.

CHAPTER 12

ABDULLAH BIN MUHAMMAD
(888–912 A.D.)

Almunzir had no male issue. The throne of Cordova therefore fell to the lot of his treacherous brother Abdullah.

Amir Abdullah, a very incapable ruler could not cope with the situation and worsened it all the more. No quarter was free from disorder and revolts. The Arabs and the neo-muslims of Seville and Elvira were fighting among themselves. The old tribal hatred and disputes cropped up with full strength. The Syrian and the Hijazians were at daggers drawn. It was beyond the timid nature of Abdullah to rise to the occasion.

Revolt of Elvira: Elvira was situated in the district of Regio. It was inhabited by the Christians. Muwalladun and Arabs, who lived mostly in the countryside. The Arabs were the descendants of the jund or exclusive aristocracy. In their eyes, the Spaniards, whether Christians or Neo-Muslims, were a "dirty rabble." Although among themselves, these Arabs were very courteous towards each other, but they showed great contempt for the Neo-Muslims (Muwalladun) when they visited Elvira on Friday to attend Juma prayers. Naturally, no love was lost between the two Muslim groups of the inhabitants of Regio. They had already fought a war during the reign of Muhammad I. A war again broke out between them soon after

Abdullah ascended the throne, it was a racial war, with the Arabs on one side and the Spaniards, both Muslims and Christians, on the other. The Spaniards besieged the Arabs in a castle, called montexecar, situated near Granada, and forced the Arabs to surrender. Their commander, Yahya ibn Sokala, was put to death by the victorious Spaniards.

Though the Arab situation was perilous, they started fighting among themselves at various places in the district of Regio. The reason was the revile of their old tribal hatreds and hostilities. In the city of Elvira, the Yemenites, who were in majority, began to fight with the Modarites (or Qaisites). But then the Yemenites realised the danger they were confronted with and agreed to choose a Qaisite, Sauwar, as their leader. Though od, he proved to be a valiant leader. He summoned as many Arabs as he could and laid siege to Montexicar and captured it from the spaiards. He then captured many other castles in the province of Regio from the Spaniards and put many of them to the sword. They appealed to the governor of Regio, Jad. In hotly contested battle, the Arabs defeated Jad and the Spaniards, killing seven thousand of them.

After his victory, many other Arab tribes of Regio joined his forces. He then attacked the Spaniards of other cities. They appealled to Sultan Abdullah for protection. The Sultan offered the Governorship of Regio to Sauwar. Peace was made between the Arabs and the Spaniards.

Battle of City : But it was a temporary peace. Sauwar attacked Umar ibn Hafsun and his allies and vassals. Then all the Spaniards of Elvira rose against the Arabs, who were defeated. They took shelter in an old and ruined fortress of Alhambra, where they were besieged by the Spaniards. The Arab's condition was critical. But Sauwar led them out into the open, where they fought furiously with the larger army of the

Spaniards. Sauwar attacked them with a band of picked Arabs from the rear and routed them. Nearly twelve thousand Spaniards were killed fighting at the gates of Elvira. The battle was known as the Battle city. Ibn Hafsun was obliged to fall back from the city. He blamed the people of Elvira for his reverse. After this he returned to his stronghold, Bobastro. A short time after, Sauwar died in an ambush. The Arabs then chose Sa'id ibn Jad as their new leader. He was of noble birth and possessed all the qualities which the Arabs prozed in a leader. Even Ibn Hafsun was afraid of engaging him in a battle. In an engagement once he had almost killed Ibn Hafsun, but he was saved by his man. So the Arabs were able to hold their own under Sa'id Ibn Jad's leadership. The Sultan recognised him as the governor of Elvira.

Arab's Revolt in Seville:

Seville was inhabited by two strong groups, the Spaniards and the Arabs. The Spaniards were Banu-Anjilono. There were two hostile Arab families Bani Hajjaj and Bani Khaldoon. Bani Hajjaj traced their origin from Umar a Yamanite of the Lakhmi tribe from father side and from Sarah the grand daughter of king Witiza from mother side. They had fiefs in the Sened, a distinct between Seville and Niebla. Banu Khaldoon tracing their origin from the Yamanite, were connected with Hadramoot. They had extensive agricultural lands in Axarafi. Both Banu Hajjaj and Banu Khaldoon were big landlords and businessmen. They were called kings of the sea-trade. They had a number of forts in Seville and virtually half of Seville was in their possession.

Quraib, the chief of Banu Khaldoon and a sworn enemy of Abdullah, tried to overthrow the Umayyad rule. He got to his side Ibrahim-ibne-Hajjaj the Yamanite chief of Niebla and Sidona. He also formed league with the Berber chief of Carnova.

The Berbers of Merida and Medellin were also instigated to attack and plunder the neo-muslims of Seville. The Berbers captured Talyata. The march of the governor of Merida (891 A.D.) against the Berbers was ineffective. Quraib feigning his loyalty to the governor, planned a severe defeat for the governor at the hands of the Berbers who returned to Talyata with large booty. Ibne Marwan Jaliqi a neo-muslim independent chief of Badajoz attacked Talyata and plundered the city and its vicinity.

Umayyad-bin-Alghafir the new governor of Seville also failed to suppress the marauders. The governor being pressed by circumstances allowed Muhammad-ibne-Ghalib a neo-muslim to build a fortress near the village of Siete Torres on the border of Seville and Ejica, provided he would keep the robbers under control. Permanent peace however could not be resorted.

The complaint of Banu Khalfoon against Ibne Ghalib, for murdering a person of Banu Khaldoon, was not well met by the Amir. The situation became so serious that Prince Muhammad could not decide the case.

In the meantime Quraib, who was still hostile to the Umayyad rule, taking the murder episode as a pretext, captured Coria, and Carmona with the help of the Lakhmite of the Sened, the Hadramites of the Axarafa and Banu Hajjaj of Seville.

The situation became all the more worse due to the timid and hopeless policy of Amir, who instead of quelling the rebels by force, deputed Jad the governor of Elvira to annex Carmona and kill Ibne Ghalib.

Jad got killed Ibne Ghalib treacherously. Ibne-Hafsoon, and ally of Ibne Ghalib demanded the head of Jad who fled away from Cordova to Seville with his brothers Hashim and Abdul Ghafir. Jad however alongwith his brothers was killed on the way by the supporters of Ibne Ghalib. Ummayya the Governor of Seville took the revenge of the murder of his brother by ordering Bani Khaldoon and Bani Hajjaj to exterminate the Spaniards. About 20 thousand were killed in the affray and a large number of them were drowned in the river while trying to escape.

After the extermination of the Spaniards of Seville the Banu Hajjaj and the Banu Khaldoon became the master of Seville. Amir Abdullah knew all about the condition of the province but had no courage to challenge the self-made masters. Umayya the governor of Seville failed to create discord and hatred between Quraib and his party. He however got Abdullah-bin-Hajjaj killed by a Berber chief Junaid, Banu Hajjaj nominated lbrahim-bin-Hajjaj, Abdullah's brother, as their leader and chief. The Governor tried to win over Quraih bin-Khaldoon, but he saved himself from the trap. The Arabs were watching the movements of Umayya. One fine morning they attacked the palace and killed the Governor and informed the Amir saying that the governor was punished with the loss of his life, for his plan to rebel against Cordova. The Amir who was well conversant with the facts, was helpless and sent another governor with his uncle Hisham to cope with the situation. Both Hisham and the governor failed to crush the power of the Yamanite chiefs.

They requested the Amir to draft a strong force to admonish Mahdi and Banu Khaldoon. Unfortunately the latter was intercepted by Banu Khaldoon. The palace servants of all ranks were the agents of Banu Khaldoon and the governor was helpless. After the interception of the letter the governor was thrown in prison (891 A.D.) Seville was controlled by the Arabs while other places were dominated by the African and Spanish chiefs, Jaen and Elvira were in the possession of the Berbers.

The neo-muslims controlled Silves, Santa maria Beja, Metrola and the hills of Priego.

It was in 286 A.H.; 895 A.D. that prince Mutrif attacked Seville. Mutrif somehow or other arrested Ibrahim-bin-Hajjaj and Khalid-bin-Khaldoon. Quraib, was compelled to surrender. Prince Mutrif returned to Cordova after plundering the fiefs of Quraib. After some time the Amir released Ibrahim and Khalid but Abdul Rahman the son of Ibrahim was kept as a hostage in Cordova.

After reaching Seville both the released persons revolted openly. Ibrahim-bin-Hajjaj and Quraib-bin-Khaldoon divided Seville into two equal parts for themselves. This was fatal for them in as much as both of them struggled for supermacy. Ultimately Ibrahim killed Quraib and Khalid became the sole master of Seville. He submitted to the Amir on condition of his being approved as the governor of Seville. The Amir sent Qasim to work jointly with Ibrahim as governor but Ibrahim annoyed him so much that he had to go back to Cordova. Failing in his efforts to release his son Abdul Rahman from the custody of Amir, Ibrahim allied himself with Ibne-Hafsoon (900 A.D.), Amir Abdullah however released the son of Ibrahim who being indebted to the Amir, submitted to him and paid the government revenue with all arrears. He was however virtually an independent chief of Seville. He administered his principality wisely. Peace and order was restored. Learned men flocked in his court. Poets of reputes including the witty poetess Qamar who came from Baghdad, adored the company of the chief.

The army was regularly paid and was satisfied. Many poets and learned men of Cordova came to Seville and were well-rewarded by Ibrahim. Ibne-Abde-Robbehi an eminent scholar, a great literary figure and the poet laureate, left Cordova for Seville and was received with respect and honour by the chief of Seville. (860 A.H 940 A.D.).

Amir Abdullah's misrule and incapability caused disorder in the empire. A sort of tribal government was formed by the Arabs, neo-muslim and Berber Chiefs. Mentesa, Medina Sidonia, Lorca and Saragossa were occupied and administered by Arab Chiefs. Algrave, Beja, Jaen and Murcia were held by the Berbers and neo-muslims. The authority of the Amir was broken up and the authority was wielded by his own nobles and vassals. Abdul Rahman-ibne-Merwan al-Jiliqui, a neo-muslim founded an independent principality in the south west of Galacia. He had the support of Alfanso III of Leon.

Death of Abdullah:

After a reign of twenty four years Abdullah died on October 15, 912 at the age of sixty eight. Only the last nine years of his reign were free from any danger to his throne. His grandson, Abdul Rahman, son of Muhammad, his eldest son, ascended the throne.

Abdullah had come to power by poisoning his brother Munzir to death. He had kept himself, on his tottering throne in cowardly behaviour towards his enemies, whether of his kingdom his religion or of his race. He was cruel, vile and despicable. He was feeble in policy and governance. But a lucky turn in the battle of Polei saved his kingdom for him and for his descendants a century more to come.

CHAPTER 13

HAKAM-II
(961–976)

Accession : Al Hakam II ascended the throne on the death of his father. He ruled for fifteen years. His rule was one of peace and prosperity at home, submission of the Christian kingdoms of the north, the extension of Umayyad power into North Africa and the blossom in and fulfillment of the arts.

Raids of Christians:

Sancho the king of Leon and Garcia the king of Navaree encouraged by the literary persuits of Al-Hakam II, broke the treaties which they had concluded so humbly with Abdul Rahman III. They were confident of their success even in the war field hoping the incapability of AI-Hakam to rise to the occasion like his illustrious father.

Sancho refused to surrender the fortresses which he had to do according to the terms of the treaty. Garcia the king of Navaree also refused to hand over to the caliph, Ferdinand (Fernan Gonzalez) the Count of Castile, who was in his custody and who had forced his daughter to divorce Ordono IV of Bargos, an ally of Cordova. Ferdinand on being rescued by Garcia, drove away Ordono IV out of Bargos who took refuge in the Cordovan territory.

Al-Hakam therefore marched in person against Ferdinand in 351 A.H., February 962 A.D. and drove away the Christians out of the Undulisian Frontiers.

Ordono IV of Leon being ousted by Sancho and Ferdinand was trying to win back the favour of the Umayyad Caliph through Ghalib the governor of Medina Celi. Ordono IV being escorted to Al-Zahra by Abdullah-bin-Qasim the Metropolitan of Seville, was received honourably by the caliph.

He requested the caliph to help him in regaining his lost territory. General Ghalib was ordered by the caliph to re-instate Ordono on his throne, who in return agreed to keep his son Garcia in Cordova as a hostage and not to keep alliance with Ferdinand.

Sancho was not liked by the people of Leon. He realizing his position, implored the caliph to renew to the former treaty and that he was prepared to surrender the fortresses according to the clause of the previous treaty. Al-Hakam therefore accorded to the request of Sancho. Ordono IV who was then staying in the Qasre-Naoora, at Cordova, died of heart failure (962 A.D). Being encouraged by the death of Ordono IV, Sancho refused to abide by the terms of the previous treaty. General Ghalib the governor of Medinaceli invaded Castille. He defeated the Galicians and captured the forts of San-Stevan-de-Gormaz (Shant Ishtiban Gharmaj.)

The combined forces of General Ghalib and Yahya-bin-Ahmad Tajibi, governor of Saragossa attacked the territory of the Basques. Garcia of Navaree was defeated and the famous city Calahora was captured. Sancho had no other alternative but to submit. Ferdinand (Fernan Gonzalez) of Castile also had to submit (966 A.D.) The counts of Borrel and Miron also followed suit. Other Christian chiefs, namely the chiefs of Catalonia, the count of Barcelona and other Christian lords entered into a treaty with the caliph and agreed to demolish all their fortresses and towns on the Cordovan frontiers and not to help the Christians against the Muslims.

Sancho, the traitor, was poisoned to death by Count Gonsalvo, in a conference on the bank of the Duro (966 A.D.) and thus Castile was brought under subjugation.

The successful campaigns of the caliph against the Christians proved that Al-Hakam was not only a man of pen but a man of sword as well.

Fatmids and Sanhajas:

The danger of the Fatimide Caliph of North Africa was not fully averted. They were planning to rule the entire Muslim world, especially Spain. They had spread the net of their spies in Spain so cleverly that neither the army nor the court and the chamber of Al-Hakam could be freed from the snares. The transfer of the Fatimide capital to Cairo (972 A.D.) averted the Fatimide danger to a sufficient degree.

The entire territory of North Africa was left under the control of Abul Fatah Yusuf-bin-Ziri, a chief of the Sanhaja Berber tribe.

Abdul Fatah compelled Hasan-bin-Chanun the last Idrisid ruler of Tangier and Arzila to submit to him and cut down his loyalty to the caliph of Spain.

The Ummayyad General Ibne Talmus, though successful in the first battle, fell fighting in the second one. This defeat brought the Ummayyad vassals in Mauritania to the side of the Fatmides. Barring a few of the towns, all were in the possession of Abul Fatah.

It was in 972 that General Ghalib landed at Qasre-Masmudah between Centa and Tangier. General Ghalib very skilfully broke up the concentration of the Berbers through rich presents and gifts to the officers and the soldiers. The result was that many supporters of Ibne Ghanum worked secretly for General Ghalib. Ibne Ghanum being defeated took shelter in Centa. Al-Hakam deputed Muhammad-bin Abi-Amir the master of the mint of Cordova to take over as the chief judge of the African territory and to look after the finance.

It was in 363 A.H., 973 A.D. that the caliph Al-Hakam sent Yahya-bin-Ahmad Tajibi with a string force to punish Ibne-Ghanum, who had to enter into a treaty with the Caliph Al-Hakam. Ibne Ghanum was sent to Cordova along with his family. He was however permitted to go to Tunisia on condition that he will never visit Mauritania. He Berber tribes of Zanat Maghrawa and Iknasa acknowledged the suzerainty of Al-Hakam. Thus Al-Hakam was able to establish peace, to let the people and the country grown more and more prosperously,

Death

Al-Hakam II died of paralysis at the age of 61 after a rule of 16 years (3rd Safar 366 A.H; 30th Sept., 976 A.D.). Before his death he had nominated his son Hisham as his successor, who was then only 12 years old. He had also appointed Mus'hafi and Muhammad bin Abi Amir as his guardians.

Character

The caliph Al-Hakam II Al-Mustansir-be-Allah (Help seeker from God the Almighty) was courteous, mild, kind, just and humble by nature. A highly learned man as he was, he respected the people of learning and felt elated to sit with them and hear them on different topics of the various subjects.

He followed the Shara and Sunnah very strictly. He said the Juma prayers in the grand mosque of Cordova with the public and not in the pew. Wine was strictly prohibited. The taxes levied by the provinces were for the good of the people. He encouraged philosophical discussions like a free thinker. He felt pleasure and satisfaction in granting amnesty and pardon to the seeker. He did not like to indulge in war for aggressive designs. He fought like a hero and commanded the army like a seasoned General until the enemy surrendered or crushed. He won because of his own extraordinary capabilities. Thus he was the illustrious son of the illustrious father.

Achievements:

To the dismay of the Christians and the intriguers, Al Hakam was not only a man of letters but also a man of sword. He was always ready to quell the inroads and risings and solidified the country with peace and prosperity. He kept at bay the Fatmids and the Christians from the Muslim frontiers.

The office of Hajib or Grand Vazir, abolished by his father, was revived by him.

There is no denying the fact that Al-Hakam inherited a vast consolidated empire from his illustrious father Al-Nasir the great. He therefore found time to devote his energy to the development of learning and culture which he imbibed instinctively.

Dr. Imamuddin is right to remark that "Modern conceptions of cleanliness, drainage system, use of soap, heating of rooms, street lighting, use of handkerchiefs are taken from the Muslims. Ummayyad rulers like Abdul Rahman II, Abdul Rahman III, and Hakam II raised the living conditions of the people and taught the unique idea, had dazzled the then Europe, and the modern world has to bow to them.

The use of fine soap was very common in public and private baths. The Harem of Al Hakam II and of the nobility were very fond of soaps. At that time the European world had no idea of even taking regular ordinary baths.

The tournaments of valour, vigour and strength in the modern European society owe their origin to the days of Al Hakam.

A prophetic tradition "cleanliness is a part of faith" has been very strictly adopted and followed by every Muslim in all times. It is interesting to note that according to Al-Khatib, Baghdad had 27,000 public baths (Hammam) in the time of Al-Muqtadir (908-32 A.D.) which rose to 60,000 in other times. The Moorish traveller Ibne-Batutah after his visit to Baghdad in 1327 A.D. found baths with regular supply of hot and cold running water through lead pipes. Undulusia ran parallel to Baghdad.

Al-Hakam II, a great patron of education, left no city, village or sub-village without a school. Elementary schools (Kuttab or Maktab) an adjunct of the Mosque had special attention of the Khalifa Al-Hakam II Al-Mustansir-be-Allah. The three "Rs", reading, writing and arithmetic were taught very carefully. Pieces of poetry served as the writing matter. Penmanship, Arabic Grammar, Quran and Hadith were taught by able teachers. Special emphasis was laid on memory work, a very important item of the curriculum.

Humanities, ilmul-adab, was yet another important clause of the curriculum. Institutions of higher education were numerous. All the educational institutions imparted free education. Hostels were available with unlimited seats with free lodging and boarding. The Khalifa's brother Munzir-bin-Abdul Rahman was the director to Ibne-Idhari three "27 free schools" of the highest standard in Cordova, where selected students were admitted and cared for, by eminent teachers, to prepare them for higher research works.

Al Hakam brought the university of Cordova, founded by his father in the Grand Mosque to a place of such an eminence which rivalled the "Baitul Hikmat" (The House of Wisdom) of Al Mamoon (830 A.D.). The Jamia of Al-Azhar, Cairo, and the Nizamiah of Baghdad founded by Nizamul Mulk the Persian Prime Minister of Malik Alp Arsalan Saljuqi (1065-7 A.D.) had to grow on its inspirations. Seville, Malaga, Saragossa, and Jaen had institutions on the Cordovan pattern and achieved distinction in later periods.

The Khalifa had raised the level of education to such a pitch that "every one could read and write whilst in Christian Europe only a few ever acquired learning and that also mostly from among the Clergy". Quoting Qazwani through Nicholson, "Even a labourer behind the plough would improvise verses on any subject extempore." Cordova was a beacon-light for the then Europe. The German poet Hrokswitha rightly described Cordova as the ornament of the world.

The Grand Mosque which housed the university of Cordova was enlarged by the Khalifa Al-Hakam and decorated with mosaics spending 2615137 Dinars and 1-1/2 dirham on it as quoted by Ibne-Idbari. The University and other educational institutions were open for all the students of the world. Muslim and non-Muslim students thronged in the university and were welcomed with no preferential treatment.

The notion that there existed special academies for the rich class is groundless. Al-Hakam, a strict follower of Sunnah and Shariah would not tolerate any distinction in the sacred domain of education. There were of course practising schools of high standard which admitted meritorious students only, irrespective of class or community to be trained and educated for purposeful achievements. The income of the Zin-Bazar, saddlers' Market of Cordova was reserved for the maintenance of schools. The rich also had to contribute to the education-fund. The salaries of the teachers and professors were disbursed from the Khalifa's own private fund.

He invited eminent professors from the East and other places to the university and employed them on rich salaries.

Ibnul-Qautia, the historian taught grammar, Abu-ali-Al-Qali the philologist of Baghdad, taught ancient poetry, proverbs, language and literature. His book "Amali" (dictations) is still a very popular book. Abu Abdullah Muhammad-bin-Abd al-Udri, the chief physician of the Khalifa's court and Muhammad Abu Al-Zubaidi the author of Kitabul-ain, a fine Arabic dictionary, were on the pannels of the professors. Abu Ibrahim the renowned Faqih (theologian) and Abu Bakr-bin-Muawiah taught hadith, theology, Muslim laws, and oriental sciences.

A large number of lecturers and professors of different subjects adored the university.

AI-Hakam II was a biblophile and so was his brother Abdullah. Their personal libraries were turned into a huge one by amalgamating them with that of Abdul Rahman Ill.

The agents of Al-Hakam ransacked the book-stalls and libraries of Alexandria, Damascus and Baghdad either to copy the rare manuscripts or to purchase them at fancy prices. Rare collection of books and manuscripts, thus gathered, numbered 4,00,000. The figure has been raised by some to 6,00,000. The catalogue of the library covered 44 volumes, with 20 to fifty sheets denoting the author's names and titles of the books.

Al-Hakam read almost all the imported books and manuscripts and put his own marginal notes which testified his knowledge and scholarship. He sent Abul Faraj Al-Ispahani the author of Al-Aghani, one thousand dinars to secure the first copy which was then composed in al-Iraq.

Separate rooms were reserved for copyists and book-binders.

In Cordova alone there were 20,000 book-shops besides a large number of copying shops.

Muhammad-bin-Abi-Al-Husain-al-Fihri of Cordova the eminent litterateur and lexicographer and Muhammad-bin-Mamar of Jaen, famous scholar of Arabic literature were deputed by the Khalifa to collect manuscripts and copy the rare books in his library.

Yousuf-al-Albaluti, Abul Fazal-bin-Haroon of Sicily (d. 379 A.H,, 989 A.D.) were famous copyists. The personal library of Ibne-Futais of Cordova, which ranked first, was sold by Public auction for 40,000 dinars in the early period of the 11th century.

Foreign scholars like, Ibne Saban of Egypt: Ibne-Yaqoub-al-Kindi of Baghdad, were employed by the Khalifa for the collection of rare books and manuscripts of any subject.

Laubanah (d. 394 A.H: 1004 A.D.) chief secretary to Talid the librarian of Khalifa's library, and Fatimah an eminent writer travelled to many places in search of rare books and manuscripts to add to the collections of the royal library.

Book shops like jewellery and cloth stalls had a brisk business. The books were printed on papers manufactured by the Arabs themselves. The books were sold at the lowest price to encourage the library and scientific persuits.

The kitabul Auqat-al-Sanat (memoir on calendar) by Abul Hasan Arbi-bin Saeed and the Tarikh Qudat-al-Qartaba by Mohammad-bin-Haris-bin-Asad-al- Khushani of Qirwan were standard books, dedicated to Al-Hakam. The dynastic history of the Umayyads by the eminent historian Ibnul Qautia (d. 977 A.D.) and the works on theology by Ibne-Zamanin (d. 1007-9 A.D.) specially written for the royal library, were also dedicated to the Khalifa, Mufarraj of Cordova, Mutarrif-bin-Isa of Elvira,

Ahmad-bin-Faraj of Jaen compiler of anthology of poems-Al-Hadaq, were among those writers who had dedicated their works to the Khalifa. Alzubaidi (d. 989 A.D.) the tutor of the Khalifa's son Hisham was known for his research work on poems. Books on belesletters were greatly admired.

The Khalifa was a serious scholar and no book of his library was beyond the reach of his study. It is said that a mobile library accompanied him, on journey and even in battle camps. After he received the first copy of Al-Aghani, he never missed the opportunity of studying it several times.

His patronisation of learning attracted eminent learned men and scholars and a large number of philosophers, theologians, historians, geographers, astronomers, astrologers, mathematicians, physicians, scientists, joined the university and settled down in Cordova.

The Khalifa was master of various sciences the study of which he owed to his eminent teachers, Qasim bin-Asbagh, Ahmad-bin-Dahim, Muhammad-bin-Abdul Salam Alkhushani, Zakarya-bin-al-khattab and Sabit bin Qasim. He was author of several books on various subjects and was an authority on history, which unfortunately could not escape the atrocities of the Christians.

The Khalifa's respects and regard for the Ulema can be very well judged from the fact that Bab-al-Sana the gate between the Chief Mosque and the palace reserved for the Khalifa only, was opened for Abu Ibrahim the theologian to attend the conference in the palace. The Khalifa with his courtiers awaited the arrival of Abu Ibrahim and rewarded him amply for his valuable services to education even at an age which had rendered him too weak even to walk on feasibly. There was no compulsory retirement for an educationist on age limit as we have today. A learned man was expected to give out the best of his even at the death-bed.

Knowledge was being sought from every corner of the world and imparted vice versa, in obedience to the behest of the Holy Prophet, (peace be upon him).

The Greek works on philosophy and other subjects were translated into Arabic and edited accordingly. The works of Socrates, Plato and Aristotle were translated into Arabic for inclusion in the curriculum.

Geology was a popular subject and several books on the subject were written by the Arabs. A separate college of agriculture was started which admitted a fair number of students.

Hakam's love of Literature and Science:

S.K. Rohilla says "Although other rules of Islamic Spain were also fond of literature and poetry, but al-Hakam excelled them all in his love for literature and sciences. He was not only a patron of the learned, but was himself a man of great learning. There was no field of learning and scholarship which he did not develop. We shall first describe his method of study then how he developed libraries, next how he promoted education, especially of the children of the poor, and lastly his patronage of scholars and scientists".

His weakness was lack of understanding of the realities around him.

Hakam's love of learning and books was really a weakness and a flaw in his understanding of the realities around him. Writes Stanley Lane-Poole, Hakim II was a bookworm, and although bookworms are very useful in their proper place, they seldom make great rulers. A king cannot be too highly educated: he know everything under the sun, and like several of the Cordovan Sultans, he may employ his leisure in music and poetry, but he must not bury himself in his library, or care more for manuscripts than for campaigns, or prefer choice book binding to binding, up the sore places of his subjects. Yet this was what Hakam did. "Al Hakam II was undoubtedly, not a weak ruler, he conducted his military campaigns successfully. But he could not see what would happen to his kingdom after him. And the collapse of his kingdom began soon after his death. With the death of his good and virtuous Khalifa ended the glory of the Ummayads of Spain. The reason was that though he repeatedly over-ran the Christian kingdoms yet he never thought of uprooting them altogether.

CHAPTER 14

THE FALL OF THE UMAYYADS
(1002–1009 A.D.)

Al-Mansur had virtually established a dynasty, viz., the Amirids. They were the defacto rulers of Muslim Spain. But the dynasty barely seven years after his death due to its unpopularity among the people of Cordova.

Hajib, Abdul-Malik 1002-1008: On the death of al-Mansur, his surviving eldest son, Abdul Malik, was appointed Hajib by the pliant Caliph, Hisham II. The new ruler remained faithful to the last instructions of his father. He continued to administer the country as did his father before, and like him, he led yearly expeditions against the refractory christians of the north. It is said that he led eight such campaigns, in all of which he was victorious. After campaigns, he was conferred the title of *"Al-Muzzafer"* the victorious, by Khalifa Hisham. However, he died in October, 1008, on his return from a campaign against Sancho, the Count of Castile. He ruled for about six years : his reign was one of peace and prosperity at home and of victories abroad.

Al-Muzzafer died in mysterious circumstances when he was still in the prime of youth. Abdul Rahman sanchelo was said to have poisoned him to death. According to the rumours current in Cordova, Sanchelo had half of an apple poisoned.

When the two brothers were having their dinner together, Sanchelo cut the apple in two and offered the poisoned half to his brother, Al Muzzafer, who died a couple of hours after. His mother, adh-Dhakhla, charged Sanchelo for the murder of her son.

Abdul Rahman 1008-9 : On the death of Al Muzaffar, his younger brother, Abdul Rahman, was appointed the Khalifa as Hajib, Abdul Rahman was nicknamed by the resentful people as Sanchelo or little Sancho, for his mother was the daughter of Sancho, the Count of Castile.

Sanchelo had inherited none of the qualities of his father, Al-Mansur; nor did he possess the qualities of his brother, Al Muzzafer. Instead, he had all the evil habits, which soon incited the people of Cordova to rise in revolt against him. He was impudent, foolish and cowardly and a pleasure loving profligate, given to the pleasures of the harem and wine. He had even no reluctance to drink in public. Once he was drinking wine with his boon friends, the muezzin's call to prayers was heard. When the Muezzin said, "Hasten to prayer!". Sanchelo remarked impudently, "Why not hasten to carousal". The Amirids had become virtual rulers of Spain, and left Hisham Khalifa in name. Even then Sanchelo decided to do what his father and brother had not dared to do at all : he aspired to the caliphate. He discussed this matter first with his Qazi, Ibn Dhakwan and his minister, Ibn Burd, who supported him in his design. Then Sanchelo approached Hisham with the request to designate him as his successor. Though virtually his puppet, Hisham was shocked to hear of it. But he was persuaded to consult some theologians. They also supported Sanchelo's proposal, for they were under the influence of the Qazi, Ibn Dhakwan.

Sanchelo proclaimed heir presumptive : After listening to the please of his advisers, Hisham agreed to nominate

Sanchelo as his successor. A document was accordingly prepared by Ibn Burd, which said:

> "After searching among high ranks as well as low, the Khalifa Hisham has found none more deserving to be appointed his successor, to become the heir to the Caliphate after his death, than the trustworthy, honest, and beloved Abu'l Motrif Abdul Rahman, son of Al Mansur ibn Abi Amir Mohammad. And the Khalifa has been induced to make this choice owing to the brilliant qualities which grace the said individual, the generosity of his soul, the greatness of origin, and the nobility of his descent; his piety, his prudence, his wisdom, his talents, all of which he knows him to possess, as he has watched him, and put him more than once to the trial, and has upon every occasion found him ready to do a good act. But are we to wonder that a man who had Al Mansur for a father and Al Muzzafer for a brother should surpass every one in virtue, and exceed all in generosity?
>
> "Another no less weighty consideration has moved the Ameer ul Momineen to take this step, namely, that whilst perusing works on the occult sciences he has discovered that he was to be succeeded, in the command of this country, by an Arab of the race of Qahtan, respecting whom there exists a well authenticated tradition preserved by Abdallah ibn Amr al As and Abu Horayrah, both of whom ascribe the following words to our

Prophet, 'The time shall come when a man
of the stock of Qahtan will drive men before
him with a stick'. Finding, therefore, no
person to whom those words can be better
applied; that he has no rivals and opponents,
but, on the contrary, every one in this country
looks up to him for direction, the Khalifa
entrusts to him the administration of affairs
during his lifetime, and bequeaths to him the
empire after his death".

The document was read in a solemn ceremony, attended
by the Wazirs, the Qazis and other people present and their
signatures were affixed to it. From that day, in November, 1008,
that is, only a month after he became Hajib, Sanchelo was
called *Wali 'l Ahd* or heir presumptive to Hisham, and then his
name was proclaimed from the pulpit of the Grand Mosque.
But, with this proclamation, the dam burst.

Conspiracy against Sanchelo : Soon after the
proclamation, a conspiracy against the heir-presumptive was
formed by all those who hated the Amirids. They included the
theologians, faqihs and qazis, many a noble of the Court, the
Princes of the Umayyad dynasty who saw the government of
Spain slipping out of the hands of their clan, and the common
people of the capital and the, country. Moreover, it provoked
the old hostility of the Modar tribe against the Himyar. They
all united their counsels, visited each other and entered into a
conspiracy to rid themselves of Abdul Rahman Sanchelo.

At the time when conspiracy was brewing up against him,
Sanchelo led an expedition against the Christians of Leon. On
the advice of Hisham, he ordered his troops to don on their
heads turbans in the manner of the Berbers, so hated by the
Cordovans. This was regarded as an act of sacrilege, for turban

was then wore only by the faqihs and qazis, and not by the soldiers who wore the traditional cap, called qualanswah. Wearing of the turban by the troops was adding an insult to injury, for besides the divines, it was worn by the hated Berbers.

Sanchelo left Cordova on his expedition in the middle of January, 1009 and reached Leori a month later and tried to defeat Alfonso V who had taken refuge in the mountains. Snow and mud obstructed the advance of Sanchelo's troops so much that they could achieve nothing. The campaign came to be known as the battle of the mud. When Sanchelo reached Toledo news reached him that a revolt had erupted in Cordova and a new Khalifa had been proclaimed there.

Revolts of Cordova : Conspirators were led by an Umayyad prince, named Muhammad. He was a great grandson of Abdul Rahman Ill. By distributing his wealth lavishly, he won over many other members of the Umayyad clan as well as several faqihs and divines. He had thus collected a band of four hundred bold and resolute desperedos and hardened criminals around him and fixed February 25, 1009, as the day they would rise in revolt. The rumours of the conspiracy, however, reached the ears of the Amirid ibn Askeleja, whom Sanchelo had made the governor of the capital during his absence. He made a thorough search for the conspirators, but could find none.

On February 12, 1009 Muhammad chose thirty of his men and ordered them to go to the terrace of the palace with their arms concealed in their cloaks, and wait for him. At about sunset, he rode on a mule and reached the place where his thirty desperedos were posted, They attacked and overpowered the palace guard, and entered in the palace. They went straight to the part of the palace where Ibne Askeleja was enjoying life with two singing girls of his harem. Muhammad rushed at him, and before he could get up and defend himself, he killed him.

The Fall of Amirs:

The fall of the Amirids led to a civil war, which ultimately ended in the collapse of the Umayyad Caliphate. A French author E. Levi Provencal has succinctly summarised this last scenerio in the history of Umayyad Spain as thus:

"In the whole history of Muslims Spain, no period was more troubled or tragic. Cordova raised the flag of revolt: the civil war soon spread to the provinces and the more distant parts of the Marches. At the beck and call of rival factions, sovereigns came and went their reigns is almost every case, ending in bloodshed and lasting more often for months rather than years. At times certain of these ephemeral monarchs disappeared into the shadows, only to reappear. In brief this was the chaos which endulged and irretrievably wrecked the patient work of the great princes of the dynasty and ended the political unity they had made so many efforts to achieve"

Let us see how all this came about.

CHAPTER 15

MUHAMMAD II

While Abdul Rahman IV was away from the capital to chastise Alfanso V of Leon in the Acturias, the people of Cordova forced Hisham II to abdicate in favour of Muhammad II bin-Hisham-bin Abdul Jabbar bin-Abdul Rahman III. The people offered homage to Muhammad II the newly installed Khalifa who assumed the title of Al-Mahdi in 399 A.H., 1008 A.D. The new khalifa, demolished the Amirid palace of al-Madinatul-al-Zahira and the city was plundered for full four days to make the Hajibat oblivious. Abdul Rahman Sanchol being helpless sued for peace and amnesty but he was killed with his ally the count of Carrion (4th March 1009 A.D.) Thus ended the Amirid caliphate so zealously founded by Al-Mansoor.

AI-Mahdi was a worthless man. He preferred to remain indulged in vices. He dismissed seven thousand Cordovans from the army and excommunicated the Saqaliba of Amir from Cordova. He drank openly and insulted the Ulema in public. The Berbers were also put to humiliation. Fearing the installation of Hisham II to the throne he proclaimed his death and burried another man in his place. He then imprisoned Hisham in the house of a minister of his. He also imprisoned Sulaiman bin AI-Nasir. He however released Sulaiman after the attack of Sulaiman's son Hisham on the palace of AI-Mahdi. Hisham then claimed the caliphate but Sulaiman and Hisham both were defeated by the Berbers.

Zawi bin Manad Sanhaji the leader of the Berbers proclaiming Sulaiman bin Hakam-bin-Abdul Rahman III as Khalifa and offered Baiat to him. He assumed the title of Al-Mustain-be-Allah. The Berbers, under the new Khalifa captured Calatrava and Guadaljara. They marched to Cordova. Al-Mahdi was defeated in the battle of Cantich (Rabi-ul-Awal, 400 A.H. November 1009 A.D.).

Sulaiman was however defeated by AI-Mahdi near Akba-al Bakr (Castilo De Bakar) who was helped by the Counts of Raimendo of Bercelona and Ermenigild of Lerida and Wadih the chief of Tortossa. The Berbers in their counter-attack killed count-Ermanifild but they were so much disheartened by finding Sulaiman absent from the battle field that they retreated leaving the win for Al-Mahdi who recaptured Cordova.

Mahdi however was killed by Wadih the Slave leader and Khalifa Hisham was proclaimed Khalifa for the second time in Zilhaj 400 A.H; July 1010 A.D. Wadih became the Prime Minister but the Berbers did not like him and kept on plundering the city. Wadih sold away rare collections of Al-Hakam's library to meet the government expenditure, as the treasury was almost empty.

It was in 1012 A.D. that Sulaiman was re-installed on the throne by the Berbers. Hisham II became untraceable. Perhaps he died in obscurity which ended the glory of the Umayyad dynasty.

The Cordovans being disgusted with Sulaiman for his raising the Berbers to the coveted posts of Hajib and Vazir, invited Ali-bin-Hameed Governor of Ceuta to capture the crown. It was in 405 A.H; 1015 A.D. that Hameed having killed

Sulaiman occupied the throne of Cordova. But he was assassinated shortly and the affairs of the kingdom became all the more confused and precarious. His brother tried to control the situation but was expelled from Cordova (1018 A.D.) endangering the affairs all the more.

CHAPTER 16

HISHAM II

For three miserable year, from July 24, 1010 to April 20, 1013, Hisham again became the Khalifa. But, whether in prison or on the throne, he was a plaything in the hands of the more powerful personalities. This time the Slaves, Khairan and Anbar, were his masters. However, his authority was confined to Cordova, which was even then threatened by the Anti-Khalifa Sulaiman with his Berber troops. They had virtually besieged the capital. The siege lasted for nearly three years, during which the Cordovans were unable to gain any advantage over the Berbers, who ravaged their farms, fields and lands outside the city.

In the capital itself, the slaves ruled the roost. Their leader was Wadith, the Hajib. He was the former client (mawla) of al-Mansur and hoped to play his role, but had not al-Mansur's talents. He sent envoys to the Anti-Khalifa and his Berbers, carrying the severed head of Mahdi, in order to persuade them to recognise the authority of the new Khalifa, Hisham. The Berbers rejected his offer angrily and pounced upon the envoys, whose lives Sulaiman saved with difficulty. However, he took Mahdi's head and sent it to Obaydullah, Mahdi's son, who was then at Toledo. Disappointed with the Berbers, Wadhih then turned to his formerly, the Count of Castile, promising him that if he would help him against the Berbers, he would return to him the castles taken from him by al-Mansur. At the same time, the Anti-Khalifa, Sulaiman, also approached the Count with a similar promise. The crafty Count informed Wadhih that if he did not deliver the castles to him, he would go to the help of the Anti-Khalifa and his Berbers. This threat was sufficient to bring the Hajib and his Council of Wazirs to their knees. They decided to hand over two hundred fortresses to the Count. This provided a handle to the Christian rulers of the north. By threatening to go to the help of the Anti-Khalifa and his dreaded Berbers, they wrested more and more castles and lands from the Muslims in northern Spain. Thus, as Dozy says, without lifting a finger, the empire of the Spanish Muslims was being snatched bit by bit, castle by castle, by the Christians, while the Khalifa and his Cordovans, thanks to the civil war among them, were unable to check them. Well might they rue the day they had overthrown the Amirids! "In a word" adds Dozy, "the lot of the Cordovans was that of every nation (sic!) which, without clearly defined aims, without the guidance of some exalted political or religious principle, blunders into the vortex of a revolution."

In 1010, the Anti-Khalifa's Berbers besieged the Capital once again. But finding it difficult to capture, they turned towards the old royal palace, az-Zahra, situated a few kilometres to the west of the Capital. An officer in the palace, who was in league with the Berbers, opened one of its gates to them on November 4, 1010 and a massacre followed. The garrison was butchered by the Berbers. Then they fell upon the defenceless people and massacred them even when many of them took refuge in the grand mosque, where the Berbers put to the sword all the men, women and children mercilessly. Afterwards they set fire to the town, which had grown around the old palace. Az-Zahra was reduced to ashes. Thus what the Cordovan mobs had done to al-Mansur's Az-Zahira, the Berbers did to Az-Zahra of Abdul

Rahman III, which were then the two most beautiful palace-towns in the whole of Europe. The destruction of Az-Zahra was a foretaste of what the Berbers would do soon to the Capital itself. It was to be the Mongol-like devastation, which the famous historian, Ibn Khaldun, had aptly called "Berberiyyah".

Cordova's Plight: Like frightened deers, the Cordovans lived on for three more years, while the Berbers were stalking around them all the time. They were reduced to very hard times: their farms and lands had been captured by the Berbers, and their supplies of food cut off. The villagers around the capital had taken refuge in the Capital, thus increasing its population which further strained its meagre resources. The Government itself was short of money, which the Hajib, Wadhih, tried to collect by selling the books of the library of Hakam II. The distress of the citizens increased from day to day: only the dread of the Berbers outside prevented them from falling on each others' throat. At last, the soldiers also began to complain of mismanagement of the affairs by Wadhih, The slave rivals of the Hajib, especially the Slave general, Ibne Abi Wada'a, incited the soldiers against him. At this Wadhih decided to send a messenger to the Anti-Khalifa with proposals of peace. When the envoy returned to report Sulaiman's reply to the Council of Ministers, the soldiers fell upon him and killed him before he could utter a word. All this happened in the presence of the Khalifa Hisham, and the Hajib. Wadhih now planned to go over to the Berbers. But Ibn Abi Wada'a got wind of it. Collecting his slaves, he attacked Wadhih's palace and killed him on October 16, 1011. His severed head was then paraded in the streets of Cordova.

After Wadhih's death, his killer, Ibne Abi Wadhih'a, became the supreme authority in the capital and he ruled it with an iron hand. The theologians supported him, declaring that the war against the Berbers was a Jihad. In this manner, he ruled the city for a year and a half more. But the Berbers continued to besiege it. In the meantime, they captured other cities in the provinces. Thus the Christians in the north and the Berbers in the south were shattering Umayyad Spain to pieces. An-Nuwayri writes about the Berbers:

> "No town, however great or strong, escaped their ravages, with the exception of Toledo and Medinaceli (Medina Salim); and the desolation was so great that a man on horseback might travel for two consecutive months without meeting a single person on the road."

Sack of Cordova: In the beginning of 1013, the Berbers, led by the Anti-Khalifa, Sulaiman, laid siege to the doomed Capital in right earnest. At last, after bribing an officer, who opened the Secunda gate on April 20, 1013, they poured into the city, destroying all before them with fire and sword: they killed all they met in the streets, entered the houses, ravished the women, and then burnt down the houses after looting all in them. The massacre was general regardless of age or sex, status or learning: the innocent citizens were butchered as mercilessly, as the soldiers or slaves, or men of learning. "Doctors, theologians, Imams, Kadis, men distinguished by their virtues, or eminent for their piety and their learning, were involved in the general massacre." The wealthy families were reduced to poverty and the poor families to misery. In short, the "Berberiyyah" was in full cry. "The most inoffensive citizens fell victims to their blind fury. Here lay the venerable Sa'id ibn Mundhir, who had been Imam of the Grand Mosque since the days of Hakam II and was renowned for his virtue and piety; there lay the helpless Merwan, scion of the noble family of the Beni Hodair, who had been crazed by unrequited love. The learned Ibn al-Faradi, author of an erudite biographical dictionary, and Kadi of Valencia under Mahdi, met a like fate. After two days of massacre, when the Berbers became satiated with blood, they put the unfortunate city to fire. The fairest palaces of the Umayyad princess and grandees, the splendid mansions of the middle classes and the humble dwellings of the poor were all reduced to ashes. Ibne Hazm, the famous writer of these unhappy times, wrote:

> "I have at last learned the condition of my splendid mansion in the Bilat-Mughith. A refugee from Cordova has told me that it is a heap of ruins. I also know, alas! the fate of my wives. Some are in the grave: some are vagrants in distant lands."

CHAPTER 17

SULAIMAN
(1013-1016)

While Cordova was yet burning, the Anti-Khalifa Sulaiman entered it and went straight to the royal palace. On arriving there, he summoned Hisham II before him. "Traitor," he cried, "Did'nt you abdicate in my favour and didn't you promise never to lay claim to the throne again?"

"Alas!" replied poor Hisham, "You know that I am the slave of others. I do what they bid me. I entreat you to spare my life and I declare again that I abdicate and appoint you as my successor."

Thus the Anti-Khalifa Sulaiman became the Khalifa Sulaiman and assumed the royal title of al-Musta'in. He remained in power for three years, 1013-1016. But he ruled a truncated Caliphate, for there were revolts on all sides not only by the Christians, and governors of the provinces, but also by his Berber chiefs. Indeed, the Umayyad Spain had started disintegrating into what the Spanish historians called "Muluk at-Tawaif". For the time being, however, Sulaiman enjoyed what was really a semblance of sovereignty. He appointed governors and officers, who went to their provinces or districts, where, instead of obeying him, they became virtually independent rulers. One by one, the provinces in eastern Spain came under the control of the Slav chiefs, such as Khairan and Anbar; and in the south, the Berber chiefs established their hold where the Amirids had given them fiefs or provinces to govern. At last, Sulaiman's authority came to be limited to Cordova, Seville, Niebla, Beja and Oksonoba, which he ruled for about four years. Though for several years he had been the rebel chief of the savage horbes, he was a peace-loving, mild and just ruler. What he longed most was a peaceful unification of the Caliphate. But this was what he could not secure. Muslim Spaniards outside his rump Caliphate hated him as a usurper placed upon the throne by the dreaded Berbers, and by the infidel Christians. When he threatened their towns either to submit to him or face the same fate as he had inflicted on Cordova, they poured in reply curses upon him. Said a post to an envoy of Sulaiman, "How far different is he from the Sulaiman of the scriptures: the one put the devils in chains, but the other has let them loose, Strange sight! A descendant of Abd Shains has become a Berber and is crowned in spite of the nobles. Never will I obey thee monstres! The sword shall decide. If they fall, life will have in store joys for me; if I perish, I shall at least be gone from the scenes of their crimes."

Such were the sentiments of the Muslim Spaniards and the Slavs, they were still loyal to Hisham. They believed him to be alive, though thrown into a dungeon by Sulaiman. The end of the unfortunate Hisham was a mystery. But his name had become a rallying-cry for the Slavs, who continued to fight in his name. One of their chiefs, Khairan, championed his cause most, He was a client of Al-Mansur, who had appointed him as governor of Almeria on the sourthern coast of Spain, When the Berbers occupied Cordova, he fled eastwards. After many vicissitudes, he succeeded in collecting many Slavs and Spaniards under his banner and then re-captured Almeria. There a general of Sulaiman, Ali ibn Hammud, became his ally. But before we relate their story, let us see what had happened to the deposed Khalifa.

Hisham's disappearance : The end of Hisham became a mystery. According to some contemporary historians, he was put to death by Sulaiman soon after he had captured Cordova. According to others, Sulaiman had again cast him in a dungeon, where he languished till death. But according to the eunuche and women of the royal harem, Hisham escaped one day from his prison and went away to "Asia", by which they probably meant some unknown city in the East. Perhaps, he then spent his last days peacefully, devoting himself to his prayers and to the study of the books on astrology and other occult sciences, unknown to his neighbours about his royal origin, but speaking Arabic with Spanish accent. So, dead or alive, Hisham remained a mystery nonetheless, his name became a rallying-cry for all those who aspired to the Caliphate throne in his name. Indeed, so great was the loyalty of the Muslim Spaniards towards the Umayyads that they flocked around any scheming aspirant to the Caliphate, who raised his banner of revolt in the name of the real or fictitious Hisham.

Beni Hammudh : Among the Berber chiefs who enabled Sulaiman to capture Cordova were two brothers, Qasim and Ali, sons of Hammud. They belonged to a Berberized Arab family, who had descended from Hasan, the elder son of Hazrat Ali. They had lived for so long among the Berbers of North Africa that they now passed for Berbers. The two brothers came to Muslim Spain in the days of al-Mansur, who employed them in his armies. They fought with their Berber troops against the Christians with distinction. When the civil war broke out, they along with their troops fought for the overthrow of the Amirids. When Sulaiman became the Khalifa, he divided his Caliphate among the Berber chiefs. To Ali ibn Hammud he gave the governorship of Tangier, Ghomarah and other places in Africa, where he acknowledged himself to be a vassal of Sulaiman. When other governors renounced their allegiance to him, he also did the same. He then conceived a plan to become Khalifa himself. The motivation for this plan was an astrological prophecy of the Khalifa Hisham, who predicted, one day, so it was rumoured, that the Umayyad dynasty would be overthrown by a descendant of Hazrat Ali, whose name would begin with the letter "*ain*". When Sulaiman overthrew Hisham and cast him into a dungeon, he came to know that among Sulaiman's Berber chiefs was one whose name began with "*ain*", he was Ali ibn Hammud. Hisham sent him a message secretly, "You will be the king of this land of Spain, as my heart tells me: I shall die at the hands of this man (Sulaiman): I make you my successor and entrust you my revenge on him" Whether such a prophecy was ever made or not, Ali ibn Hammud became a champion of the ex-Khalifa Hisham. He joined hands with the Slav chief of Almeria, Khairan, against Khalifa Sulaiman. The Slav chief was sincerely for Hisham, while Ali ibn Hammud merely pretended to be so, for at heart he was betting on his death. The two, however, made a pact between themselves: if Hisham was alive, they would both proclaim him Khalifa once again after overthrowing Sulaiman; but if Sulaiman had really killed him, the Khairan pledged that he would help Ali Ibn Hammud to the throne.

After appointing his son, Yahya, in his place at Tangier, Ali ibn Hammud crossed the Strait and landed near Almunecat, where Khairan joined him. Both then marched towards Cordova. On the way, the Berbers also joined Ali. They did not like the mild rule of Sulaiman, while they supported Ali, for he was not only a brave leader but also a fellow-Berber. Zawi, Governor of Granada and the most powerful of the Berber chieftains, declared for Ali soon after he landed on the Spanish coast. On hearing of Ali's landing, Sulaiman collected his best troops and sent them against the rebels. But they were defeated in a battle near Seville. On July 1, 1016, Ali and his allies entered the Capital. Soon after entry, Khairan made a search for Hisham. But, in spite of his efforts, he could not find him anywhere. Ali then asked Sulaiman, in the presence of the viziers and theologians, what had become of Hisham. "He is dead", replied Sulaiman curtly. "In that case" said Ali, "show us where have you buried him?" On Sulaiman's pointing of his grave, it was dug and a corpse was exhumed. Ali asked a servant of Hisham to tell whether or not it was of Hisham's. He replied affirmatively and pointed out a black tooth in the jaw of the corpse as a proof of his identification, while others around confirmed the servant's statement. Ali then ordered Sulaiman, his brother, Abdul Rahman, and his aged father, al-Hakam, to be put to death. However, when the aged Hakam was led to execution, Ali said to him, "Have you killed Hisham?" The pious old man replied, "No, we have not killed Hisham. He is still alive and...." But before he could utter the name of the place, Ali made a sign to the executioner, who promptly beheaded him. The putative corpse of Hisham was again buried with regal pomp. Ali ibn Hammud was then proclaimed Khalifa. Thus the Hammudites, the half-Berberized Arabs, replaced the Spanish Umayyads in their Capital.

CHAPTER 18

ALI

Ali ibn Hammud ruled for twenty-two months, from July 1016 to April, 1018. During the first sixteen months of his rule, he was a just ruler and kept the unruly Berbers under control: he even punished them for their lawless behaviour. It was his custom to sit at the gates of his palace on certain days of the week where the Cordovans put their complaints before him against the excesses of the Berber soldiers. He administered speedy justice, even ordering a Berber culprit to be headed for his crime. For instance, he met a Berber horseman, carrying a basket of grapes on his saddle. He enquired from where he got them, the Berber replied, "I liked the grapes and took them." Ali ordered the Berber to be executed there and then for his theft.

But, during the last six months of his rule, he became a tyrant. The reason was the hatred of the Andalusians for his rule and their love for the Umayyads. Even his erstwhile friend and supporter, Khairan, the governor of Almeria, turned against him. He had aspired to play the role of al-Mansur. But Ali was no Hisham II. He, therefore, decided to replace Ali by an Umayyad: namely Abdul Rahman, a great-grandson of the great Abdul Rahman III. Many Andalusians promised their support among whom was Mundhir of Beni Hashim, who was the governor of Saragossa, in the north-eastern Marches. He also won the support of Raymond the Count of Barcelona. In November, 1017, the rebels threatened to march on Cordova. Ali set out against them. But returned to the Capital due to rains and snow. In April, 1018, he was again making preparations to march out against them. But, one day, on April, 1018, when he was in his bath, three Slavs assassinated him.

CHAPTER 19

QASIM

The citizens of Cordova rejoiced greatly on the death of Ali. But seven days after, the Berbers chose his elder brother. Qasim, as the new Khalifa at Cordova. He was, however, opposed by three enemies, viz., the Slavs, led by Khairan, the Muslim Spaniards, led by Mundhir, and Yahya, the eldest son of Ali, who was supported by a faction of the Berbers. Khairan and Mundhir had already chosen Abdul Rahman IV as Khalifa, who had assumed the title of al-Murtaza. Angry letters were exchanged between the Umayyad and Hammudite Khalifas, in which they frequently quoted verses of the Quran in their favour. In the meantime, Khairan and Mundhir got tired of Abdul Rahman, the pretender Khalifa, due to his arragonce. While he was near Granada, the emissaries of Khairan killed him. So Abdul Rahman IV's caliphate was stillborn. Khairan then made peace with Qasim. To reconcile other Slavs, Qasim made them governors of Jaen, Calatrava and Baeja. Moreover, he treated the Cordovans with moderation and justice, at which there was hope that the Hammudite rule would endure. But the Berbers were alienated by his favouritism for the black African slaves, whom he recruited in large numbers to counterbalance the power of the Berbers. He formed them into regiments and entrusted important posts to their leaders. The Berbers were irritated by this favouritism. They began to support the cause of his nephew,

Yahya, who crossed the Strait and landed at Malaga, where his brother, Idris, was the Governor. He too supported Yahya. The Slav governor of Almeria, Khairan, ever ready to change sides, also wrote to Yahya to support him. He then set out for Cordova.

Hide and seek game then began between Qasim and his nephew. On hearing of Yahya's advance on Cordova, Qasim sought safety in flight to Seville on August 12, 1021. A month later Yahya entered Cordova and became Khalifa.

CHAPTER 20

YAHYA

The reign of Yahya ibn Ali lasted for about one year and six months, from August 12, 1021 to February 2, 1023. He had the support of none except his Berbers. But he angered them also by his arragance. On Februay, 1023, Qasim advanced upon Cordova, from where his nephew, Yahya, fled to Malaga.

CHAPTER 21

QASIM
(SECOND REIGN)

Second reign of Qasim, was shorter still. The Cordovan had taken no part in the hide and seek game of the uncle and nephew. They hated the Africans, whether Berbers or Negroes. They still yearned to place an Umayyad on the throne. When Qasim came to know of their search for an Umayyad prince he took fright and resolved to search Umayyad princes in Cordova in order to put them to death so that no revolution might take place. At this the Cordovans rose in revolt and expelled Qasim and his Berbers on September 6, 1023.

Qasim pitched his tents outside the city and laid siege to it, which lasted for fifty days. At last, on October 31, the Cordovans attacked the besiegers so furiously that Qasim lost all hope to regain power. His Berber officers also deserted him. Yahya captured him and threw him in a prison in Malaga, where he languished for thirteen years, when he was strangulated to death by the orders of Yahya, who was then lord of Malaga.

CHAPTER 22

ABDUL RAHMAN V

The country was a prey to disorder, confusion and chaos. Peace was unknown. Risings were rampant. The vassals and governors were almost independent.

It was at this critical moment that the sober and impartial personalities of Cordova intervened to solve the problem. They in a representative meeting decided to select a Khalifa by election. Through the good offices of Munzir the governor of Saragossa, Abdul Rahman V the great grandson of Abdul Rahman III was elected Khalifa on April 3, 1018 A.D. Zilhaja 11, 408 A.H. He assumed the title of Al-Mustahzir. Ali-bin-Hazam became his Prime Minister. He had an advisory council which consisted of able persons like Abdul Wahab-bin-Hazam, Abu-Amir-bin- Shubayd and others. They being disliked by the orthodox Ulema for their laxity in religious views, could not appease them which resulted into a fresh chaos.

Muhammad-bin-Abdul Rahman bin Ubaidullah a great grandson of Al-Nasir incited the people against the Khalifa. The employment of the Berbers as the royal guards infuriated the people all the more. The people of Cordova rose in open revolt and proclaimed the Khilafat of Muhammad who had killed Abdul Rahman V (414 A.H; 1028 A.D. or 1024 A.D.) Muhammad III who occupied the throne under the title al-Mustafi was killed by one of his own officers for his folly of appointing a weaver as his Prime Minister.

Neither Yahya the chief of Malaga nor the Slav chief Khairan and Mujahid of Almeria and Dinea could control the Cordovans and had to save their lives by leaving the capital city one after the other.

On December 1, 1023, the Viziers summoned the nobles, soldiers and the populace of Cordova to assemble in the Grand Mosque for the election of a Khalifa. They were convinced that Sulaiman would be elected. Sulaiman, who was confident of being chosen, entered the gate of the Mosque fully attired for the occasion. His friends greeted him and seated him on a dais prepared for the successful candidate. Shortly after, Abdul Rahman also entered the Mosque by another gate. He was surrounded by a large crowd of soldiers and common people. As soon as they stepped in the Mosque, they loudly shouted their candidate as Khalifa. So impressed were the electors, the Viziers, by the "majority voice" that they stepped forth and kissed Abdul Rahman's hand as Khalifa. Their example was followed by Sulaiman also and so did the third candidate, Muhammad ibn Iraqi. The Secretary of State then erased the name of Sulaiman from the Proclamation and entered that of Abdul Rahman.

However, the reign of Abdul Rahman V lasted for barely two months. He was a lover of poetry and literature. He appointed Ali ibn Hazm, one of the most renowned men of letters of Umayyad Spain, as his Hajib, that is, his Prime Minister. The older nobles of Cordova, who had favoured Sulaiman, did not forget or forgive Abdul Rahman's success at the election. They conspired against him. He arrested some of the aristocrats and threw them into prison. He did the same to his two rivals, Sulaiman and Muhammad ibn Iraqi. At this critical juncture, the economic conditions of Cordova deteriorated and many workers were thrown out of employment. Social discontent increased. An Umayyad prince, Muhammad by name, who was displeased with the election, for his name was not even put in the list of candidates, became the leader of the discontented working classes. At this critical juncture a band of Berber soldiers came to Cordova and offered their service to the Khalifa, who accepted it. This infuriated his body-guard, Abdul Rahman had then put Sulaiman to death. At this a mob attacked his palace and the guards allowed them to enter the palace. Confronting with the mob, the Khalifa asked his Viziers about the line of action. But one by one, they quitted the palace, and left the Khalifa alone. He then mounted a horse in order to flee the palace. But the guards stopped him. He returned and hid himself in the gutter of a bath.

The mob, not finding the Khalifa anywhere, hunted down the Berbers mercilessly. They also captured the harem of the Khalifa and divided the women among them. Then they chose Muhammad as Khalifa.

CHAPTER 23

MUHAMMAD III

For the second time, an Umayyad prince had again become a Khalifa in Cordova. To win popularity among the masses, Muhammad III lavishly distributed money and honours among them. He even appointed a weaver, as his Hajib. Knowing his position to be weak so long as Abdul Rahman V lived, even in hiding, a search was made and at last, he was found out and put to death on January 18, 1024.

Muhammad III's reign lasted for a year and half. His favours towards the poorer classes aroused the anger of the middle and aristocratic classes against him. He threw some of the nobles into prison and even ordered one of them to be strangulated. He also arrested the counsellors of his predecessor, including Ibn Hazm, his Hajib, and Abu'l Hazm, who later on became the King of Cordova. To avoid similar treatment Abu Amir ibn Shuhaid and other nobles quitted Cordova and fled to the Hammudite Yahya, the Governor of Malaga and urged him to put an end to the anarchy in Cordova. When it became known in Cordova that Yahya was preparing to attack the city, a riot broke out in May, 1025. The rioters killed Muhammad's Hajib and surrounded him in his palace. His guards told the Khalifa that they were unable to protect him and advised him to leave the city secretly. Seeing that all was lost, Muhammad accepted their advice. Putting on the clothes of a singing-girl and a veil, he left the city along with two women and took refuge in a village on the frontier, but was soon poisoned to death by one of his officers.

For six months there was no ruler in Cordova. The citizens were disgusted with the Umayyads, but feared the Hammudites due to their Berbers. After some time, however, the mob rue in the city frightened the patricians. At last, in November, 1025, they decided to invite Yahya ibn Ali, the Lord of Malaga, to come to the city. He had, however, no faith in the loyalty of the Cordovans. He consented to send a Berber general to the city as its governor in November, 1025, with the Berber guard. As Yahya had feared, the Cordovans again began to conspire against his governor with the Slav leaders, Khairan of Almeria and Mujahid of Denis, who had assured them to guarantee their freedom from the Berbers. In May, 1026, Khairan and Mujahid marched on the city. Its populace rose into revolt against Yahya's governor and drove him and his Berbers from the city, and opened its gates to the two Slav leaders, Khairan and Mujahid. But they failed to establish any new government. Fearing treachery from his ally, Khairan returned to Almeria on June 12, 1027. Mujahid also failed to set up any prince as a ruler and left the city after some time. The patricians made a search for an Umayyad prince to be declared Khalifa. After great efforts, their leader, Abu'l Hazm ibn Jahwar, the moot influential member of the patrician Council of State, and the leaders of the Slav party offered the throne to Hisham, the elder brother of Abdul Rahman IV. In April, 1027, the Cordovans took oath of allegiance to him.

CHAPTER 24

HISHAM III

At the time of his election as Khalifa, Hisham was at Lerida in the North-Eastern March (Aagon) and, was in no mood to repair to Cordova in a hury. He wandered from place to place, because many chiefs barred his way to the city. He was an elderly man, pleasure loving and indolent in habits. As a matter of fact, he had accepted Caliphate not because he wanted to rule the unmanageable Cordovans, but because of the riches and comfort of the city. At last, after two years, on December 18, 1029, he entered Cordova amidst greetings of the people and of the Council of State. But they were greatly disappointed by Hisham's appearance and undignified behaviour. Nevertheless, they welcomed his arrival, for it signified the end of disorder. Though the patricians were disappointed with his person and habits, they had to bear with him because there was no other alternative. Hisham appointed Hakam ibn Sa'id as his Hajib, which further disappointed the patricians. Hakam was by profession a weaver, with whom, however, Hisham was long acquainted. Hakam, had become a soldier during the civil war and was personally a brave man. On becoming Prime Minister, Hakam's primary duty was to keep the Khalifa in good humour by providing him dainty dishes, best wines and singing-girls and dancers. On these terms, Hisham relinquished the affairs of the government heartily to his Hajib.

Hisham remained Khalifa for another two years. During this time, Hakam administered the business of the state in such a manner as to incur the hostility of the patricians, who controlled the Council of State. Hakam first displeased the faqihs by confiscating the properties of the mosques. Although the patricians incited the theologians against him, but he did not take their complaints into consideration, for they had no influence with the common people of the Capital. The nobles hated him because of his lowly origins and could not accept that a weaver should rule over them. The President of the Council of State, Abu Amir ibn Shohaid, whom Hakam sought as his friend and confident, repulsed his advances with contempt, and showed open hostility. The patricians first tried to arouse the populace against the Hajib. But they failed, for the common people had no complaint against him. Next, they turned their attention towards the Andalusian soldiers, whom the Hajib had displeased by recruiting the Berbers in his troops. Hakam was an astute minister. He anticipated the intrigues of the patricians and punished the ringleaders of his troops. Then they approached Ibn Jahwar, the President of the Council, who had some influence on the old Khalifa. Hakam asked the Khalifa, to dismiss the President again and again. At last, he succeeded in his efforts.

Before Hakam could take any action, Ibn Jahwar struck first. He and his patricians decided to do away with both the Prime Minister and the Umayyad Caliphate, and to proclaim Cordova a republic. At first they kept their plan secret, for they knew that the common people would not welcome the abolution of the caliphate, even though they would welcome Hisham's deposition. So the patricians, led by ibn Jahwar, feigned to aim at substituting an Umayyad prince, named Omayya, for Hisham. The Councillors told him that if he would lead an insurrection against Hisham, they would make him Khalifa. Being unaware of their design, Omayya became their willing tool. By liberally distributing money among the soldiers, Omayya collected a band of conspirators. In December, 1031, they ambushed Hakam, as he left the palace and, before he could draw his sword, assassinated him. Then Omayya led the soldiers and the mob that had joined them, into the palace. On hearing the horror-stricken cries of the dying Hakam, Hisham fled up a tower in the palace alongwith his harem and four Slavs.

When the soldiers and the mob found that Hisham was perched high on the tower beyond their reach, they started to plunder the palace, while Omayya cried, "Help yourselves to these riches, all are yours and then climb the tower and kill that wretch for me." But, in spite of their efforts, the soldiers could not reach Hisham for the tower was too high. Omayya then let him alone and went to the throne-room, where he seated himself on the throne and began to issue orders as if he had actually become a Khalifa. The reckless prince had no inkling what was being decided in the house of Ibn Jahwar.

After the murder of Hakam, Ibn Jahwar, the President of the Council summoned his colleagues to his house. They came with their clients and servants, all well-armed. After resolving to put an end to disturbances, they marched to the palace and called upon the mob to desist plundering, which gradually ceased, for the mob was awed by the resolute look of the patricians and the soldiers with them. Then they addressed Hisham, "Descend from the tower and abdicate; we assure you that your life will be spared." Hisham came down the tower and was conducted to a vault of the Grand Mosque along with his wives. He beseeched the Viziers, "Do what you like to me, but spare my wives."

Next day, the patricians led Hisham to a fortress outside the city and the Viziers issued a proclamation to the Cordovans that the Caliphate was abolished for all time and that the Council of State had assumed the powers of government. Then they went to the palace, where Omayya was still lording over as Khalifa. He had summoned the officers in order to make them take oath of allegiance to him. The Viziers reproached the officers for so hastily acclaiming a mere adventurer as Khalifa and declared, "The notables have abolished the monarchy, with the approval of the people." They warned the soldiers not to cause any trouble and then asked the officer, "Arrest Omayya and banish him from the borders of our republic." Their orders were promptly carried out.

CHAPTER 25

CAUSES OF THE FALL OF THE UMAYYADS

For about three centuries, the Umayyad dynasty ruled Muslim Spain and then it fell. Before we study the causes of its downfall, one thing should be borne in mind: the fall of the Umayyad Caliphate was not the end of the Muslim Spain. It came more than four centuries later. Of course, the causes which led to the destruction of Muslim Spain were, in general, already at work during the Umayyad Rule, as we shall explain in a later chapter. But here we shall confine ourselves to the specific causes of the Umayyad downfall.

1. The Caliphal State had passed through two stages before it became that of the Spanish Umayyads. The Orthodox Caliphate of the Four Pious Khalifas was a democratic state with its structure based upon the consent of all the Muslims. When the Umayyad Caliphate was established at Damascus in 661, its base became narrower, for it was not supported by all the Muslims, such as the Mawali or non-Arab Muslims. At the end of its rule, its base became narrower still, being confined to some or the other dominant Arab tribes, and their allies, as for instance the Berber tribes. This state of affairs lasted till the end of the Umayyad rule, which included the Umayyad rule in its Spanish province. When Abdul Rahman I ad-Dakhil established dynastic rule in the Spanish province, the structure

of the Umayyad Caliphate in Spain became still narrowly based: it was no longer based on the support of all the Arab and Berber tribes which had founded Muslim Spain, but on those which were allied to the dynasty founded by Abdul Rahman. Indeed, the Spanish Umayyads regarded their Caliphate as a patrimony of their dynasty and not a democratic state of all the Muslims who dwelt in it. For example the Muwalladun or the Spaniards who had accepted Islam, were denied share in it. Strange though it may appear, it was its patrimonial structure which was the source of the strength of the Umayyad Caliphate, because the passive loyalty of the Muwalladun to the Umayyad Caliphate became its mainstay. The failure of the Amirids to supplant the Umayyads was mainly due to the loyalty of the Muwalladun towards them. The attempt of the Hammudites to supplant the Umayyads was another proof of the Muwalladun's loyalty to the latter. They always regarded the Umayyads as the legitimate rules of Muslim Spain. When this principle of legitimacy was challenged first by the Amirids and later by the Hammudiles, the Muwalladun reacted strongly against them, who now constituted about the whole population of Umayyad Spain. But, as Umayyad rule was patrimonial, the Muwalladun's loyalty was of a passive nature. They supported the Umayyads, but, they could not keep it in power, when their monarchy began to totter to a fall.

2. The basic reason of their downfall was the inability of the Spanish Umayyads to understand the realities of the situation within and without their kingdom, such as the changing configuration of social and political forces within Muslim Spain, or the winds of change which were blowing over medieval Europe and their effects on Christian Spain. During the Ninth Century, there was a revival of the Christian power in the Peninsula, when the Christians of Asturias-Leon began to conquer Muslim lands and advance towards the river Douro

and threaten the Umayyad Emirate, as for instance during the reign of Amir Abdullah (999-912). This advance was checked, apparently quite effectively, by the rise of such powerful Umayyad rulers ad Abdul Rahman III, al-Hakam II and al-Mansor. In fact, the northern Christians had been so much immobilised by the military might of these great rulers that they played no part in the subsequent downfall of the Umayyad dynasty. But this was only on the surface of things. Half the art of statemanship consists in knowing what the foreign enemies are up to and the other half in doing what is therefore necessary. The Umayyad rulers were deficient on both counts. None of them ever understood the secrets of the Christian power which lay both in the Peninsula and also beyond the Pyrenees, as for example the military potential of European feudalism, the rise of New Christianity in the beginning of the tenth century and the potentialities of the Spanish Christians' policy of repopulation in the conquered Muslim lands. Of course, the Umayyad Khalifas did build fortresses, called rabits, on the borders with the Christian kingdoms of the north and garrisoned them with troops. But they never thought of repopulating the border lands, which they had conquered, with Muslim settlers who could undertake agricultural and other activities there. This was exactly what the Christians did in the lands they had conquered from the Umayyads. Had the Umayyads; done so, they would have turned every newly conquered land into a base for further advance both economically and military and would have thus repopulated the whole Peninsula with the Muslims. The Muslim Spain, both in political and in demographical sense of the term, would have been invincible no matter what developments would have occurred beyond the Pyrenees. By their failure to do so they brought about not only their own downfall but they were also responsible for the ultimate destruction of Muslim Spain, for they were the only Muslim rulers who conquered and ruled the whole Iberian Peninsula. When the rulers of a State fail to understand the nature of the confrontation with its rival states and to strive to overcome it, is doomed to vanish from the pages of history. This was, in a real sense, basic cause of the downfall of the Umayyad Caliphate.

' 3. Umayyad Spain was a multi-racial society with ethnic and tribal divisions and rivalries. Paradoxical though it was, these divisions were at once the cause of the rise and fall of the Umayyad State: it rose to power due to Arab tribalism and fell when it was replaced by that of the Berbers. Had the Umayyad detribalised their society, not only their political power would have lasted longer, but it would have been replaced by another all-Peninsular Muslim power. The detribalised society would have been a new unifying force in the Peninsula as a whole. But as the Umayyad rulers did not create such a new social force and continued to rely upon another tribal people, the Berbers, whom they brought from Africa, they introduced new divisive tribal forces in their Caliphate, which became one of the most powerful elements in their downfall. At last, the tribal rivalries not only destroyed the Umayyad power, but also enabled the tribal chiefs and governors to capture power in the various provinces and districts where they were in power, which led to the anarchy of the Taifa kings.

4. By introducing disintegrative forces into their Caliphate, the Umayyad Khalifas were, in a very real sense, responsible for its downfall. These forces were the new Berber tribes whom they recruited into their armies and the Sclavonian slaves whom they employed in their civil, military and household services. The reasons were firstly, their dissatisfaction with the tribal *junds* of the Arab and secondly, their reluctance to rely on the native Muwalladun for these purposes. Thus they themselves disregarded the new configuration of social and political forces in Umayyad Spain. During the last century of the Umayyad rule, the Muwallad community constituted about eighty percent

of the Muslim population of the Umayyad State. By favouring the Berbers and Slavs, they deliberately kept this burgeoning Muslim majority out of the politico-military edifice of their State. Its narrow base was, therefore, unable to preserve its shaky superstructure for long. When the Khalifas were strong, they kept the Berbers and Slav officers and troops under control, but when their weak successors ascended the throne, the Berber and Slav officers controlled them. This fact was very well illustrated by the life-story of the Slav, Wadhih. He remained a loyal governor of the Marches, when al-Mansur was in power. But when the Khalifas like al- Mahdi or Sulaiman came to power, he controlled them. Another Slav Khairan, not only tried to control the weak Khalifas, but became an independent ruler of Almeria. Thus the civil war provided the leaders of these ethnic groups with the opportunity to capture power first within the framework of the Caliphal System and then, for themselves. This was the genesis of the *Muluk al-Tawaif*

5. Besides the ethnic disruption, the Umayyad Caliphate had also two weaknesses built into its political system. Firstly, its law of succession was imprecise and disruptive. Conforming to the unwritten custom of the Arab tribes, the succession to the throne was determined by one consideration: the successor should be an adult, preferably a son of the deceased Khalifa. Al-Hakam II disregarded this rule by designating his minor son, Hisham, as his successor. It enabled the Hajib, Ibn Abi Amir, to concentrate supreme authority into his own hands. Thus he and his sons became contenders for the caliphal throne and thereby they unleashed the disruptive forces which led to the *fitna* or the civil war and the consequent downfall of the Umayyad Caliphate.

The seclusion of the Caliph in his palace was another factor which weakened the caliphal authority and provided its rivals to aspire for it. This practice was first started by Abdul

Rahman III. In order to enhance the pomp and power of the Khalifa, he withdrew his person from the eyes of his subjects: no one could approach the Khalifa except through the intercession of the Hajib. Naturally, the Hajib became more powerful. His enhanced authority enabled an ambitious Hajib like, Ibn Abi Amir to arrogate the Caliphal authority to himself. But when his son and successor, Abdul Rahman Sanchelo, tried to usurp Caliphal sovereignty also, he unleashed the *fitna* of 1009, which ended in the downfall of the Umayyad Caliphate. The Arab aristocracy was opposed to the sovereignty of the upstart family of the Amirids. The Berber's were loyal to no one except to their tribal chiefs who had ambitions of their own, while the Muwallad majority regarded the Umayyads as the only legitimate sovereigns and revolted in their centres of power, like Cordova, to uphold their power and thus added a new element of disruption in the Caliphate. But the Amirids were mainly responsible for the fall of the Caliphate by thus disrupting the equilibrium of social and political forces on which it depended.

6. Slavery was not so much a disruptive as a degenerative force. It made the Umayyad rulers and the ruling classes effete and degenerate and also distroyed their family structure. This degenerative influence affected them due to the fact that the Umayyads filled their harems; and homes with slave-girls, concubines and eunuchs. It may be mentioned that all the Umayyad rulers were born of slave-girls or concubines. Thus slavery and concubinage affected the brain-centres of the Caliphate, and undermined their family system and, in conjunction with polygamy and the lack of a law of succession, disrupted their dynastic system. Under the early Amirs, the old principle of designating an adult son or brother as successor, kept the degenerative forces in check. But the deluge was let loose when al-Hakam II nominated his minor son, Hisham II,

as his successor, which provided al-Mansur, an opportunity to aspsire to sovereignty. Had an adult succeeded al-Hakam, he would have kept the ambitions of men like al-Mansur in restraint. So, between the puppet-Khalifa, Hisham II, and the incompetent Amirid, Abdul Rahman Sanchelo, the affairs of the State became so bad as to lead to the civil war, which ultimately led to the dismemberment of the Umayyad Caliphate and the rise of the Petty Kings all over the Muslim Spain.

7. The influence of geography on history is a question that is often mooted. The fact is that when the body politic becomes weak, the geographical factors begin to influence the course of history. This was amply illustrated by the course of events during the decline and fall of the Umayyad Caliphate and the ensuing civil war. The Iberian Peninsula is divided into various regions cut off from each other by plateux and mountain ranges and deep valleys, all of which foster in their isolated population and inaccessible regions particularist tendencies and aspirations. So long there was a strong centre, it kept them united. But as soon as the central authority became weak and incompetent, the centrifugal ambitions of a governor or a rebel asserted themselves. Indeed, the rise of the Taifa Kings or Muluk at-Tawaif, was the inevitable consequence of the local particularism and geographical inaccessibility, coupled with the unruly nature of the Berber and Slav military leaders.

8. Spain reached the zenith of its power and prosperity during the first few Khalifahs of the Umayyads in Spain. But after the death of Hakam II, there were no effcient Khalifahs. The weak successors of Hakam II could not cope with the growing situation of the empire. During the reign of his successor Hisham II, Hajib al Mansur, the wazir of the empire ably piloted the ship of the Staew. Under him, Spain reached its highest water mark. He was succeeded by his sons, Muzaffar and Abdul Rahman, one after another to the wizirate of Muslim spain. In

the regime of the latter, there was a serious disturbance in the city of Cordova and this led to the execution of Abdul Rahman. The gross inefficiency of the successor of Hakam II and Hajib al Mansur hastened the fall of the empire.

9. Mansur's military ability and wonderful talent for organisation was a source of constant terror to the neighbouring countries. He undertook fifty two campaigns and came out successful in all these expeditions. He reduced Leon and Navare to the condition of tributary provinces and garrisoned their capitals. He turned against Catalonia, sacked Barcelona and drove out the French Counts. A large part of Western Africa was also reduced to subjection by his generals. These created bitterness against the rule of Mansur and led to the rise of insurgents who were trying to overthrow the Muslim rule.

10. The Hijaz Arabs and the Yaman Arabs were at dagger's drawn with one another. Their continued jealuosy and hostility prevented them from standing united under one banner to defend their country from foreign aggressions.

11. The newly converted Muslims could not tolerate the aristocratic rule. So, they stood against the Khalifahs. After the death of Abdul Rahman III, Hakam II and al-Mansur, the different sections of the nation formed themselves into different sections of their own. Among them the Berbers and the Slaves became the most powerful. They quarrelled with each other for their supremacy in Spain and to set their nominees to the Spanish throne. This kind of anarchy and confusion largely diminished the strength of the Umayyad power. Moreover, the Berbers and Slaves became very powerful in the empire. The influence of the Slaves reached such a pitch that they took advantage of the decay of the central power and set up independent dynasties for themselves. The Berbers overthrew the last Umayyad Khalifa Hisham III from power. Thus the

enmity of the Berbers and the Slaves constituted one of the factors for the fall of the Muslim power in Spain.

12. The Muslims confiscated the properties of the wealthy Spaniards. They also confiscated the properties of the lords and clergies who helped the Galicians against the Khalifa. The Muslims could not satisfactorily handle the properties and consequently incurred the loss of revenue. The Slaves who were given the right to vote and the propriety of the lands subject to a fixed revenue to be paid to the Khalifas withheld payments of revenue to the Muslims. There were terrible famines in Spain during Muslim rule. The hated and disturbance between the proletariat and the industrialists also led to the decline of revenue. These chronic shortages of revenue paralysed the system of administration and contributed to the fall of the empire.

13. Besides internal foes, who were many in number, the Khalifas had to fight with external foes. The Christian tribes of North Spain wanted to expel the Muslims in order to establish their own authority. They massacred a large number of Muslims and elected their own king.

14. The Berbers of North Africa who has a prejudice against Islam raided into the territories of the Muslims and, harried the defenceless Muslims with fire and sword. These gave a death blow to the Muslim rule in Spain.

15. The Muslim empire in Spain had no national sentiment. Its army were constituted of the Christians, the Berbers and the Spaniards. These ingredients regarded the Arab Muslims as foreigners. The Arabian rule in Spain could not establish the ties of nationalism among the component races and consequently the whole empire was divided into integral parts. This completely paralysed the Muslim rule in Spain.

CHAPTER 26

GOVERNMENT AND ADMINISTRATION

Government of Muslim Spain passed through two stages; firstly, when it was a province of the Umayyad Caliphate of Damascus, from 711 to 756 : we shall call it the period of Dependent Emirate : and secondly, from 756 to 929, when it was independent Emirate, and as from 929 to 1031 Umayyad Caliphate.

Dependent Emirate : For about half a century, Muslim Spain was a province of the Umayyad Caliphate of Damascus. The Province was ruled by a Governor, called *Wali* or *Emir*. He was appointed by the Governor General of Qayrowan, whose armies had conquered the province, or by the Caliph at Damascus. It was an ad hoc arrangement, due to the proximity of Spain to Qayrowan. But often the choice of a new governor was made by the dominant party of the Arab tribes in the province, which was later confirmed by the Governor General of Qayrowan and approved by the Khalifa at Damascus. Owing to tribal intervention and dual control, no governor could hold office for long, and often not more than few months. The seat of government of the Province was at first at Seville. But it was soon transferred to nearby Cordova or Qurtaba, which remained the capital of Umayyad Spain for the next three centuries.

The internal administration of the province remained more and less the same as it was under the Visigothic kings, which, in its turn, was the same as under the Romans before them. The province was divided into three main regions, central, eastern and western. The central region included Cordova, Granada, Malaga, Almeria, Jaen and Toledo; the western region included Seville, Jerez, Gibraltar, Tarifa, Geja, Badajoz, Merida, Lisbon and Silves; and the eastern region consisted of Saragossa, Valencia, Murcia, Cartegena and albarracin. Each of the region was further divided into districts. Each district was under an officer, called *Amil*. He was appointed by the Governor of the Province.

The dual system of control was abolished by Abdul Rahman I ad Dakhil in 756, when he established in Muslim Spain an independent Emirate of his Umayyad dynasty.

Muslim Spain as an Independent Umayyad state : Although Abdul Rahman I had broken away from the Abbasid Caliphate, he and his successors till 929 A.D. styled themselves as Emirs, as the provincial governors were called before them. They were independent rulers, but they did not assume the title of "Khalifa". It was due to their loyalty to the concept of Islamic unity as represented by the Abbasid Khalifas. However, they styled themselves as "sons of Khalifas", which was, of course, a historical fact. When the Abbasid Caliphate began to disintegrate and an independent Fatimid Caliphate was established at Mahdiyya, near Qayrowan, and declared itself as the true Islamic Caliphate, Abdul Rahman III also assumed the titles of *Ameer-al-Momineen* and *Khalifa* in 929. He asserted caliphal power particularly against the Fatimids and thus justified Umayyad rule in the eyes of the theologians and faqihs. Umayyad Caliphate, however, lasted for a century more.

The Amir (or Khalifa) was the supreme temporal and

spiritual head of the State. As a symbol of his supreme authority, the name of the Emir of Khalifah was always mentioned in the Friday Khutbah in all the Mosques of Muslim Spain. As the spiritual head, he as also called the Imam. But popularly, the Umayyad ruler was always known as *Sultan*. As the supreme commander of the Muslims, he was called *Ameer-ul-Momineen* or the Commander of the Faithful. From the days of Abdul Rahman III, it became a tradition among the Umayyad rulers to adopt a throne name. At first, it was done so on the occasion of a successful campaign against the Christians, as for instance Abdul Rahman III assumed the honorifec surname of *al-Nasir li-din-Allah*, i.e., the Defender of the Religion of Allah. But later it became customary to assume a throne name at the time of accession, e.g. Muhammad II assumed the title of *al-Mahdi*. One reason why Muhammad ibn Amir and his sons became unpopular among the people was their violation of this royal tradition by assuming throne names, although they were only hajibs. For example, ibn Amir took the title of *al-Mansur billah* or *Victorious through God*.

The Amir held a hereditary office, but the later Umayyads were sometimes elected by the nobles. The Emir or Khalifa lived in pomp and grandeur in his royal palace away from his subjects who could have access to him only through the Hajib or Prime Minister. At first, the Emirs lived in Alcazar in Cordova, but Abdul Rahman III built a new palace for himself a few kilometres to the west of the city, called az-Zahra, as his seat of government.

The Amir was the supreme head of the State and wielded absolute power over his subjects. He appointed and removed at will all state functionaries : he acted as the supreme judge; he was the commander-in-chief of the army, and, as *Imam*, he was the leader in public prayers. He was solely responsible for maintaining the integrity of the Law of Islam or Sharia and for ensuring the well-being of his subjects. As the arbiter of all governmental affairs, he did not tolerate any intrusion on his rights and he toured the provinces. His court was attended by the nobles and also by the poets, philosophers, scientists and other men of learning and religion. In actual fact, only strong Emirs or Caliphs exercised the panopoly of their powers, while the weaker ones fell under the control of their Hajibs or of their harem-women.

Whether Amir the Umayyad ruler nominated his sucessors during his lifetime : usually he was his son, but in some cases a brother or a grandson was also thus designated. The successor was called *wali-ahd* or heir presumptive. He was always an adult, for a minor would necessitate a regency which would cause troubles later, as for example, the regent might arrogate sovereignty to himself. Moreover, as an Umayyad ruler was always at war with his enemies, internal and external, the existence of the monarchy might be threatened during the troubles caused by a regency. It was well illustrated by the events following al Hakam's nomination of his minor son, Hisham, as his successor, which led to the rise of the Amirids to power, and the subsequent fall of the Umayyad Caliphate. The historian Ibn Sa'id attributed the success of the Umayyads to the splendor and magnificence they displayed in public and to their impartial administration of justice. "When the salutary awe and impartial justice vanished, the decay of their empire began.

Although all powerful, the Amir had also the right to delegate his authority to his officers. The most important among them was called Hajib. Literally, the word means a doorkeeper or chamberlain, but actually it meant the prime minister of the royal administration. He was the inermediary between the ruler and all his officers and subject. Being the supreme officer, he controlled all other ministers and officers in the royal administration and was the only one to deal directly with the

Khalifa. He carried on the civil administration. Ibn Khaldun has summarized his function as thus : "In the Umayyad dynasty in Spain, the office of the Hajib was that of the person who guarded the ruler from his encourage and from the common people. He was the liaison officer between the ruler and the *wazir* and lower officials. In the Umayyad dynasty the officer of chamberlain was an extremely high position". The high position of the Hajib enabled al Mansur to rise to power and so did his sons. Later the petty Taifa kings also used this title to justify their exercise of public authority.

Wazirs : Below the Hajib, there were a number of high officers who used the title of wazir. Sometimes, however, the title of wazir was more honorary than functional. The wazirs constituted a Council of Ministers, presided over by the Hajib Each wazir was in charge of a government department. There were four principal departments; viz., Finance, Justice, Foreign Affairs and War. Once a lower officer was made a wazir, he joined the ranks of nobility. But such an officer would not necessarily give up his previous office. He would, however, receive a higher salary. Sometimes an officer could be given two offices and then called *Dhu'l Wizaratayn*, the holder of two Wazirates. Ibn Khaldun described the functions of a wazir as follows:

"The Umayyads in Spain at first continued to use the name *wazir* in its original meaning. Later they subdivided the functions of the wazir into several parts. For each function they appointed a special wazir. They appointed a wazir to furnish an accounting of government finance (Finance Minister); another for official correspondence; another to take care of the needs of those who had suffered wrongs; and another to supervise the situation of people in the border regions. A special house was prepared for all these wazirs. There they sat on carpets spread out for them and executed the orders of the ruler, each in the field entrusted to him."

Later on, however, the office of the wazir became an honorary title and was assumed even by military commanders and was sometimes even given to men of learning.

Government Departments : There were four principal departments; namely those of royal correspondence, called *Diwan ar-Rasail*, of Finance, called *al-Dhimam*; of Justice; and of War. They were combined under the Chancery, called *Kitaba*, headed by a wazir.

Each Department was under a Secretary, called *Katib*. The two most important secretaries were *Katib al-rasail* or the secretary of (royal) correspondence and the *Kitab al-Dhimam* or the secretary of finance. The secretary of correspondence or chancery was of the rank of a wazir under Abdul Rahman III. He excelled in the espistolary art, drafted and wrote official documents. The Chancery documents were stylized pieces of literature, written in rhythmic prose and full of citations from the Quran, indicating that the secretaries were men of learning and high culture. He was also the officer-in-charge of the postal organisation.

Next in importance was the Department of finance. Its secretary was called *Khazin* or *Sahib al-Makhzan* or *Katib al-dhimam*. The finance secretary was usually drawn from the Arab aristocracy of Cordova, while the lesser functionaries in 'the Department of Finance were often Mozarabs, or Jews. The finance secretary was also called *Sahib al-Ashghal*. His duties were to organise the collection of revenues, impose taxes and make disbursements. In the provinces, he appointed tax-collectors and overseers, who kept the local officers under strict supervision and awe.

All the government departments were housed near the royal palace, at first, at Alcazar, then at az-Zahra, and finally at az-Zahira.

Effective government of the Amirs (or Khalifas) was their royal household. It was more important than the government departments, for its functionaries had direct access to the Amir (or Khalifa). Most of these functionaries were eunuchs and slaves.

They served as royal bodyguard or as domestic servants. The more important household officers were the constable, responsible for royal stables, the chief of the kitchen, the custodian of the palace and other buildings, and the royal falconer. Many of these slaves were later given their freedom, allotted large estates and became rich and powerful people. This was one reason why the Slavs or the white European slaves, were so much hated by the Arab aristocracy, and later by the people of the capital, Cordova.

As we said above, originally Muslim Spain was divided into five provinces. But when independent Umayyad Emirate was established, they were reorganised into twenty-one provinces. They were called *Kuwar*, plural of *Kurah* or a province.

Governor : Each province was under a governor, called Wali. He was appointed by the Amir (or Khalifa) at his pleasure, and exercised the same powers as the Amir (or Khalifa) did at Cordova. At the time of a governor's appointment, the Amir (or Khalifa) issued detailed instructions regarding the performance of his duties. For instance al-Hakam II instructed a governor as thus: "Ask God's help; temper your authority with mercy; don't be ambitious; don't favour certain persons to the prejudice of others. The Khalifa has decided to entrust you with command of half the province of Rayyu (Regio), in his eyes, one of the most important in all al-Andalus, on account of its sea-coast, its territory, its tributes and estates. Watch what sort of servant you prove to be." The provinces were usually known after the name of their capital city or town. There the governor had his residence, maintained his court with secretarial and financial departments just like those of the royal court.

The Marches : In the beginning, when the Muslim administration was strong and powerful, Muslim Spain was divided only into provinces. But when Umayyad military power became weak and the Christians could challenge it successfully in the north, the administration was re-organised in order to check the Christian raids, and it became a sort of no-man's land. These areas were called *Thughur* or marches. They were military districts or *kuwar mujannada*. At first, these military districts were created in the southern regions. But when the south was thoroughly pacified, these Thughur were converted into regular settled provinces, mostly occupied by the Syrian troops, who had come into Spain with Balj ibn Bishr in 742.

In the north, when the Christian raids became more frequent and the Berber tribes, who had settled in the valleys of the rivers Douro and Tagus, had left these regions under the pressure of the Christian raids, these northern regions were converted into *Thughur* or Marches during 900 to 981. There were three Marches, called the Upper, Middle and Lower. The Upper March (Thagr al-Aqsa) included Catalonia and Aragon, with Saragossa as their capital; the Middle March (Thagr al-Aust) comprised the areas along the borders of Leon and Castile, with Medinaceli (Medina Salim) as their capital, and the Lower March (Thaghr al-Sharqi) bordering Galacia, and Lusitania (modern Portugal), with Toledo as their capital. In the tenth century, the Lower and Middle Marches were merged into one.

Qaid : Every March had a military governor, called Qaid, who exercised much greater power than the governor of a settled

province. Moreover, the distance between these marches and
Cordova was great, which enabled the military governors or
Qaids, to act independently of the central government. At times,
these governors became quite independent princes, for example
the Upper March became independent under the rulers of Beni
Qasi for a long time. When the anarchy of the Taifa kings began,
the military governors of the Marches were the first to break
away from the Central Government.

Administration of Justice : Law in Islam is the will of
God, immutable and permanently binding on the faithful. It is
revealed by God in the Quran and in the *Sunnah* or practice of
the Holy Prophet (PBUH) and transmitted by his *Ahadith*. The
third source of Islamic Law is the consensus of the Muslim
community, called *Ijma*. The science of interpreting the three
sources of the revealed Law was called *Fiqh* or jurisprudence,
practised by the jurists, called faqihs. Ibn Khaldun defined fiqh
as "the knowledge of the classification of the Laws of God
which concern the actions of all responsible Muslims, as
obligatory, forbidden, recommendable, disliked or permissible."
The faqihs explained the meanings of the religious texts,
established the authenticity of the Prophet's traditions, resolved
contradictions, and determined the applicability of specify rules
of law. In most cases the literal interpretation of the legal tax
was sufficient. But when it was not possible, the jurists resolved
the difficulty by analogy (qiyas). Although there were four
schools of Islamic Jurisprudence or Fiqh, but in Muslim Spain
the Maliki school, founded by Malik ibn Anas (d. 795) gained
official recognition during the reign of Hisham I (788-796).
Thereafter the Maliki faqihs dominated the religio-legal thought
in Muslim Spain, suppressed all other schools of jurisprudence
and upheld a strict orthodoxy and dogmatic unity. The result
was that Muslim Spain never witnessed juristic quarrels and
theological dissensions throughout its history, which were so
much common in all other parts of the Islamic World.

The Judicial System : The Amir was the supreme judge and was responsible for the administration of justice. For this purpose, he held a court in his palace during weekly audience, at which anyone could seek justice. But regular justice was dispensed by the *qazis* or judges.

The Qazis : The qazi or judge was appointed by the ruler. At first, when there were no Muslims in Spain except the Arab troops, the qazi was known as *Qazi al-Jund* or the judge of the regiments. But when there were other Muslims than the troopers, the judge was known as Qazi al-Jama'a or the judge of the people. He was the supreme judge. The supreme judge was also known as *Qazi al-qazat* or the judge of the judges.

In every city in Muslim Spain, where Muslims dwelt, there were also qazis, which in *small towns* the judges were called *hakims*.

All judges belonged to the Maliki school of jurisprudence. They were highly influential among the people. If a ruler was involved in a case, the qazis could also summon him to appear in his court. The importance of his office was so great in the eyes of the Muslims that few persons came forth to shoulder this onerous function. Al-Khushani, a tenth century author, explains its importance as thus:

> "Inasmuch as the post of judge of Cordova became the highest dignity in the empire, after that of the Caliph the responsibility of this authority before God have made it a very serious post, a terrible, imposing task. Some men were fearful that something unfortunate would happen to them in the after life and they feared God, because they had to answer not only for their personal conduct in their own affairs, but also in other matters

entrusted to their decision. There were in al-
Andalus, especially in the capital, men
distinguished for their wisdom and piety, to
whom the office of judge was offered, but
they did not wish to be appointed; though
urged, they were unwilling to accept, solely
for fear of God, considering the consequences
that their souls might suffer in the future life.'

The qazi was usually qualified in the Maliki fiqh or
Jurisprudence. He was always a man of high moral integrity
and habits, who insisted on his freedom of judgement in
accordance with the law and did not tolerate interference or
influence even by the Amir or Khalifa. Al-Khashani explains
the qualities of a qadi as follows:

"He should take God's Book and the *sunna*
of the Prophet Muhammad as guides whose
light will direct him on the right path. In
mediating between litigants he should
examine, question and inquire by the most
skillful and well-intentioned methods and
listen attentively to the testimony of witnesses
and carefully attend to the arguments and
proofs presented by each party. His ministers,
counsellors and aides should be men wise in
religious law. The baillifs and attendants who
help him in fulfilling his judicial functions
should be honest and continent men totally
divorced from corruption, because whatever
they do will be imputed to the judge they
serve and the people will cast blame on the
judge. When the judge has reached thorough
certainty and is sure of the truth, he ought
not to delay his judgement."

Although in Islamic Jurisprudence there is no distinction between civil and criminal law, but in broad terms, the qazi's jurisdiction was limited to civil cases, such as the questions relating to inheritance, divorce, wills, the rights and property of the orphans, religious endowments or *waqf*, (pl. *auqaf*) and *bayt al-mal al-muslimin.*

The qazi held court in a corner of the mosque, where he was assisted by assessors, scribes and doorkeepers. The litigants pleaded their cases either personally or through their representatives, presented documents or witnesses whose testimony was recorded by the scribes. Before passing judgement the qazi might consult the faqihs or legal scholars, called *muftis* who issued their written opinions or *fatwas*, declaring what was lawful according to the Divine Law. The *fatwas* was compiled in a book by Ibn Sahl (d. 1093) and referred to as precedent in cases later on. The qazis had no judicial means to enforce their decisions or compel anyone to appear before them. But their moral influence was so great that no one dared to disobey their summons or decisions, including the Umayyad Amirs (Khalifas).

In most cases, the decisions of the provincial qazis were final and could not be appealed to in a higher court. But occasionally the Qazi of Cordova could review cases decided by other judges. In theory, the Qazi of Cordova could appoint the qazis in the provinces, but in practice he rarely exercised this power. The Umayyad armies had their own judges, called *qazi'l-Asakir.* It was the post which Ibn Abi Amir once held, when he was posted by al-Hakam II to the army in Africa.

Magistrates and Police : Criminal cases were dealt with by the magistrates and police officers. Among them was the *Sahib al-Mazalim* or the administrative judge of *mazalim* or injustices. He dealt with cases of abuses of power and corruption by public officials, and also against the judges. Sometimes the ruler also dealt with the cases of injustices.

In the capital, Cordova, the police (*Shurtah*) was under the prefect of police, called *Sahid al-Shurtah*. Common people called him *Sahib al-Layl*. He was directly under the control of the central government. He was both a police officer and a magistrate and was responsible for the maintenance of law and order in the city. For the punishment of crime, he could use more direct methods than those available to the qazis. In order to prevent violence and disorders, could use such measures as might be necessary to compel people to appear before him. At first, he was also called *Sahib al-Madina* or the lord of the city. But in the tenth century, the two offices were separated. His duty was to detect crimes against public morals and to punish them. The shurtah or police force also existed in the provincial capitals, which was called *Ahdath*. Its chief was called *Sahib al-Ahdath*.

Mohtasib : In the capital and in other cities and towns, there was an officer to supervise public morals and examine the weights and measures in the bazars and markets, so that shopkeepers and others might not use sub-standard ones. He was called *mohtasib* or public censor. He performed multifarious functions. It was his duty to prevent cheating and swindling in commercial transactions, to fix and maintain price of bread and other articles of consumption at scheduled rates, to check such crimes as gambling, prostitution, indecency in dress and other immoral behaviour. In special cases, the *mohtasib* could inflict severe punishment such as cutting of hands and even lapidation or death by stoning. As the mohtasib was a kind of commercial magistrate, the people also called him *Sahib al-Suq*, the market officer.

Christian and Jewish Judges and Magistrates : In

Muslim Spain, as in other Muslim lands, the Christians and Jews had their own magistrates and judges, who applied the personal laws of these religious communities. Thus, in Spain, the Mozarabs and Jews had their own judges and laws. But in those cases in which both Muslims and non-Muslims were involved, Muslim courts, mentioned above, had jurisdiction.

The Finance Department : In Muslim Spain there were three kinds of treasuries, with each having its own sources of revenue and expenditure. They were:

1. State Treasury, called *Bayt al-Mal;*

2. Special Royal Treasury, called *Khassiyat Bayt al-Mal* and

3. *Byt al-Mal al-Muslimin* or the communal treasury for the Muslim community.

State Treasury : The State treasury, called *Bayt al-Mal*, had existed in all Muslim States, as it was instituted under Islamic injunctions. Its sources of income were the traditional Islamic taxes, viz. *kharaj* or land revenue, *Ushr* or tithes and one-fifth share of the State in warbooty, called *khumis*. Besides these taxes, the State also levied some other direct and indirect taxes and tolls also, such as toll on ferries, forests, etc. All these taxes and revenues were deposited in the Bayt al-Mal. In Muslim Spain, the Bayt al-Mal was kept in the Alcazar of Cordova, which was under the care of *Khazin al-Mal*. The incomes of the State treasury were meant for the purposes and functions of the State, such as administration, law and order, military campaigns, payments of the troops and public servants and for the poor and needy and the wayfarers. It was the most important branch of the financial department. The revenues of the State were variously estimated under various Amirs or Khalifas. Under al-Hakam I (788-796) the annual revenues of the State were 6,00,000 gold dinars; under Abdul Rahman II

(822-852) they increased to 10,00,000 dinars and under Abdul Rahman III (912.961) to 62,45,000 dinars. Of the last estimates, 54,80,000 dinars were received from kharaj or land-tax and the rest from indirect taxes. The public revenues were divided into three heads, for the payment of the salaries and maintenance of the army, the upkeep of public buildings, and for the needs of the Khalifa.

Special Royal Treasury or Bayt al-Mal was meant for the personal expenses of the Amir or Khalifa. It was managed by *Sahib ad-Diya*. It had its own sources of income and expenditure, which were separate from those of the public and communal bayts al-mal. It received incomes from legal or authorized and extra-legal or unauthorized sources, that is, not sanctioned by Islam. The extralegal incomes were often condemned by the people and by the faqihs, which occasionally led to riots by the people. The Khalifa however, tried to assuage public protests by abolishing or reducing the condemned taxes. For instance, al-Hakam II abolished one such tax and ordered that it should be publicised "so that the people might know the favour he had bestowed on them, and that the ignorant, the wise, the stupid as well as the clever, should be equally well-informed," Its sources of income were from the royal lands. It may be mentioned that the Umayyad Amirs (or Khalifas) were the biggest landlords in their country, they possessed vast estates in various provinces of their kingdom. Gifts and presents given by the nobles and other people, lands confiscated from the nobles, etc. were deposited in the Royal Treasury. The royal princes and ladies of the harem also owned their own lands and estates. Abdul Rahman III had in his royal treasury twenty million dinars: his son, al-Hakam II had double of this sum.

Bayt al-Mal al-Muslimin or the communal treasury of the Muslim community, was a unique financial institution in Muslim Spain. In it were deposited the revenues derived from the waqf properties, which were endowed by the Muslims for this purpose. The communal treasury was kept in the mosque in the custody of the qazi. The revenues of this Bayt al-Mal al-Muslimin were meant for the up-keep of the mosques and other public building and for charitable purposes. In exceptional, cases however, the Amir or Khalifa could utilise a definite portion of the moneys from the communal treasury. Later on, when the Christians conquered Muslim Spain, this system of communal services of the Muslims impressed them very much.

Sources of revenue : Umayyad State derived its revenues from two kinds of sources: those which Islam had authorised five kinds of revenues to the State, namely Zakat Jizya, Kharaj, Ushr, and Khums. Zakat was the tax levied on Muslim on capital goods such as animals, merchandise, gold and silver, etc. It was a major source of revenue. Muslim also paid ushr on landed properties, which varied from 10 to 20 per cent of the produce, depending on whether land was irrigated or unirrigated. It was the main source of revenue. Christians and Jews paid Jizya or poll tax. It was levied on all able bodied, adult freemen and varied from 12 to 48 dirhams, depending upon the tax payers social status. There were, however several exceptions : women, children, the crippled, the blind, the aged, monks, beggars and slaves did not pay jizya. Kharaj or land tax was originally levied on the non Muslim landlords, who were left in possession of their lands at the time of conquest. This tax was about 20 per cent of the produce and was paid in kind. When Muslims became owners of these lands, they continued to pay kharaj also. Those lands which were confiscated at the time of the conquest were treated as booty of war and the State received one fifth share of the produce, called khums. It was also collected in kind.

Extra legal sources of income, called *magharim*, were sales taxes, tributes from Christian rulers of the north, from the Berber of North Africa, from the semi-independent Muslims rulers of the Thaghur or Marches, sadaqat from the Muslims. Sadaqat were voluntary alms, but they were collected so regularly from the Muslims that they became a sort of income tax. Besides these taxes, the State also collected import and export customs duties, and excise on goods brought in or taken out of a town or city.

Tax-Collection : The taxes were collected both in kind and cash. As matter of fact, payment in kind was convenient for the tax payers. But it created a storage problem for the State. The State usually sold the produce thus collected to the people. In times of scarcity or famine, the State distributed food grains freely among the distressed from its granaries. The taxes paid in kind were stored in the provincial headquarters, only the sale proceeds or cash receipts were forwarded to Cordova.

In the provinces, the governors were responsible for the collection of the taxes, imposts and duties. After paying their own expenses, they forwarded the surplus to the Capital. The department of tax collection, called *Khuttat al Ashghal*, had its branches in the villages. It was supervised by an officer, known as *Amil*, who resided in the provincial headquarters or in important towns. Market dues or excise were collected by another officer, called *Mutaqabbil*.

Total income of the State varied from reign to reign, depending on the strength and stability of the State under various rulers. When the Amirs (or Khalifa) were powerful and efficient, their incomes were great, but under weak rulers, they were much lesser. When the *fitna* or civil war erupted in 1009, State income became so little that the Khalifas could not pay salaries to their soldiers, and civilian officers. Their army therefore became small and their administration weak, which became one of the main reason of the decline and fall of the Umayyad

Caliphate. Thus, as Ibn khaldun said later on, the strength and, stability of a State depended not so much on its army as on its finances.

The Military : Military Organisation of Muslim Spain passed through two changes : at first, it was based on tribal feudalism. But when Arab tribes ceased to be a force under the Umayyad Amirs, their armies mainly consisted of mercenary and slave troops.

Feudalism : After the conquest, Muslim Spain was settled by the Arab and Berber who had conquered it. Instead of cash salaries the tribes were allotted fields in various districts of the country "where they had the usufruct of properties on condition that they perform military service when summoned. These rights and obligations passed by hereditary right to their descendants," Thus each tribe acted as a military united and fought under the command of its own chief. These units were called *junds*, and each soldier *jundi*. When new Syrian troops came into Spain under Bab ibn Bishr, they too were settled in southern districts in the same manner. They were called *shamiyyun* or Syrians. After a century or so, the original Arab and Berber tribes deteriorated as fighting units. It was due to inter tribal and intra tribal rivalries and disputes among them : the chiefs quarrelled with each other over the command of their tribes, while the tribes quarrels among themselves over lands, booty, and other privileges. Moreover, their loyalty to their chiefs and tribal interests made the tribes to revolt against the Amirs, who, therefore, began to rely more on slave and mercenary troops. Thus the tribal feudalism came to an end.

Troops : Dissatisfied with the tribal *junds*, the Umayyad Amirs relied on foreign troops, who were paid by them and maintained on regular permanent basis. This step was first taken by Abdul Rahman I. He recruited a highly trained army of

40,000 Berbers as mercenary troops. Afterwards, the employment of foreign troops became a regular element of the Umayyad armies. They were recruited from various sources, such as the Berbers and Negroes from Africa, and Christians from the northern Spain and even from the lands of the Franks. As corps of professional soldiers paid regular salaries in cash, they proved to be more reliable troops than the tribal *junds,* but only so long as the rulers remained strong.

Another element of foreign troops were the Slavs. They were mostly slaves and even eunuchs, who were purchased while still young or children, in the slave markets, such as Pechina, near Almeria they were then trained for military service or for service in royal households and palaces. Because they were brought mostly from eastern Europe, they were called Slavs or *saqaliba*. For instance, al Hakam I had a palace guard of 3000 horse and 2000 foot, most of whom were slaves or freedmen. They became a regular feature of the Umayyad palace life, both as guards and as household servants. In spite of their slave origin, the Saqaliba soon acquired great political and military influence over the Amir (Khalifa) and his household. Owing to their behaviour and outlandish speech, they were bitterly hated by the people, especially of Cordova. These anti-Slav feelings became an important factor in the overthrow of the Umayyad Caliphate.

Religious Volunteers : *Jihad* or holy war is one of the religious obligations of the Muslims Spain, however, this obligation for almost on voluntary basis. The opportunity for it was limitless, for almost an endless state of warfare existed between the Spanish Christians and Muslims. The religious volunteers were stationed in garrisons of the frontiers in the northern regions, which were called *ribats*. Hence the volunteers were known as *murabitun*. When not engaged in fighting, the *murabitun* adhered to strict ascetic life. Isaal Razi writes that during al Hakam II's reign, in 975, "bands of volunteer soldiers from the citizens of Cordova set out for the Upper Marches. Day after day, desiring to participate in the Holy War, they set out. The government was astonished by the bravery of the volunteers, who were not obliged to do this, and praised their holy courage. "The name of the garrison towns of the volunteer soldiers, ribat, is still found in modern times in a place called La Rabida. Unfortunately, when the Spanish Muslims became degenerate, the tradition of volunteering for holy war ceased among them. On the contrary, from the twelfth century, the European Christians adopted the Muslim tradition and organised a number of military holy orders, e.g, the Templars or the Hospitalers in Palestine and in Spain and the knights of Calatrava in Spain, as we shall describe in a later chapter.

Al-Mansur's military : Al-Mansur completely reorganised his armies. He abolished the tribal organisation on which the armies were then based. Instead, in his new army, men were organised into regiments without regard to the ties of family, tribe or patron. Many Muslims were exempted from military service on payment of money. With the money thus received, he recruited Berbers and other foreign troops and trained them intensively for war. The Berbers were trained almost exclusively as horsemen and became his first rate cavalry force. As we have said in a previous chapter, al Mansur's troops, including the Berbers, were staunchly loyal to him and to his sons. This was one reason why the people of Cordova, who were greatly oppressed by the Berbers, bitterly hated the Amirids.

Army's Internal Organisation : Like other Muslim armies in the Middle Ages, the Spanish armies were arrayed in five divisions. They were called the centre (*qalb*), two wings (*ajnab*) on left and right sides, vanguard (*muqaddimah*) and rear-guard (*saqah*). Each army corps also had archers and light and heavy cavalry. The archers also included naphtha-throwers, whose arrows were dipped in naphtha (a sort of coal-tar) which was burnt and then hurled on the enemy. The commander-in-chief, called *amir*, was always at the centre, and rarely left his position. This order was maintained on the battle-field and also during the march. In sieges, they used the *manjaniqs* or catapults to hurl rocks and such other missiles on the besieged town or fort. The horsemen wore helmets on their heads and armour on their bodies. They also used coats of mail for their horses and mules.

Their army formation differed from time to time. A corps of troops consisted of 5000 soldiers. They were commanded by a general, called *amir*. The corps was divided into five regiments of 1000 men each. It was commanded by an officer, called *qaid*. The regiment was again divided into five groups of 200 men each, commanded by an officer, called *naqib*. Each group was again divided into five sections of 40 men each, commanded by an officer, called *arif*. Each section was divided into five units of 8 men, under the command of a minor officer, called *nazir*. Ibn Khaldun has given a different formation. According to him, the amir commanded 10,000 men, a qaid 1000 men, a naqib 100, and an arif 10.

Umayyad Spain was, throughout its history, in a state of almost permanent warfare with its Christian neighbours in the north. Muslims undertook annual expeditions against them mostly in summer, but sometimes also in winter. The summer expeditions were called *al-saifa* (which in Spanish became *aceifa*) and the winter ones were called *shitayah*.

Navy : During the ninth and tenth centuries, the coasts of Umayyad Spain were raided from across the sea by the Norsemen and the Fatimids, which compelled the Umayyads to organise their naval forces in order to defend their coastal regions. They constructed fleets of warships for this purpose, first during the reign of Abdul Rahman II. Later, Addul Rahman III built a still larger fleet of 200 warships. His main naval base was on the eastern coast at Pechina, near Almeria. His navy became the most powerful in the Mediterranean. The Umayyads had their shipyards for building and repairing ships, called *marsa* and *dar-i-san'a*. They existed at several places, for example at Barcelona, Malaga, Seville, Alicante, Algeciras, etc.

The naval fleet was commanded by *amir al-bahr* or admiral. Interestingly enough, many Arabic military and naval terms were adopted by the Spanish Christians, from where many of them passed into French, English and other European languages. We give here a list of some of those words which have become current in modern English, e.g. *amir al-bahr* became admiral, *dar-i-san'a* became admiral, *dar-k-san'a* became arsenal, *al-makhzan* became magazine.

Cordova

Description of the government and administration of the Umayyad Caliphate would not be complete without a brief description of its capital, Cordova, called *Qurtabah* in Arabic and *cordoba* in modern Spanish. The word is, however, derived from its ancient name Corduba, as it was known in Roman times. It was said to have been founded by the Carthagians or Greeks, long before it was conquered by the Romans, who also constructed its famous bridge.

Under the Visigoths, Cordova was only a provincial town, not even a provincial capital, which was Seville. Under the Dependent Amirate of al-Andalus, Seville also remained its capital from 714 to 719. In 719, the governor, as-Samh, shifted the capital from Seville to Cordova. When Abdul Rahman I ad-Dakhil captured al-Andalus, he also kept Cordova as the capital of his independent Emirate, and ıt remained the capital of the Umayyad Emirate/Caliphate till its fall in 1031.

Like most capitals in the history of the world, Cordova expanded by three distinct stages: from a small town to a city and from a city to a metropolis or capital city. In its growth both natural and human factors played their part. Cordova was situated on the banks of the river Guadalquivir, the Wadi al-Kabir or the great river, as the Arabs called it, with its fertile valley around the city. To its north-west was the mountain range of Sierra Morena. The river Guadalquivir was navigable upto the city itself, which linked it with the sea, a great advantage in the eyes of its Arab conquerors, for it connected it to North Africa and the eastern lands of Islam. Its other advantage for the Arabs was its mild climate, as compared to Toledo the Visigothic capital, which they found to be too cold for them, —a fateful decision which became an important cause in the ultimate destruction of Muslim Spain. The human factors in the growth of Cordova were the construction of the palaces, pleasure-gardens, castles etc., by the rulers, mansions by their courtiers, commanders and officers and houses by the common people, the building of the mosques and market places, the growth of arts and crafts, factories and mills, bazaars, and the like, the foundation of schools and the University of Cordova, and the construction of walls and fortifications for the defence of the city and security of its inhabitants.

Description of Cordova : Ibn Said, a man of learning and a native of Cordova, wrote:

> "Cordova surpasses all cities of the world in
> four principal features: its bridge over the
> Guadalquivir, its (grand) mosque, its palace
> of az-Zahra, and above all, the sciences
> cultivated herein."

Said ar-Razi, an Andalusian historian who died in 935, wrote:

> "Cordova the mother of cities, the navel of al-Andalus, the seat of royalty in ancient and modern times, in pre-Islam and Islam; its bridge over the Guadalquivir in its architecture and design; its mosque second to none in al-Andalus, even in Islam."

A native historian, al-Hijari, who died in 1188, wrote:

> "Cordova is a fortified town, surrounded by massive and lofty stone walls, and has very fine streets. It was in times of old the court and residence of many infidel kings, whose palaces are still visible within the precincts of the walls. Cordova, under the Sultans of the dynasty of Umayyah, became the citadel of Islam, the place of refuge for the learned, the foundation of the throne of the Bani Merwan, the place of resort of the noblest families among the tribes of Ma'd (modar) and Yemen. To it came from all parts of the world students anxious to cultivate poetry, to study the sciences or to be instructed in divinity or the law. Cordova was to Andalus what the head is to the body, or what the breast is to the lion. From its horizon rose stars for the world, notables for the age. In it were composed exquisite books and issued unsurpassed writings. The explanation of the superiority of Cordovans over all others past and present lies in the fed that the city's climate is one of research and investigation in the variety of sciences and literature."

A poet said of Cordova:

Talk not of the court of Baghdad, and its glittering magnificence
Praise not Persia and China and their manifold advantages,
For their is no spot on the earth like Cordova,
Nor in the whole world men like the Bani Hamdin.

(Bani Hamdin were the independent rulers of Cordova during the Second Taifa Spain).

During three centuries of its existence as the capital of a vast kingdom, Cordova expanded rapidly. Originally, it was a small town, situated on the right bank of the Guadalquivir at the head of a Roman bridge, which contained a castle and palace, called Alcazar, a Christian church and the town. Soon after the conquest, half of this church was converted into a mosque, while Alcazar became the residence of the governor. Abdul Rahman I converted the whole church into a Jami mosque or Grand Mosque, which was later further enlarged, as the population of Cordova increased. Abdul Rahman also built the Russafa palace, near Alcazar. On the opposite bank, at the other end of the bridge, was the small town of Secunda. When Cordova expanded, Secunda became its suburb in the south. In course of time, a large city, called al-Madina, sprang up to the north of Alcazar and the Grand Mosque, which in the tenth century had a population of about 300,000 people, surrounded by a wall which had seven gates. At the same time, twenty one districts or suburbs came into being around the Old City or al-Madina and also the palaces of az-Zahra and az-Zahira to its west and east. In the suburbs and two palaces lived another 200,000 people. Thus in the days of its glory Cordova had a population of five lakh. It was nearly five times larger than Paris in those days, which was then the capital of the vast

Frankish Empire. Ibn Said, quoting ash-Shakandi, says that the city of Cordova, including its palaces of az-Zahra and az-Zahira, extended to about twenty kilometers with streets paved and lit at night with lamps all along its length at a time when the capitals of other European countries had muddy streets, and were shrouded in darkness at night. The city was supplied with water which was brought from the mountains by aquaducts. It was conveyed to the palace and "thence distributed into every comer and quarter of the city by means of leaden pipes and into the fountains." The city had about nine hundred mosques, more than eight hundred baths, hundreds of libraries, the biggest among them was the palace library of al-Hakam II, which contained 400,000 books.

The Grand Mosque : Soon after the conquest, the Arab governors purchased from the Christians half of the church of St. Vincent and converted it into a mosque. Late, Abdul Rahman I purchased the whole church and constructed the Jami or Grand Mosque, on which he spent a sum of eighty thousand dinars, derived from the fifth or *khums* of the war-booty. The construction began in 784 but was not completed in the Amir's lifetime but by his son and successor, Hisham I, in 794. But, as the population of Cordova increased, later Umayyad rulers, like abdul Rahman, II his son, Munzir, Abdul Rahman III and lastly, the Hajib al Mansur, constantly enlarged the Mosque, improving it and making new additions to it in order to accommodate more and more worshippers. The mosque was then 148 meters long and 112 meters wide, divided into the court of open space, nineteen aisles, and tiled porticos. The number of doors, big and small, was twenty one, placed nine to the east side, including one for women, three to the north, including one for women, nine the west, including one for women. On the south side, there was no door, expect one, which was reserved for the Sultan and connected the *maqsurah* or royal enclosure in the Mosque with the palace. All these doors were covered with the finest brass in the most beautiful manner. The roof of the mosque was supported by columns. The number of these columns, large and small, was one thousand four hundred and seventeen. It was veritable forest of columns.

Al-Rusafah : Abdul Rahman ad-Dakhil, the first of the Umayyad Amirs, still nostalgic of his beloved Syria, especially remembering his grandfather, Khalifa Hisham who had brought him up, built a palace, which he named ar-Rufsafa after the name of Hisham's palace of the same name. It was built to the north of Alcazar. In this palace, Abdul Rahman planted trees and plants whose seeds were brought from other countries, especially from Syria. His love for plants was so great that he sent agents to Syria and other countries to procure him all sorts of seeds and plants. Two such trees, which he nourished with great care were a rare variety of pomegranate and a palm tree. As the pomegranate was brought from Khalifa Hisham's Rasafa garden in Damascus, it came to be known as Rasafi in Muslim Spain. The Amir encouraged his courtiers and nobles to cultivate these exotic plants and seeds in Spain.

Al-Zahra : The palace of Madinat az-Zahra was constructed by Abdul Rahman II an-Nasir in 936. He had many concubines. One of them died leaving large wealth which he did not know where to spend. Another of his concubines, named Zahra, said, "Build with this wealth a city and give it my name." The idea caught his fancy and he ordered for the construction of a beautiful palace on a site eight kilometres to the west of the city of Cordova on the bank of the river Guadalquivir, under the foothills of Sierra Morena, the Khalifa spend twenty-five years on its construction, employing 10,000 labourers daily and 3600 beasts of burden. Once the Khalifa was so much absorbed in its construction that he could not attend three consecutive Friday prayers, for which the faqihs blamed his favourite concubine. The annual cost of construction was 300,000 dinars. After its completion, the Khalifa ordered all the departments of the government to be shifted to it. Consequently, his ministers, officers, commanders bodyguard and other functionaries constructed their mansions and house around the palace, and thus a city came into being in it. As the palace was called az-Zahra (the Bright-faced), the city also came to be known as *Madinat az-Zahra* or the City of the Bright-faced.

The palace was a splendid edifice. It was 1215 metres long and 675 metres wide. It had four thousand and three hundred columns, made of gold and marble brought from Carthage, Rome, etc. "The Carthage columns may be looked upon as a gift from a mother to embellish her daughter", for Cordova was reputed to be founded by the people of Carthage in the antiquity. It had fifteen thousand door. The reception hall had walls and roof of marble ornamented with gold, windows of transparent alabaster, eight gilded doors set with ivory and with precious stones inlaid. It contained a large basin full of quicksilver. When, the sun-rays fell upon the quicksilver, it reflected them throughout the hall, which gave the impression as if the hall was shaking all over.

Abdul Rahman III and his successors used the reception hall to receive the envoys of the foreign kings. He also received Queen Theuda of Navarre, her son and grandon, Sancho the Fat when they visited Cordova for the treatment of his obesity by the court's Jewish physician, Hasday bin Shaprut, in 960.

The Zahra palace accommodated a large harem of the Khalifa which had about 6314 women and female servants, who were guarded by 3752 Slav eunuchs and bodyguards. The Khalifa had his own bodyguard of 100,000 men, mostly Slavs. Fifty years later, the palace of az-Zahra was neglected when the Ḥajib, al-Mansur, shifted the seat of government to his palace, az-Zahira, and soon after destroyed during the civil war.

Az-Zahira : For the reason which he have stated in a previous chapter, al-Mansur decided to shift the offices of the government from the royal palace of az-Zahra. He constructed his palace about a couple of kilometers to the east of Cordova on the banks of the river, Guadalquivir. He called it az-Zahira or the brilliant-faced. Its construction began in 978 and was completed within two years. In 980, al-Mansur took up his residence at the new palace along with his family, servants, guards and adherents. Soon a city also sprang up around the new palace, which was called *Madinat az-Zahira*, when al-Mansur established in it the offices of his government, built granaries and mills and factories for his large household and stables. He also granted adjoining lands to his ministers, katibs, generals, favourites, who constructed their houses and mansions around it. Al-Mansur's palace had vast gardens on the banks of the river.

Al-Mansur had premonitions of the destruction of his splendid palace. It is said that one day he was sitting in his palace reflecting on its beauties, when he suddenly burst into tears. "O az-Zahira: he cried, "May God save thee from the demons of war who would destroy thee". One of his favourites, who saw his weeping, asked the cause of his lamentation. Al-Mansur said, "God grant that my prediction would be wrong. But my presentiments tell me that then fire of civil war would soon sweep over this palace, destroy all its beauties and convert it into a heap of ruins, its gardens would be turned into dreary desert; my treasures would be scattered and what was once a scene of pleasure and mirth will be changed into a spot of desolation and ruin." Al-Mansur's predictions were fulfilled only a decade after when the *fitna* broke out after the attempt of his son, Abdul Rahman Sanchelo, to be proclaimed as the Khalifa in 1009 and the Cordovan mobs furiously burnt the palace down to ashes.

University of Cordova : The University of Cordova was founded by Abdul Rahman I in the Grand Mosque in 784. It was the first university not only in Europe, but also in the Islamic World. Abdul Rahman's successors added to it more departments. They invited professors and scholars from other Islamic countries. The University provided instruction in both Islamic and secular sciences, such as mathematics, astronomy, philosophy and medicine. Al-Hakam II established his palace library, containing 400,000 volumes. It was the biggest university library. His agents collected books for it in other Islamic lands.

Al-Hakam also founded twenty-seven free schools in Cordova.

SOCIAL LIFE

Society in Umayyad Spain was fragmented by various kinds of differences among the people. Primary difference was between the Christians and Muslims. Immediately after conquest, Christian opposition to the Muslims subsided at first. But it gathered strength during the middle of the eighth century and threatened the Umayyad rule at the end of the ninth century, as for example by Ibn Hafsun and the kings of Asturias-Leon. The great victories of Abdul Rahman III and Al-Mansur during the tenth century not only crushed the Christian opposition but contained them so much that the Christians played practically no part in the decline and fall of the Umayyad caliphate. It were the differences and disputes among the Muslims which led to the fall of the Umayyad Caliphate.

Although Islam had united the Muslims of Spain into one community of believers, but in practice they were split into various groups due to differences of race, riches and kinship, social status and slavery. These differences divided them into hostile and often warring clans and tribes and urban communities. In the beginning, there were only two ethnic groups among the Muslims, namely Arabs and Berbers. Later on, when the native Spanish Christians adopted Islam, a new Muslim group, the Muwalladun, also came into being. The three Muslim groups were further divided by class differences between the feudal landlords and the tillers of soil and between the industrial employers and their workers. The revolt of the Cordovans during the reigns of the later Umayyad Khalifas was mainly due to the industrial groups of the employers and employees. In the rest of Spain, religious, ethnic and kinship animosities played dominant role in the social and political life of the country.

The Societal Pyramid : The structure of the Umayyad society was like a pyramid. At the apex stood the Amir or Khalifa, alongwith his sons and other relatives, who formed the ruling Umayyad clan. Next to them were the grandees of the Umayyad State, viz., the hajibs, viziers, judges, generals or commanders of the armies, courtiers and governors of the provinces and marches. Along with these high dignitaries stood the feudal nobles, and aristocrats, mostly Arabs, and rich merchants and traders, both Muslims and Jews. All of them constituted the *Ahl al-Khassa* or the elite classes. Below them came the *amma* or common people, comprising both the middle and poorer classes. The middle classes consisted of small merchants and traders, industrial employers and artisans, who were Muslims (Muwalladun), Christians (Mozarabs) or Jews. They dwelt in towns and cities inside the country and on its coasts. The middle classes, however, constituted *a weak force in the social life and politics of Umayyad Spain*. At the base of the social pyramid were the poorer classes, namely the farmers and cultivators in the villages, who constituted the greater majority of the population, and the workers and labourers in the commercial and industrial towns and cities. At the lowest levels were women and slaves. However, they could five with the richer classes as their wives and concubines and as their household servants. Some of the slaves, however, became freedmen and clients of their masters and sometimes became as rich and powerful as their former masters.

Arab and Berber Tribalisms : The Arabs and Berbers, who conquered Spain, did so not as individual warriors but as members of organised tribal groups. Each tribe consisted of several hundred families or tents. All relation in a tribe were agnatically determine, that is, they were related through the male members. Women did not count at all in this male dominated or patriarchal kinship system. It was a male society for all ends and purposes. In marriage, they preferred endogamy, that is, marriage within the family group on the male side, especially between parallel cousins, that is, with the paternal uncle's daughter. The purpose was that the family property, power and prestige might not be shared with or go to cognate or other family groups and lineages. Each family group, therefore, tended to became a large extended family group, for it took women from other groups, while it did not give away its own in marriage to others. Several family groups, linked on male side, formed a clan, called *qowm*. Thus a tribe consisted of several clans, who were related together, being decended from a common male ancestor. Clans in a tribe were hostile to each other, just as the tribes were hostile to each other. Anthropological scholars of Arab and Berber tribal societies describe these tribal units as segments. The segmentary society was a sort of Hobbesian state of nature, in an which the hands of a members of one segment were on the throats of the members of the other segment. Robert Montagne characterised the segmentary tribal organisation as an "organised anarchy". In ancient Arabia, the segmentary warfare led to two tribal groupings, Modarites (Qaysites) or Northern tribes and the Himyarites (Kelbites) or Southern tribes. The Arabs carried their tribal divisions and warfare from the Arabian Peninsula to the Iberian Peninsula. The Berber tribes also did the same, transferring their hostilities from Africa to Spain when they settled in it after the conquest. Owing to their segmentary nature, the Arab tribal societies were subject to two contrary tendencies of atomization and amalgamation: the tribal groups constantly split into smaller groups, and also united into larger ones. A tribal group lived in social isolation from others. But at the same time, these groups were ready to join in political or military federations with related groups, because it was embedded in larger solidarities.

> "The essence of this kind of political organization is that politics is viewed as a zero-sum game. The wealth, power, and prestige of one's own group are increased only by decreasing those of a rival group, leading to a more or less permanent state of conflict between neighbouring groups as well as to characteristic patterns of alliance."

Much of the political history of Muslim Spain was filled with the tribal in-fighting between the Modarite and Yemenite Arab tribes. Though their rivalries were as old as pre-Islamic Arabia, but they were kept afresh in the distant Iberian Peninsula. If a forty-year war broke out between two Arab tribes in Central Arabia over a horse race in the Jahiliyya period, a seven-year war was fought between the Modars and Himyars in the ninth century Spain over the picking by a Modari of a grape-leaf from a Yemeni's vine. The segmentary principle of tribal warfare characterised even the Muwallad family of the Bani Qasi (or

Banu Qazi) of the north eastern province of Saragossa in the ninth century. The Bani Qasi allied themselves with the Modarites in order to oppose the power of the more numerous Yemenites in the province. It was by such an alliance that Bani Qasi established a semi -independent principality in the Upper March. During the tenth century, the Arab and Berber tribes broke up into lesser units and clans till they lost their political supremacy during the reigns of Abdul Rahman III and al-Mansur. This change, among other reasons,, was brought about by the numerical superiority of the Muwaladun. The hostility of Abdul Rahman III and al-Mansur towards the Arabs also contributed to the ousting of these tribal systems from the social and political life of Umayyad Spain. Nevertheless, the influence of Arab tribalism continued to exist in the culture and social ethos of Muslim Spain. Even the Muwalladun, who were really a non-tribal people adopted Arab genealogies and cultural ethos. During, the Taifa period, a couple of Arab families establishes their petty principalities.

We shall now describe the various social elements in Umayyad Spain.

The Arabs : During the time of the dependent Emirate, nearly 18,000 Arabs came in two waves, first with the armies of Musa bin Nusayr and later with Balj ibn Bishr. The Arabs of the first wave were called *Baladiyyun*, or country Arabs, while those of the second wave were known as *Shamiyyun* or Syrians. In course of time they lost this distinction. They settled as *junds* or tribal regiments mostly in the valleys of the rivers Guadalquivir in the south and Ebro in the north past of the Peninsula as well as in the coastal districts, from Valencia to Almeria and Algeciras. Many Arab settlers, especially of the Umayyad or Quraysh tribe, were granted large estates or latifundia in the south and north-east and in Toledo district. Moreover, the Arabs were given preference in government service and appointed to high post by almost all Umayyad Emirs/ Khalifas. Thus they became the new aristocratic class in Umayyad Spain, and enjoyed great wealth, prestige and power. They did not bring their women with them and intermarried freely with the local people or took slave-girls as their wives and concubines. Partly because of their riches, but mainly because of their ancient animosities between the Modarite (Qaysite) and Himyarite (Yemeni) tribes, they were always inclined to fight with each other and/or revolt against the Umayyad rulers. "Strong individualism' rivalry and envy characterized inter-Arab relationships to the extent that an Arab group would ally itself with Christians or Berbers against its fellow-Arabs." Thus they indulged in he same kind of inter-tribal warfare in the Iberian Peninsula as they did in the Arabian Peninsula before. We may say that these Arabs learnt nothing new and forgot nothing old. Their tribal culture and ethos were indeed, too strong to overcome their ancient enmities and rebellious propensities. This was the reason why Abdul Rahman III was the first Umayyad Khalifa to suppress the Arab nobles to a great extent and to curb their influence on the Umayyad State. Afterwards, in the Taifa Spain, only a couple of Arab families succeeded in establishing their independent principalities.

Berbers : At the time of the conquest, twelve thousand Berbers came into Spain with Tariq ibn Ziyad and settled mostly in the western provinces of Galacia and Lusitania (modern Portugal) and a few in the eastern province of Murcia. They were mostly a pastoral and transhuman people. They kept large flocks of sheep which they drove to the mountains in summer and into the valleys and plains in winter. Their transhuman mobility and Arab hostility were the reasons why some Berber tribes quitted Spain during the famines and inter-tribal struggles of the Dependent Emirate and returned to Africa. Thus the influence of the Berbers diminished in Umayyad Spain. Nevertheless, the Berber influence did not vanish altogether, because fresh Berber tribes were constantly recruited in Africa by the Umayyad Amirs/Khalifas into their armies. They were then brought into Spain, where they became a terror for their subjects, who hated them for their unruly behaviour and oppression, especially by the citizens of Cordova. Thus the anti-Berber feelings became a cause of the downfall of the Umayyad Caliphate.

Muwalladun : The third Muslim group was called the Muwalladun or the native converts to Islam and their descendants. Owing to intermarriages, between the Arab and Berber settlers and the native populations many of the Muwalladun were also the descendants of these mixed marriages. Many others were freedmen and clients of the Arab tribes. Although many Muwalladun were of the same Gothic and Hispano-Roman stock as were the Mozarabs and northern Christians, they assimilated themselves to the patriarchal and agnatically based social structure of the Arabs and Berbers and adopted even their tribal genealogies and culture. However, there were still some Muwallad families who preserved the maternal genealogies of their Visigothic forefathers and were even proud of their Gothic ancestry, e.g. Banu Angelino and Banu Salaries of Seville, Banu Qasi of Aragon, or Ibn'l Qutiyya of royal descent. Nevertheless, the Muwalladun were devout Muslims and often volunteered for *jihad* against the northern Christians. The Christians of the Reconguista called them "*renegados*" or renegades, a term which even some modern Western historians of Muslim Spain use for them. The Spanish Arabs and Berbers called them 'musalimah'.

At first, the number of the Muwalladun was very small. With the passage of time, however, as more and more Spanish Christians adopted Islam, their number continually increased.

At the time of the downfall of the Umayyad Caliphate, the Muwalladun constituted more than eighty per cent of the population of Muslim Spain. Originally, they were mostly serfs. But when they became Muslims, they left their villages and settled in towns and cities, where they became workers, artisans, traders and merchants and many of them joined government service as its functionaries, to became judges, katibs (secretaries), viziers, and military commanders, while others became faqihs theologians, scholars, historians and men of letters, for example the historian Ibn Qutiyah and the literary writer, theologian and thinker, Ibn Hazm were Muwalladun. In spite of their versatile achievements, no love was lost between them and the Arabs and Berbers. The Arabs hated them because of their lowly origin and called them "sons of slaves" or "sons of white women." The Muwalladun hated the Berbers for their rude and uncultured behaviour as well as for the oppressive acts of the new Berbers whom the later Umayyad Khalifas had recruited in their armies and palace guards.

Christian Mozarabs : The Christian population in Muslim Spain were called *Mozarabs*, derived from the Arabic term *musta'rib*, which meant Arabicized. They were so called because they had adopted the dress, customs and even language of the Arabs, though they also spoke among them their ancestral tongue, Roman. Thus, like many other religious communities in Muslim Spain, the Mozarabs were bilingual. At first, they were found all over Muslim Spain. But as conversions increased among them and many became Muslims, they were confined mostly to important urban centres like Cordova, Seville, Toledo and Merida and probably also in some rural areas. Their numbers also decreased, for many of them were enticed by the northern Christian kings and rulers to migrate to the north and repopulate the lands which they had conquered from the Muslims.

Yet the Christians had no cause of complaint against their Muslim rulers whose treatment was most tolerant. They enjoyed complete freedom of worship in their churches; they were governed according to the *Liber Judiciorum* which was enacted by Visigothic kings, and they had their own judges and magistrates. They were represented before the caliph by their own officers, called *the comes or defensors*; their cases were adjudicated by their own officers, called *censors* and the jizya or poll-tax was collected by their own tax-collectors, called *exceptors*. This tax was levied only on able-bodied individuals at a graduated rate from 12 to 48 dirhams, as explained above. Moreover, the Mozarabs were also employed in the government service, especially in revenue department. At first, they led two movements against the Muslim rule; firstly the Zealats Movement and then Ibn Hafsun's revolt. After their failures, the Mozarabs, who had not left for Christian lands in the north, led a more peaceful life and even found employment at Umayyad court.

Jews : The Spanish Jews benefited not from the transition to the Muslim rule. They were a highly persecuted community under the Visigothic rulers. With the establishment of Muslim rule, their condition changed dramatically from an oppressed people to the most favoured non-Muslim group. Like the Christians, the Jews also enjoyed complete freedom of worship and had the right to live under their own laws and customs. Their chief rabi was responsible for their community to the Umayyad ruler. Very few Jews accepted Islam. But many of them spoke Arabic and adopted it as their language and participated in the intellectual activities of the Umayyad Muslims. They were a highly prosperous community of traders and merchants: the slave trade was their monopoly. They brought black slaves from Africa and fair coloured Saqaliba or Slavs from Europe. Some of them became prominent in the service of the Umayyad rulers, e.g. Hasday ibn Shaprut who was the treasurer and a vizier under Abdul Rahman III. Like the Christians, the Jews lived in separate quarters in the towns and cities, but, unlike the Christians, they freely mixed with the Muslims. They lived in large numbers in Cordova, Malaga, and Granada.

Slaves : At the lowest rung of the social pyramid were the slaves. However, like women, their social position was contradictory. In Muslim Spain the slaves were not treated so harshly, as they were in the Roman Empire. Islam had condoned slavery, but enjoined the masters of the slaves to treat them kindly and equitably. In Muslim families, therefore, the slaves were often regarded as members of the family. It was considered a pious act to free the slaves, when they became clients or freedmen of the family or tribe. Sometimes, the master even gave away his daughter in marriage to his former slave. The Umayyad Emirs or Caliphs had very large number of slaves. They were usually divided into two kinds: the African Negro slaves and the European Slavs or *Saqaliba*. Slav was a generic term, used by the Spanish. Muslims for slaves brought from Europe and included not only the Slavs of eastern Europe, but also slaves from other European peoples such as Germans, Franks, etc. They were fair in colour, blue-eyed and with blond hair. They were therefore, more prized by the Spanish Muslims and often fetched higher price than the African slaves. The Umayyad rulers employed them for various purposes, such as their household servants, ad appointed some of them to high posts in civil and military services. Many of the slaves were castrated when still young. They were employed in the royal harems as eunuchs to guard their women. The female slaves were not only employed as household servants, but were also made concubines by their masters. When a slave-girl born a son to her master, she was often freed and was, then, called *umm-al-walad* or mother of the son.

Abd Rahman III was the first Umayyad Caliph who employed the Saqaliba as soldiers. He had 3750 of them. Some of the Slavs were appointed to high posts. He preferred the Slaves over the Arabs and Berbers who were unruly and rebellious. Afterwards, the number of the Slavs increased to more than fifteen thousand. Though staunchly loyal to the Umayyads, yet they became an important cause in the downfall of the Umayyad Caliphate.

The Slaves were captured from their tribes or communities in Europe or Africa while still of tender age. The European slaves or Saqaliba, were first brought by Jewish merchants to Verdun in the lands of the Franks and then transported to Pechina post of the eastern coast of Muslim Spain. While still young they were trained in various professions so as to fetch high prices, while the female slaves, who were highly prized for their beauty, were often trained as singers, etc. The male Saqaliba were also valued for their fair colour and beauty. When freed, the slaves often settled in towns. Moreover, while still young, the captured slaves were converted to Islam. In this respect, the Spanish Muslims had violated an injunction of Hazrat Umar, the second Caliph, who had ordained that no Muslim would be held as slave.

Women : In the life and society of Muslim Spain, the position of the women was not only contradictory in itself, but also contrary to Islam. The Holy Prophet (PBUH) had repeatedly enjoined upon the Muslims to treat women considerately, and Islam did not deny them equality of opportunity and rights alongwith men. In reality, condition of the women in Muslim Spain was quite different and often miserable. Polygamy was universally prevalent, justified on the ground of shortage of men due to incessant wars. Women were of two kinds: free and slaves. Owing to the control and domination of men over them, the free women were only legally free, but were socially servile. Their husbands chose them, or were chosen for them and marriage could be easily dissolved by the husband. He was free to take four women as his canonical (sharai) wives and also any number of concubines. The family life was, consequently, full of discord and tension not only between several wives and concubines but also between their children and descendants.

Spanish Muslim women observed Purdah or seclusion. But it was not so strictly enforced upon them due to several reasons. First of all, purdah system evolved gradually among the Muslims during the first three centuries of Islamic history. Even in the Abbasid Caliphate it was strictly and universally enforced only at the end of the tenth century. It was the period during which the Umayyad Spain flourished. Another factor was the remoteness of the Umayyad Spain from the central lands of Islam. Naturally, the full impact of the Abbasid institutions was not felt in the distant land of Spain. Moreover, the Spanish Muslims lived in close proximity to the Christians: intermarriages with the Christian women were all too frequent. Muslim husbands allowed their Christian wives the kind of freedom to which they were accustomed. In spite of all this, Purdah restrictions were imposed on women, especially on free Muslim women and on those slave-girls who had become concubines of their masters.

> "For instance, Andalusian priority required that women should not be allowed to walk alone, to follow a funeral or to visit cemetries; they should be kept whenever possible from the company of men at weddings and other gatherings unless accompanied. They should not wash in streamlets or sit at the edge of a wadi (river), for they would provoke men. Moreover, women should not enter churches

because of the corruption attributed to priests, who were said often to cohabit with more than one women."

THE CHRISTIANS BEFORE 1008

The northern regions of Spain gave shelter to the vanquished band of Christians. They settled in the hilly and natural strongholds to prove a menace in future.

The vanquished soldiers of Roderick along with the bishops and chiefs assembled in the mountains of Asturias and formed a tribal council in the village of Cangas-de-Onis, Pelayo, a guard of Roderick was elected as the successor of Roderick. He raided the Muslim territory but was repulsed by Alqama. Pelayo was encouraged by extending his territory in the eastern part of Asturias with the help of Charles Martel.

The Civil wars among the Muslims, encouraged Pelayo and his successors to extend their frontiers to the south of the Duro. Hajib Al-Mansoor however established the Muslim authority by overrunning the entire Christian Spain except a few places in the North.

After the death of Pelayo (737 A.D.) Alfanso I (739.757 A.D.) and Alfanso II (791-842 A.D.) formed a strong Asturian State. Alfanso devastated Sevogia, and Avila. Alfanso II taking the advantage of internal disorders during the rule of Hisham I and Hakam I, raided as far as Lisbon in the West. His conclusion of the treaty of alliance with Charlimagne, the Frankish Emperor, Louis the Pious, the king of Aquitain against the Umayyads did not prove effective.

The Muslim stronghold of Saragossa controlled the fertile valley of the Ebro. The combined forces of Austrians, Cantabrians and Basques encroached upon the Muslim territory and settled themselves in the upper valley of the Ebro. Primarily the area of land was given to the monastries by the Muslims. The monks, forgetting the tolerance of the Muslims, invited Christian chiefs to settle there and construct castles and forts, naming it as Castile (800 A.D.) to check the advance of the Muslims. Thus the gothic monarchy was established at Oviedo or Ovetao as its capital by Alfanso II. The new capital had palaces, churches and baths on the Muslim pattern.

The Christian rulers of Oviedo and Leon made no progress until the fall of Cordova.

The creation of the state of Navaree by Sancho Garcia (905-925 A.D.) was against the Frankish protectorate.

Later on there existed three states of Navaree Castile and Aragon between the Asturian Kingdom and the Spanish March, Aragon was a buffer state between the Franks and the Navarees.

The hold of the Muslims on the north-eastern part of Spain being loose, the Frankish rulers established a semi independent principality (798 A.D.) round the Gothic March or Spanish March. It was a military outpost to defend the France and invade the Muslim territory. The reigns of Hisham I and Hakam I saw the clashes of arms till the Franks were compelled to conclude a treaty known as the treaty of Aixla-Chapelle (816 A.D.).

Alfanso III (866-910 A.D.) married a Basque lady, Imina and thus strengthened his hold on Navaree. He invaded the Muslim territories but had to abdicate, with the result that his wife revolted against him and his kingdom was divided among his sons. Leon was given to Garcia; Galicia to Ordono, and Asturias to Fruela.

The Muslim influence in the north was increased by the successful attacks of Abdul Rahman III who had subjugated all the Christian kingdoms except Galicia. The Christian kingdoms were turned into Muslim protectorates. They used to pay annual tribute. They were independent for internal affairs but not for external affairs.

Sancho the fat the king of Leon was able to regain his throne with the help of Abdul Rahman III and had agreed to demolish some fortresses and to surrender some cities to the Khalifa.

Alfanso V (994-1027 A.D.) of Leon and his uncle Sancho the Great (970-1035 A.D.) of Navaree taking advantage of the weakness of the Muslim rulers invaded the Muslim territories and pushed their frontiers southwards. Leon was occupied by Sancho the Great. Sancho had extended his suzerainty to Aragon, Navaree and the Basque provinces of Spain and France. He had thus established a strong kingdom to devastate the Muslim territories.

CHAPTER 27

THE TAIFA SPAIN MULUK-AL-TWAIF

The establishment of the Umayyad dynasty in 756 A.D. in the west after its final fall in the east in 750 was the most heroic event in the Arab's history in the middle ages. Under the able leadership of vigorous rulers it foiled the malicious designs of the Abbasides and the Fatmides on one hand and crushed the Christian powers on the other, to mark a beacon for the then world.

The Umayyad flag hoisted on the Christian land, gracefully. The Christian world looked towards the Umayyad rulers as their supporters and arbitrators. Muslim Spain was a well organized and well established state.

The domestic troubles, absence of Islamic brotherhood, and civil wars, mutual hatred and suspicion backed by foreign troubles and intrigues destroyed the integrity of the state which took quarter of a century to collapse.

Cause of decay:

The decline of the Umayyad dynasty was actually perceived with the accession of Hisham II (976 A.D.). The authority which centred round the Khalifa fell a victim to the palace intrigues. The rise of Hajib al-Mansoor of course kept up illuminating the light of the Umayyad authority in Europe, but converted the caliphate to a tutelage which heralded decline and decay in the near future.

The events which followed the death of Al-Mansoor brought about the disintegration of the kingdom. All the Muslim provinces proclaimed their independence. The Arabs, the Spanish, the slaves and Berber chiefs formed a number of small kingdoms called Muluk al-Twaif. There were about 30 independent small kingdoms by 1031 A.D. Cordova was just a province instead of a capital.

It may also be noted that no ruler was capable of restoring peace and order in the country. The later rulers were more worldly and indulged in luxury. Taxes were, numerous. The people groaned under repression and tyranny. The Ulema and Fuqaha were disrespected. The Christians of the North and the Mozarabs rose in open revolts. The high sense of the racial superiority of the Arabs caused a general apathy of the people for them.

The establishment of feudalism and the distribution of wealth to the selected families of Arab princes and nobles created hatred among the neo-muslims, traders and industrialists who actually maintained the economy of the country. Internal risings were therefore rampant.

The materialistic outlook of the aristocracy and the creeping of self-interest made a headway after AI-Nasir and could not be crippled down for good by Al-Mansoor whose successors broke up the very solidarity of the empire.

Stages in the History of Taifa Kingdoms

There were thirty or more Taifa kings, some big, others small and not a few of them only little kinglings. One or two were even robbers who had perched themselves up in a hill castle and looted the peaceful villages around or the unwary passers-by. On the whole, the Taifa kingdoms evolved in four stages as below:

1. Establishment of an independent Taifa Kingdom.

2. Struggle for retaining independence against Sevillean expansionism.

3. Struggles for retaining independence against Christian revanchist designs: and therefore,

4. Submission to the Al-Murabitun of North Africa.

In this chapter we shall deal with the first two stages, while reserving the third and fourth stages for the two later chapters. Moreover, we shall narrate only the history of the bigger Taifa States, partly because of their importance, but mainly because their history encompassed those of the lesser ones, which were mostly conquered bigger ones. The big Taifa States were:

(i)   Banu Hammud of Malaga and-Algeciras.

(ii)   Banu Ziri of Granada.

(iii)   Slar rulers of South-eastern Spain, especially of Denia and Balearics.

(iv)   Banu Hud of Saragossa.

(v)   Banu Dhu'l-Nun of Toledo.

(vi)   Banu Jahwar of Cordova

(vii)   Rulers of Badajoz

(viii) Banu Abbad of Seville.

BANU HAMMUD

Hammud ibn Maimun had fled from Mauritania

(Northwestern Africa) to Spain and had taken refuge in Cordova, where Hajib al-Mansur had appointed him to a high military post. He traced his descent to the ldrisids of Mauritania. He, had two sons, Qasim ibn Hammud and Ali ibn Hammud. Actually, Banu Hammud were Berbers, but claimed to be descendants of Hazrat Ali, in order to legitimize their claim to the Spanish Caliphate, as we have said in a previous chapter.

At first, Ali ibn Hammud was appointed governor of Tangier and Ceuta and his elder brother, Qasim, as the governor of Algeciras. When the Umayyad Caliphate began to totter to a fall, Ali ibn Hammud captured Cordova and ruled it for some time. In March, 1018, he was killed by his negro slaves. Then his elder brother, Qasim, became a Khalifa. But three years later he was driven out of Cordova by his nephew, Yahya ibn Ali. Qasim then fled to the south where he captured Malaga, which he ruled for seven years, from 1021 to 1025. Granada and other Taifa States in the south were the vassals of the Hammudite Khalifas, as they always styled themselves.

After the death of Qasim ibn Hammud, his nephew, Yahya ibn Ali ibn Hammud, recaptured Malaga. He was already the ruler of Algeciras. He then became the Khalifa and ruled Malaga and Algeciras for ten years, from 1025 to 1035. Once Yahya had also been a Hammudite Khalifa at Cordova. In 1035, he tried once again to capture Cordova and Seville to become the Khalifa of Spain. But he was defeated and killed by Ismail, the son of Qazi Abu' Qasim, the ruler of Seville, in November, 1035.

On the death of Yahya, the Hammudite Caliphate split into two: Idris ibn Ali, Yahya's brother, was proclaimed Khalifa by the Berbers at Malaga at Algeciras by his negro supporters. We first turn to the Hammudite kingdom of Malaga, which was the more powerful and prosperous of the two.

Idris-I found the kingdom of Malaga no bed of roses. Though a Berber State, it contained Slavs also and great jealousy and hate existed between the two ethnic groups, since their disputes over the Caliphate in Cordova. But they remained united out of the fear of their common enemies, the rulers of Seville. However, when Idris-I died in 1039, a dispute broke out between the Berber, Ibn Bakanna, and the Slav Hajib, Naja, over the successor of Idris-I. The Berber chief favoured Yahya, the elder son of Idris-I, while the Slav Naja wanted to proclaim Hasan ibn Yahya the Khalifa. At first, Yahya ibn Idris was successful. He remained Khalifa for a year. In 1040, he was overthrown by his rival, Hasan, who put his rival, Yahya, to death soon after. However, in 1042, Hasan was poisoned to death by his wife, who was a sister of Yahya. She thus avenged the death of her brother. His Hajib Naja, the Slav, who was really the kingmaker, now dreamed of himself becoming the Khalifa. He quietly put to death the minor son of Hasan. Although the Berbers strongly resented the sacrilegious act of the Slav for murdering a Hammudite, whom they regarded as a descendant of Hazrat Ali and therefore a Syed, but for the time being they remained quiet and waited for their opportunity. When Naja led an army of the Berbers against the Hammudite kingdom of Algeciras, they killed him in February, 1043. Then they rushed back to Malaga and proclaimed Idris ibn Yahya ibn Ali (Idris-II) as Khalifa. The Slav party was crushed at Malaga soon after.

The new Khalifa, Idris II, ruled Malaga peacefully for the next three years, 1043-46. He was a man of saintly character. He loved to converse with the common people of his capital and mixed with them freely. His egalitarian attitude was, however, at odds with the ostentatious etiquette of his Court, in which it was the custom that the ruler would not appear before the common people except from behind a curtain. Moreover, Idris II was so generous that he would never say "No" to any request for anything by anyone, be it for example a castle or a vizier of the Khalifa himself. This weakness irritated the Berbers, who were accustomed to be ruled by a strong man. At this time, a cousin of Idris II, Muhammad ibn Idris ibn Ali, marched on the capital, Malaga. The common folk of the capital rose in support of their kind-hearted and egalitarian Khalifa. But he stopped them with the words, "Return to your homes for I would not have a single life lost on my account" He then willingly went into prison, while his rival, Muhammad, became the new Khalifa.

The new Khalifa, Muhammad, was of war-like bent of mind. The men around him soon got tired of him and plotted to overthrow him. Idris, who had rid himself of his peaceful habits in the prison willingly joined the conspirators against Muhammad. But Muhammad defeated his enemies and compelled Idris to flee to Africa. While these troubles were happening in Malaga, the Zirid ruler of Granada, Badis ibn Habbus, joined hands with the discontented and in 1057, annexed Malaga to his kingdom. Thus Malaga ceased to exist as an independent Taifa Kingdom.

The fate of Algeciras, the other Hammudite Kingdom, was also the same. After the death of Yahya ibn Ali ibn Hammud, it had separated itself from Malaga and became an independent Hammudite Kingdom. At first, it was ruled by Muhammad ibn Qasim ibn Hammud. He ruled it till 1049, when he was succeeded by his son, Qasim ibn Muhammad. Ten years later, Algeciras was annexed by Seville and thus it also ceased to exist as an independent Taifa Kingdom.

THE ZIRID KINGDOM

Ziri ibn Atia belonged to the powerful Berber tribe of Sanhaja, who lived near Qayrowan in North Africa. He was a very shrewd, energetic and resolute leader of his tribe. Owing to some dispute, he and his followers were forced to leave their ancestral homeland and come to Muslim Spain in the days when al-Mansur was the all powerful Hajib at Cordova. Al-Mansur welcomed Ziri and appointed him to high military posts and allotted him estates in Elvira. Ziri and his Sanhaja Berbers were the "new Berbers", and were the powerful supporters of al-Mansur and his sons and successors. But the new Berbers were hated by the people of Cordova because of their unruly and oppressive conduct. During the civil war which broke out against the Amirids in 1009, the Berbers and their leaders were driven out of the capital. Zawi, a son of Ziri, was then the leader of the new Berbers. He proclaimed Sulaiman the Khalifa as against the reigning Khalifa al-Mahdi. In November, 1009, Mahdi was defeated by the Berbers under Zawi and Sulaiman became the Khalifa. In recognition of his services, the new Khalifa; Sulaiman al-Mustain, granted Elvira as fief to Zawi. Finding Elvira not a defensible place, Zawi made Granada, near Elvira; as his capital in 1010, and ruled it as virtually independent king. When Ali ibn Hammud invaded Spain, Zawi went over to his side and fought against the Umayyad Khalifa Abdul Rahman IV al-Murtaza. Granada became a vassal of the Hammudites of Malaga. Zawi ruled Granada till 1020, when he, for some unknown reason, left his Kindsom under the care of his nephew, Habbus ibn Maksan ibn Ziri and returned to Africa.

HABBUS

Habbus ruled Granada as an independent ruler. But he styled himself as Hajib Saif al-Daula. Habbus ruled Granada for about eighteen years, during which time he constructed a palace in it, called al-Qasr and improved his capital in many ways. He annexed the neighbouring cities of Jean and Cabra into his kingdom. He also established friendly relations with other Taifa rulers. As he was threatened by the expansionist

Abbadids of Seville, he joined with Zuhair of Almeria and defeated the Abbadids of Seville. A Jew, named Samuel, was his counseller. Habbus too prided himself upon his scholarship and even claimed to be an Arab. Nevertheless, he could not trust on Arab as his confidential vizir and counsellor. This was the reason why he appointed the Jew to such a high post. Habbus died in June 1038. He left two sons Bodis and Bologguin. A civil war threatened to break out between the two brothers. But the younger brother, Bologguin voluntarily withdrew from the contest and thus his elder brother, Badis was proclaimed new king of Granada.

SAMMUEL

Sammuel Ha Levi-bin-Nagdela (Ismail-bin-Nagdela) was a Jew of Cordova. He was a petty shop-keeper of grossary in Cordova. He moved to Malaga after the subjugation of Cordova by Sulaiman al-Mustain. Abul Qasim-bin Arif, the minister, being impressed by his talent, appointed him as his assistant. He created a good impression upon Habbus who after the death of Arif appointed him as his minister. His life can be very well compared with that of Hajib al-Mansoor. He was a man of knowledge and learning. He edited the Talmud in Hebrew, which earned a name for him. His book entitled 'The Riches' along with other 22 books on grammar made him known in Persia, Palestine, Egypt and other places. He died in 1055 A.D.

Yousuf (Joseph) the son of Sammuel was bestowed the position of his father. Unlike his father he was faithless and wanted to establish the Jewish Kingdom by poisoning the heir apparent. He was however killed at the order of the famous Faqih and poet Abu-Ishaque of Elvira (30th December, 166 A.D.)

CHAPTER 28

BADIS-BIN-HABBUS
(1038-1073 A.D.)

Badis Abu Manad-bin-Habbus was a very strong ruler of Granada. He was not a just ruler. He cared only for his own self and always kept himself indulged in vices.

Zuhayr the ruler of Almeria was his rival. His prime minister Ibne-Abbas was as talented as Sammuel, the Prime Minister. Both Badis and Zuhayr were diametrically opposed to each other in character and accomplishment. Zuhayr was a great patroniser of learning and had a collection of 1,00,000 books in his royal library whereas Badis hated the educational persuits.

Once Badis invited Zuhayr to continue the friendly alliance with him, but Badis forces, lying in the ambush, killed Zuhayr in the Alpuents pass while returning to Almeria. Ibne-Abbas was also killed.

Abul Fatah, an educationist of Granada instigated Yazir the cousin of Badis to occupy the throne. The plot being unearthed, Yazir fled away to Seville but Abul Fatah was caught and killed in 1039 A.D. He did not spare the life of his younger brother Bulughin for his making delay in killing Ibne-Abbas.

Badis invaded Valencia and Seville and occupied some of

the territories. He also annexed the dominion of Malaga in 1058 A.D. Badis inspite of his cruel deeds and unjust actions cannot be ignored as a successful ruler.

He extended his capital city and built a palace Dardik-al-Rih (House of the weather cock) still known as "Casa de-Gollo". He constructed a bridge on the Durro in 1055 A.D. called Peunte-de-Cadi at the instance of Qazi Ali-bin-Muhammad-bin-Awbah. Badis died in 1073 A.D. after a long rule of 35 years leaving a strong kingdom for his successors. Tamim and Abdullah, his grandsons, who were no match to their grandfather brought the Zirid rule to a close.

The independent principalities of Slavs in the Southeast Spain and the Balearic Islands (1013-1115 A.D.) did not last long. Khyran (d. 1028 A.D., 419 A.H) of Almeria, Zuhayr of Murcia (d. 429 A.H; 1038 A.D.) and Mujahid of Denia (d. 436 A.H; 1045 A.D.) were all hopeless rulers and caused the rise of the Christian power.

Mujahid of Denia

The slaves were the slave commanders and functionaries of the Umayyad and Amirid rulers of Cordova. When their Caliphate was coming to an end, the Slav leaders tried to restore them to power. But the new Berbers under the rival Hammudites proved to be too strong for them. So the Slav leaders withdrew towards the eastern regions, of the Peninsula and established their little kingdoms there. One of them was set up by Mujahid the Slav at Denis. He also controlled the nearby Mediterranean islands of Majorca and Minorca, and Balearis collectively called Balearics. He also invaded Sardinia and ruled it for some time. He died in 1044 and was succeeded by his son, Ali ibn Mujahid and ruled it till 1075, when his petty kingdoms was annexed by Muqtadir ibn Hud of Saragossa.

Almeria

Another Slav leader, Khayaran al-Saqlabi had captured Almeria in 1013 after the Slav leaders had despaired of restoring the Umayyad-Amirid Caliphate. In 1028 Almeria came under another Slav chieftain, Zuhair who was the ruler of Murcia. Ten years later, an Amirid prince, Abdul Aziz captured Almeria. Finally, in 1091, Almeria was taken by the Almoravids.

Other Slav chieftains, like the Amirid Zuhair of Murcia, or Mubarik of Valencia were worthless rulers. They enabled the northern Christians to extend their dominions upto Valencia and other eastern cities.

THE BANU HUD
(1010-1118 A.D.)

After the conquest of Spain the Berbers were settled in the hilly tracts of North Spain to check the inroads of the Christians. Mohammad bin-Hashim-al-Tajibi was appointed governor of Aragon by Abdul Rahman III. The governorship had become heriditary in the Tajibi tribe because of its loyalty to the empire.

Munzir-bin-Mutrif-bin-Yahya the governor of Saragossa declared himself independent and made an alliance with the Christian chiefs of Barcelona and Castille. His successors could not retain the independence of Saragossa and succumbed to the power of Sulaiman-bin-Muhammad-bin-Hud, who founded the Hud dynasty and ruled Saragossa under the title of al-Mustain. He appointed his sons as governors of the various provinces. His son Ahmad assuming the title of al-Muqtadir-be-Allah ascended the throne of Saragossa in 437 A.H. 1046 A.D. His rule of 37 years is marked for the expulsion of the Norman pirates and recapturing the Fort of Bobastro. He was a good administrator and statesman. Peace reigned supreme in his time. He constructed a number of public buildings of which the palace

"Darul-Suroor" the house of joy and comfort' earned the admiration of all. Learning and culture also improved to a considerable degree. He died in 474 A.H; 1082 A.D.

BANU DHUN NUN

Toledo constituted the Middle March or *Thaghr al-Aust* during the Umayyad rule. The province of Toledo, one of the biggest in territory, was mostly inhabited by the Berber tribes since early times. One of the Berber tribes was called Banu Dhu'n Nun. They had acquired influence during the reign of Amir Muhammad I of the Umayyad dynasty. Al-Mansur enhanced their influence by appointing them to high military posts. When the civil war, which ushered in the anarchy of the Muluk at-Tawaif, began, the Qazi family of Toledo, under its leader, Abu Bakr Ya'ish ibn Muhammad ibn Ya'sih, captured power in Toledo in 1012. Six years after, in 1018, he was overthrown by the leader of Dhu'n Nun, named Abu Muhammad Ismail, who assumed the title of al-Zafir. Abu Bakr ibn al-Hadidi was his Hajib. He died on 1043.

Yahya ibn Ismail : Ismail's son, Yahya, ascended the throne in 1043. He assumed the title of al-Mamun and ruled Toledo till 1075. He was the most powerful ruler of Toledo. In a war with Sulaiman ibn Hud, he was defeated and fled to Talavera. Being wedged in between the Christians of Castile and Aragon and Banu Hud of Saragossa, he preferred alliance with the Christians. He accepted the suzerainty of Ferdinand I of Castile and Leon. He then became a sort of tool of the Christians to wage war against his fellow-Muslims. With the aid of Ferdinand, he captured Valencia, in 1065. Next he attacked Cordova, but was repulsed by Abdul Malik ibn Jahwar. However, in 1075, he succeeded in capturing Cordova with the help of a Berber chief, Ibn Okkasha. But within a few days after, Ibn Okkasha poisoned him to death.

Yahya was succeeded by his son, Yahya al-Qadir. But he was driven out of Toledo by al-Mutawakkil of Badajoz for some time. He was restored on the throne by the Christian protector of Dhu'n Nun family, Alfonso VI of Castile. However, in 1085, Alfonso VI drove out al-Qadir from Toledo. He took refuge in Valencia, where he died as a forlorn refugee. Toledo was then annexed by the king of Castile and made a capital of New Castile. Thus the Middle March, vanished for ever and Toledo became a Christian city.

THE AFTASIDS OF BADAJOZ

Badajoz was the capital of the western March. A slave chieftain named Sabur-al-Saqlabi, established himself at Badajoz as an independent ruler in 1012. But he was overthrown Abdullah son of Muhammad ibn al-Aftas in 1022. Ibn Aftas became ruler. After his death his son Mohammad bin Aftas ascended to throne in 1045. Muhammad attacked Ibn Yahya of Nielbla, who was defeated and Niebla was captured by Muhammad. In 1067, Badajoz was captured by the Christian king of Castile and Leon Ferdinand I.

BANU JAHWAR OF CORDOVA

Ibn Jahwar abolished Caliphate and declared Cordova a republic in 1031. Abu'l Hazm ibn Jahwar was elected as the first president of the republic. He refused to accept the office except on the condition that Muhammad Ibn Abbas and Abdul Aziz Ibn Hasan were also associated with him as the members of the Council. The Assembly of the people accepted his condition. The President of the Cordovan Republic was an able and wise ruler and administered it with justice and wisdom. Ibn Jahwar removed the Berbers from the city and thus satisfied the old complaint of the people. He set up a National Guard to maintain law and order in the much-troubled city. Though virtually a ruler of Cordova, he always carefully preserved its republican constitution. Whenever anyone, asked for a favour, the President would reply, "It is not in my power: the matter concerns the Council of State; I am only its agent." If an official letter was addressed to him, he refused to acknowledge it, saying that it should be addressed to the viziers. He always took a decision after consulting his Council of Viziers. He never assumed princely titles, and continued to live in his own modest house. Nevertheless, his power was unlimited, for the Council of Ministers never opposed his decisions. He was an honest and scrupulous ruler. The state treasury was not kept in his house, but was kept in the custody of the most honourable citizens. He always endeavoured to enhance the welfare and prosperity of the people of Cordova. Consequently, arts and crafts soon revived in the city and trade and industry flourished. The prices of commodities fell, while peace and security encouraged people to rebuild the houses and quarters which had been demolished by the Berbers, the Christians and other marauders who had ravaged the unfortunate city before. Ibn Jahwar patronised education and respected the faqihs and theologians. He was a man of peace and maintained friendly and peaceful relations with his neighbours. His love of peace was illustrated by the fact that he did not oppose Qazi Abu'l Qasim, the ruler of Seville, which he tried to win the public opinion in favour of the pretender, Hisham II.

Abd al-Walid : After the death of Abu Hazm, his son, Abul Walid ibn Jahwar, was elected to the office of the President of the Council of State in 1045. He continued the just administration of his father. He was also an able ruler and a patron of the learned men, faqihs and ulema. His minister, Ibrahim ibn Yahya was equally able and good administrator. Administration was divided between the President's sons, Abdul Rahman and Abdul Malik. However, Abdul Walid resigned his office in 1064 for some unknown reason. He was succeeded by his son, Abdul Malik, but the administration was in the hands of his minister, Ibn Saqa. Later, however, Abdul Malik, killed ibn Saqa at the instigation of the ruler of Seville. Cordova was then annexed by Seville. But in 1069, the city was conquered by the ruler of Toledo, AI-Mamun ibn Dhu'n Nun till Toledo itself was conquered by Alfonso VI the King of Castile and Leon.

THE BANU ABBAD
(1023–1091 A.D.)

The Banu Abbad who claimed their descent from the ancient Lakhmide royal family of Al-Hira, actually belonged to the Lakhmide tribe of Yaman. The Lakhmide precursors of Banu Abbad had their homeland Arish, on the borders of Egypt and Syria. Itafbin-Nuaym, the ancestor of Banu Abbad had joined the army of Balf-bin-Bashr and had come to Spain to settle down at Yaumin, a village on the Guadalquiver.

The dynasty was founded by Abul Qasim Muhammad I-bin-Ismail who was great grandson of Abbad. Abul Qasim was both a soldier and a jurist. Qazi Abul Qasim, at the request of the people of Seville formed a popular government with Muhammad-bin-Yasin Hamzani, Ibne-Hajjaj Al-hani and Abu Bakr Zubaidi, the tutor of Hisham II. He raised an army of 500 soldiers and captured the Christians' fortresses known as the two Brothers "Ikhwan".

It was in 418 A.H; 1027 A.D. that Yahya-bin Ali of Malaga invaded Seville, but Qazi Abul Qasirm saved Seville by giving his son Abbad as a hostage to Yahya. It was a great sacrifice which made him very popular and the people were convinced of his sincerity to the kingdom. He dismissed his councillors for their cowardness and insincerity. Zubaidi was exiled to Qirwan. Qazi Abul Qasim, in the meantime having increased his force, captured Beja and Badjoz, and also threatened Cordova, then under the chairmanship of Jahwar.

By 1034 A.D. Yahya of Malaga was accepted as the leader of the Berber chiefs and became a menace for Cordova and Seville. Abul Qasim, in order to foil the evil designs of Yahya, united the Arabs, the Slavs and the Berbers by presenting before them a man named Khalaf, a mat-maker as Hisham II who resembled the untrace Khalifa. The people accepted him for Hisham II without any suspicions. Abul Hazam bin-Jahwar also accepted him for the time being, in November, 1035.

Ismail-bin-Al-Qasim defeated Yahya and killed him and occupied Carmona. Abul Qasim however failed to create confusion in Granada through Al-Fath, a very influential personality of Granada. Abul Fath was killed in 1039 A.D.

ABU-AMR ABBAD

Abu Amr Abbad succeeded his father Qazi Abul Qasim in 433 A.H.; 1042 A.D. at the age of 26, as the prime minister. He assumed the title of al-Mutazid-be Allah (seeker of strength from Allah).

He was a very able administrator, a poet and a patron of art and learning. He believed in sorcery and adored wine. He used the skills of his enemies as his wine goblet which had the named of the victims fully inscribed on them. He also took pleasure in planting flowers in the craniums of his enemies. Though ruthless and violent, he was energetic and a vigilant ruler. He did not spare the life of his own son Ismail for his complicity in a treason. He had a strong espionage system, spread over entire Spain. He suspected his minister Habib and got him killed by his agents. He annexed Carmona at the cost of a Barber dynasty Banu Birzal. The ruler of Carmona Hakim Muhammad bin Abdullah was killed in the battle. He waged war against Ibne Tayfur the Berber chief of Mertola, and his ally Muhammad bin Yahya al-Yahsoobi, the Arab chief of Niebla (Labla) and captured Mertola (1044 A.D.; 436 A.H.)

Muhammad-bin-Yahya the Arab chief of Niebla had allied himself with the Berber Block which was comprised of the Badis of Granada, Muhammad of Malaga, Muhammad of Algeciras and Muzaffar of Badajoz. Al-Mutazid was defeated by Muhammad-bin-Yahya of Niebla with the help of Muzaffar. The attack of the combined forces of the Arabs and Berbers of Seville was foiled by Mutazid. Ibne-Yahya of Niebla was in the meantime, won over by Mutadid. Muzaffar of Badajoz was defeated and thus Ibne-Yahya was saved. After the defeat of Muzaffar the ruler of Beja was defeated by Ismail bin Almutadid. Peace was concluded in July 1051. Niebla was however annexed by al-Mutadid, soon after the peace treaty was concluded Abdul Aziz the Bakrite ruler of Huelva also surrendered his territories to him and took refuge in Cordova. Mutadid's youngest son Muhammad, only 13 years defeated the Arab chief of Banu Muzayyab at Silvas (1051 A.D.). The young prince defeated Muhammad bin Said and annexed Anta Maria-de-Algarva (Shantamariyah al-gharb) now known as Faro. The young prince was appointed as governor of Silvas and Santa Maria (1055 A.D.).

Most of the Berber chiefs of the south also acknowledge his suzerainty. The Berber chiefs of Morona and Ronda made a conspiracy to kill al-Mutazid while he was asleep. Muadh, a relation of the chief of Ronda saved the guest out of the sense of hospitality. Mutadid after his return to his capital sent valuable presents to the chief of Ronda and Morona. He also invited 60 chiefs of Ronda, Morona and Jerez to Seville in 1053 and killed all except Muadh, the saviour of his life.

Later he conquered Morona, Arcos, Jerez and Ronda. Badis the leader of the Berbers invades Seville with a strong army of the refugees of Morona, Arcos, Jereza and Ronda, but he was defeated. The invaders reached Ifriqiah where most of them perished in a famine. Qasim, the Hamudid chief of Algeciras was defeated by Almutazid in 1058 A.D. and took shelter in Cordova. Almutazid removed the pretender Hisham II from the throne and declared himself as the Amir of Spain in 451 A.H; 1059 A.D. He therefore deputed his elder son Ismail to capture Medina-al-Zahira (455 A.H; 1063 A.D.). His son Ismail at the instigation of Abu Abdulah Bazlyani a chief of Malaga rebelled against his father. Ismail and Bazlyani were arrested and killed, the former by his father himself.

Prince Abul Qasim Muhammad taking advantage of the civil risings in Malaga, captured it but was later on defeated by Badis and had to escape to Ronda.

It was in 1055 A.D. that the Christian powers taking advantage of the disorder in the Muslim fold planned to attack the Muslim territories. Fernandes I King of Castile and Leon captured Badjoz defeating Muzaffar, in 1067 A.D. Mamoon the king of Toledo offered no resistance and acknowledged his suzerainty. Fernando then invaded Seville in 1063 A.D. Al-Mutazid being unable to resist concluded a treaty and agreed to pay an annual tribute and also to deliver the carcass of St. Justa to the envoys of Fernando. The carcass being not traceable they took away the caress of St. Isidor.

Maqtadir the ruler of Saragossa recaptured Barbastro in 1066 A.D.

Fernando I was defeated badly by Abdul Malik of Valencia and had to return to Castile well beaten.

It was after the annexation of Carmona in 1066 A.D. that Al-Mutazid died on February 28, 1069 A.D.; 461 A.H.

CHAPTER 29

ABUL QASIM MUHAMMAD II
(1069–1091 A.D.)

Abul Qasim Muhammad II succeeded his father in 461 A.H., 1069 A.D. He was a great poet and an intellectual. He was a patron of art and literature but not a statesman. His wife Itemad al-Rumaykiyah was reputed for her beauty and elegance. He was so much devoted to her that he tried to satisfy her desire and fancies in all possible manners. He had planted a garden of almond trees on the Sierra of Cordova with a bathing pool of perfumed rose water and other aromatic spices for the queen. The queen was well-versed in poetry. His minister Ibne-Amar was also a talented poet.

Al-Mutamid had shown his administrative talents and qualities as the governor of Silvas when a boy of 12 only but in the company of his minister he simply loved to visit the silver field on the banks of the Guadalquiver and hold poetic discussions.

It was in 1078 A.D. that Mutamid, taking advantage of the rivalry between Ukkaasha and Mamun of Toledo, reoccupied Cordova and also annexed the lands of ade-al-Kabir and important places of the Kingdom of Toledo between the Guadilquiver and the Guadiana.

Although strong among all the petty kings of Spain, he

could not retain his chivalry against Alfanso VI, of Castile and Leon because of the intrigues of other Muslim chiefs against him.

Ibne Ammar with the help of Ibne Rashiq the Arab chief of the Castile Balj (Vilches) declared himself independent and ruled over Murcia. He however had to escape to Saragossa on the approach of Mutamid. Being betrayed by Ibne Rashiq he was arrested by Banu Suhayl and sold to Mutamid the fort of Sequra.

He was imprisoned in Seville but later on set free by Mutamid. Ibne Ammar having the displeasure of Mutamid was killed and Abu-Bakr-bin Zaidoon was appointed prime minister in his place.

Dispute however arose between Mutamid and Alfanso VI on the threatening words of Ibne-Shalib the Jewish officer of Alfanso VI who was deputed for the collection of tribute from Seville. Mutamid killed him forthwith to the consequences of his bad words.

Alfanso VI who was very restless to conquer the whole of Spain, invaded Seville. The Muslims realising the ambition of Alfanso VI united themselves to meet the common foe. Yusuf-bin-Tashfin the Murabitun King of Ifriqiah was invited to fight. Alfanso the common enemy. Yusuf defeated Alfanso VI in the battle of Zallaqah (Sacralias) (23rd October 1086 A.D.) Yousuf had to return to Ifriqiah on account of the death of his eldest son at Centa. The Christians started attacking the Muslim territories.

Yousuf was invited again to crush the Christians. He responded well and annexed Seville (1090 A.D.) and the whole of Undulusia upto the Jagus to his own Moroccan kingdom. Mutamid was exiled to Aghmat near Morocco.

Death of Mutamid

Mutamid died in his prison in 1095 at the age of fifty five after a long illness. He was buried in Aghmat, where his tomb became a place of pilgrimage for several centuries after. "Everyone loves him, every one pities him-and even now he is lamented.

Mutamid, though not a great ruler, was not a bad one. He was a poet-king and a brilliant one among a long list of poet-kings who ruled Muslim Spain. He represented as Dozy says a people and a culture that loved poetry as an expression of its genius and its humanism. With his death came to an end the tragi-comic first Taifa period in the history of Muslim Spain. The fate of those Taifa kings and kinglets was no less tragic, but we shall describe it in a later chapter on Yusuf Tashufin. In the next chapter we shall see how the Spanish Christians had become so powerful.

CHAPTER 30

WINDS OF CHANGE OVER CHRISTIAN SPAIN

The year 1000 A.D. marked a dramatic reversal in the history of Muslim Spain: while it began to disintegrate after the civil war of 1009, Christian Spain became ascendant as it had never been before. Al-Maqqari writes:

> "We have already alluded in several chapters of this work to the deplorable revolution and disastrous events by which the mighty power of the Bani Marwan (Umayyads) was overthrown, and their extensive dominions in Africa as well as in Andalus, became a prey of ambitious chieftains, thus affording an opportunity to the cruel enemy of Allah to attack in detail the divided Muslims, and to expel them at least from those countries (kingdoms) which they had so long held in their power"

Ferdinand Lot in his book, *Christian Spain from 711 to 1037*, writes of this reversal of fortunes more significantly as thus:

> "Towards 1000, the destiny of Christian Spain, whose capital had been destroyed and

> her shrine, Compostela, burned seemed
> desperate. The fact is that, beneath a
> deceptive appearance of power and
> prosperity, Muslim Spain was consumed with
> incurable internal illnesses, while the
> Christian State, backward and humiliated,
> contained within herself a perennial youth
> and vigour."

What were the causes of the reversal of the fortunes of these two peoples? What were the factors which enabled the Spanish Christians to invade Muslim Spain ?

The "perennial youth and vigour" of the Spanish Christians was only one factor in their victory over the Spanish Muslims, just as, on the other side, the tendency of the Spanish Muslims to disintegrate into *Muluk at-Tawaif* again and again was an important factor in their defeat. Besides these reasons, there were several other factors in the success of the Spanish Christians. They were the effects of the winds of change which were blowing over medieval Europe and, from the tenth century, began to cross the Pyrenees and the seas around it into Christian Spain, invigorating and instigating the Spanish Christians to a war with the Spanish Muslims *outrance*. These changes transformed Europe, including Christian Spain, into modern Europe by the fifteenth century. They were, in chronological order, briefly as thus:

(i)   Evolution of Europe feudalism;

(ii)   The emergence of New Christianity, which began with the foundation of the monastery of Cluny in 910, and culminated in the Gregorian Reforms at the end of the eleventh century;

(iii)   Social changes, such as the abolition of slavery and of its necessary concomitant, concubinage; institution of monogamy, Church ban on cousin marriages upto fourth degree, etc.;

(iv) The rise of new towns and of the burgher class of mercantile bourgeoisie as the new social, economic and political forces;

(v) New technologies of peace and war, e.g. new agricultural implements and techniques which enhanced agricultural production, use of water-mills and windmills for both agricultural and industrial production, cross-bow, gunpowder and fire-arms, printing press, etc. (some of these new technologies were really not European inventions, but adoptions and innovations by them. For instance, gunpower was a Chinese invention, which was first used as a weapon of war by the Muslims and then adopted by the Europeans: however, they devised several kinds of new fire-arms and made artillery an important weapon of war, which they used more effectively and efficiently on the fields of battle: indeed, gunpowder and the printing press transformed Europe into a modern international phenomenon);

(vi) The rise of highly centralised and absolute monarchies;

(vii) The rise of nation-states and of nationalism; and

(viii) A sociological factor, namely the ever-increasing interactional opportunities and conditions in European life and society, the very basis of its dynamism.

The causes of these historical changes were conditions of freedom of action and thought which existed in medieval Europe, but did not exist in non-European countries and continents, except during particularly dynamic periods of their histories.

These conditions were:

1. Growth of consultative and legislative democratic institutions in European countries, which resulted in the formation of cortes in Christian Spain, and parliament in English, based on the principle of no taxation without representation.

2. Growth of municipal self-government in new towns and cities: corporate and interdependent town-life.

3. Institution of monogamous family system by the Catholic Church, in the ninth century.

4. Abolition of slavery and of its necessary concomitant, concubinage which took place during the thirteenth century.

5. Greater freedom of European women to participate in all social, cultural and political activities; absence of any purdah like institutions; rise of chivalry and respectable seating arrangements for women at the tournaments and other marks of higher opinion towards them from above the twelfth century.

6. Maintenance of effective law and order conditions by the kings who became strong enough to curb feudal lawlessness, usually called 'king's peace' as in Aragon and England.

7. Lastly, growing consciousness of and respect for the human individual, for his/her capabilities and potentialities and for his/her rights and responsibilities.

The consequences of these winds of change were historically tremendous; they transformed the civilisation and culture first of Western Europe and later of Christian Spain and Portugal, and ultimately modernised them all. Their characteral effects were equally great. They made first the European and later the Spanish and Portuguese Christians ever more energetic, adventurous, enterprising, inquisitive and community-conscious peoples: and they also became more aggressive, acquisitive and expansionist peoples. On the contrary, Muslim Spain, during the same period, became more, degenerate, and more divisive and stagnant. Consequently, Spanish Muslims became incapable of resisting Christian aggression and advance, although only a few decades earlier, they had thoroughly subdued the whole of Christian Spain. Obviously, if these changes had not swept over Christian Spain, it would never have been able to defeat the Spanish Muslims. And if similar, though not identical, changes had also occurred in Muslim Spain, it would have remained as invincible as ever before, and survived into modern times. The case of the Jews is relevant here. They retained their religion but adopted many of these changes and survived in Europe down to the modern times, in spite of countless pogroms against them.

The effects of these developments varied from one to the other. Take, for instance, the case of European feudalism. Feudalism as such was a world-wide phenomenon since the ancient times. But in non-European countries, it did not evolve beyond its initial stages. In Arab countries of Asia and Africa including Muslim Spain, it remained embedded in tribal feudalism. In India of both the Hindu and Muslim periods, it remained hide-bound in the caste system. The Indian caste feudalism was really a variant of the tribal feudalism. In medieval Europe, however, feudalism evolved from the tribal feudalism of the Germanic tribal settlements into the seigneurial feudalism from the ninth to the thirteenth centuries. In the tribal and caste feudalisms, the agricultural surplus, extorted by the metayage or *batai* system, was consumed locally by the landowning tribe or caste, with the tribal chiefs or caste leaders taking the lion's share.

In seigneurial feudalism, the agricultural surplus was extorted by labour-exploitation of the serfs on a manor and consumed locally by the seigneur or feudal lord, who moved from manor to manor along with his household vassals and their retinues. From the fourteenth century onwards, seigneurial feudalism was replaced by agricultural capitalism thanks to the application of new agricultural tools, implements, and techniques, first in England and then in other West European countries. What made it agricultural capitalism was that all agricultural produce was sold in the market, far and near. With the growth of market-oriented agriculture, feudalism in Europe died a natural death. In Christian Spain and Portugal, however, it remained embedded in its seigniorial stage due to the absolutist and autocratic nature of their monarchies. Even the French Revolution of 1789 could not abolish the Iberian feudalism.

The New or Gregorian Christianity was, by its very nature, not an evolutionary phenomenon. However, its influence declined in western Europe, though not in the Iberian Peninsula, due to the Renaissance and Reformation, while the Age of Reason and especially the French Revolution in the eighteenth century delivered *a coup de grace* to it: Christianity remained, but its intolerant militancy and totalitarianism declined. This metamorphasis was, however, not due to Muslim efforts or influence.

The last six "winds of change" were really the waves of the future. Their effects are still going strong in modern Europe and the West. In Christian Spain and Portugal, however, these six "winds of change" produced effects only from the tenth to the sixteenth centuries. Then these countries became rotten with decadence and stagnation due to feudal and Catholic Church oppressions and their autocratic and unbridled monarchies. Their decline and decadence were caused to no small measure by the extirpation of the Spanish Muslims, as we shall see later on.

Europeanisation of Christian Spain

Paradoxical though it may appear, before the eleventh century, Spain was a European country only in a geographical sense; but not so in social, cultural and economic terms. What made it a European country in these senses also was due to the winds of change which blew over medieval Europe and began to influence Spain also from about the middle of the tenth century. Thus change began first with European Feudalism.

Feudalism came into Spain in two ways : Feudalism came directly into the 'Spanish kingdoms and countries near the Pyrenees, which were for long under the domination of the Carolingian Kingdom of the Franks and remained under French influence long afterwards. In the kingdom of Leon-Castile, however, it came by marriage which its rulers contracted with French and Burgundian princesses, who brought with them large numbers of French and Burgundian nobles. When the Crusades began at the end of the eleventh century, a flood of French, English, German and other feudal nobles and knights came into the Iberian Peninsula, as Christian holy warriors, and many of them settled in it. However, the exigencies of the constant warfare with the Muslims rendered feudalism in Christian Spain into "State Feudalism." It was so, firstly because it was not of the contractual and limited nature as it was in medieval France. Instead, the Spanish king, as the feudal overlord, was all powerful and not the first among equals. Secondly, the king directly controlled the lesser nobles and knights and not through the feudal magnates, as was the case in the classical French feudalism. It was the Spanish custom to grant feudal estates to the nobles in the Muslim territories long before they were actually conquered, as an inducement to them to invade and conquer Muslim lands. Sometimes, the Spanish nobles and knights themselves offered their king to allow them to invade Muslim territories on the condition that they would be granted to them as their fiefs once they had been conquered. Thus Spanish feudal classes were always orientated towards war and conquest of Muslim lands, especially after the downfall of the Umayyad Caliphate, when the Muslim south was divided into several petty Taifa kingdoms, which were unable to resist Christian advance.

Christian kingship : Christian kings of Spain and Portugal were strong rulers. Their powers were, however, checked by the Catholic Church and the ancient laws called *fueros*; and they were also subject to others institutional limitations. When Spanish cortes (parliament) came into being, it exercised some restraint on royal authority. But it lost its powers at the end of the Middle Ages. With the support of the Catholic Church, the kings claimed their authority not to be sanctioned by any human individual or parliament. Moreover, the Christian kings conquered lands from the Muslims, the more they became autocratic and absolutist. A good example of royal autocracy was how Alfonso VI, the king of Leon Castile (1065-1109) changed the Church music and liturgy. His wife was French princess, who did not like the Mozarabic music and liturgy, which was till then used in Church service in his kingdom. When the Queen tried to replace it by the French music and liturgy, a Castilian knight resisted the change by areas, which however, were constantly advancing south into Muslim Spain. Much of the conquering energy of the Christians came from their small, non kinship, nucleated bilateral family system, in which property was inherited from both agnatic and cognatic sides, but it was inherited as a single patrimony to the exclusion of all other kinship relations on both parental sides. This type of family structure generated acquisitive, individualistic and aggressive attitudes among the Christians of all classes, whether they free peasants cultivating their small pieces of land on the borders and looking hungrily across the frontier towards Muslim lands, or they be the big or small feudal lords, eager to enlarge their estates by conquering more lands in Muslim Spain, or they be the Christian kings themselves out to conquer Muslim Spain itself. On the other hand, the large, kinship based extended family system among the Spanish Muslims made them not only inward looking, but it also generated disintegrative propensities among them by inclining them towards infighting within the family members and their relative and neighbours. The extended family structure was a product of the tribal society. But the tribal society had weakened in Muslim Spain, though not vanished altogether, while no wider consciousness of community emerged among the Muslims which could override the disintegrative tendencies among them.

Catholic Church introduced several changes in the social and family life in Christian Spain. It condemned slavery and also concubinage which go with it. Consequently, both of them began to vanish from Christian Spain after the eleventh century. The Church also enforced monogamy as the only permissible form of marriage. In Christian Spain, women did not observe purdah : they mixed freely with men at all levels of society. Though a Christian man could not marry another woman during the life time of his first wife, he could, however, take mistresses. Children of such mistresses were illegitimate, yet they were not socially ill treated. Among the ruling and feudal classes, the illegitimate sons and daughters were often granted fiefs, even kingdoms, appointed as bishops and archbishops in the Church hierarchy or joined monasteries as monks and abbots, or nuns and abbesses. The founder of the Spanish ruling dynasty of Trastamaras, Enrique II (1369-1360), was a natural son of Alfonso XI (1312-1360), the king of Leon Castile.

Free towns in Christian Spain : In Muslim Spain, towns and cities grew up rapidly due to flourishing agriculture, trade and industry. In the Christian North, the growth of towns and cities was consequent of the warfare with the Muslim south. During the first three centuries, the struggle between the two was a sort of ding dong warfare; if one day the Christians took a town or a district from the Muslims, it was recaptured by the latter the next day. But from the eleventh century, the scales of war turned definitely against the Muslims. This change was brought about, among other factors, by the rise of free towns and by the repopulation policies of the Spanish kings. In Christian Spain, free towns, enjoying freedom or franchise of municipal self government under the charters granted by the kings, grew up much earlier than in Western Europe. These towns were always set up on borders with Muslim Spain and acted as first line of defence against Muslim attacks. They were occupied by two kinds of populations, brought there particularly for this purpose. They were the mountaineers who came from the barren mountain ranges in the north to settle in the fertile valleys and plains in the South, and secondly, The Mozarabs or the Christians who had lived for generations in the Muslims south and were now enticed by the Christians kings to settle in the newly-conquered lands. The Mozarabs undertook the same arts and crafts which they had carried centres of arts and crafts, trade and industry, which Christian north had lacked utterly before, and also provided new sinews of war to the castles or fortresses along the borders of Muslim Spain. The towns and castles acted as barriers against Muslim advance. The policy of repopulation was first adopted by Alfonso III (866-910), the king of Asturo-Leon in the Douro tableland. It became the first step in the continuous southward advance of the Christian kingdoms.

Christianity and Spain : The real conqueror of Islamic Spain was the New Christianity, preached by the reforming and crusading popes, among whom the most important was Pope Gregory VII (1073-85): the Christian kings, nobles and knights were only their tools, though very faithful and fanatical tools at that. The Christian Church in the Middle Ages was always a highly intolerant, militant and aggressive organisation. Its dogma was simple: the Muslims were infidels; therefore, they must be converted to Christianity; if not, they must be driven out of the Christian land, Spain, they had conquered, and better still, they must be extirpated root and branch. A modern author writes, "For the Church there was only one possible and permissible view of the Muslems. It was a doctrinal question. The Muslims were infidels; and though Christians might trade with them or even learn from them (the fact that a man had studied with the Muslims at Cordova was no bar to his election as Pope, namely Pope Sylvester II, (999-1003) the first duty of the Church and of its followers was either to convert them or, if not, to destroy them". Another author writes, "The stress on violence was particularly marked in the West. Not only could violence be justified; it was particularly meritorious when directed against those who held other religious belief or none."

The rise of New Christianity had particularly violent effect on Muslim Spain. At first the Catholic Church in it, though not friendly, was not hostile towards the newly-established Muslim kingdom in the Iberian Peninsula. The reason was the tolerance which the Muslim rulers and people showed towards the Christians and their Church. In fact, many bishops welcomed the tolerant and benevolent rule of the Muslims. But a century or so after, the relations between the Muslims and Christians began to be strained, resulting from the movement of the Cordovan Zealots and the ceaseless insurrections of the Christians of Toledo.

But the real opposition to the Muslims came from outside the boundaries of Islamic Spain, where three centres became particularly vociferous in their propaganda of mass violence and war on Islam and the Muslims. They were, firstly, the

Christian kingdoms of Western Europe, secondly, the abbots and monks of Cluny, and thirdly and most importantly, the Popes, the heads of the European Christendom and the leaders of the New Christianity. So far as Muslim Spain was concerned, the monks of Cluny became its most active and inveterate enemies. Indeed, without these European influences, Muslim Spain could not have been overthrown by the native Christians, whether of the north or south. However, these developments in Western Europe transformed the whole geopolitical situation in the Peninsula. "The effectiveness with which the Moorish generals, when they put their minds to it, crushed forays from the northern kingdoms was only matched by the latter's capacity for self-preservation. Their inhabitants melted into the protective hills and valleys to emerge once again when the Moorish raiders withdrew. Nor can one legitimately point to anything blinding of a developing cultural life. Christian nobles fought as mercenaries for Moorish rulers–sometimes against their co-religionists–and at times carved out ephemeral areas of personal authority which persisted only because of the capricious balance of power between fluid frontiers. The political pattern in the north could well have remained thus indefinitely if it had not been for the continued and growing transformation of Europe beyond the Pyrenees, examplified in the wide-reaching reforms of the Church instigated by the Benedictine abbots of Cluny in France."

The monastery of Cluny was founded in 910 in Burgundy in south-eastern France with the avowed purpose of waging war with Muslim Spain. It established a large number of its branches, called priorips, at various places in Christian Spain and helped in the Europeanisation of the Spanish church and kingdoms. It organised the pilgrim road to Santiago de Compostela, the greatest shrine in, Christian Spain, as we have described in a previous chapter. It introduced French clerics in the Church hierarchy of Spain, and replaced the old Mozarabic liturgy by the rites of the Roman Church. At the same time, the Cluny-trained bishops and monks advised the Christian rulers of Spain and even controlled and directed their policy decisions, especially of the kings of Leon-Castile. Cluny supplied most of the bishops particularly in reconquered areas–the advancing line of the victorious Christian Spain.

The Iberian Peninsula in the eleventh century was mostly a Muslim country. Hence it became a special target of the crusading New Christianity: it was, indeed, its target a quarter of century before the Crusades actually began against the eastern lands of Islam. The influence of the Catholic Church increased over the Spanish Christians from the eleventh century till it reached its highest under the Catholic rulers Ferdinand and Isabella, in the fifteenth century. "It was the bishop whose voice called the Christians to war and who led the fighting". Thus the Catholic Church in Spain grew in power along with the Reconquista till it controlled every Spanish Christian from the king and queen at the top down to a commoner in the market-place and the knight on the battlefield.

The monks of Cluny, inspired by anti-Islamism, were especially active in the Christian kingdoms of the north. They first entered Spain 1033 and established their priories in the kingdom of Navarre. But they soon moved on to the kingdom of Leon-Castile, which had more aggressive designs on Muslim Spain. Fernando I (1035-65), the king of Leon-Castile, became a vassal of Cluny. He started paying stipend of one thousand gold dinars every year to this monastery" from the tributes (called parias in Spanish) which he forced the Taifa kingdoms of Toledo, Saragossa and Badajoz to pay him. Later, his son and successor, Alfonso VI, who had conquered Toledo in 1085, forced many other Taifa kings to pay large tributes and, accordingly, he doubled the yearly stipend of the monastery of

Cluny. At the same time, Aragon, another Christian kingdom in the eastern region of the Peninsula, became the vassal of the Popes of Rome. At the instigation of the Pope, Alexander II, it led a crusading army against Barbastro, a city on the borders of the Taifa kingdom of Saragossa, as we shall presently describe. In short, from the eleventh century onwards, both the Popes and the monks of Cluny were inspired by a predatory and colonialist interest in the Reconquista wars of the Spanish Christians. In the twelfth century, the Popes established military orders of the Church to wage wars against the Spanish Muslims along with the armies of the Christian kings of Spain.

The "holy wars" against the Muslims in Spain gave the Popes the idea of the Wars of the Cross or Crusades against the Muslims in the East. It occurred to them as thus: in 1063, Ramiro I, the king of Aragon, was murdered by a Muslim. As Aragon was already a papal vassal, Pope Alexander II granted an indulgence or remission from sin, to all those Christians who would fight for the cross to avenge the king's murder. This idea was further developed in 1073 by Pope Gregory VII who organised an all-European army for Spanish campaigns "guaranteeing canonically that any Christian knight could keep lands he conquered from the Muslims." In this manner, the idea of conquering Muslim lands in Spain led only twenty years later to the idea of conquering Muslim lands in the Middle East. This was the genesis of the Wars of the Cross or Cursades which lasted from 1097 to 1217.

The Christian clergy and the monks infused a deep hatred of the Spanish Muslims in the hearts of their followers in every way. "In every thing the Christians aspired to be unlike the Muslims–in their mode of life, their dwellings, their dress, their pursuits, exercises and amusements. Thus if the Muslims detested the flesh of the swine, the Christians considered it the sweetest of the meats: the Muslims loved frequent ablutions, the Christians hated to take a bath at all."

Characteral and Military : At this critical juncture in the history of Muslim Spain, the Taifa rulers and their elite classes presented a sorry picture of the characteral and military deficiencies. They were luxury-loving, easy-going and wasteful. Their level of understanding of the realities of the situation confronting them was far more limited than that of the Umayyad Amirs/Khalifas before them. They constantly quarrelled with each other. But when defeated by the stronger ones among them, they did not join with other Taifa rulers to from a larger union. Instead they sought the help and protection of the Christian kings of Leon-Castile, who imposed tributes upon them and then conquered or threatened to conquer them with the money provided by their victims themselves. Though patrons of poets and musicians, and some of them even poets themselves of no mean order, but in view of the life-and-death struggle which the Taifa rulers had to wage with the northern Christians, their love of poetry was really a very good example of escapism and of their effete character,—a way of self-delusion of a degenerate class.

In contrast their Christian enemies were a hardy people. Culturally crude and simple, they and their soldiers were filled with the zeal and fanaticism of their revived faith and with the righteousness of their cause. They were resolved to avenge centuries of Muslim domination, for which the internal divisions and quarrels of the petty Taifa kings presented them with a very good opportunity. Egged on by the popes of Rome and the monks of Cluny and supported by their co-religionists of feudal Europe, the Christian kings, such as Alfonso VI, the king of Leon and Castile, took full advantage of the inernecine warfare of the Taifa kings and kinglets.

Militarily also, the petty Taifa rulers were no match to the northern Christians. Not only they were deficient in men, money and materials of war, these petty tyrants were also lacking in military capabilities and tactics. As opposed to them, the Christian kings possessed better and more loyal troops, which consisted of greater and lesser nobility as well as the freemen of the towns. While the Taifa kings depended on foreign mercenary troops, the Christian nobles and their vassals were bound to their liege-lords by ties of personal fealty and homage. The Christian kings could, therefore, depend upon dedicated and reliable armies. The heavy cavalry of the feudal warriors provided the Christian kings with a force which could run down the enemy troops and could thus always decide the outcome of the battle in their favour. The military superiority of the Christians lasted till the light cavalry of al-Murabits under Yusuf ibn Tashufin came on the scene.

Christians on the Move:

Ideology of Reconquista : Three elements constituted the ideology of Reconquista : New Christianity, Gothic irredentism, and Christian revanchism. The Spanish Christians had since long claimed to be the descendants of the Visigothic Germans, as did for example the three hundred Christians who had fled with pelayo into the mountains of Asturias. The Asturians and afterwards, other northern Christians dreamed of recovering the lands lost to the Muslims, whom they regarded as foreign intruders and infidels. These sentiments were, for example, expressed by the *Cronica Albeldense;* written in the ninth century, "They (i.e. the Muslims) took the kingdom of the Goths, and they still hold on firmly to part of it. The Christians are at war with them day and night, and struggle with them continuously, but they are unable to take Spain away from them completely, until divine providence ordain that they be expelled from there with (great) cruelty. Amen !" This early document expresses those sentiments of the Christians, which became the motive forces of the Reconquists, namely that Spain was once a Gothic kingdom which the Christians had lost, but they were struggling continuously to recover it and that the Spanish Muslims would be expelled from it with cruelty.

The dream of the Spanish Christian's of reconquering Muslim Spain would have never seen the light of the day but for two contributory factors : the impact of New Christianity and Europeanization of Christian Spain on the one hand, and the simultaneous degeneration of the Spanish Muslims and the disintegration of the Umayyad Caliphate. Indeed, the rise of the petty Taifa kingdom in Muslim Spain encouraged the Christian kings of the north to go on the offensive against them, armed as they were now with new influences from Western Europe. This confident attitude was first expressed by Fernado I, who had initiated the Reconquista, campaigns against Badajoz on the northern frontiers of Muslims Spain, and took Viseu and Larnego from the Toledo, seeking his help against the Huded rulers of Saragossa, he said :

> "We seek only our own lands which you
> conquered from us in times past at the
> beginning of your history. Now you have
> dwelt in them for the time allotted to you
> and we have become victorious over you as
> a result of your own wickedness. So go to
> your own side of the straits (of Gibraltar)
> and leave our lands to us, for no good will
> come to you from dwelling here with us from
> today. For we shall not hold back from you
> until God decides between us.

A decade later, the same Reconquista expectations were expressed by Count Sisnando Davidis, a Mozara, who was born in the Umayyad Seville and then went to the kingdom of Leon Castile. Alfanso VI sent him as his envoy to Abdullah, the King of Granada to demand tribute from him. Justifying the demand he said to him:

> "Originally al-Andalus belonged to the Tumis
> (Christians) until the Arabs conquered it from
> them and placed them in the most terrible
> places, Galacia. But now they have power
> and they want to redress the outrages done
> to them. There is no other way to do this but
> to weaken your position over a long period
> of time, until when you have no money and
> no men left, we shall take it without any
> expense or effort."

In short, the Reconquista did not aim at mere subjugation and domination over the Spanish Muslims: instead, it aimed at a demographical transformation of the conquered lands by exterminating the Muslim population and expelling the survivors from the Iberian Peninsula altogether. As such it was quite different from the Muslim conquest of Spain more than three centuries earlier: during these long centuries, not a single Christian was killed or driven out his home or hearth for reasons of religion or race, even though the Christian kings had driven out his home or hearth for reasons of religion or race, even though the Christian kings had driven out large Muslim populations from the newly-conquered lands under their policy of repopulation.

What was the reaction of the Muslims of Taifa Spain to the Christian threats? This question would explain the real cause of the Muslim defeat, viz., the decadence and degeneration of the Taifa Muslims. For the next fifty years after the fall of the Umayyad Caliphate, the Christians would advance and capture large chunks of Muslim Spain, while their rulers would openly proclaim their irredentist claims to the whole Peninsula, while the Muslim rulers and intellectuals would make no efforts to assert their claims on it or to justify their presence in it. Passivity of thought and action was their only response to Christian challenge. The attitude of the Muslim rulers was to appease the Christian aggressors by readily paying tributes and to accommodate themselves to the Christian conquest of large chunks of their territories. This was, perhaps, a natural reaction on the part of the luxury-loving rulers. But what about the intellectuals, including the renowned philosophers, scholars, writers, theologians and faqihs of Muslim Spain? They too failed to explain the reason of Muslim presence in Spain and to find out the ways to defend it. Instead, when the Christians would threaten to conquer the whole Peninsula and thus threaten the Muslim rulers and ruled alike with utter destruction, their only response should be to look towards the African al-Murabits to help them, but they would never rouse their own people to defend themselves.

Kings' Methods of Reconquest : No sooner did the Umayyad Caliphate of Cordova fell than the Christian kings launched their offensive against the petty Taifa kings, who had divided the Caliphate among them. The five odd Christian kings, however, did not conquer them in a single leap forward; instead, they did so gradually in course of several decades, lasting from about 1055 till 1085. During this period, however, they perfected their policies of reconquesta with the malacious thoroughness which characterise the policies of modern imperialists, of whom the Spanish reconquistadores were, indeed, forerunners and preceptors, as for example the subsidiary system of the British Imperialists in Mughal India. We may analyse their methods as follows:

1.   The basic weakness of Taifa Spain was its political fragmentation and their reluctance or inability to unite against their oncoming Christian enemies. Indeed, the Christians were secure in their knowledge that they

could attack one or the other Taifa king with impunity, for he had little or no resources to resist them and no other Taifa ruler would help him. And yet these weak rulers were rich enough—indeed, far richer than their Christian enemies—to pay them tributes (parias in Spanish), whose amount was increased each time the Christian tribute collectors came to demand it. The petty ruler paid the tribute, at first, from his own treasury, which he had filled with taxes and imposts on his subjects or from what he had looted from other Taifa rulers. When the treasury was exhausted, he imposed more taxes on his defenseless subjects and thus alienated them. The result was disaffection and revolt against him. This "softening" of a Taifa kingdom was the moment when the Christian king would invade and conquer it.

2.   With the tributes thus collected, the Christian kings equipped their armies with more and better sinews of war in order to invade and conquer the Taifa kingdoms one by one, that is, hunt them like sitting ducks,—and very fat ducks at that.

Once a territory or a kingdom was conquered, then began the period of consolidation, which the Christians called the policy of repopulation. It meant that, first, the Muslim population was killed or driven out of their lands and ancestral homes, which were then repopulated with Christian settlers. In the beginning, these settlers were the hungry but warlike mountaineers from the barren mountains of the north, but later came the Mozarabs or Christians from the Muslim South, who were induced to come and settle in the newly conquered lands. Later on, especially during the second and third rounds of reconquista, came still more ferocious Christian settlers, such as the feudal magnates and knights (called caballeros in Spanish), Christian fighting bishops priests, and monks, (called *milites Christi* or the soldiers of Christ) and the villagers and townsmen, merchants and traders, etc. In fact, the reconquista became a collective adventure every Christian, whether a king or a mendicant, Clergy or layman, rich or poor, high or low, was out to have his, and even her, share, big or small, in the conquered Muslim lands and cities.

Rising colonialist of the Christians : But reconquista was not the end of the story : it was the beginning of a new one. Eventually, at the end of the third round of reconquista, it carried them beyond the confines of the Iberian Peninsula. It was really the Spain Christian's drive to the south with a vengeance. As a matter of fact, the reconquista marked an important step "in the development of both a Spanish and a European mind. The Spanish kingdoms, constantly preoccupied with the need to occupy and colonise new territories, had avoided that static society traditionally associated with the growth of European feudalism, and the settlement of the Peninsula was already, a progressive undertaking which was to prepare communities for the future expansion overseas. Henceforth Castilians looked forward not merely to the acquisition of land but to the domination of alien states, and the granting of expectancies became a special feature of Spanish life. By the following century the Christian kingdoms were regulating by treaty not only their own future frontiers within the peninsula, but also their claims to zones of influence in Africa, thus anticipating the system by which the New World was to be divided between Spain and Portugal.

Christian Kingdoms : Paradoxical though it may appear, Christian Spain was also in a Taifa like situation. During the tenth century, when al Mansur's armies had conquered the whole of the Peninsula, there were nearly a dozen big and small Christian kingdoms. However, in the early decades of the eleventh century, their number was reduced to half a dozen, thanks to the conquest of the Catalan counties by the rising power of Aragon and Barcelona. These kingdoms were, from west to east, Galacia, Leon, Castile, Navarre, Aragon and Barcelona or Catalonia. But the events of the Reconquista during the eleventh and later centuries made three of them more important and powerful, viz Galacia, which sprang out of Leon and became modern Portugal during the Second round of Reconquista, and Castile and Aragon. During the first and second rounds of Reconquista, both Castile and Aragon, populated with more adventurous people, divided the Muslim Spain into their respective spheres of influence and conquest, but, after the third and last round, they merged, matrimonially, into the united kingdom of modern Spain. This was, in a nutshell, the evolution of modern Portugal and Spain.

First Round of Reconquista : Alfonso V (999-1082), the king of Leon, was the first Christian king to advance upon the Taifa kingdoms of Toledo and Badajoz on the Central and Western Marches of Muslim Spain. He pushed the borders of his kingdom from the river Douro southwards. He was the first Christian king to assume the title of emperor, perhaps to indicate his importance among rival Christian kings or because of his designs against the Muslims. When he died in 1028, his kingdom of Leon was incorporated by Sanchoel Mayor—"the Great" (1000-1035) into his kingdom of Navarre. Navarre was a tributary kingdom under al-Mansur. But with his death, when Sanchoel Mayor also came to the throne, Navarre became a leading state in Christian Spain. Sancho brought Aragon under his authority and, by marriage, got control of Castile also. His family was already the rulers of the small Catalan countries of

Sobrarbe and Ribagorza, while Roman Berenguer I (1018-1035) the count of Barcelona, had recognised him as his suzerain. Moreover, Sancho el Mayor was the first Christian king to open Spain to European influences, for which reason the modern Spanish historian, Menendez Pidal, calls him the first "Europeanizer." On his death, however, he divided his large kingdom among his three sons: Garda, his eldest son, got Navarre; his favourite son, Fernando I (1035-65) got Castile, while his illegitimate son, Ramiro, got Aragon.

Fernando I : With Fernándo I, the king of Castile, the reconquista began in right earnest. But first he turned against Bermudo III, the king of Leon, the son of Alfonso V. He was childless. Fernando attacked and killed him in 1037 and took over his kingdom, thus uniting Leon and Castile. Next, he attacked his brother Garcia, the king of Navarre. He too was defeated and killed in a war in 1054 and his kingdom incorporated into Fernando's kingdom. Fernando then turned upon the little Muslim kingdoms with great religious zeal. In 1055, he seized Lamego and Viseu in the western parts of the Peninsula. As yet he was not ready to launch full scale invasion of other Muslim Taifa kingdoms. Instead, he and other Christian kings were at present more interested in compelling the Muslim kings to pay tributes and thus to fill their treasuries with Muslim gold in preparation for the day when conquest and colonization would be more feasible.

While Fernando was busy in the west of the Peninsula, Roman Berenguer I, count of Barcelona, was active in the east. Between their territories lay the Taifa kingdom of Saragossa and Lerida, then ruled by al Muqtadir of Beni Hud. His Christian neighbours were preparing to attack him. Roman Berenguer had his eyes on Lerida, the eastern part of his kingdom, while Ramiro I of Aragon threatened Saragossa itself. In his predicament, al Muqtadir offered tribute to Fernando I, whose troops then defeated the Aragonese in 1063. Al Mutazid, the Amir of Seville, anticipating Christian attack, also offered tribute to Fernando, who then demanded the Amir to send him the body of St. Isidore to be reburied in his capital, Leon, in a church built for this purpose. It was, apparently, an act of Christian piety. But, really, it was a political ploy to win the favour of the Christians, among whom hagiolatry was then rampant and thus to arouse their fanatical zeal against the Muslims. Anyhow, the Christian chroniclers called him *rex magnus*, the great king. Next year, in 1064, Fernando captured Coimbra from the Muslims. It was the first important city to fall to the Christians. As usual, they drove out the Muslims from the city and the region around it in order to repopulate them with the Christians. Fernando I died in 1065. Before his death, however, he divided his kingdom among his sons and daughters : Sancho II (1065-72) received the kingdom of Castile and the tribute of the Muslim king of Saragossa; his second son and his favourite, Alfonso VI (1065-1109) became the king of Leon and got the tribute of the Muslim ruler of Toledo; his third son, Garcia (1065-72) got the kingdom of Galacia as far south as Coimbra and the tribute of Badajoz while his daughters, Urraca and Elvira, got the monasteries of Zamora and Toro respectively.

Massacre of the Muslims of Barbastro : Crusade or the war of the cross was launched against Muslim Spain in 1064, long before the Crusades in the East began. It was led by the French knights, namely Guilaume of Montreuil, Robert Crespin of Normandy, Duke William VIII of Aquitaine and Count Aremengol III of Urgel. It was commanded by Sancho I, the King of Aragon and included monks of Cluny. They were all in the service of Pope Alexander II (1061-73), who had granted them plenary indulgence, i.e. complete remission of sins, which became the usual practice in all crusades. The Pope said, "By the authority of the Holy Apostles, Peter and Paul, we relieve them of penance and grant them remission of sins." Thus authorised to commit all barbarities, the crusading army crossed the Pyrenees and besieged the city of Barbastro on the river Ebro on the borders of the kingdom of Saragossa. Yusuf ibn Sulaiman ibn Hud, who was then the king of Saragossa, instead of hastening to the relief of the city, left its inhabitants to defend themselves as best as they could. The siege lasted for four months. In August, 1064, the garrison surrendered on the condition that their lives should be spared. But when they came out of the fortress, they were all massacred. Then came the turn of the defenceless citizens of Barbastro. They too had obtained an amnesty. But when they were leaving the city, the commander of the Christian horde ordered his troops to cut them down. The carnage ensued then and did not end till six thousand Muslims were massacred. After this, the Christians ravaged the whole city. Al-Maqqari writes, "The spoil made by the Christians on this occasion, whether in money, furniture or apparel, exceeds all computation; since we are assured that the share of one of their chiefs only, who was the general of the cavalry (the Knights of St. John), amounted to about fifteen hundred young maidens, besides five hundred loads of merchandise, dresses, ornaments and every description of property, the whole of which he carried to his stronghold." The number of Muslims who perished or were made captives was between fifty thousand to one hundred thousand persons.

Christian custom : Ibn Hayyan, quoted by al-Maqqari, writes, "It was an invariable custom with the Christians, whenever they took a town by force of arms, to ravish the daughters in the presence of their fathers, and women before the eyes of their husbands and families. But on the taking, of Berbastro the excesses of this kind committed by them pass all belief; the Muslims had never before experienced anything like it. In short, such were the crimes and excesses committed by the Christians on this occasion, that there is no pen eloquent enough to describe them."

Alfonso VI : Western historians have criticised the frequent partitions of Christian kingdoms by their kings among their sons, as did Sancho el Mayor and Fernando I. But these partitions orientated Castile and Aragon towards the Muslim South by dividing it into two spheres of influence, Castile taking the western half of Taifa Spain as its sphere of influence and conquest, while Aragon took the eastern half as its sphere of advance and conquest. This orientation was mainly due to the fratricidal wars which broke out among the brothers after the death of Sancho el Mayor and again after the death of Fernando I. As we have said above, Sancho II became the new King of Castile. He first marched upon Saragossa to extort its tribute. He then challenged his brother, Alfonso VI of Leon over the title of 'emperor'. He defeated Alfonso in a battle in 1068. Thereupon, Alfonso attacked his younger brother, Garcia, the king of Galacia, in order to snatch from his share of *parias* or tribute of Badajoz. Garcia seemed to have resisted him successfully. Alfonso, then joined with Sancho II and the two drove Garcia from Galacia in 1071. But a year later, they fell out and Alfonso was again defeated by Sancho in a battle at Golpejara. He fled to Toledo and took refuge with Al-Mamun, king of Toledo and his tributary.

Alfonso stayed in Toledo for about a year, from January, 1072 to the end of the year. During this time he developed close friendly relations with al-Mamun, the Dhul Nunid monarch. Though he came as a refugee, but became a spy, closely observing the situation in the Nulnid capital, which would later enable him to capture it. One day, while he was dozing in a palace-garden, he overheard two courtiers of al-Mamun conversing about how easily the city could be captured. The details of the conversation remained in his mind and stood him in good stead when, a decade later, he laid siege to the capital.

His exile was soon brought to an end by his sister Urraca, who seemed to have for him more than sisterly love. She revolted at Zamora against her brother, Sancho, her suzerain lord, who besieged the town. During the siege, Sancho was assassinated by a man, who was reputed to be an agent of Alfonso. As Sancho had no child, Alfonso was summoned from Toledo to be proclaimed as the King of both Castile and Leon. However, the Castilean nobles, suspecting Alfonso's complicity in the murder of his brother, compelled him to take an oath of purgation. The oath was administered by a Castilean knight, named Rodrigo Diaz, better known as El Cid. Relations between Alfonso and El Cid remained strained afterwards; Alfonso never forgave him for the humiliation of subjecting him to the oath. Soon afterwards, El Cid left Alfonso's service and became a free-lance adventurer, fighting his own wars against the Muslims, as we shall see later.

Alfonso VI and Pope Gregory VII : During Alfonso's long reign, the Europeanization of Christian Spain increased all the more. French knights came into it to seek fame and fortune in the wars against the Muslims; and the Cluniac priors and monks poured in to incite the Spanish Christian kings and nobles against the Muslims. With the active support of Alfonso's French queen, they made the King to substitute the old Mozarabic rite by that of the Roman-Church.

More significantly, the Popes of Rome become directly involved in the wars in Spain against the Muslims. They even laid claim to the sovereignty of Spain. As we have said above, a crusading army had invaded Muslim Spain and captured Barbastro in 1064, which had the sanction of Pope Alexander

II. His successor, Pope Gregory VII (1075-85), went a step further. He was a proponent of the universalist claims of the Roman Church over the Western Christendom. Like his predecessor, he believed that the papacy had a definite responsibility to conquer Muslim Spain. Soon after his accession to the papal throne in April, 1073, he addressed a letter to "all the princes of Europe wishing to proceed on a crusade to Spain", in which he claimed, "We believe that it is not unknown to you that the kingdom of Spain belonged from ancient times to St. Peter in full sovereignty (*proprii iuris*) and, though occupied for a long time by the pagans, since the law of justice has not been set aside it belongs even now to no mortal, but solely to the apostalic see". Another crusading army, under the command of French knight, de Roucy, was despatched into Spain, but it did nothing more than to plunder the Muslims. In June, 1077, Gregory VII again wrote to the "kings, counts and other princes of Spain", reminding them that "the kingdom of Spain was given by ancient constitutions to Blessed Peter and the Holy Roman Church in right and ownership". The ancient constitutions to which the Pope referred were really the forgery, known as Donation of Constantine, which he has now utilizing to assert the universalistic claims of the Roman Church. Anyhow, Alfonso VI, the most powerful of the Christian rulers of Spain, paid no heed to the papal claims, and the Pope did not press them. Instead, he recognised Alfonso as the Christian crusader in Spain.

At first, Alfonso VI imposed tributes upon the Taifa, Kings of Toledo, Badajoz and Saragossa, constantly increasing his demand. Then he set one Taifa, king against another, thus weakening them both financially and militarily. Although they realised his ulterior motives, they were too weak to resist his demands. Yet they were too complacent and shortsighted not to unite together to face his challenge. Had they done so, they would have met his challenge successfully, averted their doom and learnt so much from the emergent Europe that they would have changed the course of Spanish, even European, history. History is not an immutable law of nature, but what people make of it by facing the challenges of their times. To return to Alfonso VI, his strategy towards the Taifa kings was clear from what his envoy, Count Sisnando Davidis, told Abdullah, the King of Granada, as he mentioned in his Memoirs: "Al-Andalus belong to the Christians from the beginning until they were conquered by the Arabs. Now they want to recover it. To this end, it is necessary to weaken you and waste you away with time. When you no longer have money or soldiers, we will seize the country without the least effort."

The Fall of Toledo : Al-Mamun was the ruler of Toledo, who had given refuge to Alfonso VI, when he had fled from his brothers. Mamun was a patron of scholars and poets. He had made his kingdom prosperous. He had captured Valencia and Cordova. After his death in 1075, his grandson, al-Qadir (1075-85), succeeded him. He was unable to resist his neighbours, who took Valencia and Cordova from him. The people of Toledo revolted against him and he fled from the city in 1080. He took refuge with Alfonso and sought his help. In the meanwhile, the Toledans invited al-Mutawwakil, the Kings of Badajoz, to rule over them. Alfonso captured Coria, which was his important conquest beyond the river Tagus. He promised al-Qadir to restore to power but on the condition that he would deliver Toledo to him, while his armies would conquer Valencia for him. Accordingly, Alfonso besieged Toledo. Its citizens resisted the Castilians for four years. During the siege, al-Mutawwakil fled from the city and in 1084, the renegade Al-Qadir returned to it, with Alfonso's assistance. As the price of his restoration, al Qadir paid tribute to Alfonso VI and also delivered some castles around the city to him. The people of

Toledo, however, refused to accept the, renegade. He again appealed to Alfonso for help, who besieged the city once again in the middle of 1084. For nearly a year the citizens of Toledo resisted the Castiliants. But when no relief came from other Muslim kingdoms, they surrendered the city to Alfonso on the condition to retain the possession of the grand mosque. When the Christians took possession of the city, the first thing they did was to seize the grand mosque and convert it into a church on the instigation of Alfonso's French queen, Constance. Alfonso did not resist his queen's wishes. Toledo became the ecclesiastical capital of Christian Spain, as it was before the Muslim conquest. So far Alfonso VI was concerned, after the fall of Toledo, he assumed the title of *Emperator Todua Hispaniae* Emperor of All Spaniards, i.e. of Christians, Muslims and Jews. Before the fall of Toledo, he had also raided the Kingdom of Seville, after which Mutamid, the Amir of Seville, paid tribute to him regularly. On this occasion, Alfonso penetrated upto the coast of southern al Andalus without meeting any resistance from the Amir of Seville or from any other Taifa king.

Alfonso now renewed his demands for tribute from the remaining Taifa kings, treating them with increasing contempt. When the Muslim ruler of Albarracim sent him a rich present, Alfonso in return sent him a monkey. When an ambassador of al Mutamid of Seville waited upon him, he shouted at him "Why should I leave these puppets in power: They are all caliphs like the high sounding princes of the East; one calls himself Mutamid; the another Mutawwakil, another Mamun, another al Amin but no one of them is capable of unseathing his sword to defend of Castilian marauders into different of Taifa Spain, plundering and killing the Muslims at will. One such band established itself in a strong castle, called Aledo, between Lorca and Murcia, which became a permanent base of further Christian depradations.

Reactions : The fall of Toledo sent a wave of fear and fright throughout Muslim Spain. A new fear came over them of not only losing political power but of being driven out of the Peninsula altogether. For instance, Abdullah al Ziri of Granada wrote in his Memoirs:

"The fall of Toledo sent a great tremor through al Andalus and filled the inhabitants with fear and despair of continuing to live there."

Feelings of despair and despondency were now common in Muslim Spain. A poet, Abu Muhammad al Assal cried with bitterness :

Take to your horses, men of Andalusia.

To remain is pure folly.

Garments begin by fraying at the edges,

But our Spain has ripped down the centre.

The poet had, indeed, rightly hinted at the strategy of Alfonso VI. Like Tariq ibn Ziyad, though in a reverse order, Alfonso intended to rend Muslim Spain from the middle. Tariq first took the city of Cordova and then marched straight upon Toledo : Alfonso took Toledo first and then threatened to advance upon Cordova and Seville: afterwards, he hoped to mop up the Muslim remnants and thus to finish off Muslim Spain one and for all.

After first, the Taifa rulers were reluctant to seek the assistance of the Al Mumbits of North Africa. They feared their revivalist ardour, which threatened their luxurious way of life. But Alfonso's rising ambitions compelled them to change their attitudes. In 1081, when Toledo was first threatened by Alfonso, al Mutawwakil, the ruler of Badajoz, sent an envoy to Yusuf ibn Tashufin, the ruler of the Al Mumbits, for help,

However, on his part, Yusuf was reluctant to do so. He put off these requests on one excuse or another. The situation of the Taifa kings was, indeed, pitiable. They were sandwiched between Emperor Alfonso VI, virtually the master of the northern half of the peninsula and the revivalist Al Murabits across the Strait of Gibraltar. However, when in 1085, after the fall of Toledo, Alfonso demanded Mutamid to hand over Cordova to him, the latter over came his hesitation and decided to appeal to the Al Murabit ruler, Yusuf ibn Tashufin, for help. When his son, Rashid pointed out the danger of introducing the Al Murabits into Spain, Al Mutamid replied, "That is true; but I hate to be cursed by my posterity for delivering Andalusia to the infidels; and for my part, I would rather be a camel driver in Africa than a swineherd in Castile!

Al Mutamid was, however, reluctant to make a single handed appeal. He requested his two neighbours, Abdullah al Ziri of Granada and al Mutawwakil of Badajoz, to nominate their Qazis to be sent to Yusuf ibn Tashufin as their envoys. Four persons were chosen as envoys : they were Abu Ishaq ibn Mohana, Qazi of Badejoz, Abu Jafar Kolai, the Qazi of Granada, ibn Adham, the Qazi of Cordova and Abu Bakr ibn Zaidun, the vizier of Seville. Each envoy was to invite Yusuf bin Tashufin in his sovereign's name, to land in Spain with his army. One condition was imposed : Yusuf was to promise on oath that he would not seize any one of the Taifa kingdoms. When Yusuf asked Algeciras to be ceded to him, the Sevillean envoy hesitated to agree. The envoys then returned to their kingdoms without any firm promise of help. In the meantime, Yusuf asked his faqihs about his expedition to the Peninsula. They approved of his expedition against Alfonso and by a fatwa authorized take Algeciras for this purpose. Accordingly, Yusuf ibn Tashufin sailed for Spain with his troops. However, before hoarding ship he prayed devoutly to Allah : "O God, if this crossing will help

Islam, make it easy for me; if not, rouse the sea and force me to return." The wind was, however, favourable and Yusuf set foot on Spain on June 30, 1086.

When Yusuf and his troops reached Algeciras, Razi, the son of Mutaraid and governor of Algeciras, evacuated the town and retired to Ronda on the orders of his father. After fortifying the town, Yusuf stocked it with the munitions of war. He then marched towards Seville, where Mutamid received him with royal honours. Al-Murabit army camped outside Seville, where small contingents of Mutasim of Almeria and of the Berber rulers of Granada and Mala also joined his army. It then marched towards Badejoz, where it was joined by al-Mutawwakil and his troops. The Muslim army, now numbered about twenty thousand men. It then marched towards Toledo. But a few miles from Badejoz, it met Alfonso's army near a village, called Zallaqa (or Sagrajas, as the Christians called it).

Battle of Zallaqa : Alfonso was besieging Saragossa when he heard of Yusuf's landing on the Spanish coast. He raised the seige and at once marched against Yusuf. He collected a large army, numbering forty thousand, in which many French knights had also joined. It marched towards Toledo and from there towards Badajoz. It met the Muslim force near Zallaqa. For three days the two armies camped within four kilometres of each other on opposite banks of a small tributary of the Guadiana, drinking, as the chroniclers report, water from the same stream. Yusuf wrote Alfonso a letter, inviting him to become a Muslim, or pay tribute, or he would make war on him. Alfonso replied that it was the Muslims who paid tribute to him, and that he had a larger army and would punish him for his presumptuous conduct. Yusuf wrote his reply on the back of Alfonso's letter: "What will happen you will see" and returned the letter to him.

To mislead him, Alfonso wrote to Yusuf that he would

begin fighting on Saturday, being a day which was sacred neither
to the Christians nor to the Muslims. But Mutamid saw through
his trick and told Yusuf that he would begin fighting on Friday,
the Muslim day of prayers. It proved to be true. On that day,
Alfonso ordered his troops to begin fighting. They put the
Muslim vanguard, consisting of the Andalusians, into disarray.
But Mutamid's Sevillan troops stood fast. When Yusuf saw his
vanguard under attack, he sent his general, Sair ibn Abu Bakr,
to their aid, while with his main army, he made a detour and
fell upon Alfonso's army from the rear. Though Lie Christians
fought courageously, they were confronted with Yusuf's new
tactic of compact and well-ordered infantry, supported by lines
of Turkish archers and maneuvering to the command of
thundrous rolls of massed drummers. By nightfall, victory lay
with the Muslims. Most of the Christian soldiers and knights
were killed or wounded. While others fled from the battlefield.
Even Alfonso, who was wounded in the thigh by a negro's
dagger, could save himself with difficulty with the support of
his five hundred elite horsemen. Yusuf intended to pursue the
fleeing Christians and to take Toledo. But, on receiving the
news of the death of his eldest son and their apparent, he returned
to Africa, leaving three thousand of his troops under the
Command of Mutamid of Seville.

    With the defeat of Alfonso VI at Zallaqa ended the first
round of the Reconquista. Yusuf ibn Tashufin, like Julius Caesar,
could say: "I came, I saw, I conquered". But his task was
half-done. Four years later, he was to come to Spain once again,
but under changed circumstances.

CHAPTER 31

MURABITUN
(1091–1146 A.D.)

After Hajib al-Mansoor the hold of Muslim Spain had become so loose that the Berbers established their sway over the whole of north-western Africa right from Algeria to the Niger or the Senigal river. They had their spiritual leader called Murabit (the holy) and hence they were called Murabitun.

A branch of the Sinhaja Berber tribe used to wear "Lashm" veil to protect their faces against the burning sands of the Sahara. They were therefore called Mulasemoon "The veil wearers".

Arabic word Al-Mumbit stands for the Spanish word Al-Moravid denoting a monk living in Ribat, a fortified convent. A large number of the Mulmethun had fought with General Musa-bin-Nusair both in Africa, and Spain and were very popular.

It is said that the Mumbitun migrated to Al-Maghrib, North Africa from Yemen during the days of Hazrat Abu Bakr the first Khalifa and thus belonged to the Ashab-Suffa who were monk soldiers like these.

It was at the instance of Yahya-bin-Ibrahim, a Jaddala chief of the Sinhaja tribe that Abu Imam-al-Fasi, a Malikie Faqih, preached Islam in the tribe.

Abdullah bin Yasin al-Jazuli of Nafis, near Morocco constructed a ribat, a fortified convent on one of the Niger or Senegal islands. His chief disciples, were Yahya-bin-Umar and Abu Bakr-bin-Umar of Lanthuna tribe. Abdullah-bin-Yasin became the religio-political leader. All the Berber tribes including the Lanthuna, and Masmudah, acknowledged his sway.

His chief disciple Yahya-bin-Umar advanced upto the Wadi-e-Dara and captured Sijilmash. He penetrated to the very interior region of the Sahara which could not be crossed by Musa-bin-Nusair even. He died in 1059 A.D. fighting against the Barghwata Berbers.

Yahya's brother Abu Bakr defeated the Burghwata, and struck coins in his name after annexing the former Idrisid kingdom. Thus the Almoravid state with its capital at Mamqash (Marrakesh) was founded in 1062. Abu Bakr, after entrusting his cousin Yusuf-bin-Tashufin went to the desert for unifying the Murabitun. He was however deprived of his kingdom by Yusuf and had to die in exile (1087 A.D.)

CHAPTER 32

YUSUF-BIN-TASHUFIN

Yusuf ibn Tashufin extended the Almoravid rule over the fertile western region of the Maghrib. In 1062, he founded the city of Marrakesh, after which the western North Africa came to be known as Morocco. He then marched to the north and conquered Ceuta, Algiers and other towns near the Mediterranean by the year 1082, and subdued all the Berber tribes there, including the Lamtuna and the Masmuda. He thus transformed the Almoravid kingdom into an empire. He then planned to march towards Qayrowan and to conquer Ifriqiya. But he was diverted from this plan by the events in Muslim Spain. As we have said in the previous chapter, in 1086, he was invited by Mutamid, the Amir of Seville, al-Mutawwakil, the king of Badajoz and other Taifa kings of Muslim Spain, to defend them against the all-conquering Christian king of Leon-Castile, Alfonso VI. Not only Yusuf defeated him in the battle of Zallaqa, but he also became acquainted with the military weakness of the Taifa kings, while he was charmed by the riches and fertility of Al-Andalus. However, after the victory at Zallaqa. Yusuf returned to Marrakesh, as he had promised the Taifa kings to do so leaving a small contingent of three thousand Almoravid troops in the command of Mutamid, the ruler of Seville. In the meantime, Alfonso VI, baulked in western Spain, let loose his war-hounds on the Muslims in eastern Spain.

El Cid and Valencia : As we have said above, Rodrigo Diaz de Bivar, commonly known as El Cid, was in the service of the King of Castile. But relations between him and Alfonso VI became strained soon after his accession to power, and El Cid left his service. At first, he became a free-lance adventurer. He sought service with the Banu Hud of Saragossa, whose kingdom was threatened by its three Christian neighbours, Kings of Navarre, and Aragon and the Count of Barcelona. So effete was the Muslim ruler that he sought the help of a Christian warrior like El Cid to defend himself. Anyhow, El Cid defeated the Christian force in 1082. In January, 1087, Alfonso VI, who had suffered the defeat at Zallaqa, met El Cid at Toledo and he was restored to royal favour. Alfonso then sent him to Valencia, in the eastern region of Muslim Spain to prevent its conquest by the Almoravids. Valencia had been conquered by the Christians and handed over to the renegade al-Qadir in lieu of Toledo, which he had surrendered to Alfonso in 1085. Al-Qadir was driven out of Valencia by al-Mustain and Count Berenguer of Barcelona. Alfonso V sent El Cid not only to re-capture Valencia, but also all other cities, towns and territories in eastern Spain. Soon Valencia and other cities, and towns were captured by the Christians.

At the same time, Alfonso sent another of his warriors, named Garcia Jimenez, to conquer Muslim towns in the south. This Christian force occupied the stronghold of Aledo, from where it threatened Murcia, Almeria and other important Muslim cities, which Mutamid of Seville had claimed as his own. Thus, Alfonso, though defeated in the west, threatened to conquer eastern regions of Muslim Spain. Again the eyes of the Taifa kings turned towards Yusuf ibn Tashufin to intervene on their behalf. A deputation from the Kings of Seville, Murcia, and others waited upon Yusuf at Marrakesh and requested him to save the Spanish Muslims from destruction at the hands of the Christians. Yusuf consented and ordered his troops to cross the Strait second time.

Siege of Alego : In June, 1090 Yusuf ibn Tashufin landed at Algeciras once again and marched with his troops towards the Christian-held Aledo. He summoned the Taifa rulers to join him with their troops in a war against the Christians. Mutamid of Seville, Abdullah of Granada, his brother, Temim of Malaga, Ibn Rashik of Murcia, Mutasim of Almeria and other princes responded to his summons. Muslims then laid siege to Aledo, which was defended by about thirteen thousand Castilians. The fortress was built on a hill top and was well-fortified. Although the Muslims had siege weapons, they could not capture it for four months. The reason was that the Taifa kings were more interested in intriguing against each other than in fighting the Christians, and each of them expected Yusuf ibn Tashufin to help him against his enemy. Mutasim of Almeria hated Mutamid of Seville. But he concealed his feelings from him. One day, while the two were having a friendly tete-a-tete, Mutasim expressed his uneasiness over the long stay of Yusuf in Spain. To this Mutamid replied boastfully, "Nodoubt, this man is making a long stay in our country, but what is this despicable prince and his troops. In their own country, they are half-starved beggars: we invited them into our country so that they may have their fill. But whenever I like. I need lift my little finger and they would all be sent back, from where they have come". These words were enough to provoke a most patient man. When, Mutaism reported them to Yusuf, he flow into violent rage and decided to carry out the plan which-he was already prompted to do so. Mutasim had really dug a grave not only for Mutamid but also for himself and all other Taifa princelings.

The Taifa rulers accused one another before Yusuf, Mutasim, the ruler of Almeria, tried to ruin the ruler of Seville while the latter endeavoured to over throw Ibn Rashik, the ruler of Murcia told Yusuf that Ibn Rashik had been an ally of Alfonso and was even then in league with the Christian Emperor. Moreover, he claimed that Murcia was in his possession and that Ibn Rashik was a traitor who had revolted against him. He demanded that Murcia should therefore be delivered to him. Yusuf appointed a committee of Faqihs to decide the claims of the two. They decided in favour of Mutamid. Ibn Rashik was arrested and handed over to Mutamid, but he was forbidden to put him to death. Aggrieved at the decision, the Murcian contingent left the Muslim camp along with the siege engines which they had supplied Yusuf. At this juncture news came that Alfonso was marching towards Aledo with a large army. On his part, Yusuf had already come to the conclusion that the luxury loving Taifa kings would not be able to resist Christian advance, but felt that time was not suitable to put an end to them. Accordingly, he raised the siege and returned to Africa. When Alfonso relieved Aledo, he found the condition of the defenders so deplorable that he considered it not worth holding. He ordered its fortifications to be razed to the ground and then returned to Toledo. Apparently, Alfonso had won. But the faqihs painted Alfonso's retreat as a victory for Yusuf. In fact, Yusuf had withdrawn to deliver a finishing stroke to Taifa Spain.

Revolutionary situation : Yusuf ibn Tashufin was an Islamic revolutionary and conditions in Taifa Spain provided him with a situation in which he could bring about a revolution by a kind of class war. The country was divided into three classes, viz: the effete aristocratic class of the Taifa rulers, their courtiers, poets and other hangers-on; the Muslim Ulema class, consisting of the faqihs, qazis and theologians; and thirdly, the common people. The degenerate Taifa rulers, addicted to wine and other luxuries, had filled their treasuries with many taxes, imposts and levies, imposed on their helpless subjects and yet they could not defend their little kingdoms against Christian attacks and depredations. Instead, they paid huge tributes to the Christian kings, which ranged in amount between ten to thirty thousand dinars in gold, collected as taxes from the common people. The Ulema class objected to these taxes, because they were not sanctioned by Islam. But they were too weak to oppose their Taifa masters. So the common people suffered grievously at the hands of these petty tyrants, while the faqihs and qazis could not change their ways. The rise of the Murabitun, however, offered them an opportunity to put an end to the oppressive rule of the Taifa kings. Throughout Muslim Spain the faqihs incited hostility against the Taifa kings, charging them with immorality and subservience to the Christians. They rightly asked whether such impious libertines and corrupters of public morals should have the right to rule over the Muslim community. A poet, al-Sumaisir, reproaching these kings, declared:

> *To revolt against you is a duty,*
>
> *For you make common cause with the Christians.*
>
> *To withdraw from your allegiance is no crime,*
>
> *For you yourselves have withdrawn your allegiance to the Prophet.*

The siege of Aledo provided the faqihs an opportunity to directly approach Yusuf. One of them was Abu Jafar Kolai'i the Qazi of Granada. In the Muslim camp around Aledo, his tent was next to that of Yusuf, whom the Qazi met frequently, and constantly impressed upon him to do away with all the Taifa kings, and incorporate Muslim Spain into his Berber Empire. On his part Yusuf had also come to the same conclusion, due to the experience he had of them during the siege of Aledo. As we have said above, the Almoravid fundamentalists had condemned all ways of life which were un-Islamic. They had further declared the Muslim rulers could collect only five kinds of taxes as sanctioned by Islam. During the siege of Aledo, the faqihs impressed upon Yusuf that it was his duty to remove all Taifa rulers for their un-Islamic ways and to bring Muslim Spain within his dominions. But Yusuf desisted from acting on the faqih's advise, for he had promised the Taifa kings that he would not deprive anyone of them of his kingdom. He had, however, lost all hope in the worthless Taifa rulers and decided to withdraw from Spain. Accordingly, he returned to Morocco and waited for an opportunity to intervene and bring about the revolution on which he had now set his heart.

Almoravid Revolution : During the siege of Aledo, the Taifa rulers resented the secret meetings of Abu Jafar Kolai'i with Yusuf ibn Tashufin. After his departure, the Qazi was arrested and thrown into prison. But the people of Granada, including the mother of the Granadan king, interceded on behalf of the Qazi, who was therefore set free. He fled to Cordova, where he joined other fuqaha. They issued a fatwa, denouncing the Taifa princes in general and things of Granada and Malaga in particular, who had forfeited the right to rule due to their misdeeds and ill-treatment of Qazi Abu Jafar Kolai'i. Soon after, they issued another fatwa, in which they called upon Yusuf ibn Tashufin to order the Taifa princes to adhere to the Shariat and to demand no other taxes than those prescribed by the Quran. Armed with the two fatwas, Yusuf commanded the prince to abolish the statute of forced labour and imposts which they had levied upon their subjects. In the meanwhile, the Taifa princes got suspicious of Yusuf and once again they began to kotow to Alfonso VI, the inveterate enemy of Muslim Spain. This filled Yusuf's cup of patience. He at long last decided to inflict a condign punishment upon them.

On March 5, 1090 Yusuf ibn Tashufin crossed the Strait and landed in Spain for the third time, in order to wage war against Alfonso. He marched on Toledo, the capital of Alfonso, and laid siege to it. Though he had summoned the Taifa princes to join him, none of them did so. Yusuf was so much incensed by their pusillanimous behaviour that he decided to remove them from power for ever. He raised the siege of Toledo and marched against Abdullah of Granada. He was easily overpowered and sent in chains to Aghmat in Morocco. His brother, Temim of Malaga, was similarly disposed of. Yusuf then returned to Africa, leaving his general, Sair ibn Abu Bakr, to deal final blows to the remaining Taifa princes. Sair requested as to how he should treat them. Yusuf said: "Order them to accompany you to the enemy's country: if they obey you, well and good; if they refuse, attack them one after the other, lay siege to their cities, and destroy them without mercy. You shall first attack those princes whose kingdoms border on the enemy's frontier, and you shall not attack al-Mutamid until you have reduced the rest of Muslim Spain. To every town or city which may thus fall into your hands, you will appoint a governor from among the officers of your army."

In fact, the two fatwas had already had their effect on the common people. They were alienated from their masters. Therefore, wherever Sair led his troops, the people were ready to welcome them against their own rulers. First, the Almoravid general marched against Cordova and captured it. He next laid siege to Seville. Although Mutamid resisted the Almoravid besiegers stoutly, but his own people were secretly in league with them in September, 1091, he himself surrendered his city to Sair. He too was arrested and transported to Aghmat, where he died a few year after in captivity. Then, by the end of 1091, several smaller towns passed into Sair's such as Murcia Almeria, Ronda, etc. Thus southern Spain was incorporated into the Almoravid Empire. In 1094, Badajoz, the biggest Taifa state in the west was captured, where Sair put al Mutawakkil, its ruler and his two sons to death. Next came the turn of Valencia. El Cid, the Castilian lord of Valencia, had died in 1099 but his inapt widow, Jimena, continued to hold the city against his enemies. When besieged by the Almoravid troops, she appealed to Alfonso for help. But he was much afraid of the Almoravids and did not render her any aid. Valencia was then capture in 1102. The Almoravid general, however, failed to take Saragossa in the north, east of Muslim Spain, ruled By Bani Hud. The last Taifa kingdom La Sahla, ruled by Bani Razin, also submitted to Yusuf.

Death : Yusuf ibn Tashufin died in September, 1106, at the age of 100. He had styled himself as *Ameer al Muslameen*. Before his death he had designated his son, Ali ibn Yusuf, as his successor. Before his end approached, he summoned Ali and recommended three things to him : he was not to disturb the Berber tribe, inhabiting the gorges of the Atlas or the deserts of Morocco, such as Masmudah and others; he was to conclude peace with Ibn Hud, the Sultan of Saragossa, so that he might carry on war against the Christians; and lastly, he was to fix his court at Seville, not Cordova. Yusuf had, however, bequeathed his son a vast empire extending from the borders of Sudan right across North Africa to Spain.

Ali, 1106-1143 : Ali ibn Yusuf was the paragon of Almoravid fundamentalism. Like his father, he was extremely devout, and like him also, he held the faqihs in great honour. He consulted them on all occasions and in all matters and did nothing without their approval. He spent his days in prayer and fasting. But, unlike his father, Ali was not a capable military leader. However, his deficiency was compensated by his brother, Temim ibn Yusuf. He and the old general, Sair ibn Abu Bakr, continued to win victories in Muslim Spain.

His conquests : During the early period of Ali's long

reign, there were several military successes. In 1110, Temim, the brother of Ali, forced Imad al-Daula, the ruler of Saragossa, to surrender his kingdom to Ali. He took refuge in Ruenda, where he died in 1130. Temim also captured large territory of Castile, where civil war raged between the successors of Alfonso VI, who had died in 1109. In the western region of the Peninsula, the old Murabit general, Sair ibn Abu Bakr, continued his victorious advance and captured Lisbon, Santarem and Oporto.

Administration : Nothing illustrates the fundamentalist ideology of the Almoravids more than their administrative system. The Maliki faqihs, who had welcomed their rise to power, had full control over it. They had become the dominant class in the State and had dislodged the former Ambo-Andalusian aristocracy from their position of power and riches. But, unlike the aristocracy, the Maliki jurists and theologians had their roots among the common people and enjoyed their favour and support. This was, indeed, the secret of the Almoravid power. On the contrary, the poets, scholars and philosophers had hard times under the new dispensation. They were the hangers-on of the luxury loving Taifa kings and princelings, who, with all their faults, were champions of freedom of thought and patrons of science, poetry and philosophy. The revivalist Almoravids, supported by the Maliki faqihs, condemned all this. The poets had but few patrons. Though the faqihs had now the riches, but unlike the Taifa princes, they were too parsimonious to shower dirhams and dinars on the panegyrics of the poets and sychophants, who were, therefore, reduced to poverty. Moreover, philosophy was an anathema to the Almoravids and their faqihs. Anyone found indulging in the study of this forbidden science was hounded like a common criminal. However, in their abhorrence of philosophy, the Maliki faqihs went to an, unjustifiable extreme. Along with other books on this subject, they condemned al-Ghazali's renowned book, *Ihya-al-ulum* *wad-din* or the Revival of Sciences and Religion. The Qazi of Cordova, Ibn Hamdin, along with other Faqihs, drew up a fatwa, consigning all copies of the book to the flames and declaring anyone possessing a copy of it to be condemned to death and his property confiscated. All copies of the book were burnt in public in Cordova and also in all other cities of Muslim Spain. Dozy had aptly remarked, "One must go back to the times of the Visigoths to discover another example of a clergy so powerful as the Muslim clergy were under the Almoravid rule." They had seized the administration and they now dispensed offices and honours.

The Almoravids had established a strong and very effective administration. The result was that peace and order prevailed throughout their empire. The common people wanted internal tranquillity, security from external enemies and abolition of excessive taxes. This was what they got from the reign of Yusuf ibn Tashufin and early years of Ali's reign. Muslim Spain witnessed a period of great prosperity which it had not known since the halcyon days of Abdul Rahman III and Al-Mansur a century ago. All illegal taxes were abolished. Once Yusuf tried to levy a war-tax, which he called *ma'una* or aid. The citizens of Almeria refused to pay it and the Qazi of the city supported them. He wrote a letter to Yusuf in which he took him to task, 'You claim that you are following the precedent of Hazrat Umar, the Second Caliph. But you know that Umar did not demand the contribution *Ma'una* until he had sword in the mosque that not a dirham remained in the treasury; if you can do the lie, you have the right to call for it; if not, you have no right. Greetings!". In fact, the taxation was much lower during the Almoravid rule than it had been under the Taifa rulers. It enhanced public welfare. A high level of prosperity prevailed: bread was cheap and vegetables could be obtained for next to nothing.

Persecution of the Christian minority : A sea-change had occurred in Muslim Spain: it was now a predominantly Muslim country. The formerly Christian majority had been reduced to a small minority, partly due to conversions to Islam and partly due to emigration of the Mozarabs to the northern Christian kingdoms. Under the Umayyad and Taifa rulers, the Christians enjoyed complete freedom of life and worship. But the Almoravids deprived them of their former freedoms. Instead, both the Christians and Jews were subjected to many prohibitions and restrictions. An Andalusian historian, Ibn Abdun al-Tujibi, who was a minor official in Almoravid administration, writes about these restrictions as thus:

> A Muslim must not give massage to a Jew or a Christian, nor empty rubbish or clean latrines, because Jews and Christians are better suited to these jobs, which are for the unclean. A Muslim should not entrust the care of his hair to a Jew or Christian, nor serve him as a multeteer or help him into the saddle. If he hears of anyone who does this, he should reprimand him.

> Muslim women must be forbidden to defile themselves by entering a Christian church, since the priests are libertines, fornicators and sodomites. Similarly, free women may not enter a church except for services and festivals, because the priests eat, drink and fornicate with them; and there are none of them who do not have two or more women to sleep with them.

> The ringing of bells must be suppressed in Muslim territory as something which should

only be heard in the land of the infidel.
Scientific books must not be sold to Jews or
Christians, except those dealing with their
law, because they translate them and attribute
them to their own people and bishops,
stealing work of Muslims. It is better not to
allow a Jewish or Christian doctor to treat a
Muslim, because they are ill disposed and
should confine themselves to people of their
own faith. If some one has no sympathy for
him, how can a Muslim entrust his life to
him ?

Polarisation : The seeds of anti Muslim hatred which
New Christianity had sown were now bearing fruit in the
increasing polarisation in Spain between the Muslims and
Christians. Thanks to Islamic tolerance, Umayyad Spain had
been a mixed country. Not only Muslims and Christians
frequently intermarried, but even in warfare, they often joined
with each other even against their co religionists. But with the
emergence of New Christianity and its preaching of crusades
against the Muslims from Spain to Syria, and its influence on
the kings and feudal classes of Christian Spain led to a bifurcation
in Spain on Religious grounds. In response to Christian
aggressivity and exclusivity, the Muslims began to shun the
Christians in all walks of life. It resulted, however, in a mass
exodus of the Christian (Mozarabs) to the north. Thus two
separate and distinct Spains, Muslim and Christian, came into
being. History has, however, its peculiar developments. The
Spanish Christians' intolerance of everything Islamic engendered
in them national consciousness of their being a separate people
organised for aggression against the Muslims, first of Spain
and later, of other lands. Spanish Muslims, on the contrary,
could not attain the higher level of national consciousness,

because they remained victims of tribal and other internal divisions.

Generation Gap : Like other medieval Muslim countries, Muslim Spain was also a prey to the generation gap in the achievement capabilities of its people from the beginning of the eleventh century. Succession of one generation by another is a law of life or biological necessity. But the achievements of one generation may not be continued or attained by those who come after it. This leads to the falling off or gap in the achievements capability of people or society. It signifies degeneration of human character and the cause of social decline and decadence. It was this phenomenon which ibn Khaldun, the great Muslim philosopher of history enunciated as the four generation theory of the rise and fall of a ruling dynasty. His theory, however, had one serious flaw. The cause of the decline and fall of a state, culture and civilization did not merely lay in the declining capabilities of a ruling dynasty : it was also due to the decline in the achievement capabilities of the non ruling classes, e.g., of the intellectual, commercial and such other classes. A dynasty, even a ruling class may come to an end. But if the people remain vigorous and dynamic in the qualities and capabilities of their heads and hearts, the state and its society, culture and civilisation would accordingly continue to flourish and progress from one generation to the next, of course, amidst changing condition, and environment of achievement and progress. In other words, the historical continuity and viability of a state or people does not depend so much on the ruling dynasty or classes as ibn Khaldun believed, but on the political, social, legal, cultural intellectual and ideological institutions. They orientate the people including the ruling classes, towards achievements and expertness by infusing in them such qualities and capabilities which would enable every new generation to ever greater and ever newer achievements in all fields of endeavour and in all walks of life. In such a society and people, one dynasty may fall, but another will arise from among the people to take its place. Such a people will be a self perpetuating community. On the contrary, if their institutional system is of debilitation and inhibitory nature, due to political, social, cultural, ideological or other reasons, then a general deterioration in the achievement capabilities of the people, not merely of the ruling dynasty or class, would begin, which will clearly manifest itself in the next generation. In a state of general decadence, the people are exposed to such enemies from outside who would not merely dislodge the degenerate dynasty, but would also replace the old decadent and ideological system, which would gradually dislodge the degenerate dynasty, but would also replace the old one by a new social, cultural and ideological system, which would gradually misplace the old decadent people. This is the "*drang*" or drive phenomenon in world history replacing one people by another. If such rulers are motivated by demographic expansionism, e.g. by a repopulation policy, the "*drang*" process would lead to extirpation of the vanquished. It was this kind of general decline, which ibn Khaldun could not visualise, although he was literally born in it. The decadence of Muslim Spain had become perceptible from the days of Abdul Rahman III, as for example shown by his employment of foreign Berber and Slave troops to fight his wars. The same was also true of Al Mansur's victories. The increasing decadence of the Spanish Muslims inevitably led, from the middle of the eleventh century, to the Christian reconquista. Rise of the Berber powers only staved off their ultimate tragedy : it did not remedy their basic malady. The causes of the institutional basis of the general decline, which led to the achievemental generation gap, we shall analyse at the end of our study. Here it is enough to mention that the general decline of the Almoravid Empire was further aggravated by the anti-intellectual fundamentalism and socio-legal rigidism of their Malikite jurists. Negative factors, that is, not to do what is necessary, play as determinative a part in the decline and fall of a state as do the positive ones of lethargy, love of luxury, pusillanimity, dereliction of duty, etc.

Moral Deterioration : Until 1119 the Almoravid armies were victorious everywhere. As we have said above, they had captured Saragossa on one end of the Peninsula, and Lisbon, on the other. But from the middle of the reign of Ali ibn Yusuf, moral decadence had set in the Almoravid State, which led to their decline and fall. It afflicted their army and administration first.

Almoravid generals and soldiers of Yusuf's days had come from the deserts of North Africa, where they were accustomed to the simple and frugal ways of the desert-dwellers: they were pious, brave, honest, and inured to the hard life of the desert. But enriched by the gifts which Yusuf showered upon them, they deteriorated with surprising rapidity, and speedily lost their earlier virtues. They were dazzled by the brilliant civilisation and culture of Muslim Spain. They began to hate their earlier nomadic ways and to ape the luxurious tastes and habits of the Andalusians. The degenerative effects became visible in the succeeding generation of Almoravid administrators, generals and soldiers. For instance, Ali's brother-in-law, Abu Bakr ibn Ibrahim, governor successively of Granada and Saragossa, gave up the austere habits of his early life in the Desert and training of his kinsmen. He now surrounded himself with the wine-bibbing crowd of sychophants, while he donned the crown and royal robes of the dethroned Taifa princes. The degeneration of the common soldiers was as great as that of their officers. Inspite of their orthodoxy, they behaved insolently towards the Spanish Muslims, while pusillanimity on the battlefield became their chief characteristics. Their cowardice was so great that Ali was obliged to enrol Christian captives in his armies. Thus the *Saqaliba* of the Umayyads was reproduced in the form of the *Roumis* of the Almoravid armies. (The Almoravids called the European Christian captives as *Roumis*.). In Muslim Spain itself, the Almoravids behaved like a foreign army of occupation: they seized whatever they liked. It was, indeed, the old Berber weakness to capture whatever caught his fancy. The government had become too feeble and helpless to restrain its soldiery. Ali ibn Yusuf was dominated by his wife, Qamar. In fact, the ladies of the royal household decided everything from the appointment of high officials to the pardon of a brigand, provided their favours were purchased with large sums of money. But the royal ladies were wayward in their methods of administration : they countermanded an order today which they had issued yesterday. The result was that incompetent men filled important posts and the whole administration suffered. The people groaned and complained that their Amir was interested, not in government, but in fasting and prayer. And all this happened when the Almoravids were confronted with enemies on two fronts: in Spain, by the resurgent Christians and, in North Africa, by the new Berber power of the Al-Muwahhidun.

Second Round of Reconquista : After his reverses at Zallaqa and Aledo, Alfonso VI had lost the will to resist. Yusuf ibn Tashufin. He died broken-hearted in 1109. Though he had married several times, he had only a daughter, Urraca, to succeed him. She married Raymond of Burgundy, who had come to Spain in response to her father's call to European nobles to fight against Yusuf ibn Tashufin. After Christians defeat at Zallaqa, while others returned to their homes, Raymond remained in Spain to seek his fortune. In 1091, he married Urraca and both succeed Alfonso on his death in 1109. Alfonso had also an illegitimate daughter, named Teresa. She married another Burgundian noble, named Henry. Alfonso VI allotted them a part of his Kingdom around Coimbra. This territory later came to be known as Portugal. After Alfonso's death, Teresa revolted against her sister and forced her to grant her independence. Thus a new independent kingdom of Portugal was founded. During their interal disputes, the rulers of Leon-Castile waged no war against the Spanish Muslims for more than two decades. But, in the meanwhile, two other Christian rulers renewed the Reconquista wars. They were, firstly, Ramon Berenguer, the count of Barcelona in the extreme north-eastern corner of the Peninsula and Alfonso I, the King of Aragon.

Ramon Berenguer III, the count of Barcelona, was the first to start the war against the Muslims, in 1113. By this time, however, the Spanish Reconquista had become a part of the Crusades, which had already started in 1095. Christian Europe, headed by the Popes, the rising commercial cities of Italy and the feudal classes of France, Germany and England, had launched the wars of the Crusades on the Muslims all along a transcontinental front, extending from Muslim Spain, in the west, the island possessions of the Muslims in the Mediterranean, to Syria in the east. The Italian cities of Pisa and Genoa proposed to conquer the Muslim island of Majorca, near Spanish coast, ruled by Mubashir Nasir-ud-Daula. The Pope, Paschal II, granted crusading indulgences to the participants. They chose Ramon Berenguer as their leader and several French nobles joined the expedition, which was launched in 1114. They quickly overran the islands of Majorca and Ibiza. But the Almoravid force from Saragossa soon liberated the islands, which remained as Muslim possessions for a century more. Although the expedition failed, but it aroused the interest of the Catalans and later of the Aragonese, in the Mediterranean trade and islands.

Soon after, Alfonso I, the King of Aragon, became the spearhead of the Christian counter-attack against the Spanish Muslims. Owing to his constant warfare against the Muslims, his co-religionists called him *El-Battalador* or the Battler. Like his brother and predecessor, Pedro I, he had also his eyes on

Saragossa. His brother had already captured Huesca in 1096, an important fortress on the borders of Saragossa and had thus paved the path to its capture. In the meantime, the Almoravids had taken Saragossa. Alfonso I appealed to the feudal nobility of southern France for his campaign against Saragossa. The nobles who responded had already taken part in the First Crusade, 1095-1099. Pope Gelesius II granted crusade indulgences to the participants. He added a new element in the crusading zeal of the European Christians. He granted indulgence even to those who contributed to the reconstruction of the church in Saragossa in anticipation of its capture. Accordingly, a large army of the Aragonese, Catalans, Castilians and Frenchmen advanced on Saragossa and laid siege to it in May, 1118. The siege lasted for nine months, during which the Muslim population was reduced to starvation. The Almoravids sent an army of relief, but it was repulsed by the Christian besiegers. At last, in December, 1118, the city was captured and after sometime, its Muslim population was driven out of the city. The conquest of Saragossa was another important achievement of the Christians. Like Toledo, it remained permanently in Christian hands. Soon Alfonso I granted special concessions to the Christians who chose to settle in Saragossa. Three years later, he founded a military order, which became the forerunner of the military Orders of the Templars in Christian Spain and also added a new dimension to the Reconquista. Afterwards, Alfonso-I captured Tudela, Tarragona, Boija, Alcaniz and other towns and finally, captured Calatayud in 1120 and then Daroca. He thus pushed the Christian borders well to the south of the river Ebro. These successors of Alfonso I revealed the declining strength of the Almoravids. A few years later he repeated the earlier exploit of Alfonso VI by dashing south through the Muslim Spain. In 1125, the Christian population of Granada, which was then in majority in this city, rose into revolt and appealed to Alfonso for help, promising to provide him 12,000 warriors. Attracted by the prospects of quick victory and great booty, Alfonso dashed to the south. in September, 1125 and reached the out-skirts of Granada early in January, 1126. But the Mozarabs did not rise in his support, probably out of fear of the Almoravid reinforcements from Africa. Though Alfonso, remained in the Muslim south for some time, he at last returned to the north empty-handed. Emir, Ali ibn Yusuf, punished the Granadan Christians by ordering them to be transported *en masse* to Africa. Most of them settled in various towns in western Africa. Granada became a predominantly Muslim city. Polarisation between Spanish Christians and Muslims increased further with every success in the Reconquista.

In 1133, Alfonso I again renewed his campaign against the Muslims. He captured Mequinenza in 1133. But when he advanced towards Lerida, he was thoroughly defeated by the Almoravid army at Fraga on July 17, 1134. A few months later, he died. The feelings of relief which the Muslims expressed at his death were expressed by the Muslim historian, Ibn al-Athir, as thus:

> No Christian prince was more valorous than he or possessed so much ardour for fighting the Muslims or such powers of resistance. He slept in his armour and scorned a mattress, and when once asked why he did not bed with the daughters of the Moorish petentates he had made captive, he replied, 'A true soldier ought to live only with men and not with women.' With his death Allah allowed the faithful to breathe again, free from his hammer blows."

Ali died in 1143. His son Tashufin ruled only two years and died in 1145, fighting against Muvahhidin.

CHAPTER 33

THE MUVAHHIDIN
(1146-1248A.D.)

A politico-religious movement in the beginning of the 12th century, led by Muhammad-bin-Tumart of the Masmudah tribe brought a new dynasty on the soil of North Africa to overthrow the Murabitin. He preached the doctrine of the Unity of God and the spiritual conception of Him, among the tribes of the Moroccan Atlas. Assuming the title of Al Mahdi he proclaimed to restore the true Islamic spirit in life and to suppress all evils than prevailed in society. They called themselves Muvahhidin.

His father was a mosque lamp lighter and was called "Sarraj". He led an ascetic life right from his boyhood and opposed all sorts of laxity. He did not even refrain from assaulting in the street of Fez (Fas) the sister of Ali-bin-Yusuf, the Murabit ruler, simply because she walked unveiled.

Abu Abdullah Muhammad-b-Tumart actually belonged to the Berber tribe of Masmudah, but to justify his claim for the title of al Mahdi, he traced his lineage from the house of Hazrat Imam Hasan.

He visited Cordova, Cairo, and Baghdad and studied religion, Quran, Hadith, jurisprudence and philosophy under eminent scholars like al Ghazali, Abu Bakr of Tortosa and Imam Azri of Mahdiya. Being a true desciple of Imam Ghazali he was greatly annoyed with the unwise step of the Ulema of Cordova for prescribing the works of al Ghazali.

In order to achieve his aim he started preaching Tauhid (Oneness of God) and to lead a pious life. He reformed the life of the Berbers and prevailed upon them to shun immoral life. He condemned Taqlid and believed in Quran, Sunnah, Ijma and al-Sahaba. He preached the doctrine of Tawhid to the passengers and the crews on the ships and the towns he visited. After his death between 1128 and 1130 A.D. he was succeeded by his chief lieutenant Abdul Momin-bin-Ali, who was nominated by ibne. Tumart before his death.

Having being expelled from Fez by Ali-bin-Yusuf for assaulting his sister, he settled in Tirmal not very far off from Fez. His mosque on the river Nafis was the centre of his activities.

He had formed a sort of hierarchy with a council of 11 of his devotees the chief being Abdul Mumin his successor. Another council of his consisted of 50 devotees from the various Berber tribes. The hierachy of the unitarians had two houses - the house of Lords composed of 11 most in influential Berber devotees and the house of commons composed of 50 devotees from the common communities of the Berbers. He then started a sort of civil disobedience movement stopping the payment of taxes to the Murabit ruler.

The defeat of the Murabit Governor of Sus increased the number of his followers. Bin Tumart the Mahdi attacked Morocco with 40000 Muvahidin but was repulsed by the Murabit ruler.

The defeat of the Mahdi by the Moroccan ruler had caused disintegration in his fold which was further tarnished by his one most trusted deputy Abdul Momin. His death therefore was kept a secret by Momin who was paving a clear way for his own self, and it took about 3 years to make the secret open to all his followers.

Abdul Momin : For three years after Ibn Tumart's death, his chief lieutenants kept his death secret from the community of Tinmall, during which one of his lieutenants, Abdul Momin, came to the forefront. He became the chief of the Almovahhids with the title of caliph, obviously, of the Mahdi. His rival, al Bashir, had been killed in the battle of al Buhayra. His main task was to wage war upon the Almoravids, which he carried out in three stages:

1. From 1133 to 1144, when he subdued the mountain ranges or the High and Middle Atlas and of the Rif near the Mediterranean coast.

2. From 1145 to 1147, when he conquered Marrakesh, the capital of the Almoravids and the Moroccan plain between the Atlas and the Atlantic and

3. From 1151 to 1159, during which he subdued the eastern Maghrib and the Ifriqiya or North Africa to the west of Egypt.

Being a shrewd strategist, Abdul Momin realised that direct attack on Marrakesh was not possible, as the defeat at Buhayra had shown him. Instead, he first consolidated Almohad power by conquering all the Berber tribes in the mountains of the High and Middle Atlas. This campaign lasted from 1133 to 1144, during which he subdued the powerful Zanata tribes, to which his own Kumia tribe also belonged. After this, he marched on the towns in the coastal region along the Mediterranean, where he first came into clash with the Almoravids. In the meantime, the Almoravid Amir, Ali ibn Yusuf, died in 1143 and his son, Tashufin, ibn Ali, had become the Amir. He rushed to defend the Almoravid base at Tlemsen. But the commander of his Christian regiment, count Reverter, was killed in an engagement. His death weakened the march in 1145, Tashufin ibn Ali also died when his mare he was riding fell down a precipice. A few days later, Abdul Momin captured Oran and next he took Tlemsen. He then turned towards Marrakesh, left to succeed Tashufin ibn Ali, Marrakesh was captured in 1147, which then became the Almohad capital. A general massacre of the Lamtuna Berbers was carried out, because they were the mainstay of the defeated Almoravids. Thus Abdul Momin crushed the Almoravids completely. He destroyed their palace in Marrakesh and built the Kutubiyya a mosque on its foundations.

At this time, Abdul Momin received delegation from the petty rulers of Muslim Spain seeking his help against the Christians. They had revolted and other thrown the Almoravids and requested the Almohad ruler to take over their country and to protect them from the Christians. But Abdul Momin had a different plan. He intended to conquer Ifriqiya. He contented to send a small force to help the Spanish Muslims. In Iftiqiya conditions were critical. Norman Christians from Sicily had taken Mahdiya and other coastal towns in Tunisia, whom the Berber Zirid rulers had been unable to resist. Their Muslim subjects strongly resented Christian rule. Moreover, two Bedouin Arab tribes, Benu Hilal and Banu Sulaym, had overran greater part of Ifriqiya and in conjunction with the native Sanhaja Berbers, were advancing towards Bougie. Although Abdul Momin had, in 1151, advanced on Ceuta with the intention to cross the Strait into Spain, how changed his plans and rushed to the aid of Bougie, where once had stayed with Ibn Tumart. He advanced against the Arabs. He defeated them after three days of stiff resistance at Setif and captured all their possessions, women and children. Then something unexpected happened.

Instead of treating the defeated Arabs cruelly, as he had treated the defeated Almoravis at Marrakesh, he induced the Arabs, with all their families and possession, to settle in the plain of Morocco between Rabat and Casablanca. Later, more Arab settlers came in the reign of his grandson. Abu Yusuf Yaqub during 1187-88. The result of the deportations of the Arabs was the Arabisation of Morocco. Abdul Momin's purpose was to counter-balance the influence of the Masmuda tribe, with whose help Ibn Tumart's two brothers planned to overthrow him and to oppose the designation of his son as his successor, as Abdul Momin intended to do. After settling these affairs, during 1158 and 1159, Abdul Momin again led his battle-hardened Al-Muwahhid army against the Normans in Ifriqiya. His army defeated the Normans and drove them from their possessions in North Africa. The Almohad troops then captured Ifriqiya as far as Tripoli (now in modern Libya). Thus the whole of North Africa west of Egypt came under the rule of the Almohad Berbers, something which even their predecessors, the Almoravid Berbers, could not achieve. The result of the conquest of Ifriqiya was that the trade route between Sudan and Bougie came under the control of the Almohads, which enhanced the prosperity of their empire.

Death : Abdul Momin died in 1163 at Rabat, when he was preparing to cross over the Spain. The task of conquering Spain was left to his successors.

His Personality and Achievements : Abdul Momin was a sturdy Berber of medium height. He was a good soldier, with great courage and endurance. Though of patient nature, he could be, if necessary, harsh and cruel. On capturing Marrakesh from the Almoravids, he put several thousand of them to death. He was the founder of an empire which was the largest the Berbers ever built. Even when he was pursuing his conquests, he established a strong government and a powerful army. His central administration was based on the clan or *qabila* organisation of the Masmudah and other Berber tribes. He patterned his government on the model of that of the Spanish Umayyads. Indeed, he and his successors, employed increasing number of the Spanish Muslims in their administration. In order to provide enough finances for his administration and his Almohad troops, he imposed land tax, *kharaj*, on all his subjects, excepting the Almohads. A land register was prepared for this purpose after land survey had been carried out in the whole empire. After his victory over the Bedouin Arabs in 1152, Abdul Momin assumed the caliphal title of *Amir al-Momineen*. In fact, he was the first non-Arab ruler in the history of Islam to do so. His rivals, the Almoravid rulers, contented themselves with the more modest title of *Amir al-Muslimeen*, the commanders of the Muslims. Abdul Momin also built the military might of the Almohads. As the Almohad community was exempted from taxes, it became the aristocracy of its empire. But it preserved its puritanic austerity. Nevertheless, Abdul Momin issued instructions that his sons should be addressed as *sayyids,* so as to distinguish them from the Shaikhs, the Almohad nobles. He also appointed his sons as governors of the provinces of his vast empire. Moreover, in 1154, he designated his eldest son, Muhammad, as his successor. But he proved to be an incompetent person. On his death, therefore, his other son, Abu Yaqub Yusuf, ascended the throne in 1163. He was the first Almohad ruler to incorporate Muslim Spain into his empire.

CHAPTER 34

ABU YAQUB YUSUF
(1184–1199 A.D.)

After the death of Abdul Momin, his son Abu Muhammad Abdullah ascended the throne, but he was deposed for his inefficiency, by the courtiers, and Abu Yaqub the third son of Momin was elected in his place.

Abu Yaqub was both a soldier and a statesman. Just after his accession, the tribes of the Atlas rose in revolt but Abu Yaqub compelled them to submit and surrender.

Unlike his predecessors, he personally advanced to Spain with 2000 soldiers and encamped in Seville. Ibne Saad the king of Valencia was defeated and killed in the battle of Minorca. His sons could no stand the attack of Abu Yaqub. Thus the whole of Valencia, Murcia and Lorca were subjugated by Abu Yaqub Yusuf. A daughter of Ibne Saad was married to Yousuf.

His brother-in-laws were given, large estates in North Africa in exchange of the estates in Spain. They then preferred to settle in the new estates in North Africa.

The Tagus valley up to Toledo was devastated and plundered. The frontier fort of Alcantara was annexed.

During his short stay of one year in Seville he raised its prominende by building palaces, mosques, public baths and bridges. The boats-bridge on the Guadalquiver was very conspicious. He built a beautiful mosque on the site of a church destroyed and raised to the ground by the Normans, with a beautiful minaret, now known as the Giralda which was completed by his successor.

The outbreak of a deadly epidemic (571 A.H. 1176 A.D.) in North Africa, compelled him to return to his capital to share the calamities of the people. His absence from Spain for about eight years gave an opportunity to the governors to declare themselves independent.

Abu Yaqub Yusuf raising a strong force, seventy thousand infantry and thirty thousand Cavalry, in Centa, advanced to crush the rebels. The entire force marched under the commands of the tribal chiefs with their own flag. Yusuf joined the army at Seville where the Berbers of Spain also joined him.

The rebels were helped by the Christian chiefs. A very severe battle was fought at Santare. Yusuf was fatally wounded and the defeat was thus ordained. Yusuf ultimately succumbed to the fatal wounds in 594 A.H./1184 A.D.

CHAPTER 35

ABU YUSUF YAQUB, AL-
MANSOOR-BE-ALLAH
(1184–1199 A.D.)

Abu Yusuf Yaqub, born of slave girl, succeeded his father
Abu Yaqub Yusuf in 1184 A.D. under the honorific title of
al-Mansoor-be-Allah.

He being generous, just and pious, steered the wheel of
the government with prudence for the good of the people. He
reduced the taxes and declared the acceptance of bribes, presents
and gifts a serious offence. The efficiency of the police
guaranteed the safety of roads, high ways and houses. Inns and
wells were built at intervals for the comfort of the travellers.

The fall of Cordova was replaced by Seville in importance,
fame and grandeur under the golden period of Yaqub.
Agriculture and irrigation systems were improved which made
the country self sufficient in food.

Sahebul-Madina governed the country assisted by Qazi in
the judiciary and muhtasib in municipal affairs. The ports bustled
with large ships and ferry bats. The construction of aqueduct
for the supply of fresh water to the city was a great achievement.

Seville flourished much under the Almuvahhidin, in all
fields specially art and architecture. The Jamia Masjid of Seville

and the famous Giralda Minaret 30 thousand feet high, and also the observatory spoke well of the grandeur of Seville. The construction of the minaret was planned by Abul Lais the chief engineer in 567 A.H./1172 A.D. which was completed in 591 A.H./1195 A.D. Great stress was laid on education and medicine. Schools and hospitals were innumerable and all were run by the government. According to Marakabi, Morocca had such a well-equipped big hospital which had no equal in the then world.

The court of Yaqub was flocked with eminent scholars like Ibne Zuhr (Avenzor) and Ibne Baja (Avempace) the physicians, and Ibne Rushed (Averroes) the philosopher who was Qazi of Cordova also.

The quot Hole "the Muvahhidin adored Seville with the Giralda, which still stands guard by the Cathedral, but the Christians have added a stupid revolving stature of a Saint on top. Students from Christian Europe came to Muslim schools to study alchemy, medicine, mathematics astronomy and astrology. They were taught, accommodated and treated at par with the Muslim students. The Muslims gave Europe without prejudice, all that they had in their stores of learning, culture and civilization, as a manifestation of the true Islamic spirit of tolerance and the recognition of human brotherhood. Yaqub was a mujahid and after, welcoming the embassy sent by the great Salah-ud-Din, headed by his nephew Usamah-bin-Munqiz, he readily despatched 180 well equipped ships to fight for the Muslims against the Christians.

It may however be noted that inspite of his prosperous rule, Yaqub had to face the rebels. The chiefs of the Balearic Islands who favoured the Murabitun tried to overthrow the Muvahhidin. They were joined by the brother of Yusuf. They were however crushed and the Balearic Islands were annexed.

The third crusade (1189-1192 A.D./685-588 A.H.) was on. The English knights on their way to Jerusalem taking advantage of the disturbed condition. Plundered Evora, Beja and Salwis and made a general massacre of the innocent Muslim citizens. They played unprecedented havoc and spared none of the Muslims to breath life.

Being greatly distressed with the sad news, Yaqub advanced from Morocco with 300,000 Berbers. Alfanso VIII leader of the Christian army met at Alarcos (al-Ark). The Christians were crushed in as much as one hundred and forty six thousand Christian soldiers were killed and thirty thousand were made prisoners of war. This grand victory established the generalship and war insight of Yaqub and his general Sanani.

Alfanso fled to Toledo while a portion of the routed army took refuge in Calartave (Fort of Rabah). Yaqub and his general Sanani sparing no time followed the cowards and crushing them well and reconquered Calartava, Guadalajara, Escelona and Salamanca. The kings of Navaree and Leon had no other alternative but to submit. Toledo was also beseiged (1196 A.D./ 592 A.H.) but on the mercy appeal of the mother and wives of Alfanso VIII the siege was lifted and the approved enemy of the Muslims was left to play treachery later on. Had Yaqub and General Sanani, been not moved by the crocodile tears of Alfanso and his family, Muslim Spain would not have been wiped out from the map of Europe.

The Aragonese who had raised their heads, were also crushed. The Sultan then returned to Seville and staying there for a year reorganised the entire administrative machinery. He however returned to Morocco in November 1197 A.D./593 A.H. to breath his last in 594 A.H./A.D.

ABU ABDULLAH MUHAMMAD

In the beginning, the reign of Muhammad an-Nasir was one of peace and prosperity in Africa. As the Banu Ghaniya were again giving the Almohads trouble, the new Khalifa first marched against them. In 1204, he captured Majorca in the island-group of the Balearics, from where Banu Ghaniya had established links with Aragon, Genoa and Pisa, all hostile to the Almohads. He then marched towards Ifriqiya, where Banu Ghaniya had captured Tunis, Mahdiya and extended their power deep into the Great Sahara. He defeated Ibn Ghaniya and took Tunis and other towns from him. Ibn Ghaniya then went deep into the desert and appeared in the west, where he sacked Sijilmasa and devastated the whole of the central Maghrib so terribly that, two centuries later, Ibn Khaldun wrote, "Not one fire still burns there, and cockcrow is heard no more." Ibn Ghaniya was finally tracked down and captured in 1233. Thus came, to an end the opposition of this surviving Almoravid dynasty against the Almohads. But Bani Ghaniya's long-drawn struggle exhausted the resources and weakened the military power of the Almohadi. Their defeat at al-Aqab (Las Navas de Tolosa) in Spain in 1212 would not have produced such disastrous consequences, as it did, if their struggle with Banu Ghaniya had not weakened their empire in Africa.

Alarcos was a cruel blow to the Spanish Christians at a time when they were confident that they would soon finish off Muslim Spain forever. Ever Christian Europe was shaken by this victory of the Muslims. Never before in the whole history of the world a whole continent was aroused so aggressively by a defeat in one corner of it, as Western Europe was by the Christian defeat at Alarcos in 1195. It was the first indication of how far Europe, including Christia Spain, had been integrated into one political unit by the influences emanating from New

Christianity. Rodrigo Jimenez de Rada, the Archbishop of Toledo, travelled the length and breadth of France, and Italy to recruit troops, while Pope Innocent II declared a crusade against Muslim Spain. A large number of foreign knights, chiefly English and French, took the road to Spain to engage in this holy war: some sixty thousand crusaders came from beyond the Pyrenees. They consisted of the Archbishop of Narbonne (France) and a horde of ruffians, cut-throats and the like. In Christian Spain itself, Alfonso VIII of Castile cemented his friendship with Alfonso IX of Leon by marrying his daughter to him. He also patched up his quarrel with the King of Navarre who was a little before planning an alliance with the Almohads, while the king of Portugal also joined this grand alliance of the Christians. At the same time, the military orders and the bishops in Spain, led by Rodrigo Jimenez de Rada, had become increasingly insistent to resume hostilities against the Muslims. The Pope Innocent III threatened with excommunication any prince who attacked his Christian neighbours. In short, by 1210, the European Christendom was all set for a war with Almohad Spain, and in 1211 they started raiding it.

On being informed of the Christian raids, Muhammad an-Nasir crossed the Strait in May, 1211, with a large army, estimated to be more than a hundred thousand strong, including sixty thousand Andalusians. He marched against the castle of Salvatierra, held by the knights of the monkish order of the Templars since 1195 after they lost Calatrava. It took the Almohads four months to reduce it. As winter had set in, the Khalifa decided to renew war in the spring next year. Thus he wasted valuable time, as the Christians had not yet mustered their forces in full strength. The reverse at Salvatierra made all Castile to prepare for war during the winter months. The kings of Aragon and Navarre also rallied to support the Castilian king. The king of Portugal, Alfonso II held aloof, because

Alfonso IX of Leon had attacked his kingdom. The Almohad khalifs, remained inactive during these quarrels between the Christian kings and missed an opportunity to weaken the Christians further. At last, on June 20, 1212, a large Christian army of all-European composition marched out from Toledo towards Cordova, capturing on the way Alarcos and other towns which the Muslims had taken years ago. It reached al-Aqab, which the Christians called Las Navas de Tolosa, on July 13. At the same time, Muhammad an-Nasir also advanced from Cordova and blocked the Christian advance. The size of the Muslim army had been differently reported. According to al-Maqqari, it amounted to six hundred thousand warriors, while others thought it to be a little more than one hundred thousand. It was, however, not a united force due to internal dissensions. The Andalusians in it were disaffected. On reaching the battlefield, the Muslims took a strong position on the heights of the Sierra Morena.

After preliminary skirmishes, the battle began on July 16. It lasted for only one day. The Christians advanced upon he Muslims in three waves. The first one was repulsed and thrown into confusion. But Alfonso VIII, who was in supreme command, rallied his troops and, with Archbishop Rodrigo who was fighting by his side, launched an attack on the Muslim centre, where an-Nasir had posted himself with the cream of his army. The Muslims fought back fiercely, but at the end they wavered and broke. Their defeat turned into a rout. An-Nasir fled from the battle-field to Cordova and then feeling unsafe there, he crossed the Strait into the safety of Morocco. Behind him he left his whole army butchered almost to the last man. In his letter to the Pope Innocent III, Alfonso VIII wrote exultantly: "on their side 100,000 men or more fell in the battle, according to the estimate of the Saracens whom we captured. But of the army of the Lord, incredible though it may be, unless it be a miracle, hardly 25 or 30 Christians of our whole army fell. O what happiness! O what thanksgiving! though one might lament that so few martyrs from such a great army went to Christ in martyrdom".

The consequences of the Muslim defeat were disastrous. It was the real cause of the rapid disintegration of the Almohad empire, while Muslim Spain again lapsed into Taifa Syndrome, that is, it disintegrated into several petty kingdoms, which were destroyed utterly during the next forty years by their relentless enemies: only little Granada survived for another two centuries and a half.

The immediate causes of the Muslims' defeat lay in the dissensions among their troops and commanders and the purge of his commanders which Muhammad an-Nasir undertook after landing in Spain. He ordered the execution of Yusuf ibn Qadis for evacuating the fortress of Calatrava when he was confronted with Alfonso's army. It was a hasty and injudicious action which disheartened his troops. His Andalusian troops were disaffected. Another cause was the valuable time the Almohad Khalifa wasted in capturing the fortress of Salvatierra. A war had broken out between the Christian kings of Leon and Portugal, of which he took no advantage.

But there were other causes which lay deeper than the immediate reasons of the Muslim defeat. The Almohads were already involved in a dilemma: they were confronted with enemies in Africa and in Spain and they now did not possess those resources in men and materials to wage war on two fronts as did the early Almohads, like Abdul Momin or Abu Yaqub Yusuf. Had it not been so, they could have raised new troops to confront their enemies once again and wipe out the disastrous effects of their defeat at al-Aqab. The Almohad Empire was large in size, extending from the borders of Sudan in Africa to the borders of Castile and Portugal in the Iberian Peninsula, but it had become hollow within since long. It did not enjoy the same economic resources as did its founder, Abdul Momin. Two factors played important role in the decline and disruption of the economy of the Almohad Empire. Muslims had enjoyed the monopoly of the international trade across the Mediterranean sea-lanes from the eighth century, which linked the Islamic West with the lands of the Islamic East. It was now lost.

From the tenth century, Muslim monopoly was challenged and disrupted by the emergent trading powers of the Christian Europe, as for example, the Italian commercial cities like Genoa, Pisa etc., and the rising Christian kingdoms of Catalonia and Aragon in north-eastern Spain and the Frankish rulers of southern France. In course of time, they not only destroyed Muslim-monopoly of the Mediterranean international trade, but also diverted it to Europe, i.e. to themselves.

While the Christian sea-dogs (to borrow a term from the Elizabethen England) were causing havoc to the Mediterranean trade of the Muslims, various rebels against the Almohads were consequently doing the same to the carvan trade across the Great Sahara which linked Egypt, Sudan and Sub-Saharan Africa with the Maghrib (Morocca) and Muslim Spain. It deprived the Muwahhids of the Sudanese gold, on which their economy mainly depended.

Modern Western writers, with the French in the lead, have laid the blame for the disruption of the trans-African caravan routes on the two Arab bedouin tribes, Banu Hailal and Banu Sulaym who had burst into Ifriqiya in the eleventh century and caused great havoc to this caravan trade by their depredations. However, the Hilalian "catastrophe", as the Western writers call it, was really a myth devised by them in order to conceal the real facts. The bedouin depredations were really the first

effects of the diversion of the international trade from the shores
of the Muslim countries in the Mediterranean to those of the
Christian countries of southern Europe. More of such effects
were to come in the form of revolts against the Almohad Empire
and against the African kingdoms which rose to power
afterwards. They were the effects of the economic ruination
caused by the disruption and diversion of the Mediterranean
trade from the Islamic world to Europe by the rising sea-power
of the European Christians. This economic ruination, in its
turn, provoked the depradations of the tribes and rebels in North
Africa both against the Almohad Empire and its successor-states.
It was, indeed, a vicious circle: the more Europeans dominated
the Mediterranean trade routes, the more the tribes and rebels
destroyed the caravan trade routes in North Africa, the greater
was the political instability in North Africa and Muslim Spain.
The Almohad Empire was the first to suffer the effects of this
vicious circle. The revolts of Banu Ghaniya, Banu Marin and
other rebels caused widespread devastations during the reigns
of the later Almohads.

The economic ruination of the Almohad empire was a
slow but a continuous and irreversible process, for it led to the
depopulation of the vast regions of North Africa. The
demographic decline of North Africa was evident from the
middle of the eleventh century and reached its low point in the
middle of the fourteenth. Consequently, "agriculture, especially
arboriculture, diminished." Nomadism spread. Cities and
villages disappeared or became depopulated. Qayrowan, which
had hundreds of thousands of inhabitants in the ninth and tenth
centuries, was now a small town. Leo Africanus says of Bidjaya
(Bougie) that the town had only 8000 household and could
easily have sheltered 24000." On the other hand, during this
period, when the Muslim West was becoming depopulated, the
Christian West was undergoing a real population explosion. Of

course, the reason of all this was one and the same: *diversion of the Mediterranean trade from the Muslim World to the Christian West*. With it began the downturn in the history of Medieval Islam, which ended six centuries later in the global expansion of Christian Europe and in the enslavement of nearly the whole Islamic world and in the destruction of several Muslim peoples and countries, the first among them being Muslim Spain itself, as well as Sicily and other Mediterranean islands, then ruled by the Muslims.

To return to the Almohads. The increasing economic ruination and depopulation of their empire led to the decrease in their revenues. As we have said above, Abdul Momin had imposed land-tax on all his subjects, except his Almohad community. When the Almohad revenues decreased, they imposed newer and greater taxes, which caused hardship to their subjects. Hence more revolts against them. At the same time, the Almohad army had lost its original fighting spirit and were more and more replaced by mercenaries of Arab, Zanata and even Christian origin, who were unable to hold its many fronts in Africa and Spain. It ended by giving way to the attacks of the conquistadors in Spain, the Christian sea-dogs in the Mediterranean and to the numerous rebels in North Africa. Herein lay the reasons why the Almohads were not able to mount another attack on the Spanish Christians after their defeat at al-Aqab (Las Navas de Tolosa).

If the Muslim rulers of Spain and North Africa had defended their Mediterranean trade lanes the very first day the Christian intruders appeared on the scene, their history would have been quite different: the emergent Europe's drive to the south would have been arrested at the very start. Of course the struggle would have been hard and bitter, for the Europeans were organised and led by the New Christianity and by their highly war like feudal classes, who were then tasting the first fruits of the rising commercialism of their trading cities and kingdoms. Before all this, however, the Muslim rulers had first to nab the plundering instincts of their tribes. But the Almohad rulers, like other Muslim rulers before and after them had no idea of how to crush the predatory propensities of the tribesmen in North Africa or of the Christian seamen in the Mediterranean.

DECLINE AND FALL OF THE ALMOHADS

Death of Muhammad an-Nasir : Muhammad an-Nasir did not live long after his defeat at al-Aqab. He died a year after, in 1213, perhaps poisoned by his courtiers, or just accidently. His empire had already began to decline from the day he was defeated. It is worth mentioning that while Muslim Spain suffered grievously from this defeat and began to disintegrate soon after, Muslim North Africa showed no reaction or shock at this defeat. On the contrary, there was an attitude of passivity and even indifference, which was exemplified by the Khalifa an-Nasir himself.

Abu Yaqub Yusuf II : An-Nasir as succeeded by his son, Abu Yaqub Yusuf II, who took the title of *al-Mustansir billah* (he who implores the help of God). He was a mere boy of about sixteen when he ascended the throne and gave himself tip to pleasure and repose. He was too incompetent to save his tottering empire. Owing to his incompetence, the power came into the hands of the Shaikhs, the aristocracy of the Almohads. Al-Mustansir died in January, 1223.

As al-Mustansir died childless, the Shaikhs chose his father's uncle, *Sayyid Abu Muhammad Abd al-Wahid*. During his short reign, the Almohad princes and governors in Spain became practically independent. He was strangled to death in 1224. The Almohad empire was then divided between two claimants. A relative of him, Al-Adil ibn al-Mansur, proclaimed himself Khalifa at Murcia and captured some towns in al-Andalus. He fought a battle with the Christians, but suffered a severe and shameful defeat. He fled to Morocco, leaving a brother, named Abu'l Ala Idris, who ruled at Seville. In the meanwhile, Banu Marin, who dwelt on the borders of the Almohad empire in the Sahara, entered Morocco and began to contend for sovereignty with Banu Ghaniya. The Almohad Shaikhs proclaimed Yahya ibn Nasir as Khalifa at Marrakesh. After the assassination of Abdul Wahid, the Shaikhs supported the claim of al-Adil and proclaimed him Khalifa. But he was killed by the rebels in 1227, who chose an inexperienced youth, Yahya ibn an-Nasir, also known as Yusuf III. But he ruled for one year only.

Abu'l Ala Idris al-Mamun : When Yahya was proclaimed as Khalifa at Marrakesh, Al-Adil's brother Abu'l Ala Idris, proclaimed himself Khalifa at Seville. He now styled himself as al-Mamun. He did two things. Firstly, he denounced Ibn Tumart's doctrine of Mahdism, and began to favour Maliki faqihs, who were still very popular in Muslim Spain. Secondly, he adopted a policy of friendship towards the Christians and sought alliance with them, especially with Alfonso VIII's son, Fernando III, by surrendering to him several fortresses on the borders of Muslim Spain. In reward for this, the Christian king allowed him to recruit Christian mercenaries. Their recruitment was the first indication that the Almohad army, the mainstay of their political power, had ceased to be a military force. Anyhow, with Christian mercenaries, Idris al-Mamun crossed the Strait for Morocco in 1228 and left Muslim Spain for ever, where Bani Hud captured power. With the aid of the Christian mercenaries in Morocco, al-Mamun defeated his rival, Yahya, and became Khalifa. He granted concessions to the Christians to open trade with Morocco. He thus became the first Muslim ruler to grant commercial concessions to European Christians, with all the other consequences which affected the Maghrib and other Muslim lands later on. He died in 1242.

He was followed by half a dozen weak Khalifas, who were unable to keep the Almohad empire intact even in the Maghrib. Their names we need not mention here. When the Almohad dynasty ceased to exist in 1274, its empire in Maghrib came to be divided into three independent kingdoms. They were: the Marinids (c. 1250-1472) who ruled Morocco in the western parts of the Maghrib; the Zayyanids (1235-1554) who rose to power in the region of Tlemsin or central Maghrib; and the Hafsids (1228-1574) who captured Ifriqiya, the eastern province of the Almohad empire. For our purposes, these successor-kingdoms of the Almohad empire are important for two reasons. They played supportive role in the history of Granada, the only Taifa kingdom which survived in Spain. Secondly, the great Muslim historian and philosopher of history, Ibn Khaldun, served all these three kingdoms, studied their political, social, economic, cultural, intellectual and religious life, on the basis of which he expounded his cyclical theory of the rise and fall of states, cultures and civilisations.

CHAPTER 36

THE THIRD AND LAST TAIFA SPAIN
THE THIRD TAIFA SPAIN

The defeat of the Almohad Khalifa, Muhammad an-Nasir, at al-Aqab (Las Navas de Tolosa) in 1212 was not so disastrous as the subsequent collapse of the Almohad Empire made it so. Almohad empire soon became a victim of double Taifa disintegration, i.e. of both its Spanish and African possessions, which resulted from the precipitous flight of an-Nasir across the Straits of Gibraltar into the security of his capital, Marrakesh. In Muslim Spain, his flight unleashed two forces which had always been its bane, namely, the recrudescence of the Taifa Syndrome and the consequent ease with which the Christians could conquer the petty Taifa rulers. In Muslim Spain, the disintegration of the Almohad empire started about 1224, when al-Adil, the Almohad governor of Murcia, was attacked by the Christians. In a pitched battle with them, he suffered a severe and shameful defeat. Like an-Nasir before him, instead of continuing the struggle, he fled to Morocco.

Ibn Hud : The growing weakness of the Almohad rulers perturbed the Spanish Muslims, who had though no love for them and their religious innovations. Indeed, as Ibn Khaldun wrote, the Muslim Spaniards detested the domination of the Almohad Berbers and their "oppression weighed heavily upon them and their hearts were filled with hate and indignation against these aliens". However, in this perilous situation, they began to look for a man who would save them from the merciless Christians, who were now eagerly sharpening their sword's to attack and destroy them. The man who came to their rescue was Muhammad ibn Yusuf al-Jodhami, commonly known as Ibn Hud. He was a descendant of Banu Hud, who were the rulers of Sargossa till they were driven out from there by the Al-Murabits. Ibn Hud raised the standard of revolt in the province of Murcia, the eastern province of Muslim Spain in 1226. He made a popular appeal by proclaiming to abolish Al-Mawwahid innovations and to restore Islam in Spain. Abu'l Abbas Al-Muwahhid governor of Murcia, marched against him, but was defeated by him with great loss and fell back on the city of Murcia. Its inhabitants, however, rose against the governor and drove him out and proclaimed Ibn Hud as their king, who soon entered the city amidst public rejoicings. Ibn Hud then captured Granada, Malaga and Almeria. By the year 1229, Cordova, Jaen and other important cities also rendered their allegiance to him. In these cities he massacred the Almohads as heretics. Seeing himself the sole master of virtually the whole Muslim Spain, he assumed the title of Amir al-Muslamin (the Commander of the Muslims). He sent an embassy to the Abbasid Khalifa, al-Mustansir, at Baghdad, declaring his allegiance to him and holding power in Spain in his name. The Khalifa replied favourably in 1233, investing in him all the dominions he had or would conquer in Spain. Ibn Hud then began to mention the name of the Abbasid Khalifa in the Friday khutbahs. He also assumed the royal title of al-Mutawakkil ala'illah (One who relied on God).

Revolts : Ibn Hud did not long enjoy his newly-acquired sovereignty. Perturbed by his popularity among the Muslim masses, a new crop of Taifa kings rose into revolt against him. Either they assumed the same authority and title as he had, or they preemptorily refused to acknowledge him as their sovereign. The story of the Taifa disintegration of Muslim Spain is painful even in outline. The disintegration was, moreover, so confusingly kaleidoscopic that the mere retelling of it involves repetition. It was disintegration within disintegration: with one local lord after the other gone haywire, if I may use this awkward but accurate description of the Taifa Syndrome. Each Taifa ruler jostled for power and territory with his rivals, till he was himself attacked and even destroyed by newer and even lesser Taifa rebels, while they as well as their Almohad overlords sought peace with their Christian enemies by paying tributes and handing over strategic castles and cities to them, in order to fight their Muslim rivals more single-mindedly.

After Ibn Hud, the second Taifa ruler to rise to power was Abu Jamil Zayyan ibn Mardanish. He was a descendant of Ibn Mardanish of the second crop of the Taifas, who had fought for so long against Al-Muwwahids. Zayyan ibn Mardanish had made himself master of Valencia and the surrounding country in 1231. Another Taifa chief was Ahmed al-Baji, who was a descendant of the famous theologian, Abu'l Walid al-Baji. He had revolted at Seville where he had overthrown the rule of Ibn Hud. But he was killed in 1231 by another Taifa king, named Muhammad ibn Yusuf ibn al Ahmar, also known as Ibn Nasr. Ibn al-Ahmar was a leader of the aristocratic counter-revolution against the populist propaganda of Ibn Hud. His revolt began at Arjuna, a town near Seville, on October 28, 1231. He soon made himself master of Jaen, Granada, Malaga and even of Cordova and Seville, flying the red flag of his counter-revolution over Granada, which became the capital of his little kingdom. As we shall see in the next chapter, he was the only Taifa ruler to survive the Christian onslaught. He founded the Nasrid Kingdom of Granada. In the meanwhile, Ibn Hud lost his all but a small portion of his Spanish kingdom till he was murdered

by one of his lieutenants in 1238. By this time, however, Taifa
Spain was sinking into a welter of uprisings, "punctured by a
dizzying succession of assassinations, beheadings, reprisals,
depositions, intrigues, betryals, restorations, riots, ephemeral
lesser rebellions, vindictive massacres, noisy tumults, bloody
battles, paying of tributes to the Christian over-lords and
disconcerting losses of territory to the armies of Portugal, Castile
and Aragon". Such were, in short, the bitter fruits of the Taifa
Syndrome.

　　　　Obviously, the third Taifa Spain was smaller in size and
had fewer Taifa rulers in it than the two earlier ones. Moreover,
it lasted only for a decade or two. The reason was that the
Christian aggression against it began soon after the Taifa kings
rose into rebellion in various parts of Almohad Spain. "The
whole of Andalusia" writes Ibn Khaldun, "now became a prey
to civil war when every castle and its city was in the possession
of an independent ruler". The Christians did not fail to take
advantage of "the divisions and perversity" of the Taifa chiefs.
In short, the pattern of the Taifa Syndrome remained the same
as before: first the petty rulers, oblivious to the Christian peril
hovering around them, fought against each other, then one or
the other Taifa sought the help of the Christians against his
rivals, paying tributes to them for this purpose and thus providing
them an opportunity to capture one of the other of them, and
lastly, the Christians on their own account attacking and
conquering them all except Granada, because its ruler knew
how to combine duplicity with defiance towards his Christian
overlord of Castile.

The Reconquista completed

　　　　At this time, three Christian kingdoms were in the forefront
of anti-Muslim campaigns, egged on by the Pope and the Catholic
Church behind them. They were the Kingdoms of Portugal,

Castile and Aragon, extending from the west to the east on the Peninsula. By various treaties among them, e.g. the treaty of Cazola in 1179 and of Almizra in 1244, they had already divided Muslim Spain into their respective zones of conquest: Portugal was to capture western region of Taifa Spain, Castile its central region, a lion's share, while Aragon to get its eastern region, including the islands of the Balearics off the Levantine coast of the Peninsula. As before the Christian armies consisted of the feudal knights and magnates, fighting bishops and prelates, urban militias as foot-soldiers and bowmen, the various Military Orders of the Templais, Hospitallers, Calatrava, and the crusaders from various countries of Western Europe, whom the Pope had incited to fight against the Spanish Muslims. One reason which had particularly infuriated the Popes against the Spanish Muslims was the failure of the fifth Crusade in the eastern lands of Islam. In short, the Spanish Muslims had to face the combined forces of the fanatical New Christianity and the feudal classes of Europe, financed by the Italian commercial cities, like Pisa, Genoa, etc.

Thirteenth century was, indeed, a very dark period in the history of Islam. While the Spanish Christians had conquered practically the whole of Muslim Spain and the European crusaders renewed their efforts to reconquer the Holy Lands, Changiz Khan's Mongol hordes had overran the Muslim kingdoms in Central Asia, Ghaznah and Persia. What was more, the Pope and rulers of Christian Europe, e.g. Jamed I of Aragon and Alfonso X of Castile were in contact with the Mongol chief in order to launch a combined attack on the Islamic World from both east and west. Their unholy alliance, however, did not materialise: Mongol advance on Egypt was repulsed and the crusaders thrown back. However, this defeat impelled the Spanish Christians to try hard to overwhelm and destroy the Taifa-ridden Muslim Spain.

The Portuguese were the first to launch aggression against the Muslims. As before, the Portuguese advance was preceded by the invasion of the Crusaders. In 1217, a fleet of two hundred ships from Germany and Low Countries (modern Belgium and Holland appeared off the western coast of the Iberian Peninsula. The Bishops of Lisbon and Evora persuaded the Germans and Flemings to lay siege to Aleacer do Sal, which lasted from July to October, 1217. The city fell to the Christians on October 18, and was followed by the usual loot, rapine and massacre of the Muslims at the hands of the besiegers. Soon afterwards, various towns in the extreme south of the Portuguese kingdom were captured. Among them was the town of Moura, which was commemorated by the supreme sacrifice of brave Muslim girl. Her name was Saluqiyya. She was the daughter of the Muslim lord of the Alentejo. On her wedding day, she wait in vain for her betrothed to come. While coming towards her town, his wedding party was ambushed by the Christians, who strippe the dead of their clothes, entered the town in the disguise of Aral and seized the town. Finding her all lost, the courageous maide flung herself from the top of a tower and killed herself. Since then the place came to be known as the Tower of The Moorish Maiden.

A few years later, Sancho II, the king of Portugal, captured Elvas in 1230 with the help of the knights of Santiago and afterwards, he captured Silves, where war had raged for long. His successor, Alfonso III (1248-79), completed the conquest of the remaining Muslim lands in Algrave, the south western corner of the Peninsula. Thus was established the modern kingdom of Portugal. As we shall see later, the Portuguese became a great sea faring nation during the early Modern Age.

Conquests of James I : The next to advance against Taifa Spain was James I (1213-76), the king of Aragon Chatelaine. (He was also known as Jaime, Jaume, Jacme, etc., thanks to various dialects spoken in his kingdom) Long after his death, his people called him James the Conqueror, because of his conquests of the Muslim territories of Balearics and Valencia which were then two Taifa kingdoms. Like his father and grandfather, who had conquered Saragossa and the Ebro valley from the Muslims, James I had also his eye on these Taifa kingdoms to the south east of his territories. James I has been aptly described as "a passionate defender of the Christian religion, a notorious womanizer, and a formidable crusader." But his eagerness to conquer Muslim lands was also ardently shared by his people. He ruled a federated kingdoms, known as the Crown of Aragon. It consisted of two distinct parts, Aragon and Chatelaine. Aragon was a feudal country, whose nobles and knights sought to acquire fiefs in Muslim Valencia to their south. Chatelaine, whose capital was Barcelona, a city on the coast of the Mediterranean, had become a mercantile country: its merchants and traders were more interested in conquering Balearics, a group of islands situated off the eastern coast of Valencia. Majorca, the biggest of the Balearic islands, was ruled by Muslim king, Abu Yahya. These islands were inhabited by Muslims, who had close trade relations with Tunis and other Muslim countries of North Africa.

Besides King James and his Catalan merchant community, the Pope and the mercantile cities of Genoa and Pisa in Italy and the merchants of Marseilles in southern France, were also deeply interested in capturing Muslim Balearics and ousting the Muslims from the Mediterranean trade.

Conquest of Balearics : In December, 1228, James I declared his intention to invade Majorca, which was hailed by all parties concerned. The Catalan cortes (parliament), meeting at Barcelona, supplied men, money and materials of war to the King, while Pope, Gregory IX, granted crusade indulgences to all who accompanied the crusading King, and the mercantile cities of Italy and France provided him with ships, funds and fighters. Thus commanding a large military force and a fleet of 150 ships. James I sailed from Barcelona in September 1229. The invaders laid siege to Palma, the capital of Majorca. The Muslims were soon starved into surrendering their city, on December 31, 1229, but were massacred by the victorious Christians. By the end of 1230, all the islands of Balearics came under Christian control. The Muslims who survived the Christian massacres, fled to Tunis and other North African countries. The fall of the Balearics was a mortal blow to the Muslim naval supremacy and commercial monopoly of the Mediterranean. The victorious King granted Barcelona the freedom of trade with Majorca, while Genoa, Pisa and Marseilles were rewarded for their collaboration with the grant of trading privileges and establishing trading houses in the island. The conquest of Balearics also enabled the King to invade the Taifa Kingdom of Valencia, whose coast was now controlled by the Christian naval ships.

Conquest of Valencia : Considered from the standpoint of geography and economist, the Christians could not conquer the "Kingdom of Valencia" as it was called then. It was a coastal land, nearly 320 kilometres long and 60 to 80 kilometres broad, with the Mediterranean Sea on its east and a mountain range on its west, which separated it from the rest of Muslim Spain. Its fertile plain was intersected by several rivers and stream,--the biggest of which was the Guadalaviar, a corruption of *Wadi'l Abyad* or White River of the Arabs, and a large number of canals were taken out of these rivers and streams to irrigate the fertile farms, fields and orchards, which were called *huertas* or intensively cultivated irrigated fields. Its farmers and cultivators were hard-working people and ingenious in developing a highly intensive and flourishing agriculture. They had evolved a wonderful system of distributing water, which irrigated their huertas. Moreover, a great number of prosperous and populous towns and cities, along with their castles and fortresses existed all over the Kingdom of Valencia. The Muslims called it the Garden or Paradise of al-Andalus. And it was a thoroughly fortified garden. Yet it was conquered by the Christians! The reason was that like other Taifa kingdoms, it lacked politico-military strength and stability to resist the Christian invaders. Internal disputes and dissensions weakened its defences. Ibn Hariq, one of its poets, who died in 1225, a little before its conquest, said, "Valencia is a paradise surrounded by two misfortunes: famine and war". Famine was due to internal disorders and war was due to its Christian enemies,

When the Muwahhid power was crumbling to pieces in Muslim Spain, Valencia was ruled by Abu Zayd, as its governor. He was a Muwahhid prince, a descendant of Abdul Momin, the founder and the first Khalifa of the Muwahhid empire. On the fall of the Muwahhids in Spain, he became an independent ruler of Valencia in about 1214, and styled himself as its King: hence Valencia became known as a Kingdom. He was attacked by James I in 1225, who tried to capture Peninsula in its north, but failed. Next year, James again ravaged Valencian northern territory of Teruel. Abu Zayd bought peace by offering to pay tribute to the Aragonese King. In 1228, Abu Zayd was attacked and overthrown by Zayyan ibn Mardanish. He then fled to Aragon, where he offered King James to become a Christian on the condition that his feudal possessions in Valencia were restored to him on its conquest. The shrewd Christian King accepted his offer and thus turned him into a tool to invade and conquer Muslim Valencia. He was given the Christian name of Vincent. He then became a crusader and fought against his erstwhile co-religionists in Valencia.

Valencia had a special attraction for King James and his feudal nobles who expected to acqqire large feudal estates in its fertile huertas. They conquered it in three stages. First stage (1232-35) began in 1232, when active preparations for invasion started. The King took the crusader's vow at Monzon, in which he was joined by the nobles, the bishops, and chiefs of the Military Orders of the Temple, the Hospital, Santiago and Calatrava. Many crusaders came from Languedoc or southern France and as usual, Pope Gregory IX preached crusade against the Spanish Muslims. The invasion began soon after. In 1233, the Aragonses King captured Burriana Peninsula and other towns to the north of Valencia city, which constituted its outer defence boundary. After these successes, the King returned to Aragon. Soon after, he divorced his first wife and took another, who was a princess of Hungary. She urged her husband to capture Valencia soon, so that her children, yet to be born, could inherit it after the King's death.

Prodded by his new wife, King James renewed war with Valencia. Thus began the second stage, (1236-38). Again James I, took the crusader's vow at the cortes (parliament) of Monzon in 1236, which provided him with funds for the campaign against the city of Valencia, which was the main objective of war at this stage. As before, French and English crusaders joined his army. The Christians advanced upto the city and occupied a hill overlooking the city. Zayyad ibn Mardanish tried to dislodge the Christian from the hill, but failed to do so. The tight investment of the city from land and sea began. Zayyan sought the aid of Abu Zakariya, the Hafsid Amir of Tunis, who sent a fleet loaded with men, arms and relief supplies for the Muslims of the beleaguered city. But the fleet failed to reach the city because it was blockaded by the Christian navy. The siege lasted for more than a year, till faced with starvation, Zayyan ibn-Mardanish agreed to surrender the city. According to the terms of capitulation, dated September 29, 1238, "all the Moors both men and women, who wish to leave Valencia, may leave and go safely and securely with their arms and all their movable goods they can carry on their backs.........We also wish and grant all those Moors who wish to remain in the district of Valencia shall remain in it on our safely and securely........We also give you a firm truce." Thus Muslim Valencia ceased to exist.

James I entered the city on October 9, 1239, where his first act was to convert its grand mosque into a cathedral and to set up an episcopate. He next distributed the houses and fields around the city among his victorious troops. This method of distributing conquered lands and houses was called *repartimiento,* to distinguish it from the older method, called *presura,* as we shall explain later on.

Grief of the departing Muslims : While the Christians were rejoicing over their victory, the Muslims of Valencia sank into grief and despair. They had five days to leave. With grief writ large on their faces and over their body bent under the load of the movables they were allowed to take, fifty thousand of them left for ever "their green country, their houses, bazaars, farms, graveyards, mosques and places holding memories," Tears showed in every eye and cries of sorrow rose on all sides. "What crime has Valencia committed," asked Ibn al-Abbar, the wazir of Zayyan ibn Mardanish, "that such should be its fate?" Abu'l-Mutariff ibn Amira, a Valencian intellectual cried, "O Valencia the beautiful, the elegant, the brilliant! The infidels have silenced in it the call to prayer and have stifled the breath of Islam's faith." Several centuries later, al-Maqqari, after describing the capitulation of Valencia, wrote, "May God Almighty restore it to the Muslims!"

The third Stage : The third state of the conquest of the Kingdom of Valencia lasted from 1239 to 1248, during which the Christians conquered the southern sector of the Kingdom, including such cities as Jativa, Gandia, Denia, Alicante, Orihuela and others, till they reached the borders of Murcia. There they came across the Castilian forces, who had already subdued Cordova and other cities of al-Andalus. According to their treaties, the Christian kings had already allotted zones of conquest to each other and Murcia was allotted to the Castilian King, Ferdinand III. As Murcia was not within his reach, due to Granada, Fernando's successor, Alfonso X, requested James I to conquer it for him. In 1266, the advancing armies of James captured it and the city was handed over to the Castilian King. At the time of its conquest, Muslims of Murcia requested James not to convert the grand mosque of their city, adjacent to the Alcazar, into a church, but the Christian King replied preposterously, "Do you think I would allow you to cry early morning into my ears, Allah lo Sabha O'Allah, when I am fast asleep in my palace?" As the victor has always his way, the Christian King converted the grand mosque of Murcia into a church.

With the fall of Murcia was completed the conquest of Valencia by James I. Before the advancing Christian armies waves upon waves of Muslim refugees left their homes in the cities, towns and villages as they passed into Christian hands. But still a great majority of them chose to remain under the Christian rule. They were called "tamed" Muslims or *Mudejars*. We shall deal with them presently.

Ferdinand III : Castile, the oldest and the greatest enemy of Islamic Spain, was the last to act against it. The reason was that its rulers were involved in dynastic troubles. Alfonso VIII, the victor of Las Navas de Tolosa in 1212, died two years after his victory. He was succeeded by a minor son, Henry I (1217-17), who died soon after his accession. His sister, Berenguela, was married to the King of Leon. Her son, Ferdinand III, became the King of Castile. But he too was a minor. So during his minority, the Castilian advance against Muslim Spain halted till he became of age in 1224. Then he too began to fish in the troubled waters of the third Taifa Spain. In 1224, he captured Quesada and devastated adjacent districts of al-Andalus. The Muwahhid governors of Baeza, named Abdullah, and of Seville, named al-Idris, were ready to make peace with him in order to have a free hand in Morocco, for which purpose Ferdinand III supplied al-Idris with Christian troops. He thus pushed the Muwahhid princes out of Spain, so that he too would have a free hand against Ibn Hud and other Taifa rulers who were rising to power in various parts of Muslim Spain. In the meantime, Ferdinand III strengthened his position by becoming the King of Leon also on the death of its last King, Alfonso IX, who was his father. So at this critical moment in the history of Muslim Spain, two of its oldest enemies. Leon and Castile, were united into a single kingdom of Castile- Leon under Ferdinand III. This union doubled his resources in men and materials against the tiny Taifa rulers. In their internecine wars, however, the Taifa rulers were ready to become vassals of Ferdinand in order to fight their rivals more furiously. In fact, this short-sightedness was one of the secrets of the ultimate Christian victory. Christian clergy were also as eager to conquer Muslim Spain as the Christian kings. In 1231, Rodrigo, the archbishop of Toledo, reoccupied Quesada and other castles. In 1233, again, Ferdinand III invaded al-Andalus where the Taifa kings were busily engaged in their interminable civil wars. He retook Ubeda and Baeza from Ibn Hud, who was also menaced by Muhammad ibn al-Ahmar. Ibn Hud made peace with Ferdinand by surrendering several border castles to him. During 1233 to 1235, several towns in al-Andalus passed into Christian hands.

Cordova : Assisted by the bishops, feudal magnates, Military Orders in Castile and Leon, and the militias of the towns, Ferdinand 1235 III marched against Cordova in 1035, which was then in Ibn Hud's hands. In his advance on Cordova the Castilian king found a band of Muslim traitors within this ancient Muslim city who were ready to help the Christians to gain control of a suburb of Cordova. They appealed to Ferdinand III to come to their aid, who was then away in Leon. In spite of his truce with Ibn Hud, who had agreed to pay him tribute, Cordova was too great a prize for Christian monarch to respect the truce. He at once marched on Cordova. Ibn Hud tried to stop his advance, but was defeated. He returned to Seville, leaving Cordova to its fate. The Christian besieged the city, destroyed the fields around the city and tightened the siege around it. Realizing that no help was forthcoming from Ibn Hud and their situation becoming worse everyday, the defenders offered to surrender.

In June, 1236, Cordova, wrote al-Maqqari, "the seat of the Umayyad Caliphate, respository of the theological sciences, and abode of Islam, passed into the hands of the accursed Christians. (May God destroy them all)!"

Like James I of Aragon, Ferdinand III also offered the usual terms of capitulation: those Muslims who wanted to leave could go with all their movables on their backs, while those who chose to stay could do so. As usual, the elites of the city left Cordova, while the poorer classes mostly stayed behind. When Ferdinand III entered the fallen city, his first act was to convert its grand mosque into a cathedral. He also ordered the bells of Santiago, which al-Mansur had brought from there and had hanged in the grand mosque as lamps, to be carried on the backs of the Muslims again to the church of Santiago.

The conquest of Cordova opened the whole valley of the Guadalquivir to Ferdinand Ill. He quickly captured all the towns which traditionally depended upon it. Another result was that

Ibn Hud was discredited in the eyes of his followers. One of them murdered him at Almeria in 1238.

Jaen : After the death of Ibn Hud, Muhammad Ibn Ahmar remained the chief Taifa ruler in al-Andalus. He had already established his capital at Granada in 1237. But, unlike Ibn Hud, he could not become the supreme ruler of Taifa Spain, for he was unable to resist the Castilian advance. When he tried in 1244 to raid the territories of Andujar and Martos in Castilian possession, Ferdinand III retaliated by attacking and taking Arjuna and then besieged Jaen, one of the important cities in his Kingdom, and the best fortified in al-Andalus. The siege of Jaen lasted from August 1245 to April, 1245. Al-Ahmar tried to relieve the city, but a revolt in Granada, his capital, compelled him to make peace with the Castilian King and surrender Jaen to him. He further agreed to pay tribute to him and to become his vassal. He attended the Castilian Cortes and served him with his troops. He even agreed to help Ferdinand III with his army in the conquest of Seville, the last important Muslim city in Taifa Spain.

Seville : The fall of Jaen in 1246 opened the road to Seville to the Castilian King. The fall of Carmona brought the Christians nearest to Seville. Seville had, indeed, great attraction for Ferdinand. It was the most opulent city in Taifa Spain. Being situated on the lower reaches of the Guadalquivir, it was really a seaport with direct access to the Atlantic and the Mediterranean. As a matter of fact, the Kingdom to Castile had, upto now, no direct outlet to the Mediterranean. Moreover, Seville was situated in the fertile basin of the Guadalquivir and was the capital of Muslim Spain since the days of the Abbadid kings of Seville of the first crop of the *Muluk at-Tawaif.*

By July, 1247, the Castilian army had approached the walls of Seville and laid siege to it. But the sea link was still open with Triana on the west bank of the Guadalquivir by a bridge of boats. Realising this, Ferdinand III ordered a fleet to be raised in his ports in the Bay of Biscay in order to blockade Seville. The Castilian fleet reached the mouth of the Guadalquivir, where it repulsed the fleets of Seville and of Ceuta and Tangier, and broke the pontoon bridge at Triana. Seville was now surrounded on all sides. Its defenders appealed to the Muwahhid Khalifa, al-Said (1242-48). He died before he could send help. During the summer of 1245-48, the condition of the defender worsened. The siege weapons of the Christians battered the walls of the city, while it was completely cut off with the outside world by land and river. Running short of provisions for the winter, the city capitulated on November 23, 1248.

Under the terms of capitulation, the whole population of Seville departed, carrying their movable goods with them. Among these refugees were the ancestors of Ibn Khaldun, who had dwelt in it for more than five centuries. Like most other refugees, they settled in Tunis. On December 22, 1248, Ferdinand III entered the fallen city. His first act was to convert the grand mosque at Alcazar into a cathedral, its lofty tower became church tower, called Giralda. He also established a bishopric in it. He then distributed the lands and houses among his victorious troops. Without further fighting, about a dozen other towns and cities of al-Andalus surrendered to the Castilian King.

With these Christian victories, Muslim Spain, with the exception of the small Kingdom of Granada, had ceased to exist and its old glories vanished. Despair, dejection and resignation to the Will of God were the feelings of the departing Muslims. One of their poets, ar-Rundi, expressed the feelings of his countrymen as thus:

A curse smote her Muslims and the bane gnawed her,

Until vast regions and towns were despoiled of Islam.

Ask Valencia what became of Murcia,

And where is Jativa, or where is Jaen ?

Where is Cordova, the seat of great learning.

And how many scholars of high repute remain there?

And where is Seville, the home of mirthful gatherings,

On its great river, cooling and brimful with water?

This misfortunate has surpassed all that has preceded,
And as long as Time lasts, it can never be forgotton!

Diaspora of Muslims : The collapse of the third Taifa Spain sent waves after waves of Muslim refugees across the Straits of Gibraltar, as each city, town or district fell into the hands of the all-conquering Christians from 1217 to 1250. The waves of emigrants consisted of those Muslims who chose to leave their ancestral homes and lands either under the terms of capitulation laid down by their victors or due to the terror of the Christian revanchis. They consisted of all classes of people, rich or poor, high or low, although the richer or elite classes were preponderant among them. These classes consisted of the ex-rulers, wazirs and governors, military officers and soldiers, landlords, merchants, traders, ulema, faqihs, scientists, scholars, poets, writers, etc. They left their palaces and homes along with their wives and concubines, children and slaves, family dependents and relatives. Ethnically, the majority of these emigrants were white Muslim Spaniards, while there were also a few Berbers and still fewer Arabs who had long settled in Muslim Spain, but they all spoke Arabic. Their total number was estimated to be about three millions. Most of them settled in Tunis, Morocco and other Kingdoms of North Africa (al-Maghrib) but a few of them went as far as Cairo, Makkah,

Madinah, Baghdad and Damascus. They brought with them
not only the Islamic and secular sciences and learning, poetry
and literature of Muslim Spain, but also the knowledge and
skills in agriculture and industry, and in many kinds of arts and
crafts and architecture, which they imparted to the peoples of
Tunis, Morocco and other Muslim countries. The educated
people among the emigrants soon filled posts of distinction in
the north- west African states, becoming, for example, wazirs,
katibs (secretaries), governors of provinces and districts, and
holding various administrative offices, and they also became
scholars, writers, theologians, etc. At the same time the poorer
people among them became labourers, craftsmen, artisans,
farmers and cultivators, taking to the same occupations which
they had practised in Muslim Spain. In the villages, they
developed the art of irrigation, planted new kinds of trees, and
introduced water-mills, while in the cities like Tunis, Tlemsin,
Algiers, Fez, Marrakesh and others, they worked as architects,
masons, bricklayers, carpenters and gardeners, building splendid
palaces, gardens etc. In short, the impact of these emigrants on
Tunis and al- Maghrib was so great that, for the next three or
four centuries, they became great centres of Islamic civilisation
and culture which rivalled with those of the older centres of the
Islamic East.

Modejars :

Large populations of the Spanish Muslims, who chose to
remain in their ancestral cities, towns and villages, now came
under he domination of the Christian conquerors. They were
known as the "tamed" Muslims of *Mudejars* (In Spanish
Mudejares). This term was derived from the Arabic
"*Mudajjan*", which means "tamed", 'domesticated' or allowed
to remain'. For two more centuries, i.e. thirteenth and
fourteenth, the Mudejars constituted an Islamic element in a
highly hostile and aggressive Christian environment.

Surprisingly enough, no Muslim historian or writer, contemporary or of the later ages, has written anything about their "lost brethren" who were now under Christian heels. Whatever information we have about them has come to us either from Christian sources or archaeologically. The Christian sources were, however, indirect, for the dominant Christians were too arrogant and too disdainful to write anything about the Mudejars. But, as exploiters of the Mudejar labour and skills, they had mentioned them in their land deeds, royal edicts municipal or governmental laws (fueros) and in such other documents. The second, and a silent source of information consists in the 'wonderful artifacts of the Mudejar skill and craftsmanship, which the Spanish and even European Christians had bought from them as articles of daily use, and many of which are now preserved as museum pieces. Centuries later, modern lovers of art, archaeologists and historians have studied them as specimens of Mudejar art.

Vanquished Muslims : So far as the treatment of the vanquished Muslims by the victorious Christians was concerned, it varied from one stage of the Reconquista to the other. As such, it had three distinct stages. During the first stage, which lasted from the middle of the eighth century to 1085 when Alfonso VI of Castile conquered Toledo, the Christian conquerors showed no mercy or humanity towards the vanquished Muslims. Those of them who did not flee from the newly-conquered Christian lands were put to the sword to the last man, woman and child or sold as slaves by the Christians. It was, indeed, an essential part of their "depopulation policy" so that the 'unoccupied land's could be repopulated by the Christian settlers, who were either northern mountaineers or Mozarabs, who came from the Muslim south. During this bloodthirsty period, Christian Spain expanded from the northern mountains of Asturias to the river Douro. As a result of this colonialistic policy, no Muslim minority existed in the Kingdom of Leon-Castile during the early centuries of the Reconquista, as also in other northern Christian kingdoms, which were then coming into existence.

During the second stage, which lasted from the end of the eleventh to the middle of the fifteenth century, things changed a bit. After the defeat of the petty kings of the three Taifa Soains, the Christian kings conquered large chunks of Muslim territories, and those Muslims, who did not like to leave their ancestral homes, were allowed to remain and came under the protection of the Christian conquerors. They came to be known as Mudejars. Only the Kingdom of Portugal was an exception. Its conquerors continued the old policy of depopulation or extirpation of the Muslims in the territories they had conquered, such as Lisbon or Algrave. The reason was that the Portuguese conquerors were prompted in their campaigns by the Popes and the crusaders from France, England, and other countries of Western Europe.

The third and last stage of the Reconquista began at the end of the fifteenth century, when the surviving Muslim Kingdom of Granada was completely destroyed by the Spanish Christians. As usual, the richer and more educated Granadan Muslims fled or emigrated to North Africa, while the poorer classes among them continued to live under Christian dispensation for another century or so. These new Muslim minorities were known as *Moriscos*. We shall describe the fate of these unfortunate Muslim communities in a later chapter, for the old Christian fanaticism and colonialist brutality had become ascendant once again in their treatment of the defenceless Moriscos. Indeed, they met a more cruel fate than did the Mudejars, their earlier co-religionists.

Why were the Mudejars treated more leniently by their

Christian masters ? Did these Christians become more tolerant and liberal-minded than the other two ? Not so. The reasons lay in the demographic, economic and cultural advantages which the Mudejars possessed and which their Christian masters wanted to exploit. In other words, the then Christian colonialism had become more exploitative than exterminative, at least for some time.

One of the strange anomalies in the history of Muslim Spain is that when the Muslims were demographically weak, they were militarily strong, but when they became demographically strong, they became militarily weak. In other words, when the Muslims in Spain were much fewer in numbers, they were victorious over the more numerous Christians but when they became more numerous than the Christians, they were defeated and conquered by them. The result was that large Muslim communities in the cities, towns and villages of the quondam Muslim Spain came under Christian domination. In fact, the Muslims were in majority in the provinces of Andalusia and Valencia in the Kingdoms of Castile and Aragon respectively. It took their masters more than two centuries of oppression, pogroms, conversions and expulsions to destroy Muslims completely. The same tragic story was repeated, when the Kingdom of Granada was conquered by the Christians. The Moriscos were in majority till the genocidism launched by the Christian State and Church, turned the tables on them in much shorter time than it did in the case of the Mudejars.

Why were the Mudejars so fortunate as to survive so long?

This question leads us to the second anomaly in the history of Muslim Spain. In the modern theory of international power politics, it is generally averred that economically and technologically advanced countries would conquer or dominate those which are economically backward or under-developed.

Muslim Spain was industrially, agriculturally and technically far more advanced than the Christian north. Yet it was defeated and conquered by the latter. What were the reasons for this anomalous situation? This question we shall discuss in a subsequent chapter. Here we shall consider its effects on the Mudejar situation. In a very real sense, the Mudejars were heirs to five-centuries of the splendid progress and achievements of the Spanish Muslims in agriculture, industry, arts and crafts. Naturally, it was not sensible for their Christian master, their murderous fanaticism notwithstanding, to kill the hen that laid golden eggs. So the Mudejars continued to practise their ancestral arts and craft under Christian dispensation. They manufactured such useful and beautiful things as tiles and ceramics, fabrics am textiles, Cordovan leather goods, etc. and built palaces and churches for their Christian masters. The richer classes in Christian Spain and even in Europe, bought these goods very eagerly. Thus the unknown Mudejar men and women helped in raising the standard and quality of life of the dominant Christian classes who formerly lived a drab and dreary life in the barren mountains of the north.

Secondly, the Mudejars also played an important role in the cultural and intellectual life of their Christian masters. In this respect, however, the Spanish Christians were more selective or choosy. Though they rejected, on religious grounds, much of the literature and poetry of the Spanish Muslims of the earlier ages they employed many Mudejar singers and performers in their churches, till the Council of Valladolid in 1322 condemned the employment of the Muslims in church service.

Mudejar Zones : The areas where the Mudejars lived were called Mudejar Zone. First of the Mudejar Zones was the country around Toledo, which was conquered by Alfonso VI in 1085, at the end of the first Taifa Spain. Next was Saragossa and the Ebro valley, which were conquered by the Aragonese

. kings at the end of the second Taifa Spain. The third and biggest
Mudejar zone came into being after the third Taifa Spain was
so speedily overran by the Christians of Leon-Castile and of
the Crown of Aragon. During this period, the whole valley of
Guadalquivir, the heartland of Muslim Spain for centuries, was
conquered by Fernando III of Leon-Castile and re-christened
as Andalusia, and became one of three provinces of the Kingdom
of Leon-Castile, containing such cities as Cordova, Seville,
Jaen, etc. Although large numbers of Muslim elite classes had
fled or emigrated from it, still its Muslim population was much
larger than the Christian settlers and remained so for about a
century and more. The same was the case of the "Kingdom of
Valencia" on the east coast of the Peninsula, which had been
conquered by James I, the King of Aragon. Similarly, the
province of Murcia in the south of the Peninsula, annexed by
Castile, remained for long a predominantly Muslim region.

Christian settlement : Soon after a Muslim territory was
conquered, Christian colonisation began. During the first stage
of the Reconquista, the method of re-settlement, known as
presura, was simple: as the Muslims were either killed or driven
out of the conquered lands, the Christian settlers occupied the
so-called "unoccupied lands" as they liked. During the second
stage of Reconquista, the Christian conquerors adopted a more
systematic policy of colonisation. In the conquered cities and
towns, they ordered the Muslims, who preferred to stay on
under the Christian rule, to quit their homes and houses along
with all their goods and relocated them in special reservations
outside the city or town, called *morerias*. The houses and lands
thus vacated were then distributed among the victorious
Christian by a method which was called *prepartimiento*, i.e.
they were apportioned among the victorious Christians.

In the villages, however, the repartimiento was
impracticable, partly because the Muslim population was too

large to be shifted around, but mainly because the Christian conquerors allotted these villages to their nobles as large feudal estates, thus reducing the Muslims to the position of serfs. Anyhow, for the rural Muslim communities, servitude was no new experience. As we have said above, Muslim Spain had a rudimentary and chaotic form of feudalism. Whenever central authority in it weakened, as did under the later Umayyads or under the Murabits and Muwahhids, and the Taifa disintegration broke out once again, the lot of the Muslim peasantry became very hard. They passed from the hands of one Muslim land-holder into those of another, who extorted as much out of them as he could during the short period before he too was supplanted by his rivals. The Christian domination, on the contrary, was more stable and permanent: hence they exploited their Muslim serfs more systematically and thoroughly. In some places, e.g. Murcia, however, repartimiento was applied even in villages, Muslim proprietors were driven out and vacated lands apportioned among Christian settlers.

Mudejar communities : Every Mudejar community, called *Aljama*, lived in a walled-enclosure, called *moreria*. The Christian rulers had organised the Muslim aljamas on the same lines as they had in their towns. The Christian towns or cities had a municipal corporation, called *universitas* or commune. It elected its officers, made its own laws, collected its own taxes and governed its affairs, without much interference or control by the king or central authorities. The Mudejar aljamas were not such autonomous corporations. Although they had the power to elect their officers, like the qazis, amins, etc., but such powers were rarely exercised. The taxes were imposed on them by the Christian rulers. They had their own laws, called *cuna* (i.e. sunnah). But even in this case also, the Christian kings and cortes interfered and made laws for the aljamas.

The Mudejars lived in an apartheid-like situation. They

were confined within their walled morerias and were prohibited from living outside them. The walls of the morerias were built and maintained by its aljama. If they failed to do so, the Christian authorities punished them with fines and forced them to build or repair them from time to time. A Muslim could go out of his/her moreria only under a licence. If he was found outside the moreria walls without such a licence, he was captured by the Christians and sold as a slave and his property, such as his goods or animals, like a donkey or mule, confiscated. The Muslims were not allowed to butcher animals, for the sale of meat was a state monopoly. Meat was sold by licensed butchers, who were always Jews. The Muslims could not buy it from any other place or person. Moreover, the Christian authorities fixed the price of the meat at much higher rates than the meat sold to the Christians. It was a real hardship for the Muslims, for meat was their staple food.

Every aljama had its own officials. The most important among them was the qazi. He was a judge and decided all cases in which the Muslims were involved or which were brought before him for his decision. He was also a censor, supervising the moral life of the Muslims in his aljama. He supervised the markets in the moreria. He also settled theological disputes among the Muslims. In short, the qazi's jurisdiction was extensive. He was a central figure in the Mudejar life. In spite of it, many qazis were appointed by the Christian authorities. Sometimes, a Mudejar Qama had no qazi or he was an absentee, which caused much hardship and resentment among its Muslim population.

Another officer was known as *amin*. He was the tax-collector and financial officer of the moreria. He kept accounts of its community and received salary for his job. In small towns, he had also judicial powers.

In very aljama, there was also a *faqih* or jurisconsult.

An officer, called *mustasaf* collected taxes on meat, both royal and local, and fines for fraud or other market offences.

In theory, the Mudejar aljamas were municipal corporations, like the Christian Universitases. But, in practice, they did not enjoy the same autonomy and independence as did the Christian Universitases. In time of crisis, such as a war, the king took away all their authority and appointed a Christian officer, called *commissarius, administrator* or *rector,* who exercised absolute powers over very aspect of life in the moreria. He could impose any tax, or penalty, decide all cases and order the Muslims as he liked.

Within the walled enclosure of a moreria, the Muslims enjoyed many amenities of life, though under the herrenvolkic domination of the Christians. They had their own markets and bazaars, their Islamic schools and centres of learning, and their well kept mosques, where they enjoyed the liberty to call the faithful to prayers. Though the greater majority of the Mudejars, were poor and many awfully so, there wee also some rich ones among them, especially those who held some judicial or official position in their aljamas, or those who were the favourites of the Christian king or queen, as for example the Belvis family in Valencia. The condition of the Mudejar women was most deplorable. They could be ill-treated by any Christian any time, They could be captured and sold as slave or kept as concubines. In fact, any free Mudejar woman could be made a concubine and allotted to a royal favourite. "We therefore direct and command you" said a royal order, "to grant and release the said Stephen one of the first female Saracens to be confiscated by you (i.e., King's official) for our Court in the manner mentioned before, with which Saracen he may do as he wishes." Moreover every moreria had one or more prostitution houses, where, both Muslim and Christian prostitutes plied their trade, among whom the Muslim prostitutes were in majority. They were visited even by the Christians, who were otherwise reluctant to enter the morerias. Prostitution was one reason why the dominant Christians held morerias in utter contempt as places of low repute.

Kinds of Mudejars : All Mudejars were divided into the broad categories, free and slaves. Even the free Mudejars were held in various degrees of servitude. So far as the Aragonese Mudejars were concerned, they were divided into four categories:

> the Mudejars of the King (and also of the Queen)
> the Mudejars of the feudal lords;
> the Mudejars of the Catholic Church and
> the Mudejars of the moneasteries, convents and military orders.

These distinctions were for the purposes of servitude, labour taxes and fines, otherwise they were all considered as the king's Mudejars. The king taxed them all, imposed fines on them violation of many laws, e.g. of dress or diet, and got his share of fines and penalties imposed by the other three categories of their masters. The Mudejars who changed lords, lost all real property and also, all but personal goods (just like their vanquished forefathers who had to part with their all except what they could carry on their backs at the time of their capitulation). Faithful Christian bequeathed their Mudejars to the church or monastic orders as the serfs or slaves Majority of the churchmen, monks and nuns regular oppressors of the Mudejars. It was with them both an act of faith and of financial gain. "Bishop of Valencia was best known to the Muslim population there by his jail, in which very large numbers of Muslims were kept waiting trial or sale as slaves. The Bishop of Tortosa enslaved many Muslims whom he had pardoned and tortured and extorted money from Mudejar officials.

Mudejar serfs : Spanish Muslims had developed agriculture greatly both in the basin of the Guadalquivir, where their agricultural production was based on the *norias* or Persian wheels and in the fertile canal-irrigated huertas of Valencia. When they were conquered by the Christians, they became their serfs, called *exaricos*. Like the serfs in contemporary feudal Europe, the Mudejar serfs were tied to the land of their Christian lords (i.e. kings, queens, feudal lords, ecclesiastical lords, etc). When their lands were transferred from one lord to another, the Mudejar serfs also changed hands. On the death of a lord, his heirs inherited the Mudejar serfs as they did his lands. Like their European counterpart, the Mudejar serfs worked on their lord's lands, paid him fees and fines for the use of his mills or ovens and fulfilled other feudal duties. There were also some free farmers in the village morerias. But in course of time, they too passed into servitude and then eased to be distinguished from the hereditary serfs.

Mudejars slaves : Technically, a distinction was made between the free and slave Mudejars. But it was more on paper than in reality. Any foreign Muslim in the Kingdom of Aragon was legally enslaveable. So too the so-called free Muslim subjects of the king. "Any Muslim found by the Christians who could not or would not identify his lord or owner was automatically enslaved by the Crown." Such enslaved Muslim were called *res vaccantes* or "unclaimed objects." Even a free Mudejar who was not an "unclaimed object" could be enslaved for violating laws or dress codes. This sort of enslavement was so common that the king could allot a Muslim to anyone of his favourites even long before he or she was enslaved as "the next Saracen confiscated by the Crown," to put it in the words of a royal edict. There were many Mudejars who were thus enslaved without any given reason. John Boswell has calculated that during 1255-65, there were 59 Mudejars who had been enslaved without giving any reason for their enslavement by the King. The kings sometimes imposed heavy fines on the Christians for enslaving free Mudejar but after collecting the money, he did not set the unfortunate Mudejar free. Moreover, the king received one-fifth of the sale price of every Muslim sold into slavery. Hence "it was obviously in the King's interest to see as many Muslims as possible confiscated and enslaved.

Mudejar arts and crafts, etc : Whether free or slave, Mudejars were the backbone of the economy and prosperity of the Christian Spain, and remained so till she become a rich an powerful imperialist nation in the early modern Europe. The Mudejars could engage in all occupations and professions except priesthood for obvious reasons and butchering, for reasons because meat trade was a State monopoly. Christian kingdoms had a thriving urban culture which required craftsmen, labourers, and professionals of all types in ever-greater numbers. Pottery was virtually a monopoly of the Mudejars. It was Mudejar art *par excellence*. They had developed the art of applying coloured glazes to earthenware, which fetched high prices not only in the Peninsula but also in Europe and gave rise to the pottery industry at Piotiers in France and spread later as far as Holland in the north and Italy the south of Europe.

The Mudejars also worked in the construction industry as masons, bricklayers, carpenters day labourers etc. Paper-making was their important occupation. They were also traders in grain and salt. They also maintained the canal irrigation system, which was developed by the Spanish Muslims of the earlier ages and on which the agriculture and prosperity of Christian Spain now depended. The Mudejars also practised medicine, but under strict regulations of the Crown of Aragon. However, they could not treat Christian patients, except in the presence of a Christian physician.

The Mudejars of both sexes were also found, almost exclusively, in the entertainment industry as jugglers, jesters, dancers, musicians, etc. "Probably the Christian majority found such positions unappealing and gladly left them for the Mudejars."

The Mudejars also worked as shoemakers, tanners, transporters, vintners and the like.

But their greatest achievements were in the arts of ceramics and mosaics. They distinguished in the making of tiles and blue faience. Coloured tiles, now known as *azulejo* in modern Spanish, are still popular in Spain and Portugal, which are a legacy of the Mudejar age. Cordova and Toledo in the Kingdom of Castile and Calatayud, Malaga, and Manises in Valencia were the chief centres of the lustre pottery of the Mudejars.

In architecture, the Mudejar combined the horseshoe arc and the vault with the Gothic architecture of the Spanish Christians which became the Spanish national style.

The influence of the Mudejars can be seen today in the fact that numerous terms of these trades and industries are still found in the modern Spanish language, especially in the arts and crafts of pottery, ceramics, fabrics, architecture, carpentary, etc.

Under their treaties of capitulation, the Muslims had been guaranteed by their Christian conquerors the right to govern their lives according to their Islamic Law or Sunnah, administered by their own judges or qazis, and equality before the law along with the Christians. But within a century, all the Mudejars were deprived of these rights and guarantees first in criminal and then in civil cases. The Christian rulers ceased to appoint qazis to decide Mudejar cases. Instead, they appointed Christian judges even in those civil cases in which Muslims alone were involved, such as those of marriage, divorce, inheritance, etc. In criminal cases, the Christians adopted most draconian laws for the Muslims. By the order of October, 1364, the Aragonese King appointed a Christian judge with criminal jurisdiction over the Muslims who was entrusted with "the power to burn or brand hands, feet, noses and other members, or to remove or amputate them, to incarcerate or banish or inflict any other punishment or type of sentence . . . . . . as should seem fitting, without any appeal, complaint, supplication or recourse by the accused Muslims.

Thus, by the end of the fourteenth century, all Muslims cases, civil or criminal, came under the jurisdiction of the Christian judges, known as bailiffs, who controlled the Mudejar morerias within their jurisdiction. Moreover, the Muslims could not be lawyers. They had therefore to depend upon Christian lawyers to defend their cases, even when both parties were Muslims. Of course, the Christian lawyers charged exorbitant fees from the Muslim litigants. Even laws became instruments of Mudejar oppression. In spite of the equality before the law, the Muslims could be plundered by the Christian with impunity and the laws would not protect them. "Loss of property was probably the single greatest problem of Aragonese Mudejars. They provided a ready source of plunder for any official or citizen, who was in dire need of food, animals, cash, or even a slave." The aggrieved Muslim could neither had the Christian punished or his property restituted even by the King. Thus "severe laws and certain retribution (by the Christians) made physical resistance by Muslims unheard of."

After nearly two centuries of Christian domination, the "tamed" Muslims vanished from the pages of history, leaving behind no written records or traces as to how all this happened. Indeed, so effective was their destruction that, by the fifteenth century, the term "Mudejar art" referred not to persons but to objects of art. We know that in such Mudejar zones as Andalusia and Valencia, their populations were much larger than those of the Christians. How were then these large populations eliminated from their ancient lands ? The disappearance of a whole people is not something unknown to human history. Apparently, the Mudejar disappearance occurred so silently and yet so effectively as to leave no clue behind it. As usual, however, we have indirect evidence of their extirpation. Some of the causes of their disappearance are discussed briefly, follows :

1. Christian oppression, and State pressure, e.g. over taxation, reduced great majority of the hard-working Mudejars to abject poverty and misery;

2. Mudejar revolts, which occurred frequently during the thirteenth and fourteenth centuries, were, however, easily crushed by the overwhelming political and military power of the Christians and, consequently, many thousands of the Mudejars were either killed or exiled by their victors;

3. Plagues, like Black Death and famines took a heavy toll of the Mudejar lives in disease, death and misery, for they lived under extremely insanitary conditions in their morerias;

4. Widespread enslavement of the Mudejar men, women and children, who were then sold to foreign European masters or were afterwards absorbed into Christianity by living in Christian families;

5. Expulsions of the Mudejars as exiles etc., from Christian Spain;

6. Their emigration to Granada and other Muslim lands in North Africa, which took place sometimes as a trickle of emigrants and at other times in large groups e.g. a Muslim, his family or a group left on pilgrimage to holy places in Arabia and then never returned to

their Spanish homes;

7. The anti-Muslim pogroms or riots by the Christians of Castile and Aragonese Kingdoms, which resulted in reducing the Mudejar population by death and destruction or by consequent emigration to other Muslim lands.

8. Conversion to Christianity was, of course, rare among the Mudejars. But their assimilation into the dominant Christian culture became quite common, which later on paved their path to the adoption of the Christian faith. Their cultural assimilation was noticed by Ibn Khaldun, who visited Christian Spain in 1364 on a diplomatic mission. He wrote, "the vanquished always want to imitate the victor in his distinctive marks, his dress, his occupation and in all other conditions and customs," and he then added, "At this time, this is the case in Spain. The Spaniards (i.e. the Mudejars) are found to assimilate themselves to the Galician (i.e. Christian) nations in their draw, their emblems and most of their customs and conditions. This goes so far that they even draw pictures on the walls and (have them) in buildings and houses." Cultural assimilation was the path by which the surviving Mudejars adopted Christianity.

To sum up: the despised and harassed Mudejar communities were constantly decimated and reduced in numbers by both man-made (Christian) and natural calamities till they were smothered out, of existence by the ambient political; military and cultural superiority of the Spanish Christians.

But no sooner did the Mudejars disappear from the pages of history than a new crop of Muslim victims fell under the Christian heels. They wore the Moriscos for the fallen Kingdom of Grenada whose rise and fall we shall consider next.

CHAPTER 37

NASRID DYNASTY
(1232–1492 A.D.)

The Banu Nasr claimed their descent from Sad-bin Abada, a companion of the holy Prophet and the chief of the Khazrah tribe.

It was in the first century of Hijra that two notable persons from the family of Hazrat Sad-bin-Abada entered Spain, one stayed in Takarna and the other in village near Sarqasta (Saragossa) which was later on termed at Khazraj.

According to Ibne Khaldoon the Banu Ahmar lived in the fort of Arjuna, a fort of Cordova and were nicknamed Banu Nasr, tracing their descent for Hazrat Sad bin Abada. The predecessors held high military posts under the Umayyads.

Foundation : Of the several petty kingdoms of the third Taifa Spain, the small and shrunken kingdom of Granada was the only one to survive the onslaught of the Castilian conquistadors. It was founded by one of the Taifa kings, named Muhammad ibn Yusuf ibn Ahmed ibn Nasr, popularly known as Ibn al Ahmar (or son of the red one). He traced his descent from Hazrat Sa'd bin Abada, the chief of Banu Khazraj of the Ansars of Medina. Two of his descendants came to Spain at the time of its conquest: one of them settled at Takarna in the south, while another at Sargossa in the north of the Peninsula.

According to Ibn Khaldun, the family of ibn al Ahmar, known as Banu Nasr, were the *Shaikhs* or Chiefs of Arjuna, a castle near Cordova and held military positions under the Muwahhid rulers of Spain. When their rule in Spain began to disintegrate and Ibn Hud raised the standard of revolt against them, several chiefs also revolted against Ibn Hud. One of them was the Shaikh of Arjunah, named Muhammad ibn Nasr ibn al Ahmar. He raised the standard of revolt on October 28, 1231 with the support of his clan, Banu Nasr, and the family of Ibn Ashqilulah, and cause himself to be proclaimed Sultan of al Andalus. Next year, in 1232, he captured Jaen and Xerez. In the pandemonium which broke out in Taifa Spain over the populistic policies of Ibn Hud, ibn al Ahmar joined hands with another rebel, Abu Merwan al Baji, the chief of Seville and formed an alliance with him against ibn Hud. But with duplicity which characterised ibn al Ahmar, he soon marched on Seville, captured it in September, 1234, and put al Baji to death. Angered by his double dealing, the people of Seville revolted against him a month later and drove him out of the city and again proclaimed ibn Hud as their Sultan. Ibn al Ahmar returned to Jean where he received the news that the people of Granada had proclaimed him as their Sultan. In 1235, he went to Granada and received the allegiance of its people and took up his abode in it. He built a fortress on a hill in Granada, which was called Al-Hamra (The Red) or Alhambra, as it is known even today. In this manner Granada became the capital of his small kingdom. Afterwards, Ibn al-Ahmar also acquired possession of Malaga and Almeria in 1245 and of Lorca in 1264.

CHAPTER 38

MUHAMMAD I

Muhammad I and Fernando III : The rise of ibn al-Ahmar or Muhammad I to power could not go unchallenged by Ferdinand III, the King-Emperor of Castile-Leon. So he became a vassal and tributary of the Christian King against his fellow-Muslims. He assisted the Christian King with his troops in the capture of Cordova, Seville and other Muslim towns. In return for his assistance, the Christian King helped him in capturing Granada, Malaga, Almeria and Lorca, as we said above. When Ferdiand III died in 1252, Muhammad I renewed his tributary vassalage with his successor, Alfonso X (1252-1284). Naturally, a question arises: Why did the Castilian Kings, who had great imperialist ambitions and had conquered all the petty Muslim kings of Taifa Spain, allow the petty Kingdom of Granada to exist on the soil of Spain, which they could otherwise easily wipe off the face of the earth? The situation, however, was not so simple as it might appear.

Compared to the Christian Kingdom of Castile-Leon, which surrounded it on all three sides, Granada was a very small kingdom. But two things ensured its survival for two and a half century more: the character and policies of its founder Muhammad I and its peculiar geo-political situation.

Character : Muhammad I might well be described as a

prototype of a Machiavellian prince. He knew the art of double dealing. He knew also where lay his strength and weakness. He could bow before the strong one day, but would defy him the next day when opportunity made it possible. Indeed, he performed a remarkable feat in establishing his Kingdom when Castilian power appeared so invincible, and, by skillful diplomacy, he preserved its independence on one side and also avoided dangerous entaglements with the Muslim kings of North Africa, on the other.

Geo-political Situation : From Ronda in the west to Almeria in the east, the Kingdom of Grenada was about three hundred kilometres long and about a hundred kilometres broad. It lay in the mountainous region in the south-eastern corner of the Iberian Peninsula, on the coast of the Mediterranean, with Gibraltar, Malaga, Almeria and others as its ports and had links with the Muslim Kingdoms of North Africa. The little Africa was thus sandwiched between two mighty ones, namely the Christian Africa of Castile to its north and the newly-established kingdom of the Marinids in North Africa, who both of them aspired to conquer it. The Mierinids dreamed of reviving the Al-Muwahhid Empire of Spain of the recent past, in which Grenada could be both their tool and target. The Castilian danger was, however much greater and closer. Ferdinand III was eager to conquer Grenada, but Muhammad I stayed, him off by becoming his vassal and by paying him a large tribute. Moreover the mountain range of Sierra Navada near Granada was the first line of defence against Castilian aggression, just as the Strait of the first line of Gibraltar was defence against African advance. Furthermore, Muhammad I and his successors also by allying with one of their enemies against the other. Thus, by playing this deadly game of hide and seek, the Granadan Sultans protected their petty Kingdom effectively for more than a century and half from 1232 to 1400. During this period, however, the

Castilian rulers were also involved in their internal troubles
and in their ambitious plans to become the Holy Roman
Emperors in Central Europe.

The collapse of the third Taifa Spain had given place to
three Christian kingdoms in the Iberian Peninsula, viz., Portugal,
Aragon and Castile. Portugal was too small to challenge its
powerful neighbour, Castile. James I of Aragon and his
successors had also imperialist ambitions. But, Aragon was
only a Mediterranean naval power, while the Mediterranean
Sea was fast losing its ancient importance as the highway of
mighty empires. That was the reason why Aragon, in the long
run lost to Castile in its race to build an empire of its own. On
the contrary, Castile, which had captured a lion's share in the
conquest at Muslim Spain, had greater advantage, in men and
materials and also in its control at both the Mediterranean and
Atlantic coasts. Moreover, in their long-drawn struggle against
Muslim Spain, the Castilian kings had learnt one lesson that
either Spain must control North-West Africa (Morocco) or
North-West Africa would control Spain. This was the reason
they had learnt from the domination at Muslim Spain by the
Al-Murabits and Al-Muwahhids. That was the reason why the
Castilian King, Ferdinand III, planned to bring Morocco under
his domination soon after he had completed the conquest of the
third Taifa Spain. However, there was one obstacle: the ports of
Taifa, Algeciras and Gibraltar, which were nearest to the African
coast, were in the hands of Muhammad I of Granada. Though
he was his tributary vassal, yet he was reluctant to part with
them. When Ferdinand III died in 1252, he left unfinished the
conquest of Granada and also his projected invasion of Morocco
to his son and successor, Alfonso X *el Sabio* or the Leanred
(1252-84)

On his accession, Alfonso X was confronted with four
tasks: to control the Mudejar majority in Andalusia, to get

himself elected as the Holy Roman Emperor, to launch the invasion of Morocco, and to conquer Granada. The first task was easiest to achieve and also most attractive to his nobles and common Christians. Immediately after his accession, he began the colonisation of Seville and the territory around it, whose the subjugated Muslims or Mudejars were still in a great majority. He distributed houses, lands, vineyards, olive groves and the like, belonging to the Mudejars, among Christian settlers who came from all over the Peninsula, according to the method of repartimiento. In his book, *Libro del Repartimento,* drawn on his orders, he gave a list of grantees and of the Muslim properties given to them as fiefs, taking care, of course, to reserve a larger share to himself. Thus he became the richest king in whole Europe. However, he wasted this wealth in trying to be elected as the Holy Roman Emperor. He failed in this endeavour. His people, especially the feudal nobility, resented his attempt, because they were burdened with more taxes. His second adventure, the invasion of the Marinid Morocco, was also not a great success. In early September, 1260, he sent a fleet to attack the port of Sale on the Atlantic coast of Morocco. The Muslims of the city, who took the fleet to have come for purposes of trade and were just breaking the fast of Ramzan, were taken aback when the Christians attacked their city. After capturing the city, the Christians, as usual, gave themselves up to killing, rape and loot. When the Marinid Amir, Abu Yusuf Yaqub ibn Abdul Haq, sent a force against the Christians, they hurriedly withdrew from the city after setting it to fire. Thus Alfonso's crusade against Sale was also a failure. But it provoked the enmity of the Marinids.

Muhammad I and Alfonso X : The next target of Alfonso X's crusade was the Kingdom of Granada. His adventure against Sale had shown him that for the invasion of Morocco he must first possess the ports of Gibraltar and Tarfia, which were in the possession of Muhammad I of Granada. He demanded the Granadan King to hand them over to him. Although Muhammad I visited Seville, the Castilian capital, every year and paid tribute to Alfonso X regularly, but he refused to comply with his orders. He knew that these ports were his links with Muslim Africa. If they fell into Castilian hands, he would be unable to get military aid from the Marinids of Morocco. His little kingdom would then be swallowed up the Christians. Not content with mere refusal, Muhammad I prepared his counter-crusade against Alfonso X. In conjunction with Ibn Hud, the king of Murcia and a vassal of Alfonso X, he incited the Mudejars of Andalusia against their Castilian king. They revolted in 1264. The Mirinid ruler of Morocco also sent a contingent of 3000 troops to join the holy war (*jihad*) against the Christians. They were welcomed by the Granadan King. They fought bravely against the Castilians. However, to counter- balance his relations with the Marinids, Muhammad I renewed his homage to the Hafsid Amir of Tunis, so that his dependence on the Marinids might not threaten his sovereignty at any time later on.

The Mudejar revolt began in May, 1264. The "tamed Muslims" soon liberated several cities, like Arcos, Vejer, Rota, Medina Sidonia Sanlucar, Murica, Moratalla, and Lorca from the Christians. But Seville, Cordova, Jaen, Cartagena and Orihuela could not be thus liberated. Moreover, in several town the Christians formed *hermandad* or brotherhood unions to defend them against the Muslims. Six months later, in October, 1264, Alfonso X struck against the Muslims. His troops re-captured Medina Sidonia, and other towns, while Cadiz and Sanlucar were captured in 1265. Thus the Mudejar revolt was crushed and waves of Muslim refugees fled to Granada and North Africa. In the meanwhile, troubled Granada provided Alfonso X with an opportunity to strike against Muhammad I. The members of the family of Banu Ashqilula, who were close associates of Banu Nasr, and were governors of Malaga, Guadix and Comares, revolted against the Sultan because of the favours he had shown to the Moroccan troops. In response to the appeal of Banu Ashqilula, Alfonso X invaded Granada and occupied the vega or plain of Granada in May, 1265. Realising that further continuation of conflict would not be in his interest Muhammad I offered truce to Alfonso X in August, 1265, who accepted it. Muhammad pledged to pay the annual tribute of 150,000 *maravedis* and to assist the Christians in the conquest of Murcia. On his part, Alfonso X promised not to support the rebellious Banu Ashqilula. But the two monarchs had no mind to stick to the terms of the truce. The Christian King did not stop supporting Banu Ashqilula against the King of Granada, although he paid his annual tribute regularly in 1266 and 1267.

Castilian Nobles : Alfonso X was a mixture of the old and new. Being a faithful Christian, he supported the Church and the clergy in every manner. He also favoured the rising class of the burghers or the mercantile bourgeoisie of the towns, and with its support sought to restrict the powers and privileges of the feudal nobles, who had grown very rich by plundering the "tamed" Mudejars. Moreover, he sought to become the Holy Roman Emperor, for which purpose he spent huge sums of money. At the same time, influenced by the Roman Law, he tried to enhance his royal authority, and to make a single code of law (fueros) for his whole realm. He demanded more and more taxes from the nobles and the merchant classes, which they resented very much, The Castilian nobles were particularly incensed by his attempt, to centralised all authority into his own hands and thus upset the delicate balance of European feudalism in which both the ruler and the ruled (i.e. the nobles) had equal rights and authority in the business at the State. Angered by his pro-clergy and pro-burgher inclinations, the nobles began to conspire against their King in 1270. They own received the support of Muhammad I of Grenada and of Abu Yusuf, the Marinid Amir of Morocco, whom they appealed for help, though the Amir contented himself with mere verbal sympathies. In the meantime, the rebellious nobles, led by the King's brother, Felipe, repudiated the bond of vassalage and threatened to go over to Muhammad I, the King of Grenada. Alfono, X reproached his brother bitterly for siding with the King of Granada, "the enemy of God, of the faith, of the king and of his kingdom". "You" he said to his brother, "as the son of King Fernando and queen Beatriz, and as the brother of King Alfonso, ought better to safeguard the lineage from whence you come and the duty that, you owe to it." On his part, Muhammad I welcomed the royal rebel and the Castilian nobles and concluded an alliance with them against Alfonso X. But before he could take further steps against the Castilian King he died shortly after in September, 1272.

By his energy and tactful policies, Muhammad I had saved his little Kingdom from the depredations of the Castilian rulers. Had he lived a little longer, he would have perhaps utilized the Castilian rebels to inflict a grievous injury on the Castilian Kingdom. Soon after accession to power, Muhammad I had assumed a royal title of *Al-Ghalib billlah* (the conqueror by the grace of Allah). He built for himself the castle and palace at al-Hamra (Alhambra) which was enlarged and further embellished by his successors. He was man of the people; he invited them to lay their grievances before him twice every week. His court was flocked by posts and men of learning. He consulted the fuqaha and the Ulema, in matters of the State. Although in his Friday Khutbas, he mentioned the names the Abbasid caliphs as his suzerains or if the keystone of his policy was his alliance with the Marined of Morocco.

Abdullah Muhammad : After overcoming some opposition to his accession, Muhammad I's son, Abdullah Muhammad ascended throne at the end of 1272, as Muhammad

II. Like his father Muhammad II was an energetic ruler and continued his father's policies. Being well versed in Islamic fiqah, he was known as *al Faqih*. He was also a great patron of learning.

Alfonso X opened negotiations with the Castilian rebels who had taken refuge in Grenada and at last, in 1274, he won them over to his side by promising to accede to their demands, such as restoring their feudal by fueros or laws, etc. Thus the revolt of the Castilian nobles came to an end. The Castilian king also renewed his pact with Muhammad II who agreed to pay homage to Alfonso X and pay the annual tribute, of 300,000 *maravadis* and even promised to contribute money to Alfonso X to get him elected as the Holy Roman Emperor. For this purpose, the Castilian king left his kingdom for southern France. But pope Gergory X did not favour his candidacy. Instead, he got elected Rudolf of Hapsburg as the Emperor of Holy Roman Empire. Deeply saddened, Alfonso X returned empty handed to his kingdom, which was threatened by the invasion of the Marinids of Morocco.

In spite of his peace treaty with Granada, Alfonso X did non stop supporting the Granadan rebels. Moreover, he continued to strengthen his naval fleet, and develop the ports of Cadiz and others on the coast of Atlantic against the Marinids and appointed a high ranking officer as the admiral of Castile. These naval preparations incensed the Amir of Banu Marin. Moreover, his continued support to the Granadan rebels provoked Muhammad II to repudiate his treaty and to join hands with the Marinid Amir against him. The Mirinid Amir, Abu Yusuf Yaqub, demanded Muhammad II to surrender the ports of Tarifa and Algeciras to him, so that he could have a ban from where he could invade Castile. Though reluctant, Muhammad II had to accede to the demand of the Marinid Amir.

The Marinid Sultanate of Morocco was a successor-state of the AI-Muwahhid Amir and, like the Muwahhids, the Marinid Amir, Abu Yusuf Yaqub, also aspired to re-establish a Muslim State in the Iberian Peninsula. His invasion of Castile was, indeed, the first step towards the revival of Muslim Spain. But, in this respect, Muhammad II of Granada was his unreliable ally. He was reluctant to part with the ports of Taifa, Algeciras and Gibraltar to him and began to suspect the Marinid plan to establish the Marinid Empire in Spain. However, the Marinid invasion of Castile was really the opening phase of the long-drawn confrontation between Christian Spain and Islamic Maghrib. Really it was initiated by the Castilian Kings. They aimed at the domination of North Africa in order to forestall for ever all attempts by the Muslims to reconquer Spain. It was a logical conclusion to their Reconquista wars which they had waged for centuries against the Muslims of Spain.

After making peace with the ruler of Tlemcen, with whom he was at war, the Marinid Amir, Abu Yusuf Yaqub, landed at Tarifa in August, 1275 and confirmed his agreements with Muhammad. While Muhammad II advanced upon Jaen. Abu Yusuf led his troops along the river Guadalquivir towards Cordova. Alfonso X was still far-away in France. But his heir, Infante Fernando de la Cerda, who was the governor of Castile in the absence of his father, led Castilian troops against the Moroccans. But he died suddenly soon after. His place was taken by Nuno Gonzalez, *adelantado de la frontera* or the frontier governor, and a groundee of the Castilian Kingdom. On September 7, 1275, a battle took place between the Castilians and the African Muslims near Ecija, in which the Muslims won as decisive a victory as they had won at Alarcos in 1195 under the Muwahhid Khalifa. Nuno de Conzaiez, the Castilian commander, was killed along with 18,000 of his troops. A month later, another Christian army commanded by the Archbishop of Toledo was defeated near Jaen by Muhammad II. When Alfonso X returned from France at the end of the year, he offered truce to the Muslims who accepted it. But a year after, in 1277, Abu Yusuf Yaqub again came to Spain and advanced as far as Seville, Cordova and Jerez. But Alfonso X remained on the defensive, avoiding any confrontation with the Muslims on the battlefield. However, he induced his allies, Banu Ashqilula, to cede Malaga to the Marinid Amir, Abu Yusuf. Muhammad II, who was already suspicious of the Marinid intervention in Spain, got frightened. He proposed an alliance with Castile in order to drive out the Marinids from the Peninsula. Accepting the alliance, Alfonso X sent a fleet to blockade Algeciras in 1278. But a Marinid fleet broke the blockade and drove away the Castilians.

CHAPTER 39

ABDULLAH MUHAMMAD II
(1272–1302 A.D.)

Muhammad II succeeded his father AI-Ghalib with a resolve to fulfil the mission of his father which was left over, due to his sudden death.

He was a great patron of learning and a linguist. Being a renowned juris himself, he was popularly known as Faqih. He conducted the affairs of the government with justice, prudence, and statesmanship.

Rebellion broke out first after his accession which he faced boldly. The rebel governors were made to surrender at Anti-quera. He thus cleared the dirty political atmosphere of Granada and established confidence in the people.

He concluded a treaty with Alfonso X who agreed to reinstate his rebel brother Don Filipe to his fief and recall his force from the territory of Granada.

Muhammad II, in the meantime, assessing the magnitude of the internal strife in the kingdom of Alfonso and his keen desire to conclude a peace treaty with him, prevailed upon the Marinid king of Morocco. Abu Yaqub-bin-Abdul Haque to join hands with his against the Christians. Abu Yaqub responded well to the call and invaded the Christians Spain with 50000 soldiers.

The Christian Leader Nuno Gonzalez de-Lara invaded Granada in 1274 A.D. The General with 8000 Christians was killed in the battle.

Sancho son of James I of Aragon was killed in a battle near Jaen. Muhammad II in recognition of the services of Abu Yaqub, donated Al-jazirah Algeciras and Tarifa to him. After the departure of Abu Yaqub, the Christians invaded al-Jazirah and Granada, but were repulsed by Muhammad II. Al-Jazirah was later on purchased by Muhammad II from the king of Morocco for 100,000 Misqlals (468+3/4 seers) gold to strengthen his kingdom.

After a rule of over 30 years Muhammad II died during his prayers in April 1302 A.D./701 A.H.

CHAPTER 40

MUHAMMAD III
(1302–1309 A.D.)

Muhammad III succeeded his father Muhammad II in 1302 A.D.

Just, after accession he faced several rebellions. The Governors of Almeria and Guadix revolted but they won crushed by Muhammad III. He, however could not face the rising force of the Christians who captured Gibraltar and laid siege to al-Jazirah, with the result that the frontier towns of Quesada, Bedmar and Quad Kos were ceded.

Muhammed III had to abdicate in favour of his uncle Abdul Juyush-Nasr-bin-Muhammed (1309 A.D.). He remained in prison for five years in the fort of Almunicar.

CHAPTER 41

ABUL JUYUSH NASR
(1314 A.D.)

After compelling Muhammad III to adbicate, Al-Nasr occupied the throne.

He was a patron of learning. He took keen interest in scientific research. A number of books on philosophy and science were written and published. The invention of the clock marked the scientific research. The construction of various public buildings gave evidence of his interest in architecture.

Inspite of his efforts to keep the kingdom peaceful, he failed to do so. He had to buy peace with Ferdinand IV the king of Castile on agreeing to pay annual tribute.

Muhammad III tried to regain his lost throne but he was killed.

Ferdinand IV was succeeded by his son Alfonso XI, a child 13 months only. The kingdom of Castile then was running in chaos and confusion. It was an opportune time for the Muslims to reconquer their lost territories but the influential chiefs of Granadan court instead of uniting themselves against Christians, fell a prey to their own rivalry. Al-Nasr had to abdicate in favour of his nephew Abul Wahid known as Ismail. There was thus no chance for Muslims to mend their fate.

ISMAIL I

According to al-Maqqari, the reign of Abu'l Walid Ismail-I was one of the most prosperous that the Muslims of Granada had ever had. During his reign, the Christians of Castile twice invaded Granada with the resolve to capture it and destroy the Muslim Kingdom for ever. Castile was then ruled by Maria de Molina, the grandmother of the infant King. Alfonso XI, as a regent, alongwith her son, Don Pedro and her brother-in-law, Infante Juan. Taking advantage of the civil war in Granada, Pedro led an army against it and captured several frontier fortresses, including Tiscar.

Three years later, in 1319 Pedro and Infante Juan again led a large army to attack Granada with the intention to capture it. The Christian army included several princes from other Christian kingdoms of the Peninsula and had the benedictions of the Archbishop of Toledo, whom al-Maqqari called the "Baba" of the Spanish Christians. On hearing of Christian preparations for war, the Muslims of Granada appealed to the Marinid Amir, Abu Sa'id, for help. But he refused. When the Christian army appeared in sight of Granada, Sultan Abu'l Walid Ismail first tried to parley with the Christians. He offered them huge amount of gold. But the Christians refused. At this the Sultan resolved to fight. He divided his army into two. Placing one division under Abu'l Jiyush, he ordered him to lay in ambush, while with the main army he marched against the Christian horde. Though the number of the Muslims was very small, but they made so desperate an attack that the Christian began to retreat. At this moment, the division under Abul Jiyush attacked the Christians, who were then completely routed. All the Christian princes, including Pedro and Infants Juan, lay dead on the battlefield, while several thousand Christian soldiers and knights were killed or captured. Afterwards, the Granadans captured several towns and fortresses, such as Baeza, Galeria and Martos, sixteen miles west of Jaen, in July, 1324.

Abu'l Walid Ismail returned to Granada victorious. But he did not survive long. One of his cousins, Muhammad, killed him in his Palace with the help of his relatives and friends on July 18, 1325.

MUHAMMAD IV

In the history of Granada and its Christian enemy, Castile, fourteenth century was, on the whole, a period of confusion and civil wars, started by the powerful nobility. In the case of Granada, they were caused by the assassinations of the ruling sovereigns and in the case of Castile, due to the minorities of the young kings and regencies, which provided enough opportunities for the powerful Castilian nobles to cause civil disturbances. Nevertheless, the Christian rulers of Castile realised the strategic importance of the Strait of Gibraltar for their overseas expansion and succeeded in acquiring control of it. Though the Muslim rulers of Granada and Morocco were also aware of its importance but their hold on it weakened due to civil commotions, murders of the rulers and the decline of the Marinid dynasty.

After the murder of Ismail I of Granada in 1325, the conspirators chose his little son, Muhammad IV as the Sultan. Though only a boy of twelve years, the new Sultan showed great energy. So after his accession, he marched in person against the Christians and took from them the city of Cabra. Owing to his being minor. Al-Mahruq, the Prime Minister, was appointed his guardian. On coming of age, he dismissed him and put him into prison and appointed Ibn Yahya as his Prime Minister. In spite of his energetic rule, the traitors were at work in Granada. They invited the Castilians to invade it. But the young Sultan marched against them and defeated the Christians at Casares. The Castilian king, Alfonso XI, planning a major assault upon Granada, joined with the forces of Aragon and Portugal. The war with Granada lasted from 1325 to 1330, during which both sides captured each other's fortresses. Confronted with the combined forces of the Christian kings, Muhammad IV journeyed to Morocco to seek the aid of the Marinid ruler Abu'l Hasan (1331-51). The Marinids, who were also perturbed by the loss of Gibraltar, willingly sent a force to re-capture it. Both the Moraccan and Granadan armies besieged Gibraltar for about five months, and finally captured it in June, 1333. Alfonso XI tried hard to relieve the besieged fortress of Gibraltar, but due to his troubles at home and his allies' reluctance, he failed to do so.

The return of the Marinids and their occupation of Gibraltar displeased influential Granadan nobles. A conspiracy was hatched against the Sultan. Muhammad IV was killed by a band of conspirators while he was inspecting the defences of Gibraltar on August 24, 1333. The conspirators at once proclaimed his brother, Yusuf, as the Sultan.

CHAPTER 42

ABUL HAJJAJ YUSUF I
(1333–1354 A.D.)

After the assassination of Muhammad IV his brother Abul Hajjaj Yusuf was raised to the throne of Granada by the Prime Minister Rizwan.

Yusuf I proved himself a very able and enlightened sovereign.

Abul Hasan the king of Morocco sent General Abdul Malik with a strong force to capture Spain. He conquered Algeciars and Gibraltar but was defeated at Pagans by the Christian. Abdul Malik was killed in the battle. Abul Hasan personally attacked the Christians and devastated the whole of the eastern Mediterranian region.

Yusuf I also joined Abul Hasan and laid siege to Tarifah. A very fearful battle was fought near the mouth of the Salado on October 30, 1340 A.D. Aragon, Portugal and Castile had a well-knit force to fight against the Muslims. The Muslims lost the field. Alfonso XI died of plague during the war. After the death of Alfonso Yusuf I of Granada adopted a defensive policy at Morocco and refrained from renewing the attack on the Christians.

A peace treaty for ten years was concluded with Yusuf I by the Castillians after the capture of Tarifah and Al-Jazirah.

Yusuf, after the conclusion of the treaty engaged himself in building up the administration. He devoted himself to art, architecture, literature and science. He beautified and enlarged Al-Hamra. He also constructed the Babal-Shari (the great gateway) of Al-Hamra. Banu-Regio, Puerta-de-la-justica and Casa Real, even today are the reminiscene of the glorious period. Alcazar, now in ruin, was built by him. Granada was supplied with sweet water from the Scierra Nevada through lead pipes stored in marble reservoirs. A mosque with orphanage and alms house was built in every locality which accommodated 12 Muslim houses.

Every village had schools where free education was imparted to all, irrespective of creed and belief. The famous college of Granada was built in 749 A.H./1349 A.D. where full research facilities were available in physics, physiology, botany and natural science. The renowned physician Ibne Baytar was the famous botanist of the time.

Yusuf being himself a poet, encouraged poetry to a greater degree.

He reorganised the police department and instituted night-patrols. Municipalities were also re-organised to guarantee better service. He loved peace and hated unnecessary bloodshed. He was magnanimous by nature and mourned the death of his bitter enemy Alfonso XI who died of plague during the siege of Gibraltar, and permitted the funeral procession to pass through Gibraltar to Seville.

The country as a whole was flourishing and Granada had hopes with him but he was stabbed to death while praying in a mosque on October 19, 1354 A.D.

It is yet to be authenticated whether the murderer was really a mad man or he fell a victim to the Christian conspiracy.

CHAPTER 43

MUHAMMAD V

On his accession to the throne, Muhammad V assumed the title of '*Al-Ghani b'illah*' (He who is contented with God). Ibn al-Khatib, the historian of the Nasrid Kingdom who was Prime Minister under Yusuf I, continued to hold the office under his son, Muhammad V. He was a brave ruler. But he was surrounded by many conspirators. They were in the pay of the Christians, who were always trying to subvert the Muslim Kingdom from within. Two of them were the Sultan's step-mother and her son Ismail. Muhammad V had hardly reigned for five years, when the conspirators, Ismail and his relative, Abu Sa'id, revolted against him in Granada. Muhammad V was then out of his capital. They captured Alhamra, the royal palace, on august 23,1359. Muhammad V left for Guadix, and then for Fez to seek the help of the Marinid Amir, Abu Salim. He stayed at Fez for three years. During this period, he met the great Muslim historian, Ibn Khaldun, who was then in the employ of the Marinid Amir.

During Muhammad V's absence, his step-mother made her son, Ismail ibn Yusuf, as king. But he was soon killed by his brother-in-law and chief adviser, Abu Sa'id, who ascended the throne as *Muhammad VI*. He ruled only for three years, during which the condition of Granada deteriorated further. At last the people revolted against him and invited Muhammad V from Fez to occupy the throne in 1362 once again. On his arrival, Muhammad VI fled to Seville, where the Christian king, Pedro the Cruel, killed him and his 37 companions for the treasures, they had brought with them. Pedro, while attacking Muhammad VI with his lance, cried, "Take this because of your evil pacts with the king of Aragon." As he fell, Muhammad said "O, how little chivalry you display".

On his return to Granada Muhammad V invited Ibn Khaldun to his capital. He reached Granada in 1362 and became a wazir. A year after, Ibn Khaldun went on a diplomatic mission to the Castilian king, Pedro the Cruel, at Seville, which was then the capital of the Kingdom of Castile.

The Castilian king was deeply influenced by Ibn Khaldun's learning and invited him to stay in Seville permanently and promised to restore to him the lands of his ancestors. But he refused. After completion of his mission, Ibn Khaldun returned to Granada. Soon after, his relations with Ibn al-Khatib, the Prime Minister, became strained, for the later became jealous of Ibn Khaldun's popularity with the Sultan. In 1368, Ibn Khaldun returned to his native city, Tunis.

Ibn al-Khatib, the Prime Minister, remained in the confidence of Muhammad V after his return to Granada in 1362. But four years after, relations between the two became strained. To escape the wrath of his master, Ibn al-Khatib fled to Fez, where the Marinid Sultan, Abdul Aziz, welcomed him. On his instigation, the relations between Marinids and Muhammad V became hostile over Gibraltar and Ceuta. When the new Marinid Amir, Abu'l Abbas, ascended the throne, he was friendly towards Muhammad V. On his request, Abu'l Abbas put Ibn al-Khatib to death in 1374.

Muhammad V ruled Granada till his death in 1391. His reign had been a period of peace and prosperity to his kingdom.

Commerce and industry flourished and agriculture prospered due to a great network of irrigation canals, especially in the Vega or plain of Granada. With the death of Muhammad V the glory of Granada came to an end. Weak and almost obscure sultans ascended the throne, while its Christian enemies were constantly sharpening their swords to rich on it and destroy it.

CHAPTER 44

YUSUF II

On Muhammad V's death, his son Yusuf II ascended the throne. Although he successfully resisted two attacks on Granadan territory by the Castilian commanders, but he could rule only for a year. He died of eating a poisoned gift sent by the Masinid Amir of Fez. He was succeeded by his son Muhammad VII. During his reign began the life-and-death struggle for Granada which lasted for about a century and ended in the utter destruction of the kingdom of Granada by Castile.

CHAPTER 45

MUHAMMAD VII
(1392-1408 A.D.)

Yusuf II was succeeded by his son Muhammad VII. His first unwise step was to imprison his elder brother Yusuf in the fortress of Salobrena.

The Christians who played prominent part in developing the mutual hatred among the rulers and the people, and hatching successful conpiracies, called a war council under Henry Ill to end the kingdom of Granada. Henry III died and his plan was left unmatured. The Castillians however invaded Granada in 809 A.H./1406 A.D. and captured the fortress of Zahra, at present in the province of Cadiz.

The Muslims therefore attacked Bedat and laid siege to Alkadet (Haz-ataca). The Christians had to bear a heavy loss but the battle was left undecided.

Muhammad VII, died in the meantime in 811 A.H./1408 A.D.

CHAPTER 46

YUSUF III
(1408-1417 A.D.)

After the death of Muhammad VII his brother Abu Abdullah Yusuf III was placed on the throne by the people.

The Castillians refused to renew the peace treaty which end, in 1410 A.D. and Ferdinand the guardian of the young Castillian king captured Antequera. A treaty was then concluded which got to release of all Christian prisoners of war. The terms of the treaty were not favourable to him but he could not help accepting it due to his own weak conditions and circumstances.

Sultan Fayd of Fez sent his brother Abu Saeed, on the invitation of the people of Gibraltar, with a large force to conquer it. The African force was routed by Ahmad bin-Amir Yusuf III and Abu Saeed was made a prisoner. The Sultan of Fez instead of rescuing his brother left him to the mercy of Yusuf III who set him free and helped him with strong force to invade Fez. The Sultan was defeated and the throne of Fez was occupied by Abu Saeed. Peace and friendly relations were thus established between Granada and Fez.

Yusuf was a just and benevolent ruler. He was so popular that the Christians came to him to got their disputes settled by him. He encouraged military sports and acted as a judge of the tournaments

The frontier provinces were managed well and were brought under control.

Granada flourished well and peace reigned supreme. The people however played in wealth and lost all their chivalrous qualities to stand shy before the Christians.

CHAPTER 47

MUHAMMAD VIII AL-YASAR
(1417-19; 1427-29)

On Yusuf III's death, his son, Muhammad VIII became the King. He was known as al-Yasar or left-handed. He was a very rude, arrogant and worthless ruler. Eunuchs and slaves were appointed to high places while learned courtiers were dismissed and humiliated. The people rose in revolt against him. He was soon overthrown by the family of Banu Sarraj, whom the Castilians called Aben-cerrajes. Then began a sort of tug-of-war between various princes of the Nasrid family, with each of them a puppet in the hands of the king-makers.

CHAPTER 48

MUHAMMAD VIII AND MUHAMMAD IX

He was succeeded by Muhammad (1427-1429 A.D.). He expelled the Banu Sarraj from Granada who with the help of the Castillian king and the Amir of Tunis deposed him and restored the throne to Muhammad VIII (1429-32 A.D.). John II of Castile being enraged at the refusal of Muhammad VIII to acknowledge his suzerainty attacked Granada in July 1431 A.D. A severe battle was fought at Hinguervuda. Muhammad VIII being unable to resist had to escape to Malage.

CHAPTER 49

YUSUF IV AND MUHAMMAD VIII's THIRD REIGN (1432–1445 A.D.)

A grandson of Muhammad VI Yusuf IV bin Al-Ahmar userped the throne of Granada with the help of John II of Castile, after the flight of Muhammad VIII to Malaga. Yusuf IV died after a few months and Muhammad VIII occupied the throne for the third time. The frontiers of his kingdom were shrinking fast. Civil strife was the regular feature of the day. Jimena, Huesca (Granada) Humela (Jaen) and other towns were captured by the Christians.

His nephew Muhammad X bin Usman having imprisoned him, occupied the place of Al-Hamra in 850 A.H./1445 A.D.

CHAPTER 50

MUHAMMAD X AND SAD BIN ALI

Muhammad who occupied the throne in 850 A.H./1445 A.D, was equally hopeless and was deposed by Sad a son of his father's cousin in 859 A.H./1454 A.D.

Granada, then, was passing through a very critical time. Civil war was on. The treasury was empty. The country represented a desert. The unguarded frontiers and forts were in the hands of Christians. Sad could not check the advance of Henry IV the kinds of Castile and in 1462 A.D. important forts like Archidona Gibraltar fell into the hands of Rodrigo, Poncede Leon (Lazriq) and the Duke of Medina Sindonia. Sad used for peace and agreed to pay 12 thousand dinars as the annual tribute.

He died in 870 A.H./1465 A.D.

CHAPTER 51

ABUL HASAN ALI
(1465–1483 A.D.)

Abul Hasan was a better substitute of his father, but lacked statesmanship.

His brother Abu Abdullah AI-Zaghal who had established himself in Malaga, refused the Christians to rise against his brother. He instead, went straight to Granada and offered Baiat at the hands of Abu Hasan.

In the beginning of his reign Abul Hasan improved the condition of Granada. He reorganised the Civil and military departments and raised a strong army. He defeated the Christians, in a number of battles and proved his superiority.

He had two wives, one of the Nasrid family and the other a Christian named Isabella. The Christian wife in a way dominated Abul Hasan and got him indulged in luxury so much that he became indifferent from the affairs of the kingdom and earned the displeasure of the people.

The Christian wife was compelling to him to nominate her son as his successor. The nobles and the courtiers were divided on the subject. The murder of the nobles of the Banu Sarraj family, in the Palace of Al-Hamra created a great disorder in the country.

The Christians were watching the internal strife and the palace intrigue very closely.

The marriage of Ferdinand (The Catholic) of Aragon with Isabella (the Catholic) 1469 A.D. strengthened the position of Christians to a greater degree.

Thus in 1482 A.D. the Christians captured the fort of the Sierra-de-al-Hamra to the southwest of Granada. Fighting was on even in streets and the Christians killed even infants in mothers' laps. Houses and mosques were burnt to ashes.

CHAPTER 52

MUHAMMAD XI
(1482–1483 A.D.)

While Granada was shrinking day by day and the Christians were capturing town after town, the palace was shrouded with selfishness, dynastic interests and civil war. Muhammad Abu Abdullah (Boadil) (Sp) at the instigation of his Arab mother Aisha revolted against his father Abul Hasan who favoured his son by his Christian wife Isabella (Zahra). He seized Al-Hamra in 1482 and his father Abul Hasan had to take refuge in Malaga which was the independent principality of his brother Abu Abdullah Mohammad al-Zaghal.

Abul Hasan reoccupied the throne of Granada but retired in favour of his brother al-Zaghal. He had the rest of his life in Almunicar, where he breathed his last.

CHAPTER 53

MUHAMMAD XII AL-ZAGHAL
(1483–1487 A.D.)

AI-Zaghal was a wise ruler and it was hoped that the decaying condition of Granada would improve, but Ferdinand very cleverly won over Abu Abdullah to fight against his uncle AI-Zaghal for the throne. Abu Abdullah a tool for the destruction of Granada acted according to the instruction of Ferdinand and Queen Isabella, hoping the throne of Granada for himself. In spite of the appeal of AI-Zaghal (891 A.H./1486 A.D.) in the name of Islam, to unite against to Christians, Abu Abdullah did not respond to his call. The Banu Sarraj opposed Abu Abdullah for his playing a stooge in the hands of the Christians, who in the meantime captured Alora, Qasr Bonila, Ronda and other cities. The Muslim population was either killed or sold in the market by the order of Ferdinand and Isabella.

CHAPTER 54

ABU ABDULLAH MUHAMMAD XIII

The last Nasrid King, Boabdil, a stooge of the Catholic Monarchs now played the role he had secretly promised them : he pretended to fight the Christians in order to surrender the remaining independent cities to them on the promise that they would allow him to retain grands as a vassal of Castile. The Catholic kings knew that Boabdil might be their pliant tool, but the valiant people of Granada would not submit to the Christians without a long and hard struggle. So they let Boabdil play the role of a defender of the remaining cities of the Nasrid Kingdom so that he could befool his people into an easy submission. Hence the year of 1488 was year of minor combats. The year 1489 saw more serious fighting. A Castilian army of thirteen thousand cavalry and forty thousand infantry, fighting under the eyes of Isabella and Ferdinand, besieged the city of Baeza in the eastern province. Its defenders fought valiantly. As usual, the Christians destroyed the fertile gardens, orchards and olive trees outside its walls. Finally it surrendered to the Christians. Soon after Almeria, Guadix and other eastern cities followed suit

By the year 1490, only a third of the Nasrid kingdoms, with the Vega of Granada in its centre, remained in the hands of Boabdil, who had, however, no heart to fight. Though Boabdil was a secret ally of the Castilians, the people of Granada were not willing to submit without fighting. With the characteristic short sightedness. Banu Sarraj, the old king makers, not knowing what role Boabdil was playing, at long last came out in defence of Granadan Independence. The Castilian army with Isabella and Ferdinand at its head, marched into the Vega of Granada in the winter of 1490-91 and surrounded the city on all sides. The Castilians built a contravallation or a permanent military ban against the walls of Granada, which they called *Santa Fe*, meaning Holy Faith. The siege lasted throughout 1491. But actual fighting was minimal, confined mostly to hurling of arrows and missiles by each side. The reason was that Boabdil was secretly negotiating terms of capitulation with his Christian overlords. The terms were finally settled on November 25, 1491. Under these terms, the city was to be surrendered to the Christians in March, 1492. But as news of his surrender leaked out to the citizens and fearing that a revolt might brake out against him, Boabdil surrendered the city to Ferdinand and Isabella on January 2, 1492, and on January 6, the Catholic monarchs entered the city of Granada through the gates of the Nasrid place of Al Hamra, which became Alhambra thereafter amidst immense Christian rejoicings, Inigo Lopez de Mendoza, the count of Tendilla, was appointed captain-general of Granada. With this Nasrid Granada ceased to exist.

Some of the important terms of capitulation were:

1. On the surrender of the city, Boabdil, his courters, officers and all his former subjects would become the loyal vassals of Ferdinand and Isabella.

2. Abu Abdullah Boabdil would be awarded a fief in al-Bushara (Alpujarras) on the coast south of Granada.

3. All Muslim property and rents would be respected and Muslims who wished to emigrate would be allowed to sell their possessions. Safe passage would be guaranteed to those who wished to emigrate.

4. The Muslims would retain their own customs and religious freedoms and would be held accountable only to their own judges. Disputes between Muslims and Christians would be settled by mixed courts.

5. For three years after the surrender, the Muslims would pay no taxes, and after this period they would pay the same amount of taxes as they paid to the Nasrids.

6. No Christian would be allowed to enter a Muslim house forcibly and would be punished if he did so.

7. There would be no forcible conversion of Muslims to Christianity. Muslims desirous of adopting Christianity would have to declare their final decision before two judges.

8. Christian women married to Muslims and those who had become Muslims would not be reconverted against their will.

9. Hostages would be returned at once and Muslim and Christian prisoners will be set free.

10. Muslims who wish to emigrate from Spain within a period of three years would be allowed to take with them their movable property, including gold and arms, and they could also return within this period. But if they do so after three years will have to surrender one-tenth of their property to the Christian State.

11. Muslim merchants would be free to trade within and outside Spain on the payment of the usual customs duty.

12. Christians of good character would be appointed governors of Granada and would be punishable for violating any of the terms of capitulation.

Apparently, the terms of capitulation were very liberal. But we shall see presently how did the Moriscos, or the Muslims who opted to remain in Christian Granada, fare under them.

"The Last Sigh of the Moor" : The treacherous Boabdil, who was granted a fief under the terms of capitulation, and had intended to live in Christian Granada ever after, changed his mind soon after the surrender. When departing from the city, he burst into tears. His mother, Ayesha, who had herself played no little part in his treachery, remarked, 'Now weep like a woman what you could not defend like a man'. The malicious Spanish Christians called the spot where Boabdil cast his last mournful look at Granada as *el ultimo sospiro del Moro"*, "the last sigh of the Moor." Boabdil left Granada for Fez, where he lived in prosperity. But his descendants as al-Maqqari writes, were reduced to poverty and were nothing more than mere beggars.

THE MORISCOS

Hardly had the ink on the paper on which the terms of capitulation were written dried then the Christian masters of the Moors, as they called the Muslims, began to violate them. The trouble began with the collection of revenues. But it soon assumed the questions of conversion to Christian religion and reason of the state, that is, the need of the Christian state to make all its peoples to conform to its laws and religion. Though the subjugated Muslims remained staunchly loyally to Islam and Islamic culture, language and customs of their ancestors, powerful forces of Christian domination were arrayed against them. These were the forces of victorious Christianity, in itself a highly militant and aggressive religion, of a monarchy which had been fighting with the Muslims for the last eight centuries and was now carrying on its wars of conquest into Muslim North Africa and beyond, and of a people who were organised

into a warlike nation. Their emergent nationalism was based
upon the principle of One State, One Religion and One People.
It created such a hostile environment that the survival of the
Muslims in it was only a question of time. In fact, the old
colonising instincts of Castilian monarchy had been revived on
a much larger scale under the new-nationalism and imperialism
of Christian Spain, which was now a united kingdom of Castile
and Aragon.

The persecutions, however, first began with the Moriscos
of Granada. The Catholic Kings were deprived of their share
in the spoils of victory in the form of the revenues from the
estates of the former Nasrid Sultans, because they had been
appropriated by the Christian nobles and royal officials after
the fall of Granada among them Gonzalo de Cordoba and the
Count of Tendilla, the first governor of Granada, had managed
to acquire enormous estates. The Monarchs received a very
small share, so that the benefit to the royal treasury was
negligible. This was the reason why the Catholic rulers appointed
a *converso* or a newly-converted monk, Hernando de Talavera,
as the first Archbishop of Granada. He relied more on
propaganda than persecution to convert the subjugated Muslims
to Christianity. But he failed in his mission even eight years
after, for the conquered Muslims showed no inclination to accept
Christianity. When the Catholic Monarchs visited Granada a
second time in 1499, they appointed the bigoted Archbishop of
Toledo, Cardinal Ximenez de Cisneros as it governor. He was
really Isabella's representative in Granada. He was to assist the
Archbishop Hernando de Talavera, whose policy of peaceful
persuasion was soon replaced by the policy of forcible
conversions of the Muslims. He was an apostle of the Church
Militant and believed that the third degree methods were more
appropriate to convert the adamant Muslims of Granada to
Christianity than the persuasive ones of his predecessor. He

brought with him a number of toughs to help him in converting the "infidels" whether they liked it or not. Thus on a single day, 3000 Muslims were forcibly baptized by the fanatical Cardinal. He made his clergy to treat the Muslims so cruelly that "no matter how staunch and sceptical they might be, after being at his mercy for four or five days they emerged saying that they wished to be Christians." Moreover, the Cardinal burnt as many books of the Muslims as he could lay his hands on, called "*outos de fe*" or acts of faith by burning books or persons. Furthermore, in spite of the terms of surrender, he ordered the conversion of the grand mosque in the Albaycin, a quarter in Granada, into a church. These acts of highhandedness aroused the Muslims of Granada to a revolt in 1500. It was, however, speedily crushed. But the rebellion spread to the mountains of Alpujarras to the south of Granada. It too was savagely suppressed.

These revolts provided the Catholic Monarchs with a pretex to suspend the terms of capitulation in 1502, ten years after the surrender of Granada Muslims were offered two alternatives: either to become Christians or to face severe punishment by the combined powers of the Christian State and Church. Another rebellion took place in the mountains of Ronda in February, 1502. But it too was suppressed cruelly. They give one example of Christian brutality: when storming a Muslim town, the Christian commander, count of Serin, "blew us the mosque in which the women and children of a wide district had been placed for safety." Many of the Muslims fled to North Africa. Still three millions of them remained in Castile. The Catholic Monarchs issued a decree, ordering the Muslims to become Christians within three months or face expulsion. Then began a veritable Christian reign of terror. Many hundreds of thousand of Muslims were deported from Granada, where they were in majority, to other parts of Castile, where they were soon constrained to become Christian by the pressure of Christian majority. Many more of them were forcibly converted to Christianity by the strong arm methods of Cardinal Ximenez. The remainder, who continued to live in the inaccessible parts of Granada, such as the mountains of Al-pujarras, were officially declared to be Christians, whether or not they had, actually become so. Such outwardly Christian, but inwardly Muslim Moors were called *Moriscos* by the Old Christians.

Inquisition was the instrument of the Catholic Church to root out heresy by the third degree methods of torture, burning on the stakes, etc., in the garb of judicial inquiry. In the hands of the Church Militant, it became a powerful instrument to extirpate Muslims, whether Mudejars or half- Christian Moriscos or Marranos. It was the most inhuman institution of the most intolerant religion. The Spanish branch of the Inquisition was first established by in Catholic Monarchs in 1478 under the papal bull to root out the Marranos in Seville. (Marranos were Jews who wee outwardly Christians but secretly practised Jewish faith). Later, the authority of the Spanish Inquisition was extended to the Mudejars in Valencia and the Moriscos in Granada. Like the Nazi Germans of the modern times, the Inquisition developed a technique of finding out the purity of faith by the "purity of blood", called *limpieza de sangre*. According to it, every Christian in Spain had to prove by documents that he was a descendant of Christians on both paternal and maternal sides. If a Spanish Muslim or Jew could produce no such documents, as obviously many could not, they were hauled before inquisitors and tortured to death or condemned to *outos de fe* by being burnt to death. The fanatical cardinal, Ximenez, became the head of the Inquisition of Castile in 1507 and extended its operations to the Americas and Philippines where large territories had meanwhile come under Spanish and Portuguese domination. Its methods of trial were harsh. Torture was used as a means of obtaining confessions. The accused was kept utterly apart from his family and friends, who could come to know of his whereabouts if only he or she was set free, a rare occurrence or was to be burnt in an *auto de fe*. Penalties were usually harsh and even brutal, and varied from imprisonment to burning to death. *Auto de fe* literally means the public declaration of the judgement passed on heretics in Spain and Portugal by the Inquisition. In practice, it meant the burning of the heretics in a public place on the orders of the inquisition. The burning took place on Sundays or such other holidays, which were truly "holy days" in the fanatical Christian country like Spain or Portugal. A procession was taken out in which the functionaries of the Inquisition took part, who led the condemned person or persons to the place of burning. It was not the living who alone were thus punished, but even the dead and the fugitives were similarly treated, by means of the burning of the effigies of the dead and of those who had succeeded in fleeing. Death alone did not quench the fanatical zeal of the inquisitors, for they also punished the accused with heavy fines and confiscation of their properties. In this respect, however, the Catholic Monarchs and their successors, shared the proceeds with the Church. Indeed, the practice became so common that even good Christians were accused of heresy and burnt and their properties shared by their accusers. For instance, the estate of a wealthy victim of the Inquisition was divided between Cardinal Carvajal, the inquisitor Lucero, the royal treasurer Morales and Ferdinand's private secretary, and later on, a professor of theology and even a prime minister were burnt on the stakes by the Holy Office, as the Inquisition was known in Christian Spain.

The first victims of the Spanish Inquisition were the Mudejar serfs and slaves in Valencia. Charles V (1517-58), the clergy with the Inquisitors at their head, and the Christian traders

and artisans were all in favour of forcible conversion of the
Mudejars, but the nobles were not, because they were their
hard-working peasants. The opposition of the noble was,
however, easily overcome when the Pope also gave his approval
to the forcible conversion of the Mudejar serfs, on the pain of
enslavement or expulsion. The objections of the nobles were
thus overruled. In 1525, the Spanish king, Charles, ordered
that the pope's instructions were to be carried out. The Mudejars
revolted at various places in Valencia, but their rebellions were
put down. Many thousands of them fled to Africa, but many
more accepted Christianity. Even then they were subjected to
the Inquisition, and many of the half-hearted conversos were
put to death. Thus vanished in Valencia, Catalonia and Aragon
the last remnants of the Muslims.

The Problem : We now come to the last region in Christian
Spain where Muslims were legally and officially declared to be
Christians, but at heart they were not. They were the Moriscos
of Granada. Since 1525, the Spanish rulers had issued decrees
that all the Muslims must either be baptised or they be expelled
from Spain. Thus legally and officially all Muslims who did
not leave the country became Christian. These christianized
Muslims or Moriscos behaved publicly or outwardly as
Christians, but within their families and friends they continued
to behave as Muslims in many ways even to the extent of showing
their repugnance of baptism. For example, when a Morisco
child was baptised by a Christian priest in the church, his parents
would bring him home and wash him to clean him of Christian
taint. What was more, the Moriscos, still remained loyal to
many Islamic customs, beliefs and practices. They spoke Arabic:
or they did not learn the Roman language of the Spanish
Christians. After a Morisco couple was married in the church,
they returned home and solemnised their marriage according
to Muslim rites. They continued to wear the same old Muslim

dress and costumes as before and did not take to the hats and breeches of the Christians. The Morisco women wore the veil or hysos and did not appear in public, although as Christians they were expected to discard veil and move freely in public. Being accustomed to Muslim cleanliness, their habit of bathing was particularly hateful to the Christians. In other countries and societies, which were not nationalistic in social and cultural sense, such customs and habits as those of the christianized Moriscos would not have excited any reaction or led to any persecution. For instance, in Mughal India many Hindus accepted Islam, but they preserved their caste relations, customs, beliefs and practices for centuries afterwards. But it was not to be so in a highly nationalistic Spain where Christian religion, beliefs and practices were to be uniformly observed by all people, rich or poor, high or low, born or baptised as Christian. National unity meant uniformity of social and cultural life and behaviour. So nationalism in Christian Spain and also in Christian Portugal meant not only one state, one religion and one people, but also one society, one law, one idealogy and one culture. The existence of the Moriscos, or the christianized Muslims, was, therefore, as intolerable to the powerful Christian Church, Kings, and the relentless Inquisition as it was repugnant to the Christian masses. Their national spirit demanded that either the totalitarian Christianity must be thrust down the throats of the half-Christian and half-Muslim Moriscos or they be extirpated.

Extirpation : The problem of the total conversion of the Moriscos, though not intractable, was a difficult one. Hundreds of thousands of Moriscos lived in the inaccessible mountains of Alpujarras in southern Spain. When they were subjected to the totalitarian Christianity and State they revolted in 1568. It lasted for two years-the longest of the Morisco revolts. It was partly due to the inaccessibility of the Alpujarras mountains and partly due to the Muslim volunteers from North Africa

who had come to fight along with them against the Christian
armies. Th revolt started when the Christian tax-collectors
demanded taxes hated by the Moriscos. Led by a descendant of
Banu Sarraj, named Farax, they revolted and killed some
Christian soldiers, who were billeted in the houses of Muslim
peasants. The rebels then fled to the hills where they chose a
descendant of the Umayyads of Spain, Mulay Muhammad ibn
Umayya. Soon the Moriscos of the whole Alpujarras rose in
revolt in 1568. Village after village rose against their Christian
oppressors; killed the priests and burnt the churches and drove
the Christians from their areas. The Christian commander,
Morquis of Mondejar, was unable to suppress the revolt. In
1569, the new Morisco leader, Mulay Abdullah Aben Abu,
assumed the title of king. Philip II, the King of Spain, appointed
his half-brother, the young Don John of Austria, as a new
commander of Christian forces. The war on Moriscos then
began in right earnest. Superior weapons of the Christians and
their greater numbers turned the scales of war against the
Moricos, Don John carried the war most mercilessly. His motto
was "No quarters". "Men, women and children were butchered
by his order and under his own eye; the villages of the Alpuxarras
were turned into human shambles". The survivors who took
refuge in caves were smoked to death. Thus ended the last
revolt of the Moriscos in 1571. Muley Abdullah Aben Abu was
also killed and his severed head was nailed on a gate of Granada
for thirty long years. His followers suffered and equally terrible
fate.

Many thousands of Moriscos still survived in Valencia
and Murcia. The now Spanish king Philip III, completed the
work of extirpation began by his father. In 1609-1610, he ordered
the deportation of about two million Moriscos to Africa or to
other lands of Islam. But the cup of the sufferings of the Moriscos
seemed not be full yet. Many thousands of the refugees were

killed in Africa because to the native Muslims they appeared to be Christians and Spaniards. Many thousand more returned to Spain only to be mercilessly driven out once again. They went to France where the French welcomed them because they were at war with Spain and were absorbed into French society. In Christian Spain also those Moriscos who, were deported to other Christian-majority areas were distributed among Christian families as their slaves and servants: they too were absorbed into Christian society. Thus by 1612, vanished from the soil of Spain the last vestiges of a peaceful and industrious people whose only crime was that though they professed Christianity but spoke Arabic and lived like Muslims something which Christian fanaticism, combined with a new fanaticism of national uniformity, could not tolerate, based as it was on the Nazi-like concept of *limpieza de sangre* or the purity of the blood.

"The Moors were banished;" writes Lane-Poole, "for a while Christian Spain shone, like the moon, with a borrowed light; then came the eclipse, and in that darkness Spain has grovelled ever since." This was, *inter alia*, the reason why modern Spain and, modern Portugal, in spite of their plunderings for centuries of their colonial possessions in the Americas, Asia and Africa, have remained since the 18th century down to the present times as the most underdeveloped of the developed countries of modern Europe. This was perhaps the reason why the later Western Imperialisms, as those of Holland, France and Great Britain, relied not so much on Christian zeal to build their Empires as on commercial and economic exploitation of their subject peoples and countries.

CHAPTER 55

CAUSES OF THE DECLINE AND DESTRUCTION

In the history of Muslim Spain, seven kingdoms rose and fell including the tiny kingdom of Granada, till at last the Christians succeeded in conquering the whole of it. The specific causes of the rise and fall of these kingdoms, we have already considered in previous chapters. In this chapter, we shall consider the reasons why the Muslims could not hold the Iberian Peninsula permanently even after nearly eight centuries of rule and why were they driven out of it root-and-branch? That kingdoms and empires rise and fall is very common occurrence in human history, but that a whole people should be extirpated from a country, in which they had lived for ages, is something rare. There must be some special reasons why happened so in Muslim Spain.

This question is significant for yet another reason. The decline and destruction of Muslim Spain occurred in an anomalous situation, for otherwise the conditions in it were far more favourable and advantageous for its survival than they were for its Christian enemies. These conditions were a larger population and a more developed economy. We shall now consider this anomalous situation.

Population : It has been estimated that at the time of

Muslim conquest the population of the Spanish Christians was about seven million, while that of the Muslims, including both Arab and Berber settlers, was a little more than thirty thousand. A century after, about 700,000 native Christians accepted Islam. The law of numbers then came into operation: the more the Muslims, the greater the number of conversions. The conversion process then became both continuous and cumulative. "This is a self-generating process, and the rate of conversion increases without the necessity of any specific social or political policies, or of any factor extrinsic to the process. Accordingly, about two million native Christians accepted Islam during the ninth century and about three millions during the tenth century. By the end of the eleventh century,–the first Taifa period in the history of Muslim Spain, more than eighty percent of the total Christian population had become Muslims, calculated to be about 5.6 million, while two million Mozarabs had fled to the North during this period. Thus by 1100, Muslim Spain had truly become a Muslim country: only a few per cents of Jews and Christians remained in it at this time. And this demographic preponderance of the Muslims lasted upto the fall of Muslim Spain: even the kingdom of Granada was overwhelmingly a Muslim majority country.

Economic : Economic development of Muslim Spain was also a continuously upward movement till by the end of the Umayyad Caliphate, in 1031, Muslim Spain had become the most advanced and prosperous country not only in the Islamic West (Maghrib) but far more so in the whole of Europe. And it remained so under the Taifa, the Murabit and Muwahhid rulers. Even the kingdom of Granada was as much prosperous as its Christian enemies.

However, the economic development of Muslim Spain suffered from one serious flaw: it was organised for the production of luxury goods for the degenerate elite classes.

This was one reason why it was so easily exploited, by means of tributes, by Christians.

Political instability : Surprisingly enough, political instability of the Umayyad Spain was simultaneous with the rising curve of conversions: the more the Muslims, the greater the political instability. And the Umayyad Caliphate fell when virtually its whole Christian population had accepted Islam. Afterwards, political instability became a malaise, which afflicted the Taifa kingdoms and of the Berber empires in al-Andalus so much that none of them remained in power for more than two or three generations. This state of affairs indicated a deep-seated malady in the political and social life of Muslim Spain, and became a basic cause of the success of Christian reconquista. Not only the Spanish Muslims were afterwards unable to set up a single, united all-Peninsular State, but their Taifa and Berber rulers were also unable to resist the Christian invaders successfully. The reason was that the Andalusian ruling and other elite classes were afflicted with political and social decadence and moral degeneration, which seemed to be an irremediable and irreversible condition of their political, social and cultural life.

Why were the Spanish Muslims so degenerate and decadent? What were the reasons that when Muslim Spain was almost a hundred per cent Muslim country and also a highly developed one, it became so weak and vulnerable ?

Briefly, the reasons lay in the following:

1.   Its rulers' failure to de-tribalize their governmental system;

2.   Their limited awareness and comprehension of the situation confronting them;

3.   Muslim family system and the degraded position of Muslim women;

4.   Kinship society: inhibitions at grass-roots level of social life.

5.   Slavery and concubinage;

6.   Ethnic divisions and disputes;

7.   Minority governments in Muslim Spain;

8.   Taifa Syndrome; and

9.   Expansionist Dynamism of the Iberian Christians.

Failure to de-tribalise their governmental system : Iberian Peninsula was conquered by the Arabs and Berbers. They had come, not as individuals, but as organised tribal groups. Consequently, the political and military systems which they set up in Spain was based on tribal lines. As the Arab tribes were politically and culturally more advanced, they monopolised the governmental system. The Berbers had no say in the government of the Umayyad Emirate and in its settlement policies. Conditions, however, began to change under the Caliphate.

The Arab, as well as Berber, tribalism was of segmentary nature. It was a conflictive-cooperative system of organisation. A tribe was divided into clans, called *"banu"*, which were always in conflict with each other over pastures and other good things of life, including women. But when in conflict with a rival tribe, all the clans would co-operate to oppose it. Similarly, every clan was divided into a number of families, who quarrelled with each other over good things of life, but would also co-operate when confronted with a rival clan. Lastly, brothers in a family would quarrel with each other over their family possessions, but would also co-operate when confronted with the families of their cousins. This segmentary or conflictive cooperative nature of their societies was the reason behind all the feuds and wars in the Arab and Berber tribal societies and also the reason why they co-operated when confronted with a common enemy. It has been aptly described as a "system of organized anarchy". It was a binary system of fission-fusion, which characterised all segmentary tribal societies. The Arabs, seeing only its co-operative of fusion aspect, called it their tribal "*asabiya*" or group solidarity. But "asabiya" was a dual process: they co-operated with each other when confronted with a common enemy, but fell out when the enemy danger vanished or their thought it had vanished.

So the Arab and Berber tribes co-operated with each other during the conquest of the Visigothic Spain. Once it was conquered and the process of settlement on the conquered lands began, they, led by the Arabs, began to quarrel over the division of governmental offices and privileges and the distribution of the conquered lands among them. Thus were revived the pre-Islamic rivalries of the Modar (Qaisite) and Himyar (Kelbite) tribes of the Arabs, which were further aggravated when the Syrian (Kelbite) troops under Balj bin Bishr arrived on the scene. The Berber tribes were also ready to side with one or the other Arab faction. But the Kelbite governor, Abu'l Khattar Hassam, resolved the issue by settling the Syrian tribes on various lands in southern regions of Muslim Spain. Thus come into being what we have called Arab tribal feudalism.

Feudalism : Owing to its segmentary structure, Arab tribal feudalism in Umayyad Spain was subject to two contrary tendencies loyalty towards the tribal interests and loyalty towards the Umayyad State they had set up and for which they were duty-bound to fight and defend it against its enemies, internal and external. At first, the loyalty of the Arab tribes towards the Umayyad Emirate was stronger than their tribal loyalties. Herein lay the strength of the independent Umayyad Emirate during the early period of its history. But afterwards, the tribal loyalties became preponderant, which led to incessant revolts of the Arab tribes during the reign of Hisham I (796-822). These revolts compelled him to adopt a new measure to lessen his dependence exclusively on the Arab tribes for military purposes. He recruited new troops whom he paid regular salary. However, he did not abolish tribal feudalism or the system of feudal levies of the Arab tribes. Thus began the dual system of paid and regular troops, on the one side, and the tribal feudatories, on the others. This system lasted throughout the ninety century. The Arab rebellions, however, continued. In the tenth century, from the reign of Abdul Rahman an-Nasir (912-961), a radical change took place; the payment of the tribal levies in the form of fiefs stopped altogether, with the result that tribal feudalism came to an end. Instead, the Umayyad Khalifas now relied upon the mercenary and slave troops. They consisted of the Berber tribes from North Africa and the slave troops of the European Slavs and African Negroes.

Even this change did not save the Umayyad Caliphate from downfall, which led to the rise of the Taifa kings. The reason was that the later Umayyad Khalifas could not command the loyalty of their mercenary (Berber) and Slav troops, while the old tribal feudal troops of the Arabs had ceased to exist since long. But not the internal kinship loyalties or the "asabiya" of the Arab and Berber tribes. Had it been so, there would have been no *Muluk at-Tawaif* and no Taifa Syndrome. Instead, the fall of the Umayyad Caliphate would have led to the rise of a new unified power in Muslim Spain under a new dynasty on all-Peninsular basis as before.

The Umayyad rulers could have checked the divisive tendencies of the tribal "asabiya" by granting fiefs to the Muwalladun on the same condition of military service, as they had granted to the Arabs. They would have thus transformed the tribal feudalism into a State-based feudalism of the type which later sprang up in the Christian kingdoms of the north.

This development would have brought several advantages to the Umayyad or to any other all-Peninsular Muslim State.

Firstly, the Muwalladun, whose numbers were constantly increasing, would have been closely integrated with the all Peninsular Muslim State;

Secondly, all ethnic differences in Umayyad Caliphate or its successor Muslim state would have been wiped out from its body politic, which would have made the whole society politically and socially homogeneous, though, of course, it would have still been stratified into fief-holding and peasant classes, but not on ethnic or racial grounds;

Thirdly, the incipient Christian kingdoms would have been nipped in the bud in the eighth century; and

Lastly, the Umayyad rulers would have no need to recruit the Berber mercenary and Slav troops, for they or their successor state in Muslim Spain would have their own native fief-holders to fight their wars against internal or external enemies.. This full-fledged feudalism would have also provided loyal and devoted warriors and also with inexpensive administration, because the fief-holders, even of the outlying districts and provinces, would have themselves administered them.

Why did they not de-tribalise their socio-political system and institute full-fledged feudalism? The reason was that the social and political life and thought of the Umayyad rulers, as also of the Murabit and Muwahhid rulers after them, were embedded in kinship ideology, which stunted their understanding and knowledge of the realities around them, as we shall consider next.

The limited knowledge and understanding : Muslims of Spain, whether rulers or ruled, always lacked the necessary awareness and understanding of the Christian world around them, As we have said in previous chapters, the Umayyad rulers could never visualise what effects the depopulation and repopulation policies of their Christian enemies would have on their Emirate/Caliphate. They had also no understanding of the consequences of the northward flight of their Christian subjects, the Mozarabs, although they saw thousands upon thousands of them fleeing from their ancestral homes in Muslim Spain and settling on the lands newly conquered from the Muslims, often in the fortified towns on the advancing frontiers of the Christian -kingdoms. The same was true of the Murabit and Muwahhid rulers of Muslim Spain afterwards.

The intellectual elites of Muslim Spain also did not take any interest in the language, customs, culture, arts and sciences of the Christian lands in the Peninsula and also in Europe. Perhaps they believed them to be intellectually and culturally too inferior to be worth studying. But not so the Christians of Spain and Europe. After the conquest of Toledo by Alfonso VI, Raymond, the Archbishop of Toledo, established a school of translation during 1126 and 1151, in order to translate Arabic books on various arts and sciences of the Muslim thinkers and scientists into Latin and Roman. Thus the Arabic books in Latin garb soon spread throughout Western Europe. In spite of their deep-seated prejudices and hatred of the Muslims, the writers, scholars, thinkers and philosophers of medieval Europe, many of whom were at first Christian clergy monks, eagerly studied and discussed the writings and philosophies propounded by the Muslims. At first, their purpose was, in fact, merely to carry on anti-Islamic propaganda among fellow-Christians. But later, they developed a more scholarly and secular attitude towards the achievements of Muslim writers and thinkers. They became then eager to learn about the Muslim advances in mathematics, astronomy, botany, agronomy and other arts and sciences. On the contrary, no such corresponding effort was ever made by

Muslim writers', scholars and thinkers about the European achievements, especially when about had been founded in Europe from Montpellier in the Kingdom of Aragon in Christian Spain to Oxford and Cambridge in distant England during the first half of the thirteenth century. Of course, by that time, most of Muslim Spain had ceased to exist, by the Muslim kingdoms of Granada and of North Africa were still flourishing. Even Muslim historians of these kingdoms, including Ibn Khaldun, showed little or no interest in the events and achievements of the Spanish and European Christians, although they lived under the very shadows of their expansionist kingdoms.

Muslim Family System : Family system has always a great influence on the evolution of the society, economy, culture and state. On the other hand, social attitudes, customs values, and beliefs of the people, as well as the state and its law and policies also have great effects on the evolution of the family system.

In Muslim Spain, polygamy and concubinage had highly deleterious effects on the family life and structure and on the position and role of women. First of all, the family relations and kinship structure among the Muslim narrowed and constricted their social consciousness and understanding. They could not conceive of wider social and political relations and loyalties. That was the reason why Muslim Spain tended to disintegrate into the anarchy of the Taifa Syndrome. Moreover, their polymous family structure also affected their laws of inheritance, especially of the feudal lands or fiefs of the conquering tribes. They were divided among many heirs born of several wives and concubines of a fief- holder. These, divisions affected the growth of feudalism by arresting it at the level of feudal tribalism, by inciting feuds in and between the tribes. The most disastrous effect of the polygamy and concubinage was however on the succession to the throne on the death of a reigning amir or sultan. There were always two or more claimants to the throne on such occasions. In the case of the kingdom of Granada, as we said in the previous chapter, polygamy became the immediate cause of its downfall and destruction by the Catholic Monarchs Compared to the anarchic law of succession in Muslim Spain, in medieval Europe the law of primogeniture had regularised the succession to the throne: the eldest living son, and if none, the eldest living daughter, ascended the throne on the death of the reigning king or emperor. It made the Christian feudal and state systems very stable, strong and viable.

Position of Muslim Women : Though the position of Muslim women in Muslim Spain was comparatively much better than that of their sisters in other Muslim countries due to its peculiar social environment, nevertheless they suffered from various kinds of restrictions as well as animosities arising from its patriarchal family structure. Purdah confined them in their houses, while polygamy, concubinage and male domination made them highly docile, servile and passive inmates of the harem, ready to suffer any injustice inflicted on them by their husbands or masters. Their husbands chose them or were chosen for them. Once married or purchased, the husband became their master in name as well in fact. A woman was an object of love and chivalry, but never a comrade in social life, activities and adventures. The docility of the Muslim women always made them "of their own free will" as the legal formula put it, to allow their husbands to take a new wife or concubine. Ibn Rushd, the twelfth century philosopher of Muslim Spain, who had first-hand knowledge of the deplorable condition of the Muslim women, wrote:

> Our society allows no scope for the development of women's talents. They seem

to be destined exclusively to child birth and
the care of children, and this state of servility
has destroyed their capacity for larger
matters. It is thus that we see no women
endowed with moral virtues; they live their
lives like vegetables, devoting themselves to
their husbands. From this stems the misery
that pervades our cities, for women
outnumber men by more than double and
cannot procure the necessities of life by their
own labours.

Comparison with the women in Christian Spain would
reveal the reason why the suppressed and lowly position of
Muslim women became, for no fault of theirs, an important
factor in the decline, defeat and destruction of Muslim Spain.
Christian society knew no purdah and no polygamy. Instead,
its women moved freely among men and participated in all
social, economic, cultural and political activities, while its
monogamous family system provided them with an assured and
respectable social position.

Moreover, their laws, prohibiting cousin-marriages upto
fourth degree, also compelled the people to seek wives from
remotely-related or non-related families, which greatly widened
their social and political relationships. R.W. Southern writes,
"Nothing was more effective in giving men the sense of
belonging to a society beyond the horizon of their ordinary
interests than the recollection of their distant kinsmen. Women
were less rooted in the soil than men; they brought new
influences from distant parts and established bonds between
men of little or no identity of purpose or of interest." He adds
further, "At a time when the spread of ideas was achieved more
through the movement of people than through the impersonal
circulation of books, the migration of ladies of noble birth and

the small company of advisers who surrounded them was a potent factor in drawing together remote parts of christiandom. In Christian Spain, the matrimonial alliances among the ruling dynasties often led to the unification of their kingdoms, which helped them to overcome their Taifa like situation and led to the emergence of modern Christian Spain. Furthermore, among the ruling classes in Christian Spain, many of the Christian queens and other women played a very active role in the governance of their kingdom and in the Wars with Muslim Spain: among them the best (or the worst?) example was that of Isabella, one of the Catholic Monarchs. Jimena, the wife of El Cid, the conqueror of Valencia, ruled it for several years after the death of her husband. We may say, therefore, that historically the Spanish Christian women played an important and decisive role, though secondary and supportive to their menfolk, in the defeat and destruction of Muslim Spain.

Kinship society : Kinship structure of the Muslim society and the segregation of women deeply affected the morphology and sociology of the urban life in Muslim Spain. Unlike the Christian town and cities, no Muslim town or city had a municipal organisation where the towns-people could assemble and settle their civic affairs by mutual consultation and decision. They had also no public squares and other civic facilities where men and women, young and old, could gather civic affairs by mutual consultation and decision. They had also no public squares and other civic facilities where man and women, young and old, could gather together to participate in civic functions and public festivals regardless of tribal and ethnic differences. In fact, all rest and recreation activities and occasions were celebrated privately or within family and kinship groups. Moreover, every kinship and ethnic group lived separately in its own urban quarters. In these quarters, all streets were laid out as cul-de-sacs or blind alleys, called *darub* (sing. *darb*) in

Arabic. The houses in them were so built that their backs were
turned towards the streets. The walls of the houses along the
streets had no windows opening, on them, so as to ensure the
segregation and seclusion of their female inmates.

In short, the community life in the towns and cities of
Muslim Spain was characterised by ethnic isolation and social
fragmentation. The absence of municipal organisation, of public
squares and other public facilities for cultural and social activities
as well as the division of town life into isolated quarters and
darub were factors which disintegrated social and collective
life in Muslim Spain. They inhibited the very possibility of the
growth of national consciousness among the Muslim people at
the grass-roots level of their social existence. Though, the
civilisation of Muslim Spain was urban, but it lacked the
dynamism and energy of an urban society.

The result was obvious. During ordinary public
disturbances or civil wars, the isolated cul-de-sacs and quarters
in Muslim towns and cities provided some security to their
inhabitants. But when it came to a war or a siege by the norther
Christian invaders, the fragmented and isolated communities
in these towns and cities could not unitedly defend themselves
against their enemies. This was the fate of Toledo first and then
of all other towns and cities in Muslim Spain afterwards. As
against this, the Christian cities had their own brother-hood
unions to defend themselves.

The influence of the slaves and concubines of the life,
society, economy, culture and state system of Muslim Spain
was morally degenerative and historically disastrous. Urge
number of slaves, both males and females, made the women
idle and their masters luxury- loving. The employment of slaves
by the Umayyad rulers as civil servants and soldiers alienated
the incipient feudal classes, which became a powerful factor in

their revolts and in the ultimate downfall of the Umayyad Caliphate, from which even the loyalty of their Slav troops could not save them. And when the Umayyad ship of state was sinking, the Saqaliba were the first to run away from Cordova and set up independent principalities in the eastern regions of the moribund Caliphate. The harem life of the Muslim rulers distracted their minds and attention from the affairs of the state. Talking of the Taifa rulers, El Cid said to the Valencians on the surrender of their city to him:

> If you have urgent business come to me and
> I will listen to you.
>
> For I do not shut myself up with women to
> drink and sing, as do your lords, of whom
> you never have an audience.

The austere Murabit ruler, Yusuf bin Tashufin also reproached the Taifa rulers for their debauchery and libertinism. But his own successor, Ali bin Yusuf, left the affairs of the state to his wife, who established a sort of Harem Rule, which ushered in the speedy downfall of the al- Murabitun.

Ethnic divisions : Muslim Spain was literally a hotbed of ethnic divisions, disputes and rivalries. As we have already explained, it was mainly due to the shortsighted and wrong policies of the Umayyad rulers. The main ethnic groups were:

1. The Arabs : they constituted a dwindling group;

2. The Berbers: they also constituted a dwindling group but for the wrong policies of the Umayyads;

3. The Muwalladun: they constituted an ever-increasing element due to the rising curve of conversions, but were politically unimportant again due to the Umayyad policies;

4.   The Mozarab Christians : they too were a dwindling element due to the rising number of conversions to Islam and their flight to the Christian north; and

5.   The Jews: they constituted a very small element in the population of Muslim Spain. They had welcomed the rise of Muslim Rule in the eighth century. But when Muslim Spain began to crumble to pieces under the hammerstrokes of the northern Christians, they also fled to the north. They were a money-making community and would go where they could make more money.

Before we study the quarrels and wars between the tribal and ethnic groups in Umayyad Spain which led to its downfall, let us first probe into the roots of tribal and ethnic differences and rivalries which resulted in the large-scale political struggles among them.

The agnatic, polygamous and endogamous family structure was mainly, even exclusively, responsible for the perpetuation of the tribal and ethnic differences and cleavages in Muslim Spain under the Umayyads, as it was also during the Murabit and Muwahhid times later on. Most often a Muslim married his first-degree parallel cousin, i.e., the daughter of his paternal uncle, not only to keep the family lands and properties within the family, but also to preserve the cultural and social customs, beliefs and values of its tribal and ethnic group. Consequently, an Arab family remained Arab and a Berber remained Berber from generation to generation. Of course, he did marry other women as his wives and concubines who were not so directly related or, even not related at all. But in such families, the children of the parallel cousins, being descendants of the original stock, considered themselves as true descendants of their patrilineages and regarded themselves as superior to their half brothers, born of distantly related or non-related wives and concubines. The children in such families were conditioned into aggressive attitudes, prejudices and hatreds due to sibling rivalries of half-brothers and cousin hostilities of related families, which they later extended or transferred to those outside their family groups such as the rival clans, and tribes and ethnic groups. Thus the tribal "asabiya" and tribal relations, prejudices and enmities were perpetuated from one generation to the next.

The result of the tribal loyalties and hostilities was the bifurcation of the Society of Muslim Spain into rival tribal and ethnic groups. There were no institutions in it, like seignorial or state feudalism, monogamy, abolition of slavery, freedom of women, which would have created a homogeneous and integrated society. Instead, its rival tribal and ethnic groups were, like paralled streams, always flowing side by side but never mixing and fusing into a new, homogeneous people. Their socio-political situation, created by internal divisions and dissensions, proved to be disastrous for the survival first of Umayyad Caliphate and later of Muslim Spain itself. The bane of the ever divisive segmentary society of Muslim Spain became a boon for its Christian enemies.

During the period of the Dependent Umayyad Emirate, the total population of the Arabs in Muslim Spain was about 18, 000. Compared to the then Christian population, the Arab population was almost microscopic. But they became at once the ruling and land owning feudal elites, and enjoyed the two advantages of political domination and demographic expansion for the next two centuries. Their population exploded and their wealth and influence increased. Consequently, they became an arrogant people, who believed that they were a superior race. But, in spite of their perillous situation, the Arab tribes did not forgot their ancient hostilities between the Modars and the Himyars of pre Islamic Arabia. Soon after their settlement, they renewed their tribal hostilities and wars, which lasted throughout the Umayyad Rule. Although they were surrounded by both Muslim and Christian enemies. But due to their arrogance and insouciance, they remained oblivious to these dangers and challenges. Instead they behaved as if they still dwelt, not in the Iberian, but in the Arabian Peninsula.

At the time of the conquest, the Berbers constituted the second kinship group of about 12,000 settlers. Although co-conquerors, the Berbers never enjoyed the same political advantages in the Umayyad state as did the Arabs. It was due to this and after the conquest. The Berbers were mostly pastoral people, who settled in the arid regions of the Peninsula.

After nearly two centuries, from the middle of the tenth century, a new wave of Berbers came into Muslim Spain. They were the warriors recruited by Abdul Rahman III and his successors into their armies. They were the New Berbers. Their numbers constantly increased. Unlike the Old Berbers, they were unruly and uncultured people and a cause of civil war and the downfall of the Umayyad Caliphate.

Like the Arab group, the Berber group of both old and new Berbers had also the agnatic, polygamous and endogamous family structure and segmentary tribal organisation, which constantly stoked the fires of inter- tribal and intra-tribal quarrels among them and with the rival Arab clans and tribes. The unruly, violent and avaricious habits of the Berbers have been aptly described as Berberiyya" by Ibn Khaldun. In Muslim Spain, these traits of the Berbers became the cause of civil war and of the downfall of the Umayyad Caliphate.

Muwalladun were the native Spaniards, the pre-Islamic Gothic and Hispanic inhabitants of the peninsula, who for one reason or other had accepted Islam. Literally, the term means a "born Muslim". It was a pejorative term, reflecting the contempt the other Muslim kinship groups, especially the Arabs, showed towards these New Muslims. As we have said earlier, the population of the Visigothic Spain at the time of conquest was about seven million. A great majority of this population became Muslims or Muwallads in three different ways:

(a) as clients of the Arab tribes, who assumed the genealogies of their patron tribes;

(b) children of the mixed marriages between the Arabs (and also the Berbers) and their native-born wives, who were Christians, but their children usually became Muslims. In fact, the children of the mixed marriages were the real Mawalladun or "born Muslims". But later they gave their epithet to the whole group of converts, no matter what was their origin.

(c) From about 800 A.D., more and more of the Christians began to accept Islam of their own accord: some wanted to escape the payment of Jazya, but bulk of them wanted to escape oppressive serfdom, in which their forefathers had been held since the Visigothic times. So they left their ancestral villages and settled in neighbouring town and cities and became Muslims. Most of them became artisans, craftsmen and labourers but a few of them became traders and merchants and became rich and influential. In course of time, they began to speak Arabic.

The Muwallad population was far greater than the combined populations of the Arabs and the Berbers, old and new. Yet there was no love lost between the three ethnic groups. The Arabs and Berbers hated them, and the Muwallads reciproctated these feelings. They loved to speak Arabic, but hated the Arabs. For instance, Abdullah ibn Umar of Seville, who died in 889, spoke Arabic beautifully, while he detested the Arabs. The Arabs called them sons of the slaves", or "sons of the white women" and stigmatised them as "cowards". Thus a wide gulf separated the three ethnic groups. The Muwallads were non tribal people, but they had also adopted the tribal genealogies owning to the highly tribalistic ethos in which they lived. They even adopted the agnatic, endogamous and polygamous family system of the dominant Arab culture. Though the Muwalladun were devout and dedicated Muslims, yet the gulf between the three Muslim ethnic groups remained unbridged due to Arab arrogance, exclusivity and the Muwalladun's Berber-phobia. However, the main reasons why these ethnic groups did not merge into one homogeneous people were the wrong and shortsighted policies of the Umayyad and other Muslim rulers.

However, all this could have been transformed, if the Umayyad rulers had been loyal to the basic teachings of Islam. Islam teaches three great nation-building principles:

(i)   Egalitarianism

(ii) Brotherhood of Believers; and

(iii) *Adl* and *Ehsan* of justice and common good.

If the Umayyad amirs/Khalifas had been guided in the policies and other acts of State by these great teachings of Islam they would have brought about a radical transformation in the emergent society and culture and, therefore, in the political balance of forces in Muslim Spain. They would have, first and foremost de-tribalized the Arab and Berber settlers by abolishing slavery polygamy and concubinage. Like charity, social change begins at home. The Muslim rulers could have easily done so by instituting monogamy. It would have released their family structure from the agnatic unilaterality and exclusivity and would have also one "justice and common good" to the women. After all, equality a brotherhood of believers as well as *"adl wa'l ehsan"* were, under Islam, not the prerogatives of men only: women were entitled to them as much as men.

Secondly, these noble principles would have undermined the Arab and Berber tribalism thoroughly. It was no equality a brotherhood of all believers to grant all benefits and favours to the Arabs and Berbers, e.g. lands, government employment and enrollment in the army, etc. and to deny them to the Muwalladun, who constituted a far greater majority of the Umayyad subjects than did the other two groups. As the Muwalladun were, really non-tribal people, their induction into the fief-holding classes, and into government offices and armies, would have given further impetus to the de-tribalizing tendencies in Umayyad state and society and created a more homogeneous people. Thus after a few generation of these three antagonistic ethnic groups would have ceased to be Arabs, Berbers or Muwallads and would have, instead, become single, unified and homogeneous Spanish Muslim people. All tribal and ethnic differences would have vanished, if only the Umayyad rulers had shed their Arab prejudices against the Muwallads and would not have discriminated against them in matters of State. They would have then no need to recruit new Berber mercenary troops of Slav and Negro slave troops at all. Instead, they would have relied only upon the native-born Spanish Muslims for all their military and governmental purposes. Thus these three Islamic principles would have transformed their social and political system and welded the warring ethnic groups of Arabs, Berbers and Muwalladun into a single, united Spanish people-on the way to become a nation-state the first in Europe and in world history.

Why did the Umayyad rulers not do so ? This question leads us to yet another drawback in the Umayyad State System.

Minority government : Umayyad Emirate/Caliphate was

always a government of a small Umayyad kinship group. It consisted of the kinsmen of the Umayyad Amir or Khalifa and of his clients or freedmen. At first, they had the support of the Arab tribes which had settled in Spain, especially of the Yemenites, and of the Berber tribes who had come into Spain with Abdul Rahman I. After a century, however, they, lost the support of the original Arabs, especially after the reign of Abdul Rahman II. Then they began to rely more and more upon their own kinsmen and clients, whose numbers had by then increased, and also on foreign mercenary and slave troops.

During the reign of Abdullah (888-912), the Umayyad Emirate touched the nadir of its fortunes, when the Arab tribes and the Muwallad and Christian communities, led by Umar bin Hafsun, were in revolt against it all over the Peninsula. The Amir saved himself with the support of his kinsmen and freedmen. Even then he would have faced hard times, if Ibn Hafsun had not renounced Islam and proclaimed himself a Christian, which cost him the support of his Muwallad and Arab allies. After his death, his grandson, Abdul Rahman III, restored the glory and power of the Umayyad by going all-out for the recruitment of the New Berber mercenaries and Slave troops. Neither he, nor his successors, ever sought support of the Muwallads or of the Arabs or old Berbers, except of those who were their clients, like general Ghalib. It was, therefore, inevitable that, when later the weak Umayyad rulers could not keep the lawless New Berber troops under control and the Muwallads and Arabs revolted against them, the minority government of the Umayyad Caliphate collapsed like a house of cards.

De-Ethnicization : The Christian kingdoms of northern Spain were, never confronted with the problems of ethnic cleavages and rivalries, although they had, at first, a number of such groups. For instance, in the kingdom of Leon-Castile, there were the Basques, the Franks (i.e. Western Europeans from France, Germany, England, etc.) and the fugitive Mozambs. But, after a couple of generations, their ethnic differences vanished and they merged with the native Christians to form a new and homogeneous people. Writing of the eleventh century Leon-Castile, Glick says:

> "Three Christian groups characterized by substantial ethics differentiation–primarily linguistic–did evoke special responses, but were handled more in accord with the special statutes governing religious minorities as a more or less transitional measure to enhance peaceful intergroup relations during the period of acculturation. None of the three groups-Basques, Franks, and the Mozararbs, of Toledo-suffered the long-term stigmatization that the religious minorities did."

The reasons of the de-ethnicization in Christian Spain were, firstly, their bilateral, exogamous and monogamous family system. There was, therefore, little or no ethnic hostility among these groups, because they were not conditioned to such reactions in their family environment, even when these groups lived near each other. Secondly, and equally importantly, the Christian rulers did not discriminate one group against the other in such matters as the grant of fiefs, or government offices, military command, or in the grant of municipal charters and other civic and economic privileges. Lastly, the Christian rulers were always closely linked with their peoples; they never ruled as minority governments over alienated majorities. Thus they had always a homogenous and unified peoples behind them, which was the secret of their strength and success over the Umayyad and other rulers of Muslim Spain and the cause of the ultimate destruction of Muslim Spain.

Taifa Syndrome : The immediate cause of the Christian victory over the Spanish Muslims was the socio-political pathology of Muslim Spain, which we have called Taifa Syndrome. It was the real bane of Muslim Spain, an inevitable result of its ethnic divisions. It again and again afflicted the united State System in Muslim Spain and disintegrated it into a number of petty kingdoms and principalities. We have already studied the causes of the rise and fall of these mini- kingdoms in earlier chapters. None of the great rulers of Muslim Spain, Umayyads, Murabits or Muwahhids, ever tried to understand why their great States tended to disintegrate into the anarchy of *Muluk at-Tawaif,* nor did anyone among the intellectual elites of Muslim Spain–its writers, poets, scholars, scientists, historians, thinkers, philosophers, theologians, fuqaha and others, ever try to explain the reasons why Muslim Spain was so prone to Taifa Syndrome, although many of them suffered from the tragedy and trauma of the resultant defeat and destruction of Muslim Spain. Their intellectual inanity and also their sycophancy were, indeed, the real bases of the Taifa Syndrome and the consequent destruction of Muslim Spain.

Expansionist Strategies of the Iberian and European Christians : The expansionist strategies of the Spanish and Portuguese Christians played a very decisive role in the defeat and destruction of Muslim Spain. Organised by the New Christianity and its fiercely intolerant militancy and armed with the seigniorial feudalism and later by the adventurous mercantile bourgeoisie, the Iberian Christians always aimed at the total extirpation of the Spanish Muslims. To this end, they always adopted a systematic policy of consolidating every one of their conquests by first killing and driving out the whole Muslim population from the newly conquered city or territory and then repopulating the "unoccupied lands" with Christian colonisers. Lack of such a consolidation policy was, the important reason why the brilliant victories of Abdul Rahman III and of al-Mansur turned into dust a couple of decades after. Moreover, the Christian expansionist strategies not only inspired the Crusades, but also gave rise to the nation-states, colonialism and imperialism first in Christian Spain and Portugal and later in France, and England during the early modern period of the European history, i.e. from fifteenth to seventeenth centuries.

Confronted with the genocidal expansionism and dynamism of the Spanish and Portuguese Christians, the question of the survival of the tolerant, tribalistic and traditionalistic Muslim Spain was an impossible proposition, especially when its great rulers, like the Umayyads, the Murabits or the Muwahhids, had no idea or comprehension of what they were confronted with, or what their Christian enemies were up to and when their rule was so prone to the forces of the disintegrative Taifa Syndrome, which their statecraft never knew how to overcome. On the contrary, the Spanish Christians never suffered from this socio political malady, although during the tenth and eleventh centuries they lived in a Taifa like situation. However, they had several integrative forces among them which overcame this situation, such as the seigniorial Feudalism, the Catholic Church, the emergent mercantile bourgeoisie and the custom of matrimonial alliances. Some time such an alliance united two warring Christian kingdoms into a new political entity against the Muslims, e.g. between Aragon and Castile which gave birth to modern Spain. Among the Spanish Muslims such a custom could never arise due to the widespread prevalence of polygamy, purdah, slavery and concubinage. Consequently, marriage among them could not acquire such a sanctity or importance as to be the basis of a permanent political alliance between two warring dynasties. These were the reasons why Taifa Syndrome was an incurable malaise of Muslim Spain.

CHAPTER 56

INTELLECTUAL ACHIEVEMENTS, CONTRIBUTIONS AND CULTURAL PROGRESS

"Muslim Spain wrote one of the brightest chapters in the intellectual of medieval Europe. Between the middle of the eighth and the beginning of the thirteenth century, Arabic speaking peoples were the main bearers of torch of culture and civilization through out the world. Moreover they were the medium through which ancient science and philosophy were recovered, supplemented, and transmitted in such a way as to make possible the renaissance of western Europe. In all this, Arabic Spain had a large Share" Hitti.

LANGUAGE AND LITERATURE

Al-Qali (901-67 A.D.) was born in Almeria and educated in Baghdad. He was one of the eminent professor of the University of Cordova. His book 'al-Amali' is very famous. Among his disciples Mohammad Ibnul Hasan al-Zubaidi (928-89 A.D.) was the chief. He was born in Seville but his family came from Hism. Primarily he was appointed by al Hakam as the supervisor of the education of his son Hisham and later on was appointed as Qazi and Chief Magistrate of Seville. Allama Jalal Uddin al Sayuti used very extensively his book which had the exhaustive list of the grammarians and philologists who flourished up to his age. Sayutis book *Muzbir* is mostly based on the book of al Zubaidi.

It may be mentioned here that the Hebrew grammar based on Arabic grammar had its birth in Muslim Spain. Hayyuj Judahbin David (Abu Zakarya Yahya-Ibne Dawud) the "father of the scientific Hebrew grammar belonged to Cordova where he died in the eleventh century.

Ibn Abde Rabbih (860-940 A.D.) of Cordova, the poet laureate of Abdul Rahman III, descended from an enfranchised slave of Hisham I. His books al *iqdul Farid* (the unique recklace) earned the first place after *al aghani*, among the works on the literary history of the Arabs. Ali Ibne Hazam (994-1064 A.D.), the original thinker and philosopher of Muslim Spain, was noted for his fertile mind and prolific writings. His descendency is controversial. He himself claimed his lineage from a Persian client but he is also said to be "the grandson of a Spanish Muslim convert from Christianity". In his youth he held the post of vazir of Abdul Rahman al Mustazhir and of Hisham al Mutab but later on he retired to a life of seclusion and literary persuit. According to Ibne Khalikan and al Qifti he wrote four hundred volumes on history, theology, tradition, logic, poetry and other allied subjects. He expounded the Zahirite (literalist) school of Jurisprudence and theology. He glorifies platomic in his *Tawq al Hamamah* (the doves necklace) an anthology of love poems. Among his surviving works, *al fask fi al Milal* wal ahwal Nihal (the decisive word on sects, hetrodoxies and denominations) "entitles him to the honour of being the first scholar in the field of comparative religion.

The periods of the party kings specially of the Abbadies, Murabits and Muwahhids were noted for the history of literature. The cultural seed well-sown in the Umayyad period flourished in Seville, Toledo and Granada to remined the greatness of Cordova. The Arabicized Christians, Mozarabs who were educated in the Muslim Universities, had communicated many elements of Arabic culture to the kingdoms of the North and the South. The fables, tales and apologues which began to flourish in the western Europe in the thirteenth century had complete analogies with Arabic works. *Kalilah-wa-Dimnah* was translated into Spanish for Alfonso the wise (1252-1282 A.D.) of Castile and Leon. It was also translated into Latin, shortly afterwards by a baptised Jew. "But the most significant contribution of Arabic to the literature of medieval Europe was the influence it exercised by its form, which helped liberate western imagination from a narrow rigid discipline circumscribed by convention."

The science of philology attained its peak under eminent writers like Ismail bin-Qasim, Ibnul Qatia, Abu Taman bin Ghalib, Ahmad-bin- Ahan bin-Saeed, Abu Ali Ismail-bin-Qasim, Abul-Abbas and others, Books like *alif Maqsoora, wa-mamdooda, wa-Mahmooza; Kitabul-afal, Kitabul-alam-fl-lughat* (100 volumes, *kitab al-nawadir, Al-Kamil* successively spoke of the literary grandeur of the days.

Poetry:
The euphonic character of Arabic language, its music and exquisite diction, formed the characteristic of Arabic speaking people to use the poetical composition as a passion intensively. This characteristic was therefore fully manifested on the Spanish soil.

Poetry like other subjects was regarded an essential feature of culture and civilization. A number of sovereigns were distinguished poets. Besides the first Umayyad ruler and several of his successors, Mutamid ibne-Abbad was a notable poet. Cordova, Seville and Granada were seats of accomplished poets.

Keeping aside Ibne-abd-Rabbih, Ibne Hazam, Ibne-al-Khatib for a while, Muslim Spain produced renowned poets like Abu-al-Waheed Ahmad bin Zaideen (1003-1071 A.D.) who belonged to the Makhzum family of the Quraysh. He was a confidential servant of Ibne-Jahwar the chief of Cordova but later on he was exiled for his profession of love with Walladah the daughter of the kahlifa al-Mustakfi. He was later on appointed by al-Mutadid al-Abbadi as grand wazir and commander of the army. He was conferred the title of dhul wizaratain (of the two vizarats i.e. sword and pen). He was a distinguished letter writer also. His epistles which denounced Ibne-Abdus, minister of ibne-Jahwar became very popular.

His verses for Princess Walladah, the renowned poetess, and Qasre-al-Zahra depict the characteristic of Spanish Arabic poetry.

Abu Ishaque-bin-Khefajah (1139 A.D.) "peoples' poet" of Valencia was greatly admired by the people. His Diwan was published in Cairo in 1286 A.D.

Muhammad-ibne-Hani (937-73 A.D.) was a licentious poet of Seville. He composed several panegyrics for the Fatmid Khalifa al-Muiz.

Muhammad V the ruler of Granada awarded route permit to Ibne Khaldoon in a well-composed verse.

Princess Aisha the daughter of Prince Ahmed and Princess Walladah the daughter of Khalifa al-Mustakfi were accomplished poetesses. Mariam-bint-Yaqub was not only a poetess but a literary figure also. Labana of Cordova was an accomplished poetess and also highly skilled in mathematics. She was personal secretary of al-Hakam II.

Muwashah

With the popularity of poetry, the poets of the later period tried to popularise a new form which had emancipated itself from the conventional fetters. It had developed a new metrical form in which the verses of a poem were divided into several pieces or *misras* with corresponding *"Qafia"*, to complete a verse *"Sher"* unifying the pieces. The various pieces did not correspond to one metre. Generally *Misra* was composed of four pieces and the fourth *misra* had its own separate *Qafia*. It was something like the "free style" poetry of today. Muqaddam bin-Muafir Alazizi the court poet of Amir Abdullah-bin-Muhammad Umvi was very proud of his invention. Abbada the court poet of Al-Motasim of Almeria was an exponent of this form.

Both the forms, *Zajal* and *Muwash-shah*, were very popular. Abu Bakr Qazman of Cordova sang *Zajal* for the first time in Cordova, which gained much popularity in every street. *Muwash shah* travelled from Spain to North Africa and to the East. The blind poet Abul Abbas of Toledo was a popular poet of the form.

Ibrahim-bin-Sahl the Jew (1251 or 1260 A.D.), and Muhammad bin Yusuf Abu Hayyan (1256-1344 A.D.) of Granada composed several *Muwash-shah* poems. Abu Hayyan wrote Persian Turkish, Coptic and Ethopic grammars of which only the Turkish survived.

Both the forms *Zajal* and *Muwash-Shah* were developed and adopted by the Castillians in their popular form Villancio. Arabic poetry in general and this lyric type in particular was so popular that even the ploughmen at Shille (Silves) in Southern Portugal did improvise verses extempore. In modern Lebanon, Qawalun extemporaneously produce such folk-poems which they called *Zajal* and *Muwash-Shah*. The pattern can be very well symbolised with the Qawwals of this sub- continent, who very artfully combine the various verses of different metres with other verses, of different languages even, in majalis to invoke stirs, emotions and admiration.

In Southern France Provencal poets followed and adopted the form. The troubadours (Ar. Tarab) (Qawal) of the twelfth century imitated their southern contemporaries, the Zajal-singers.

Paper : Books were almost the sole means of acquiring knowledge. The book-markets of Cordova held first place in Spain. Libraries flourished side by side with the Universities of Cordova, Seville, Malaga and Grenada. Private libraries were numerous and contained large number of books on various subjects. Translation and printing works were on, which necessitated the manufacturing of writing-paper–the most beneficial contribution of Islam to Europe. The invention of movable type by Germany in the middle of the fifteenth century owed its success to the invention of printing paper by the Muslims.

Religion:

Maliki fiqh remained dominant in Muslim Spain throughout its history. Nevertheless, there were several original thinkers of religious thought. Among them Ibn Hazun was the most important.

Ibn Hazm :

We have already considered Ibn Hazm's contribution to the Andalusian literature. His contribution to religious thought was both original and great. He rejected the four schools of fiqh for he was a follower of the school founded by Daud al-zahiri. According to the Zahiri Schools, Quran and-Hadith should be interpreted in the strictest literal sense, and by analogy, deduction, or innovation, as was done in other schools of Islamic Jurisprudence. According to Ibn Hazm, instead of depending on the interpretation of the sacred text by others, every Muslim should study the Quran and Hadith for himself. Ibn Hazm thus pleaded that the direct study of the original texts of the Quran and Hadith neglected under the influence of Imams of the other fiqh schools, would be revived once again.

In ethics, Ibn Hazm contended that good and evil depend on the will of God, without which there was no objective standard of good and evil. As action is wrong only because God forbids it. Thus God's approval or disapproval is the only standard of right or wrong. But God's, will is not arbitrary, instead it is consistent with His own nature.

Ibn Hazm was the founder of the science of comparative religion. He was the first thinker who undertook a system atomic study of the old, and new testaments, and came to the conclusion that Islam was a better religion than Christianity.

Astronomy and Mathematics:

The rulers of Cordova, Seville and Toledo had greatly encouraged the astronomical and mathematical studies.

Most of the Andalusian astronomers endorsing the views of abu Mahshar believed in "astral influence as the course underlying the chief concurances between birth and death on this earth. The study of astrology (astral influence) necessitated the determination of the location of the places with their latitudes and longitudes throughout the world. Astronomy was thus helped by astrology. The Latin west drew its inspiration in astronomy and astrology through the Spanish channels. Abul Qasim Maslamah al Majriti (1007 A.D.) of Cordova edited and corrected the planetary tables (Zij) of al Khawarizmi, the first Muslim composer of the tables. He converted the basis of the tables from the Yazdgirdera into that of Hijra is also known as meridian of 'arin' by that of Cordova, al Majriti is also known as "the Mathematician". The Latin version of the tables was made by Adelard of Baith in 1126 A.D. Another Zij of Al Battani, composed about, 900 was rendered into Latin by Plato of Tivoli.

The writings of the Ikhwan al Safa, were introduced in Spain either by al Majriti or his disciple Abu al Hakam Amer al-Karmani.

Abu-Ishaque Ibrahim-lbn-Yahya al-Zarqali (L. Arzachel) was a prominent astronomer whose observations and studies formed the basis of the Toledan tables. The tables comprised geographical information from Ptolomy and al Khawarizmi. It was in the 12th century that these tables were rendered into Latin by Gerad of Cremona. Raymond of Marrius (1140 A.D.) drew chiefly from the astronomical canons of al-Zarqalio improved type of astrolob called "Safihah" was a great invention. He took the lead in proving the motion of the solar apogge with reference to the stars. It amounted to 12.04 according to his measurements, whereas its real value is 11.8.

Jabir-bin-Aflah of Seville, sharply criticised Ptolemy in his famous book Kitabul-Hayah (book of astronomy) and rightly asserted that the Mercury and Venus had no visible paralaxes. His book is noted for a scholarly chapter spherical and plane trignometry. "The science of trignometry, like algebra and analytical geometry was founded by Arabs."

Nur-al-din-abu-Ishaq al-Bitraji (alpetragious 1204) a pupil of Ibne-Tufyal is noted for his book "Kitab al-Hayah" on the configuration of the heavenly bodies in which the theory of homocentri spheres has been revived in a modified form. He believed in the aristotalian system and opposed the Ptolemic system.

Arab astronomers have left their immortal traces on the sky which can be discerned even today by the stars.

Star-names in European languages are mostly of Arabic origin such as Acrab (aqrab, scorpion), Algedi (al-jadi, the kid) al-tair (al Tair the flyer) Dench (dbanah tail), pherkad farqad, retained such as a "Zimuth" (al Samut), "Nadir" (Nazir) Zenith (al-Samt) which "testify to the rich legacy of Islam to Christian Europe."

The mathematical vocabulary of Europe is also indebted to the Arab scientific influence, other than "algebra and "algorism" the, algebraic term "surd" (deaf root) in trigonometry "sine" (L. sinus) is a translation from an Arabic word jayb (pocket)

The Arabic "cipher" or zero is the most valuable and interesting contribution of the Arab scientists to the world. This has facilitated the use of arithmetic in every day life.

Alkhawarizmi was the first to use numericals including zero in place of letters. The zero and Arabic numericals lie in the root of the science of calculation of today.

Botany and Medicine:

The Andulusian Muslim scientists enriched the world by their researches in the field of natural history specially Botany pure and applied as in the fields of astronomy and mathematics. Their observations of sexual difference between various plants and palms and hamps were not only correct but unique. Further, their classification of plants into three categories those that grow from cutting or grafting from seeds or spontaneously was a new idea.

The famous physician of Cordova abu Jafar Ahmad-bin-Muhammad Ghafiqi (1165 A.D.) having collected plants in Spain and Africa, named each in Arabic, Latin and Berber with full description. His book *al Adwiyah al-Mufrida* (samples) was appropriated by Ibn-al-Baitar.

Abu Zakariya Yahya ibne-Muhammad of Seville wrote his famous book, towards the close of the 12th century, *al Filaha*. It was an outstanding medieval work on agriculture. The book primarily based on earlier Greek and Arabic sources, was mostly based on the experience of Muslim Farmers of Spain. It treated 585 plants and explained the cultivation method of more than fifty fruit trees. It presented new observations on grafting method, the properties of the soil and manure. It also discussed in detail the diseases of trees, vines and plants and prescribed medicines for curing the diseases. It is wonder, how and why the book was left un-noticed by ibne-Khalikan, Yaquiti and Hajji Khalfah. It is all the more curious how ibne-Khaldoon could call it a recension of ibne-Wahshiyah.

Ibn-al Baytar:

The most renowned Botanist and pharmacist of Spain, rather of the Muslim world was Abdullah ibne-Ahmad ibne-al-Bayta (Veterinary doctor), a worthy successor of Dioscorides (Ca. 50 A.D.) the author of Materia medica. He was born at Malaga. He travelled in Spain and North Africa as a herbalist. Throughout his travels a group of artists accompanied him to sketch out the various herbal plants with full accuracy.

Later on he was attached with the court of al Malik al Kamil Ayyoubi as chief herbalist. He also visited Syria and Asia Minor. He died in Damascus in 642 A.H. 1248 A.D. His two celebrated works, dedicated to his patron al Saleh Ayyoubi *Al Mughni-Fi-ladwiyah al-Mufridah*, added to his eminences.

Both the books are regarded as wonders in the field of Botany and medicine.

Al-Jame is a collection from simple remedies from the animal, vegetable an mineral, with the Greek and Arabic data duly supplemented by his personal experiments and researches.

"Some 1400 items are considered of which 300 including about 200 plants were novelties. Parts of the Latin various in of Ibne-al-Baytar's "somplicia" were printed as late as 1758 in Cremona.

Medicine was a favourite subject for almost all the learned persons of Andulusia as a hobby. Many philosophers were noted physicians. Some of them were physicians by vocation and some by hobby. Ibne Rushd, Ibne Maymun Ibne-Bajjah and Ibne-Tufail were known as philosophers but medicine was a hobby for them. Ibne-Khatib the noted historian stylist was one of those physicians who held the office minister of health. He was specialist in gyanaceology.

"In connection with the "black death" which in the middle of the 14th century was ravaging Europe and before which Christians stood helpless, considering it an act of God, this Muslim physician of Granada composed a treatise in defence of the theory of infection" in his *Maqna-a-Sale-an-almaraz-al-hael*. He proved that "the existence of contagion is established by experience and evidence of the senses and the trustworthy reports. The fact of infection becomes clear to the investigator who notices how, he who established contact with the afflicted, gets the disease, whereas he who is not in contact remains safe and how transmission is effected through garments, vessels and ear-rings. "

Al-Zahrawi:

Abul Qasim Khalaf ibne-Abbas al-Zahwari was the greatest surgeon of the Arabs. He was the court physician of al-Hakam II (961- 76 A.D.). He was born in Al-Zahra, the famous suburb of Cordova. The Latin writers called him Abulcasis or Abbucasis a corruption of Abul Qasim.

His distinction in the field of medicine rests on his book

al Tasrif-li-man : Ajaz-an-al-Talif (an aid to him who is not equal to the large treatise). He has introduced a new idea in the surgical world of cantrization of wounds, crushing stones inside the bladder and kidney and the necessity of vivisection and disection. The surgical chapter of the book was translated into Latin by Gerard of Cremona. Its various editions were published at Venice in 1497, at Basel in 1541 and at Oxford in 1778. It was the chief manual of surgery in Salerno, Montpellior and other early schools of medicine. His book contained full illustrations of surgical instruments. The Arabs laid the foundation of Surgery in Europe.

A colleague of al-Zahrawi was Hasady-b-Shaprut the Jewish minister and physician of Abdul Rahman III translated in Arabic the Materia medica of Dioscorides.

Ibne-Zuhr:

Abu Marwan Abd-al-Malik ibne-abi-al-Ala surnamed Ibne-Zuhr (L. Through Heb. "Avenzoar") was born in Seville between 1091 and 1094 A.D. and died there in 1162 A.D. He served as court physician and vazir of abdul-Mumin, founder of the Muvahhid dynasty. Ibne Zuhr's ranking in the science of medicine was paralleled by that of Al-Zahrawi in the art of surgery. Three, out of his six medical works are extant. *Al-Taysir-fi-al-Mudawah-wal-Tadbir* (the facilitation of therapeutics and diet) a counterpart of al-Kulliyat of Ibne-Ruslid, his friend and admirer, was his most valuable work. Ibne-Rushd, in his "al- Kulliyat" has declared ibne-Zuhr as the most renowed physician since Galen. He was the greatest clinician after al-Razi. Ibne-Zuhr was the first to discuss feeling in bones and describe the itchmite (Su'abat-al-Jarah). Ahmad al-Tabri (second half of 10th century) had anticipated the itchmite in his *al-Mualeja-al-Bugratiyah*.

Ibne-Zuhr was very fortunate to leave behind six

generations of physicians in direct descent, who maintained his prestige in the field of medicine. His son Abu-Bakr was of course a noted physician but his distinction was more due to his extraordinary control on Literature than to his medical activities. He was appointed as court Physician at Morocco by Abu-Yusuf Yaqub al-Mansoor of the Muwahhid dynasty but he was poisoned to death by a jealous vazir. His funeral sermon was read by the Khalifa himself.

Among other Hispano-Arab physicians, Ubaidullah ibne-Al-Muzaffar al-Bahili of Almeria who entered the service of Muhammad ibne-Malikshah Sabuqi of Baghdad (1127 A.D.) and provided a mobile dispensary transported on 40 camels, indicated the importance of the Health services. He died at Damascus in 1154 A.D.

The science of Pharmacy was at the zenith of its achievements in Andulusia, specially in Cordova. Pharmacopaeta, was complete in all respects. Muhammad bin Fatah of Cordova, and Al-Hassani were noted pharmaceutics. The two brothers Ahmad and Umar were also noted physicians. Yahya ibne-Ishaque the author of *Tib-e-Kabir* was a favourite of Khalifa Al-Nasir.

Saeed-bin-Abde-Rabbih of Cordova, the great astronomer, and physician was noted for his treatment through tablets (Qurs) His books *"Ta-aliq-wa-Mujarrabat-fi-Tib"*, earned a name.

Ahmad-bin-Jabir, during the reign of Al-Hakam II earned a name in medicine and philosophy in the whole of Europe. Muhammad bin Abdoon of Cordova's book '*Kitab-fi-al-Taksir*' was a valuable work on medicine and general treatment .

The research work of Abdul Rahman-bin-lshaque-bin-al Haisham *"Ilmul-Basr wa-al-noor"* (opthalmology) was greatly honoured in Europe. He was authority on eye-diseases and treatment. He was the first to make researches on twilight. He invented the theory of Ether and proved that the Ether-world is beyond the vision-limit.

Muhammad-bin-Qasim was yet another renowned eye specialist whose work on eye-disease and treatment was authority. Physicians and specialists like Jawad, Khalid-bin-Yazid, ibne Muluka, Ishaque, Abul-Fazal-bin-Yusuf, Ishaque-bin-Qaisar Talitali and others have contributed much to the medical world.

It is worthwhile to note that right from the first century Muslim domination in Spain, Eastern culture flowing from higher level to Andulusia, flowed very generously into Europe in all ranks of society. Medical science, of which Europe was quite ignorant, was transmitted there so perfusely that the Arab physicians earned the title of "Saviours of humanity" Many Arabic works on medicine were translated into Latin and other languages and introduced in medical schools, established on Arabic pattern.

The surgical part of Ali-ibne-al-Abbas' work "al-Kitab-al-Maliki" was translated into Latin by a disciple of Constantine, John the Saracen (1040-1103 A.D.) a Salernitan physician. Constantine the African (1087 A.D.) himself had translated the theoretical part of the book in Latin.

"To Constantine, to Gerard of Cremona, (1187 A.D.) translators of Al-Zahrawis' Tasrif, al-Razi's al-Mansuri, as well as ibne-Sina's al-Qanun, and to Faraj ben-Salim (Fasarius Fasagut), the Silician Jew who translated al-Razi's al-Hawi in 1297 A.D. and ibne-Jazlah's Taqwim-al-Abdan, medieval Europe was chiefly indebted for its knowledge of Arabic medicine."

The introduction of Arabic technical terms into European languages, "Julep" (Ar. Julab) for a medical aromatic drink; "Roh" (Ar. Rubh) for a conserve of insipissated fruit juice

with honey; " syrup" (Ar. Sharab, sherbet) "Soda" (Ar. Suda)
spilitting pain in the head "Duaramater" and "piamater (Ar.
al-Umm al-Jafiyah), (the coarse mother) and al-Umm-al
Raqiqah, (the thin mother) "Alcohol" (Ar. al- Kull) "Alembic"
(Ar. al-inbiq) "Alkali" (Al-qali) "Antimon" (Ar. Itmid) "Aludel
(Ar. al-uthal, vessels) "Realgar" (Realgar" (Ar.rabj al-ghar the
powder of the cave) and "Tutty" (Ar. Tutiya" clearly testify the
domination of the Arabic medicine.

PHILOSOPHY

Al-Farabi describes the different grades of being in a
descending order. According to him the forms of things existed
in God, who exists from all eternity. The series of spiritual
existence consist of six grades of being. The first three of these
grades remain spirit *per sec*. But the last of these enter into
relation with the body.

The ethical and political teachings of al-Farabi are also
very much enlighting. According to him ethics deals with the
fundamental rules of conduct. He emphasised that reason should
decide whether a conduct is good or bad and that the highest
virtue consisted in knowledge. A man who knows the moral
principles and acts accordingly, is better than one, who does
not know them but practises blindly. Man has the freedom of
choice which depends on rational consideration. Thus freedom
depends on motives determined by reason. But the freedom of
man is imperfect because of the opposition of the body. Only
when the rational soul becomes completely free from the
bondage of the body, it becomes completely free. The *summum
bonum* or the highest aim of life is to attain such freedom.

In politics al-Farabi holds that morality can reach
perfection only in a State and State is either good or bad as is
the ruler. The State thus determines the lot of the people not

only in this world, but also in the world to come. Al-Farabi also earned reputation as a fair physician, mathematician, an occult scientist and an excellent musician. His treatise *Kitab al-Musiqi al-Kabir* (the Great Book of Music) was highly appreciated by the then world. He breathed his last in 950 A.D. at the age of about eighty.

Though Ali al-Husayn Ibn Sina (980-1037) achieved the greatest fame in the West as a renowned physician, yet he was equally honoured in the Arab world as a brilliant philosopher. During his early life, some Isma'ilian missionaries arrived in Bukhara from Egypt and converted his father to their beliefs. This conversion had an important effect upon the education of Ibn Sina for the Isma'ilian movement of Islam was closely associated with the translation of Greek philosophy into Arabic. From the Isma'ilian missionaries, he learnt Greek philosophy, arithmetic and geometry. The writings of al-Farabi, another original thinker of Islam, inspired this young scholar towards the intensive knowledge of Aristotle. His interpretation of Aristotle was mostly based on the writings of Farabi. In this respect he may be called a pupil of Farabi.

Ibn Sina was a great commentator on Aristotle and Plato. His teachings on philosophy, particularly his commentaries on Aristotle and Plato, later exerted a tremendous influence on European philosophy during the Middle Ages. Most of the later philosophers both in the East and the West were greatly influenced by his writings. According to Syed Amir Ali, Ibn Sina, "was unquestionably the master spirit of his age, and inspite of the opposition raised against him by fanaticism and self-interest, he left his impression of an undying character on the thoughts of the succeeding ages. His voluminous works testify to the extraordinary activity of his mind. It is he who systematised Aristotelian philosophy and filled the void between God and man in Aristitotle's fragmentary psychology by the doctrine of intelligence of the spheres conceived after a scientific method."

Some orthodex Muslims regarded Ibn Sina as heretic. He was never an atheist but in some points he disagreed with the orthodox section of the Muslims. He believed in the existence of God and in the prophethood of Muhammad (P.B.U.H.). According to Ibn Sina, God is the original cause for all existence. All the material universe depends ultimately upon God, for without this original cause there would be no forms of existence. Existence itself is classified by Ibn Sina into three types of souls: the vegetative, whose activity is limited to nutrition; the *animal* which possesses vegetative faculties but adds higher faculties of sense and the *human* soul which possesses vegetative, animal and rational faculties. It is man's power of reason or *aql*, which brings him closest to God–the Supreme Intellect.

Ibn Sina wrote that all human intellect is defective, for pure knowledge exists only in God. Nevertheless, because of his power of reasoning man can conceive of universal–ideas which he has abstracted from experience through the study of the world. In the effort to achieve more perfect knowledge. Ibn Sina, recommended that men follow the rules of logic. He says, 'The end of logic is to give a man a standard rule, whose observance will preserve him from error in reasoning.'

Regarding the problem of the creation of man Ibn Sina differed sharply with the prevalent opinion of his day. According to the Platonic theory, souls originally existed in the upper realm close to the Supreme Being. Then as a result of committing some fault, these souls fell to earth and became united with material bodies in punishment for their sin. This theory of Plato was accepted by most of the Arab philosophers. But Ibn Sina could not accept this. If the souls would have been sent from Heaven to earth to learn the secrets of the world, one cannot explain the fact that some infants die shortly after birth and that, at least, a soul can learn little in the relatively few years it may reside in one human body. The great philosopher eventually concluded that the souls are prepared from all eternity. Every time a body is ready to revive life.

On the question of a future life after death, Ibn Sina was concerned in the Islamic doctrine of "Return". In his *Shifa* he wrote, "The true religion which was brought to us by our Master and Prophet Muhammad (P.B.U.H.)....has explicitly described the pleasure and pain of the future life". Thus he believed in the future of the physical body as well as the spiritual soul of man after death.

Although he was a student of Aristotle, Ibn Sina disagreed with the Greek philosopher on the important relationship between God and the universe. Aristotle maintained that the world is eternal and its movements transient. God, he believed, was not the Maker of the universe but only of its movements. Ibn Sina, on the other hand, declared that the universe is both eternal and a creation of God, the Primal Cause. This thesis resulted in the simultaneous timing of cause (God) and effect (the universe), but Ibn Sina reasoned that cause does not invariably precede its effect in time–i.e., the movement of a key is the cause of the opening of a lock, although the action of cause and effect takes place simultaneously.

Ibn Sina wrote a number of books on various subjects, such as Physics, Metaphysics, Mathematics, and Philosophy. His *Kitab al-Shifa*, (Book of Healing), a philosophical encyclopaedia based upon the Aristotelian tradition as modified by Neo-platonic influences and Muslim theology has been divided into three parts, namely, *al-Muntiq* (Logic), *al-Tabiyyat* (Physics) and *al-Ilahiyyat* (Theology). In the theological section of his book, Ibn Sina discusses the nature of the existant things–

Divinity and the world-and says that the existence of the former is necessary while that of the latter is contingent. With regard to the proof for the existence of God, he maintains that God is the ultimate cause or the uncaused cause of everything in the world, inasmuch as the argument in this connection through infinite regress as well as through circle leads us nowhere. He further holds that the religious laws have one significance for the masses and quite the other for the learned.

Ibn Sina died at Hamadan at the age of 53. With his death there passed away from the arena of this world a personality who held an undisputed leadership in the world of both letters and science not only of his own time but of the centuries to follow him.

Abu Bakr Muhammad Ibn Yahya, popularly known as Ibn Baja, was one of the most celebrated philosophers in Muslim Spain. He was born at Saragossa towards the end of the 11th century A.D. Living in Seville for some time he proceeded to Africa and was appointed to the higher post under the Almoravids. Ibn Baja was not only a philosopher, physician, mathematician and astronomer, but also a musician of the first rank. When the study of philosophy had become extinct after the demise of Ibn Sina, he being the disciple of Farabi took up the task of developing the system of his master and introduced the Neo-Platonic interpretation of Aristotle in a conservative line. He wrote many original works on different subjects. He died at Fez in 1138 A.D.

Ibn Tufayel (Abu Bakr Muhammad Abdul Malik Ibn Tufayel al-Kaisi) was born at Wadiash in the province of Granada in the beginning of the 12th century. He was a distinguished philosopher, physician, mathematician, poet and was held in high respect at the court of the Almohad dynasty. His teaching is akin to that of Ibn Baja but with an additional stamp of a mystic strain. According to him ecstasy is the means of attaining the highest truth and knowledge. His famous work called *Hai Ibn Yaqzan* represents the gradual and successive development of intelligence and the power of perception in a person wholly unassisted by outside instruction. He died in Morocco in the year 1185 A.D.

Ibn Rushd (Averroes in Latin) who came of an illustrious family of Cordovan jurists, remained for centuries a beacon light in the ocean of darkness in which medieval Europe lay engulfed. He was the greatest Muslim philosopher and the prfoundest commentator of Aristotle. His father and grandfather, like himself, had graced the chair of chief judge (*Qazi ul-Quzzat*) at Cordova. He devoted his early life to the study of Theology, Law and Philosophy most of which he mastered at the feet of Abu Ja'far Harun of Truxilo, an eminent scholar of the day. In philosophy he came under the influence of Ibn Tufayel.

Ibn Rushd's chief contribution to philosophic literature is his commentaries on Aristotle's work and he put his heart and soul to this work befitting a true lover of Aristotle. It is needless to say here that he was a devoted student of Aristotle. Ibn Rushd had the highest regard and admiration for him. "Aristotle for him was the supreme perfect man, the greatest thinker, the philosopher who was in possession of an infalliable truth", says a famous historian. The chief work of Ibn Rushd on philosophy apart from these commentaries is *Tahafut at-Tahafut* (Destruction of Destruction), rejoinder to al-Gazzali's *Tahafut al-Filasfa* (Destruction of Philosophers) in which he defends the philosophers against the charge of free thought and unbelief levelled against them be orthodox theologians. He further develops them in his *Kitab al Filasfa* (Book of Philosophers) and his *Fasl-ul-Maqali fi Muwafaqatil Hikmat wal Sharia* (A true and critical discussion on the question of agreement between philosophy and revealed religion). His other works include a commentary on Plato's *Republic*, "Criticism on a Farabai's Logic", "Discussion on certain theories of Ibn Sina" and "Glosses on the 'Aqida of Mehdi Ibn Tumrat". He also wrote on Law and his contribution in this is *Kitab Badiyat al Mujahid wa Nihayal al- Maqasid*. But a large part of his work in original Arabic is lost.

Ibn Rushd has for centuries been represented both in the Muslim East and the Christian West as the author of the thesis that philosophy is true and revealed religion is false. And there is hardly any truth in this imputation, for he held that philosophy and revealed religion both preached eternal truths and that conflict between philosophy and revealed truth as enshrined in the Holy Quran was unthinkable. "He also held that prophetic revelations were necessary for spreading among mankind the eternal verities proclaimed equally by religion and philosophy; that religion itself directs their search by means of science; that it teaches truths in a popular manner comprehensible to all people; that philosophy alone is capable of seizing the true religious doctrines by means of interpretations; but the ignorant apprehend only the literal meaning'.

Ibn Rushd dealt with this subject at full length in his book. *Fasl-ul-Maqali fi Muwafaqatil Hikmat wal Sharia*. But it is an irony of fate that, in spite of his role as a champion of the unity of Islamic faith with philosophy, his name has been associated with a grossly anti-religious school of thought, which goes under the name of Averroism. This Averroism is the product of the genius of Siger of Brabant and his fellow- scholars who dominated the intellectual circle at Paris in those days.

The main doctrines which brought Ibn Rushd in conflict with Muslim theologians concern the question of the eternity of the world, the nature of God's apprehension. His fore-knowledge, the universality of the soul and of the intellect and the nature of resurrection. The great philosopher does not deny the eternity of the World and other imputations but gives different explanations from the theological one.

Ibn Rushd was far ahead of his time when he made his appearance on the stage of the world. "His political theories," in the words of Sayed Amir Ali, "were directed against human tyranny in every shape." He regarded the Republic under the four pious Caliphs as the model Government. He considered women to be equal in every respect to men and 'claimed for them equal capacity in war, in philosophy, in science.' If they were placed in the same position as men, they would become equals of their husbands in every field of works. Ibn Rushd died in 1198 A.D.

About the middle of the 4th Muslim century there grew in Basra an interesting eclectic school of popular philosophy which is known in the history of Islam as Ikhwan al-Safa (the Brethren of Purity). The aim of this school was the reformation of the Isma'ilian doctrine and the revival of its original form. The brethren wanted to keep alive the lamp of knowledge among the Muslims, to introduce a more hearty atmosphere among the people, to arrest the downward, course of the Muslims towards ignorance and fanaticism and thereby to save the social fabric from utter ruin. To this school none but men of unsophisticated character and the purest morals were admitted. The brethren formed branches in every city of the Caliphate wherever they found a body of thoughtful men willing to work according to their scientific method. "This scientific and philanthropic movement was led by five men who with Zaid at the head were the life and soul of the brotherhood. Their system was eclectic in the highest and truest sense of the word. They gave to the world a general 'resume' of the knowledge of the time in separate treatises which were collectively known as the *Rasail-i-Ikiwan as-Safa wa-Khullan-ul-Wafa* (Tracts of the brothers of purity and friends of sincerity) and these risalas cover almost every subject of human study- mathematics, including astronomy, physical geography, music and mechanics, physics, chemistry, meteorology biology, zoology, grammar, ethics, metaphysics, the doctrine of a future life, etc. In fact, they formed a popular encyclopaedia of all sciences and philosophy then existing.

Besides the above philosophers, there were other philosophers whose contributions to philosophy were of great importance.

HISTORIOGRAPHY

Before the advent of Islam, there was no systematic way compiling history among any nation of the world. It was the Muslims who recorded in writing the sayings of the Prophet and the revelations revealed on him. "The Muslims achieved a definite advance beyond previous historical writing in the sociological understanding of history and the systematisation of historiography". The abundance of historical tales in the Quran and the life of the Prophet of Islam created an incentive for the Muslims to study history. In the initial stages, historical events were mostly committed to memory but later on, large volumes of history were compiled. History has always been considered the most important subject in the educational curriculum of Muslims. The traditions of the Prophet collected to some of the celebrated historians of Islam formed the greatest biographical history that had ever been compiled.

The writing of history began in the reigns of the Umayyads and was developed during the Abbasid period. The early historians depended on the continuity of the chain of reports, more particularly on the authenticity of the reporters. The early historical works were mostly based on legends, traditions, biographies and genealogies.

The writing of history really started in the second century A.H. Ali bin Muhammad bin Abdullah Madani (b. 136 A.H.), a copious writer, occupies an outstanding place among early Arab historians. He made a tour of Basra and Madain and later settled in Baghdad where he was patronised by the renowned musician Ishaq al-Mawsuli. He wrote a number of works which had been divided into groups of books–the first dealing with records of the Prophet, the second with the records of the Quraysh, the third with the marriage of the nobles and the records of women, the fourth with the records of the Caliphs, from Abu Bakr to Mutasim, the fifth with historical events in Islam, the sixth with Islamic conquest, the seventh with the records of the Arabs and the eighth with poetical history. Madaini is quoted as an authority by later historians. Hisham bin al-Sayyib al-Kalbi of Kufa was another famous historian during the second century of Islam. He wrote more than 150 works and is considered an authority on genealogies. Muhammad Ibn Ishaq of Madinah (d. 151 A.H.) wrote the biography of the Prophet (*Sirat Rasul Allah*) at the behest of the Abbasid Caliph al-Mansur. The work of Ibn Ishaq on the life of Muhammad is collected in three volumes. His work has been preserved by Ibn Hisham who knew the book through a pupil of Ibn Ishaq. Ibn Hisham took from the first part only the history of Muhammad's ancestors since Ibrahim but combined the two independent parts with occasional considerable abridgements into the *Kitab Sirat Rasul Allah*.

Muhammad bin Umar-al-Waqidi (130-207 A.H.) was the most outstanding historian of the second century of the Islamic era. He was a prolific writer on various subjects. His special attention to chronology has been commented upon by western writers. He wrote *Maghzi* which dealt with the conquest of

Uqbah in West Africa, Al-Waqidi is considered an authority on tradition, Islamic jurisprudence and history. The secretary of al-Waqidi wrote a history dealing with the life of the Prophet and his Companions.

The third century was a century of intellectual attainments in the history of Islam. It was in this period that some of the brightest luminaries appeared in the horizon of Arab learning. Ahmad Ibn Yahya al-Baladhuri of Iran was one of the earliest and leading historians of the third century. He travelled extensively in quest of historical knowledge. The main works of this historian are *Futuh al-Buldan* and *Ansab al-Ashraf* (Book of the Lineages of Nobles). The *Futuh al-Buldan* deals with the record of Muslim conquests and also describes the subsequent history of the countries concerned. He received the designations, *Baladhuri* because he died (279 A.H.) of mental derangement after drinking baladhur (Indian bhang). Al-Baladhuri was not only a great historian but also a famous geographer. Abu Hanifa Ahmad al-Dinawari who flourished in Dinawar (in Persian Iraq) was an authority on astronomy and botany and also left behind valuable works on mathematics, geography, philosophy, literature and history. He wrote a work in 13 volumes on the Quran. His famous work entitled, *al-Akhbar al-Tiwl* (long narratives) is a universal history up to the history of Mutasim. Abdullah bin Muslim bin Qutayba (213-270 A.H.) was another historian of this period. He was the Qazi of Dinawar and wrote several important treatises on literary subjects. His historical work entitled *Kitab al-Ma'arif* (Book of Knowledge) is a store-house of information about the holy Prophet and Arab genealogical table. Ibn Wadi Al-Yaqubi was a famous historian and geographer whose compendium of Universal history contains 'the ancient and unfalsified Shi'ite tradition.'

Abu Jafar Muhammad Ibn Jarir al-Tabari (838-923 A.D.) who was born in Tabaristan, the mountainous district of Persia, is regarded as the father of Islamic history and as one of the greatest historian of the world. Tabari is said to have learnt the Quran by heart at the age of seven. He travelled all over Asia and Egypt in quest of knowledge and to collect data for historical works. According to Yaqut, Tabari wrote 40 pages daily for 40 years. Among his works on diverse subjects, the two most outstanding which influenced later writers are the exhaustive commentary on the Quran and his universal history known as *Tarik al-Rasul wal Muluk* (Annals of the Apostles and Kings). According to George Sarton his history is "remarkably elaborate and accurate." His history begins with the creation of the world and goes down to 915 A.D.).

This was the first elaborate and complete historical treatise in the Arabic language. The later historians including Abul Fida, Ibn Athir Miskawayh and Ibn Kamil used this work as a chief source of information and guidance. Abul Faraj Ispahani (897-967 A.D.) who was of an Arabian descent wrote a famous book named *Kitab al-Aghani* in which he had discussed the lives and activities of Arabian poets and musicians. It is an invaluable work on Arab antiquity which has been called the "Register of Arabs" by Ibn Khaldun.

The historical composition of the Muslims in Arabic reached its highest point in Tabari and Masudi. Abul Hasan Ali al-Masudi (912-957 A.D.) is famous both as a historian and a geographer and was one of the versatile of the 5th century writers. Barnes describes him as 'the Herodotus of the Arabs for he possessed the same avid curiosity and zeal for information as did the father of history.' He belonged to an Arab family and was born at Baghdad. In his youth, he travelled all over the Muslim countries in quest of learning. His *Muruj al- Dhahab wa-Ma'adin al-Jawhar* (Meadows of Gold and Mines of Precious Stones) is a record of his travel experiences and observations. "He was also one of the first to make use of the historical anecdotes".

Ibn al-Athir was a distinguished historian of the thirteenth century, who wrote Kamil, a history of the world up to 1231 A.D. He produced another important work *Asa al-Ghabah* (the Lions of the Thicket), a collection of 7,500 biographies of the Companions. Ibn Khallekan wrote an important geographical dictionary, often quoted by European authors.

The Muslim Spain witnessed a host of historians. Among them Ibn Qutiya, Abu Marwan Hayyan Ibn Khalif, surnamed Ibn Kayyan, Ibn al-Farabi and Ibn Khalfun were the prominent. The last one flourished in the 14th century of the Christian era. Born in Tunis in 1332, he was in the midst of all the revolutions of which Africa was the theatre in the 14th century. "His magnificent history is preceded by a Prolegomena, in itself a store-house of information and philosophical dissertations. In the Prolegomena, he traces the origin of the society, the development of civilization, the course which led to the rise and fall of kingdoms and dynasties; and discusses among other questions, the influence of climate on the formations of a nation's character." Ibn Khaldun asserts with justice that he has discovered a new method of writing history. No historian had ever taken a view at once so comprehensive and so philosophical; none had attempted to trace the deeply hidden caused of events to expose the moral and spiritual forces at work beneath the surface or to divine the immutable laws of national progress and decay. He owed little to his predecessors, although he mention some of them with respect. The fame of Ibn Khaldun rests on his *Muqaddamah*, the first volume of his well renowned book, *Kitab al-Ibar* in which he had discussed the history of the Arabs, Persians and Berbers. "Ibn Khaldun was the greatest historian-philosopher Islam produced and one of the greatest of all times," says Prof. Hitti.

GEOGRAPHY

The institution of the holy pilgrimage, the orientation of the mosques towards Makkah and the need for determining the direction at the time of prayer give religious impetus to the Muslim, study of geography.

The Muslims made great strides in geography and their contributions to it were of immense value in the history of the world. They demonstrated the spherical shape of the globe at a time when the scientists of Europe emphatically asserted that it was flat. The interest of the Muslims in geographical matters was largely born of the environment in which they lived. The children of the desert had to have a knowledge of the fixed stars, the movements of the planets and other heavenly bodies and the change of weather. These were carefully observed for the purpose of travel over the vast expanses of the desert. The knowledge about the position of the stars led to the determination of latitude and longitude.

The scientific study of geography in Islam began under the Greek influence. The Muslims translated the Greek works into Arabic and the result of the widespread activity in translating Greek works was that they became acquainted with the geographical works of Ptolemy. The Greek contribution of geography reached its high watermark with the work of Ptolemy. But the Muslims not only translated Greek works into Arabic but they also preserved, cultivated and on a number of important points developed it.

Muhammad bin Musa al-Khwarizmi (d. 847 A.D.) was the outstanding geographer whose work laid the first foundation of geographical science in Arabic. His *Kitab Surat al-Ard* (The Book on the Shape of the Earth) which served as a basis for later works was written in the first half of the 9th century A.D.

Prof. Minorsky says that it is a work, the like of which no
European nation could have produced at the dawn of its scientific
activity. He was one of the earliest map-makers in Islam. The
first map of the world was executed during the reign of Mamun
by many scholars among whom al-Khwarizmi was one of them.
Muhammad bin Musa made a measurement of the earth at the
inspiration of al-Mamun.

One of the earliest geographical works of this period is
that of Ibn Khurdadbih who was of Persian descent. His famous
book entitled *Kitab al-Masalik al-Mamalik*. (On Routes and
Kingdoms) gives a summary of the main trade routes of the
Arab world and the descriptions of distant lands, such as China,
Korea and Japan. This work was used by many later geographers.
Ibn Wadeh al-Yaqubi was a distinguished geographer. He was a
Shi'ite and flourished in Armenia and Khorasan. He made an
extensive tour of India and the Maghrib (N.W. Africa). His
book *Kitab al-Buldan* (Book of Countries) which gives details
about numerous places and attempts have been made to state
facts of physical geography, explaining the human geography
of many areas was written in 891 A.H. Yaqubi was specially
interested in the statistical and topographic aspects. He was
sometimes known as the 'Father of Muslim geography.'

Ibn al-Faqih al-Hamadani who was born in Hamadan, a
famous city of Iran, is generally known as the author of a
geographical miscellany. His works *Kitab al-Buldan* is often
quoted by Masudi and Yaqut. Another geographer of Persian
origin Ibn Rustah flourished during this time. He was the author
of an encyclopaedia, the seventh volume of which deals with
geography.

Abu Zaid al-Balkhi was a famous scholar at the court of
the Samanid dynasty. He stood in high favour with the Vazier
al-Jaihani who is like-wise the writer of a voluminous

geographical treatise. Al-Balkhi is one of the early Muslim map-makers and his work, *Surat al-Aqalim* (Figures of Climes) consists of explanations of charts. He also wrote 'Routes and Kingdoms' *Kitab al-Masalik wal-Mamalik* which was compiled in 921 A.D.

Al-Istakhri, an Iranian, wrote a similar work named *Kitab al-Masalik wal-Mamalik*. In his work maps play an important part. His work is based upon Balkhi's works of the same name. Ibn Hawqal was a widely travelled man whose travels lasted no less than 30 years. He travelled throughout the Muslim world gathering store of knowledge and experience. He at the request of al-Istakhri revised his maps and text of his geography. But later on he re-wrote the same book and issued it under his own name.

Al-Maqdisi, a native of Palestine, was the most celebrated geographer the Islamic world has ever produced. His reputation as a geographer has been widely recognised in the West. He was a famous traveller who visited all parts of the Muslim world except India and Spain. 'In his writings he reveals himself as a very close observer of life and professions and seems to have a great insight into the literature of the lands which he visited. In 985 A.D. he embodied an account of his twenty years of travel in a book named, *Ahsan al-Taqasim fi Ma'arfat al-Aqalim* (the Best of Divisions for the Knowledge of the Climes). Al-Maqdisi divided the lands of Islam into fourteen divisions or provinces. He prepared separate maps for each division and in these maps he used symbols and method of representation of relief, etc. for their proper comprehension by all.

Al-Beruni (Abu Raihan Muhammad bin Ahmad) has been regarded as one of the greatest geographers of the Muslim world. His keen sense of geographical observation reveals through famous work, *Kitab al-Hind*. Detailed discussion about this man has been made under Mathematics.

Yaqut Hamavi (Ibn Abdullah ar-Rumi) was one of the celebrated geographers of the Eastern Muslim. He came of a Greek parentage and was born in Asia Minor in 1179 A.D. While yet a boy he was bought in Baghdad by a merchant from Hamah (hence his surname al-Hamavi) who gave him good education. He served his master as a travelling clerk but after the third journey to the Island of Krish (in the Persian Gulf) he left his benefactor. He became bookseller and writer to support himself. His great 'Geographical Dictionary' (*Mujam al-Bulban*) is a veritable encyclopaedia containing valuable information on history, ethnography and natural science. Yaqut's another monumental work, *Mujam al-Udaba* (Dictionary of Learned men) gives useful geographical information in addition to the literary notices. He was a self-made man of wide learning and experiences.

Al-Qazwini, a renowned geographer of Arab family, was born at Qazwin in Jibal (North Iran). He wrote a cosmography and a geography and gave in the latter many curious and fabulous details about the places he mentioned. Another original geographer who flourished in the 14th century A.D. was al-Dimishqi. He is an important authority for Arab's knowledge of South India.

Spain produced a good number of geographers of outstanding merit. Al-Bakri who was born in 1040 A.D. at Cordova wrote a 'geographical dictionary' and a book on 'Routes and Kingdoms'. Muhammad bin Abu Bakr az-Zuhri and al-Mazini are the next two notable geographers of Granada. Abu Bakr az-Zuhri was one of those writers who gave to their work the name of geography.

Al-Idrisi was perhaps the best known geographer in the West. He came of an Alid family and was born at Ceuta in 1099 A.D. He attracted our attention more than any other

Spanish geographers, first, because he worked at the court of a Christian king, Roger II of Sicily, secondly, because he long passed for the sole representative of Islamic geographical knowledge. The fact that King Roger II entrusted the composition of a description of the known world to a Muhammadan scholar indicates clearly how far the superiority of Muhammadan learning was acknowledged at that time. Being persuaded by the King of Sicily, al-Idrisi settled down at the court of Palermo and there he wrote a treatise, 'Amusement for him who desires to travel round the world' also known as 'Kitab Rugari' (Book of Roger). At the same time "he also made a celestial sphere and a representation of the known world in the form of a disc, which gives him an outstanding place among the Muslim cartographers." The work of Idrisi is certainly the most notable example of the fusion of ancient and modern geography.

The geographical literature after al-Idrisi cannot claim any originality, except the narrations of travellers. Among best known are the Spaniard Ibn Jubair and Ibn Batuta, a man from Morocco. The former's work under the title, 'Rihlat Ibn Zubair (Travels of Ibn Jubair) became very very popular both in the East and West. His writings were utilised by later geographers.

Abu Abdullah Muhammad Ibn Batuta was the famous medieval traveller who travelled throughout the lands of every Muslim ruler of his time. He gives a fine description of every country he visited. He is rightly remembered as a distinguished descriptive geographer.

Besides, there were many geographers of outstanding merit. The great number of geographers after Idrisi shows clearly that the knowledge of geographical matters was still widespread at that age. "But after the Mongol invasions the Muhammadan world lost for ever its ideal and even its scultural unity", says H. Kramers.

CARTOGRAPHY

The Muslims opened a new chapter in the history of cartography, the science of map-making. They made much progress in cartography. Their wide range of knowledge in geography and their original contributions to it along with the translation of Greek works have been highly recognised by the civilised world. They got inspiration from the Greek writers, and most of them based their writings upon Ptolemy's works. But they did not follow them blindly and slavishly. They developed many of their points with their own contributions. The Muslims discarded the idea of the Greeks on several points. They refused to accept Ptolemy's idea of the connection between Africa and South-Eastern Asia, making the Indian Ocean a landlocked Sea. Though they were not successful like other departments in attaining a higher standard in cartography, yet none can deny that they represented the world on a map when the western scholars could not think of it. This clearly shows their advancement of knowledge in cartography which may be regarded as one of the divisions of geography.

Ptolemy was undoubtedly the greatest and by far the best cartographer in the ancient world. But the fundamental error he made in making the maps was his under estimate of the earth's size. In his estimation Europe and Asia extended over one-half the surface of the globe while in reality they cover only about 1300 degrees. In the same manner he counted the length of the Mediterranean sixty two degrees whereas in reality it is only forty two degrees. The Arab geographers and the marine chart-makers of the 13th century had corrected this distortion; but yet it continued to figure in European cartography until 1700 A.D. The Muslims constructed celestial globes and their maps of those areas which had come under Islam were superior to those of Ptolemy.

Among the earliest map-makers of the Islamic world was al- Khwarizmi whose *Kitab Surat al-Ard* was written in explanation of the maps. It is supposed that he copied it from Syrian copy of Ptolemy's maps. He also made a map of the Nile. He participated in the scientific activity in which no less than seventy scholars took part for the preparation of the map of the world during the reign of Mamun. Some of the orientalists have given an indication that there had existed a collection of maps of some parts of Iran and a map of the world in pre-Abbasid period which may be called an 'Iran Atlas'.

Al-Balkhi was the next distinguished map-maker in Islam, His "Atlas' contained a world map, a map of Arabia, the Indian Ocean, maps of the Maghrib (Morocco, Algeria, etc.) Egypt, Syria, the Mediterranean and about a dozen other maps of the central and eastern Islamic-world. His geographical works written in explanation of his maps. Mr. K. Miller calls it 'the Islam Atlas'. In later years, maps of Istakhri and Ibn Hawqal were based upon the works of Balkhi. The closing stages of the Balkhi School were represented by the famous geographer al-Idrisi who says, "In the making of maps we have done our best to bring out correct representations of the different parts of the empire after carefully studying a number of drawings and also the drawings of Istakhri which come nearer to fact and are worthy of reliance although confused and imperfect in many places." He divided the lands of Islam into fourteen divisions and showed each one in a map. In his maps routes were coloured red; the golden sands, yellow; the salt seas, green; the well-known rivers, blue; the principal mountains, drab so that everybody understood the descriptions.

Art and Architecture

The Arabs in Spain did not neglect to carry with them all the arts, minor and practical introduced or developed by Muslims in other lands. They studied the various regional or local arts and blending them with their own, brought a new pattern so exquisitely that it could claim the Arab Character in all respects. The grand mosque of Cordova, a fine blend of the Gothic and Zionist architecture with the Muslim architecture represented purely the Spanish art which in the course of time was widely known and accepted as the Spanish art outstanding all other arts of Europe.

Minor Arts

The Hispano-Mosque School excelled in metal work which involved fine decoration with varied patterns in relief. Engravings inlaid with gold and silver. It was generally known as damascening, from the European association of the work with Damascus. The specimen of a relic of Hisham II (976-1009), preserved in the Cathedral of Gerona in the form of a wooden Casket sheatted with silver gilt embossed plating with scroll-like foliation, bore an Arabic inscription which stated the names of two craftsmen Badr and Tarif.

Toledo and Seville were specially famous for the metal work such as cutlery, sword blades and astrolobes. Their blades were next only to the damascene blades in temper and elasticity. The astrolobes an astronomical instrument of the ancient Greek invention, was perfected by the Muslims and introduced in Europe in the twenty century. The astrolobe of the Muslims determined the Prayer time and the geographical position of Mecca. It was very valuable for the mariners and an essential adjunct for astrologers. It was a beautiful piece of art-work by itself.

Ceramics

The Muslims were the past masters from an early period in the application of coloured glazes to earthen wares and so was with the enamel work. Valencia was the centre of this industry in the west. Poetiers was Centre of pottery industry.

Holland imitated the Muslim Pottery industry in the 15th century. It was also introduced in Italy. Later Spainish Vessels could be noticed with their pseudo-Arabic inscriptions. The Spanish Muslim School distinguished itself in various forms of Ceramics as well as mosaics particulary tile and blue faience. Azulejo (Ar. al-zuiayji) indicates the favourite choice of modern Spain and Portugal of colored tiles as a legacy from the Arabs. Toledo and Cordova manufactured exquisite pottery in the third quarter of the eleventh century Calatayud (Qalat Ayyub) Malaga and Manises in Valencia were very famous for the industry. Muslim Spain was second only to Syria in glass industry, and run almost parallel to China in pottery.

Textiles

The Arabs of Spain share well in the development of textile arts with the Arabic speaking peoples who were leading fabric-makers and silk mercers in the medieval age. They could not however compete with Persian Carpet-making. Cordova was the centre of weaving industry. Almeria had 4800 looms according to Allama Maqqri. Al-Mawsil exported mussolina or muslin to Italy and Baghdad supplied the Italian market with fine silk cloth under the Italianised name "baldacco" and "baldachin" the silken Canopies suspended over the churches. Granada supplied Granadines to the European dress shops. Silk cloths with rich colouring of floral and geometrical designs were in demand for church Vestments and royal robes. The 12th century witnessed the adoption of Islamic designs by the European Weavers, with Arabic Script. Not only in metal and glass-work, pottery, architecture and decorative art but in textiles also the European work had the stamp of Islamic Style in the 14th and 18th centuries. To this day even, the Spanish Carpenter prefer Arabic trade marks.

Ivories

The School of Ivory Carvers at Cordova, flourished well in the 10th century. It produced beautiful Ivory caskets and boxes decorated with carved, inlaid or painted ornaments which represented musical performances and hunting scenes. The Cylindrical Casket made in 353 A.H./964 A.D. for a gift to the queen of Khalifa al Hakam II was the puzzling example of the art.

ARCHITECTURE

The Mosque of Cordova

The foundation of the grand mosque was laid by Amir Abdul Rehman al-Dakhil in 170 A.H./786 A.D. It was completed by his son Hisham I in 177 A.H./793 A.D. He added to the mosque the famous wonderful square minaret, which indicated the Afro-Syrian Style. Azan was called from the minaret. The place where the Muazzin called the Azan was 54 ft. long in area and the area of the extreme top floor was 73 ft. long and 18 ft. broad. Additions to the mosque were made by the various rulers from time to time. The area of the mosque during the reign of Abdul Rehman al-Nasir was 225 in length and 205 yards in breadth Al-Hakam II added 105 yards to it in length whereas Hajib al-Mansoor added 85 yards to it in breadth. Its roof was supported by 1293 columns which spoke of the exquisite workmanship of the Arabs.

Brass lanterns illumined the entire mosque. "One chandelieri held a thousand lights the smallest held twelve."

The mosque had twenty one gates, nine each on the western and eastern sides and three on the northern side. It was however the wonder of the world which is now a cathedral.

The Alcazar of Seville and the Al-hambra of Granada are the most superb remains of al-Undulusia.

Madinat-al-Zahra, now called Cordova-la-Vieja built by Abdul Rehman III and his successors stood for the topmost architecture of then world. The columns were imported from Rome, Constantinople and Carthage. A fountain decorated with human figures was brought from Constantinople and fixed in the place. The Berbers (1010) had sacked the Madinah and set it on fire which damaged a fair portion. Al-Mansoor had built a similar palace called Madinah-al Zahira, east of Cordova, which was also damaged by the Berbers.

The Alcazar of Seville built by a Toledan architect for the Muvahhid Governor in 1199-1200 A D. was renovated in the Muslim style by Madejor workmen for king Peter the cruel in 1353 A.D. as royal residence. The Alcazar of Seville excelled all other Alcazars in Cordova Toledo and other Spanish towns. The Giralda tower of Seville erected in 1184 A.D. originally the minaret of the great mosque stood for one of the finest Muvahhid monuments.

Alhambra

The construction of Alhambra was begun by the Nasrid ruler Muhammad al-Ghalib in 646 A.H./1248 A.D. and was completed by Abu-al-Hajjaj Yusuf (1333-54 A.D.) and by his successor Muhammad V al-Ghani (1354-59 A.D.). The Alhambra palace has been accepted as the last word in the architectural workmanship. One would hardly believe that such a magnificent building could be the achievement of the decaying period of the Muslims in Spain. The interior decorated inscription, on the walls, mostly ascribed to Abul Hajjaj and the Court of Lions represent the highest imaginative art. The twelve marble lions standing in a Circle in the Centre of the Court, spouting a jet of fine water from their mouths, presented a heavenly scene.

The floral decoration of the Hall of Justice spoke of the

excellence of the Muslim Culture. Various scenes painted on leather in the ceiling illustrated the historic Muslim Chivalry with ten rules seated on an oval bench. The motto of *al-Ghalib Wala Ghalib illa-Allah* (there is no Conqueror other than Allah) was exquisitely inscribed on the wall to stir Character, dedication and belief in God.

The Arch

The Pointed arch, a very unique and beautiful invention of Muslim architecture eclipsed the old horse-shoe form of arch of northern Syria, Ctesphon and other places which existed before Islam. The pointed arch of the Muslim architecture became the distinctive feature of the Western Gothic architecture. The Umayyad mosque of Damascus and Qusayr Amra had pointed arches, first. It was known as the Moorish arch in Spain. The Vaulting system based on intersecting arches and "Visible intersecting ribs , was the original contribution of the Undulusian Arabs which manifested the highest engineering skill. Such architectural features developed at Cordova were taken to Toledo and other places in the north by the Mozarabs. The Mudejar engineers made it very popular with some improvements in the style.

The Morisco's persecution

General Musa-bin-Abdul Ghazzan objected to the terms capitulation as he knew the astute diplomacy of Isabella and Ferdinand. The persecution of the Jews at the hands of the Christians stood for a clear example. Having failed to enlist support of the Muslims, he left Elevira for all times to come, with a challenge, to the shortsighted, selfish and treacherous Muslim chiefs that their existence will not be tolerated in Spain by the Christians and their persecution will be an unparallel episode in their history of the world. Their Catholic majesties Ferdinand and Isabella did not wait for long to unsheath their malicious, designs against the Muslims by setting aside all the terms of the Capitulation. The royal words promises and assurances in the name of the holy Christ proved baseless. They were simply hollow diplomatic utterances just to prepare grounds for the savage and inhuman treatment with the innocent Muslim people.

The Queen's confessor Cardinal ximenez led a campaign of forced conversion in 1499. He ordered for the withdrawal from circulation all Arabic books, dailies, weeklies, magazines both Islamic and general and burnt them all. Shops and libraries and private, were burnt to ashes. Al-Undulusia was the scene of a "bonefire of Arabic manuscripts for months together on the various subject of Arts and science. The inquisition was then instituted simple to torture the innocent Muslim people regardless of age and sex.

The Muslims who remained in Spain after the fall of Granada were called Moriscos (S.P. little Moors). The Romans called the people of Western Africa Mauretanisa as "Mauri " meaning Western, a Phrocnician origin, whence S.P More and English Moor. The Berbers were the Moor proper, but the term "Moor" was applied to all the Muslims of Spain and north western Africa. The half million Muslims of Philippines are still called Moors. They were so named Spaniards after the discovery of the islands by magellan in 1521 A.D.

The Romance dialect, a regional spoken language of the Muslims Spaniards employed the Arabic script. Their literature termed al jameado (al-ajamiah, foreign tongue was rich and interesting. A collection of such manuscripts escaped the cruel eyes of the officer of the inquisition for their being hidden under the floor of an old house. The Mudigares (Mudajjamn domesticated were the Muslims of Castile, Leon and Aragon who lived under the Christian rulers before the fall of the

Muslims in the south. They were called Morisco from the 16th century onwards. It was 1492 that after the fall of Granada all Muslims were called moriscos just to humiliate them. The Moriscos were forcibly baptised. The Royal decree (501 A.D.) declared that all Muslims should either accept Christianity or leave Spain on pain of the confiscation of properties moveable or unmovable. The law of Philip II (1556 A.D.) required the remaining Muslims "to abandon at once their language, worship, institutions and names of life." Philip II also ordered the demolition of all Muslims Spanish baths as a relics and pauper. "Between the fall of Granada and the first decade of the seventeenth century not less than three million Muslims were executed. It is now for the modern world either to appreciate or condemn the unthinkable tortures to the Muslims who gave light, civilisation, culture education and above all. "Life" to Europe, the dark Europe of the day without any racial or religious discremination. Peace had always been the demand of the day and even in the antique period of history peace reigned supreme and the treaty whether oral or written were abserved honorably even by the so called uncivilized warriors and chiefs who actually much honest, true and superior to the civilized group of untrue and selfish rulers. The terms of capitulation were nothing more than the elephants tusks. How far the royal words of their catholic majesties, to quote Luis Bertrand, "We (Ferdinand and Isabella) swear by our faiths and royal word that we will observe and make observed every thing herein contained; everything and every part, now and hereafter now and for ever" stood true, simply to prepare ground for the total extermination of the Muslims. Further, the Christian masters could not afford to cultivate their lands without the Moriscos who were not only hard and honest cultivators but also men of skill. They were so skilful in agriculture that every piece of sterile alpujharah was brought under cultivation by their deligence which enhanced the economy of the country. They were excelled in manual work disliked by the Christians. They were famous tinkers, soap makers, rope makers, sandle-maker, shoe makers, matress makers, weavers, tailors, potters, gardeners, olive oil peddlers, muleteers, gold smiths and iron smiths. Their living was simple and moderate and were willing tax payers. Their living was simple and religious and believed in the religiuos unity of the entire country. Their catholic majesties, Ferdinand and Isabella took only six or seven years to go back to their royal words by appointing Fransico Jimenez de Cinceros as incharge of the missioary work for the conversion of the Muslims by force. In the meantime Fernada de Talavera the first Archbishop of Granada carried out mutual exchange between the Moriscos and the lazy Christians and thereby accelerated pace of conversion. The Moriscos had to surrender their wealths and property to the lazy Christians through the Archbishop. The switch of forced conversion was on at full speed. They were not to be given any social status and were called perros moros (Moorish dogs). The acrhbishop cineros burnt a large number of rare Arabic books on science philosophy and other important subjects heathen works.

The Moriscos of Granada revolted on account of the forced conversion. The Christian legislation passed a law which compelled their Morscos either to accept. Christianity or to pay 50000 sucats of Gold. The law was a naked negation of the terms of capitulation. Holy Water of Christianity was forcibly sprinkled on them which confirmed the heinous plan and mind of the Christians. Any one who refused to abide by the church law was put to death on the charge of heresy even after accepting Christianity. The registration order (Ist January 1568) for the Morisco children between the ages of 3 to 15 years for education (in Christian lines compelled the Moriscos to protest strongly under the leadership of Fernando di valor (Maulvi Abdullah Muhammad bin Umiaya known as abu Humeya) in December

1568. The Christian royal force under the command of Dan Juan de Austria an illegitimate son of Emperor Charles V expelled the Moriscos from Granada to Seville (1569).

The Moriscos were true Muslims and were proud of their nationality ancestors and their past glory. Their leader Abu Humeya, a true Chivalrous Muslim said "Dont you know that we are in Spain and that we have owned this land for 900 years. We are no band of thieves but a kingdom nor is Spain less abandoned to vices than was Rome. It is our natural father land. I know and feel the sweet of the fatherland." It is said that the Moriscos would have driven out the Christians from Granada but as ill luck would have it family quarrels arose and leader was killed by his own treacherous followers in October 1569. The table turned and the Moriscos fell a prey to the heinous conspiracy of the Christians aided by quislings of their own fold and were expelled from their fatherland in 1609. The Muslims who gave light to Spain and the rest of Europe, were put to unthinkable torture and humiliation and were denied by Law the basic human rights even.

To quote Hole "The 13th century vevro or statute of Zorita, a village in the Guadalajara, provides that men shall frequent them (baths) on Tuesday, Thursday and Saturdays, women on Monday and Wednesday, Jews on Friday and Sunday." No mention was made of the Muslims who were in the habit of taking baths daily in the public baths. The Muslim were prevented by the Christians from bathing and in 1567 the church closed down baths at Granada for the Muslim.

The 4th of August 1609 passed the inhuman and merciless law of expulsion of the Moors which being enforced in September 1609 expelled not less than 467, 500 Moors from their own homeland. The Muslims were denied their birth right to live in country, even as subjects and citizens whose precursor had founded the great empire and lived there for centuries together as sons of the soil and had developed the country on humanitarian grounds for all the citizens whether Muslims or non-Muslims.

Decline and fall of an empire is a natural process which is experienced only when the manifesto which binds the nation in to one collective whole, gets loose or broken aided hypocracy, coersion, dishonesty, mistrust, parochialism and unwholsome physical and mental curbs on the inmates of a country. Decline is guaranteed all the more when the "Head" cares more for his "chair" than the good of the country. Instead of scanning his own deeds he prefers to be surrounded and guided by such yes men who make country affairs so complicated and problematic that the "Head" is forced to play in the enemy's hand and develops hatred, dissension and confusion among his own people against him. Instead of studying the causes of the success of his own ancestors carves out a policy based on tribal hatred and superiority which makes the bondage of love and mutual understanding so weak and loose that his own chair is broken to pieces. The great social order, the chief vehicle of solidarity was polluted with injustice, short sightedness, ill will and doubts. The great Social Order responsible for the political success advocated vehemently the religion national unity and ego free from all discrimination was cornored injudiciously by the rulers, the vazirs and omara, just to create a new Order" which guaranteed the 'fall." The New order literally crushed down the Islamic culture and civilization based on Universal brotherhood, justice and equity parochialism, social superiority, blood pride rained their heads. The entire society was bathing in vices caring little consequences.

The Muslim culture which was one and one alone was divided parochialised culture due to the selfishness of the later rulers which gave rise to civil wars and provided a golden opportunity for belonging to the Humari, Muzari, Shami, of their family line with the Zanata, Maknasa, Sanhaja etc. This gave rise to serious regular civil wars which weakened the empire and prepared the round for the expulsion of the Muslims from their fatherland when the Muslims ignored to abide by the Divine Command.

"Hold tight the Divine chord and do not put yourselves to divisions" the decay downfall and annihilation was destined. Spain was divided into pieces. The Berbers in the south the Saqaleba in the east had established their own independent kingdoms. The new Muslims and the Christians in north had their own independent principalities in the north. The central government of Cordova was too weak to control the situation. There was no strong centre at all to repair the broken sheet.

The birth of petty dynastic clearly indicated the fate of Muslim Spain. Each dynasty right from the Jawahirites of Cordova to the Banu Abbad of Seville were at daggers drawn. The Murabetin, the Muvahidin and the Nasrids, were all following a policy suicidal to themselves and to the country.

It is very tragic to point out that between 1010 A.D. the formation of the petty dynasties and 1492 A.D. the final surrender date, there was no capable political leader or ruler who could handle the situation effectively and save the empire. How could the various rulers reconcile themselves to be subjugated by the foreigners without making any genuine effort to solve their disputes on their own table ?

The Muslim rulers and powerful chiefs instead of taking lesson from the battle of Tours or poiters in 732 and the heroic advent of Abdul Rehman I in 755. break off all chords of unity *ukhuwat* and farsightedness, and fell a prey to disunity and tribal jealousy which weakened the government with economic deadlock. The economy of the country was so deplorable that the Royal treasury or State bank was empty.

The people who had to say in the government were subjected to heavy taxes which naturally resulted in open revolts. There was no constitution to balance the society and bring the people closer to the government. The true spirit of democracy and tolerance enunciated and practiced by Pious Caliphs were deliberately ignored. The people who were put to stresses and strains by the ruling class had no other alternative but to raise their heads against the selfish group and erode the authority. The rulers and Umara of Undulusia failed to realize that the people drew inspirations from Imam Ibne Hanbal who though subjected to the inquisition and put in chains by al-Mamun, scourged and imprisoned by al Mutasim stubbornly refused to recant and allowed no modification in the traditional form of confession, and adhered to the truth. Khaja Nasir Uddin Tusi (b. 591 A.H.) the great scholar fell a prey to red-tapism and remained in prison for 15 years by Amir Nasir Uddin Hasham, governor of Qabistan, for submitting a Qasida to the Khlifa al-Mutasim-be-allah-Abbasi on the eve of his accession. The Qasida was actually submitted to the Prime Minister Abu-Alqami to be forwarded to the Khalifa. But al-Alqami, a worthless minister, was jealous of Khaja Nasir Uddin's potent knowledge and reared his nearness to the Khalifa and got him imprisoned on the plea that the Qasida was not submitted through proper channel an excuse which was unique then. History is replete with such injudicious selfish steps of other rulers and the umara which toppled down a number of empires Muslim or non Muslim. There being no definite programme, political or economic, the entire government machinery ruled round personal whims. Neither the Mosque nor the Church once emblim of peace, could save the kingdoms from decay and ruins. Muslim Spain therefore could not be an exception. The universal brotherhood, the chief security of life honour and peace was set aside, simply to guarantee disaster and annihilation. Flowers of different kinds, species, colours and odours which once bloomed and blossomed together were made to wither away by the gardeners themselves.

Could the rulers, the Umara and the Ulema, have settled their disputes and differences at their own table of piety and justice in the light of the saying of the Holy Prophet, (peace be upon him).

"A Muslim is the mirror of a Muslim" no power on earth could have obliterated them from Undulusia, their celebrated fatherland.

CHAPTER 57

AGRICULTURE AND INDUSTRY

Agriculture

One of the greatest achievements of the Spanish Muslims was the all-round development of agriculture and irrigation, which made their country self-sufficient in cereals, vegetables, fruits and all other kinds of agricultural produce. While the Christian North was barren and bleak, relying mostly on "dry farming" or herding, the Muslim South was a land of smiling *vegas* and lush green *huertas*, in the valleys of the Guadalquivir, Ebro and other rivers and in the coastal region of the peninsula. It was partly due to the interest its rulers took in planting gardens, but mainly due to the labour and skill of its farmers and cultivators, landlords and agronomists.

Irrigational systems : The achievements of the Spanish Muslims in agriculture were mainly due to their system of irrigation. Although they had inherited it from the Romans to some extent, but they greatly developed it by introducing several new technique and innovations, mostly brought from the Islamic East. The Iberian peninsula can be divided into two parts, the wet north and the dry south; though some rain falls in the north, but the south remains mostly dry. Yet it has a number of perennial rivers and streams, while there is also underground water. These were the two sources of water which the Spanish Muslims harnessed for agricultural purposes. Hence there were two kinds of irrigational systems, viz. the canal- based irrigation and the well irrigation

Canals : Canal-based system of irrigation was established in the eastern (Valencia) and in the south-eastern (Alicante) regions of Muslim Spain. The Valencian system consisted of eight canals, taken out of the river which the Arabs called **Wadi al-Abyad** or the White River. The canals were of the gravity-flow type. Every canal was supervised by an officer, known as *sahib al-saqiya* or master of the canal. The water was distributed to each irrigator on equal time units of the day. The result was that when supply of water in the river was abundant, each irrigator received larger share, while in times of scarcity, its share was lesser. This canal system was first set up by the Umayyad Amirs, probably during the reign of al-Hakam I (788-796), when his cousin Abdullah al-Balansia (or Valencian) was the governor of Valencia. But later, the region came to be inhabited by the Berbers, as was shown by the canals known after the names of Berber clans, e.g. Favara canal was named after the Hawwara Berbers. In the south-eastern (Alicante) region, the canals were taken out of the springs, and were privately owned.

There were also canals or aqueducts to supply water to the palaces and gardens of the rulers and to the mosques and houses of the citizens in the city. Such canals were first built by Abdul Rehman I to supply water to the Grand Mosque of Cordova. Abdul Rehman III built a canal to supply water to his newly-built palace of az-Zahra. It was taken from the mountain of Sierra Morena to the north-west of Cordova.

Qanats : Qanat meant a chain of wells, linked by underground channals. This technique was of Persian origin since ancient times. Its advantage was the prevention of evaporation. The qanats were first built by the Romans in the lberian peninsula, which the Muslims rehabilitated. They existed in Murcia region in southern Spain.

Dams : Another remarkable irrigation technique was the construction of a dam, called *sudd* by the Arabs, who were accustomed to build dams even before the rise of Islam. In Muslim Spain, however, they had, so to say, ready-made dams constructed by the Romans, In ancient Arabia (Yemen) there were storage dams. In Muslim Spain, they constructed diversion dams to serve the canals of the huertas in the Valencia region. They dammed up narrow gorges into reservoirs. They also invented the de-silting sluice gates, so that the dams would not be choke up with silt.

Well-irrigation : Well-irrigation was introduced in the Iberian peninsula by the Arabs to utilise its unerground water It was supplement to the river supplies which were not sufficient for the growing needs of agricultural production in Muslim Spain The wells were known as "naurahs" in Arabic and "norias" in Spanish. Before the coming of the Arabs, cultivation in Spain, like other Mediterranean countries, was only possible in winter, as there was no rainfall during summer months. But the introduction of well irrigation enabled the Spanish Muslims to undertake cultivation both in winter and summer. The winter crops were wheat, barley and the summer crops, which the Arabs introduced for the first time in the Iberian peninsula, were sugar-cane, cotton, rice, etc. The well irrigation was undertaken by three kinds of water-lifting devices as described below:

The Naurah : The *na'urah* was an adoptation of the Persian Wheel (which is known as *rahat* in Urdu). It was in use in the eastern Muslim countries, and was introduced into Muslim Spain by the Arabs as early as the eighth century. Though there were several varieties of the norias, their general plan was as follows; a horizontal wheel, to which was attached a shaft, to which an animal, usually a donkey, was hitched; a vertical wheel whose teeth were geared to the horizontal wheel on whose rim were affixed a number of pots which lifted water from the river or canal, or from a well. The three parts of the noria were made of wood. It could be easily repaired by the farmer himself or by a local carpenter.

The norias were set up by the farmers to irrigate their fields and farms by the river or canal water, or from the well There were five thousand norias on the river Guadalquivir alone, as al Shaqundi wrote in the 13th century. They were also installed in the royal gardens. Abdul Rehman III had installed a noria in his royal garden in Cordova, which was known as *munyat al-naura* or the garden of the naura. A Taifa king, al-Mamun, had installed a noria in his garden in Toledo, which was called *majlis al-naura*. It raised water from the river Tagus. These norias were driven by the current of the river or canal or by the animals.

The Water-Wheel : The water wheel, also called na'ura, was a single, ungeared wheel, compartmented, or with pots affixed on its rim, to lift water from a river stream or a canal. It was also made of wood. It was driven by the current of the river, stream or canal, from which it lifted water. It was, therefore, a sort of self-propelled device. It was usually of a very large size. For instance, a great water-wheel, ninety cubit (50 metres) high was installed on the river Tagus at Toledo. It supplied water to the people of the city and to the gardens and fields around it. Another large na'ura was installed at La Nora in Murcia. It was driven by the current of the Aljufia canal, The water-wheel had one advantage: it supplied water even when the river or canal ran low.

Another water-lifting device was called *Khattarah*, or swape. It consisted of a single pole of wood. It worked on a pivot and had a bucket on one end to lift water from a river or stream. It was an ancient Egyptian invention. It was also installed in various parts of Muslim Spain, e.g. at Malaga.

There were also many other kinds of water-wheels; some of them were driven by animals called dawlabs. Others were really water-mills to grind flour, or were utilized for other industrial purposes.

The Arab "Green Revolution : The increased supply of irrigation water enabled the Arabs to introduce a great many summer crops, which brought about what Thomas F. Glick has aptly called, the Arab Green Revolution. It may be added that the Arab Green Revolution did not produce harmful side-effects and hazards for human health, environment and ecology as are produced by the modern Green Revolutions, e.g. pollution caused by the use of pesticides, etc., yearly decline in the yields of the HYV (high yielding-vaneties) crops, their lower protein contents, etc.

Agricultural development began with the interest shown by the Umayyad rulers. Abdul Rehman I the Enteror was the first to do so. His nostalgia for the trees and plants of his native country Syria, made him introduce several eastern species in the garden of his palace, Rusafa, in Cordova, such as the palm-tree, the safari pomegranate, etc. A new variety of the fig tree was introduced by al-Ghazal which he brought from Constantinople, during the early years of the ninth century. It came to be known as donegal or dunaqal. The method of introducing new varieties of trees and plants was that they were first acclematised in the gardens of Toledo, Almeria, etc., and then their cultivation spread in other regions of Muslim Spain.

Among the new kinds of summer crops which required

more heat and water were cotton, sugar-cane, and rice. Their cultivation was made possible with the increased supply of irrigation water. Other trees introduced by the Arabs were olive, apricot, lemon, naranja (orange), toronja (grapefruit), jujube, etc., and, the vegetables like carrot, egg plant (or badhinjan), artichoke and others. Several regions in Muslim Spain specialised in the cultivation of particular crops according to the suitability of the local climate, water supply, etc. Among them was the famous region; called al-Sharaf, to the west of Seville. It was about sixty kilometre square area, covered with millions of olive and fig trees "which can be traversed walking always in the shade of olive and fig trees". So much olive oil was produced in this region that it was also exported to North Africa. Several varieties of figs were also cultivated, some of the best in the world. Malaga area in the south specialised in the cultivation of the figs, which were also exported to other countries. Among the cereals, wheat was cultivated in areas around Cordova, Lisbon, Valencia. Rice was cultivated especially in Valencia where irrigation water was abundant, and in the southern coastal regions, such as Malaga, Seville. Other cereals introduced by the Arabs were pulses, beans, lentils and tares.

Besides olives and figs, several kinds of fruit trees were also cultivated, such as apple, almond, peaches, apricot, quince, pears, while such new fruits as banana, dates, melons, etc., were first introduced by the Arabs. Mulberry trees were grown for rearing silkworms.

As a Science : Agriculture was made a science by the Spanish Muslims. They did so by means of systematic management of land, gradations of soils and by an extraordinarily great application of hard work, skill and knowledge. Thus they developed the agricultural resources of the country in a wonderful manner. Arab Ibn Saad in the reign of al-Hakam II

(961-976) and Ibn Bassal who lived in the second half of the eleventh century, contributed to the development of the agricultural science. Ibn Bassal, wrote a treatise on agronomy or practical agriculture. He divided the soils into ten kinds according to their capacities for producing crops in different seasons of the year. The Spanish Muslims were able to raise four crops a year. They also applied manures to regulate the heat and moisture of the soil. They also "corrected the land" i.e. levelled the field so that water would reach every place in the field. For cultivating vegetables, they planted them on raised ridges and furrows. With such applications, 'they made the most sterile tracts bloom into luxuriance." 'Where fields," writes Thomas F. Glick, "that had been yielding one crop yearly at most prior to the Islamic invasion were now capable of yielding three or more crops, in rotation; and where agricultural production responded to the demands of an increasingly sophisticated and cosmopolitan urban population by providing the towns with a variety of products unknown in northern Europe. "Such were the achievements of the Arab's Green Revolution.

Livestock : While the Arab settlers concentrated mostly on agricultural production, the Berber settlers, who were a pastoral people, undertook herding of sheep, goats and cattle on a large scale in the central and western regions of the Peninsula. They were a tranhurnant people, that is, they took their herds to the mountains ill slimmer and brought them into the valleys and plains during winter Berbers introduced the merino breed of sheep, which was, and is even today famous for its wool. The Arabs also kept several other kinds of animals, such as cows, horses, mules. The horses were kept mostly for war purposes. Al-Mansoor had large stables of horses near his al-Zahira palace. He bought 8,000 horses every year. Mules were for riding and transport purposes. The Spanish Muslims always used mules for riding. Though they kept camels also, but the climate of the Iberian Peninsula was not suitable for this animal.

"**Calendar of Cordova** : Mozarabic bishop Rabi bin Zayd also known by his Latinised Visigothic name Recemund, lived in the days of Abdul Rehman III and was his envoy to the German emperor, Otto I. He compiled a calendar of Cordova, which contains information about the condition of agriculture at the time when Umayyad Caliphate was at its zenith. It was dedicated to al-Hakam II. As agricultural operations and activities were carried out on the basis of the solar year, the *Calendar* explains them according to it. Concerning the month of January, it says:

> The sap rises in the wood of the trees. Birds mate. The falcons of Valencia build their nests and begin to mate. Horses feed on young shoots. Cows calve, and the milk yield increases. The young of ducks and geese are hatched. Now is the time to plant gain and the mallow and to put in stakes for the olive trees, pomegranate trees and similar fruit trees. The early narcissi bloom. Trellises are put up for the early vines and other, non-fruiting climbing plants. Purslane should be planted, a sugar cane harvested, beet preserved, and syrup prepared from bitter lemons."

In February, it says"

> "The young birds hatch. The bees propagate. The sea creatures stir. The women begin to tend the silkworm eggs, and wait for them to burst. The cranes make for the liver islands. Saffron bulbs should be planted and spring

cabbage sown. Some trees already break into leaf Truffles can be found now, and the wild asparagus grows. Mace begins to send out shoots. This is the time to graft pear and apple trees and to plant saplings. Where necessary and possible without harmful effect, people are bled, and take medicine. This is the month to send out and swallows return letters to recruit summer labourers. Storks and swallows return to their homes.

About March it says"

Fig trees are grafted in the manner called *tarqi*, the winter corn grows up; and most of the fruit trees break into leaf. It is now that the falcons of Valencia lay eggs on the islands of the liver and incubate them for a month. Sugar cane is planted. The first roses and lilies appear. In kitchen gardens, the beans begin to shoot. Quails are seen: silkworms hatch; grey mullet and shad ascend the rivers from the sea. Cucumbers are planned, and cotton, saffron and aubergines sown. During the month the government sends orders for the purchase of horses to its agents in the provinces. Locust appears and must be destroyed. Mint and marjoram are sowed.

Regarding May, it says:

The ears of wheat have already begun to form. Fruit appears on the olive trees and vines. Bees prepare honey. The early varieties of pars and apples ripen as well as the black grapes, known as cow eyes, apricots and cherries. Now is the time for preserving nuts, and the juice is extracted from the *sh'abiyi* apple. Poppy seed is gathered, and syrup is made from it in the Orient, the sycamores ripen at this time. Fumitory, celery, dill, house-leek, black poppy seed, mustard, watercress, and *tarathit* are gathered, and the juices extracted from them. Cantomile flowers are also gathered and oil made from them.

The Reconquista and Agriculture : The Christian *reconquista* dealt a severe blow to the agriculture, as developed by the Muslims. For some time, the Mudejars and Moriscos continued agricultural production on the old scale. But after their expulsion and extirpation agriculture came to be restricted both in area of cultivation and in scale. Spanish and Portuguese Christians were more interested in war than in peaceful occupations. Moreover, the Spanish Christians were more interested in keeping large flocks of sheep and goats. Their sheep owners set up an organization in 1284, called mesta. Its large herds literally ate away thousands of villages and drove away settled communities to other regions of the Peninsula and to their colonies in the Americas. The Christians believed wool production to be a more profitable activity than agriculture. Indeed, war and wool were the bases of Spanish Imperialism.

Industry And Technology

As in other medieval countries, industry and technology in Muslim Spain were closely related and interdepedent. Though some agricultural and industrial techniques were invented or devised by the Spanish Muslims, but most of them were adopted or borrowed from the Muslims of Egypt, Iraq, Persia and other eastern lands of Islam, or from the Chinese, Byzantines and other peoples. Later on, these technologies passed on to the borthern Spanish Christians and, still farther to the West European countries, especially from the eleventh century onwards, either by technological diffusion, or by migration of artisans and craftsmen, or by conquering Muslim territories. Industrial production was undertaken mostly by hand operated tools and implements. Nevertheless, current of a river, stream or canal and the muscle power of the animals. They also installed wind mills in the Valencia and Gibraltar regions in the later period of their history. Unlike the ancient Greeks and Romans, the Spanish Muslims never employed slaves for any kind of economic production.

Urban growth and Industrial development : Nothing helps the economic development of a country more than urbanisation. During the Umayyad period, the towns in Muslim Spain expanded very quickly; first to expand were Cordova and Seville in the valley of Guadalquivir, next Malaga and Cadiz and the ports of the Strait of Gibraltar and then Toledo and Saragossa. These were, however, old urban centres in the Iberian Peninsula, which had a new lease of life under the Muslims. However, new towns also came into being in Muslim Spain, which had not existed before. They were Almeria on the Mediterrean coast, founded in 756 and Qasrabi Danis on the Atlantic coast south of Lisbon, traders and merchants. They started the industrial activities and production of consumer goods and luxury articles, while trade in slaves, gold and silver and in other luxury goods enriched the new trading and mercantile classes, which consisted of Muslims as well as of Christians and Jews.

Paper : Paper was invented by the ancient Chinese. From China paper making technique reached Central Asia, which the Arabs had conquered in 704 and acquired this technique. Paper making mills were, first set up in Baghdad, from where this technique spread into other parts of Islamic world, including Muslim Spain. Jativa in Valencia region became the first paper making centre. Afterwards, Valencia also became a paper manufacturing centre. Cotton, and linen were the two raw materials used for manufacturing paper. Later on, the art of making paper passed on to Castile and in the twelfth century, to France and other European countries. Andalusian paper was also sold in North Africa.

Textile : Cloth making is one of the oldest arts of mankind. Cloth making techniques were first introduced into Muslim Spain in the eighth century in the two port cities of Almeria and Malaga. It was probably of Egyptian or Persian origin. Soon after, it spread all over Muslim Spain. Historians record cloth making in such towns and cities as Cordova, Seville, Saragossa, Valencia, Beza, Murcia, Alicante, Elche, Malaga, Santarem, etc., Cotton, linen, silk, and wool were the main raw materials of the textile industry. It was really a cottage industry : every weaver worked on the loom in his house with the help of his family members and sometimes employed non family workers. Hatching and rearing of silk worms was mainly the work of women, while dyeing was carried on by both men and women. Later on, collective workshops or manufactories were also set up, where several weavers and workers worked together.

Cloths of many varieties and types were manufactured. Each class of people and every occupation had its own kind and style of dress and costumes. Silk fabrics were highly priced. Among them were *tiraz, jurijani* and *isfahani* (of Persian origins), *attabi* and *dibaj*. *Attabi* was also make of cotton and linen. It was first manufactured in Baghdad and was later imitated in Muslim Spain. In the city of Almeria, tiraz was manufactured "in eight hundred workshops, and one thousand for (manufacturing) excellent tunics and brocade and as many for ciclaton; the same was for jurjani and isfahani".

The Umayyad rulers had their special workshops for manufacturing tiraz and other costly cloth within the precincts of their palaces not only for themselves and their household, but also for donating as royal gifts and presents to their courtiers, officers and bobles. Tiraz was a royal monopoly, manufactured in the workshop called dar al tiraz. Specially trained weavers worked in the royal workshops. The example of the Umayyads was followed by the Taifa kings and also by the Christian rulers of the north. Spanish fabrics became famous in North Africa and other Mediterranean countries for their delicacy and craftsmanship.

The *Mahtasibs* or market inspectors regulated the manufacture of all kinds of fabrics very strictly. Dimensions of the looms for the manufacture of silken, cotton and other kinds of fabrics were controlled. Similarly the conditions and prices of the cloths were also regulated by the *mohtasibs*.

Carpets, prayer mats tapestries, and robes of honour were also manufactured.

Flour : Mills for grinding flour were of different varieties and sizes, which ranged from the hand quern to the water mills. They were mostly the adoptation of the na'ura or water wheel, They were operated by hand or paddle or by the flowing water of the rivers and canals. They were fixed at one place and run by water-current, animals, or wind. The hand querns were so small that they could be earned from place to place. The Berber soldiers always carried besides their weapons two things viz a small hand quern and an oven and would grind their flour and cook their meals while on the march. The water mills were usually installed on the banks of a river, where a diversion dam was built so that water could be diverted into the mill. In Muslim

Spain, all kinds of mills were called *raha* (plural *arha*), but the mills which were driven by animals were called *tahuna*. The mills were of both horizontal and vertical types. Besides wheat, various kinds of cereals, henna and other things were ground in their special mills. In Cordova there were four mills run by the water power, derived from a dam on the Guadalquivir. The milling technology was later copied by the Spanish and European Christian in the eleventh and twelfth centuries.

Leather : Leather was abundantly available in several parts of Muslim Spain. Beja was famous for tanneries because its water was particularly suitable for tanning all kinds of hides and skins. Tanneries and leather work were always set up outside the walls of the cities. Several cities in Muslim Spain became famous for the manufacture of various kinds of leather goods, e.g. Saragossa for jackets of *sammur* or beaver-fur, while the leather industries of Cordova became so well-known in the eleventh century France and then in England that "Cordova" itself became an antonomasia for leather. In France, for instance the shoemakers were known as *cordoanaires*, while in England the term *cordovan* stood for special kind of leather, and cordwainer meant a shoemaker. Leather was also used for the manufacture of several other kinds of goods, such as belts sheaths, shields.

Besides leather, the Spanish Muslims also made shoes with cork soles. As oak-trees grow abundantly in the Iberian Peninsula, the Romans had developed a number of oak-based industries including the making of cork-soled shoes. The Muslims inherited these industries. The shoes made of cork-sole were called *qurq*, the Arabic form of cork. The artisan who made cork-soled shoes was called *qarraq*. Seville, Malaga, Granada and Madrid were the centres of this industry.

Glass : Glass-making was a Chinese invention which the

Arabs had acquired from them. Throughout the Islamic world in the Middle Ages, glass was either cut from crystal or blown in moulds. In Muslim Spain, glass vessels were manufactured in Almeria, Malaga and Murcia. The technique of cutting crystal was introduced in Muslim Spain by Abbas Ibn Firnas, who was a courtier of Abdul Rehman II (822-852) and of Muhammad I852-886. A large variety of glass and crystal vessels were manufactured in various towns and cities of Muslim Spain, such as goblets, jars with two, four or eight handles, bowls with handles, rose-water sprinklers, glass lamps, etc. The technology of glass-making was later copied by the glass-makers of Barcelona and other Catalan towns and from there it spread to various French towns in the later Middle Ages.

Pottery and Ceramics : Pottery is another ancient invention of mankind. It evolved from the hand made earthenwares to that of turntable and kick wheel. Ceramics was the art of hardening the earthenwares in fire. All these techniques were practised by the Spanish Muslims from the very beginning of their history. Almost every village, town and city in Muslim Spain had its pottery and ceramic shops and centres. In the villages, the water carrying pots of the na'ura were made by the local potter. But the glory of Muslim Spain lay in its golden pottery and lustre ceramics. It was carried on at such places as Toledo, Cordova, Elvira, Jativa, Murcia, Malaga, Calatayud, etc. Abu Jafar Ahmad Ibn Muhammad. Ibn Mughith (died 1066) wrote about the golden pottery of Toledo. The Arab geographer, al-Idrisi, mentioned in 1154 about the manufacture of golden ceramic wares in Calatayud. The art of lustre-painting of earthenwares, tiles, mosaics, flower-pots, vessels, and *azulejos* was developed during the period of the Umayyad Caliphate. The glazed wares or *azulejos* were painted with the glaze of cobalt oxide. They were decorated with plants, animal figures and kufic inscriptions. This art was introduced from the Islamic East into Malaga during the Taifa period. From there it spread to Murcia and then to Christian Spain. The potters of Malaga also first developed the art of enamel glazes. The lustre-ware with golden metallic glaze on a white ground became famous from the eleventh century. The earthenwares were hardened in ordinary kilns. The lustre kilns were comparatively smaller in size. After the Christian conquest, the arts of pottery and ceramics also spread in the northern Spain, when many of the Muslim artisans and craftsmen were employed by the Christian masters. However, these arts spread slowly into Europe, because the medieval Europeans imported the wares of the Muslim craftsmen from Muslim and Christian Spain.

Mines : The Romans had developed mining in the Iberian Peninsula. They used to dig up many kinds of metals such as gold, silver, iron, lead, copper, tin and cinnabar from the mines. The Visigoths, who came after them, neglected the Roman mines completely. The Arabs began to exploit them again, though on a smaller scale than the Romans. It seems that the Spanish Muslims did not improve on the Roman mining technology.

The Muslims exploited all kinds of mines. The gold mines were at Lisbon, Almaden, Tudmir and Elvira. Silver was mined near Beja (in Portugal), Badajoz, near Toledo and Cordova, in Murcia and Jaen. Iron was mined in the mountains of Valencia, Elvira and near Almeria, Denia, Jativa and in Navarre. Copper was mined in Elvira and in the mountains of Toledo. Lead was mined in Elvira, Beja, Almeria and Almaden.

Non-metals, like mercury, alum, glass-sand, antimony, white salt and black vitriol were also found in many places in Muslim Spain.

Pearls, and precious stones, like rubies, juaspers, agate and others were also found abundantly and of great varieties.

Marble of soft and hard quality was quarried for building palaces, mosques and houses of the rich.

Metal : Gold and silver were used for making ornaments, decoration and for various other purposes. They were used for making coins, utensils, and crowns. Ornaments like ear-rings, necklaces, bracelets, which were worn by women, were made and also gold and silver boxes and caskets. Gold and silver were also used for decorative purposes in palaces, mosques, churches. For instance the roof of the maqsurah or royal enclosure in the Grand Mosque of Cordova was made of silver plates.

Weapons : Warfare was almost a daily need of the medieval peoples. Weapons of war were therefore as necessary as any other article of daily use. Weapons were of great variety, such as swords spares, bows, javelins, etc. Moreover, a warrior on horseback needed different kinds of weapons than a foot-soldier. In fact, the stirrup for riding a horse played as important a role in warfare as the sword on spear. As a matter of fact, Charles Martel's victory in the battle of Poiters (or Tours) was mainly due to the use of stirrup by his horsemen, whose use the Arabs had not yet acquired. Similarly the victories which the Berbers won over their enemies were greatly due to the short stirrups which they used. The Spanish Muslims however, soon learnt all kinds of weapons which the Spanish and European Christian warriors used. For instance, the armies of al-Hakam II (961-976) used both Christian, Arab and Berber swords, Arab and Frankish bows, long and cross respectively, and javelins of Christian origin. In fact, war technologies were more quickly adopted by the Muslim and Christian examines than were more peaceful technologies, as for example the use of fire-arms or cannons by them in fifteenth century.

Almost all the weapons were manufactured in Muslim

Spain, such as swords, shields, spears, breastplates, bows and arrows etc. Almost every town had its metal industries, where weapons was also made. There were arms factories in the royal palaces amirs and Khalifas.

Statues : Although the Spanish Muslims were not idol-worshippers, but the Spanish Christians were. Statues were made for Christian churches. Muslim rulers had made figures of animals and humans to decorate their palaces. During the excavation of the Zahra, the palaces of Abdul Rehman III, a figure of stag has been discovered.

Clocks : Although mechanical clocks of modern times were not yet invented, non-mechanical clocks of various kinds were extensively used by the Spanish Muslims. Indeed, their irrigational system, which require proper distribution of water-share to each farmer, could not operate without these clocks. Two kinds of clock namely the sinking bown and the outflow clepsydra, were used for this purpose.

Spanish Muslims had made five kinds of time-measuring devices for both astronomical, irrigational and other purposes. These were :

1. a sundial divided into quadrants;

2. the "Palace of Hours" which was a cupola with windows so arranged that sun shone from each of them at different times of the day;

3. a clepsydra in which the water, whose flow was regulated by siphon, turned an astrolabe;

4. a candle clock whose indicator was moved by a counterweight regulated by the candle; and

5. a compartmented, cylindrical mercury clock. The mercury clocks and water clocks were really

chronometers to measure the movements of the heavenly bodies.

Organizations : At first, industrial production was undertaken by an artisan or craftsman within his workshop in his house. He had the help of his family members and sometimes of an apprentice. Later on, two or more artisans and craftsmen worked together by enterting into a contract. They pooled their resources and shared the profits according to the shares contributed by each of them. Still later, guilds of workers and artisans came into being. They were industrial associations which regulated the quality of the products, raw materials used, working conditions and prices of their products. For instance, they tried to compensate a partner who had suffered loss due to the neglect of the other partner.

Trade and Commerce

From the ninth to thirteenth centuries, Muslim Spain was a leading industrial country in North Africa and Europe. It was far more developed and prosperous than any other in these regions. It had extensive trade links with the countries in North Africa and Europe, which extended as far south as Sudan and as far into Europe as Germany and England. As the European countries were very poor and backward, Spanish Muslims' relations were much greater, not with Europe, but with the lands of Islam in North Africa and as far as Egypt, and Iraq. As we have said above, Muslim Spain had an urban civilisation: the riches and property of its towns and cities and even of its villages, depended on both internal and foreign trade. It provided not only consumer goods for the common people but also luxury goods for the rulers and the rich.

Internal Trade : Muslims of Spain had inherited wonderful network of the Roman roads. The Arabs also added some roads of their own, especially in the western regions of the Peninsula where the Romans built very few roads. Roads were necessary for travel and trade, especially in a mountainous country as the Iberian Peninsula. For internal trade and transport, the Spanish Muslim mostly relied on mules, donkeys and to some extent on camels. Unlike the Romans they did not use oxen-drawn carts very much.

The factors which led to the growth of internal trade were the increased agricultural and industrial production, the increase in the population of Muslim Spain and the foreign trade demands. So great were its productive activities and prosperity that Ibn Hawqal, who visited Muslim Spain in the tenth century, declared it to be the cheapest country in the world.

Spanish Muslims were highly commercial-minded people. There were markets (*suqs*) everywhere in towns, cities and villages. And there were daily markets, weekly markets, periodical markets and permanent markets. Rural markets dealt in local agricultural produce and did not possess the sophistication of the urban markets. Rural markets were usually held on Wednesday, hence called *suqa al araba'a* or Wednesday markets.

In towns and cities, various kinds of markets existed, namely the *funduqs* where traders and merchants from abroad brought their goods; suqs, which were smaller and covered markets and less protected than the funduqs. There were also shops almost in every quarter and street. The shops were owned by the artisans, traders and merchants, mosques and also by the rulers. Each town was divided in to different quarters and each quarter was usually inhabited by one class of artisans and traders. For instance, in Cordova there was street of al Bazzazin or cloth merchants, Bab al Attarin or gate of the spice merchants, or Bab al Tawwabi or the gate of bricklayers in Granada. Almeria was a commercial centre for the sale of slaves, including both the Saqalib from Europe and the negro slaves of North Africa. Seville was famous for the sale of musical instruments, while Cordova for the sale of books and slaves.

The Muhtasib : No account of the internal trade in Muslim Spain would be complete without mentioning the *muhtasib*. He was a market officer *par excellence*. He was appointed by the ruler or governor, but was answerable to the qazi for his duties. In the early period of the Umayyad Emirate, he was known as *sahib al-suq* or master of the market. The Muhtasib worked under the supervision of the qazi. His main function was the inspection of the markets within the area of his jurisdiction, called *hisba*. Accordingly, he regularly checked the quality of the goods offered for sale, and controlled their prices. His main duties were to check the weights and measures and the inspection of artisan manufactures and of the eatables for adulteration. For these purposes, he daily went round the markets, accompanied by an assistant who carried a balance to test the weights of the articles on sale. When he found a shopkeeper, trader or merchant indulging in any malpractice or fraud, he would punish the culprit on the spot and order the destruction of the adulterated goods or articles. He also looked after the security of the safety of the traders and merchants and supervised the organisations of the artisans, shopkeepers and producers, such as partners in a business fulfilled their contractual obligations. He also looked into the violations of law regarding buildings, and disposal of household rubbish and saw to the cleanliness of the bazaars, especially around the mosques. He supervised the traffic in the bazaar and market places. So important were the functions of the *muhtasib* that this officer was also appointed by the Christian conquerors in the Mudejar areas for the proper functioning of their market economy.

Foreign Trade : Like the internal trade, the pattern and turn over of the foreign trade of a country are very good criteria of its internal prosperity and political stability and strength. The opposite is equally true. Muslim Spain was the hub on which the international trade of the Islamic west revolved during the glorious days of the Umayyad Rule, just as Iraq was that of the Islamic East during the early period of the Abbasid Caliphate. Muslim Spain held this position even during the post Umayyad period, though with declining fortunes, due to the repeated rise and fall of rising power of the commercial cities of Christian Spain, Italy, France and of other European countries.

Muslim Spain traded with Africa to its south and with Christian Europe to its north. With Africa its trade consisted of gold from Sudan, Negro slaves from Senegal to Chad in Central Africa and gum from West Africa for use in the manufacture of silk. From the Christian countries of Europe, it bought slave (the *saqaliba*), mostly from the Slav countries of eastern Europe, furs from Scandinavian countries of the far north and Frankish swords. To Africa it exported various consumer goods as well as mercury which was used to produce gold amalgam. To Europe it exported mainly, gold and silver currencies (dinars and dirhams) and a costly silken cloth known as *spanisca*.

Slav slaves were captured while still young in eastern Europe mostly by German raiders and sold to the Jewish merchants who brought them to Almeria. It may be noted that all commercial dealings with the European Christians were through the Jews. Animosities between the Christians and Muslims were too great for any direct commercial dealings between the two.

Foreign trade of Muslim Spain was as brisk as it was extensive. It was undertaken by both land and sea routes. From the tenth to twelfth centuries, the Mediterranean was really a trade link between Muslim Spain and the Muslim countries of the East as far away as south Asia (i.e. Sind, Hind and Ceylon).

The ports in southern Spain, from Seville to Almeria, were really 'transit ports for trade with Africa and the East. At first, traders and ships from Muslim Spain had to go to Qayrowan and other ports on North African coast and between Alexandria and Seville and Alexandria and Almeria. A voyage from Alexandria to Almeria took 66 days. But if the wind was favourable, it took even few days. The period of favourable trade winds was called mausim or "season" (from which the English word "monsoon" is derived).

Foreign Trade and Political Instability : As we have said above, the pattern of foreign trade has a great effect on the stability of a state. At first, the foreign trade of Muslim Spain brought great riches and prosperity to the country. But from the eleventh century, it produced a number of deleterious effects. Most of its imports consisted of gold and slaves. Though they enhanced economic activities in the Umayyad Caliphate, but they also produced degenerative effects on its ruling and immense riches attracted the aggressive designs of the Spanish Christians. When the puny *Muluk at-Tawaif* rose to power, the Christian invaders imposed *parias* or tributes on them, which they paid in gold with all the disastrous consequences which we have explained in previous chapters.

At the same time, Christian merchants and sailors of Europe threatened the shipping lanes of the Muslims in Mediterranean so much so that by the thirteenth century the centre of gravity of international trade in the Mediterranean shifted from the shores of the Islamic countries to those of southern Europe. Two factors contributed to this transformation. In Muslim Spain, as also in all other contemporary Muslim countries, there was no middle class in the sense of a politically powerful or effective bourgeious class, as it had come into being in various countries of Christian Europe. In Muslim Spain, there were only two classes, the rich and the poor, the upper

556 History of Muslim Spain

and the lower. Unlike the emergent bourgeois classes in Christian Europe, the merchant class in Muslim Spain was not independent political force : it could not defend its economic interests against the excesses of the ruling classes. It had no say or power in the conduct of the state. It was subservient to the ruling classes. Secondly and equally importantly, the Muslim ships remained tied to the shipping lanes along the coasts of the Mediterranean, while the Christian merchants and navigations had invented new kinds of ships which were ocean going and were armed with better weapons. Moreover, European merchants were searching for new trade -routes both on land and sea, e.g. Marco polo went to China in search of land trade route and Herry the navigator organised sea routes on the Atlantic Ocean. Consequently, by the fourteenth century, "despite violent alternations between buoyancy and depression, it now became clear that economic power, the force of material expansion, and creative activity, were to be for centuries the privilege of Western Europe." On the contrary, the decline in foreign trade produced economic disruption in Muslim Spain which, in its turn, caused political upheavals, revolts and rebellions against its central authority. Thus post-Umayyad Spain disintegrated again and again into *Muluk al-Tawaif* which finally paved the way for its conquest by the Spanish Christians in the first half of the thirteenth century.

COMMERCE AND TRADE

Arabia is a land of barren and desert and hence the inhabitants could not fully depend on her for their livelihood. They were to seek their fortune elsewhere in the open world. The economic factor was unquestionably the main cause which brought them into close contact with many nations of the world. It was for the solution of the economic problem, that the Arabs risked the sea voyage as far Coromondal, Ceylon and further east in the Indian Ocean.

Before the rise of Islam, the Arabs used to carry on business transaction with many parts of the globe. They had established several colonies in the East African coast. The southern Arabia called by Ptolemy *Arabia Felix* w s the center of trade in those days. Job, a Jewish writer, has said that the Arabs imported balm, spicery, myrrh, and other articles from western India and exported them to Egypt and Palestine. The ships of the ancient Arabs used to sail in the Rea Sea, the Iranian Gulf and the Indian Ocean. Gherra was the, chief port for Indian trade in East Arabia. The Indian Ocean was which became the rivals to the enterprising state of Yemen sounded the fall of the Yemenite ascendancy. The Yemenits lost their influence and supremacy in the sea. But the rise of Islam brought new courage and vigour and the Arabs again became the famous trading nation in the East. They commanded the Mediterranean, t   Indian Ocean and the Red Sea for several centuries.

Commerce has been highly encouraged by our Lord in the Holy Quran. The Prophet of Islam (P.B.U.H.) not only encouraged trade but himself set an example by starting business. Early in life he accompanied his venerable uncle Abu Talib in mercantile expedition to Syria. In his youth he took up the charge of Khadija's business and showed his intelligence and ability as a business man. At the advent of Islam most of his early converts were traders. Abu Bakr, Usman and Abdur Rehman bin Auf were the leading merchants of Arabia. On their coming to power they were engaged in conquests and administration of the state and hence they could not get the time to run business independently. But when they were free from the cares and anxieties of the empire they turned their attention to business again.

Madina, Kufa, Basra, Damascus, Egypt, Mosul and Baghdad were the centres of trade and commerce. The caravan routes were repaired, roads were made, a postal system was established and developed and all sorts of facilities were given to the traders. Commercial information was gathered through the travellers who used to travel all over the world. The writings of the travellers helped greatly the traders in their business. Industry was fostered, mines were opened out' paper was manufactured, silk worms were reared, procelain, earthenware, iron, steel and leather goods were made and exported to different parts of the globe.' 'The tapestries of Cordova, woollen stuffs of Mercia, silks of Granada, gold work of Toledo, sword blades of Damascus and Ispahan were famous in the then known world. Fine carpets were also made by the Muslims. The textile industry reached its high watermarks under the Muslims. The names of *Muslin* (from Mosul) and *Demask* (from Damascus) show that these textiles were imported from Muslim countries.

From the 10th century A.D. to the rise of the European maritime activity the Muslims were the masters of the Mediterranean, the Red Sea the Indian Ocean, the China sea and the Pacific Ocean. Their trade and journey extended over a great area comprising the whole of the Northern and a part of the Central southern and Eastern Asia, as far as the China. They established colonies from the Atlantic to the Pacific Oceans. Malaga (60 miles off north Mediterranean). Alexandria, Basra, Baghdad, Barcelona (situated on the Mediterranean) and Cadiz (Spanish port of the Atlantic) became the flourishing ports of the Muslims. The ships of the Spanish Muslims amounted to one thousand. They established factories on the Danube. Prof. Shustery says, "This grand work of civilization was not limited to Arabs who were the earliest members of the Muslim brotherhood. It was the combined efforts of Arabs, Iranians Turks, Indians, Chinese, Africans and Spanish Muslims". The commercial interest led the different nations of the Muslim world to establish an universal brotherhood. The unity and amalgamation of so many nations under one flag gave birth to a new culture which was called Islamic culture. This Islamic culture was far superior to all ancient culture of the West.

The Indian Ocean was the great field of trade. Its base was the Persian Gulf, where ports like Siraj and Basra with its suburb Uballah and those on the Uman coast had been even in pre Islamic time very important centres of trade and navigation during the 9th century A.D. About the middle of 10th century A.D. the Muslim traders carried their business on such a scale that their ships had reached the Chinese town of Khanfu, now Canton. From here the traders proceeded further north and it is believed that they knew Korea and Japan. In the south Muslims discovered Sumatra, Java. Malacca sailors were long before familiar with the Indian Ocean. When Vasco da Gama, the Portuguese traveller, could not find out his way in 1748 on reaching Malindi on the east coast of Africa, it was a Muslim sailor named Ahmed Bin Majid who showed him the way to India. Ibn Majid is regarded as the inventor of mariner's compass. He is also known as the writer of a sailing manual for the Indian Ocean, the Red Sea, the Persian Gulf, the south China Sea and the East Indian archipelago. The ships of the Muslims used to keep regular traffic with Malabar and Ceylon. Muslim colonies were established on the Malabar coast and Daibul in Sind became an emporium for the Indian Trade. During this time, Several wonderful voyages of Sindbad, the sailor will speak highly of the maritime activities of the Muslims. Muslim sailors imported silk, camphor, cinnamon wood coconuts, musk, aloe and other Indian and eastern commodities to Iran, Iraq Egypt and Mediterranean ports.

Basra was the chief port on the Iranian Gulf, from which ships sailed via Muscat to the coast of Western India, Ceylon and the islands of the Indian and Pacific oceans in the East.

Iranian trade centres were famous for fine carpets, silk, precious stones, textile manufactures, wool, cotton, household furniture, dried fruits, etc. These articles were carried to Russia and through the European and Jewish merchants to England, Norway and Sweden. Through Khurasan and thence to Khiva merchants entered into the mouths of the Volga as far as Kazam and the Don (river of Russia). Russian goods, such as fur, wax and honey were exchanged for silk, cotton and linen. Merv became the centre of trade and learning during the rule of the Saliuqs. It was famous for its textile fabrics and silk. Herat was noted in manufacturing carpets, sword blades and other warlike weapons. Balkh and Badekshan were remarkable for their precious stones.

Spain was the centre of trade and industry during the Middle ages. Cordova, the capital of Spain, was famous for its leather trade, silversmiths and filigree works. Its industry could support 'two hundred thousand families.' The Muslims of Spain were noted as weavers and dyers of silk and wool. They were also masters in metal work. Qairowan was the centre of trade for the west, east and central Africa. There were other places in Africa which became the emporium of trade. Fez in Morocco was famous for manufacturing red caps and fabricating silk, and gold thread. Africa exported gold dust, ivory, ostrich, etc. to different parts of the country. Alexandria and Fustat were the important ports through which the trade of the East passed to the West. Sicily was a prosperous centre of trade. It had flourishing industries. Eastern goods were imported to it and it passed then on to the European countries. It obtained wheat, vines olives and fruits from Europe and exported them to the surrounding seaports of Africa, Asia and Europe.

Trade was carried on by land and sea. In the centuries when the Islamic empire flourished, caravan traffic was the most common means of travelling and trading between the different Islamic countries. At the same time, 'there were some important overland routes that led out of the Empire, first those to India and China, secondly, those to southern and central Russia and thirdly, the African trade roads' India and China could also be reached by sea. That was why the carvan trade was not so important on this side as in other directions.

It has been marked that the Muslims made much progress in education and rendered invaluable contribution to the culture and civilization of the world. Their thirst for knowledge was so great that on many occasions they sold out their shirts, for want of money, to purchase books. Islam gave tremendous impetus and encouragement to the advancement of learning and it was Islam that raised some of the most backward nations to the highest pinnacle of moral and material progress. Wherever the Muslims conquered a country they gave them a new light, inspired them with new ideals of Islam and raised them to a level of civilization. Thus they transformed many uncivilized and uncultured tribes into civilized and cultured people. To whatever land they went, they made it their home, absorbed the culture of the conquered people and strove their best for the intellectual and moral progress of the land of their adoption. Wherever the banner of Islam was hoisted, remarkable centre of learning soon sprang up. Damascus, Cordova, Baghdad and Cairo became, from time to time, renowned centres of culture and held the torch of light and learning, art and science bright and shining before the Western world when all Europe was sunk in ignorance and superstition.

The contribution of the Muslims to science is greater than that of Europe. But the Western world does not care to admit here indebtedness to Islam. Europe remained barren of all intellectual progress as long as she was under the heel of the church. It was the Muslims who, when all Europe was emerged in ignorance and strife, led the vanguard of intellectual progress in the world. There was a time when learning in Europe could be obtained only through the medium of the Arabic tongue. The Europeans are now proud of their mastery over astronomy, mathematics and philosophy but the knowledge of these subjects was originally derived from the Saracenic schools. Mr. Draper says, "In whatever direction we look, we meet in various pursuits of peace and war, of letters and science, Saracenic vestiges," Another renowned British scientist, Dr. Campbell, remarks, "When Europe was lying torpid in the depth of intellectual obscurity and gloom in the dark ages, culture and civilization were spread in the Islamic states under the high patronage of the Khalifas of Baghdad and Cordova and at a time, when the barons and ladies of medieval Europe could not even sign their names, almost every adolescent boy and girl in Islam could read and write freely and with ease." The Muslims made important contributions in medicine and created modern chemistry. They also made valuable researches in botany, geography and other brandhes of natural philosophy. There can be no doubt that Europe is deeply indebted to Islam for all its scientific discoveries. In fact, it was Islam that produced scientists, who anticipated Bacon, Newton, Kepler and other great scientists of Europe. The condition of Europe in respect of science and civilization would have been today what it was 1,400 years ago if the Muslims had not introduced paper, gunpowder, Mariner's Compass into Europe.

SOCIAL GRADES

The social grades in Islam during the Middle Ages were also worth admiration. Though the Arab Muslims were all powerful in the State and the Mawalis (non-Arab Muslims) were never put into any difficulties. They enjoyed the security of honour, life and property under the Muslims. Women and slaves occupied an exalted position in the society.

Position of Women

During the Middle Ages the position of women in Islam was far better than that of any other women in the history of the world. No religion before Islam did anything for the betterment of women. Nowhere in the world did they get the treatment they were entitled to as men's partners in life: They were looked down with bitter contempt and treated as chattels in society. Among all nations of antiquity, the wife was the slave of every caprice and whim of her husband. She was marketable and transferable to others at the sweet will of the head of the family. She had no right in the property of her father as well as of her husband.

It was Hazrat Muhammad (peace be upon him) who raised women from the depth of lowliness to the position of respect and dignity. He was greatly moved by their miserable condition of half the human race. The reforms introduced by him effected a marked improvement in the social position of women. He enforced respect for women as one of the essential teachings of his creed. He said that 'paradise is at the feet of the mother'. He also said, "The best of you is he who treats his wife best." The pre-Islamic Arabs used to burn their daughters alive. The Prophet of Islam prohibited this fearful custom under severe penalties. The killing of daughters was stopped for ever.

Some of the institutions of Islam, such as polygamy have become, subjects of criticism among the western people. But they have forgotten the necessity and circumstances under which it was introduced. Polygamy originated out of sheer necessity from the decimation of the male population as a result of frequent tribal wars and the numerical superiority of women.

Among all Eastern nations of antiquity, polygamy was a recognised institution. It was prevalent among the Hindus, the Medes; the Babylonians, the Assyrians and the Persians.

Polygamy also existed among the Israelites before the time of Moses. The Athenians, the most civilized of all nations of the past, treated the women as chattels, looked down upon them with hatred and contempt. An Athenian could have more than one wife. So the history of the then world shows that until very recent times, polygamy was not considered so reprehensible as it is now.

The Prophet of Islam found polygamy practised among his people as well as the people of the neighbouring countries. In the neighbouring countries it assumed some of its degrading aspects. The Christian world made attempts to correct the evil but to no effect. Besides the plurality of wives, there existed a marriage of temporary contracts called 'Muta' marriage among the Jews and the ancient Arabs.

The Prophet disliked the custom of 'Muta' marriage. He allowed woman such rights and privileges as she had never enjoyed before. She was placed on an equal footing with man in the exercise of all legal powers and functions. He took steps for the gradual abolition of the evil of polygamy limiting the number of contemporaneous marriages and by enforcing absolute equality between all the partners of life. In this respect the Quran says :

> "You may marry two, three or four wives.
> But if you fear that you cannot deal equitably
> and justly with all, you shall marry only one."
>
> (4: 3).

It is clear from the above verse that polygamy is opposed to the very teachings of Islam. As complete equity (*adl*) is not possible for a man, "the Quranic prescription amounted in reality to a prohibition." It should also be borne in mind that the necessity of polygamy cannot be overlooked altogether. Its practice depends on certain conditions of society which make the institution absolutely necessary for the preservation of women from starvation or utter destitution. "If reports and statics speak true, the greatest portion of the mass of immorality prevalent in the centres of civilization in the West arises from absolute destitution." It is time that in those countries where the circumstances, which once made its practice necessary, are absent, polygamy has become an evil but where the conditions of the society are contrary to the interest of women, polygamy is a necessity.

With the progress of civilization and the advancement, of ideas, the necessity of polygamy is disappearing. Steps are being taken in some of the Muslim countries to put it down. It is believed that polygamy in near future will disappear from Muslim countries.

Divorce is another important subject which has been misunderstood by the Europeans. Among many nations of antiquity, a husband could divorce his wife for any reason but the wife was not entitled under any circumstances to demand a divorce from her husband. Among the Arabs, the power of divorce possessed by the husband knew no limits. The Prophet looked upon the custom of divorce with extreme disapproval. He emphatically declared that nothing more displeased God than divorce. He made a new departure in this respect. "He restrained the power of divorce possessed by the husbands and gave to the women the right of obtaining a separation on reasonable grounds." In order to obtain divorce, men have to go through different stages in course of which his mind may change. About the divorce laws enforced by Muhammad (peace be upon him) M. Sidillot says, "Divorce was permitted, but was made subject to formalities which allowed a revocation of a hurried and not well-considered resolution. These successive declarations, at a month's interval were necessary in order to make it irrevocable." Like men, women have the right to divorce their husbands on the ground of ill-usage, want of maintenance and various other causes.

Though the seclusion of women is regarded as a bar to the progress of society in the present century, the Prophet of Islam realised the advantages of the observance of privacy and recommended it to the womenfolk probably in view of the widespread laxity of morals among all classes of people in Arabia. He saw the *Purdah* among the Persians and other Oriental communities. Regarding the importance of the Purdah the Holy Quran says:

> "And speak to the believing women that they
> refrain their looks and observe continence;
> that they display not their ornaments except
> those which are external and that they draw
> their kerchiefs over their bosoms."

The Prophet of Islam gave women the fullest liberty to choose her husband. A woman who has come of age cannot be married without her consent. If a girl is married in her minority, she can repudiate the marriage on attaining the age of maturity. After her marriage a Muslim woman does not lose an independent business of her own. As long as she is unmarried, she remains under the care of her parents. But as soon as she is married, the law gives all sorts of privileges to her as an independent being. She is entitled to enjoy property. Thus in many respects she occupies a decidedly better position than any woman of Europe.

Muslim women in medieval society evinced a keen interest in all educational activities and in public life. Some of them are stated to have distinguished themselves as scholars and poetesses. A'ishah, the wife of the Prophet, was noted for learning and courage, intelligence and generous, she held a high position among the earliest traditionalists. Many learned Muslims including the Companions used to learn the law of Islam from her. She was a good orator and a poetess. Regarding the eloquence of A'ishah, Mu'awiya, the first Khalifa of the Umayyad dynasty, said, "I have never heard an orator more elegant than A'isha." Fatimah, the daughter of the Prophet, was celebrated for her pious life. She was a poetess of reputation and composed verses on several occasions. Zarqa, daughter of 'Ali, was a good orator and took part in the battle of Siffin against Mua'wiya, Asma, daughter of Yazid Ansari, was a well-known orator and poetess. Sukaynah, daughter of Husayn, was one of the most remarkable women of her age. "Her rank and learning combined with her fondness for song and poetry and her charm, good taste and quick wittedness to make her the arbiter of fashion, beauty and literature in the region of the sacred cities." Khansa was celebrated as the greatest poetress of Arabia. Her birth-place was at Najd. She came to Madina and embraced Islam at the hands of the Prophet. In the days of ignorance, Khansa won fame as a poetess all over Arabia.

Layla, daughter of Abdullah, was a renowned poetess who flourished at the beginning of the Umayyad rule. Umm-ul Banim wife of Walid, was another talented and accomplished lady of the time. She exercised great influence over her husband and the State. Zainab, daughter of Tathriya, was a prominent poetess in the Umayyad period. Saint Rabiah was one of the most eminent of holy persons of the time. These accomplished ladies of the Umayyads maintained the genuine spirit of culture.

The Abbasid women enjoyed an exalted position in society. But towards the end of the tenth century, the system of strict seclusion and absolute segregation of the sexes had become general. During this period many of the Abbasid ladies, such as Khayzurar Ulayyah, Zubaidah, the wife of Harun al-Rashid, and Buran, the wife of Mamun, excelled in handling the machinery of the state and too active parts in politics. Many of

them also evinced a keen interest in literary pursuits. Zubaidah
was a talented women and an accomplished poetess. She won
national fame in the days of Khalifa Mutasim and is described
by the author of the *Kitabul Aghani* as woman of great beauty,
virtue and talent. She was also famous as singer and a musician.
Umm-ul-Fazl, Mamun's sister, was a gifted poetess in the reign
of Mutawakkil. Umm-ul-Habib, Mamun's daughter, was noted
for her scholarship. Shaikha Shuhda was another talented lady
who lectured at the Cathedral Mosque at Baghdad on literature,
rhetoric and poetry. Jainab Umm-ul-Muwayyid was a
distinguished lawyer. Taqia, daughter of Abdul Faraj, was a
renowned poetess. Besides these, there were women during the
Umayyad and Abbasid periods who made contributions in
different spheres of cultural activities to the world.

Slavery

Slavery was one of the important institutions of pre-Islamic
Arabia. It was not an unmitigated evil. It was, on the other
hand, rendered necessary by certain social and political
conditions of ancient society. Slavery was prevalent among the
Greeks, the Romans, the Jews and the ancient Germans who
treated the slaves most inhumanly. Christianity retained slavery
as a recognised institution and did nothing for the welfare and
betterment of the slaves. Under the civil law, slaves were treated
as mere chattels. Christianity made no protest against this
institution nor did adopt any measure for the mitigation of the
evil.

Islam had to deal with two kinds of slaves those who were
in the position of the Muslims before their conversion to Islam
and those who were taken captives in wars. The object of Islam
was first to better the conditions of slaves, to educate them, to
make them aware of the dignity of human nature and conscious
of the necessity of labour and work, and then to emancipate

them. The sudden abolition of slavery in Arabia was fraught with immense danger to the social order of the country and such a step would have severely injurious not only to the masters but even to the slaves themselves. The vast slave population whose independence of spirit had been crushed by an abject subjection would, if suddenly set free, have proved dangerous to society. The slaves who would not have themselves gained from such freedom would have been turned into vagabonds and impecunious beggars. It was for this reason that Islam established a perfect brotherhood between master and slaves so that the degradation which attached to the position of a slave might be removed. In this connection the Holy Quran says:

> "And to those of your slaves who desire a
> deed of manumission, executed for them, if
> you know good in them and give them a
> portion of the wealth of God which he has
> given you." (24: 33).

This verse requires two conditions for the manumission of a slave. Firstly, the slave who wants manumission should not be a worthless fellow. If the master knows that he would be a useful member of society, he should be freed. But if his freedom is likely to prove harmful to himself and to society, he should better fill the position in which he is of use. Secondly, the slave should not be turned out peniless into the world but the master should give him a portion of his property so that he might be able to make a start in the world as a respectable person. If these two conditions are not fulfilled, the emancipation of slave would bring more harm than benefit. There is also a tradition to this effect. It is reported that Abu Zarr, one of the companions of the Prophet, asked him, "which slave is the most excellent to emancipate?" The Prophet replied: "The one that is highest in price and most highly estimated and loved by his master." It was such a slave whose emancipation could be a substantial gain to society. A freedom which turned a working slave into a beggar or a thief was not recommended by Islam, for it brought benefit neither to society or to the individual. The object of Islam was to better the conditions of slaves and along with it to arrange, for this gradual emancipation. It was of no use to set the slaves free at once. In consideration of other betterment of the slaves and the then circumstances, Islam adopted the method of gradual emancipation.

The injunctions of the Quran and the traditions of the Prophet tend to the gradual emancipation of the slaves. The Prophet freed every slave that came into his possession. Besides, oft-repeated words as found in traditions lay stress upon the freedom of slaves. He is reported to have said: "Verily my friend Gabriel continued to impress upon me the necessity of kindness to slaves, until I thought that people should be no more taken as slave." The authenticity of his tradition cannot be questioned, as he himself acted upon these words. The Holy Quran also enjoins the emancipation of slaves in the following words:

> "And (notwithstanding all these blessings
> upon him) man, does not attempt to ascend
> the difficult mountain road at what knowest
> thou that mountain road is that which it is
> difficult to ascend? It is the emancipation of
> slaves."

Here the Holy Quran has attached much importance to the emancipation of slaves. The Quran at the same time has realised the insurmountable difficulties in the attainment of this object and hence it has described it as the mountain road which it is difficult to ascend.

The emancipation of slaves was, therefore, a religious duty and it was faithfully performed by the Companions of the

Prophet. Many of his Companions spent money in purchasing slaves for the sake of emancipation.

The emancipation of slaves was also a duty of the state. The Holy Quran says:

> "Alms are only for the poor and needy and those who are appointed for their collection and distribution and those whose hearts are reconciled and for emancipating slaves, and for those in debt and for the cause of God and for the wayfarer. This is an ordinance from God and God is Knowing and Wise."
> (9:6).

This chapter was revealed at a time when a Muslim state with full authority had been established.

It has already been said that the Prophet did not enjoin a wholesale enfranchisement of slaves at once, for such a step would have proved highly injurious to the peace and well-being of society. But he did not like slavery to be continued for ever. Emancipation of slaves was one of the highest forms of virtue in his teachings. The Prophet is reported to have said: "Whoever frees a Muslim slave, God shall protect every one of his limbs from fire for every limb of the slave set free."

It was Hazrat Muhammad (peace be upon him) who brought a complete change into the social life of the slaves. He realised the miserable fate of the slaves in the hands of their cruel masters and did all that was possible to raise their status. The Prophet asked his followers to treat them with kindness. He says,

> "And as to your slaves, see that ye feed them as ye feed yourselves and clothe them as ye clothe yourselves."

CHAPTER 58

SCIENTIFIC PROGRESS

Brifault, a great scientist, says, "Science owes a great deal to Arab culture. The ancient world, as we saw, was pre-scientific.The astronomy and mathematics of the Greeks were a foreign importation never thoroughly acclimiatised in culture. The Greeks systematised, generalised and thoerised but the patent ways of investigation, the accumulation of positive knowledge, the minute method of science, detailed and prolonged observation and experimental enquiry were altogether alien to the Greek temperament. What we call science arose in Europe as a result of the new spirit of enquiry, of new methods of investigation, of methods of experiment, observation and measurement, of the development of mathematics in a form unknown to the Greeks. That spirit and those methods were introduced into the European world by the Arabs."

Thus it is fully recognised that science in its modern sense owes its origin to the Islamic spirit of enquiry and that the scientific method is one of the most fruitful contributions of Muslim culture. The Arabs made outstanding contributions to every branch of art and science. It is said that when they first entered into the heritage of an ancient civilization, they brought with them, apart from their religious and social ideals, no spiritual contribution save their music and their language. But within a short time the Muslims, by virtue of their intellectual labour, became the masters of science and learning during the Middle Ages. Among the masters of science who shone like luminous stars in the horizon of Muslim sky were Hasan ibn Husayn, Abul Wafa, Abu Yunus, Al-Beruni, al-Khwarizmi, Umar al-Khayyam, Jabir bin Hayyan, Ibn Musa, al-Razi, ibn Sina, Muhammad Damiri and Zakariya Qazvini. The following subjects will speak of their contributions to different branches of science.

Medicine

The Pre-Islamic Arabs possessed a certain knowledge of animals, plants and stones of their vast peninsula. They knew the medical value of these things. Of the earliest physicians who lived in Arabia just before the advent of Islam, the names of Harris bin Kalda, and Nasir bin Alqama may be mentioned here. These physicians studied medicine and philosophy in the college of Jundi Shahpur in Iran. The great Muhammad (peace be upon him) was not only a teacher, a theologian and a prophet but he was also a physician. He understood the use and value of medical arts. He recommended the practice of medicine arts. He recommended the practice of medicine to his followers. The Umayyad Khalifas encouraged the study of medicine but real progress in Arabian medicine began with the coming of the Abbasids. The Greek, the Iranian, the Syrian and some of the Indian students and teachers had filled up the seats and chairs of the medical college at Jundi-Shahpur. The work of translation from Greek into Syriac and Pahlavi had commenced in the fifth century A.D. and in the sixth century the works of Hippocrates and Galen were translated into Syriac language. A large number of Greek, Iranian and Indian works were translated during this period. The College of Jundi-Shahpur continued to be the scientific centre of the Islamic empire. Masaijawaite, an Indian Jew, translated the work of Ahron into Arabic.

The rise of the Abbasids inaugurated the epoch of the greatest power, splendour and prosperity of Islamic rule. The development of Islamic medicine may be mainly divided into four periods. The first period is the age of translation from 750 A.D. to 900 A.D. in Arabic and the following men were the translators who shed lustre on the Abbasid court as distinguished physicians. It should be borne in mind that many of the translators made original contribution.

Jabir ibn Hayyan called as Sufi was a physician of good reputation but no record of his work has come down to us. He is famous as father of Arabic alchemy.

During the reign of al-Mansur the task of translation of Greek science was taken up in right earnest at Jundi-Shahpur. He invited Jujas, son of Bakht Yishu, the chief physician at Jundi-Shahpur to his court. Another member of this family, was the physician of the Khalifas al-Hadi and Harun al-Rashid. This Bakht Yishu family 'produced no less than seven generations of distinguished physicians, the last of whom lived in the second half of the 11th century A.D. In the curative used of drugs some remarkable advances were made by the Arabs. It is they who established the first apothecary shop, founded the earliest school of pharmacy and produced the first pharmaeopoeia.

Yuhanna ibn Masswayh was the Christian physician. He produced a number of medical works in Arabic. His book entitled *al-Ash Maqalat fi'al'Ayn* (Ten treatises on the eye) has been published with English translation. In time of al-Mamun, learning reached the climax of its glory. The Khalifa created in Baghdad a regular school for translation. Hunayn ibn Ishaq, a gifted philosopher and physician, was one of the translators of this school. He was an Arab of the tribe of Ibad but Christian by religion. Galen's medical and philosophical books have been translated by him. It was he who gave Galen his supreme position in the Middle Ages in the Orient. Besides several works of his own, he translated the seven books each of Hippocrates and Paul of Algina. He also translated the great synopsis of Oribasius and the materia medica of Dioscorides. Among the Arabs and the Persians the most famous of his books were the Questions on Medicine and Ten Treatises of the Eye. Hunayn had several contemporaries who were considered great translators.

The Abbasid Khalifa al-Mutawakkil refounded at Baghdad the library and translation school. The Khalifas and their grandees gave the Christian scholars the necessary means to travel in search of Greek manuscripts. The Christian savants were thus allowed to bring them to Baghdad for translation. Hunayn's recently published book, 'Missive on the Galenic Translations' shows how the Twenty Books of Galen were being studied. The books of Galen were the main subjects of the students of Medical Schools at Alexandria.

Isa bin Yahya, Ishaq bin Hunayn, Hubayal and Quota bin Luqa were the translators from Greek works. Besides the works of Greek translation, the translators did some independent works. But most of the independent works are lost. One, however, was published at Cairo. The author of the work was Thabit ibn Qurra, a native of Haran (Iraq). The work is divided into thirty one sections 'on hygiene' diseases from head down to the breast, stomach and intestines, their causes, symptoms and cure.'

The second period (900-1100 A.D.) is the age of independent observation and criticism on Greek and other past authors. The period may be called the Golden Age of Muslim Medical science. The Muslims had so long been the translators of Greek science. 'Their science was the continuation of Greek science which they preserved, cultivated and on a number of important points developed and perfected.' But from this onward they began to rely upon the own resources and to develop from within. The sciences, especially medicine rapidly passed from the hands of the Christians and Sabians into the possession of Muslim scholars. The notable medical authors of this period were Persian in nationality but Arab in language. Ali al-Tabari, al-Razi, Ali ibn Abbas and Ibn Sina occupy unique places in the history of the world.

Ali ibn Rabban al-Tabari who flourished in the middle of the 9th century was an Iranian of Tabaristan. He was originally a Christian but in the reign of Mutawakkil he embraced Islam and entered into the service of the Khalifa. He became the favourite physician of the Khalifa al-Mutawakkil under whom he wrote his famous work entitled *Firdous-ul-Hikmat* (the Paradise of Medicine). This book deals not only with medicine but also includes, to some extent, Philosophy, Astronomy and Zoology and is based on Greek Iranian and Indian Works.

The next outstanding figure in the medical field was Abu Bakr Muhammad ibn Zakaria al-Razi (Europeans called Rhazes) who was born at Rayy near Tehran. Al-Razi was unquestionably the greatest physician during the Middle Ages and one of the greatest physicians of all time. He was a student of Hunayn ibn Ishaq who was well acquainted with Greek, Persian and Indian medicine. Early in life, he learnt music and could play well on the lute. In his youth 'he practised as a chemist but in his latter years when his reputation attracted pupils and patients from all parts of western Asia, he devoted himself exclusively to medicine. He wrote as many works as two hundred, half of which are medical. One of the most celebrated work of al-Razi is his treatise, 'On Smallpox and Measles' which was early translated into Latin and later into various languages including English. It was printed not less than forty times between 1498 and 1866. This treatise was considered an ornament to the medical literature of the Arabs. It served to establish al-Razi's reputation as one of the keenest original thinkers and greatest clinicians not only of Islam but of the Middle Ages. But the greatest of his medical works is *al-Hawi* (the Comprehensive Book) which was written in twenty volumes. For each disease he first cites all the Greek, Syrian Arabic, Persian and Indian authors and at the end he gives his own opinion and experiences. This work was translated into Latin under the auspices of Charles I of Anjou by the Sicilian Jewish physician Faraj ibn Salim in 1279 A.D. under the title of Contineus. It was printed several times from 1484 onwards. It influence on European medicine was very considerable.

Al-Razi was the chief physician at Baghdad hospital. He is also considered the inventor of the Seton in surgery. Besides medicine, al- Razi left writings on theology, mathematics, natural science and astronomy. The last but one deals with matter, space, time, motion, nutrition, growth, putrefaction, meteorology, optics and alchemy. One of the principal works on alchemy was the *Kitab al-Asrar* (the Book of Secrets) which was translator, Gerard of Cremona. Al-Razi had a prominent contemporary known to the West as Isaac Judaeus who became the Fatimid Khalifa's phyician in Tunisia.

'Ali ibn Abbas (Hally Abbas) was a Persian Muslim of Zoroastrian descent. He wrote an encyclopaedia named 'The Whole Medical Art' known to the Latins as Liber Regius (*Al-Kitab al-Malik*). The book deals with both the theory and practice of medicine. It begins with a criticism of previous Greek and Arabic medical treatises. This book was dedicated to the reigning Buwayhid ruler, Azad-ud-Dowla. It was twice translated into Latin but at last superseded by the *Qanun* of ibn Sina.

Abu Ali Husayn ibn Sina, more commonly known to the west as Avicenna, was the greatest intellectual giant of his age whose immortal works on Medicine and Philosophy have always remained a never-failing source of guidance and inspiration not to the students of those subjects only, but to the wider reading public as well. He achieved his greatest fame in the west as a renowned physician. While still in his teens, the young medical student earned such a higher reputation that he was summoned to treat the Samanid Sultan of Bukhara, Nuh ibn Mansur. The latter being pleased with his treatment allowed him to read in his library. The young scholar rapidly absorbed the immense contents of the royal library and embarked upon a career of writing at the age of twenty-one. He wrote a good number of books on medicine, philology, philosophy, theology, geometry, astronomy and arts. Nearly all his works are written in Arabic except a few verses. He has composed one or two treatises in Persian. His famous work on medicine known as *Canon of Medicine* was the most influential medical compendium to reach Europe from the Arab world. The Canon was a mammoth undertaking, a careful classification and systematization of all the medical knowledge known to the Arabs in the eleventh century. This medical encyclopaedia deals with general medicine, diseases affecting all parts of the body, special pathology and pharmacopoeia. As regards the importance of ibn Sina's Canon, Prof. Hitti says, "The Arabic text of the Canon was published in Rome in 1593 and was, therefore, one of the earliest books to see print. Translated into Latin by the Gerard of Cremona in the 12th century this Canon, with its encyclopaedic contents, its systematic arrangement and philosophic plan, soon worked its way into a position of pre-eminence in the medical, literature of the age, displacing the works of Galen, al-Razi and al-Majusi and becoming the text-book for the medical education in the schools of Europe. In the last thirty years of the 15th century, it passed through fifteen Latin editions and one Hebrew. In recent years a partial translation into English was made. The book distinguishes mediastinitis from pleurisy and recognises the contagious nature of phthisis and the spreading of diseases by water and soil. It gives a scientific diagnosis of ankylostomasis and attributes it to an intestinal worm. Its meteria medica considers some seven hundred and sixty drugs. From the 12th to the 17th centuries this work served as the chief guide to medical science in the west and it is still in occasional use in the Muslim East. In the words of Dr. Osler "it has remained a medical Bible for a longer period than any other work."

High tribute has been paid to ibn Sina by the Italian poet, Dante who placed him in the illustrious company of Hippocrates. Galen and Sacliger. As a psychologist, ibn Sina foreshadowed twentieth century theory on brain localization. He taught that the external sense-sight, hearing tongue, taste and smell-were centred in the brain. The Arabs emphasised upon the brain, and not the heart, as the seat of reason and sense, represented an immense step forward in medical science. With ibn Sina, Islamic medicine reached its zenith in the East.

Among the second class physicians mention may be made of Ali ibn Isa. Ibn Lazlah and Yakub ibn Akhi-Hizam. The works of these physicians were translated into Latin.

While the Eastern Islamic world was acquiring supremacy in medicine, the western Muslim world developed also as a centre of this science. The Muslims of Spain and North Africa produced a number of distinguished physicians whose works became a model to European scholars. During the reigns of Abdul Rehman III and Hakam II of Cordova, Hasday bin Shaprut, a Jew was at once minister, court physician and patron of science. He translated the splendid manuscript of the materia medica of Doscurides into Arabic.

Abul Qasim known to the Latins as Abul Casis was a court physician in Cordova. His name is associated with the great work entitled Medical Vadth Mecum (*at-Tasrif*) in thirty sections. It deals with all medical subjects including surgery. This work greatly helped to lay the foundation of surgery in Europe. It was translated into Latin and Hebrew. Among the other physicians ibn Baja, ibn al-Wadf, ibn al-Jazzar, ibn Rushd, Aven Zoar and Maimonides. Many of these physicians, were also great philosophers. Of these physicians, ibn Rushd better known by his European name of Averroes deserved a special mention here. He was a native of Cordova. He distinguished himself as philosopher and physician and was one of those who made Muslim contribution to the study of Aristotle. He earned for himself the title of the Commentator. As regards Aven Zoar, it is said that he was a great authority on pharmacy which was an institution of Muslim invention. He and others carefully studied the effect on the body of drugs obtained from various parts of the world and discovered many remedies.

The savants and scholars in the field of science were given all, sorts of facilities and privilege by the reigning ruler. Jibrail bin Bakht Yihu is Said to have received 10,000 dirham from the public treasury and 50,000 from the private purse of the Khalifa. Muslim hospitals had special wards for women and each had its own dispensary. Besides permanent hospitals in the big cities, there were travelling hospitals also. 'Some physicians had their own botanical gardens for cultivating and experimenting with plants from various parts of Asia, Europe and Africa'.

In Egypt, Syria and Mesopotamia there was much medical activity in the 11th century A.D. Ali ibn Rizwan of Cairo produced a fine medical topography of Egypt. Ibn Butlan of Baghdad, Abu Mansur Mowafiq of Herat were the famous physicians. Ophthalmology was another branch of medicine which reached its zenith (1000 A.D.) under the Muslims. The science of optics owes much to the Muslim research. Abu Ali Husayn al-Haitham (Alhazen) of Basra who understood the weight of air, corrected the misconceptions of the Greeks as to the nature of vision and demonstrated for the first time that the rays of light come from the external object to the eye and not from the eye itself impinging on external things. He discovered that the refraction of light varied with the density of the atmosphere and vice versa. Ali Husayn left several minor writings on physical optics, among them one on light. Others of his treatises deal with the rainbow, the halo and with spherical and parabolic mirrors.

The third period (1250-1650 A.D.) is the age of decline of Arabic medicine and the rise of European science in Western Asia. All important works in medical science had been translated from Arabic into European languages. The earliest religious teachers of Islam tolerated the science but from the time of al-Ghazzali onwards, this toleration gave place to persecution of these studies "because they lead to loss of belief in the world and in the Creator." This was surely an important factor to prevent the rise of great independent thinkers. As for instance, Muslim spirit of respect for the dead prevented them from dissecting dead bodies which European took up and gave the world a better knowledge of the internal portions of the human machinery. With the commencement of the 14th century magic and superstitious practices began to creep into the medical works of the Muslim writers, 'whose medical knowledge was often derived from religious writing.' This led to the deterioration of the general standard of the material. In addition to this the philosophical bias predominated among medical men and hence it worked no less important for the deterioration of medical science during this period.

As a result of suppression of Arabic writers, the European surgery began to rise. Among the physicians who flourished

during this period in the Islamic world were Maimonids, Abdul
Latif ibn al-Baytar, Zainuddin Ismail and Rashiduddin Fazlullah.

Maimonids was the great Jewish philosopher of Spain.
He was a man of immense learning. He spent most of his active
life in Cairo under the great Salahuddin and his sons. His famous
medical work in his Ahorisms in which he criticised the opinions
of Galen. His younger contemporary, Abdul Latif who travelled
from Baghdad to Cairo to see renowned scholars and the land
of Egypt, is known to have corrected Galen's description of the
bone of the lower jaw and of the sacrum. Ibn al-Baytar who
composed 'A Collection of Simple Drugs' collected plants and
drugs on the Mediterranean littoral from Spain to Syria and
has given descriptions of more than 1,400 medical drugs.
Zainuddin Ismail wrote a famous book entitled
Zakhira-e-Khawrezm Shahi which ranks as one of the most
important works on medicine. Rashiduddin was a famous
physician who encouraged the study of science in Persia.

In the fourth or present period, the east has to sit again at
the feet of the western scholars. The west 'received from eastern
scholars its knowledge of drugs, the qualities of minerals, ideas
about the science of optics and a better developed chemistry.'
But now she has managed to return all these with compound
interest. The old Arabian method of treatment, known as *Yunani*
appears to be incomplete. Its perfection is possible, according
to Mr. Shustery, only by the absorption of western methods.
Though some of the Indian leaders, like Hakim Ajmal Khan of
Delhi, are taking interest in the Yunani, there is very little hope
of their success. The other Islamic countries like Iran, Turkey,
Iraq and Egypt have adopted the western method of its solution.
The Muslims learnt many things from Greek physicians. They
extended and improved anatomy, physiology and other branches
of medicine and sent them with their original contributions to

Europe. They became the teachers of Medieval Europe but today they are the pupils of Western scholars.

Astronomy

The Muslims made a great progress in astronomy. The greatest discoveries and studies were made by them with increasing knowledge. They may be said to have established their name in heaven itself. They made wonderful discoveries about the movements of the solar system and other astral bodies. They ascertained the size of the earth, the variation of the lunar latitudes and the procession of the equinoxes. Abul Hasan discovered atmospheric reflection and al-Maimun determined the obliquity of the ecliptic. Ibn Junnus, Nasiruddin Tusi and al-Bani constructed astronomical tables of great value. It was the Muslims who first built observatories in Europe and invented the telescope, the compass, the pendulum and many other useful astronomical instruments.

Under the second Abbasid Khalifa, al-Mansur, the centre of the Muslim culture was Baghdad which was founded in 762 A.D. The plans of the town were drawn up by the astronomers, Naubakht and Mashallah. In 777 A.D. Yaqub al-Fazari, an astronomer, presented at the court of al-Mansur a Hindu astronomer named Manka who introduced an Indian work on astronomy called the *Siddhanta*. This work was translated by Muhammad ibn Ibrahim al-Fazari and used as a model by latter scholars. Al-Fazari not only dedicated himself to the theory and publishing of books on the armillary sphere, the calendar, the astrolabe but also to the making of apparatus. Ahmad ibn Muhammad al-Nehaveendi was one of the earliest astronomers who wrote from his observation an astronomical table, *al-Mushtamal* which formed a decided advance upon the nations of both the Greeks and the Hindus.

The work begun under al-Mansur developed still more

under his grandson, al-Mamun who was a man of fine intellect. He caused the works of the ancients to be translated into Arabic. Many of the Khalifas of the Abbasid dynasty connected the link between ancient culture and modern civilization. They translated the foreign works and preserved for us in their translations a number of Greek works. Their intellectual activity reached its meridian in the 9th and 10th centuries. But it was continued down to the 15th century. From the 12th century everyone in the West turned to the East and the works of the Arabs began to be translated in foreign languages. Al-Mamun established a *Bayt al-Hikmah* for the translation of foreign works. In addition to this, he erected at Baghdad near the Shamasiyah gate an astronomical observatory under the directorship of Sind ibn Ali, a converted Jew and Yahya ibn Ali Mansur. The Banu Musa brothers also established an observatory for themselves. Sharafuddin bin Azad-ud-Dowlah erected an observatory under the direction of several Iranian astronomers. The Fatimid Khalifas had one in Egypt known by the name of *Rasad-e-Hakami*. 'The system of establishing observatories was imitated from Muslims by Europeans, who improved it on a large scale.'

Arthmetic and Algebra also flourished along with Astronomy. Among the astronomer-mathematicians was the famous al-Khwarizmi whose tables revised by the distinguished astronomer Maslamah al-Majriti and translated into Latin by Adelard of Bath, 'became the basis for other works both in the East and the West. Ali ibn Isa made astronomical observation at Damascus and Baghdad and wrote treatises on the astrolabe. Yahya bin Ali Maisur has written several books on astronomy and compiled 'Mamunic' tables. Al-Farghana (Abul Abbas Ahmed al-Farghana) was one of the eminent astronomers of his time. He belonged to Farghana in Transoxina. He is known in Europe as Alfaganas. He was the author of the Elements of

Astronomy (Compendium of Astronomy) which was translated into Latin by Gerard of Cremona.

Under al-Mamun's successors, there flourished a number of scholars who threw vivid light on Arab learning. Abu Mashar Jafar of Balkh was an astronomer of great renown. Four of his works were translated into Latin. He is well known in Europe both as an astronomer and an astrologer and is often found quoted by Western writers. The *Zij-abi-Ma'shar* or the Table of Mashar has always remained one of the chief sources of astronomical knowledge. Thabit bin Qurra of Haran in Mesopotemia is regarded as the greatest geometrician. He also made astronomical observations in Baghdad, notably to determine the altitude of the sun and the length of the solar year. He recorded his observations in a book.

In the next generation these stands out one of the most conspicuous astronomers that Islam has produced. He was al-Battani whom the Latin scholars of the Middle Ages and Renaissance most admired. He made his astronomical observations from 877 to 918 A.D. He wrote a large treatise and compiled astronomical tables which show in many respects an advance on the work of al-Khwarizmi. He made corrections of Ptolemy's theory of calculation. Al-Battani substituted the sine for the chords. He used tangent and contingent and he was familiar with two or three fundamental relations in trigonometry.

Among the numerous astronomers who lived in Baghdad at the close of the 10th century, Ali ibn Amajur and Abul Hasan Ali ibn Amajur generally known as Banu Amajur were prominent. They were famous for their calculation of the lunar movements. Al-Khujandi made astronomical observations and determined the obliquity of the ecliptic. Muslama bin Ahmad corrected and replaced the astronomical tables of Khwarizmi from Iranian into Arabic chronology.

The Salijuq Sultan Jalaluddin Malik Shah patronised astronomical studies. He established an observatory at Nishapur where he summoned a conference of astronomers to reform the Persian calendar based on an accurate determination of the length of the tropical year, Umar al- Khayyam was one of the astronomers who attended the conference. The researches of Umar al-Khayyam and his collaborators resulted in the production of the calendar named after the Sultan, *al-Tarikh al-Jalali* which was more accurate than the Gregorian one. Nasiruddin Tusi was the most celebrated philosopher and eminent astronomer of Islam during the Mongolian period. He made observations in his own observatory at Maraghah and drew up the astronomical tables known as II-Khani. The instruments at this observatory were noted as the best and most perfect of his time. He is equally important as a mathematician.

Astrology

Astrology has been severely condemned by Islam, though it became an important subject of study to Muslims who followed the old tradition of Iran. In spite of this, the Khalifas or kings greatly honoured the astronomer at their courts. Astrology was based more on speculation than on scientific investigation. 'Superstition was thus made a semi-scientific subject by Muslim astrologers'. Ibrahim al-Fazari was the first Muslim who constructed astrolabes. From al-Fazari onwards the use of the astrolabe is found to be in great use throughout the Islamic world from Indo-Pakistan to Morocco. Mashallah and Naubakht were famous both as astronomers and astrologers. The works of the former seems to have reached Spain in the time of Abdul Rehman III and has served as a pattern of science, then, for all the treatises written in western Europe. Many of the astronomer-mathematicians were renowned astrologers. Abu Bakr was a famous Iranian astrologer who wrote both in Arabic and Persian. Besides these, there were many astronomers and astrologers who adorned the court of the Abbasids.

Mathematics

In the realm of mathematics the Arabs proved masters of science with few equals and they contributed considerable materials towards its advancement. They taught the use of ciphers to Europe 'though they obtained it from India and thus became the founders of the arithmetic of everyday life'. "They were indisputably the founders of plane and spherical trigonometry which, properly speaking, did not exist among the Greeks," says Prof. Arnold. The Arabs gave the Western world one of its greatest heritages, that of its numerical system, for it is the Arabic symbols which are universally used today by every nation on earth. Besides the numerical system, the Arabs invented decimal arithmetic, which is universally employed by everyone in all walks of life. Moreover, the Arabs gave the world the science of algebra in its perfect form. Algebra and the other Arabian mathematical discoveries were brought to Europe and other lands by means of the Arab sea-rovers, merchants, traders and their maritime people who carried on extensive commerce. Algebra is one of the proudest achievements of the Arabs and it was cultivated with so much absorbing interest that within two centuries of its creation it had reached gigantic proportions.

The ingenious Arab people fully appreciated the value of all sciences and did not hesitate to export and share their accomplishment with peoples of other lands and races. Algebra, statics, conic sections and other branches of applied mathematics are the discoveries of the Muslims. They were the first of all nations of the world to translate Euclid geometry. They, for the first, applied algebra to geometry. They discovered equations of the second degree and developed the theory of quadratic equations and the binomial theorem. The Arabs not only collécted and translated the works of the Greek mathematicians but they supplemented the original to a very great extent and wrote their own commentaries.

There were good numbers of mathematicians among the Muslims who shone like radiant stars in the horizon of intellectual firmament of Islam during the Middle Ages. Of the mathematicians, Muhammad ibn Musa Khwarizmi occupies an outstanding place in the history of great thinkers, who had enriched the diverse branches of knowledge during the era of early Islam. Being one of the greatest scientists of all time and the greatest of his age, Khwarizmi has made lasting contribution to the domains of mathematics, astronomy and geography. As a mathematician, he has left ineffaceable marks on the pages of mathematical history of the world. He was undoubtedly one of the greatest and most original Mathematicians the world has ever produced. About his celebrated works on algebra entitled *Hisab al-Jabr al-Muqabalah* Prof. Hitti says, "Translated in the 12th century in Latin by Gerard of Cremona, the work of al-Khwarizmi was used until the 16th century as the principal mathematical text-book of European universities and served to introduce into Europe the science of algebra and with it the name. Al-Khwarizmi's works were also responsible for the introduction into the west of the Arabic numerals called algorism after him." Al-Miawrizmi's mathematical works were the principal source of knowledge on the subject to the world for a considerable time. George Sarton pays him a high tribute when he considers him as "one of the greatest scientists of his race and the greatest of his time." He systematised the Greek and Hindu mathematical knowledge. The oldest arithmetic composed by him in Arabic was known as *Kitab al-Jama al-Tafriq* which has been lost in Arabic. Al-Khwarizmi was the first exponent of the use of numerals, including zero, in preference to letters. It was through him that Europe learnt the use of zero or cipher.

His work on the Indian method of calculations was translated into Latin by Adelard of Bath in the 12th century. Al-Khwarizmi has the distinction of being one of the founders of algebra and developed this branch of science to an exceptionally high degree. His great book, *Hishab al-Jabr al-Muqabalah* contains calculations of integration and equations presented through over 800 examples. He also introduced negative signs which were unknown to the Arabs. The translation of Khwarizmi's algebra by Rebert Chester marks an epoch for the introduction and advancement of this branch of science into Europe, "The importance of Rebert's Latin translation of Khwarizmi's algebra," says a modern Orientalist, "can hardly be exaggerated, because it marked the beginning of European algebra."

Taiyab (850 A.D.) was the first writer on trigonometry. Yakub ibn Ishaq al-Kindi (874 A.D.) was the distinguished scholar of mathematics, astronomy and natural philosophy. He is said to have written more than two hundred books on astronomy, optics, Euclid and meteorology. Muhammad bin Isa al-Mahani (884 A.D.) is credited with the invention of modern algebra. He wrote on trigonometry, astronomy, solid geometry and cubic equations. He demonstrated methods of using algebra to solve a whole field of intermediate science problems. He made observations on the solar and lunar eclipses and planetary conjunctions. Abu Mashar al-Balaki (888 A.D.) wrote on astronomy and astrology. His astronomical treatise namely *Kitab al-Makhal al-Kabir* has the same scope as Ptolemy's *al-Majest*. Al-Himsi (888 A.D.) translated the work of Appalonius. Ahmad ibn Taiyab al-Sarakshi (899 A.D.) wrote on arithmetics, algebra, astrology and astronomy. Thabit ibn Qurra (900 A.D.) revised the Greek translations of Euclid and Ptolemy and wrote extensively on astronomy, astrology, amicable numbers and spherics. He is said to have invented some new propositions in geometry and is known for using algebra in geometry.

After the completion of translation works, a period of 500 year (990 A.D.–1400 A.D.) came in which the Muslims made contributions. In this period astronomy and algebra were further developed and plane trigonometry was systematised. Afterwards the Muslim mathematicians developed the spherical trigonometry. The scholars of the ninth century realised the need of other branches of applied mathematics, such as statics, optics and dynamics in which they did the elementary kind of work. The following savants played important roles in the history of original contributions to mathematics.

Muslims ibn Ahmed al-Iaisi (908 A.D.) wrote on arithmetic and astronomy. Muhammad ibn Jabir al-Battani (929 A.D.) was the greatest Arab astronomer who first published the trigonometric ratios and determined very accurately the obliquity of the ecliptic and wrote on orthographic projections, motion of the moon and planets. Abu Nasr al-Farabi (951 A.D.), the greatest philosopher of Islam, wrote on astronomy and geometry. Abdul Wafa (998 A.D.) of Iran was one of the greatest Muslim mathematicians in the 10th century, who wrote commentaries on Khwarizmi, Diophantos and Euclid. He compiled trigonometrical tables and worked on place and solid geometry. It was he who first pointed out the generality of the sine theorem in relation to spherical triangles. "He studied the tangent and introduced the secant and consecant and showed the simple relation between the six trigonometric levers."

Abu Raihan Muhammad al-Beruni (973-1049 A.D.) was one of the greatest scientists of all times. He was the most original and profound thinker that Islam has ever produced in the domain of the physical and mathematical sciences. He was not only a scientist but also a historian, philosopher, naturalist, geologist, mineralogist, astronomer and mathematician. He had a keen geographical sense and his conclusions in that connection deserve high merit. He has written on various subjects after close investigation. Of his books, (1) Chronology of Ancient Nations, (2) History of India (*kitab al-Hind*), (3) An Astronomical Encyclopaedia entitled '*Masudi Canon*' and (4) A Summary of Mathematics, Astronomy and Astrology. Born in one of the suburbs of Khwarizm (Khiva), he was captured by Sultan Mahmood of Ghazni on the fall of Khiva. His *Kitab al-Hind* may be regarded as one of the most significant productions in the field of regional geography. He wrote monumental work *Qanun al-Masudi* under the patronage of Sultan Masud. On the mathematical and astronomical side of geography, al-Beruni discusses the antipodes and the roundity of the earth, the determination of its movement and gives the latitudes and longitudes of numerous places.

Al-Majrit Abul Qasim Maslama (1004) wrote on astronomy, geometry, and on the theory of number. Ibn Sina Abu Ali (1037 A.D.) wrote on cuclid, arithmetic and astronomy. Al-Haithan, Hasan ibn al-Hasan (1038 A.D.) was an author of about 200 books and wrote on algebra, geometry and astronomy. He is an authority on optics being the first writer on refraction and twilight. Abu Bakr Muhammad ibn Husayn (1029 A.D.) of Karkh was a mathematician who wrote on arithmetic and algebra and solved quadratic equations and disphantine equations..

Among the latter mathematicians who were influenced by al-Khwarizmi was Umar ibn Ibrahim al-Khayyam (1123 A.D.), the greatest mathematician in the 11th century. He was not only a distinguished mathematician and astronomer but also a famous poet. He had written several treatise of arithmetic, algebra and astronomy. His solution of the euluc and liquadratic equations with the help of conic sections is the most advanced work of Arabic mathematics. Abul Walid Ibn Rushd (1198 A.D.), the greatest Arab philosopher of Spain, wrote on externity of universe, planets, and eclipses. He is said to have worked on spherical trigonometry and on the theory of aeronautics also. Muhammad Nasiruddin Tusi (1247 A.D.), an all round scholar with a fine synthetic brain, was another famous astronomer and mathematician. He worked an arithmetic, geometry, plane and spherical trigonometry and on astronomy. He gave proof of Pythagorus theorem, made observation at Maraghah in which he-set up huge rings for ecliptical, solstical, equatorial armillaries purposes. He edited most of the mathematical works of antiquity to the number of sixteen which practically constituted the whole scientific knowledge of the period.

During the period of decline, the following savants closed the list of Muslim mathematicians. Jamshid ibn Masud al-Kasbi (1436 A.D.), an assistant of Ulugh Beg, wrote a short treatise on geometry, arithmetic and astronomy. Ulugh (1549 A.D.), a Persian prince, founded an observatory at Samarquand. The astronomical tables which were worked out under his personal direction are highly esteemed in Europe as well as in the East. Ali ibn Muhammad al-Qalasadi (15865 A.D.) wrote on arithmetic and has shown considerable originality in his work on the theory of number. He was the last of the great mathematicians of Spain. Muhammad ibn Maruf of Constantinople (1585 A.D.) and Behauddin al-Amili (1622 A.D.) wrote on arithmetic and spherics. After Behauddin Amili we hear no Muslim mathematician of wide fame who did any original work.

Chemistry

After metria medica, astronomy and mathematics the Muslims made their greatest scientific contribution in chemistry. Chemistry grew out of alchemy which the Islamic scientists did much to improve and advance. Their greatest contribution to the world's store of knowledge was the accumulation of scientific facts and the advancement of scientific theories and methodology. "Modern chemistry", says Mr. Humboli, "was admittedly the "Modern chemistry invention of the Muslims, whose achievement in this sphere were of unique interest." They conclusively proved the worthlessness of ancient chemistry. They found out the chemical affinities of mercury, lead, copper, silver and gold and knew the chemical process of oxidation and calculation. The Muslims were the first to teach the world distillation, filtration and crystallisation. They knew how to change a liquid into vapour. It was in Muslim Spain that chemistry was first established and had the Muslims not been defeated at Poitiers, it would have reached its zenith there.

Jabir ibn-Hayyan, known as Geber in the western world, is the father of modern chemistry. His name is the greatest in the field of medieval chemical science. He clearly recognised and stated the importance of experimentation than any other early alchemist and made a noteworthy advance in both theory and practice of chemistry. He wrote some five hundred treatises on chemistry. His works after the 14th century were the most influential chemical treatises in both Europe and Asia. He discussed scientifically the two principal operations of chemistry, calculation and reduction. Jabir improved on the methods for evaporation, sublimation, melting and crystallisation. He discovered for the first time nitric acid, sulphuric acid, aqua regia, silver nitrate and several other compounds and knew how to produce *aqua regia* in which gold and silver could be dissolved. He was the prophet and forerunner of positive and dynamic science. From his studies, he was able to predict the vast part which gases would be found to play in the makeup and composition of elements and more complex substances. He brought system and order to chemical science and made it almost a sacred art. He was followed by others whose originality and industry profoundness of knowledge and keenness of observation evoke the astonishment of readers.

Other important chemists of that era were al-Razi (Rhazes who re-discovered sulphuric acid and aqua-vitae and Ibn Sina (Avicenna), a renowned doctor, who helped to systematise medical chemistry. Later on, al-Razi became celebrated all over Europe and was considered the foremost authority and master of chemical science by all men of learning.

In spite of overwhelming evidence to the contrary, European historians have deliberately exaggerated the so-called inferiority of Arabian science. Ignorance and superstition reigned supreme in Europe while the Arab peoples were attaining a literary and scientific renaissance. When the Arabs were making epochmaking discoveries in their world, the Europeans were placing a premium upon every conceivable kind of social and political evil. A case in point is the field of chemistry which was considered one of the most significant realms of science by the Arabs. They called it "the Science of Key". As the science of chemistry advanced, the other sciences progressed space.

CHAPTER 59

INFLUENCE OF MUSLIM

During the later Middle Ages, writes Francisco Gabrieli, Arab science "flooded and fecundated Europe." But before we consider this "flooding and fecundating" of medieval Europe by Arab science, we shall consider, briefly, the reasons why the Spanish Muslims did not transmit their achievements in science, and Philosophy to their own people who came after them? Why did the springs of scientific and philosophical thought became dry in Muslim Spain?

The transmission of the knowledge of science and philosophy, like that of all other intellectual and artistic achievements, from one generation to another, is the task of three important Institutions, viz., the family, the educational institutions and the social milieu and ethos.

Family life among the alitle classes in Muslim Spain became degenerate, decadent and hide-bound a few generations after the establishment of a new kingdom or empire due to purdah, polygamy, slavery and concubminage. The same kind of deterioration occurred in the educational institutions. Their attitude towards the teaching of philosophy was always hostile, because the philosophers tried to interpret Islamic teachings according to reason and logic.

Social milieu and ethos were most hostile to the pursuit

of rational sciences and philosophy. In this respect, the Maliki faqihs, qazis, theologians and the common people were always in the forefront. If science and philosophy flourished in Muslim Spain, it was, firstly, due to the influence of the Muslim scientists, scholars and philosophers of the Eastern lands whose writings always impressed the educated elites in Muslim Spain and secondly due to the patronage of the Umayyad and afterwards of the Taifa rulers. Though they patronised scientists and scholars, but not the philosophers, who were first patronised and protected by the Murabit and Muwahhid rulers, although the faqihs and mutakalimun, who were the disciples and followers of al-Ashari and Ghazzali as well as their soldiers and military commanders always urged them not to do so. At last, the Muwahhid Khalifa, Abu Yaqub, had to comply with their wishes when he was engaged in a holy war with the Christians. It was due to such a hostile environment that rational sciences and philosophy ceased to exist in Muslim Spain.

On strictly religious grounds, Christianity was as much hostile to the pursuit of science and philosophy as were the Muslim faqihs, and *Mutakallimun*. Nevertheless, there were new forces in Christian Spain and Europe which favoured the dissemination of Muslim sciences and philosophy and thus "flooded and fecundated" Europe. The new forces were.

(i)   the ruling elites,

(ii)   the newly emergent educated elites, including both clerical and secular scholars,

(iii) the commercial and industrial classes in the new towns and cities of Europe, and

(iv) the schools and universities which were founded in the early decades of the thirteenth century.

The Process of Diffusion : In modern times, there is a

lot of talk of the transfer of science and technology from the "developed" countries of the West to the "underdeveloped" countries of third World. In the Middle Ages after the critical year 1000 A.D., such a transfer took place by a process of diffusion of science and philosophy from the developed Muslim Spain, and also from the developed Muslim East, to the underdeveloped Christian Europe. In spite of the religious, cultural and linguistic barriers, achievements of Muslim Spain began gradually to diffuse into Christian Spain and later into other lands of Christian Europe.

But, owing to the religious, cultural and linguistic barrier this process of diffusion was complex. In the case of Christian Spain was preceded by a softening of the anti-Islamic attitudes, then so rife in it. At first, the Christian rulers and the Catholic Church sought information about the Muslim achievements in order to use them as weapons of war and propaganda against the Muslims. But later a new factor came into being: it was the interest of the European scholars, scientists and philosophers in Muslim sciences and philosophy, not for any military or propagandist purposes, but for intellectual and scholastic reasons. The scholastic factor came to the fore during the twelfth to fifteenth centuries, when the influence of Ibn Rushd (Averroes, Ibn Sina (Avicenna) and of other Muslim scientists and philosophers on European mind was at its highest. Thanks to the great influence of Aristotle's philosophy in medieval Europe, his commentator, Averroes, had immense appeal to the European philosophical mind. Averroism proclaimed that reason and philosophy were superior to faith and to knowledge founded on faith. As such Averroism was different from Averroes, for he never asserted the primacy of reason over revelation.

Agencies of Diffusion : As we said above, the diffusion of Muslim achievements began with the softening of anti-Islamic attitude among Spanish Christians. Although Islam was a tolerant religion, the intolerant medieval Christianity was an inveterate enemy of Islam and Muslims. That was why the Spanish Christians were most hostile to everything Islamic. The boundary between the Muslim and Christian Spain was not only a battle-line but also a barrier to all influences emanating from the developed Muslim south to the backward Christian north. Nevertheless, two agents softened, though unwittingly, the hardened attitude of the northern Christians. First of them were the Mozarabs or Islamised Christians who lived for a century and more in Muslim south before emigrating to the Christian north. During their sojourn among the Muslims, the Mozarabs adopted the Muslim practices, sciences and arts, which they introduced into the Christian north.

The Jews, especially those who became Christians, were another agents of influence. When the Mozarab exodus to the north had virtually stopped, the Jewish emigration began which lasted from the eleventh to the thirteenth centuries. Their influence was really much greater than that of the Mozarabs, for the Jews were a tri-lingual and tri-cultural people: they knew Arabic, Hebrew and Roman and even Latin. That was the reason why they played a great role in the translation of Arabic books into Roman or Latin. Moreover, the Jews were proficient in the sciences and philosophy of the Muslims. In fact, the Jews living in the northern Christian kingdoms came to know of newly published Muslim books on science much earlier than their Christian compatriots. For instance, Ibn Zuhr's *Kitab al-Taysir* was known to the Jews in Barcelona four years after its publication in 1161, whereas the Christians came to know of its in 1281, more than a century after its publication.

Translations : Translations of the books and writings of an advanced civilization play a pivotal role in the diffusion of knowledge and in the transfer of science, technology and philosophy to the under-developed or less advanced peoples, nations and civilizations. At first the translators were Mozarabs and Jews. They, especially translation of the works of Muslim the converted Jews, helped in the scientists and philosophers into Latin and Roman for the Spanish Christians. Soon after these translated books reached other lands of Europe, because Christian Europe Latin was then its *lingua franca*.

Toledo School : The fall of the Umayyad Caliphate and the depredations which the *fitna* or civil war caused so much destruction to be a centre of learning. Consequently, in Cordova, that it ceased capitals became the centres of Toledo, Seville and other Taifa captured Toledo in 1085, its learning. When the Christians learning fell into their hands, which the Christian treasurehouse of scholars and savants soon exploited for their own ends. Translation is a creative act, as near to original writing as possible, especially when the recipient culture and people are backward and ignorant, and yet are eager to learn new thoughts. This was what the Toledan school of translators did for Christian Spain and still more importantly for Christian Europe. It must, however, be noted that it was the enterprising and dynamic spirit of the European Christians of the later Middle Ages, which made them so inquisitive and enquiring of what an advanced culture had to offer them.

Several translators, both Christians and converted Jews, worked together or separately and singly at Toledo and other cities in Christian Spain and Europe. Among them were High of Santalla, John of Seville, Domingo Gundisalvo, Gerard of Cremona, Plato of Tivoli, Rudolph of Burges and Hermann of Corinthia. Some of them worked in a cooperative manner, i.e., he who knew Arabic, usually a renegad Jews, first translated the Arabic text into Roman and then a Christian, usually a monk, would translate it into Latin. Thus John of Seville translated Ibn Sina's *De Anima*. As he said: "The book was translated from Arabic, myself speaking the vernacular (Roman) word by word, and the archdeacon Dominic (Gundisalvo) converting each into Latin." Thus the works of the Andalusian and eastern Muslim writers and philosophers were translated into Latin during the twelfth century and later.

Soon after, the Toledo school became a center for scholars, who gathered in the city from various countries of Europe. One of the first among them was the Englishman, Adelard of Bath (c. 1090-1150), who translated Euclid and also *Arithmetic of al-Khwarizmi*. A generation after came another Englishman, Robert of Chester (c. 1110-c. 1160) who translated the *Algebra* of al-Khwazimi. Then came Gerard of Cremona (1114-1187), (Cremona is in Italy). He translated the *Almagest* of Ptolemy (which became the standard medieval text on astronomy), and the voluminous *Qanun fi'l Tibb*. (the Canon of Medicine) Ibn Sina, which became the most widely studied medical text in medieval Europe for several centuries. Innumerable Arabic books were translated into Latin from the twelfth to the seventeenth centuries.

However, a change came in the "spirit" of translation of the Toledo school after Michael Scotus (c. 1175-c. 1253) came from Scotland to Toledo. He translated the works of Ibn Rushd (Averroes) and also of Abu Ishaq al-Bitruji. But he was more interested in astrology and magic than in science. The result was that in the later centuries, the school of Toledo came to be known in medieval Europe as a centre for witchcraft and black magic. This was mainly due to the fanatical spirit of Christian Spain, which was then victorious all over the Iberian Peninsula. However, the hatred towards the Muslims agitated the Spanish heart so much that they did not develop Muslim science and philosophy beyond translations of their writings. Religious fanaticism of the medieal Spanish Christians did riot favour the search for new thought or for creative writing. But this was not true of the rest of medieval Europe, where the writings of the

Muslim writers and thinkers were eagerly studied, while those of Ibn Rushd (Aerroes) gave rise to a great philosophical movement, which was known as Latin Averroism, as we shall discuss presently.

Alfonso X the Wise : "The great apostle of Muslim learning in Christian Spain was Alfonso X, *el Sabio* (The Wise), King of Castile and Leon from 1252 to 1284." He organised translation work on a vast scale. But, by his time, a shift had occurred in the kind of translations. He was not interested in Muslim philosophy and science so much as in Andalusian literature, music and other arts. He got them translated into his native tongue, Roman, which thus became the forerunner of modern Spanish. Among the works which were thus translated were *Libro de los juegos* or the Book of Games, like dice, chess, backgammon, etc., *Lapiderio,* a treatise on the virtues of precious stones, *cronica general*, a pseudo-historical writing, *Grande e general Estoria* or a great and general history, and his *Las siete* partidas, a code of Spanish laws. He also got compiled astronomical observations, known as *Alfonsine Tables*, which remained in use in Medieval Europe for several centuries.

Latin Averroism : Although the writings of Ibn Rushd were soon forgotten in the Islamic world after his death, they had great influence in Christian Europe from circa 1200 to circa 1650. The newly-founded University of Paris became the first centre of the study of Averroes' commentaries on Aristotle. This movement was led by Siger of Brabant (1240-1280/1284), professor of philosophy in the University. He was joined by several of his colleagues. This movement came to be known as Latin Averroism, because the discussion on Averroess' philosophy was carried on in Latin, which was the language of learning in Medieval Europe. Averroism was really a tendency to accept and interpret the philosophy of Aristotle in the light of Ibn Rushd's commentaries on Aristotle's works. That was why Averroes (Ibn Rushd) came to be known as the Commentator of Aristotle throughout the Later Middle Ages in Europe.

Siger of Brabant and his colleagues, however, understood Averroes's commentaries in terms more than what he had himself said. Confronted with the dogmas of the Christian Church, they propounded, in 1260, the theory of "double truth" by which they asserted that the truths of religion and reason were not only different but also contradictory, yet both were equally true. However, this concession could not placate the totalitarian Church, for its implications clearly denied many of its dogmas. Siger declared that there was only one "intellectual soul for mankind and thus one will", and that this soul was eternal, while individual soul was not immortal. Moreover, he and his colleagues further asserted the eternity of the world. Now all these views were opposed to what the Church had maintained for centuries past. The Church authorities, led by the Inquisitor in France, took Siger and his colleagues to task. Siger, however, continued to insist on the autonomy of philosophy as a self-sufficient discipline, not subordinate to the Church dogma. Obviously, this challenge to the totalitarian ideology of the Church could not go unpunished. The Bishop of Paris, the Inquisitor and Thomas Aquinas all rose to defend the Church against Siger and his colleagues. They condemned them for heterodoxy, a crime for which they could be burnt on the stake. Siger fled in 1277 to Orvieto, where he was placed in the custody of a mad cleric, who stabbed him fatally, and thus caused his death in 1281 or 1284 under highly mysterious circumstances.

The Church's reaction to Averroism was as sharp as it was merciless. Siger and his colleagues were silenced, writings of Averroes banned, while the Church poured invectives on Averroes, branding him as "the accursed", "a famous barker" and "an impious Arab". Even the world "Averroist", became a derogatory term, so much so that for about a century, no one dared to declare himself as one. However, Averroism was revived during early fourteenth century, first in Paris and soon afterwards in Padua near Venica, in Italy. A group of philosophers in the Padua university styled themselves as "Averroists".

During the Renaissance in Italy, Averroism flourished in Padua, Bologna and other Italian universities. It was then known as Paduan Averroism, it had no overriding concern for theology. Instead, it had secular orientation. Averroists like Zimara (died 1532) and Niphus (died 1546) tried to reconcile Averroism with Christian theology. At this time, the invention of the art of printing added to the popularity of Averroism: Averroes' writings were published in Arabic, Latin and Hebrew again and again at Venice in 1481, 1482, 1484, 1489, 1497 and 1500. Later his complete editions were published in 1553 and 1557. After 1580, however, the number of readers of Averroes diminished. Cesare Cremonini (died 1631) was the last philosopher who styled himself as Averroist. Averroes was finally published at Geneva in 1600. But the time revolutionary changes had occurred in Europe. Renaissance had challenged the totalitarian authority of the Christian Church; Galileo had laid the foundations of experimental physics, and Copernicus and Kepler had freed astronomy from the speculative philosophy of Aristotle. Thus Averroism, as an integral part of Aristotelianism, was discarded by the new methodology of the experimental sciences. However, Averroism had not fallen: it was superseded by the modern scientific thinking, and rationalism.

Besides Averroes, Avicenna (Ibn Sina) had also a great influence on medieval Europe, especially on the study of medical science. Avempace (Ibn Bajja) and Ibn Tufayl, the two philosophers of the Berber period of Muslim Spain, were also translated into Latin. Ibn Tufayl's philosophical novel, *Hayy*

Ibn Yaqzan, was translated into Latin as *Philosophus autodidactus* in the fifteenth century by Pico della Mirandola (died 1494) and by Edward Pocok in 1700, while the Quaker G. Keith translated it into English in 1674. It is said that Ibn Tufayl's philosophical novel greatly influenced the English adventure story of *Robinson Crusoe* by Daniel Defoe (1660-1731)

HISTORICAL CHART

8th to 10th Centuries

Muslim world far ahead of Christian Europe in a fields of human endeavour. Muslim domination over the Iberian Peninsula. Three historic developments in Western Europe: emergency of Seigneurial Feudalism, which repulsed Arab advance into the Frankish lands; Institution of monogamy by the Christian Church; Rise of the totalitarian Catholic Church or the Gregorian Revolution which made the Catholic Christianity a militant, aggressive and anti-Islamic force in the subsequent centuries.

Circa 1000 A.D.

A turning-point in East-West relations, when scales began to turn in favour of Western Europe.

Eleventh Century:

Muslims were still far advanced in philosophy, science and technology. Christian Europe launched Crusades against the Islamic World, including Muslim Spain, where the Christians captured Toledo.

Twelfth Century

Christian Europe's military power held in check by the new upsurge of Muslim power. European feudalism was successfully countered by the Berber tribalism under the Murabitun and Muwahhidun in Muslim Spain and by the Turkish tribalism in the Muslim East. Rise of the new towns in Europe and the emergency of the burgher or mercantile bourgeoisie in Western Europe; the challenge to Muslim monopoly of the Mediterranean trade by the rising commercial cities of Italy, France and Christian Spain. Muslim intellectual advances in philosophy, sciences and technology, and their transfer to Europe through the translation of the Arabic books into Latin by the scholars of the Toledo school of translators. Slavery banned by the Christian Church in Europe.

Thirteenth Century:

Christian Spain's victory over Muslim Spain was complete excepting the kingdom of Granada. Averroism became popular among the European scholastics: intellectually Muslim Past and Christian West were at par; if they could speak each other's language, Arabic or Latin, they could converse with each other in identical terms: for once at least the twins i.e. East and West could meet. But in trade and shipping, Christian Europe began to dominate the Mediterranean.

Fourteenth Century:

Christian Europe forged ahead in its military adventures on both land and sea; Portuguese geographical explorations in the Atlantic and along the coast of western Africa began, in order to by-pass the Muslim control over the eastern trade, especially in gold, slaves and spices. Although intellectually Muslim world and Christian Europe were still more or less at par; yet the Muslim East began to sink into a deep intellectual slumber, with the solitary exception of Ibn Khaldun: Muslim intellectual, especially Averroist, influence still great on Christian Europe.

Fifteenth Century:

Renaissance Europe far ahead of the Muslim world in intellectual fields. Geographical discoveries by the Portuguese in the East and by the Spanish in the New World or America. Granada, the last remnant of Muslim Spain, wiped out by Christian Spain. Ottoman Turks captured Constantinople, which gave further fillip to the Renaissance in Italy and other European countries: European intellectual advances continued, with Averroism, still dominant. Rise of National States in Europe, first in Portugal and Spain and next in France and England.

Sixteenth Century:

Copernican Revolution, based on his heliocentric theory, which upset Christian theology and philosophy; consequently Aristotelianism, along with Averroism, began to be questioned by European intellectual classes: now search for facts, not authority, became the basic principle in science and philosophy- the very basis of the *Scientific Revolution*. Protestant Revolt (Reformation) decentralised and devolved the totalitarian hold of the Catholic Church onto the national churches in Protestant countries. Portuguese Imperialism victorious in the Muslim East from the Indian Ocean to the China Sea: Portuguese and Spanish Imperialisms aroused the French, Dutch and English imperialist ambitions. With these developments, however, the Middle Ages in Europe came to an end.

But Spanish and Portuguese State Systems were not free of Catholic Church's medieval hold, which wits a necessary, or inevitable, consequence of their reconquista ideologies.

Seventeenth Century:

Modern experimental science came into being with Galilee's discoveries in physics, particuarly mechanics; Kepler's Laws completed Copernican Revolution and ushered in modern astronomy: Scientific Revolution firmly established in Europe. Secularism and humanism in Renaissance Europe undermined the totalitarian hold of the Christian Churches over European intellect, though not over European social and cultural life. (It took three centuries more to overthrow this hold of the Christian Churches, Catholic or national, when in the 20th century European society and culture became more liberal, tolerant and pluralistic.) For the Christian Church, all that was solid for centuries began to be questioned more and more by its Christian critics.

Although European scholars had long since translated and studied Muslim writings on philosophy, sciences, arts and technology, but no Muslim scholar or writer ever thought of translating into Arabic European books and writings on these new intellectual developments, inventions and discoveries. In fact, the gap in the level of development between Europe and Muslim World in respect of science and technology, philosophy and arts, as well as in economic, political and military systems, was now so great as to impel the Europeans towards the conquest of Muslim (and also non-Muslim) lands. Consequently Muslim peoples and countries

were subjected to endless invasions and conquests by
the European powers, led by the Portuguese and
Spanish empire-builders; and yet no Muslim scholar,
thinker or ruler ever tried to search for the reasons of
these developments and of the expansionist impulses
and designs of the European aggressors: they were
too degenerate to do so. In such circumstances, the
Moriscoes the last of the Spanish Muslims, were
extirpated totally by the Spanish Christians, without
any repercussions anywhere during the first decade of
the seventeenth century,--and ominous event,
portending what was to happen afterwards to many a
people the world over.

CHAPTER 60

EVOLUTION AND TRANSFORMATION OF FEUDAL EUROPE EUROPEAN FEUDALISM: c. 500 – c. 700 A.D.

During the sixth to eighth centuries, usually known as the Dark Ages, Roman Empire crumbled to pieces due to the invasions of the Germanic tribes from the north. They conquered and settled in various provinces of the Empire from Britain to Italy and Spain. In the course of their conquest and settlement the Germanic or Teutonic tribes intermingled with the vanquished Roman or Romanised people, which proved to be momentous for the subsequent history of Europe. From this mixing up of the peoples and tribes, races and cultures in course of times arose the feudal system of Europe. It was, however, such a tangled affair that historians are unable to decide whether the origins of European feudalism lay in the Germanic or Roman ways of life. For our purposes, it is enough to say that the old Germanic tribal formations and relations had broken down into smaller kindred groups due to their mixing up with the alien peoples and cultures, the intermarriages among them and the loss of continuity of the past traditions and customs of both the Germanic and Roman peoples. Two definite trends developed among them, which became the initial forms of the early medieval feudalism in Western Europe. They were, firstly, the changes in the Germanic kindred groups and, secondly, the practice of seeking Protection of a powerful chief in the neighbourhood. These trends transformed the earlier feudalism into kinship feudalism of the Germanic kindred groups.

The Germanic kinship society and its feudalisation : The Germanic tribes had retained the earlier matriarchal position of women to a greater extent than did the other patriarchal societies of the past. Among them, woman continued to enjoy both freedom and respect as well as the protection and support of her own kin group after she had been given in marriage to her husband's kin group. In fact, the descent was traced among them both from maternal and paternal sides. Every man believed himself to be related to both his paternal and maternal kinsmen. Marc Bloch, the eminent French historian of the European feudalism, writes: "Already in ancient Germany each individual had two kinds of relatives, those "of the spear side" and those "of the distaff side", and he became bound, though in different degrees, to the second as well as to the first. It was as though among the Germans the victory of the agnatic principle has never been sufficiently complete to extinguish all trace of a more ancient system of uterine filiation".

In other words, in the ancient Germanic tribes, although woman was under the *mund* or dependency of men, she was yet free and respected, and not reduced to the level of a chattel of her husband's kin group. This fact played a great part in the social evolution of the medieval European society. Intermarriages between various Germanic groups as well as between them and the vanquished Roman groups, became a decisive factor in this evolution. That was the reason why, after a century or so of the conquest, the Germanic peoples became as much Romanised as the Roman people had become Germanised. That was also the reason why the kindred groups of the conquering Germanic tribes did not become caste groups: they did not remain distinct and separate from non-German groups by differences of race, colour or military domination. This was the beginning of the long-drawn process of the disembowelment or weaning of the emergent European society from the kinship relationships. It prevented the Germanic kindred groups from being classified into castes, as it had been the case with the ancient Indian Aryans.

Nevertheless, there would have been no feudalism in Europe, if the Germanic kindred relationships had not existed at all. But there would have been no feudalism of the type that evolved in Europe if these relations had been as strong as they had been in other kinship societies. For they would have then arrested the process of further feudalisation. European feudal society would have then stagnated at the level of the semi-feudal and semi-tribal society, as did the Abbasid and post-Abbasid Muslim societies in the Middle Ages. Marc Bloch has put it aptly: "The tie of kinship was one of the essential elements of feudal society; but its relative weakness explains why there was feudalism at all". He explains further, "The ties of kinship continued to exist very powerfully in the feudal society, but they took their place beside new ties after which they tended to pattern themselves and to which they were at times considered inferior."

During the early period of the Germanic tribal settlements, the old Roman system of strong and centralised government and administration had broken down, while the new Frankish kingdoms were unable to create the same conditions of peace and order as had existed in the Roman times. Hence conditions of anarchy and disorder, violence and war prevailed all over Europe, called the Dark Ages. In these conditions, a new type of politico-military relationship grew up among the half-Romanised and half-Germanised people, based on a practice called "commendation". Under it, a man would seek the protection of a powerful man in his neighbourhood by paying homage to him and would thus become a "man of a man", as the custom of homage so clearly signified. He then joined his protector's group of kinsmen and warriors. This relation was not based on the natural affinity of blood or birth, but on the individual's voluntary action. It was a sort of personal relationship between a powerful man, who promised protection and aid, and a weak man who promised his armed support or service against his enemies. The protector became the lord or seigneur and the protected man his vassal, as the two parties soon came to be called in the language of the emergent feudalism.

It should be noted that this new type of relationship was not peculiarly Germanic. It had also arisen among the Roman peoples during the period of decline and fall of the Roman Empire. It arose, primarily, because a man sought protection of the strong for the reason that he had lost the protection of the Roman State as well as of his kinsmen in the village community. Both had become too weak or were otherwise unable to provide protection to him and his property and lands, or did not provide enough 'support and opportunities for pillage and plunder, while the protector was strong, because he still commanded the armed support of his kindred group, slaves of his household and of his armed retainers. Such a mixed group of warriors was called *comitatus*. Professor F.L. Ganshof writes, "The *comitatus* consisted of a group of free warriors who had taken service of their own free will under a chieftain, and fought with him and on his behalf as a band of close comrades. These bodies of armed retainers whom we meet with during the Merovingian period (481-716 A.D.) had thus a double origin, and it is not possible to say whether they owed more to their Roman or to their Germanic predecessors".

In other words, the strong was stronger because he still enjoyed the armed support of his kinsmen, while the weak was weaker, for he had lost it or found it insufficient for his protective or predatory purposes. This is the reason why European feudalism should be regarded as an outgrowth of a kinship society in transition, i.e., a kinship society which did not ossify into rigid caste relations. Had it been so, no man would have sought voluntary protection of a chief of another kin group on such a contractual basis. Instead of it, he would have relied on his own kin group for such a protection, or he would have submitted to the power and aggression of the strong by paying tribute to him, as long as it could not be avoided. This was what the conquered kin groups, tribes and castes, did in the countries of Muslim feudalism, whenever they found a strong man, chief or king, etc., in their neighbourhood too strong to resist. Payment of a tribute was not a contractual relation but an act of necessity, for it was imposed on the weak by the strong. One had to submit to it, just as one submits to natural calamities, like floods or fairies. Commendation, in early medieval Europe, was a voluntary relation between a strong man and his weak neighbour for the sake of mutual advantages as well as mutual obligations on both sides, that is, protection and maintenance (which meant providing food, arms, horse, etc.) by the lord and military service and loyalty towards him by the vassal. In course of time, however, the lord ceased to feed his vassals at his own table, or in his household except for a specific number of days in a year. Instead, he gave lands to his vassals, fiefs, by means of which each of them could maintain himself and also provide himself with a horse and other accout rements of war. Thus they became his tenants or fief-holders, holding lands on his behalf, for under the feudal law the lands allotted to the vassals were still regarded as of the lord's

Feudal Hierachy : At first, the practice of commendation or homage was a voluntary act; people themselves sought the protection of the strong in their neighbourhood. But soon after the kings of the Frankish kingdoms (Merovingian and Carlovingian) found it a useful method for raising armies of such armed retainers and feudatories. They distributed lands among their armed followers, retainers, relatives, courtiers and the like, on the condition of paying homage, and taking oath of fealty and rendering military service. It was strictly a personal bond, but was considered as strong as that of kinship or blood relationship. In their turn, the royal tenants or magnates, called tenants-in-chief in feudal law and ranked as dukes, marquis and counts, subinfeudated or distributed their vast lands among their vassals on the same terms of personal homage, oath of fealty and military service. They were known as lesser tenants, and did not owe allegiance to the overlord (king or empire) but only to the tenants-in-chief, their lords. It was a source of weakness and often led to revolts by the powerful feudal magnates during the succeeding age of the high feudalism. Anyhow, during the eighth and ninth centuries, the whole European society, including the Christian Church, came to be feudalised, that is, it was organized into a vast hierarchy of feudal lords and vassals, with the king or emperor, as the overlord, at its apex. As all the political relations were strictly of contractual nature the king, as an overlord, was only a suzerain and not a sovereign of the feudal lords; that is, he was not their absolute and all powerful ruler. He was as much bound by the feudal rights and obligations as any of his vassals.

The Fief : Moreover, the subordination of the persons was also the subordination of the lands or fiefs. The greater lords or magnates had aster lands or fiefs and the lesser ones had smaller fiefs, till we come to the smallest of them, called a knight's fee. The knight was a horseman and the lowest in the feudal hierarchy of warriors-on-horseback. His fee or fief was a grant of land, usually of the size of a village, but enough to maintain him, his horse, his accoutrements, his house-hold and his castle around which lay his fee lands. The knight's fee or a lord's demense was called a manor, in which he was known as the lord of the manor. In other words, a fief could be as small as a knight's fee or a manor and as large as a seigniory of a feudal magnate or tenant-in-chief, which was in some cases as large as a province. Thus the seigneurial military order was detailed to the manorial agrarian order below it. During the early stages of the evolution of European feudalism, a fief was granted, not for the revenues it would provide to the lord or his vassal, but for maintaining him or his vassal as a life-long warrior.

With these developments, the tribalistic features had ceased to exist in European feudalism, which had now become a fully developed feudal system, i.e., a politico-military socio-economic system of landholding. Muslim feudalism, on the contrary, never evolved upto this level. The reason was that it could never sever the umblical cord of the blood relationships of its kinship groups, that is, of the tribes and clans, as was the case under the Caliphates of the Umayyads of Damascus and of Cordova in Muslim Spain. Later, the comparatively more developed *iqta* or *jagirdari* feudalism of the Abbasid and post-Abbasid kingdoms and empires, e.g., of the Indian Mughal Empire, was subject not only to the kinship atavism of Muslim fief-holders as that of the Umayyad Caliphates, but also to the bureaucratic and administrative purposes of their sultans or rulers, and, therefore, suffered the same fate of the rise, decline and fall as did the ruling dynasties themselves. To return to Europe. With the growth of feudalism proper, the Dark Ages in the history of Western Europe came to an end and the feudal age began.

Early Feudal

During the early feudal ages, the fiefs were granted only on the condition of rendering military service, failing which they could be withdrawn by the lord or the overlord, as the case may be. Moreover, the fiefs were granted for life only. On their withdrawal or on the death of a vassal or sub-vassal, they could be granted to anyone else, who might not be the son or relative of the former fief-holder. But this right of the feudal lord came to be restricted during this period due to the growth of a new kind of family relations. The most important among them was the institution of monogamy as the only form of marriage in the European society, sanctioned and sanctified by the dogma of the Christian Church, and later., by the law and authority of the State, when it became powerful enough to enforce it.

Women and the Christian Church : The Christian Church, from its earliest days, had a strangely ambivalent attitude towards women and their sex, i.e., a mixed feelings of attraction and repulsion, even of repugnance. The early Christian Church Fathers held the same debasing opinion about women as the medieval Muslim Ulema came to hold later on. But their ambivalence ultimately saved the Church Fathers from the pitfalls of polygamy and purdah, which came to be so ardently and piously advocated by the Muslim Ulema and feudal classes, little realising that they were elitic, not Islamic institutions. The Christian Fathers had a deep respect for women, if they became saints and martyrs. But they had also equally deep-seated loathing for their sex and contempt for women, the ordinary mortals. They called their *sex imbecilitas sexus*, i.e., the weak and inferior sex. They believed woman to be the cause of Man's Fall, for Eve, tempted by the serpant as they put it, made man, the superior being, to taste the fruit of the Tree of Knowledge, which led to his Fall. For this original sin, woman was punished with eternal pains and sorrows in subordination to her lord: as the Bible puts it: 'in sorrow thou shalt bring forth children; and thy desire shall be to thy husband, and he shall rule over thee." Woman was, therefore, under the subjection of man. In his Epistles to the Ephesians, St. Paul declares, 'Wives! submit yourselves unto your husbands, as unto thy Lord. For the husband is the head of the wife, as Christ is of the Church".

Such was the misogyny of the early Christianity, out of which came the self-contradictory dogma of the Holy Matrimony of the medieval Church. The basic tenet of this dogma was the indissolubility of marriage, for it made a man and a women "one flesh", which ever dealt could not part. It became one of the seven sacraments on which the Christian faith was based. From this followed the principle of monogomy or "single marriage" of a man and a woman, not because it was regarded as a social ideal, but as a necessary evil, to be tolerated by the Church because of human frailty for sex. Athenogoras, one of the early defenders of Christianity against its pagan critics in the days of the Roman Emperor Marcus Aurelius (161-130 A.D.), declares: "Our rule is that each must remain as he is born, or be content with a single marriage. Second marriages are nothing more than decorously disguised adultery". This principle also condemned divorce, which the medieval Church permitted only under exceptionally rigorous conditions. From this also followed the impediments of consanguinity and affinity, which prohibited marriage between individuals related upto the seventh degree of relationship. We shall now consider the social consequences of these tenets of the Holy Matrimony.

Polygamy existed in the early medieval Europe. The Teutonic tribes were not very particular about the form of marriage. But from about 800 A.D., under Charlemagne, the Frankish Emperor (768-814), the Catholic Church began to insist on monogamous marriage among the Franks. Its concern was not with any social reform but with the salvation of the souls of the Christian believers. The Church Fathers believed woman to be a special agent of Satan, created to lure, by the guiles of her body and beauty, the unwary man from the path of virtue and eternal salvation. At first, they preached celibacy as the only guarantee for salvation. But, as it was obviously impractical for the faithful and suicidal for the Christian community, they advocated monogamy as a sort of necessary compromise between the Devil and the man, while they insisted on celibacy for the clergy. Monogamy was, however, instituted in a rather roundabout manner. Marriage was declared to be a sacrament, a mysterious but holy bond between the husband and wife, which could only be sanctified if performed by a priest in the church. Thus marriage came under the Canon Law, the law of the Church, which would not sanction a second marriage during the lifetime of the wife. This has been the marriage law throughout the Christendom down to the modern times.

The medieval law of monogamy had a great effect on the structure and life of the family group in the feudal Europe. In the early medieval period every feudal noble had a large household of his kinsmen and it was only with their armed support that he could defend and his people against his enemies and rivals who were on the prowl to attack plunder and destroy him and his But his dependence on his kinsmen hindered the transfer of his all. lands to his children, for his brothers, cousins and other relatives had an equal claim on his lands. The institution of monogamy began to transform the family structure so much that the hold of the kindreds began to loosen. It integrated the interests of the husband and wife/father and mother with each other, for there was no co-wife/co-mother to disrupt them. Thus a small family group of the parents and their children, called a nuclear or biological family by modern sociologists, began to emerge as a viable social institution. The father was now more inclined to transfer his fief or land to his children to the exclusion of his kindred, whose interests were all the more divergent as no cousin marriages were possible. Describing the effects of the prohibition of cousin marriage on European society. R.W. Southern writes: 'The wide net cast by the prohibited degrees of marriage often forced a very great man to look far afield for a wife, unless he would made a disparaging match or fall under ecclesiastical censure".

From a benefice to a heritable fief : Now the monogamous family system began to transform the structure of property relations in the feudal system of land tenure. The weakening of the kinship hold on the feudal system of land tenure. The weakening of the kinship hold on the family interests made the fief-holders to turn their fiefs into heritable patrimony. As we have said above, the fief were temporary grants by the lord (seigneur or king). It was called a benefice. He could re-grant it to any other of his vassals at any time. Indeed, in the feudal theory, all land was of the king, who could distribute it among his vassals as he liked. But the growing family interests of the fief-holder to retain it within his family inclined him to make it a patrimony, to be inherited by his children. This development took place in Western Europe, that is, in England, France, Belgium, etc., during the ninth and tenth centuries. By the beginning of the eleventh century, it became so complete that the word "fief" itself came to mean a heritable estate. A century after, writes Marc Bloch, the inheritability of a fief became a law.

These developments reveal the fact that in medieval Europe, kinship system and feudalism became, basically, two different social phenomena : the former was based on relations of blood and birth, while the latter on territorial allegiance through land-tenure. Their social consequences were also equally opposite in nature one made the social relations of the people concerned to be introvert or in-ward looking in their interests, activities and behaviour, oriented towards their family and small kinship groups, while the other to be extravert of outward-looking towards the larger interests of the society and country. Moreover, land-holding on the basis of kinship or communal ownership led to the dissipation of its productive powers as well as to parasitism of the surplus population, while the new feudal ownership with monogamous family interests led to the greater development of agriculture and other occupations, as we shall presently see. Furthermore, the inheritability of the fiefs led to a new legal development. By the end of the twelfth century, the nobles or fief-holders also acquired the right of sale and alienation of their lands. Formerly, sale of landed property was not possible under the old feudal law. But now genuine sales became a frequent affair. It clearly showed that the hold of the feudal overlord, king or emperor, as well as of the kin groups on the landed property had virtually ceased to exist and that the lands became the private property of the fief- holders.

It was a silent revolution in land ownership and, thereby, in agricultural production, which in course of time, proved to be of immense historical significance. Firstly, it led to greater and more efficient exploitation of agricultural resources, use of new tools and techniques and better use of labour power. Secondly, it led to the growth of new market towns and cities, which were dependent both on the agricultural produce as well as on the serfs who fled from the feudal exploitation. Thus a new type of artisan and mercantile classes came into being in these urban centres, which were free from kinship relations but linked by relations of production on which their guilds were based. That was the reason why these classes and their guilds never became castes, as they had in Hindu India and in some

Muslim countries in the Middle Ages. Anyhow, it was, in medieval Europe, a silent and yet a continuous and cumulative transformation of agriculture and thereby of the new urban centres of production, which gradually but progressively revolutionised the whole economy and society of Western Europe and thus set the stage for the emergence of the modern capitalist system of the West.

As we have said above, the European feudal order was a hierarchial system in which the overlord (king or the like) at the top was not an autocratic or absolutist ruler, but only a liege-lord of the greater tenants. As such, he was the *primus inter pares*, the first among the equals. As a matter of fact, in European feudalism, the concept of State, was basically contractual in nature, in which the very idea of sovereignty or the supreme authority of the State was unknown. When, however, the nation-states came into being at the end of the Middle Ages, their sovereign rulers had to struggle hard to subdue the powerful and refractory feudal magnates, while the political thinkers of the age expounded the absolutist theory of sovereignty to justify the, exercise of the supreme and unlimited authority by these rulers.

High Feudalism

Primogeniture : The heritability of the fief led to a new development. It was the prevalence of the rule of primogeniture in most of the Western Europe countries during the eleventh and twelfth centuries. It regulated the inheritance and succession to the feudal estates. Its prevalence was due to the need to protect and ensure the family interests of the feudal nobility. It arose from a conflict between the prevalent feudal law and the family interests of the fief-holders. Under the feudal law, a fief could not be subdivided or fragmented, for it would thereby undermine its politico-military purpose for which it was granted.

A fief must remain sufficiently large to enable a fief-holder to render military service and pay feudal dues. Writes Marc Bloch: "Furthermore, the original grant having been so calculated as to provide for the pay of a single vassal with his followers, there was a danger that if it were broken up the fragments would not suffice to maintain the new holders, with the result that they would be ill-armed or perhaps forced to seek their fortunes elsewhere. It was therefor important that the tenement, having become hereditary, should at any rate pass to a single heir". Therefore, it became imperative that a fief should not be divided when inherited by the children of a deceased noble. Indeed, the same was true of the small lands of the serfs, who also must have enough land on succession so as to maintain themselves in such a way that they performed their labour-service on the lord's demesne. Hence arose the need to restrict inheritance of a fief to one of the sons, preferably the eldest, on the death of a fief-holder. This was how the rule of primogeniture originated. However, the eldest son succeeded to the fief after paying homage and taking the oath of fealty to his father's lord. In case a noble had no sons, his eldest daughter succeeded him, and her husband became the vassal of his lord. This rule, which became a law in England during the twelfth century, protected the feudal estates from fragmentation, while it made succession and inheritance clear-cut and precise operations, obviating all disputes over lands and property which were, by the way, the bane of all Asian and African feudalisms, when the authority of the king or emperor in them became weak.

Thus the monogamous family system in medieval Europe streamlined the complicated questions of land inheritance and succession and also protected the productive powers of the land from uneconomic fragmentation and the relations of production from disruption. It was something never attained in the agricultural economy of the Muslim feudalism. On the contrary, one of the main reasons why the Muslim feudal society foundered after a generation or two of the dynastic rule, when every descendant among the innumerable progeny of the polygamous and multi-concubinal amirs, iqtadars, timriots, zaims, pashas, khans, jagirdars, mansabdars, etc., as they were variously called in different Muslim countries, claimed a share in the paternal estate, even after it had become, for politico-military as well as for economic purposes, too small to be of any good. The fragmentation of agricultural lands and the disputes over them undermined economic prosperity and political stability of the Muslim kingdoms and empires and became one of the main causes of their decline and fall. In medieval Europe, on the contrary, the rule of primogeniture enabled the feudal families to maintain their social, political and economic position and perform their military and other functions properly from generation to generation. Moreover, this rule also dealt a final blow to kinship parasitism, for not even a brother would expect to be maintained by his fief-holding brother. That was why there were no idlers and parasite hangers-on in the European feudal families, while their numbers became legions in the Muslim feudalism of the Middle Ages. Only the dynastic decline and downfall of a kingdom or empire cleared these Augean stables a generation or two of moral and social degeneration. In European feudalism, under the rule of primogeniture, the younger sons had to fend for themselves as best as they could for they would go, nothing from the family estate after the death of their fathers. Of course, the fathers used to provide their younger sons during their lifetime in one way or another. They would be helped to become pages or squires in the service of a powerful noble or king, in order to become knights and, in course of time, to get fiefs of their own by deeds of valour and service to their masters. Or they would be helped to join the Church as prelates or monks, while unmarried daughters would become nuns in the convents. Sometimes, the fathers of such children used to provide them new lands in their neighbourhood by cleaning the forests, of which Europe was then full.

When the Crusades (1095-1291) began, the younger sons of the nobles, the surplus population, to put it in modern jargon, eagerly joined them. They fought against the Muslims, first in Spain and later in the Holy Lands (Palestine and Syria), where they founded the Kingdom of Jerusalem and acquired vast lands as fiefs for settlement. It was the first European in colonialism. It failed, however, after a couple of centuries, for feudal Europe had no surplus left in population and wealth to sustain it. By this time, the younger scions of the nobility had found new outlets for acquiring wealth and social status in the rising towns by undertaking commercial activities at home and abroad across the high seas and intermarried into the business families of the emerging burgess classes. Thus the family system of monogamy and primogeniture, on the one hand, saved the rural economy of the feudalism from parasitism of the surplus population and, on the other, engendered new economic and demographic forces in the political and economic life of the West European feudal society.

This was equally true of the poorer classes, the serfs. Their life was full of daily toil and drudgery. "Their's dull routine of agricultural labour which monk of the eleventh century symbolized in a gialogue written for schoolboys.

Ploughman, how do you work

"....I go out at dawn to drive the oxen to the field, and yoke them to the plough. However hard the winter I dare not stay at home for fear of my lord–every day I have to plough an acre or more.–I have to fill the oxen's bin with hay and give them water and carry the dung outside.–Hard work it is because

I am not free." So the hard-pressed serfs fled to the new towns and cities to escape from the exploitation and oppression of their feudal masters. In these new urban centres, the fugitive serfs became labourers, artisans, craftsmen and even merchants and trades and joined their guilds or founded new ones. Moreover, by the end of the 11th century, slavery also ceased to exist in Western Europe.

Primogenitue as the law of dynastic succession : The rule of primogenitue led also to a political consequence of equally great historical significance. It became the law of dynastic succession, first in England after Henry II (1154-89 and then in all other European monarchies. "The law of monarchy did not at first recognise primogeniture, any more than did the feudal law......Nevertheless, the right of primogeniture was a convenient fiction; moreover, it was gradually imposed by the example of the fief itself, and in France, in spite of some opposition, it became the rule almost from the outset." It freed the royal succession from ages-old occurrences of intrigues, quarrels and wars of succession and revolts by various contenders, even pretenders, for the throne on the death of a monarch. Of course, the Muslim kingdoms and empires down the ages could not free themselves from this constitutional malaise. It caused not only political upheavals and anarchy but also hastened up their speedy decline and downfall, according to Ibn Khaldun's theory of four-generation dynastic cycle. "The Muslims", writes Dr. Anwer G. Ghejn, "who fell heir to the flourishing culture of the Near East, did not escape the unhappy consequences resulting from the unsettled state of affairs as regards the transmission of power. They were, perhaps, on of the most important causes of the decline of the Islamic State." To throw some light on the gory scenes of courtly intrigues, princely revolts and murders and wars of succession, it would be enough to refer to the history of the Mughal Empire from the days of Babar to those of the descendants of Aurangzeb. These revolts and wars of succession became one of the important causes of its decline and fall. In this respect, however, the case of the Ottoman Sultans was unique. The accession to the throne of a new Turkish Sultan often led to the cold- blooded slaughter of his brothers, usually several dozens in number. This cruel practice began after Mohammad the Conqueror (1451-81). He issued a *qanun*, enjoining his descendants as thus: "And to whomsoever of my sons the Sultanate shall pass, it is befitting that for the order of the world he shall kill his brothers. Most of the Ulema allow it. So let them act on this". And they did act–with a vengence. The qanun was obeyed up to the end of the sixteenth century. Then more humane sentiments prevailed. The royal brothers were then not killed but imprisoned for life in a pavilion in the royal harem, which was significantly called gafts or cage. Thus for another century and half, the brothers, cousins and uncles of the reigning sultans were kept in a condition of life-long, imprisonment.

In Europe, however, the law of primogeniture strengthened the monarchical rule, made the succession to the throne a peaceful and regular affair and the system of government stronger and more stable than ever before, whereas it had been hitherto exceptionally weak under the old feudal system. It helped in the evolution of a strong and centralised system of monarchy, which curbed the fissiparous tendencies of the feudal nobility, restrained its lust for plunder and lawlessness, and created conditions for the macrosocialisation of the national economy and society, law and culture. Thus came into being, in due course of time, the nation-state, the first of its kind in human history. The new national monarchies put an end to the feudal anarchy, infused respect for the rule of law, maintained the "king's peace", and fostered the growth of trade and commerce on national or country-wide scales by joining hands with the burgess classes of the new towns and cities against the 'lawless feudal nobility. In short, the socio-economic and political evolution of medieval Europe was in just the opposite direction to that of the medieval Islamic world, due to the differences of their family systems and all the other differences these systems implied.

European Feudal Nobility–a warrior class par excellence: The feudal nobility of medieval Europe was a warrior class *par excellence*

And when battle is joined,
And all men of good lineage think
Of naught but the breaking of heads and arms;
For it is better to die than to be vanquished and alive.
I tell you, I find no such savour
In food, or in wine, or in sleep,
As in hearing the shout ''On! On! "from both sides,
And the neighing of the steeds that have lost their riders.
And the cries of "Help! Help!"
In seeing men great and small go down on the grass beyond
the fosse,
With the pennoned stumps of lances still in their sides.

Thus sang, in the second half of the twelfth century, the troubadours of Southern France, who were also noblemen and warriors themselves. Warfare was a legal obligation under the feudal custom, a game of pleasure, also a matter of honour and always a source for the acquisition and re-distribution of fiefs for this warrior class. Warfare was, as Mare Block so aptly puts it, "a nobleman's chief industry." And when they had no enemy to fight–a condition we call peacetime, the feudal nobles and knights would fight mockbattles, singly or in groups (teams, as we would say). They were called tournaments. They were attended by both lords and ladies. A beautiful lady was chosen as the queen. She awarded honours to the winners of these mock-battles.

Historically, the warlike spirit of the European nobility played a very dynamic role in the evolution and transmition of Feudal Europe. This class was born, as we have said above, during the anarchy war and violence of the Dark Ages after the downfall of the Roman Empire. And it was further settled by the great struggles it waged to defend Europe against invaders from the east, south and north during the eighth and ninth centuries. Nurtured in war, it lived by war for a thousand years or so, and vanished only when outdated by the new weapon systems of the new society it had itself created by its insatiable lust for warfare. No other warlike class in human history had such a long and uninterrupted record of pugnacity and love of warfare as had the European feudal nobility. Whatever faults and shortcomings the knights and barons of medieval Europe might have had, they never became a class of degenerate effects, as, had the noble classes of the medieval Muslim feudalism again and again after a generation or two of martial valour and victory. The reasons lay in the kind of family and social life the European noble classes lived.

Family and Social Life in Feudal Europe : In all preindustrial patriarchal societies, the social role of women was necessarily secondary and supportive, provided they were not socially and morally incapacitated by such institutions as purdah and polygamy, when it became degenerative. The European women of the feudal era played their role of support and assistance, influence and stimulation to their menfolk to the maximum degree in all fields of work and achievement, whether social, economic, cultural, military or political.

The life of the feudal nobles at home was busy, lively, and

often hard and onerous, for they were mostly occupied with warlike activities and with judicial and such other responsibilities. Life in a medieval castle was always full of warlike actions and exploits, and sometimes of feasts and festivals and tournaments. The plans of early manor houses and castles show no extensive private rooms for the lord's use. "It is not seemly that a lord should eat alone", said a feudal proverb. The lord, indeed, had his kinsmen, his armed revenue, his vassals or knights, along with his servants, in attendance in the great hall, where he dined and also meted out justice. And the feasts in the hall brought together the whole village community. In such conditions, privacy was virtually non-existent. Contacts between the nobles and their ladies were often close and intimate, providing them with many "delightsome" encounters often with a "distant" lady. Sex is one of other most chaos product phenomena in human life. Had not the Church ordained monogamously regulated social life, the whole fabric of the European feudal society would have collapsed in a mess of sexual anarchy. The monogamous family system guaranteed security of life, activity and influence to the ladies of the knightly classes and ensured proper transmission of family estates and traditions from generation to generation. Much had, indeed, changed since the far-off days of the free but uncouth womanhood of the Germanic tribes, and also from the rough- and-tumble of the early feudal ages of war and violence. The life in the manors and castles of the High Feudal Age had become more orderly and cultured. But it was still the life of the isolated village communities, isolated both by geography and the lack of roads and other means of travel and transport, with the exception of the horse of the feudal lords, and of the more humble pony of the clergy and the pilgrims.

However, during the later centuries of medieval Europe,

a new type of womanhood began to emerge both in the feudal manors and villages as well as in the new towns and cities. The feudal ladies had not only preserved their old freedom and influence, but had also acquired new tastes and manners and new capacities for the management of the manors and influence over their men. Marc Block writes: "The noblewomen had never been confined within her secluded quarters. Surrounded with servants, she ruled her household, and she might also rule the fief-perhaps with a rod of iron. It was nevertheless reserved for the twelfth century to create the type of the cultivated great lady who holds a salon. The boudoir of the high-born lady and, more generally, the court, was henceforth the place where the knight sought to outshine and to eclipse his rivals not only by his reputation for great deeds of valour, but also by his regard for good manners and by his literary talents".

It was the great age of chivalry in European feudalism. But it was the last age of feudal glory, for it now began to be transformed by the winds of change which started blowing over Feudal Europe from the thirteenth century onwards.

It is a matter of tremendous historical significance that the winds of change in Europe always blow in quite a different manner than they did in the past societies of Asia and Africa, with the possible exception of the Japanese. Progress in European society, past or present, has always been an inner and organic growth resulting from the developments within the society itself. Moreover they are also continuous and cumulative they do not suffer from and kind of retrogression or reversion due to social or ideological atavism. New conditions and forces arise in it from the developments and conditions which preceded them. That was (and is) the reason why the energies of the European mind and character, life and society were always free for unlimited action, interaction, organization and achievements, unhindered by any inhabitation and or ideological actavism.

New conditions and forces arise in it from the developments and conditions which preceded them. That was (and is) the reason why the energies of the European mind and character, life and society were always free for unlimited action, interaction, organization and achievements, unhindered by any inhibition and inertia of the, whether of the Church and clergy, of sex and kinship bonds, or of the past customs and traditions, when once new conditions, new relations and needs, and new interests and ideals had arisen among them. Such were the developments which finally put an end to feudalism during the later ages of medieval Europe.

The changes which occurred during the last three centuries of Feudal Europe were too many and too varied and complex to be enumerated in details. Briefly, they were as under:

First of all, the family group began to contract to its bio-socially necessary dimensions, that is, to the size of the natural family of the parents and their children, affecting all other aspects of the European society. The contraction of the family size was due to the cumulative effects of other monogamy, prohibition of cousin marriages upto fourth degree, and the need to protect family interests in property and inheritance, especially in landed property, eliminating kinship hold on the family and its property. Marc Bloch writes, "On close examination, however, it looks as if from the thirteenth century onwards a sort of contraction was in progress. The vast kindreds of not so long before were slowly being replaced by groups much more like our small families of today." Indeed, the rule of primongeniture compelled even younger sons and brothers to seek other sources of livelihood and income than family inheritance. These changes produced a galvanising effect on the mind, character, attitude and society of Europe. They necessarily produced men and women of active and achieving habits, inclination and character. They were always in a dual state of competition and cooperation with other individuals and groups in the society, which was (and is) also non-kinship in its structure and attitude, in order to defend and enlarge their individual and family interests and properties. Accordingly, in times or circumstances of need, they could not seek or withdraw into the microsocial shell of kinship groups, such as that of clans, castes and the like, for there were none. Hence there arose the need for interaction with and orientation towards others than relatives. It was a new type of social situation, the macrosocial situation, in which every member of the small family group, man or woman, young or old, had to be active and achieving in one or the other field of endeavour, especially when the old feudal warfare for acquiring fiefs and social status became increasingly impossible in conditions of King's peace" under the powerful monarchs of the rising nation-states, while ever newer avenues for work and wealth were opened in the expanding economy, society and culture of new Europe. Thus arose the achieving personality in the European society at the end of the Middle Ages in both the urban and rural centres. Europe was thus individualized. Rise of individualism was indeed a new phenomenon of tremendous significance not only in European but also in world history.

Secondly, the urban revolution of the twelfth century brought into being new mercantile communities in the flourishing towns and cities of Europe during the Later Middle Ages. They extended their trade relations and activities not only within their countries but also all over Europe and even beyond the seas. These mercantile communities were united by the nature of their work and occupation, not by kinship bonds.

Thirdly, new centres of learning and scholarship, the universities, were set up for the teaching and study of theology, law, logic, geometry and philosophy at various places in Western Europe from Italy to England.

Fourthly, the new monarchical states rose first in England, then in Christian Spain, France and in other countries of Western Europe, which had liberated themselves from the shackles of feud decentralization of law and sovereignty. They became so strong and centralised as to maintain peace and order even against the powerful feudal Magnate throughout the kingdom. Thus originated the modern nation- state system on the basis of sovereign nationhood and not on feudal custom and parochialism.

Origins of parliamentary representative system : The contractual and limited nature of the feudal kingdom required that the king would always consult the feudal magnates on important matters of the government. These consultative royal councils were variously called *curi regis,* parliament, or cortes. In France, the consultative council did not develop further, because the French kings limited it to only judicial matters. In Christian Spain, the cortes or legislative bodies lost their powers, because the Spanish kings acquired great powers in their wars against the Muslims. In England, parliament gradually evolved from the curia regis. When King John (1199-1216) tried to impose more taxes on the nobles for the Third Crusade, the nobles considered them unjustified, and revolted against the King. They compelled him to sign a charter of their rights or liberties, called Magna Carta. One of these rights was that the King would levy taxes only after receiving consent of the nobles, given by their representatives. Later the Englishmen read the principle of "no taxation without representation" into it. Afterwards Edward I summoned the model parliament in 1297. which consisted of two Houses, the House of Lords representing the nobles and the House of Commons representing the knights and burgesses from the towns, called boroughs. In the fourteenth century, the English Parliament acquired the right to submit bills for royal assent. It thus became a legislative body. By the end of the Middle Ages, parliament as a legislative institution, was firmly established in England, bequeathed by the consultative system of the medieval feudal state. It thus became a powerful macrosocialising agency for the English nation.

Lastly, feudalism itself changed from its earlier politicomilitary seigneurialism to the new market-oriented manorialism. Again this change was at first more pronounced in England than elsewhere in Europe. None-the-less, it paved the way for the same transformation in the villages or manors as had already taken place in the earlier-established market towns and cities that is to say, the orientation of agricultural production towards the market by the profitmaking entrepreneurs.

Thus, during the thirteenth century, the last great age of the European feudal magnates, the manorial agriculture became more and more market-oriented. It was the golden age of demesne farming. But decline in wheat prices, depopulation, due to plague and famine, and the rise in wages, the farmlands were turned into pastures for sheep-farming. The money-minded feudal classes became then more and more capitalistic. The big feudal landlords rented out their lands to their stewards or to the merchants from the nearby towns and cities, while the small feudal landowners, the knights, themselves took more and more to agriculture than ever before, till they became, in England, country gentlemen, squires and yeomen. It was from their ranks that the rising royal power recruited its armies to crush the feudal magnates under the Tudors. Later on, during the fifteenth century and after, the enterprising squarishly in England and their counterparts in Flanders, France and other courtries of Western Europe, became more and more productivity-conscious. They introduced new agricultural tools, implements and techniques. Such as better ploughs, use of horses as draught animals in place of bullocks, and new types of crops animal husbandry and sheep-farming. It was this agricultural transformation which put an end to the thousand year old European feudalism. It is, indeed, a sad commentary that such a warlike class as the European feudal class had been for centuries was literally eaten away by such a peaceful creature as the sheep, when the vast estates of other old feudal lords were turned into pasturetands for them all over England, Flanders and Low Countries (Belgium and Holland), France and in other European countries. But this change was brought about by the feudal lords themselves becoming a class of reinters. They leased out their lands, further enlarged by enclosing the commons and village greens, to the profit-making squires, merchants and such other entrepreneurs, who got rich quick by wool trade and by manufacturing woollen textiles. Western Europe had, indeed gone, capitalist and modern.

This change sounded the death-knell of feudalism in Western Europe. The English feudal classes, freely intermarrying with the emergent Mercantile Classes of other new towns and cities anticipated it and adopted themselves to it readily and peacefully than did the feudal classes of several other European countries. In France, they clung to their feudal privileges in a caste-like fashion, till the French Revolution of 1789 administered to them a *coup de grace* for good. Only Christian Spain was an exception to this rule of progress. Its feudal classes had aided their absolutist rulers in conquering Muslim Spain and even the newly-discovered Americas. But then Imperial Spain and its feudal classes became stagnant and hide-bound with the exaggerated feudal notion of chivalry and romance, which the Spanish writer, Cervantes (1547-1616), ridiculed in his well-known novel, *Don Quixote*.

Expanding horizons of the medieval European mind and society : All the changes, described above, had a powerful effect on the European mind and society at the end of the Middle

Ages. Its expanding population and the need for achievement led the West European peoples to seek new sources of wealth in agriculture and industry, trade and commerce, in clearing woodlands and in conquering foreign lands -by undertaking geographical explorations in overseas countries and continents and by invasion and conquest of non-European peoples and lands. At the same time, the adventure of new ideas also began to dispel the centuries-old traditionalism of the Middle Ages. New vistas of information about the non-European world, much wider than the little world of medieval Europe, and the new knowledge of the universe, much greater than the parochial outlook and ideology of the medieval Church, began to agitate and inspire the European mind and intellect at the end of the Middle Ages. It was, indeed, a two-phased development: a process of macrosocialisation of the European peoples, on the one side, and the emergence of the achieving individual, on the other.

Passing away of Feudal Europe : We now come to the end of our survey of the evolution and transformation of Feudal Europe. From circa 1500, feudalism was dead or dying in Western Europe, first in England and then in other European countries. With this the Middle Ages came to an end and modern Europe stepped on to the world scene. But they bequeathed six things to it: firstly, a macrosociety, i.e., a society of unlimited opportunity and freedom for interpersonal interactivity, achievement orientation and inspiration. Secondly, a system of nation-states, each nation organized for peace and prosperity at home and for war and aggression abroad; thirdly, a mercantile bourgoisie, which harnessed its nation-state for its commercial activities and adventures all over the globe, and thus ushered in industrial revolution, modern capitalism, colonialism and imperialism; fourthly, a representative parliamentary system, which became a cradle of democracy, i.e., a political system of a country for organizing its whole people for internal development and external conquest, expansion and colonisation; fifthly, a small monogamous family system, which orientated its members, young and old, male or female, towards action, work and achievement; and sixthly the idea of the individual as an independent and self-reliant personality endowed with rights and freedom for self-realisation, and loyal to his nation, but not to any lesser solidary group. These legacies gave modern European peoples and nations great capacity for organization, integration and expansion, and as individuals, boundless capabilities for work, enterprise and adventure, as well as an insatisable propensity to think new thoughts, make new discoveries in various sciences and arts and to invent new tools, machines, weapons and techniques. These were and are the secrets of European dynamism. But they have also made modern Europe a problem for the survival of the non-European world, or rather of the non- Western world, for Europe has since then expanded into a Western World. Muslim Spain was the first victim of the aggressive expansionism of Europe in general and of Christian Spain in particular. And many more such victims were to come later on.

In the Middle Ages the Iberian Peninsula was divided into the Kingdoms of Castile, which included most of northern and central Spain. Aragon which included Caterlonia and Valencia in the east and south; Navarre the small kingdom astride the Pyrenees which France long coveted; Granada the last refuge in Spain of the Moors and Portugal. Castile was a monorchy whose power was limited by the numerous privileges granted to the cities founded during its expansion, and by the assembly known as the cortes. The cortes was a body representative of nobles, clergy and the third estate. Its powers over taxation and legislation and its privilege of acknowledging the heir apparent, made it more powerful in fourteenth and fifteenth century Castile than Parliament in England or the Estates-General in France. It sent elected members to the Royal Council, which was the executive of the state. It is not possible within the limits of this book to do more than mention a few salient facts in the history of Spain prior to the amalgamation of Castile and Aragon in 1469. In the thirteenth century Alfonso the wise (1252-1282) stands out in Castile for his encouragement of science and culture, and for his creation of a homogeneous legal code out of the diverse legal relics of Roman and Visigothic rule. His son Sancho, who deposed his father in 1282, began a period of steady pressure against the Moors, which continued at intervals until the Moors were finally expelled from their last stronghold of Granada in 1492. Pedro the cruel (1350-1369), who earned his title by many deeds, including the murder of his own half-brother is nevertheless remarkable for his tolerance Jews. The abandonment of this policy later in a country where the great majority of noble and middle-class families had Jewish blood, and the persecution of Jews as well as Moors by the Inquisition at the end of the fifteenth century had for the Spain the same evil effect, in a greater degree as the persecution of the Huguenots had for France, or, in more recent times, as the persecution of the Jews had for the Germans. There is an interesting connection between Pedro the Cruel and England. John of Gaunt, son of Edward III, married Pedro's daughter Constance and claimed the home in 1369, when the Henry of Trastamara another half-brother of Pedro, succeeded Pedro; but allowed himself to be bought off when he realised the futility. of the enterprise. The last ruler of a separate Castile was Isabella, who succeeded in 1474 and married Fredinand of Aragon in 1469.

Aragon

Aragon was a kingdom of different traditions from Castile. It was formed from the amalgamation, as a result of the marriage of the ruler, of the country of Barcelona with the small principality of Aragon. In 1238 James I (1213-1276) contemporary of the Alfanso the wise of Castile, took Valencia from the Moors. The policy of Aragon now turned more and more to expansion overseas, whereas Castile remained inland-minded despite access to the Atlantic gained by the capture of Seville and Ladiz in the thirteenth century. James I's son, Pedro III, opposed the French under Charles of Anjou in Sicily, and assumed the crown of Sicily after the massacre of the French called the Sicillian vespers (1282). Pedro's successor. James II, received the thrones of both Aragon and Sicily, and added Sardinia and Corgica, to which Pedro IV early in the fourteenth century added the Balearic Islands. In the fifteenth century Naples was added to this list of territories, Alfonso V succeeding in 1442 in having himself recognized as king after a long struggle against the Angevin claimants. On his death in 1458 Alfanso bequeathed his hereditary kingdom of Aragon and Sicily to his brother, John II and Naples to an illegitimate son, Ferrante. The latter succeeded in holding Naples against the French claimant, who abandoned the field in 1464. The French claim now lapsed until revived by the ambitious Charles VIII in 1494.

Union of Castile and Aragon

The final stage in the history of Castile and Aragon in the Middle Ages begins with the marriage of Ferdinand of Aragon with Isabella of Castile in 1469, though it was not till 1474 and 1479 respectively that Isabella obtained the crown of Castile and Ferdinand that of Aragon. The union between the kingdoms was purely personal, and each retained its own laws and institutions, as did England and Scotland when the two Crowns were united in the person of James I-VI in 1603. The union was, however, a necessary preliminary to a strong Spanish monarchy. It gave Isabella the power to strike successfully at the swollen privileges of the Castilian nobility, and to both rulers the chance of developing the economy of their kingdoms by judicious taxation and currency reforms, and the throwing open of the two countries to mutual free trade. Unfortunately, such liberality went hand in hand in both monarchies with extreme religious bigotry. The Inquisiton authorised in Spain by a papal bull in 1478, became a royal weapon to achieve religious uniformity at all costs. The expulsion of 200,000 Jews was followed by a final campaign 1481-1491, against the Moors of Granada, who, after being granted a liberal peace, were seven years later suddenly given the choice of conversion or exile.

Portugal

Of the early history of Portugal it is unnecessary to say much here. Portugal became a separate kingdom in the twelfth century. It underwent similar vicissitued to other contemporary states inducting an especially terrible visitation of the Black Death in 1348-1349, a period of unrest thereafter as in England and cruel civil war from 1383-1385. In 1387 John I married a daughter of John Gaunt, and their youngest son was that Henry the Navigator, whose study of navigation and cartography and assistance in the fitting out of maritime expeditions led later to the settlement of the Azores (1480) and of the Cape Verds Islands in 1496 to the rediscovery of the cape of Good Hope, and to the great voyage of Vasco da Gama to India. These and other matters relating to the discovery of the New World will be more fully dealt with in another chapter.

The Jews were the partners of the Muslims in their intellectual's progress. Most of them wrote books in Arabic and some translated Arabic book into Hebrew language. The philosophical writings of the Muslim writers are still survived due to those Jews writers. The personality of Musa bin Samon (Moses son of Simon 1135-1204) was the rising point of Jews philosophical struggle, who under the influence of philosophy of Farabi and Ibn-e-Sina tried to conform the writings of Aristotle and the old testament. On the one hand he explained the divine revelation and confirmed with the philosophy and on the other hand he limited the Aristotle's Philosophy to the worldly affairs and the affairs of sources of life thereafter left to the words of God.

During the full swing of the Muslim period, the Jews were the fond of litrary work. They were privileged class but at the beginning of Muslim down fall they were not so. The hardships created by the bigotted Muslims compelled the Jews to flow away towards the Christian countries leaving their houses especially in southern France so that they became reason between the two civilizations which the nature has trusted to them.